FREEMASONS

SOUTH DAKOTA TERRITORY

L - Z

For bulk purchases, please contact the publisher.
Enquiry@Athenaia.Co

Library of Congress Cataloging-in Publication Data
Names: Jordan, Darrell
Freemasons South Dakota Territory – L – Z, Darrell Jordan, MPS
Description: First U.S. edition. | Coeur D'Alene, Idaho: Athenaia [2024]
Identifiers: LCCN (pending) |
ISBN979-8-88556-056-6 (First Edition hardcover)
Subjects: OCC012000: SOC038000: SOCIAL SCIENCE / Freemasonry & Secret Societies |
BODY, MIND & SPIRIT / Mysticism |
PHI013000: PHILOSOPHY / Metaphysics
LC record available at https://lccn. loc.gov

On the internet: Parallel47North.com/collections/esoteric-books
Author and Managing Editor: Darrell Jordan
Original Author and Essay: Freemasons South Dakota Territory – L - Z
Executive Producer: Yuka Jordan
Book Cover Design by Yuka Jordan
Book Cover Art and Illustrations: Jessica Naomi
Image Credits: Freemasons South Dakota Territory and Darrell Jordan's personal collection
Printed and bound in the United States

Publisher: Athenaia, LLC
2370 N Merritt Crk Lp, Ste 1
Coeur D'Alene, ID 83814
The United States

It is my extreme honor and privilege to
present this work;
"Freemason's - South Dakota Territory"
to the Grand Lodge A.F. & A.M. of
South Dakota.

Fraternally yours,

Darrell Jordan 32°

Editor & Researcher

Sources:

History of South Dakota Vol II; Robinson, Doane; 1904

History of Dakota Territory Vol. IV; Kingsbury, George W.; 1915

History of the great Northwest and its men of progress; Hyde, Cornelius William Gillam; 1901

SOUTH DAKOTA

Chronology

1609. Territory granted to Virginia by charter.

1628. Granted to John Endicott and other "Joint Adventurers."

1671. Spain took formal possession of all country west of Lake Michigan and the Mississippi River.

1681. Marquette 's map, outlining principal features of state, known to exist.

1700. Mahas or Onakas occupies southeastern part of state.

Ree Indians known to be dwelling in Missouri River valley.

1703. On or before this date Charles Le Sueur published a map of the territory which is now South Dakota.

1712. French king granted the territory to Anthony Crozat for a period of twenty-five years.

1733. Reverted to king of France.

1743. Verendrye visited western part of state and took possession for France.

1750. Rees attacked by Sioux nation (date approximated) and after years of warfare are forced to retreat to the north.

1762. France ceded the territory to Spain.

1785. Pierre Dorion made an alliance with the Yankton Indians.

1790. Pierre Garreau resided with the Rees at Arikara at the mouth of the Grand River.

1796. Cedar Island, below Pierre, known to contain the trading house of Trudeau.

1800. Spain recedes the territory to France.

1803. Territory purchased of France by the United States.

1804. Attached to the Territory of Indiana, for judicial purposes.

Actual transfer of title and possession accomplished.

Lewis and Clark start on their expedition.

1805. The District of Louisiana becomes the Territory of Louisiana.

1806. Return trip of Lewis and Clark.

1807. First conflict with Indians.

1808. American Fur Company organized by Pierre Chouteau and Manuel Lisa.

1810. Loisel's post burned.

1811. Expedition of John Jacob Actor passes through state and

touches the northern point of the Black Hills.

1812. Becomes part of Missouri Territory.

1816. Trudeau's trading house burns.

1817. American Fur Company construct a post on what is now

Goddard's Island. Two years later removed to Ft. Pierre.

1821. Missouri admitted to Union, and that part of the state west of the Missouri River left without government until 1854, while the part east of that river remained without government until 1834.

1822. Rocky Mountain Fur Company organized for trade along the Missouri River.

1823. General Ashley, head of the above company, routed in an attack by Rees, while attempting to go up the river. Colonel Henry Leavenworth leads an attack upon the Rees and punishes them, this being the first military invasion.

1828. Waneta removes from Elm to Missouri River.

1831. Steamboat Yellowstone makes first trip on Missouri.

1832. George Catlin, famous Indian portrait painter, visits the state and plies his art, securing many valuable portraits.

1834. South Dakota territory east of Missouri becomes part of Michigan.

1836. Michigan admitted as state and our state becomes a part of Wisconsin.

1837. Smallpox scourge practically destroys the Mandan Indian tribe and severely injures many other tribes.

1838. Becomes part of Iowa Territory.

1839. General John C. Fremont visits state in interest of science.

1840. Rev. Stephen R. Riggs, an eminent missionary to Indians, visits Fort Pierre.

1843. John J. Audubon, the renowned naturalist, and Edward Harris, a geologist of note, made a joint expedition to the territory.

1849. Minnesota Territory erected and made to include all of South Dakota east of the Missouri River.

1851. A second smallpox epidemic visits and despoils Indians.

1854. Territory west of Missouri River included in Nebraska.

1855. The fur trade practically over.

Fort Pierre fur station purchased by national government and 1200 troops stationed there during winter of 1855/56.

1856. Western Town Company, incorporated at Dubuque, Iowa, makes settlement at the Falls of the Sioux.

1857. Dakota Land Company, of St. Paul, organized and locates townsites at Falls of the Sioux, Flandreau, Medary, Estelline and other points in the Sioux valley.

Spirit Lake, Iowa, Massacre by Indians from Dakota.

Rescue of Abigail Gardner by Christian Indians, near Ashton.

1858. Minnesota admitted to Union and territory east of Missouri River left without any government until 1861.

General Harney makes treaty with Indians, which was never ratified.

A legislature elected which met at Sioux Falls and passed a memorial to Congress praying for the establishment of a Territorial government.

1859. A new election held at which Judge J. P. Kidder for Delegate to Congress, and a full quota of Territorial officers, including a new legislature, were elected. Congress ignored the movement.

Ratification of treaty opening land to settlement lying between the Sioux and Missouri rivers and extending as far north as a line between Pierre and Watertown.

Permanent settlements made at Elk Point, Yankton, Vermillion and Bon Homme.

Dakota "Democrat." a newspaper, established at Sioux Falls.

1860. Mass Convention held at Yankton praying Congress for Territorial government.

First schoolhouse built at Bon Homme.

1861. Territory erected, embracing what is now North and South Dakota, Montana and much of. Idaho and Wyoming. The "Dakotain" at Yankton and the "Republican" at Vermillion established.

1862. First Legislature meets at Yankton, which town becomes the capital of the Territory.

Territorial (now State) University located at Vermillion and the penitentiary located at Bon Homme.

A regiment recruited for service in the Civil War Minnesota Massacre occurs.

1863. Idaho Territory formed, leaving Dakota Territory practically as it remained until statehood.

Governor Jayne runs for Congress, seems to be elected, and resigns as governor.

Newton Edmunds of Yankton appointed governor.

First Masonic lodge established; St. John's, No. 166.

1865. Treaty signed at Fort Pierre which terminated the hostilities

resulting from the Minnesota Massacre.

1866. Andrew J. Faulk appointed governor.

Beginning of Red Cloud war which continued to 1868, and prevented the government from constructing roads through the state to the gold fields of Idaho and Montana.

1868. Red Cloud war ends. Sioux Reservation, west of Missouri River and including Black Hills, created.

1869. John A. Burbank appointed governor.

1872. First railroad in state, Sioux City to Vermillion.

1873. Above road continued to Yankton. Winona & St. Peter railroad built to Lake Kampeska.

1874. John L. Pennington appointed governor.

Custer expedition discovers gold in the Black Hills.

1875. Government attempts to secure treaty with the Indians

permitting mining in the Hills.

Miners rush to gold fields in violation of treaty rights.

A.F.&A.M. Grand Lodge founded.

1876. Indians assemble for war on miners.

Battle of Little Big Horn and Custer Massacre.

Black Hills relinquished by treaty signed only by chiefs. Reservation Indians disarmed.

1878. William A. Howard made governor.

1879. Great boom begins.

Railroads start extensions.

1880 Governor Howard dies and N. G. Ordway is appointed governor.

Great October blizzard and continuous winter until middle of April, 1881.

1881. High waters in all rivers.

Springfield Normal established.

Small tract of land given to Nebraska.

Yankton College established.

Vermillion completely destroyed.

Capital removal commission appointed.

1882. Capital removed to Bismarck.

Division and statehood convention held at Canton. University buildings provided for by Clay County voting $10,000 bonds for buildings.

1883. First constitutional convention held at Sioux Falls. Brookings College established.

Madison Normal founded.

Presbyterian College opens at Pierre.

Sioux Falls College founded.

1884. Gilbert A. Pierce appointed governor and succeeds N. G. Ordway.

All Saints School founded at Sioux Falls.

1885. Law passed providing for a constitutional convention for part of Territory south of the forty-sixth parallel.

1887. Governor Pierce resigned and Louis K. Church was appointed by President Cleveland to the position.

Dakota Wesleyan founded.

School of mines founded.

Redfield College founded, and school opened in September.

1889. Territory divided and South Dakota admitted as a state.

A. C. Mellette succeeds Church as Territorial governor and later becomes first governor of the state.

Third constitutional convention meets in Sioux Falls. Beginning of new period of hard times.

Augustina College founded at Canton.

1890. The Messiah war and battle of Wounded Knee.

Death of Sitting Bull.

Lands between White and Cheyenne rivers opened to settlement.

1891. Governor Mellette enters upon second term.

W. W. Taylor becomes state treasurer.

Financial conditions somewhat improved.

1893. Charles H. Sheldon succeeds Mellette as governor.

Taylor succeeds himself.

Severe nation-wide financial panic.

1894. Financial conditions very unsatisfactory. Land values poor, many banks fail.

1895. Governor Sheldon continues as head of the state.

Treasurer Taylor, unable to settle with the state, absconds.

Later returns, is convicted and serves a term in the penitentiary.

Hard times continue.

1896. Andrew E. Lee, Populist, elected governor. Anti-prohibition amendment to constitution carries.

1897. James H. Kyle, Populist, elected senator.

1898. One regiment, the First South Dakota, and one battalion of cavalry, known as Grigsby's Cowboys, organized and mustered for service in Spanish war.

1899. First South Dakota arrives in Philippine Islands and sees service in subduing rebellion.

Governor Lee succeeds himself.

Initiative and referendum clauses added to Constitution. President McKinley visits state and welcomes First South Dakota regiment upon its return.

1900. Republicans returned to power. Charles N. Herreid elected governor.

1901. Robert J. Gamble elected senator in place of R. F. Pettigrew. Law school established at State University.

Department of History organized at Pierre, under state control.

Northern Normal and Industrial School opens.

1902. Governor Herreid reelected.

Senator Kyle dies and A. B. Kittredge is appointed to take his place.

The battleship South Dakota christened at San Francisco by Miss Grace Herreid, daughter of the governor.

1904. Rosebud Indian reservation opened to settlement by novel method of drawing for chance to file.

Mitchell-Pierre capital fight.

Period of free transportation.

Great era of settlement and abundant prosperity begins.

1905. Samuel H. Elrod becomes governor.

Legislature provides for a commission to construct a new capitol building and outlines method to finance same. Legislature refuses to place upon the ballot an initiated bill for a primary election law. Authorizes the construction of shirt and overall and twine factories at the state penitentiary.

New railroad construction both east and west of the river announced.

Plans for two, million-dollar bridges over the Missouri, drawn.

1906. Republican party split into factions. Coe I. Crawford elected governor.

1907. "Reform legislature" passes anti-pass, anti-lobby, primary election laws and also measures designed to control corporations.

1909. R. S. Vessey becomes governor. Coe I. Crawford succeeds A. B. Kittredge as senator.

1910. Governor Vessey succeeds himself.

1911. Ziebach County created.

Under census of 1910 state gets another congressman and legislature districts the state.

Return of hard times caused by almost complete failure of 1911 crops.

1912. Frank M. Byrne elected governor.

1913. Thomas Sterling elected senator.

Tax Commission created.

Bureau of Public Printing created.

Mothers' Pension Fund System established. Verendrye Plate found.

1914. Frank M. Byrne elected to succeed himself.

Peter Norbeck elected lieutenant governor.

Ed. M. Johnson, Democrat, elected senator.

1915. Capital punishment abolished.

Bank Guaranty of Deposits' Law enacted.

Haakon County created from part of Stanley. Jackson County created from part of Stanley.

1916. Peter Norbeck elected governor.

W. H. McMaster elected lieutenant governor. Constitutional prohibition of the liquor traffic enacted.

1917. Rural credit system started.

State sheriff and state constabulary provided for.

Code commission appointed.

Educational survey undertaken.

United States enters world war and South Dakota sends troops to front.

Highway appropriation made by state to match appropriations by congress.

Torrens system of land registration enacted. Workmen's Compensation Law passed.

Jones County created from part of Lyman.

EARLY SETTLEMENTS

Scarcely had the Indians removed from their old hunting grounds when settlers began to enter the territory and erect their western cabins.

In 1859 the first white families settled in the counties of Union, Clay, and Yankton. George Brown located at Vermillion in August, 1859, and erected the old "Miner Hotel." Miner Robinson, L. E. Phelps and P. H. Jewell, removed to Vermillion during the same season, and J. H. McHenry opened the first store at that town in September, 1859, and in the following spring the Van Metre ferry and Compton & Deuel's saw-mill were put in operation. In July, J. Stanage selected his claim on James River, erected a house, opened a farm, and established a ferry for the crossing of the public travel. Thomas Frek and Henry Arend located near the upper ferry, which at that time was the old government crossing, and kept by J. M. Stone, to whom the settlers' mail matter once a week was delivered from Sioux City, by the driver of the Fort Randall express, enclosed in an old oilcloth satchel. During the same season D. T. Bramble erected the first frame building in Yankton, as a store, near the levee, on the newly surveyed townsite of the Upper Missouri Land Company, consisting of J. S. B. Todd, A. W. Hubbard, Enos Stutsman, and others. Captain Todd erected his little law-office on the corner of Broadway and Second streets during the same winter. M. K. Armstrong came as the first land surveyor in Dakota, in 1859, and on the cold, blue Christmas day, H. C. Ash and wife, at the head of the pioneer family of Yankton, entered the place, and opened a tavern in a rude log house on the west side of Broadway. During the following year the old log churches at Yankton and Vermillion were erected, in which the Revs. Hoyt, Ingham, and Martin, were the first to proclaim the word of God to the pioneers of Dakota. At this time Sioux Falls, owned by the Dubuque and St. Paul Town Companies, was the leading town in the territory, and the United States survey of lands had been extended to that place in September, 1859, and in the fall of 1860 the first tier of townships was surveyed along the Missouri river, in which year Vermillion commenced its rapid strides in growth and settlement, and outstripped all its competitors, while Yankton was ranked as the third town in Dakota. The three places were aspirants for the embryo capital. At Sioux Falls the Northwest Independent was published, elections had been held, provisional officers chosen, a delegate to congress elected, and legislatures convened in 1858-59 and 1859-60.

But government appears to have looked with more surprise than compassion on these early political freaks of Dakotans. The people who had settled on the western slope of Dakota, however, were more moderate in their demands, and more successful in their petitions to congress. These pioneers, on the 8th day of November, 1859, assembled in mass convention to petition congress for a territorial organization. A memorial was drafted and signed by the citizens of the territory, which was conveyed to Washington by J. B. S. Todd, calling the attention of the government to our situation. The session passed, congress adjourned, and amid the tumultuous preparations for a presidential election and the muttering thunders of a rising rebellion, Dakota was left ungoverned and unorganized.

Not to be discouraged by this partial failure, the pioneers assembled again in mass convention at Yankton, Dec. 27, 1860, and again on Jan. 15, 1861, and prepared an earnest and lengthy memorial to congress, which was signed by 578 citizens and forwarded to the speaker of the house and president of the senate. Again, a cloud hung dark over Dakota's prayer. A new president had been elected — the old power was retiring, a new one advancing; and the rebellion which, but the year before, was muttering in smothered tones, had now burst forth in all its fury, and was bearing upon its maddening waves seven revolted states of the Union. But through the gathering darkness a ray of light was seen. The old power could organize —

the new one appoint; and on the second day of March, 1861, President Buchanan approved the bill giving to Dakota a territorial government.

The news did not reach Yankton until the 13th of the month, and on that night hats, hurrahs and town lots '"went up," to greet the dawning future of the Great Northwest.

Under its new boundaries the territory comprised all of the present Territory of Montana and the eastern slope of Idaho, and contained about 350,000 square miles, which was bounded on the north by the British line, east by Minnesota and Iowa, south by the Iowa line, and the Missouri. Niobrara and Turtle Hill rivers, up to and along the forty-third parallel of latitude, to the Rocky Mountains, thence along their snowy range to British America. Some 70,000 square miles of this territory was situated east of the Missouri river, and constituted that country which had been trimmed off from the state boundaries of Minnesota in 1858, while a vast expanse of the new territory, reaching out from the Missouri to the Rocky Mountains, was carved out of the old Territory of Nebraska, as formed in 1854. Dakota, thus established, constituted the largest organized territory in the United States, and afforded a river navigation of not less than 2,000 miles. In June the following officials, appointed by the new administration, arrived and entered upon the discharge of their duties: Wm. Jayne of Illinois, governor; John Hutchinson of Minnesota, secretary; P. Bliss of Ohio, chief justice; L. P. Williston of Pennsylvania and J. L. Williams of Tennessee, associate justices; W. E. Gleason of Maryland, district attorney; G. D. Hill of Michigan, surveyor general; W. F. Shaffer, marshal; W. A. Burleigh of Pennsylvania, agent of Yanktons; H. A. Hoffman of New York, agent of Poncas. H. A. Kennedy was appointed register and Jesse Wherry receiver, of the Vermillion land office during the same season, both of Dakota Territory. On the 6th of June the Weekly Dakotan was issued at Yankton, under the head of the Dakotan Company. In the following month The Dakota Republican was started at Vermillion by Bedell and Clark.

A census was taken, showing the population of the territory to be 2,402, and on the 13th of July the first proclamation of the governor was issued, dividing the territory into judicial districts, and assigning the judges thereto. Chief Justice Bliss was assigned to the second district at Yankton; Assistant Justice Williston to the Vermillion district: and Judge Williams to the Bonhomme district. On the 29th of July a second proclamation was issued, dividing the territory into council and representative districts, and appointing the 16th of September for a general election.

ANCIENT FREE AND ACCEPTED MASONS

Among the very first settlers of South Dakota were several Masons, and as early as 1862, during the first session of the territorial legislature, consultation began looking to the organization of a lodge, but the Indian troubles of that season suspended operations in that line for a period. However, no sooner was safety to the community assured that the matter was again taken up and Melancthon Hoyt, Episcopal missionary; John Hutchinson, secretary of Dakota territory; Henry C. Ash, the pioneer hotelkeeper, of Yankton; Nelson Miner, captain of Company A, Dakota Volunteer Cavalry; Justus Townsend, physician, and auditor of Dakota territory; Downer T. Bramble, legislator and pioneer merchant; G. N. Propper; James M. Allen, who was secretary of the provisional government established at Sioux Falls, and Frank M. Ziebach, founder of the Dakotan newspaper, petitioned for a dispensation to establish a lodge of the Ancient Free and Accepted Masons at Yankton. The dispensation was duly granted and the lodge instituted with the petitioners above named as charter members, the charter bearing date June 3, 1863. The lodge was called St. John's, No. 166, of the jurisdiction of Iowa. For six years thereafter it was the only lodge in the territory.

The genealogy of Dakota Masonry is as follows: From England to North Carolina, from North Carolina to Tennessee, from Tennessee to Missouri, from Missouri to Iowa, from Iowa to Dakota territory, from Dakota territory to South Dakota. The first officers of St. John's lodge were as follows: Melanchton Hoyt, master; Downer T. Bramble, senior warden; John Hutchinson, junior warden; George W. Kingsbury, treasurer; Moses K. Armstrong, secretary; George N. Propper, senior deacon; F. M. Ziebach, junior deacon; Bligh E. Wood, tyler.

The next lodge to be instituted in Dakota territory was Incense No. 257, of Vermillion, chartered February 10, 1869. Alpheus G. Fuller, of Yankton, who had been elected delegate to congress by the Sioux Falls provisional government in 1858, was the instituting officer. A year later, April 16, 1870, Elk Point Lodge, No. 288, was instituted, with H. H. Blair as master; Elias Hyde, senior warden; E. H. Webb, junior warden; P. E. Maynard, treasurer; John Lawrence, secretary; C. W. Beggs, senior deacon; J. A. Wallace, junior deacon; Eli B. Wixson, tyler. On June 10th Minnehaha Lodge, No. 328, was chartered at Sioux Falls, with Thomas H. Brown, R. C. Hawkins, E. Sharpe, T. Pomeroy, G. B. Sammons, W. H. Holt. J. H. Moulton, and George Hill as charter members. On June 3, 1875, Silver Star Lodge, No. 345, was organized at Canton, and W. H. Miller, Sr., M. W. Bailey, S. H. Stafford Jr., W. M. Cuppett, D. H. Hawn and others were charter members.

Delegates from these five lodges met in the hall of Elk Point Lodge on June 22, 1875. These delegates were empowered to take such measures as were necessary in order to form a grand lodge of Freemasons within and for the territory of Dakota. This convention adopted a constitution and by-laws and elected officers for a grand lodge and petitioned the Iowa grand lodge, to which they were still subject, for an organization. Pursuant to this action and petition the Iowa grand lodge sent T. S. Parvin to Dakota and at Vermillion, on July 21, 1875, the grand lodge of Dakota was duly instituted by Mr. Parvin in the old Baptist church.

The delegates who met in the convention at Elk Point on June 22d and took the preliminary steps toward the organization of the grand lodge of Dakota were as follows: St. John's Lodge No. 166, Yankton, George H. Hand, L. M. Purdy, F. J. DeWitt; Incense No. 257, Vermillion, Horace J. Austin, A. H. Lathrop, Vernette E. Prentice; Elk Point No. 288, J. A. Wallace, H. H. Blair, D. W. Hassen; Minnehaha No. 328, Thomas H. Brown, J. W. Callendar, Richard A. Pettigrew; Silver Star No. 345, Canton, William H. Miller, Sr., Mark W. Bailey, S. H. Stafford, Jr.

The first officers of the grand lodge were as follows: T. H. Brown; master; Mark W. Bailey, secretary. The grand masters have been Henry H. Blair, 1876; George H. Hand, 1877 to 1880; Thomas H. Brown, 1881; Oscar S. Gifford, 1882 and 1883; John F. Schrader, 1884; William Blatt, 1885 and 1886; Henry M. Wheeler, 1887; John Q. A. Braden, 1888; George V. Avers, 1889; Theodore D. Kanouse, 1890; George A. Johnston, 1891; Harvey J. Rice, 1892; Richard C. McAllister, 1893; William C. Allen, 1894; Frederick H. Files, 1895; James Lewis, 1896; Albert W. Coe, 1897; J. G. Bullen, 1898; Louis G. Levoy, 1899; W. H. Roddle, 1900; John A. Cleaver, 1901; Charles E. Hill, 1902; Frank A. Brown, 1903, and Byron P. Dague, 1904; Mark W. Bailey was secretary for two years until his death, in 1877; W. E. Caton succeeded him for one term and Charles T. McCoy was secretary from 1878 until 1893, when he was succeeded by George A. Pettigrew, who still serves in that capacity.

The meetings of the grand lodge have been held as follows: 1875, Elk Point and Vermillion; 1876, Yankton; 1877, Yankton; 1878, Sioux Falls; 1879, Yankton; 1880, Yankton; 1881, Sioux Falls; 1882, Watertown; 1883, Rapid City; 1884, Aberdeen; 1885, Fargo; 1886, Bismarck; 1887, Huron; 1888, Deadwood; 1889, Mitchell; 1890, Madison; 1891, Watertown, 1892, Sioux Falls; 1893, Yankton; 1894, Hot Springs; 1895, Pierre; 1896, Huron; 1897, Mitchell; 1898, Sioux Falls; 1899, Yankton; 1900, Aberdeen; 1901, Sioux Falls; 1902. Huron; 1903, Deadwood; 1904, Yankton. At the last report there were one hundred Blue Lodges in South Dakota, having a total of 5,444 members.

The institution of the York Rites in Dakota territory date from 1885, when, on the 25th of February, charters were issued to the following chapters: Yankton No. I, Yankton; Sioux Falls No. II, Sioux Falls; Dakota No. 3, Deadwood; Siroc No. 4, Canton; Huron No. 10, Huron; Watertown No. 12, Watertown; Aberdeen No. 14, Aberdeen; and on June 8th of that year Mitchell No. 15, Mitchell; Denver No. 17, Arlington; Brookings No. 18, Brookings; Orient No. 19, Flandreau, and Redfield No. 20, Redfield, were chartered. It will be observed that the above numbers do not run in regular order, this fact being due to the North Dakota chapters then in this jurisdiction.

The grand chapter was organized at Sioux Falls, July 8, 1885, the first fourteen chapters taking part in the organization. The meetings of the chapter since the first have been held at the same place and approximate time as the grand lodge. The grand high priests have been as follows: 1885 and 1886. William S. Blatt; 1887, Peter Picton; 1888, Collins D. Pratt; 1899, John F. Schrader; 1890, John Davidson; 1891. Henry S. Williams; 1891, Park Davis; 1892, William J. McMackin; 1893, Edward B. Bracy; 1894, Robert T. Sedam; 1895, Louis G. Levoy; 1896, Harvey T. Rice; 1897, George V. Avers; 1898, Samuel J. Coyne; 1899, George A. West; 1900, P. F. Ives; 1901, Martin G. Carlisle; 1902, Samuel J. Moore; 1903, Ed S. Ames; 1904, Samuel H. Jumper. The grand secretaries: Thomas J. Wilder, from organization until statehood, when the jurisdiction was divided, and since that date George A. Pettigrew has held the position. There are now twenty-nine chapters, having at the last report 1,784 members.

The commandery preceded the chapter in this jurisdiction. There are now fourteen of these bodies, the first of which is Dakota No. I, organized at Deadwood, August 19, 1880. The grand commandery was organized at Sioux Falls on May 14, 1884, by Theodore S. Parvin, of Iowa, under warrant of the grand commandery of the United States. The right eminent grand commanders since organization have been: 1884, Samuel Roy; 1885. Levi B. French: 1886, Daniel S. Glidden; 1887, Marc A. Brewer; 1888, Joseph A. Colcord: 1889, William D. Stites; 1890, John F. Schrader; 1891, Samuel H. Jumper; 1892, George W. Burnside; 1893, George H. Rathman; 1894, William J. McMackin; 1895, Frank A. Brown; 1896, J. J. Casselman; 1897, Joseph T. Morrow: 1898, William T. Doolittle; 1899, George V. Ayers; 1900, E. W. Coughran; 1901, Morris H. Kelly; 1902, Ed S. Lorimer; 1903, Fred A. Spafford, Edwin E, Sage was the first grand recorder, but was succeeded at the first election by Bruce M. Rowley, who held the office from

1885 until 1892. William H. Holt then held it for two years, when, in 1895, he was succeeded by George A. Pettigrew, who continues in the office.

For the history of the Scottish Rite bodies in South Dakota we are under obligation to T. W. Taubman, of Aberdeen, who writes: "I have had some difficulty in gathering the authentic history of the Rite in the territory of Dakota and the state of South Dakota. In 1874 Albert Pike, the sovereign grand commander, attached Dakota territory to the state of Minnesota and placed the same under the jurisdiction of A. T. C. Pearson, inspector general of that state, but it seems that he did not do any work within the territory. On January 6, 1883, the territory was annexed to Nebraska and was in charge of Robert Carrell Jordan, the inspector general of that state [and first grandmaster of Nebraska 1857-60], but prior thereto and on January 1, 1882, Arthur James Carrier, thirty-second degree, was appointed deputy for the territory of Dakota. He did the first work within the territory and established Alpha Lodge of Perfection No. I, in Yankton, on February 3, 1882, but I am informed that the date of its charter was February 8th of that year.

"Brother William Blatt writes me that Brother Carrier was an Indian trader and boarded with Mrs. Dawson on the southwest corner of Third and Linn streets in that city, where he occupied the parlor and there communicated to him and several others whose names he was unable to recall the degrees from the fourth to the fourteenth, who immediately thereafter applied for a charter, bought nine hundred dollars' worth of paraphernalia, and, in unison with the other Masonic bodies, leased the west half of the present hall, remodeled it at great expense and began work hopefully and energetically, but fearfully in debt. Brother Jordan inaugurated Mackey Chapter, Rose Croix, in Yankton, February 27, 1883, and Dr. D. Frank Etter was elected wise master, and Brother Fleming writes me that John B. Dennis was appointed deputy for Brother Jordan. About the last of July or the first of August of that year Brother Pike visited Yankton and Sioux Falls and he states in his allocution for that year that Brother Dennis accompanied him for the purpose of establishing bodies at Yankton and Sioux Falls. Brother Dennis was appointed deputy for the supreme council for the southern part of Dakota April 25, 1884. Robert B. Bruce Council of Kadosh No. I was not chartered until March 10, 1887, but I do not know by whom nor when it was inaugurated, but find that it is mentioned as paying dues in 1886. Brother Rufus E. Fleming, thirty-third degree, who had been deputy for the northern part of Dakota territory, was, on October 19, 1886, made an active inspector general for the entire territory, and Dr. Etter was his deputy until his death. He was succeeded by Brother Blatt and he by Brother Beadle. Oriental Consistory was chartered at the 1888 session of the supreme council and was instituted by Brother Fleming on December 10th of the same year, when George A. Archer was elected master of Kadosh. When first chartered it was known as No. 2, but Occidental Consistory No. I at Sioux Falls having forfeited its charter in 1889, the supreme council authorized Oriental to be known as No. I, which it now is. Other bodies of the Rite which have been instituted in the state are Webster Lodge of Perfection, June 13, 1887; Cyrus Lodge of Perfection, at Watertown, August I, 1887; Khurum Lodge of Perfection, at Sioux Falls, September 15, 1884; and Albert Pike Chapter, Rose Croix, at Sioux Falls, September 15, 1884. At the session of the supreme council in 1884 there was a petition for a consistory at Sioux Falls, but the same was rejected because there was no council of Kadosh, but one was subsequently established. The application for a consistory was again rejected in 1888, but a recess vote was taken and a charter granted and a consistory at Sioux Falls inaugurated by Brother Fleming on either the day before or after the one at Yankton. Their council of Kadosh was known as Cour DeLain No. 2 and was instituted by Brother Fleming May 2, 1888. The lodge and chapter at Deadwood was constituted May 21, 1892, the council May 23, 1892, and the consistory October 20, 1892. A lodge of perfection was located at Hot Springs in November, 1894; at Aberdeen a lodge and chapter was instituted April 6, 1894; the council February 21, 1895, and the consistory January 16, 1896, and the Albert Pike Lodge of Perfection at Eureka January 18, 1898, but the charters were never granted either to Watertown,

Hot Springs or Eureka and those at Sioux Falls were forfeited in 1892 or 1894, they never having done any work. At the present time the total membership in the state in about eight hundred."

After the division of Dakota territory, North and South Dakota remained one jurisdiction, under the supervision of Rufus Eberly Fleming, thirty-third degree, inspector general, until October, 1899, when the supreme council divided the territory and made South Dakota a separate jurisdiction and elected Edward Teare Taubman, thirty-third degree, of Aberdeen, the inspector general for the state.

There are thirty-six chapters of the auxiliary Order of the Eastern Star in South Dakota. The grand chapter was organized at Watertown July 10, 1889, delegates from the chapters at Watertown, Flandreau, Webster, St. Lawrence, Aberdeen and Madison taking part in the organization. The grand matrons have been; 1889, May H. Monks; 1890, Florence M. Mudgett; 1891, L. Leslie McBride; 1892, Lurancy W. Norton; 1893, Mary Brown; 1894, Sarah J. Clark; 1895, Hettie Downie; 1896, Fannie R. Roddle; 1897, Jennette E. Herreid; 1898, Jennie E. Bradley; 1899, Jennie Shirk; 1900, Margaret Y. Hitchcock; 1901, Eudora Z. Pettigrew; 1902, Annie Marston; 1903, Eva G. Davison, Mrs. A. C. McAllister has been secretary from the organization. At the last report there were 2,439 members.

Magnificent temples for the Masonic bodies have been erected at Yankton, Aberdeen and Deadwood. The Masonic bodies meeting at Chamberlain own a very commodious and well-arranged temple.

There are in South Dakota two temples of the dependent order of Ancient Arabic Order of the Nobles of the Mystic Shrine, El Riad Temple, at Sioux Falls, organized May 25, 1888, and Naja Temple, at Deadwood, founded September 19, 1892. An application for a charter has been made at Aberdeen for the establishment of a temple there.

* Past Grandmaster SD

‡ Past Grandmaster of another state

TABLE OF CONTENTS

REV. ULYSSES GRANT LACEY

Ulysses G. LACEY, the able and popular pastor of the Presbyterian church of Miller, claims the fine old Buckeye state as the place of his nativity, having been born near the city of Columbus, Franklin County, Ohio, on the 27th of May, 1867, and being a son of George W. and Mary J. (Patterson) Lacey, the former of whom was born in the state of Ohio and the latter in Virginia. The father of the subject was a farmer by vocation, and both he and his wife live a retired life in Maitland, Missouri. When the subject was but a child his parents removed to Holt County, Missouri, in which state he was reared to maturity. After duly availing himself of the advantages of the public schools and after serving a five-years apprenticeship as teacher, he entered Highland University, in 1893, in northeastern Kansas. After two years of college work, he was recommended by Highland presbytery to the seminary. He had in the meanwhile determined to prepare himself for the work of the ministry, and his consecration to this noble calling has been of the most insistent and objectively prolific nature. In 1895 Mr. Lacey was matriculated in the Omaha Theological Seminary, a Presbyterian institution, and there he completed his ecclesiastical course of study and was graduated in 1898. His first charge was in South Dakota, his ordination to the ministry having been subsequent to his graduation by Central Dakota presbytery. Shortly after leaving the seminary in Omaha, he became a member of the presbytery of Central Dakota and accepted the pastoral charge of the church organizations in Wentworth, Coleman and Bethel, this state. In this connection he labored zealously and effectively for nearly five years, within which time, with the devoted co-operation of his people, he effected the erection of a church edifice in each of the villages mentioned, and none of these buildings represented an expenditure of less than fifteen hundred dollars. The membership was doubled in the churches in Wentworth and Bethel, while in Coleman the roll of members was augmented by three times the original number represented. During his earnest labors in this attractive but exacting field Mr. Lacey resided in the village of Wentworth, and there the church erected for his use a beautiful cottage parsonage. In September, 1902, Mr. Lacey resigned these pastoral charges to accept the call extended by the church in Miller, and his resignation was a cause of deep regret to his former parishioners, but they released him in order that he might continue his good work in a wider field. Since assuming the pastorate of the church in Miller he has succeeded in increasing its membership near one hundred percent., while all departments of the church work have been vitalized, the progress in both a spiritual and temporal sense being most gratifying. At the time when he came to Miller Mr. Lacey also had a call to the pastorate of a church in northeast Minnesota, at a salary larger than that offered by the church in Miller. Learning of this status of affairs, the society called a meeting and voluntarily agreed to offer the same compensation as that offered by the Minnesota church, while Mr. Lacey was also most earnestly and insistently urged to remain here, which he did. He is a man of rare pulpit ability, a forceful and logical speaker and one who is thoroughly fortified and grounded in the faith which he exemplifies in his daily walk and conversation as well as in his sacred ecclesiastical functions. He is untiring in his efforts, has unbounded zeal and enthusiasm and his personality is such as to win and to retain to him the high regard of all with whom he comes in contact. While a resident of Wentworth Mr. Lacey drove thirty miles each Sunday in order to hold services in each of the three places assigned to his charge, and in all other portions of his work he has shown the same self-abnegation and the same solicitude for the uplifting of his fellow men. In politics he gives his support to the party for which his father fought for four years and received an honorable discharge in 1865.

Fraternally he is a member of the Ancient and Accepted Order of Scottish Rite Masons. On the 23d of December, 1891, was solemnized the marriage of Mr. Lacey to Miss Minnie Noland, who was born and reared in Holt County, Missouri, and to them were born two children, Glenn D. and Helen F., born February 14, 1893, and May 23, 1896, respectively.

ORATOR HENRY LaCRAFT

O. H. LaCRAFT, the honored and popular postmaster of Clark, was born in Farmington, Washington county, Wisconsin, on the 13th of August, 1850, and is a son of John and Mary E. (Klice) LaCraft, both of whom were born and reared in Ashtabula County, Ohio, being representatives of pioneer families of the old Buckeye state and of French and Puritan lineage respectively. The maiden name of the maternal grandmother of the subject was Emily Kendall, and she was a direct descendant of the progenitors of that name who came to America in the Mayflower, while she was a niece of Amos Kendall, who was at one time postmaster general of the United States. The subject of this review secured his educational discipline in the public schools of Wisconsin, completing a course in the high school. From 1871 to 1873 he was engaged in farming in the vicinity of Scott, Sheboygan County, Wisconsin, in the meanwhile teaching school during the winter months. In 1883 he came to Clark, South Dakota, where he engaged in the general merchandise business, having been one of the first settlers in the town, and he continued to be successfully identified with his line of enterprise until 1891, since which time he has been connected with the executive affairs of the local post office, while he also gives his attention to his farming interests, having a well-improved ranch of three hundred and twenty acres ten miles southeast of his home city. In politics he is a stalwart advocate of the principles and policies of the Republican party, and he has served in nearly a consecutive way as justice of the peace since 1875, while he has been a member of the board of education since 1892 and its president for the past four years. He served as postmaster from 1893 to 1896, and was thereafter deputy, while later he was again appointed postmaster and is still incumbent of the office. He served as a member of the state senate in 1900 and is also a member of that body at the time of this writing, 1904.

He is identified with the Masonic fraternity, the Independent Order of Odd Fellows, the Knights of Pythias, the Ancient Order of United Workmen, the Degree of Honor, the Knights of the Maccabees and the: Modern Brotherhood of America. On the 16th of April, 1873, Mr. LaCraft was united in marriage to Miss Charlotte R. Haviland, who was born in Scott, Sheboygan comity, Wisconsin, on the 20th of July, 1852, and whose death occurred on the 17th of July, 1883. She was a daughter of Edgar and Susan Haviland, and of her two sons one is living — William C., who was born March 1, 1871, and who is now engaged in the lumber business in Clark, O. Merton, who was born on the 4th of January, 1878, died on the 21st of March, 1898. On the 25th of February, 1885, Mr. LaCraft consummated a second marriage, being then united to Miss Clara M. Smith, who was born on the 30th of July, 1864, being a daughter of Charles and Margaret Smith. Of the children of this union, we enter the following data: Walter S. was born August 12, 1886; Delmar B. was born September 19, 1889, and died on the 3d of December, 1892: Osnier H. was born May 16, 1893; Lynn K., October 3, 1898: and Irma R., September 17, 1897.

D. L. P. LAMB, Judge Lamb is now serving his third term as county judge in Charles Mix County, maintaining his residence in the town of Geddes, and merits consideration as one of the able members of the bar of the state. He is a native of the Wolverine state, having been born in Hillsdale County, Michigan, on the 15th of June, 1852, and being a son of John and Virginia (Newkirk) Lamb, of whose nine children all save one are still living. The father of the subject was born in Pennsylvania, where he was reared and educated, having grown np under the sturdy discipline of the farm. His parents came to the United States from Holland and located in the old Keystone state, where they passed the remainder of their lives. As a young man John Lamb removed to Ohio, settling near Lancaster, Fairfield County, where his marriage occurred, his wife having been a native of Westmoreland County. West Virginia, where her father was a wealthy manufacturer and slaveholder, while eventually she and several of her brothers became residents of Ohio. John Lamb was engaged in farming in Fairfield County, Ohio, until about 1850, when he removed to Michigan and settled in Hillsdale County, where he continued in agricultural pursuits, becoming one of the substantial farmers and honored citizens of that county, in which he passed the residue of his life, his death occurring in 1881, at which time he was seventy-two years of age, while his devoted wife passed away in 1903, at the age of eighty-four years, both having been consistent members of the German Reformed church, while he was a Democrat in his political adherency.

Judge Lamb was reared on the homestead farm and his early educational advantages were such as were afforded in the public schools of his native county. In 1875 he came west to the western part of Nebraska, where he spent about a year on the ranch of his uncle, returning home in 1876, while he continued to devote his attention to study as opportunity presented, having gained much through his well-directed application. In 1880 he came to Fort Randall, Dakota, where he secured employment in a trader's store and also secured contracts for supplying wood. In 1882 he came to Charles Mix county and entered timber and pre-emption claims, in Jackson township, proving up on the same in due time, and in the spring of 1885 he located in the village of Wheeler, this county, where he was soon afterward appointed deputy sheriff, serving one year in this capacity, and at the expiration of that period, in July, 1886, he was appointed to the office of clerk, of the district court by Judge Bartlett Tripp, retaining this incumbency until the admission of South Dakota to the Union, retiring from the office in November, 1890. In the meanwhile, he had continued his study of the law, and was admitted to the bar of the territory in June, 1889, since which time he has been engaged in the practice of his profession to a greater or less extent. The winter after his retirement from the office of clerk Judge Lamb engaged in the abstract business, in partnership with Frank Adams, whose interest in the enterprise he purchased in 1892, and he still conducts an abstract business in Wheeler. In 1894 he was elected to the office of state's attorney, on the Democratic ticket, serving two years, and in 1896 the financial policy of the Democracy failed to meet his approval and he transferred his allegiance to the Republican party, being an active worker in the presidential campaign of that year. In 1896 he was the candidate of his party for the office of county judge and was elected by a gratifying majority, but in the election of 1898, he was defeated for the same office, while in 1900 he was again elected to the bench and was chosen as his own successor in 1902, being now on his third term and having proved a most impartial and fair-minded member of the judiciary of the state. After the town of Geddes was platted and its settlement was instituted, in 1900, Judge Lamb removed from Wheeler to the new and enterprising town, with whose phenomenal progress and growth he has been thus identified from the start. He was appointed United States commissioner in January, 1902, and is still incumbent of this office, being one of the most prominent and influential citizens of the county in which he has so long maintained his home and in whose welfare, he has an abiding interest. While a resident of Wheeler he served as postmaster during both administrations of President Cleveland, while for several years he has held the office of notary public.

He and his wife are members of the Congregational church, and fraternally the Judge is identified with Geddes Lodge. No. 135, Free and Accepted Masons, and Mitchell Chapter, No. 16, Royal Arch Masons. On the 6th of May, 1890, Judge Lamb was united in marriage to Miss Caroline McLain, of this county, and they are the parents of four children, Charles E., Fred. Daniel L. P., Jr., and Iril C.

WEBB LAMBERT

The great northwest with its pulsing industrial activities and its limitless opportunities for agricultural, commercial and professional advancement is constantly drawing to it men of capability and ambition who find here scope for their activities and in so doing contribute to the upbuilding and prosperity of the state. In this connection Webb Lambert is well known. He is now filling the position of states attorney for Stanley County, having entered upon the duties of the office in January, 1913. He is a native of Randolph County, West Virginia, and a son of the Rev. James W. and Susan M. (Schoonover) Lambert, the former a Methodist minister connected with the Iowa conference. The family removed to the west during the boyhood of Webb Lambert and he had the advantage of a classical course in the Iowa Wesleyan College at Mount Pleasant from which he was graduated with the Bachelor of Arts degree. He determined upon the practice of law, however, as his life work and with that end in view entered the University of Nebraska, in which he won his LL. B. degree. In early manhood he took up the profession of teaching and proved a capable educator, imparting readily and clearly to others the knowledge that he had acquired, but he regarded teaching merely as an initial step to other professional labors and after preparing for the bar entered at once upon the active practice of law. He has made continuous progress in that connection, his ability being attested by the court records which indicate his successful handling of many important and involved legal problems. In January, 1913, he became states attorney of Stanley County, and he was reelected in November, 1914, for a second term.

Mr. Lambert was married January 10, 1911, to Mrs. Ola (Ackerman) Edwards, of Williamsburg, Iowa. He is a republican in politics and his military record covers service with the Fiftieth Iowa Volunteer Infantry at the time of the Spanish-American war. Fraternally he is connected with the Independent Order of Odd Fellows, with the Benevolent Protective Order of Elks and with the Masons and has many friends both within and without those organizations, to the teachings of which he is ever consistently loyal.

J. GEORGE LAMPERT

Having come to the Black Hills region in his childhood and passed the greater part of his life in this section, J. George Lampert, of Keystone, one of the rising and prominent young business men of that portion of the state, is thoroughly imbued with the spirit of the west and in full sympathy with the enterprise and aspirations of its people. He was born on March 13, 1871, at Oshkosh, Wisconsin, and is the son of Jacob and Lena (Kresse) Lampert, the former a native of Switzerland and the latter of Germany. In 1875 the family moved to Stevens Point, Wisconsin, and in 1881 came to South Dakota, arriving at Rapid City in June. Mr. Lampert was ten years old at that time, and had been without much opportunity for schooling in his previous residences, so he received his scholastic training mainly in the schools of that town, also taking a course of special instruction in the State School of Mines, located there. Thereafter he was employed in a merchandising establishment at Rapid City until 1892, when he moved to Hill City and secured work in mills for three years, coming to Keystone in the fall of 1893. He at once secured an engagement with the Holy Terror Mining Company to work in

its mill and in that and the Keystone mill was employed as an amalgamator until February 11, 1902. At that time, he bought stock in the Hayes Hopkins Supply Company, and took a position in the store as assistant secretary and treasurer of the company. He is an active and zealous member of the Masonic order, the Odd Fellows and the Knights of Pythias, in lodges at Keystone. On June 25, 1902, at Keystone, he was married to Miss Edna M. Clifford, a native of Nebraska.

THOMAS W. LANE

Thomas W. LANE, one of the popular citizens and prominent and successful farmers and stock growers of Jerauld County, is a native of the state of Illinois, having been born in the city of Freeport. Stephenson county, on the 16th of May, 1857, and being a son of Thomas and Bridget Lane, the former of whom was born in England and the latter in Ireland. His father was for many years engaged in the grocery business in Freeport, he being now deceased. The wife is now living in Chicago, being about eighty-five years old. The subject of this sketch attended the public Schools of his native city until he was thirteen years of age. He began to shift for himself when nine years old. working on a farm until thirteen years old, when he secured a position as brakeman on the Western Union Railroad, out of Freeport. He came to the territory of Dakota as conductor on a construction train on the Iowa & Dakota division of the Chicago, Milwaukee & St. Paul Railroad, in 1879, and was conductor on the first regular train with the coaches out of Mitchell, in May, 1880. He was identified with the line until the road reached Woonsocket, in May, 1883, and then conducted trains from Sanborn, Iowa, to Chamberlain, South Dakota, until 1886, when he went to Minneapolis, Minnesota, and followed the same occupation until 1892. Then, on account of his wife's ill health, he went to his present ranch which land he secured from the government. Here he has ever since maintained his home, while he has purchased additional land and now bas a finely improved ranch of twenty-six hundred acres, where he devotes his attention principally to the raising of high-grade livestock, conducting operations on an extensive scale and being one of the leading citizens of the county.

Mr. Lane is a stanch Republican in his political proclivities and has been an active worker in its cause, while in 1902 he served with marked acceptability as a member of the state senate from the nineteenth senatorial and sixteenth representative district; he has been incumbent of various township offices, in some one of which he has served ever since coming to the state.

He is a member of the Masonic fraternity, in which he passed the commandery degrees in 1881, being now identified with Crusade Commandery, No. 39, at Cherokee, Iowa, and to the Shrine at Sioux Falls, South Dakota, while he is also affiliated with the Modern Woodmen of America and the Order of Railway Conductors. He and his wife are members of the Baptist church. On the 14th of October, 1880, Mr. Lane was united in marriage, at La Crosse, Wisconsin, to Miss Lina A. Harrington, who was born in Cambria, Columbia County, that state, being a daughter of James A. and Charlotte J. Harrington. Mr. and Mrs. Lane have no children. The town of Lane, in this county, was named in honor of the subject, who lived here sixteen years. He owns a half interest in a section of and adjoining Grove Valley and a fourth interest in the quarter section on which the town is located.

WARREN D. LANE

W. D. LANE, one of the successful attorneys of the Roberts County bar and member of the well-known law firm of Barrington & Lane, Sisseton, was born near Cresco, Iowa, May 10, 1867, the son of Abraham and Sarah (Darling) Lane, natives of Pennsylvania and New York respectively. Abraham Lane was a farmer and public-spirited citizen, and for many years enjoyed distinctive prestige in his community as an enterprising man of affairs. Of his family of seven children only three are living, Rev. Louis L. Lane, pastor of the First Methodist Episcopal church of Sisseton; Theron W., an attorney practicing his profession at Bridgeport, Washington, and Warren D., whose name furnishes the caption of this review. Mr. Lane moved to Iowa in 1851 and died in that state in 1879, at the age of forty-eight; his widow subsequently came to South Dakota and settled on a claim east of Wilmot, later changing her residence to the town of Bristol, where he departed this life in the year 1897.

The early life of Warren D. Lane was spent in Iowa, and his youthful experiences were similar to those of the majority of lads reared in close touch with nature on the farm. After attending the public schools of Cresco until the age of sixteen, finishing the high-school course the meantime, he accompanied his mother to South Dakota, settling in 1883 on the claim in Roberts County, alluded to in the preceding paragraph, where he devoted his attention to agricultural pursuits, until engaging with his brother in the furniture business at Wilmot two years later. Actuated by a laudable ambition to increase his scholastic training, he and his brother disposed of their furniture business in 1892, and entered the Northwestern University at Evanston, Illinois, from which institution he was graduated four years later with the degree of Bachelor of Science. Subsequently he took the degree of Master of Science at the University of Minnesota, and in 1898 was graduated from the same institution with the degree of Bachelor of Laws, after which he began the practice of his profession at Sisseton, where in due time he forged to the front as ap able and energetic attorney, winning a conspicuous place among the leading members of the Roberts County bar. Since then, he has been admitted to practice in the higher courts of South Dakota and the supreme court of the United States, and by unflagging industry has built up a large and lucrative legal business.

While well-grounded in the principals of the law and familiar with every branch of his profession. Mr. Lane has won especial distinction as an advocate, being regarded as one of the strong, logical and eloquent public speakers of the west, in consequence of which his services are eagerly sought in important jury trials and in cases requiring clear exposition of technical points of law and profound discussion before courts. While a student of the University of Minnesota, he represented that institution in the inter-collegiate debate with the Iowa University and at the Northwestern University he was elected class orator and won the Lyman F. Gage prize for extemporaneous debate, and was elected to membership in the Phi Beta Kappa Society, besides gaining various other honors for public discourse and scholarship.

The same year in which he opened an office in Sisseton, Mr. Lane was nominated by the Republican party of Roberts County for state's attorney to which office he was triumphantly elected and the duties of which he discharged for two consecutive terms. He has always manifested a deep and abiding interest in political questions, and since coming west has been actively identified with the Republican party, being one of its leaders in this part of South Dakota, while as an organizer and campaigner his reputation is widely known throughout the state.

Primarily devoted to his law practice, and making every other consideration subordinate thereto, Mr. Lane is also interested in various business and industrial enterprises, being president of the Iowa and Dakota Land and Loan Company, vice-president of the Roberts County Abstract and Title Company, and a stockholder in the Citizens' National Bank, besides having large and valuable real-estate interests, owning a valuable homestead near Sisseton and considerable property within the corporation.

Mr. Lane belongs to several secret and benevolent organizations, notable among which are the Masonic fraternity, Knights of Pythias and Improved Order of Red Men, in all of which he has held important official station. Mr. Lane and Miss Maude Cross, of Wilmot, South Dakota, daughter of Edwin and Lyle (Smith) Cross, of Minnesota, were united in the bonds of wedlock on June 28, 1899, the marriage resulting in the birth of two children, Everett, who died September 5, 1900, at the age of five months, and Frances F., born August 25, 1902.

NICHOLAS P. LANG

Nicholas P. Lang, living at Belle Fourche, is filling the office of auditor of Butte County. He was born at Mankato, Minnesota, July 27, 1876, and is the youngest in a family of eight children whose parents were Mathias and Hannah (Hanner) Lang, both of whom were born at Treves, in the Rhine province of Germany. The father's birth occurred May 22, 1832, and the mother's natal year was 1838. She died January 14, 1877, when her son Nicholas was but a few months old, thus terminating a married life which was begun hi Germany in 1863. Mathias Lang had come to the new world with his father in 1847, settling in Milwaukee, Wisconsin, after which he engaged in farming in that state. In 1861, however, he returned to Germany and was there married in 1863. The following year he took his wife to Canada but after a year spent in that country came again to the United States, settling at Madison, Wisconsin, among its early residents, being one of the first men to drive a team into that city. There he remained until the spring of 1876, when he traveled overland to Mankato, Minnesota, by way of Prairie du Chien. He remained at Mankato until called to his final rest in 1904.

Nicholas P. Lang pursued his education in the schools of his native city and in a normal school, from which he was graduated with the class of 1897. When seventeen years of age he started out to make his own way in the world, working for others, and subsequently he resumed his interrupted education. Later he engaged in teaching school in Minnesota for a number of years, spending three years as a teacher at Walnut Grove, one year at Blakely, in Scott County and four years at Buhl, Minnesota. He afterward removed to Belle Fourche, where he took up the profession of teaching, being chosen superintendent of the city schools, in which capacity he continued for eight years. All through this period he made continuous progress in connection with his school work, introducing various improvements in methods of study and instruction. He studied closely the opportunities for advancing the interests of the schools and his work was attended with excellent results. He resigned, however, in 1914, when he homesteaded a mile south of Newell and turned his attention to farming, which pursuit he followed until elected to his present office. In addition to owning farm lands in this state he likewise has city property in Belle Fourche but he devotes his entire time to the duties of his position as county auditor of Butte County and is making an excellent record by reason of his capability and fidelity.

Mr. Lang has been married twice. On the 27th of November, 1900, he wedded Miss Jennie Mosier, who was born at Janesville, Minnesota, a daughter of William and Julia (Beers) Mosier. The father is still residing in Janesville but the mother passed away in 1900. The death of Mrs. Lang occurred at Buhl, Minnesota, December 14, 1905. She left two children: Robert, born January 23, 1902; and Dorothy, January 12, 1903. On the 23d of July, 1907, Mr. Lang was married to Miss Mabel De Vore, who was born near Chambersburg, Pennsylvania, her parents became residents of Duluth, Minnesota, but never removed to South Dakota. The father, who was an attorney by profession, has passed away but the mother still makes her home in Duluth. To Mr. and Mrs. Lang has been born a son, James De Vore, whose natal day was June 28, 1912.

Mr. Lang belongs to the Masonic fraternity and the Knights of Pythias lodge, of which he is a past chancellor. He is president of the Belle Fourche fire department and a member of the board of directors of the Commercial Club. In a word, he is interested in all that pertains to the welfare and progress of his community and his cooperation has been an important element in advancing its interests along lines working for the permanent as well as the present good of the town.

MORITZ ADELBERT LANGE

The history of South Dakota would be incomplete if mention of the activities and achievements of Moritz Adelbert Lange were omitted as he has for many years taken a prominent part in the political, business and educational affairs of the state, particularly in the Black Hills region. He served ably in the state senate, was for eight years assistant state superintendent of public schools and is now a leading merchant of Rapid City.

Mr. Lange was born in Chautauqua County, New York, January 28, 1855, and is a son of Moritz J. and Margaret (Dawley) Lange, natives of Saxony, Germany, and the state of New York respectively. The father emigrated to the United States in the early '50s, in company with Carl Schurz, Henry Siegel and many others, who found the then existing political conditions in the fatherland intolerable. Like most of his comrades Mr. Lange had seen military service in Germany and was one of many thousands of his fellow countrymen who enlisted in the Union army at the time of the Civil war. He served for three years and five months and won an officer's commission. In 1855, soon after arriving in this country, he settled in Iowa and after the close of the civil conflict returned to his farm in that state, where he continued to cultivate the fields and raise stock until he retired from active life. His death occurred at Decorah, Iowa, in 1911, when he had reached the advanced age of eighty-two years, and his demise was sincerely mourned by those who knew him. He and his wife had four children, of whom the subject of this review is the oldest.

Moritz A. Lange received his early education in the Decorah public schools and his later training in Stamford Seminary, Decorah Institute and the Oskaloosa Institute. He taught school for a time and on coming to Dakota territory in 1878, he located in McCook County, where he resumed teaching. Shortly after his arrival he was elected superintendent of the county schools and served acceptably in that position for twelve years. He also held the office of county surveyor. For many years his name was associated with the development of the public-school system of the state and for eight years he was assistant state superintendent of schools, in which capacity he did much to advance the interests of the rural schools. He it was who organized the first county course of study in the state and was one of the committees who drew up the courses of study in use at the present time. During his long residence in McCook County, he acquired and still retains an interest in a large amount of good farming land.

In 1907 Mr. Lange removed to Rapid City and in connection with his son Arthur M., engaged in the jewelry business, to which he still devotes a part of his time. The store of which he is part owner is one of the leading establishments of its kind in the western part of the state and its trade is constantly increasing. Mr. Lange of this review has never allowed his interest in educational matters to flag and is still a regular attendant at the state teachers institutes. While actively engaged in educational work he conducted forty state teacher's institutes and kept in close touch with the teachers throughout the state, thus securing a unity of action which resulted greatly to the good of the public school system. Few men have done more to advance the interests of the schools and few are more deeply interested in their welfare today. For some years he was a member of the Rapid City school board and drew upon his great fund of knowledge of educational affairs in solving the problems that arose in connection with the development of the city schools.

Mr. Lange is a stalwart republican and for many years has been prominent in party councils, being considered one of the republican leaders in his part of the state. He has held a number of positions of public trust and responsibility and in 1912 was honored by being chosen a member of the state Benate. In that capacity he manifested a keen understanding of public needs and a broad-minded spirit that placed the good of the state above personal or merely local considerations.

On the 2nd of April, 1879, Mr. Lange married Miss Eva May Puntney, a daughter of William and Sarah (Bogue) Puntney, of Decorah, Iowa. To them one child was born, a son, Arthur Moritz, who married Miss Mary Simpson and has two children, Harry Adelbert and Arthur.

Mr. Lange of this review is a Mason and a member of the Independent Order of Odd Fellows, being held in high esteem in those organizations. He usually attends the Congregational church and has been a lifelong worker in church affairs, singing in the choir for many years. He is fond of hunting and fishing but finds perhaps still greater pleasure in the study of outdoor life. He is one of the best authorities in the state upon the plants, birds and animals of South Dakota and, has written extensively upon those subjects. His life has been a busy one and his years are crowded with worthy achievements in many lines of human endeavor, but he values most highly the respect and esteem freely accorded him by those who have known him longest and most intimately.

A. J. LARSEN

A. J. Larsen, who has lived in South Dakota for thirty-four years, is now serving as sheriff of Beadle County, having been elected to that office in 1912. His birth occurred in Republic County, Kansas, in 1870, his parents being Amund and Hannah Larsen, who took up their abode in the Sunflower state in 1860. The father still resides there, but the mother died March 18, 1914.

A. J. Larsen attended the public schools in the acquirement of an education and in his boyhood made his way to South Dakota, arriving in Hudson, where one of his uncles resided, on the 29th of July, 1881. He did work all over the state for a number of years and in 1894 embarked in the stock business at Belle Fourche, carrying on his undertakings in that connection until 1912 or until elected to his present office. In 1898 he had come to Beadle County, locating on a stock farm in Hartland township, while subsequently he settled near Wolsey. As sheriff of the county, he is proving an efficient and valuable official, discharging his duties without fear or favor and conserving law and order in a manner that is contributing greatly to the peace and prosperity of the community.

On the 28th of November, 1898, Mr. Larsen was united in marriage to Miss Lydia G. Goodsell, a native of Lincoln County, South Dakota, by whom he has three children, two sons and one daughter, Carter H., Kenneth A., and Wava K., all at home. He gives his political allegiance to the republican party and is identified fraternally with the Benevolent Protective Order of Elks, the Masonic lodge, consistory and

Shrine, the Modern Woodmen of America and the Eagles. His life has been upright and honorable in its varied relations and the circle of his friends is almost coextensive with the circle of his acquaintances.

LOUIS LaPLANTE

LOUIS LA PLANTE.

A consistent and valuable prerogative is exercised by a compilation of this nature when it enters a resume of the life history of so honored and prominent a pioneer as he whose name initiates this paragraph. Whatever there is represented in the perilous and stirring-life which marked the life on the frontier is known to the subject by personal experience in the days long since past, and then, as in the later era of development and civic and industrial progress, he played well his part, proving himself a man of courage, self-reliance and utmost integrity of purpose.

Mr. LaPlante comes of sterling French lineage, as the name implies, and is a native of the province of Quebec, Canada, where he was born on the nth of November, 1835, being a son of Louis and Sophia (Morran) LaPlante, both of whom were likewise born and reared in that province, the paternal grandfather, who also bore the patronymic of Louis, having been a seafaring man. as was also the father of the subject. He who was later to become a pioneer of South Dakota received somewhat limited educational advantages in his boyhood, and early became dependent upon his own resources. At the early age of ten years, he became identified with the vocation followed by his father and grand-father, going to sea and continuing as a sailor before the mast for the ensuing seven years, within which time he visited the principal maritime ports in England, France, Germany, Wales and America. In 1852 he arrived in the city of New Orleans, Louisiana, where he secured employment in connection with steamboat navigation on the Mississippi river, being thus engaged for two years, after which he turned his attention to coal mining on the Ohio river. In a short time, he found himself afflicted with the all-prevailing ague, and consequently returned to St. Louis, and after a trip to New Orleans, came back to the former city and there shipped on the steamer "St. Mary," plying the upper Missouri river. On this little vessel he came up the river as far as the mouth of the White River, in what is now South Dakota, this being then the head of navigation, and thence the government supplies with which the boat was laden were freighted through with teams to old Fort Pierre, where Mr. LaPlante put in his first appearance on the nth of November, 1855, his twentieth birthday anniversary. He passed the winter at Camp Pierre, on the opposite side of the river. Major Galpin being in charge of the camp, and in the following spring, in company with seven other men, started down the river with supplies, the same being transported with mule-teams. The party became disaffected because the supply train had been placed in charge of an unpopular man. instead of Charles Picotte, who had been the choice of the men and they accordingly left the supply train at the mouth of White River, their principal objection to service in the connection being that they were reluctant to work under military rules and supervision. The eight men took a small supply of necessary provisions and made their way back to Fort Pierre on foot, where they were taken prisoners and court-martialed, all being ordered out of the country. On their way up the river, they found a soldier who had deserted from Fort Pierre with two others. The three deserters had lost their way and two of them died from lack of food and from exposure, while the survivor was found in a fearfully demented condition, having entirely eaten the body of one of his companions, and partially consumed the other. He was taken back to the fort and placed in charge of the authorities, and in the following summer was sent down the river to St. Louis. When ordered to leave the country each of the eight men agreed to do so with the exception of a half-breed Indian, who told Colonel Harney, commanding the post, that he had a natural right to the country and would remain. He brought into play a knife, with which he attempted an attack on the colonel, but was disarmed. He was permitted to remain, this provision being a part of the treaty made by the Indians with Colonel (later General) Harney, in 1856. Seven of the men then proceeded down the river, but the adventurous spirit of Mr. LaPlante led him to escape surveillance and make his way up the river to Fort Clark, where he entered the employ of the American Fur Company, with which he remained engaged until it disposed of its business about 1859. He then became an employe of the company's successors, the firm of Frost, Tudd & Atkins, and was in their service until 1861, when Mr. LaPlante engaged in trapping on his own account. In the summer of 1863, he entered the employ of the government at Fort Randall, which was then in command of General Cook, who had relieved General Sully, and passed the summer in carrying dispatches between that post and Fort Sully. In the summer of 1864, he was engaged in scouting duty for General Sully, having become by this time familiar with the country and with the habits and maneuvers of the crafty Indians, while his daring and courage led him to risk the many dangers involved in the service in which he was engaged. He followed scouting during that summer and then engaged in business on his own account, trading with the Indians and raising horses and cattle. His ranch was located in Bon Homme County and there he continued to reside until 1875, when he removed to Fort Pierre, where he established his home, while he has ever since been engaged in stock raising, his ranch being located on the Cheyenne river, sixty-five miles west of Fort Pierre, and comprising one thousand eight hundred acres, in Stanley County, while he also uses the open range and conducts his operations on an extensive scale. When the Black Hills district was opened to settlement he engaged in freighting between Fort Pierre and Deadwood, in which enterprise he successfully continued until the year 1883. He gives special attention to the raising of Hereford and shorthorn cattle and Percheron and French coach horses. Mr. LaPlante is a man of broad and varied experience and strong mentality, well informed and genial and courteous in his relations with his fellow men. Though he has nearly attained the age of three score years and ten he enjoys perfect physical health and is a worthy type of the sturdy and valorous frontiersmen who aided in ushering in the era of civilization and progress, while his integrity has ever commanded to him the respect and confidence of those with whom he has come in contact. He is a pioneer of pioneers, and it is most consonant that he be accorded marked precedence in this publication. His elder sons, two of whom are individually mentioned on other pages of this work, are also numbered among the progressive and successful stock growers of the state, being likewise located on a reservation, while all of his children have been accorded excellent educational advantages and have honored the name which they bear and the state in which their entire lives have been passed.

The two eldest sons have attained the thirty-second degree in Scottish Rite Masonry, and the subject himself is a Royal Arch Mason, while he is also affiliated with the Independent Order of Odd Fellows. He is a stanch Democrat in politics, and upon the organization of Stanley County was elected a member of its first board of commissioners, serving one term, while for two years he was a member of the village council of Fort Pierre. In March, 1860, Mr. LaPlante was united in marriage to Miss Julia Abbott, who was born and reared in Fort George, South Dakota, being a daughter of Mr. Abbott, of the firm of Abbott & Cotton, who were engaged in the fur business in this section in the early days, having their headquarters in the city of New York, while their trading post was at the mouth of the Yellow Medicine River, in Pratt County, South Dakota. Mr. and Mrs. LaPlante have six sons, namely: Frederick, George. Alexander, Charles, Louis, Jr., and Ovila.

DUDLEY WILLIAM LATTIMER

Only a comparatively few years ago, save perhaps in the southeastern part, South Dakota was a great prairie district, awaiting the awakening touch of man, its lands being then unclaimed and uncultivated. The American public, however, was aroused to an understanding of the fact that within the borders of what was then known as Dakota territory there were great opportunities and here and there towns and villages sprang up, each the center of growing business activities, ready to meet the demands of the farming population that, too, was growing rapidly in its numerical strength. In the town of Thomas, Hamlin County, D. W. Lattimer is now conducting a general mercantile establishment as the senior partner of the firm of Lattimer & Meadows and is winning success in this undertaking. He was born in Fond du Lac, Wisconsin, on the 4th of December, 1872, and is a son of Isaac J. and Jennie (Hopkins) Lattimer. The father devoted his life to bridge building, and now resides at Delton, Wisconsin. The mother, however, is deceased.

In the public schools of his native state D. W. Lattimer pursued his education and when his text-books were put aside turned his attention to the occupation of farming, which he followed in that state until he reached his twenty-fourth year. Like others, he heard of the opportunities of the growing west and in 1896 came to South Dakota. He settled first in Hamlin County, where he purchased a quarter section of land on section 2, Hayti township. He had very little capital, but he made arrangements for the payments and with characteristic energy began to develop the place, which he continued to farm for twelve years, adding many improvements thereto. At the end of that time, he sold the farm for double the original purchase price, or rather exchanged it for that value for his present business. He was successful as an agriculturist and is making equally creditable progress as a merchant. The store is well appointed, a good line of goods is carried and the business methods are thoroughly reliable.

On the 5th of November, 1898, Mr. Lattimer was united in marriage to Mrs. Cinderella Meadows, widow of Joseph F. Meadows, and they have a son, George, now four years of age. Mr. Lattimer exercises his right of franchise in support of the men and measures of the republican party and at the present writing is serving as assessor of his township. On one occasion he was his party's candidate for the office of sheriff, but was defeated. In lodge circles he is well known. He belongs to Sioux Valley Lodge, A. F. & A. M., of Castlewood: to Watertown Camp, No. 145, I. O. O. F., of which he is a past grand master; and to the United Workmen lodge, of which he is a past master. He is a believer in the teachings of the Methodist church and his faith is a guiding factor in his life, making him a man honorable in every relation and at all times trustworthy and reliable. He has never been afraid to venture where favoring opportunity has led the way, and in his business affairs he has readily discriminated between the essential and the nonessential. He has made rapid advancement since coming to South Dakota and may well be termed one of the builders of this empire of the northwest.

George W. LATTIN, one of the leading lawyers and jurists of Kingsbury County, claims the old Empire state of the Union as the place of his nativity, having been born in Dutchess County, New York, on the 23d of April, 1858, and being a scion of old and honored families of that state. The original American ancestors in both the paternal and maternal lines came from England to the new world in the colonial epoch of our national history, locating in New England, from which cradle of history representatives of both have gone forth to diverse sections of the Union. The subject is a son of E. C. and Ruth (Mosher) Lattin, both of whom were likewise born and reared in Dutchess County. The father of the subject was a miller by vocation and his death occurred, in Nassau, New York, in 1865. Judge Lattin was a lad of seven years at the time of his father's death, and in 1869 he accompanied his widowed mother on her removal to DeKalb County, Illinois, where his mother purchased land, continuing to reside on this homestead farm until her children had been reared to maturity. In 1882 she removed to Franklin, Nebraska, where her death occurred in the spring of 1889. Of her four children we enter the following record: Stephen is a resident of Glyndon, Minnesota, where he is engaged in business; George W. is the subject of this review; Alma is the wife of Samuel Chriswell, of Charleston, Oklahoma; and Ella is the wife of William Mercer, of Aurora, Illinois.

George W. Lattin received his rudimentary education in the public schools of Poughkeepsie, New York, and was eleven years of age at the time of his mother's removal to Illinois, where he was reared to maturity on the homestead farm. In the meanwhile, he completed the curriculum of the public schools, and in 1876 he entered the Classical Seminary at East Pawpaw, Illinois, where he was graduated as a member of the class of 1880, receiving the degree of Bachelor of Science. In 1880 he was matriculated in the law department of the Northwestern University, in Chicago, where he completed the prescribed course and was graduated as a member of the class of 1882, William J. Bryan having been a member of the junior class at the time of the subject's graduation. Mr. Lattin secured the highest honors in his class, and upon his examination prior to graduation made the mark of one hundred percent.

In the spring of 1882 Judge Lattin came to Kingsbury County, South Dakota, and took up a claim near the present village of Iroquois, and thereafter he lived upon his farm for eight years, making gool improvements and bringing a goodly portion under a high state of cultivation. In 1890 he was elected judge of the county court, whereupon he took up his residence in DeSmet, where he has since made his home. He served on the bench until 1898, and made a most enviable record, very few of his decisions meeting with reversal in the higher courts. In 1892 he purchased the Kingsbury County Independent, a weekly paper, and retained entire control of the same until 1898, when he disposed of his interests in the enterprise. In April of that year, he was appointed captain of Company E, First South Dakota Volunteer Infantry, and preliminary to entering active service with his command he resigned his position on the bench. He accompanied his regiment to the Philippines, where he remained in command of his company during the entire term of service, participating in all the engagements in which his regiment was involved, and returning to his home in October, 1899, having received his honorable discharge on the 5th of October of that year. Since his return Judge Lattin has been actively engaged in the practice of law in DeSmet, while he makes his home on his fine farm, of one hundred and sixty acres, which lies contiguous to the town. He has attained a high degree of success in temporal affairs, and the same stands as the result of his own efforts, for through his own exertions he made his way through college, having been practically dependent upon his own resources from the age of sixteen years. In politics he was formerly arrayed with the Republican party, lint upon the organization of the Populist party he identified himself with the same, and has since been a stanch advocate of its principles.

Fraternally he holds membership in DeSmet Lodge, No. 55, Ancient Free and Accepted Masons, and in DeSmet Lodge, No. 25, Ancient Order of United Workmen. On the nth of July, 1881, Judge Lattin was united in marriage to Miss Sarah van Patten, of Lee County, Illinois, in which state she was born and reared, being a daughter of C. F. Van Patten, who was one of the pioneers of Lee County. To Judge and Mrs. Lattin have been born eight children, namely: Mary, who is a successful teacher, is a member of the class of 1903 in the State Normal School, at Madison; William, who was graduated in the DeSmet high school, is now engaged in teaching; and Herbert, Lois, Homer, Ralph, Mark and Sidney are all at the parental home.

JOHN WESLEY LAUGHLIN

John Wesley Laughlin, who retired from the office of deputy United States marshal of South Dakota in May, 1914, has since devoted his attention to his real-estate business and personal investments, including farm property. He lives in Pierre and is a man of wide acquaintance in the state, enjoying the respect and goodwill of all who know him. He was born in Mount Pulaski, Illinois, January 2, 1860, and is a representative of one of the old American families and one of the fourteenth generation of Laughlin's in a direct line. Those of the name have for several generations figured in the wars of the nation. James Laughlin, the great-grandfather of John Wesley Laughlin, was one of the heroes of the Revolutionary war. The parents of our subject are Robert H. and Susan (Jackson) Laughlin, still residents of Mount Pulaski, Illinois. The latter, a native of Logan County, Illinois, is a daughter of James Jackson, a cousin of Andrew Jackson. Robert H. Laughlin was the first to enlist in Mount Pulaski, Illinois, when Abraham Lincoln issued a call for volunteers for service in the Civil war. At the close of his first enlistment, he was honorably discharged, but when the second call for troops was issued, he immediately responded and remained in the service until the close of hostilities. When the Union men were ordered from Bolivar, Tennessee, to Holly Springs with one hundred rounds of ammunition the flag bearer was sick. After several calls for a volunteer to carry the flag Mr. Laughlin responded and also at Vicksburg, he again carried the colors.

His son, John Wesley Laughlin, was reared upon the home farm in Illinois, early becoming familiar with the best methods of tilling the soil and caring for the crops. He attended the public schools but when not busy with his textbooks worked in the fields. He came to South Dakota in March, 1883, to enjoy the agricultural opportunities offered in this state. He preempted a claim in Byron township, Hughes County, where he spent seven years, bringing much of his land under cultivation. He afterward removed to Blunt, where he engaged in raising and training horses, owning some of the best trotting stock to be found in this part of the country, but the alarm of war again sounded and with the patriotic spirit of his forebears he offered his service for active duty with Grigsby's Rough Riders in the Spanish-American war and was commissioned first lieutenant, rendering uncomplaining, intelligent and loyal service at a time when sickness, hardships and dull routine tested the soldiers' mettle. He went to the front as a member of Troop E, Third United States Volunteer Cavalry, being mustered in on the 15th of May, 1898. Three days later he was promoted to the rank of first lieutenant and was mustered out with that command on the 8th of September following. He was an efficient officer, maintaining strict discipline, yet was very popular with the boys. The regiment was known as Grigsby's Rough Riders, having as its members many farmers and stockmen of South Dakota. The organizer of the regiment was Colonel Melvin Grigsby, who at that time was attorney general of the state.

After being mustered out Mr. Laughlin returned to his home at Blunt, South Dakota, and in 1900 he was elected to the office of sheriff of Hughes County. There was a hot contest at both the primary and general elections, Mr. Laughlin being the winning man. After serving from 1901 until January, 1905, he retired, but in November, 1908, was again elected and in November, 1910, was reelected, serving for four years. The Free Press said: "He is a heavy taxpayer and as an officer and civilian his conduct has always been above reproach and his word is ace high even with his political enemies; he has none other." The capability and worth which he displayed as sheriff of Hughes County led to his appointment to the position of deputy United States marshal in 1901 and he filled that position most acceptably for thirteen years, serving until May, 1914, since which time he has devoted his attention to his real-estate business and personal investments, including farming property. During the past six years Mr. Laughlin has also been president of the South Dakota Sheriffs Association.

Fraternally Mr. Laughlin is a Mason, Knight of Pythias, an Odd Fellow, a United Workman and one of the Sons of Veterans. Socially he is popular, winning friends wherever he goes. In politics he is a stalwart republican, doing everything in his power to advance the interests of his party. In politics, as in business, he has always believed in constructive rather than in destructive measures and he seeks to annihilate anything that may be wrong by introducing that which is acknowledged to be for the public good. For three decades he has been a resident of South Dakota and throughout the entire period has labored earnestly and persistently for the welfare and progress of the community and of the state and he is justly accounted one of the popular and highly respected residents of the capital city.

On the 7th of April, 1887, Mr. Laughlin was united in marriage to Miss Lizzie Dickey, a native of Greensburg, Indiana. Their son, Robert Virgil, born February 10, 1892, was graduated from the University of South Dakota in 1914 and is now a practicing attorney of Pierre.

CHARLES J. LAVERY, M. D.

Pronounced ability has won distinction for Dr. Charles J. Lavery, for twenty-two and one-half years engaged in the active practice of medicine and surgery in Fort Pierre and now a representative of the profession in Aberdeen, South Dakota. His life, however, has been so varied in its activities, so commendable in purpose and so fruitful in results that to mention him merely as a physician and surgeon would be giving a very one-sided view of a life that has reached out in usefulness along many lines, touching the general interests of society to its material, intellectual, political and moral benefit. Dr. Lavery was born February 5, 1867, in Clinton, Clinton County, New York. His father, John Lavery, was a native of County Armagh, Ireland, but the major portion of his life was spent on this side of the Atlantic and his loyalty to his adopted country was manifest in four and one-half years' service as a member of Company A, Ninety-sixth New York Regiment, in the Civil war. He married Jane Coulter, a native of County Mayo, Ireland, and her influence has ever been the guiding spirit and the inspiration in the life of her son Charles.

After attending the country schools Dr. Lavery became a student in the high school at Cliurubusco, New York, and, having determined upon the practice of medicine as a life work, later entered the medical college at Columbus, Ohio, while subsequently he became a student in the College of Physicians and Surgeons of Chicago, Illinois. He was licensed to practice in South Dakota, at Pierre, January 21, 1891, and has since devoted his life to his profession with excellent results. Locating at Fort Pierre, he entered upon active practice and there remained for more than two decades. His ability soon won recognition and his practice steadily grew in volume and in importance.

For nearly twenty-three years he was superintendent of the Stanley County board of health and that he enjoyed the confidence and goodwill of his brethren of the medical fraternity is indicated in the fact that

15

he was elected and served for several years as secretary treasurer of the Fourth District Medical Society of the state. He was also for three years a member of the board of councilors of the State Medical Association and was appointed a delegate to the Pan American Medical Congress in 1903. He was appointed a delegate to the Anti-Tuberculosis Congress at Atlanta, Georgia, in 1895 and appointed delegate to a like congress in Atlantic City in 1907. On the 6th of July, 1907, he received appointment as United States examining surgeon in connection with the bureau of pensions and he has done much important hospital work. He acted as assistant chief of staff and visiting physician and surgeon to St. Mary's Hospital at Pierre for years; was surgeon in chief and consulting physician to the Fort Pierre Hospital when that institution was open and is a member of the American Medical Association and the American Health League. There is no profession so little commercialized as that of the practice of medicine. Physicians and surgeons everywhere are not only engaged in healing disease but are as strenuously engaged in disseminating knowledge that will prevent it. This may seem to react against themselves in their efforts to earn a livelihood through medical and surgical practice, but underneath all personal desire for gain on the part of a conscientious physician is the broad humanitarian spirit that ranks first the welfare of his fellowmen. This spirit is lacking in not the least degree in Dr. Lavery, who is in all things progressive and anxious to combine the spirit of disinterested service with the practice of medicine and surgery.

He is widely recognized, as well, as a most capable, energetic, enterprising and resourceful business man and for years was president of the Fort Pierre Business Men's League. He was a director and the vice president of the Fort Pierre National Bank from its organization until 1913, was a director and the vice president of the Great Western Telephone Company and a director and secretary of the Stanley County Creamery Association. In business matters his judgment is sound and his enterprise unfaltering and he thus contributes to public prosperity as well as to individual success. Along many other lines his spirit of devotion to the general welfare has been manifest. He represented the state of South Dakota at the conservation congress in Sacramento, California, in September, 1907, and he was appointed by the governor of South Dakota to represent the state at the international conservation congress in Washington, D. C., February 18, 1909.

He was a member of the Missouri River Navigation Congress in 1910 and was appointed by Governor Robert S. Vessey a delegate to the National Rivers and Harbors Congress at Washington, D. C., December 7, 8 and 9, 1910. It will thus be seen that he is studying the great vital problems before the country and is keeping in touch with the best thinking men of the age.

Aside from all this Dr. Lavery is a member of the Episcopal church and served as warden of his church while in Fort Pierre and is now a member of the vestry of St. Mark's church at Aberdeen. In politics he has been a republican but is now somewhat independent with progressive tendencies and he is a believer in and advocate of the single tax.

On the 20th of February, 1895, Dr. Lavery was united in marriage to Miss Matilda Isabella Widmeyer, a sister of Dr. J. P. Widmeyer of Rolla, North Dakota, and Mrs. Robert Rogers of Ottawa, Canada. For his second wife Dr. Lavery chose Margaret Ethel Whitney, a daughter of Dr. J. J. Whitney of Fort Pierre, South Dakota, whom he wedded October 14, 1897. Mrs. Lavery's mother, Mrs. J. J. Whitney, and her two sisters, Miss Mary L. Whitney and Mrs. J. A. McKillip, reside in Fort Pierre. Mrs. Lavery pursued her musical education in the Philadelphia Conservatory of Music and is very proficient in that art. By the first marriage there was a son, Ruble St. Elmo, born March 22, 1896, and by the second marriage a daughter, Margaret Anna, born January 14, 1904.

Dr. Lavery removed from Fort Pierre to Aberdeen, September 1, 1913, and a short time before his departure, a reception was tendered him by about fifty of his fellow townsmen who gathered in the

Masonic Hall and gave utterance to their feeling of regret over his departure and spoke of the high esteem in which he was uniformly held in Fort Pierre. On that occasion he was also presented with a Masonic watch charm. The local paper said: "Dr. Charles J. Lavery has for many years been one of the busiest and most self-sacrificing men of the state. He is not merely an eminent physician and successful surgeon, for, while due credit and honor are given him along these lines, he is also a broad-gauged man of affairs who has spent years in evolving plans for his state and the northwest which will mean much to future generations. It would be selfishness indeed to express regret that the sphere of usefulness for this splendid citizen is about to broaden, not only in his profession but along so many other lines for which his untiring efforts through the busy years have developed his capabilities, and the Fairplay editor, having enjoyed close association with Dr. Lavery for nearly thirteen years, and with a full realization of the deep personal loss which this move means, wishes him the success in his new field which he so richly deserves, feeling sure that the people of Aberdeen will recognize his ability and splendid qualities and that a place of prominence awaits him."

It was soon after this that Dr. Lavery removed to Aberdeen, where he is now located and there, he is meeting with the success which his talents and his ambition merit. He is widely known in fraternal as well as professional and business circles. He became one of the charter members of Hiram Lodge, No. 123, A. F. & A. M., of Fort Pierre, of which he was the first treasurer and again filled that office in 1901. He was likewise its worshipful master for two years and is now senior grand steward in the Grand Lodge of South Dakota. He is also a member of Aberdeen Chapter, No. 14, R. A. M.; Damascus Commandery, No. 10, K. T., at Aberdeen; South Dakota Consistory, No. 4, S. P. R. S., of Aberdeen, South Dakota; and Yelduz Temple of the Mystic Shrine at Aberdeen, South Dakota. He is likewise identified with Aberdeen Lodge, No. 49, I. O. O. F., and Aberdeen Encampment, No. 22; Lodge No. 30, A. O. U. W.; Camp No. 5215, M. W. A.; Aberdeen Lodge, No. 55, K. P.; and Aberdeen Lodge, No. 1046, B. P. O. E. He also belongs to Aberdeen Lodge, No. 590, Loyal Order of Moose, of which he is lodge physician and surgeon.

The specific and distinctive office of biography is not to give voice to a man's modest estimate of himself and his accomplishments, but rather to leave the perpetual record establishing his position by the consensus of opinion on the part of his fellowmen. Judged by this standard, Dr. Lavery is one of the eminent citizens of the state. His life has been so varied in its activities and so effective in its results as to leave a deep impress upon the history of the state, while the regard in which he is uniformly held attests his personal popularity and the attractiveness of his most marked characteristics.

THOMAS JAMES LAW

Thomas J. LAW, the able and popular young state's attorney of Deuel County, was born in the city of Chicago, Illinois, on the 17th of January, 1870, and is a son of Thomas J. and Josephine (Stanley) Law, the former of whom was born in the dominion of Canada and the latter in Wisconsin. The paternal grandfather of the subject came from the north of Ireland to America and settled in the province of Ontario, Canada, where he married, his wife being a native of that section. The maternal grandfather was a native of New York and a descendant of stanch old New England stock, while his wife was of German extraction and was likewise born in the old Empire state. When the subject was a child of two years his parents removed to Lafayette County, Wisconsin, where his father engaged in the practice of law, and the latter and his wife now reside in Shullsburg, Wisconsin. After completing the curriculum of the high school in Shullsburg, Lafayette County, Wisconsin, in which he was graduated as a member of the class of 1887. Mr. Shaw entered the law department of the University of Wisconsin, at Madison, where he completed the prescribed course and was graduated on the 1st of July, 1891, with the degree of Bachelor of Laws, while he was also admitted to the bar of the state. On the 28th of the following October he located at Clear Lake, the judicial center of Deuel County, South Dakota, where he has since been engaged in the practice of his profession and where he has gained prestige as an able trial lawyer and counselor, while he has proved a most efficient and discriminating public prosecutor. He is a stanch advocate of the principles and policies of the Republican party and has been a zealous worker in its local ranks. In 1894 he was elected state's attorney of Deuel County and was chosen as his own successor in 1896. while in 1900 he was again elected to this office, as was he also in 1902, his second term expiring January 1, 1905.

In 1891 Mr. Law was raised to the sublime degree of Master Mason in Amicitia Lodge, No. 25, Ancient Free and Accepted Masons, at Shullsburg, Wisconsin, and he was one of the charter members of Phoenix Lodge, No. 129, of Clear Lake, with which he is still affiliated. He is also a charter member of Clear Lake Camp, No. 1981, Modern Woodmen of America, and of Watertown Lodge, No. 838, Benevolent and Protective Order of Elks, at Watertown, this state. On the 10th of October, 1894, Mr. Law was united in marriage to Miss Ethel M. Roberts, who was born at Emsdale, province of Ontario, Canada, on the 8th of September, 1877, being a daughter of William and Elizabeth Roberts, both of whom are now deceased. Mr. and Mrs. Law have two children, Elsie M. and Stanlev R.

J. C. LAWVER, M. D.

J. C. LAWVER, established in the successful practice of his profession in the town of Spencer, McCook County, was born in Bellville, Washington County, Pennsylvania, on the 2d of January, 1862, a son of Martin and Margaret (Moss) Lawver, of whose eight children all are living save one. Martin Lawver was born in Brownsville, Fayette County, Pennsylvania, as was also his father, while the grandfather was a native of Germany, whence he came to America in an early day, being numbered among the sterling pioneers of the old Keystone state. In the maternal line the Doctor traces his ancestry back to Scotch-Irish stock. His mother died in 1882, and his father now resides in Spencer, this state, having come to South Dakota about 1883 and purchasing land in McCook County, where he was actively engaged in agricultural pursuits until 1902, when he removed to Spencer, where he has since lived retired.

Dr. Lawver may be said to have inherited a certain predilection for the medical profession, since on the maternal side of the family there have been a number of able physicians, in the various generations. His uncle, Jolin C. Moss, was the inventor of the process of photo-engraving, in which connection his name became known throughout the civilized world, while several others of the Moss family attained distinction as lawyers and educators. Dr. Lawver secured his early education in the public schools and supplemented this by a course of study in Waynesburg College, at Waynesburg, Pennsylvania. At the early age of fourteen years, he purchased medical books and began to devote his attention to careful study of the same, having determined to fit himself for the medical profession. In 1882 he went to New York city to complete his medical studies. In the fall of 1884, he entered the Bellevue Hospital Medical College, in New York City, where he continued his studies for the ensuing three years, being graduated with the degree of Doctor of Medicine. He then began the practice of his profession at Granville, West Virginia, where he remained until the fall of 1891 when he was matriculated in the Baltimore Medical College, in the city of Baltimore, where he was graduated in the spring of 1892, having thus secured the very best of preliminary training for his exacting and responsible profession. After his graduation the Doctor continued in practice at Granville for a short time, and in the fall of the same year he came to South Dakota in search of an eligible location. In February, 1893, he established himself in practice in Spencer, where his skill, devotion and personal courtesy have been the factors which have enabled him to build up a large and representative practice. In addition to his superior medical education which fitted him for active duties, since he commenced to practice twelve years ago, he has been a liberal patron and student of most of the leading medical books and periodical publications in this country and abroad, by means of which he has successfully kept posted on the latest discoveries for the cure of human afflictions and the most skillful methods of treating them. Stacks of medical magazines and a magnificent library of the best medical works, representing a cost of hundreds of dollars, attest in the most emphatic term to the educational qualifications of Dr. Lawver. Among the office equipment are nearly all the latest devices, implements and medical appliances used in testing the condition of the human system and for treating chronic diseases in the most scientific way. Very few country physicians have such a fine display of instruments and appliances as has Dr. Lawver, of Spencer, and this fact as well as the further fact that he possesses superior skill in handling them, is becoming widely known throughout this section of the country. During the past year the Doctor has erected a fine two-story brick building, entirely adapted to his own use, and it is his intention to ultimately utilize this building as a hospital in which he can treat cases of every description from different parts of the country, and give them hospital treatment at home equal to or better than what they now go to larger cities to obtain. He is a member of the State Medical Society and at all times keeps in touch with the advances made in both branches of his profession.

In politics he renders allegiance to the Republican party, and fraternally is identified with the Free and Accepted Masons and the Modern Woodmen of America. On the 2d of February, 1903, Dr. Lawver was married to Miss Margaret Theis, of Farmer, this state, she being a daughter of Jacob Theis and a native of the state of South Dakota.

JAMES MARSHALL LAWSON

James M. LAWSON, who is engaged in the practice of the legal profession in the city of Aberdeen, is a native of the Old Dominion state, having been born in Virginia, on the 5th of January, 1863, his father. Rev. Orr Lawson. D. D., having been at that time a missionary in that section, in the interests of the Presbyterian church, and was compelled to leave the south a few weeks after the birth of the subject by reason of the animosity of the southern people, the war of the Rebellion being then in progress. The father of the subject was born in western Pennsylvania, as was also his wife, whose maiden name was Mary E. Marshall, and to the old Keystone state they returned upon leaving Virginia. Rev. Orr Lawson has long been a distinguished clergyman of the Presbyterian church and is now residing in Iowa, having attained the venerable age of seventy-five years, while his noble and devoted wife was summoned into eternal rest on the 17th of February, 1903, at the age of sixty-six years. Of their four children, two are yet living. The original progenitors of the Lawson and Marshall families in America came from the north of Ireland and the north of England in the colonial days, and both settled in western Pennsylvania, while representatives of the families did valiant service in the cause of independence during the war of the Revolution.

James M. Lawson passed his boyhood days in Pennsylvania, where he secured his early educational discipline in the public schools. At the age of twenty years, he was matriculated in Princeton University, where he was graduated as a member of the class of 1884, receiving the degree of Bachelor of Arts. He then entered the law department of the University of Michigan, at Ann Arbor, where he was graduated in 1886. Shortly after his graduation in law he came to Aberdeen, South Dakota, where he exposed his professional "shingle" in July, 1886, and made ready for the practice of law. He was soon established in a satisfactory business, while he is now one of the leading members of the bar of this section, retaining a representative clientage, and having had to do with much important litigation in the state federal courts, his prestige and precedence feeing the diametrical result of the proper application of his energies and abilities. He is financially interested in farming, and in mining developments in the Black Hills, and his success in temporal affairs has been of no equivocal order. In 1884-5 Mr. Lawson was a private in the Washington Artillery of Pottsville, Pennsylvania, the same being at the time a portion of the Fourth Regiment of the Pennsylvania State Guard. This company has had a long and distinguished history, having had an uninterrupted military existence since the war of 1812.

It was in General Scott's army of occupation in the city of Mexico in 1847, and was one of the first five companies to volunteer for service in the Civil war under President Lincoln's first call, later receiving the thanks of congress for its prompt response to this exigent call. These five companies were in the city of Washington twenty-four hours in advance of all other troops. They passed through the city of Baltimore the day before the Sixth Massachusetts arrived there, and one of their men was seriously injured in a conflict with a mob of southern sympathizers, this being the first blood shed incidental to the great internecine conflict which followed. All five companies were from Pennsylvania, and served from Bull Run to Appomattox. The Washington Artillery was also with General Miles in Porto Rico during the late Spanish American war.

Mr. Lawson has ever given an uncompromising allegiance to the Republican party, and he is one of its leaders in the state. In 1893 he was speaker of the house of representatives, during the third general assembly of the new commonwealth, and since 1899 has served continuously as the representative of the thirty third senatorial district in the state senate, in which he has been an influential and valued worker, having been chairman of the judiciary committee during the sessions of 1899 and 1903, and chairman of the apportionment committee in 1901, while he has also held membership in other important circumstances of the senate. In 1899 he introduced and urged forward to enactment the bill establishing the Northern Normal and Industrial School at Aberdeen, and he has been consistently called, the father of this excellent and valuable institution. In 1893 while a member of the house, he introduced the bill providing for the state geological survey.

Senator Lawson's religious faith is that of the Presbyterian church, in which he was reared, and fraternally he is identified with the Masonic order, in which he has attained the chivalric degrees, being a member of Damascus Commandery, No. 10, Knights Templar, in Aberdeen. The Senator remains a bachelor. He has a distinctive predilection for out-door life and sports afield and afloat, while he has announced as his fad or special fancy that of tree culture.

HORACE W. LeBLOND

Horace W. LeBlond, a pioneer druggist of Chamberlain, South Dakota, and in point of continuous residence one of the town's oldest business men as well as one of the leading citizens of Brule County, was born June 28, 1854, in Celina, Ohio, and when a child of three years was taken by his parents on their removal to Minnesota, in which state he spent his childhood and youth and in the public schools of which he received his elementary education. The discipline thus acquired was later supplemented by a three years course in the University of Minnesota, after which he took up the study of pharmacy and pursued the same until becoming proficient in every detail of the profession.

In 1881 Mr. LeBlond came to South Dakota on a prospecting tour for a location, and being pleased with the new town of Chamberlain and the advantages it afforded to young men of spirit and enterprise, he decided to make it his permanent place of abode. In due time he secured a business room and stocking the same with a full line of drugs and a complete assortment of such other articles and sundries as are usually found in first-class establishments of the kind, opened his doors and announced himself in readiness to wait upon his customers. Being the only business house of the kind in the place, he soon commanded a large and lucrative patronage and his career from that time to the present day, covering a period of over twenty-two years, presents a series of continued advancements, which now place him in the front ranks of the enterprising and successful men of affairs in this part of the state. Mr. LeBlond has added largely to his stock in order to keep abreast of the steadily growing demands of the trade, and being, as already indicated, a master of his profession and at the same time a most courteous and obliging business man whose relations with the public have always been of a pleasant and agreeable character, it is not at all surprising that he has won a warm and permanent place in the confidence and esteem of the people.

Since locating in Chamberlain, Mr. LeBlond has been an influential factor in the growth and development of the place and a conspicuous figure in its political and public affairs. Although a strong adherent of the Democratic party, he was elected in the early days of the town to the office of city clerk, making the race on the Peoples' ticket and defeating a well-known and popular competitor by a very decisive majority. After serving one term with credit to himself and to the satisfaction of the public, he was re-elected his own successor on the citizens' ticket, his successful management of the office being his greatest recommendation to the suffrage of the people regardless of party or political affiliation, his second term fully justifying the support given him and adding to his reputation as an able and judicious and popular public servant.

Mr. LeBlond has a beautiful and attractive home in Chamberlain which is presided over with dignity and grace by a lady of intelligence and varied culture who, since 1893, has worthily and honorably borne his name, shared his fortunes and successes, co-operated with him in his endeavors and sympathized and assisted him in all of his aspirations. Mrs. LeBlond before her marriage was Miss Lizzie Bridgeman and she was born in Little Rock, Arkansas, and moved to South Dakota in 1880. In his business and social relations Mr. LeBlond has been actuated by the highest motives of honor and his record is that of a man of wide intelligence and broad generous sympathies, whose integrity has never been questioned and whose character has always been above reproach.

He is a Mason of the Royal Arch degree, an influential member of the blue lodge in Chamberlain and at various times has been honored with high official stations in the different branches of the order with which he is identified.

JOHN T. LEE

John T. Lee, the periods of whose residence in South Dakota covers forty-six years, is one of the well-known and representative citizens of Minnehaha County and is actively identified with business interests as manager of the S. H. Bowman Lumber Company and of the Farmers Elevator Company of Brandon, this state. His birth occurred in Christiania, Norway, on the 11th of February, 1855, his parents being Thorsten and Anna (Okre) Lee, natives of Norway, who emigrated to the United States in 1867 and took up their abode in Allamakee County, Iowa. The father, a blacksmith by trade, opened a shop in the town of Waterville. In the spring of 1870 he came to South Dakota, filing

on a homestead in Split Rock township, Minnehaha County, on which he resided until his death, which occurred in 1898. The mother of our subject was called to her final rest in the year 1906.

John T. Lee, who was a lad of twelve years when he accompanied his father and mother on their emigration to the United States, left home at the age of thirteen and came to South Dakota in 1869 — one year prior to the arrival of his parents. During the first winter here, he lived with a brother in Canton and worked in a sawmill. When his parents came to this state, he joined them on the home farm and assisted his father in the work of the fields until he had attained his majority. In 1876 he wedded Miss Christina Nelson, a native of Sweden, and after his marriage located on a farm which his brother had homesteaded, John T. Lee succeeding to the ownership of the property at his brother's death. He extended the boundaries of the place until it embraced two hundred and forty acres and continued its operation until 1891, when he left the farm and took up his abode in Brandon. There he was made buyer for the Farmers Association, serving in that capacity for six years. On the expiration of that period the Farmers Association sold out and Mr. Lee became agent for its successors, remaining with his new employers for about six years or until his election to the office of county treasurer in 1903. He served in that position for two terms or four years and some time after the expiration of his second term returned to Brandon. On the organization of the Farmers Elevator Company, he was made manager, and subsequently, when his son resigned as manager of the Bowman Lumber Company, he was offered and accepted the management of the latter concern as well. In these connections he has manifested excellent executive ability and sound judgment, and his efforts are a recognized factor in the continued growth and success of the institutions with which he is identified.

To Mr. Lee and his first wife were born four children, as follows: Edward, who acts as manager for the S. H. Bowman Lumber Company at Canton; Anthon, a member of the Frank Hyde Jewelry Company, of Sioux Falls; Hannah, who is employed as bookkeeper by the Loonan Lumber Company of Sioux Falls; and Albert, an inspector of fruits and vegetables at Minneapolis. The wife and mother passed away in 1894, and on the 31st of December, 1903, Mr. Lee was again married, his second union being with Mrs. Mary Holmes, who was formerly a Miss Hustad and is a native of Norway. Mrs. Lee conducts a successful millinery establishment in Sioux Falls, her store adjoining the Sioux Falls National Bank.

For a number of years Mr. Lee has been a factor in the local councils of the republican party. He served for twelve years as county commissioner of Minnehaha County and in that connection made a most commendable and creditable record. Fraternally he is identified with the Masons, belonging to the following organizations: Minnehaha Lodge, No. 5, A. F. & A. M., of Sioux Falls; Sioux Chapter, R. A. M.; St. Croix Commandery, No. II, K. T.; the Consistory; and the Mystic Shrine. He likewise belongs to Lodge No. 262 of the Benevolent Protective Order of Elks, while his religious faith is indicated by his membership in the Lutheran church, with which his wife is also connected. During the long period of his residence in Minnehaha County he has proven himself a public-spirited, progressive citizen, a trustworthy business man and a stanch friend, and his salient qualities of character justly entitle him to the esteem of those who know him.

MAJOR A. W. LEECH

Major A. W. Leech is superintendent and special disbursing agent of the Yankton Indian reservation. He has about eighteen hundred and thirty Indians under him and in the past three years improvements amounting to a half million dollars have been made under his supervision. He is very enthusiastic in his work and gives it his undivided attention and his best thought. A native of Ohio, he was born January 6, 1865, a son of Robert J. and Matilda F. (Hurley) Leech. The father, who was by trade a carpenter, has passed to his reward.

Major A. W. Leech attended the public schools in his boyhood and was later a student in the Kansas Normal College at Fort Scott, Kansas, from which he was graduated, on the completion of a special science course. He then engaged in school work and in October, 1900, entered the Indian service as a day-school teacher on the Rosebud reservation. He continued to hold that position until September, 1903, when he went to Oklahoma as assistant superintendent. Later he was for three years day-school inspector and on the 1st of February, 1912, he assumed charge of the Yankton reservation as superintendent and special disbursing agent. The Indians under his care number about eighteen hundred and thirty and since he has had charge of the reservation, they have made unusually rapid progress in civilization. They engage chiefly in farming and the acreage under cultivation has increased quite materially in the last three years. The water difficulty has been solved and many good wells have been drilled, including a number of artesian wells. The houses in which the Indians live are of a better type than heretofore and show marked advancement in comfort and sanitation. At the government board school there are about one hundred children, who are receiving both a scholastic and an industrial education. During the three years that Major Leech has been in control of the reservation a great deal of farm equipment has been secured and other improvements have been made, the total expenditure reaching the half million mark. He understands the Indians well, which largely accounts for his success as superintendent, and another factor therein is his love for his work, to which he devotes himself unsparingly.

Major Leech was married on the 19th of August, 1886, to Miss Mary B. Holstein, a daughter of Fred Holstein, of Fort Scott, Kansas. To this union have been born five children: Nada B., now Mrs. L. R. Divilbiss, of Kansas City; Charles A., of Chicago; Harry R., of Greenwood, South Dakota; Marie J., the wife of W. B. McCown, of Darlington, Oklahoma; and Ora A., at home. There are also three grandchildren.

Major Leech is affiliated with the Presbyterian church and his wife belongs to the Christian church. Fraternally he is a thirty-second degree Mason and he is also identified with the Ancient Order of United Workmen. All who have come into contact with his work recognize its value and respect and esteem him for his ability and his sincere interest in the advancement of the Indians under his charge. He has also gained and retained the sincere friendship and warm regard of many as he possesses those qualities of mind and heart that are associated with the highest type of manhood.

JOHN H. LeMAY

John H. LeMAY, editor and publisher of the Northville Journal, at Northville, Spink County, is a native of the city of Philadelphia, where he was born on the 27th of January, 1870, being a son of Edward F. and Nellie (Robertson) LeMay, the former of whom was born in France and the latter in Scotland and both of whom have now passed away. The father of the subject came to America as a young man, and established his home in Philadelphia, while he became a prominent contractor in the construction of railways and bridges. The subject secured his early educational discipline in the fair old "City of Brotherly Love," and thereafter completed a course of study in the Shattuck Military Academy, at Faribault, Minnesota. At the age of sixteen years, he entered upon an apprenticeship at the printer's trade, working during vacations for several years in Duluth, that state, gaining an excellent knowledge of the details and mysteries of the "art preservative of all arts," and thereafter he was engaged in the work of his trade in divers sections of the union, having come to South Dakota in 1896, while in April, 1900, he settled in Northville and purchased the Northville Journal, of which he has since been editor and publisher. The Journal is a five-column quarto and is issued on Thursday of each week, while both editorially and in matter of letter-press it is an attractive publication, while it so fully covers matters of local interest that it is a welcome visitor in the majority of the best homes in this section. In politics, Mr. LeMay is a stanch advocate of the principles and policies of the Republican party, and his paper is the medium through which he wields the greatest influence in local affairs of a public nature, while he is thoroughly progressive in his attitude and always ready to lend his aid and influence in the furthering of worthy enterprises for the general good. He is a member of the South Dakota Press Association. He has attained to the thirty-second degree of Scottish Rite Masonry, being a member of the consistory at Aberdeen, and is also a member of the Order of the Eastern Star, as well as of the Ancient Order of United Workmen. He enjoys unqualified esteem in business and social circles and is one of the popular young men of Spink County.

On the 1st of May, 1902, Mr. LeMay was married to Miss Miry Elsom, who was born and reared in Northville, being a daughter of Joseph Elsom, concerning whom a specific sketch appears on another page of this work. On February 8, 1904, a son was born to this union.

GEORGE E. LEMMON

The history of the west is a familiar story to George E. Lemmon. A native of Utah, he has spent much of his life on the frontier and was the founder of the town of Lemmon, in which he now makes his home. He was born at Bountiful, forty miles from Salt Lake City, May 23, 1857, a son of James H. and Lucy E. (Whittemore) Lemmon, who were natives of Ohio and Illinois respectively. They were married in Marengo, in the latter state, and soon afterward went to California. The father had made the trip to the Pacific coast in 1847, before gold was discovered, in the second emigrant train to cross the plains, and was engaged in merchandising, in freighting and in various other enterprises. He also participated in the Oregon Indian war from the start to the finish. Returning to Illinois in 1852, he was married and with his bride again made the trip to the far west. Their first child, Hervey, was born in an emigrant wagon when they were crossing the plains. Mr. Lemmon took with him a herd of thoroughbred Durham cattle, and being held up by the winter weather in Utah, he bought a farm at what was then Grantsville but is now Bountiful. There the family lived for six years and it was during that period that the birth of George E. Lemmon occurred. The following spring the father continued the trip to California with his freighting outfit of fifteen or twenty wagons and after spending that summer and the following winter in California returned to Utah, where he lived until 1859, when he removed to the vicinity of the present site of Hastings, Nebraska, and established a stage station at that point. In 1866-1867-1868 he was one of the sub-contractors engaged in building the Union Pacific Railroad through Ogden, Utah, to the vicinity of Salt Lake City. He died at his home in Nebraska in 1903, having long survived his wife, who passed away in 1875. He was always prominently identified with live-stock interests, raising, buying and selling cattle and horses on an extensive scale. He was also a well-read man and one of considerable influence in the community in which he lived.

George E. Lemmon was reared on the plains and was educated in the public schools of the different localities in which the family home was maintained. In 1870 he was in the employ of J. W. Iliff, the cattle king of Wyoming, and in 1877, before reaching his twentieth birthday, he purchased his first bunch of cattle and his connection with the cattle business has been continuous, while the growth of his business has made him one of the prominent cattle men of the western country. For three years he resided at Ogallala, Nebraska, and in 1880 removed to Buffalo Gap, in the Black Hills district of South Dakota, within twenty-five miles of the Bad Lands. He transferred the base of his operations to the Moreau River In South Dakota in 1888 and thence went to the Grand River in 1892, there operating prominently as a stockman until 1907, when the town of Lemmon was established. At that time, he held extensive government land script and assisted the Chicago, Milwaukee & St. Paul engineers in laying out the route for the building of the transcontinental road. Knowing that the route was the only available one through that part of the country, he bought extensive land scripts with the view of establishing town sites and the town of Lemmon was located on his holdings. Thirty days after the establishment of the first bank in the town he bought an interest in the institution and acted as president thereof until he disposed of his stock in the early part of 1914.

Mr. Lemmon was married in 1886 to Miss Bertha Reno, of Buffalo Gap, South Dakota, by whom he had three sons, namely: James H., who is engaged in the banking and cattle business; Roy E., a ranchman residing in Meeker, Colorado; and George R., who is a ranchman of Red Lodge, Montana. For his second wife Mr. Lemmon chose Miss Rosella Boe, of Deadwood, South Dakota.

Fraternally Mr. Lemmon is a Mason, belonging to the lodge. in his home town. In politics he is an earnest republican and for many years served as county commissioner of Fall River County, South Dakota, of Adams County, North Dakota, and of Perkins County. He continued in that position in Perkins County from its organization until January 1, 1915, when he refused to continue longer as an incumbent in that office. He now concentrates his attention upon his land holdings and he still operates in the purchase and sale of cattle. At one time he had the largest cattle pasture in the United States, having under fence eight hundred and sixty-five thousand four hundred and twenty-eight and one-half acres which he held under lease. He was at one time the largest cattle operator in the country and in this connection, he is widely known. Every phase of western life is familiar to him and in his chosen line of business he has taken advantage of the conditions offered by the west, finding excellent range for his cattle on the open prairies. He has keen business insight and sagacity, is ready in resource and at all times is capable of wisely meeting a situation. His operations have been carried on most extensively and his success is the merited result of his ability.

CHARLES E. LENNAN

Charles E. LENNAN, one of the successful and highly esteemed real-estate dealers of Bowdle, Edmunds County, is a scion of stanch old colonial stock, of Scotch-Irish origin, and is himself a native of the old Pine Tree state, having been born in Belfast, Waldo County, Maine, on the 14th of December, 1848, and being a son of Ansel and Mary (Maxey) Lennan, both of whom were likewise born and reared in that noble old New England commonwealth. David Lennan, grandfather of the subject, was one of the largest owners of timber lands in Maine, where he met with heavy financial losses at the time of the Moosehead Lake speculation, his loss having footed up to fully fifty thousand dollars in the connection through his endorsing security papers. The father of the subject was for many years deputy collector of customs at Belfast, Maine, was for several years a pension agent, and also devoted no little attention to the buying of raw furs, passing the last twenty years of his life in the city of Bangor, where his wife also died. The father, an old-line Democrat, wielded no little influence in political affairs in his native state and was a man of the highest integrity and honor in all the relations of life. Of his two children the subject of this review is the younger. Charles E. Lennan secured his early educational discipline in the public schools of Maine, which he attended until he had attained the age of nineteen years. He then engaged in the ship brokerage and commission business, and later as shipper and dealer in baled hay and farm produce, at Bangor, Maine, also operating quite heavily in the same lines in New Brunswick, building up a most successful business, in which he continued for some time. From 1880 he was engaged in the wholesale and produce business in the city of Boston, Massachusetts. In the spring of 1883, he came to what is now the state of South Dakota and took up government land twelve miles northwest of the present town of Blunt, in Hughes County, returning to Boston in the autumn of 1884. There he established himself as selling agent in the wholesale hay business, with the firm of Scott & Bridge, extensive operators in the line. In the autumn of 1885, he located at Crown Point, Indiana, with the intention of shipping hay from that point to eastern markets, but one month later decided to again come to South Dakota. He invested in land at Scranton, Walworth County, and found the investment entailed a total loss. He then came to the present site of Bowdle, where he in a sense brought in the first building in the embryonic village, having originally erected said building at a point one and one-half miles southwest, and having hauled the same to the new site. In this building he established himself in the real-estate business. The years 1886 and 1887 proved hard ones in the state, and all of the real-estate dealers located on the railroad at points west of Ipswich were practically starved out by reason of lack of patronage and general business stagnation, but Mr. Lennan weathered the storm and finally found his anchorage secure. He has succeeded in building up a very prosperous business and is known as one of the leading real-estate men of this section of the state. He also makes a specialty of the extension of financial loans upon real-estate security.

In politics he gives his allegiance to the Republican party and fraternally is identified with the Masonic order, in which he has received the degrees of the lodge and chapter. On the 26th of December, 1896, Mr. Lennan was united in marriage to Miss Hortense B. Kennedy, who was born in Illinois, and reared in Kansas, of which state her foster-brother is governor at the time of this writing.

LUDWIG LEVINGER

Ludwig LEVINGER, president and owner of the Aurora County Bank, at White Lake, is a native of the kingdom of Württemberg, Germany, where he was born on the 10th of April, 1867, being the second in order of birth of the four children born to Herman and Mary (Linder) Levinger. All the children are still living, but the subject is the only representative of the immediate family in the United States. He was afforded liberal educational advantages in the fatherland, where he remained until he had attained the age of seventeen years, when he decided to come to America, where he was convinced, better opportunities were afforded for attaining independence and success. Accordingly, in the spring of 1883, he embarked for the United States, landing in New York City, whence he made his way to the city of Chicago, where he secured employment in a wholesale men's furnishing-goods house. He retained this position a few months, in the meanwhile sparing no pains to inform himself in regard to American business methods and customs, and in the summer of the same year he decided to seek his fortunes in the west. He located in Mitchell, South Dakota, where he held a clerkship in a furniture establishment until the spring of 1885, when he took up his residence in White Lake, where he secured a position in the White Lake Bank. From a clerical position he was soon advanced to that of cashier of the institution, and in his executive office he continued to render efficient service until 1890, when he purchased the business of the Aurora County Bank, the oldest monetary institution in this section, the same dating its inception back to the year 1882, and as president and manager of thig bank he has attained a high degree of success and an enviable reputation in business circles. All this is the more gratifying to contemplate in view of the fact that he came to this country without capitalistic resources or influential friends, and in the short period of twenty years has placed himself well in the forefront in the ranks of financiers in the great and prosperous state of South Dakota, being known and honored as one of the influential citizens of his county. He is a stalwart Republican in his political proclivities, and for sixteen years has served as mayor of White Lake, of which office he is incumbent at the present time, while he has been also a member of the board of education for the past fifteen years.

He stands high in rank in the Masonic fraternity, holding membership in the following bodies: White Lake Lodge, No. 84, Free and Accepted Masons; Mitchell Chapter, Royal Arch Masons; Mitchell Commandery, Knights Templar; Oriental Consistory, No. I, Ancient Accepted Scottish Rite, at Yankton; and El Riad Temple, Ancient Arabic Order of the Nobles of the Mystic Shrine, at Sioux Falls. In 1896, Mr. Levinger was married to Miss Sadie Wagner and they have two children, Frank R. and Margaret.

BURRE H. LIEN

Burre H. LIEN, merits consideration in this history by reason of his standing as one of the most progressive and public-spirited citizens of Sioux Falls and as one who has been prominent in the public and civic affairs of the state. Mr. Lien was born near Spirit Lake, Iowa, on the 21 St of December, 1859, being a son of Hans and Gertrude (Burreson) Lien, both of whom were born in Norway. An uprising of the Indians in the vicinity caused the parents to leave their home in Jackson, Minnesota, in 1863, and they removed to Decorah, Iowa, where they remained until 1873, when they removed to Faribault County, Minnesota, where the father continued to be identified with farming until the time of his death.

The subject of this review received his rudimentary education in the public schools of Iowa and Minnesota, and supplemented the same by a course in the normal school at Mankato, Minnesota. In 1879 he came to Brookings County, South Dakota, where he engaged in teaching school, becoming one of the pioneer educators m that section, where he also took up government land and engaged in farming, continuing to follow the two vocations until 1883, and thereafter serving two years as deputy register of deeds of that county. In November, 1885, he was elected judge of probate and at the next general election was chosen register of deeds of the county, in which capacity he served two terms, or four consecutive years, while for three years he was a valued member of the city council of Brookings. In June, 1891, Mr. Lien took up his residence in the city of Sioux Falls.

In politics Mr. Lien gives an uncompromising allegiance to the Democratic party, in whose councils he has been an important factor in the state. In 1894 he was elected to represent the third ward of city of Sioux Falls in the municipal board of aldermen, while in 1898 he was elected mayor of the city, giving a business-like and able administration and accomplishing much in improving and extending the public utilities. In March, 1899, he was appointed a member of the state board of charities and corrections, of which he was chosen chairman, and he continued to be a member of this important board until 1901. In 1900 he was made the candidate of his party for the office of governor of the state, and while he gained that endorsement at the polls which indicated his personal popularity, he met the defeat which attended the party ticket in general throughout the state in that year. Mr. Lien has ever shown a deep interest in the welfare and advancement of his home city, and his civic pride prompted him to a most valuable and timely donation to the city in April, 1903, when he presented to the municipality nine acres of land for a city park, the same being most eligibly and attractively located and being the first and only land provided for park purposes in the city.

Fraternally he is identified with the following named Masonic bodies: Minnehaha Lodge, No. 5, Free and Accepted Masons; Sioux Falls Chapter, No. 2, Royal Arch Masons; Cyrene Commandery, No. 2, Knights Templar; Oriental Consistory, No. I, Ancient Accepted Scottish Rite, in which he has attained the thirty-second degree; and El Riad Temple, Ancient Arabic Order of the Nobles of the Mystic Shrine. He also holds membership in the Independent Order of Odd Fellows and the Benevolent and Protective Order of Elks. On the 15th of May, 1881, Mr. Lien wedded Miss Anne Udseth, of Brookings County, this state, and they have six children, namely: Henry L., George O., Florence, Agnes, Harold and Eva.

ARTHUR LINN

ARTHUR LINN.

Arthur Linn came to the territory of Dakota in December, 1869, locating at Yankton. In January, 1870, he purchased the Union and Dakotan, the only paper at the capital and the first paper issued in the territory. He took an active part in territorial affairs, political and otherwise, and was elected chairman of the Republican County committee in 1870, and took a leading part in the campaigns of 1870, 1872, 1874 and 1876. His first newspaper experience was gained in the editorial rooms of Harper's Weekly in 1858, when a boy. The editor of Harper's Weekly in 1858 was John Bonner, a warm friend of Mr. Linn, and he offered him a position, which was accepted. He remained in Harper's until the summer of 1860, going to the editorial rooms of the New York Herald, then under the personal management of the elder Bennett, with Fredric Hudson as editor in chief. During Mr. Linn's connection with Harper's Weekly, he met nearly all the prominent people of the nation, including Edward Everett, Stephen A. Douglas, Alexander H. Stephens, of Georgia, the blind preacher, Mr. Milburn, ex-President Fillmore, General Thomas, Francis Meagher, and all the prominent literary men and women of that time.

When the echoes of rebellion rolled up from Charleston. Mr. Linn was with the Herald, and had the honor of climbing the flagstaff on the old Herald building, corner of Nassau and Fulton streets, and raising the first American flag put up over any newspaper building in New York City. After the news came that Sumter had fallen, a patriotic mob composed of thousands visited every newspaper office in the city the next day and compelled every one of them to purchase a flag and show their colors. The raising of the flag over the Herald office on the afternoon of April 14, 1861, saved that office from the demonstrations which followed.

On August 23, 1861, Mr. Linn enlisted and became a member of Company H, Tenth New York National Zouaves, and joined the regiment at Fortress Monroe. It is not material to this sketch how old Linn was when he enlisted, but as a matter of record it may be stated that he was just fourteen years and eight months old when he donned his zouave uniform in New York City, but the recruiting officer was made to believe that he was eighteen, or he could not have become a soldier. He served three years in the Army of the Potomac, and was on guard on the beach at Fortress Monroe the night the "Monitor" arrived from New York and challenged Lieutenant Worden and his boat as he was seeking a pilot so that he could go to the relief of the frigate "Minnesota," which ran into a sand bar while going to the relief of the "Cumberland" and "Congress," which were destroyed by the "Merrimac" in the fatal encounter March 8, 1862. He took part in the capture of Norfolk, Virginia, May 10, 1862, which resulted in the destruction of the "Merrimac," and Linn saw her burn and then blow up in the night, after the Union troops had captured Norfolk and Portsmouth. From Norfolk his regiment was ordered to join General McClellan's army in front of Richmond, and his regiment was one of the first to meet the onslaught of Hill's corps at Mechanicsville, which opened the seven-days fight in front of the rebel capital. After the bloody campaign his regiment was sent to Washington, along with the Army of the Potomac, and took part in the bloody battles which stayed Lee's advance against Washington, and again marched to meet Lee at Antietam and again at Gettysburg.

Mr. Linn was mustered out at Norfolk, Virginia, August 23, 1864, and was offered a position with the field staff of the New York Herald, with headquarters at City Point, and the Herald was the only paper that had headquarters within the sacred circle which surrounded General Grant at City Point during the siege of Petersburg. In the fall of 1865 Linn returned to New York, and in March, 1866, left for Iowa to visit relatives at Charles City, and, strange as it may seem, he had not visited his old home on Staten Island, below the city, until February, 1904, when he was a guest of President Hill to witness the launching of the great steamship "Dakota," at New London, Connecticut, February 6th. After the launching he visited the scenes of his boyhood in New York, Brooklyn and Staten Island, and returned to his home at Canton, South Dakota, better satisfied with his home and state than ever before.

During the summer of 1872 Mr. Linn made a visit to Spotted Tail's hostile camp, half way between the Missouri river and the Black Hills, and while on that trip was shown a bag of gold by old James Bordeau, which he easily proved came from the Black Hills. On Mr. Linn's return to Yankton, he published a full account of the matter, with such proof as to convince all that there was plenty of gold in the Hills, and from that time the excitement grew and continued to develop until finally the white man had driven the Indians out and the great stampede of 1876 began. Linn's account was the first evidence of the great wealth of the Hills, and in 1873 the famous Collins expedition was organized at Sioux City, which was stopped by General Hancock. In 1874 General Custer was sent into the Hills to explore the country and Linn's account was found to be correct. In 1875 a few daring gold hunters got into the Hills, but the Indians and soldiers drove them out. In 1876 a stampede began which the Indians were powerless to stop, and the history of the famous Deadwood gulch began. In 1897 Arthur Linn was appointed commandant of the South Dakota Soldiers' Home and remained in command until May, 1901, when his successor was chosen. Mr. Linn returned to Canton and again took charge of his paper which had been in charge of his son Arthur during his absence, and he says he expects to remain in the editorial harness for the balance of his active life, and continue to promote the best interests of the state which he has done so much for. He was secretary of the territorial council during the session of 1874-75, but declined a second term in 1876-7.

Mr. Linn is a thirty-second-degree Mason and a member of Consistory No. I, of Yankton, and is also a Knight Templar. He is the editor and proprietor of the Dakota Farmers' Leader at Canton and owns one of the best printing plants in the state. On June 7, 1870, Mr. Linn married Etta Brown, daughter of Colonel and Mrs. E. M. Brown, of Montpelier, Vermont. Three children came to bless their home, but only one remains, Florence Jean Etta, born November 24, 1890. The eldest son, Arthur Edward, born May 8, 1876, died January 21, 1901. Alexander, born November 24, 1880, died May 18, 1895. Mr. Linn is a member of the Methodist church, and the oldest newspaper editor in the state. He has seen Dakota grow from fourteen thousand people in 1870, to nearly five hundred thousand in 1904, and expects to see a population of one million before he retires from the active management of the Leader.

ISAAC LINCOLN

Among those prominent in the banking and financial circles of South Dakota is Isaac Lincoln, president of the State Bank of Aberdeen, vice-president of the Aberdeen National Bank and president of the First National Bank of Webster, Day County. Mr. Lincoln is a native of the state of Maine, and is descended on both sides from colonial stock, his ancestors having come to New England in 1636, settling on Cape Cod. Mr. Lincoln was born in Brunswick, Maine, and is a son of Dr. John D. and Ellen (Fessenden) Lincoln, who were likewise born and reared in Maine, where the respective families were early established. He secured his education in the public schools of his native town and in Phillips Academy in Andover, Massachusetts. Shortly thereafter he came to the territory of Dakota, where he engaged in farming and stock raising until 1886, when he located in Aberdeen. Besides his banking interests he is engaged in the real-estate business and in farming, having one of the largest stock and grain farms in the county, which he personally supervises. In politics he is a Republican, and fraternally is identified with the Masonic order.

A. W. LINDOUIST

As the name indicates, the subject of this sketch is of foreign blood, although a native of the United States, having been born near Alma, Wisconsin, on the 4th day of September, 1869, John and Christina (Westling) Lindquist, his parents, both natives of Sweden, came to America in 1850 and settled in Wabasha County, Minnesota. Later he moved to Alma, Wisconsin, and from there to Ortonville, Minnesota, in 1877, where the father engaged in farming. He died December 24, 1902, at the age of seventy-two years, the mother being still a resident of Ortonville. John and Christina Lindquist reared a family of six children, five living, the subject of this review being the oldest of the number. A. W. spent his early years on the homestead near Ortonville, and received his education in the public schools of that place, after which he accepted a clerkship in a mercantile house, holding the same for a period of eight years. Resigning his position at Ortonville in 1891, Mr. Lindquist came to Roberts County, South Dakota, and in February of the same year established himself in the mercantile business at Wilmot, which line of trade he has since conducted, the meanwhile greatly enlarging his stock by adding a general assortment of goods, including all kinds of agricultural implements and farm machinery, and meeting with most gratifying success in his undertaking. His patronage, which includes a wide range, is quite lucrative, and in his well-stocked establishment is found every article of merchandise demanded by the general trade. As a business man he is familiar with the underlying principles of commercial life, being a careful buyer, an accomplished salesman and progressive in the management of his affairs, yet sufficiently conservative as to make few errors of judgment, steering clear of unwise speculations and being satisfied with the sure gains that come from legitimate trading.

In addition to his commercial interests, Mr. Lindquist is a large real-estate holder, owning and personally managing the farms in Roberts County, besides holding a half interest in the old family homestead in Big

Stone County, Minnesota. He belongs to the public-spirited class of men that have done much to promote the material advancement of Wilmot and Roberts counties, and he has also achieved considerable reputation as a shrewd, resourceful and far-seeing politician, having borne quite a prominent part in bringing about the re-election of Hon. J. H. Kyle to the United States senate. His influence in municipal, county and state politics has given him considerable prestige among the leaders of his party, not only in the county and district in which he resides but throughout the state as well.

Mr. Lindquist is a thirty-second degree Scottish Rite Mason, belonging to the blue lodge at Wilmot, the consistory at Aberdeen and the Mystic Shrine at Minneapolis, Minnesota. He is a zealous member of this ancient and honorable brotherhood, is well versed in its mystic work and his sterling manhood proves that its principles and precepts had not a little to do in guiding and controlling his daily life and conduct. Mr. Lindquist was married on May 31, 1893, to Miss Edna Knappen, of Minneapolis, and is the father of two children, Muriel and Phyllis.

DAVID EMANUEL LLOYD

David Emanuel Lloyd has for an extended period been active in business circles and in the public life of Yankton. He was born September 27, 1856, in Red Wing, Goodhue County, Minnesota, a son of Walrath and Johannah (Anderson) Lloyd, who emigrated to the United States in 1852 from Sweden, settling at La Crosse, Wisconsin. The father afterward removed with his family to Red Wing, Minnesota, and preempted land in that district, but lived again at La Crosse for some years. In 1863 he removed to Lansing, Iowa, and in 1878 became a resident of Sioux Falls, South Dakota, where his remaining days were passed, his death occurring in 1899, while his wife survived until 1903. Throughout the entire period of his residence in America he was identified with pioneer life and with the early development of various sections of the west. To him and his wife were born nine sons and a daughter, of whom the daughter, Clara V. Lloyd of Sioux Falls, and four sons survive.

David Emanuel Lloyd attended the district schools until thirteen years of age and the following year became a clerk in the post office. He held the position of accountant in the First National Bank at Yankton from 1881 until 1895. In 1891 he was elected a director of the Yankton Building & Loan Association and has continued to be reelected each year since that time, being still a member of the board. He has been called to various public offices, the duties of which he has discharged in a most capable and commendable manner. In 1887 he became city clerk of Yankton and was city treasurer from 1890 until 1894 inclusive. The following year he was elected county treasurer and filled that position for two years. In 1898 he was again called to public office in appointment to the position of postmaster, in which he served for four years. In 1909 he was made a member of the board of education for a term of four years and was reelected in 1913, so that he is now active in directing the management of the schools of the city. He served as treasurer of the board of education from 1890 until 1895 and in 1903 he was made a member of the city council for a two years' term.

On the 14th of June, 1882, at Mason City, Iowa, Mr. Lloyd was united in marriage to Miss Dorothea Elizabeth Kumpf, a daughter of Jacob and Mary (Eming) Kumpf, who emigrated to America from Germany in the late '50s, settling in Allamakee County, Iowa, Mrs. Lloyd being born at Dorchester, that county, in 1860. To Mr. and Mrs. Lloyd have been born the following named: Clara D., James M., Dorothea E. and William W., who are yet living; and David E., who died in December, 1900, at the age of nearly four years. All were born in Yankton, South Dakota.

Mr. Lloyd has been a Mason since 1879, always maintaining his affiliation with the craft. He is now secretary of St. John's Lodge, No. I, A. F. & A. M., of Yankton; is a past high priest of Yankton Chapter, No. I, R. A. M.; and is the present preceptor of Oriental Consistory, No. I, A. & A. S. R., also of Yankton. He likewise belongs to the Knights of Pythias fraternity and with his family attends the Congregational church.

HON. ANDREW J. LOCKHART

HON. ANDREW J. LOCKHART

On the pages of South Dakota's history, the name of the Hon. Andrew J. Lockhart is written large, because of his close and prominent connection with the upbuilding and development of his locality. He has also figured prominently in political circles as a leader in republican politics and has been a member of the state senate. He makes his home in Clear Lake, but his business activities cover a wide territory, as he is the president of the Eastern Investment Company and president of the Bank of Clear Lake, the Farmers Exchange Bank of Toronto, the Exchange Bank of Gary, the Altamont State Bank of Altamont and the State Bank of Bemis.

Mr. Lockhart has always been a resident of the middle west, his birth having occurred upon a farm in Columbia County, Wisconsin, on the 28th of March, 1863, his parents being John and Agnes (Gray) Lockhart. They were born, reared and married in Ayrshire, Scotland, and came to America in 1849. After spending eighteen months in New York, they removed to Wisconsin, where their remaining days were passed. The father devoted his life to agricultural pursuits.

While spending his youthful days under the parental roof Andrew J. Lockhart attended the public schools and also a high school in Wisconsin. When his school days were over, he entered the employ of a sewing machine company, spending a short time in that way at Baraboo, after which he went to Stevens Point, Wisconsin, where he was engaged in the same business. On the 1st of April, 1884, he removed to Brookings, South Dakota, where he was employed in a lumberyard, and in 1884, when Clear Lake was founded, he removed to this place and became manager of a lumberyard in the new town, so continuing until the following May, when the yard of which he had charge was consolidated with another business and thus he was left without a position. The recognition of his energy and ability, however, did not leave him long in that condition, for he entered the employ of an elevator company at Watertown, of which he was made manager. After nine months there spent, he returned to Clear Lake, where he was manager of an elevator for a year and then entered the grain and agricultural implement business on his own account. In order to do this, he borrowed capital at a rate of thirty-six per cent interest, payable in advance. In 1889

32

he took up the real-estate business but remained in the grain and implement business until 1894, when he became manager of the Eastern Investment Company, with offices at Clear Lake although the business was owned by people of Toronto, Canada. In 1898 Mr. Lockhart purchased their stock in the business and has built it up to its present proportions, making it financially the largest and strongest real-estate concern in South Dakota. Its present condition is attributable entirely to the efforts and energy of Mr. Lockhart, who is a man of keen sagacity, sound judgment and indefatigable diligence. Each step in his career has been a forward one, bringing him a broader outlook and wider opportunities, and from time to time he has been connected with other interests which in their extent and importance place him among the leading financiers of the state. Of six different financial concerns he is the president and the banking interests of his section of the state have largely been promoted and extended through his efforts.

On the 31st of May, 1893, Mr. Lockhart was united in marriage to Miss Clara M. Goddard, a daughter of Joseph C. and Agnes (Hunter) Goddard. Hers was an old-time family that arrived in Deuel County in 1876, settling at Goddard's Lake, where the father secured sixty acres of heavy timber, surrounded by water. This is one of the prettiest spots in all South Dakota. Both the parents have now passed away and Mrs. Lockhart recently purchased the old estate. By her marriage she has become the mother of four children: Edith M., Beatrice Gray, Fern Irene and Florence May.

Mr. and Mrs. Lockhart hold membership in the Congregational church and are interested in upholding and promoting the moral standards of the community. Mr. Lockhart is a prominent Mason, having taken the degrees of the York Rite and of the Mystic Shrine. He also has membership with the Elks and the Modern Woodmen of America. His political allegiance is given the republican party and in early days he served as county commissioner to fill a vacancy and he was mayor of Clear Lake as long as he would consent to accept the office. He has thus left the impress of his individuality upon the history of the city, its upbuilding and development. In 1909 he was elected a member of the state senate and made such an excellent record during his first term that in 1911 he was reelected. During the second term he was chosen president pro tem without opposition, a fact which indicates the confidence reposed in his integrity as a citizen and his public spirit, even by those who do not hold similar political views. It is well known that he is fair and just on all occasions, that he never takes advantage of another and that he seeks with singleness of purpose the best interests of the community at large.

SAMUEL S. LOCKHART *

Samuel S. Lockhart, member of the bar of Milbank and county judge of Grant County, was born in Tarbolton, Ayrshire, Scotland, November 20, 1850, a son of John and Agnes (Gray) Lockhart, who were also natives of Tarbolton. The father, who was born January 21, 1828, is now living at Clear Lake, South Dakota, but the mother, who was born in August, 1821, died March 6, 1900. They were married in 1849 and had a family of ten children, of whom seven are yet living, as follows: Samuel S., of this review; John L., of Pierre, South Dakota, who is engaged in the real-estate business, is also active in the ranks of the republican party and was formerly commissioner of school and public lands; James G., a blacksmith of Milbank; Andrew J., of Clear Lake, who is engaged in the real-estate and banking business and acts as president of the Eastern Investment Company; Robert S., who is in the employ of the International Harvester Company at Watertown; Margaret, with whom John Lockhart now makes his home and who is the wife of John Tower; and Thomas F., who was successfully engaged in agricultural pursuits throughout his active business career and is now living retired at Portage, Wisconsin. The father has been an active factor in the local ranks of the republican party and held a number of town offices. His religious faith is that of the United Presbyterian church.

Samuel S. Lockhart acquired his education in the common schools of Caledonia, Wisconsin, and the High School of Portage, from which he graduated. He then taught school about for four years, after which he pursued the study of law under private instruction, being admitted to the bar in 1881. Previous to this time he was called to the office of clerk of the court at Portage, Wisconsin, accepting that position in 1879 and serving until 1883. During the winter of 1883 he was clerk of the senate at Madison, Wisconsin, and in May of that year he removed to Milbank, South Dakota, where he entered upon the practice of his profession. In this field he has since been active and now has an extensive practice which is indicative of the wide trust reposed in his professional ability. He has again been called to public office along the line of his profession. In 1885 and 1886 he was district attorney for Grant County and in 1895 and 1896 he was states attorney, having served in the meantime as city attorney in 1893 and 1894. In 1890 he was made special United States agent for collecting mortgages and indebtedness for the United States census bureau. In 1900 he was elected county judge and has occupied the position continuously since save for a period of two years. He has made an excellent record as a fair and impartial judge upon the bench and his decisions are characterized by a masterful grasp of the various problems presented for solution.

On the 29th of March, 1879, at Randolph, Wisconsin, Mr. Lockhart was united in marriage to Miss Harriet L. Marvin, a daughter of George G. Marvin, a farmer and a member of the Wisconsin legislature in the year 1871. Mr. and Mrs. Lockhart are the parents of five children, namely: Harriet M., who has for a number of years been a teacher in the public schools of Duluth; Agnes G., who follows the profession of teaching in Seattle; John G., engaged in the wholesale lumber business at Sheboygan, Wisconsin; Marvin, an agriculturist of Saskatchewan, Canada; and Margaret Janet, who is attending school.

The parents are members of the Congregational church and Mr. Lockhart gives his political allegiance to the republican party. He is also a very prominent Mason. He was initiated into the order on the 24th of November, 1874, and on the 8th of May following became a Master Mason in Fort Winnebago Lodge, No. 33, of Portage, Wisconsin. He was demitted therefrom and affiliated with Milbank Lodge, No. 20, of Milbank, South Dakota, March 19, 1891. In 1895 he was elected junior warden, became senior warden in 1902 and worshipful master in 1903 and 1904. In June, 1902, he was appointed grand pursuivant and in 1906 junior grand steward, while in 1907 he was elected junior grand warden, becoming senior grand warden in 1908. The following year he was made deputy grand master and in June, 1910, at Pierre, he was chosen most worshipful grand master. He became a Royal Arch Mason in 1880 at Portage, Wisconsin, and following his removal to the west joined Milbank Chapter, No. 15, R. A. M., on the 20th of February, 1884. He was elected scribe in 1895, king in 1897, serving until 1904, and in 1906 was chosen high priest. In 1907 he was elected secretary and has since occupied that position. In 1880 he joined Ft. Winnebago Commandery, No. 4, at Portage, Wisconsin, but afterward demitted and joined the commandery at Aberdeen, South Dakota, in 1910. In 1895 he joined the Royal and Select Masters and was thrice illustrious master of the council at Milbank. In April, 1912, he became a member of the consistory and in October, 1904, joined the Shrine, of which both he and his wife are members. He is a recognized leader in Masonic circles in his part of the state and exemplifies in his life the beneficent spirit of the craft. He is now serving as president of the board of education of Milbank, having been connected with that board for about twelve years and at the same time he is upon the bench as county judge. No one questions his fidelity to duty. It is well known that South Dakota has in him a loyal champion, that he has faith in her future and that he does everything in his power to advance her interests, promote her material and moral progress and uphold her political and legal status.

HARVEY I. LOFFER

Harvey I. Loffer, a well-known and able lawyer of Sioux Falls, who in November, 1912, was elected to the office of justice of the peace for a term of two years after having previously filled out an unexpired term in that position, was born on a farm in Logan County, Ohio, March 13, 1874, his parents being Christian and Theresa Alice (Jackson) Loffer, the former a native of Pickaway County and the latter of Shelby County, Ohio. The paternal grandfather, Solomon Loffer, removed from Pennsylvania to the Buckeye state.

It was in the schools of Logan County that Judge Loffer pursued his early education and his professional training was obtained in the law department of the Ohio Northern University at Ada, Ohio, from which he was graduated with the class of 1899. He then went to Dell Rapids, South Dakota, where he remained for a year, after which he established his home in Montrose, this state, continuing there until January, 1904. On the latter date he removed to Sioux Falls and was cashier for an insurance company in that city until 1907, when he entered another insurance office, in which he continued for about three years. He afterward spent a year as head bookkeeper for a plow firm and in 1910 entered upon the active practice of law. In January, 1911, he was appointed justice of the peace and in November of the following year was elected for a two years' term. His has been an excellent record in the justice court, for out of nine hundred cases brought before his court in Sioux Falls in fifteen months only eight have appealed from his decision and stood trial in the circuit court, and on no occasion has his decision ever been reversed by the higher tribunal. His knowledge of the law is comprehensive and exact and his ability to accurately apply its principles is manifest in the foregoing statement.

In Logan County, Ohio, on the 26th of December, 1901, Mr. Loffer was united in marriage to Miss Delia Hill, a daughter of Daniel and Sarah (Young) Hill, and now have one child, Marion Wilson Loffer. The parents are members of the Methodist Episcopal church and Judge Loffer also belongs to the Masonic lodge, the Knights of Pythias and the Independent Order of Odd Fellows. His political allegiance has always been given to the republican party and it was upon that ticket that he was elected justice of the peace. He is a thoughtful, earnest man, unfaltering in the support of his honest convictions and in the discharge of his duties is at all times conscientious and reliable.

T. B. LONG

T. B. LONG, one of the representative members of the bar of Brule County, is a native of Iowa, and secured his early educational discipline in the public schools of Mason City, Iowa, being graduated in the high school, and later he was for one year a student in the law department of the Iowa State University, at Iowa City, having previously prosecuted his technical reading under an able preceptor, and was admitted to the bar. In 1880 Judge Long came to what is now the state of South Dakota and located in Mitchell, where he was engaged in the practice of his profession about two years, while he also took up a pre-emption claim adjoining the town site of Mount Vernon, in the same county. Later he came to Brule County and took up his residence in Kimball, where he has ever since maintained his home and where he has gained prestige in his profession and distinguished precedence as a citizen. He is an uncompromising Republican in his political proclivities and was elected state's attorney of Brule County. He was also elected to the probate bench, and he acceptably administered the affairs of this important office for one term. Under the administration of President Harrison, Judge Long was appointed postmaster at Kimball, and held the office four years. Since retiring from office, he has given his attention to the active work of his profession. Fraternally he is identified with the Masonic order and also the Knights of Pythias. Judge Long was united in marriage to Miss Minnie Egloff, and they have one child.

L. K. LORD

L. K. LORD, president of the First National Bank of Parker, Turner County, is a native of the state of Connecticut, having been born at Stafford Springs, on the 31st of December, 1851, and being a son of John K. and Sarah (Spellman) Lord, the former of whom was born in Maine and the latter in Connecticut, while both families have long been identified with the annals of New England history. The father of the subject was a contractor by vocation, and both he and his wife died in the state of Connecticut.

L. K. Lord was reared to manhood in his native state, in whose public schools he secured his early educational training. He continued his residence in Connecticut until 1883, when he came to the west and located in the state of South Dakota, where he was engaged in the grain business. He was one of the projectors and organizers of the First National Bank of Parker, which was founded in 1887 and of which he has been president since then. It is one of the popular and substantial financial institutions of the state, basing its operations on a capital of twenty-five thousand dollars, while its deposits have now reached the notable aggregate of nearly two hundred thousand dollars. Mr. Lord devotes the major portion of his time and attention to the executive duties devolving upon him in this connection and to the management of his other capitalistic and industrial interests.

On the 29th of October, 1872, Mr. Lord was united in marriage to Miss Nettie M. Converse, who was likewise born in his native town of Stafford Springs, Connecticut, being a daughter of Orrin and Marietta Converse. Mr. Lord is a Mason, having attained the Royal Arch degree, and also belongs to the Ancient Order of United Workmen and the Knights of Pythias. In 1902-3 he was president of the South Dakota Bankers' Association.

THOMAS QUINBY LOVELAND

T. Q. LOVELAND, one of the honored pioneers of Brookings county, is a native of the state of Ohio, having been born in Trumbull county, on the 14th of January, 1829, and being a son of Azehel and Emily (Newell) Loveland, both of whom were born in the state of Connecticut, their marriage being solemnized in Ohio, where Mr. Loveland was engaged in farming and followed the trade of carpenter until his son Thomas, subject of this review, attained such age as to make it possible for him to assume the management of the farm. When the subject was sixteen years of age his parents removed to the northern part of Trumbull County, locating near the town of Bristol, where the father turned his attention to lumbering, having owned and operated a sawmill, in which Thomas was actively employed for some time. Azehel Loveland died in the year 1851, his death resulting from an accident, — a slight cut in the knee developing into blood poisoning, from which he died nine days after receiving the injury, being survived by his wife and five children, concerning the latter of whom we incorporate the following brief record: Thomas O., is the immediate subject of this review; Emily, who is deceased, was the wife of Hiram Williams, of Trumbull County, Ohio; Martha is the wife of Smith Travis, of Bristol, that county; Mary, the widow of John Russell, is a resident of Pittsburg, Pennsylvania; and Sidney A. is a resident of Ellsworth, Minnesota. The devoted mother was summoned into eternal rest in 1881, her death occurring in Bristol, Ohio.

Thomas O. Loveland continued to be associated with his father in business until the death of the latter, and continued the enterprise one year thereafter in the interest of the family. On the 2d of April, 1850, he was united in marriage to Miss Roana House, a daughter of Alvin and Sallie (Melbe) House, who came to Ohio from Stanestead, Canada, passing the remainder of their lives in the old Buckeye state. Our subject and his wife walked side by side on the journey of life for more than half a century, strong in mutual love and confidence, and the silver cord was finally loosened when the devoted wife and helpmeet was summoned to the land of the leal, on the 19th of March, 1901, at the age of sixty-nine years. She was a woman of noble and gracious character and was loved by all who came within the sphere of her influence. Of the union of Mr. and Mrs. Loveland were born nine children, of whom two died in infancy. Of those who attained maturity we enter data as follows: Rozelia, the widow of Enos M. Hunt, is a resident of Alexandria, Minnesota; Ella is the wife of Dr. James L. Colegrove, of Brookings, South Dakota; Edna is the wife of Austin Maxwell, of Kanaranzi, Minnesota; Emma is the wife of George Thayer, of Brookings; Quimby A. resides in Fairfield, Wisconsin; Susie is the wife of Herman M. Harden, editor and publisher of the Huron Democrat, at Huron, South Dakota; and Addie is the wife of Judson R. Towne, a teacher in the high school at Duluth, Minnesota.

After retiring from the lumbering business, the subject conducted a hotel at Bristol, Ohio, about two years, at the expiration of which he removed to Baraboo, Sauk county, Wisconsin, in which locality he rented a farm, to whose cultivation he devoted his attention for the ensuing year, and he thereafter was in the hotel business in Baraboo for two years. This was about the time of the discovery of gold at Pike's Peak, Colorado, and Mr. Loveland was among those who set forth to seek fortune in the new Eldorado. He set forth for the gold fields and the company proceeded as far as Fort Carney, where they encountered persons returning from Pike's Peak, their reports being so unfavorable as to cause many of the outgoing party to abandon the trip and return home, among the number being the subject. He was thereafter engaged in farming in Sauk County, Wisconsin, for two years, within which time the dark clouds of civil war obscured the national horizon. In 1863 he tendered his services in defense of the Union, enlisting as a private in Company F, Third Wisconsin Cavalry, with which he continued in active set vice until December, 1865, when he received his honorable discharge, at Madison, Wisconsin. It was his good fortune to receive no wound while fighting for the integrity of the nation, nor was he ill at any time during his term of service. He was discharged as second lieutenant and brevetted first lieutenant of his company, having been promoted to this office within a year after his enlistment, while he proved a valiant and faithful soldier of the republic. In the spring of 1866, with money which he had saved from his pay as a soldier, he purchased sixteen acres of land at Russell's Corners, Sauk County, Wisconsin, and there began raising hops. He continued this enterprise one year, disposing of his property after gathering his first crop, for which he secured sixty cents a pound. From this source he realized sufficient money to purchase a farm of fifty-five acres, in the same township. He remained on this farm until 1872, when he sold the property and started for the west, his financial resources at the time being represented in the sum of one thousand dollars. He proceeded to Rock County, Minnesota, where he entered claim to a homestead, proving on the same and there continuing to follow agricultural pursuits until he found that his efforts were rendered futile by conditions over which he had no control. In 1878 the grasshoppers destroyed his crops, and for five years their depredations were such that he was not able to even raise seed for planting, being compelled to mortgage his farm and eventually losing the property. In 1878 he determined to try his fortunes in South Dakota, whither he came with a team, a small supply of farming implements and seven or eight head of cattle, the only vestiges of his years of toil and endeavor. He settled near the little village of Fountain, in Aurora township, Brookings County, where he took up pre-emption and tree claims, thus coming into possession of a half section of land. His first effort was to bring about the required improvement of his tree claim, which he did by the setting out of ten acres of trees, and he bent himself earnestly to the work before him and soon a definite success attended his efforts. In time he erected on his farm a commodious and substantial house, good barn and other buildings, while he brought two hundred and forty acres of the tract under a high state of cultivation, developing one of the valuable farms of this section of the state. In 1900 he disposed of his farm, having become the owner of an entire section, and from this sale he realized eleven thousand dollars, — a fact which stands in evidence of the prosperity which had been gained through his indefatigable energy and his availing himself of the excellent opportunities presented. After disposing of his farm Mr. Loveland took up his residence in the city of Brookings, where he has since maintained his home, being now the owner of four houses and lots in the city and having other excellent investments. He is now living retired and is enjoying the just rewards of his many years of honest and earnest toil.

Fraternally he is a member of the Masonic order, but is not affiliated with any of its bodies in an active way at the present time. He was reared in the faith of the Democratic party, to which he gave his allegiance until the outbreak of the war of the Rebellion, since which time he has been a stanch advocate of the principles of the Republican party. In 1894 he was elected a member of the board of county commissioners of Brookings County, serving three years, within which term the county jail and sheriff's residence were erected.

Sherman F. LUCAS, of Bonesteel, Gregory County, was born in Waverly, Bremer County, Iowa, on the 17th of September, 1864, and is a son of William V. and Sophronia M. (Lowe) Lucas, both being of Scotch-Irish lineage. William Vincent Lucas was born in Carroll County, Indiana, on the 3d of July, 1835, and was there reared and educated. In 1856 he was united in marriage to Sophronia M. Lowe, who was born in the same county, in 1835, and in the same year they removed to Iowa and became numbered among the pioneers of Bremer County. The father of the subject was a presidential elector from that state in 1876, served as treasurer of Bremer County for four years, and was a man of much influence in his community, while in 1880-81 he had the distinction of serving in the office of auditor of the state of Iowa. In 1883 he removed with his family to South Dakota and located in Brule County, of which he was treasurer for one term. He was a member of congress from South Dakota for the term of 1893 and 1894 and was for several years commandant of the State Soldiers' Home, at Hot Springs, being himself a veteran of the Civil war, and he resigned this office on the 1st of July, 1903, and removed to California, being now a resident of Santa Cruz, that state. His cherished and devoted wife was summoned into eternal rest in August, 1896. She was a woman of noble and gracious character, a zealous member of the Methodist Episcopal church and was held in affectionate regard by all who came within the sphere of her influence.

Sherman F. Lucas secured his early educational discipline in the public schools of Waverly and Mason City, Iowa, and learned the printer's trade in the newspaper office of his father, in the latter place. In May, 1883, he came to the present state of South Dakota and located in the village of Castalia, where in the following month, in association with his brother, Aaron B., he engaged in the newspaper business, establishing the Castalia Republican, the pioneer paper of the town. In 1888 he disposed of his interest in this enterprise and accepted a position as assistant cashier in the Charles Mix County Bank, at Castalia. In 1890 he was appointed clerk of the courts of that county and served one year, being defeated for re-election in the Populistic landslide of that year, though he ran eighty votes ahead of his ticket and was defeated by only eleven votes. He passed the year 1891 in Fort Randall, being placed in charge of the post trader's store by the receiver. He was chief clerk of the enrolling and engrossing force of the lower house of the state legislature during the general assembly of 1893, and during the summer of 1895 was second clerk on the Diamond Joe line of steamers, plying between St. Louis and St. Paul. In 1856 he was appointed assignee of the Charles Mix County Bank, continuing his residence in Castalia, that county, until 1899, when he removed to Bonesteel, Gregory County, and here established the Gregory County News, disposing of the same in May, 1903, to S. P. Ayres & Son. On the 1st of April, 1899, he was appointed postmaster of the town and has since remained incumbent of this office. In 1899 he was admitted to the bar of the state upon examination before the supreme court, and gives considerable attention to the practice of his profession. He was the candidate on his party ticket for county judge in 1900, but was defeated by the Democratic candidate, Edwin M. Starcher. He served two years as a member of the board of trustees of the village of Bonesteel and is known as one of its most loyal, progressive and public-spirited citizens, while he gives an uncompromising allegiance to the Republican party. as may be inferred from preceding statements. At the time of the Spanish-American war Mr. Lucas raised in Charles Mix County a company of volunteers, but they were not mustered into the United States service, by reason of the fact that the state's quota of soldiers was fully supplied from the members of its National Guard.

Mr. Lucas was affiliated with Doric Lodge, No. 93, Ancient Free and Accepted Masons, at Castalia. of which he was master for one year. A lodge is about to be constituted at Bonesteel and Mr. Lucas has been selected as its first worshipful master. He is also identified with the Royal Arch Masons, at Mitchell; is venerable consul of Bonesteel Camp. No. 4793, Modern Woodmen of America, and also affiliated with the Brotherhood of American Yeomen. Mrs. Lucas is a member of the Methodist Episcopal church, and the subject contributes to the support of the same. On the 24th of June, 1899, Mr. Lucas was united in marriage to Miss Cora B. Johnson, who was born at Fredericksburg, Bremer County, Iowa, in March, 1875, being a daughter of Marcellus M. and Ella M. Johnson, early and honored pioneers of Dakota territory. Mr. and Mrs. Lucas have two children, Vincent Lowe, who was born April 20, 1900, and Arthur Wayne, who was born May 9, 1902.

ANDREW H. LUNDIN

Andrew H. LUNDIN was born in Sweden on August 24, 1848, and remained in his native land until he was twenty, receiving his education and learning his trade as a blacksmith there. In 1868 he came to the United States, and after working at his trade for nearly five years in various parts of the East, went to California in 1873, and during the next three years was employed at his craft in San Francisco and at mines in other parts of the state. In 1876 he returned east on a visit, and the next spring came to the Black Hills, arriving in May. A few months were passed in different portions of this region, then in September, 1877, he settled at Lead, where he has since maintained his home. His first engagement here was. as a blacksmith for the Golden Star mine, and later he worked for the Highland in the same capacity. This was before these properties belonged to the Homestake Company, and when it acquired them, he accepted employment with it, remaining in its service until 1882. In that year he took charge of the shops of the Black Hills & Fort Pierre Railroad at Lead, this line at that time belonging to the Homestake Company. When it was sold to the Burlington in August, 1901, he left its employ and took a year's rest. In the fall of 1902, he built his present shop on Prince Street, and here he has worked up a large and profitable business in blacksmithing and making wagons. He has been thrifty all the while as well as industrious, and has acquired considerable real estate of value in the town and extensive mining interests. On April 19, 1882, he was married at Lead to Miss Helen Brakke, a native of Wisconsin. They have three children, Alfred, Willard and Helen.

Mr. Lundin is a devoted and zealous member of the Masonic order and the Independent Order of Odd Fellows, holding his membership in the lodges of these fraternities at Lead. No man in the town or neighborhood stands higher in the general estimation of the public, and none deserves a higher place in public regard and good will.

D. E. A. LUNDQUIST

D. E. A. Lundquist, the first settler of the thriving town of Irene, South Dakota, and in point of continuous residence its oldest inhabitant, is a native of Sweden, where his birth occurred on the 22d day of February, 1858. His father, A. G. Lundquist, a well-to-do merchant and landowner, also interested for a number of years in factories and various other industrial enterprises, departed this life in his native land in the summer of 1888. The mother, whose maiden name was Eva Wennerstrom, also born and reared in Sweden, is still living in that country, as are other members of the family, the subject and two brothers who reside in New York City being the only representatives in the United States.

Mr. Lundquist received a liberal education in the schools of his native place and after finishing the same, in the summer of 1872, took up the study of telegraphy, which in due time he mastered. For six years he had charge of a railway station in Norway, during which time he creditably filled the positions of operator, ticket agent and bookkeeper. At the expiration of the time noted he resigned his position and on December 4, 1879, left Norway for America, bound for Minnesota, reaching Delavan, that state, twenty-three days after bidding farewell to the shores of his native land. The winter following his arrival he attended a country school and after spending the next summer herding cattle, he accepted, in the fall of 1880, a clerkship in a general store in the town of Easton. During the ensuing five years he served as clerk and bookkeeper for different mercantile establishments in Faribault County, Minnesota, and in the fall of 1885 went to La Crosse, Wisconsin, as bookkeeper for a construction company which was building a branch line of the Chicago, Burlington & Quincy Railroad to that city.

Severing his connection with this company, Mr. Lundquist subsequently returned to Minnesota and for some time thereafter held the position of bookkeeper and cashier in the bank at Wells, Faribault County, which place he resigned in the summer of 1887 and went to Sioux Falls, South Dakota, to enter upon his duties as bookkeeper for a contractor who was constructing into that city a section of the Illinois Central Railroad. When this work was done, he concluded to remain at Sioux Falls, and after spending five years there as bookkeeper in a wholesale house, he again turned his attention to railroading, engaging in the winter of 1892 with the Great Northern, which at that time was being constructed between the cities of Sioux Falls and Yankton. Since the completion of this work, in the fall of 1893, Mr. Lundquist has lived at Irene, with the history of which town he has been very closely identified ever since the place was located. Mr. Lundquist came to Irene before the town was laid out, locating on the present site April 15, 1893, shortly after severing his connections with the Great Northern Railroad. When the town was, in the summer of the above year, surveyed and platted, and the proprietor, Jacob Schaetzel, Jr., of Sioux Falls, placed the lots on the market, Mr. Lundquist was appointed agent and continued as such until the fall of 1894, during which time he disposed of the greater number of lots, besides using his influence to advertise the advantages of the place to the world and induce a substantial class of people to locate in the new and rapidly growing town. He not only erected the first building in Irene and became the first permanent resident, but is also the father of the first child born in the town, besides being the first merchant, served on the first school hoard, was the first justice of the peace, and the first man in the place to be commissioned notary public. Shortly after locating at Irene Mr. Lundquist opened a general store, which he has since conducted with a large and steadily growing patronage.

Mr. Lundquist is a member of the Masonic brotherhood, belonging to Lodge No. 5, Sioux Falls, having joined the order at Blue Earth City, Minnesota, in 1885; he is also a charter member of Camp No. 2323, Modern Woodmen of America, with which society he united in June, 1894, and in addition to these fraternities, he has been identified since November, 1899, with Council No. 24, Ancient Order of Pyramids, besides belonging to the order of Home Guardians, Temple Lodge No. I, at Canton, South Dakota, joining the last named organization in November, 1902.

On September 20, 1890, at Spirit Lake, Iowa, was solemnized the ceremony which united Mr. Lundquist and Miss Etta Capitolia Cassidy in the holy bonds of wedlock. Mrs. Lundquist was born August 4, 1869, in Missouri, and she has presented her husband with five children, whose names and dates of birth are as follows: Viva Rose, January 1, 1892; Vera Maud, September 19, 1893; Elsie Ruth, November 4, 1894; Esther May, June 9, 1896, and Eva Grace, April 20, 1899, all living, and all born in Irene except the oldest, who first saw the light of day in the city of Sioux Falls.

ℳ

REV. ROWLAND OLIVER MACKINTOSH

The Rev. Rowland Oliver Mackintosh, rector of Christ's (Episcopal) church of Lead, South Dakota, is a power not only in church circles of the city but also in the larger community life, as he realizes that the clergy can serve the cause of Christianity by aiding in all those movements that seek the betterment of mankind as well as by caring for the spiritual needs of the members of their congregations. Without neglecting in the least this last duty, Mr. Mackintosh has done much for the welfare of the community along many lines of moral progress. He was born in County Donegal, Ireland, on the 20th of April, 1881, a son of John and Elizabeth (McClay) Mackintosh. The father was born in Inverness, Scotland, and the mother in County Tyrone, Ireland, of Scotch antecedents. They are now residents of Donegal, Ireland, where the father was connected with the government service.

Rev. Rowland O. Mackintosh was reared at home, receiving his early educational training in the public schools, while later he was instructed by a tutor. Upon leaving the Emerald Isle he went to Canada, where he spent two years with a brother, being engaged during that time in survey work in connection with railroad construction. Determining upon the ministry as a life work, he entered the Kansas Theological College at Topeka in 1904 and graduated in 1907. He became rector of St. John's church at Parsons, Kansas, where he remained for about two years, after which he devoted three and a half years to missionary work in California and Wyoming. In February, 1914, he was called to Lead as rector of Christ's church, which has one of the largest Episcopal Sunday schools west of Chicago and the largest church attendance in Lead. The members of the church are on the whole deeply devoted to its interests and the influence of the organization is felt throughout the city, being a strong force for moral advancement. The zeal and consecration of Mr. Mackintosh are a potent element in the development of the church, which has already accomplished great things in the name of Christianity.

He was married on the 10th of June, 1908, to Miss Helen Attrill, of Ridgewood Park, Goderich, Ontario, Canada, and to this union has been born a son, John, whose natal day was October 12, 1909.

Mr. Mackintosh is a member of Parsons Lodge, No. 183, A. F. & A. M., and Deadwood Consistory, No. 3, having taken the thirty-second degree in Scottish Rite Masonry. He believes in the wisdom of the policies of the republican party and supports its candidates at the polls. While in Wyoming he was chaplain for the National Guard of that state. His sincerity, zeal and straightforwardness and his exemplification of the spirit of brotherly kindness have won him not only the esteem of his own people, but the respect of the community at large.

Ernest Madden, clerk of the courts of Lincoln County, was born in Worthing, that county, on the 13th of December, 1877, a son of James and Mary (GerDer) Madden. The father was a native of Schuylkill County, Pennsylvania, and the mother of Spring Green, Wisconsin. They were married in South Dakota, Mrs. Madden having come to this state with her parents, while Mr. Madden arrived in South Dakota when a young man following the Civil War. During the period of hostilities between the north and south he had served as a member of Company A, Ninety-fifth Illinois Volunteer Infantry, rendering valuable aid to his country in that connection. Upon his removal to the northwest, he settled in Lincoln County, establishing his home there in 1870. He took up a homestead claim, on a part of which the town of Worthing now stands, and he is still living upon that farm.

It was there that Ernest Madden was reared and the public schools of Worthing provided him his early educational facilities, while later he attended the Brookings Business College. He was but fourteen years of age when upon him practically devolved the management of the farm, for his father, conducting a grain business in Worthing, gave most of his attention to that undertaking. Although the duties and responsibilities that came to him were heavy, he resolutely and bravely met them and early displayed marked ability and notable enterprise. At eighteen years of age, he became a member of the South Dakota State Militia, enlisting in Company I, which was later reorganized and became Company D. Mr. Madden rose from private to the rank of first sergeant of his company. On the outbreak of the Spanish-American war, he was one of fifteen members of his company who enlisted, and was mustered in as a member of Company D, First Regiment, South Dakota Volunteers. He was with that command from the 25th of April, 1898, until discharged on the 18th of August, 1899. At the time of his enlistment, he was made first sergeant of his company. The regiment was assigned to duty in the Philippines and he took part in a number of engagements, including the battle in the trenches at Manila, February 23, 1899, the skirmish at San Francisco, Del Monte, on the 25th of March, 1899, and the skirmish near Polo on the following day. He was also in the battle of Marilao River on the 27th of March, 1899, and there sustained a gunshot wound in the arm and chest. He was in line for promotion at that time and was brevetted second lieutenant. His discharge reads: "Service honest and faithful, and character excellent."

After being discharged from the army Mr. Madden returned home and pursued a business course in the State Agricultural College at Brookings. He then turned his attention to the grain trade, forming a partnership with his father at Worthing, but on account of ill health he was forced to take up an outdoor life and for two and a half years was carrier on a rural mail route. In May, 1908, he resigned and took up a homestead on the lower Brule Indian reservation in Lyman County, upon which he resided until he proved up on his claim. He then returned to Worthing and again became associated with his father in the grain business. Energy and determination have always been his and have figured largely in his success, not only in commercial lines, but also in public affairs.

It was about the time of his return to Worthing that Mr. Madden became actively interested in local politics and in June, 1912, he was nominated on the republican ticket for the office of clerk of the courts, to which position he was chosen at the November election of that year. He took his office on the 1st of January, 1913, and in the March primaries of 1914 he was nominated without opposition and was again chosen to the office, the duties of which he has ever discharged with promptness and fidelity.

In 1903 Mr. Madden was united in marriage to Miss Ella L. Raines, of Lake City, Minnesota, and to them have been born five children: Melba R., Wayne M., Norma R., James E. and Ernestine H. Mr. Madden belongs to Worthing Lodge, No. 145, F. & A. M., and has attained the thirty-second degree of the Scottish

Rite, his membership being in Oriental Consistory, S. P. R. S. He also belongs to El Riad Temple, A. A. O. N. M. S., at Sioux Falls, and he and his wife are members of the Order of the Eastern Star. He is likewise connected with the Canton Commercial Club and he thoroughly indorses its well formulated plans for the upbuilding of the city. He has never faltered in his allegiance to the republican party, yet he places the general good before partisanship and the welfare of the community before personal aggrandizement.

JAMES MADDEN

J. MADDEN, of Worthing, who has been a resident of Lincoln County for more than thirty years, was born near Newcastle, Schuylkill County, Pennsylvania, on the 9th of November, 1847, and is a son of Owen and Ellen (Tulley) Madden, both of whom were born in County Galway, Ireland, whence they came to America when young, their marriage having been solemnized at Pottsville, Pennsylvania. They were descended from stanch old Irish stock, identified with the annals of the province of Connaught for many generations. The father of the subject was employed in the mines in Pennsylvania, and met his death as the result of an accident while thus working, our subject being but eighteen months old at the time; while his mother died when he was but nine years of age, so that he was early thrown upon his resources and is to be considered as essentially the architect of his own fortunes. He attended the common schools of Pennsylvania until the death of his mother and later contrived to effectively supplement this training by doing farm work in summer and various chores in winter, during which latter period he had the privilege of attending school, receiving his board in compensation for his services in the line noted. In 1856, wishing to find some other occupation than that which had cost his father his life, he accompanied an unmarried uncle to McHenry County, Illinois, where he worked on a farm for several years, in the meanwhile attending school, as before stated. In 1864 he signalized his patriotism by enlisting in the defense of the Union, becoming a private in Company A, Ninety-fifth Illinois Volunteer Infantry, with which he proceeded to the front, taking part in the battle of Nashville, Tennessee, and the engagement at Spanish Fort, Alabama, which was captured by the Sixteenth Army Corps, on the evening of April 8, 1865, General A. J. Smith commanding the corps, Mr. Madden continued in active service until the close of the war, when he received his honorable discharge and returned to Illinois, where he remained until 1868, when he removed to Steele County, Minnesota, where he was engaged in farm work during the summer of that year and employed in the lumbering woods during the ensuing winter. In the spring of 1869 he returned to Illinois, and with the money saved from his earnings he purchased a team of horses, with which he returned to Minnesota, where he was associated with a friend in farming for one season, disaster attending their enterprise, as their crops were destroyed by a severe hailstorm. Mr. Madden then abandoned agricultural pursuits and passed the winter of 1871-2 in the south, and in the spring of the latter year he came as a pioneer to what is now South Dakota and filed on a homestead claim in Lincoln County, and on this place he has ever since maintained his home, while he has added to his holdings until he now has a valuable and finely improved landed estate of one hundred acres, being part of the town site, continuing to devote his attention to diversified agriculture and to the raising of stock, while for the past twelve years he has also controlled a prosperous business in the buying and shipping of grain. He held for several terms the office of chairman of the official board of Lynn township, and has also been a valued member of the board of trustees of the village of Worthing, which is located on his- old homestead. He gave his allegiance to the Republican party until its repudiation of bimetallic monetary system, and since that time he endeavors to support the men and measures which seem most fully American and make for the perpetuation of the principles on which our republic is founded.

Fraternally he is an appreciative member of the time-honored Masonic order, with which he has been identified since 1882, having at the time of this writing attained to the thirty-second degree in the Ancient Accepted Scottish Rite and being affiliated with Oriental Consistory, No. I, of the valley of Yankton. He has also been a member of the Grand Army of the Republic since 1885, and takes a deep interest in his old comrades in arms. He is liberal and tolerant in his religious views and recognizes the good accomplished by all denominations. He is straightforward and sincere in all the relations of life, his integrity is beyond question, and thus he has gained a wide circle of loyal friends, and ever holds this friendship inviolable. On the 12th of December, 1876, at Canton, this county, Mr. Madden was united in marriage to Miss Mary Gerber, a daughter of Frederick and Augustine Gerber, the former of whom was born and reared in Switzerland, while the latter was born in Germany. The following record is entered concerning the children of Mr. and Mrs. Madden, the respective dates of birth being given in the connection: Ernest, December 13, 1877; Cora, Alay 29, 1882; Maud, May 18, 1885; Frederick, July 2, 1886; Mary Ellen, July 3, 1894; June, October 18, 1896; and Edwin Tulley, September 25, 1903.

ALEXANDER MADIL

Alexander MADIL was born in Ogdensburgh, St. Lawrence County, New York, on January 29, 1843. He was reared to agricultural pursuits in his native county, attended the public schools at intervals during his minority, and at the age of twenty-three left New York and went to Waupaca County, Wisconsin, where he engaged in the lumber business. After remaining in the latter state until the spring of 1877, Mr. Madill came to South Dakota and during the greater part of the next year and a half devoted his attention to prospecting in the Black Hills, with Deadwood as his headquarters. In the fall of 1878, he went to Custer City and began prospecting on French creek, but the following year changed his location to the site of the present city of Keystone, where he purchased a number of mining claims, which have since increased in value. In 1880, with Dr. Hope, he located the Bullion mine, in which Benjamin Mitchell subsequently acquired an interest. Mr. Madill and the latter gentleman being principal owners of the property at the present time. This mine, which is bonded to eastern capitalists, shows great value and promises, when fully developed, to become one of the largest and richest mining properties in the Black Hills.

In addition to the above, Mr. Madill has located a number of other valuable claims in different parts of the country, several of which he sold at liberal prices, and he was also interested for some time in the Ida Florence mine, a mine of great promise, which he helped promote and develop. Mr. Madill lived at Keystone until the spring of 1891, when he came to Squaw creek and took up his present ranch, five miles from Hermosa, where, in addition to looking after his mining interests, he has since been engaged in farming and stock raising. He has a fine place which is admirably suited to agriculture and grazing, and has spared neither pains nor expense in developing and improving the property and providing his family with the conveniences and comforts and not a few of the luxuries of life. Mr. Madill is one of the progressive men of the Black Hills and manifests commendable zeal in whatever makes for the growth and development of this section of the state. Always a staunch Republican, he persistently refused to accept office from his party until the fall of 1900, when he was induced, much against his will, to consent to run for the legislature. His election followed as a matter of course and he represented the county in a very creditable manner, proving an able and indefatigable worker for the interests of his constituency, and earning an honorable reputation as a law maker. In all that constitutes intelligent and aggressive citizenship, Mr. Madill is easily the peer of any of his contemporaries, and as a kind and obliging neighbor, with the good of his fellow men at heart, he enjoys the esteem and confidence not only of the community in which he resides, but of the people of the county as well.

He is a member of the Masonic fraternity, at Keystone, and in addition thereto gives his support to all public and private benevolences, being charitable and ever ready to assist the deserving poor wherever they may be found. On January 20, 1873, Mr. Madill was united in marriage with Miss Emma Kelley, a native of Maine, but at that time living in Waupaca County, Wisconsin, where the ceremony took place. Five children have been born to Mr. and Mrs. Madill, namely: George, Gertrude, Roy, Earl and Olive.

JUDGE WILLIAM B. MALLORY

Judge William B. Mallory, attorney at law, who is now serving as judge upon the bench of the county court, is an able representative of that profession which has long been regarded as the conservator of the rights and privileges, the life and liberties of the individual. In his practice he has ever held to high professional standards and since coming to the bench his opinions have been characterized by the utmost impartiality and fairness. Judge Mallory is a native of Eaton Rapids, Michigan, born August 23, 1878, of the marriage of W. H. H. and Florence (Godfrey) Mallory. The family removed to North Dakota in 1882, when the son William was but four years of age, and there took up a homestead claim and began the development of a farm in a district which was still upon the frontier.

William B. Mallory pursued his early education in the public schools and afterward attended the university at Mitchell. Having decided upon the practice of law as a life work, he completed his law course in the State University of Wisconsin at Madison in 1904 and was admitted to the bar of South Dakota the same year. He immediately opened an office at Lennox and from the beginning enjoyed a large and growing practice. No dreary novitiate awaited him. He was the only lawyer in Lennox and he soon demonstrated his power to cross swords in forensic combat with many an older and more seasoned lawyer in the district. His ability in that direction led to his election to the office of county judge. In fact, throughout much of the period of Mr. Mallory's residence in Lennox he has been in public office and the record that he has made in this connection is a most commendable and creditable one. He is now president of the board of education and gives much of his time to advancing the interests of the schools, thinking out along broad lines which will benefit the educational system and render it more effective in the preparation of the young for life's practical and responsible duties. The present commodious, modern school building has been erected during his term of office.

On the 21st of June, 1906, Judge Mallory was united in marriage to Miss Mara Avery, a daughter of Charles Avery, and unto them have been born two sons, Paul and Beverly. The parents hold membership in the Methodist church and are earnest Christian people, who exemplify in their lives the teachings of that denomination. Judge Mallory is also a valued representative of Lennox Lodge, No. 35, F. & A. M. He takes his recreation in bird study and few men outside of the profession are better informed on ornithology. Politically be is a republican and, while he is not a politician in the usually accepted sense of the term, his fellow townsmen, recognizing his ability, called him to the office of judge of Lincoln County in 1912, since which time he has sat upon the bench, making a most creditable record in conducting the work of the courts, which he does in a most dignified manner, the proceedings being ever orderly on the part of everyone. He is seldom, if ever, at fault in the application of a legal principle and upon the bench he seems to have put aside every trace of personal prejudice that would in any way disturb the even balance of a just opinion.

JOHN W. MARTIN

Watertown owes more perhaps to the efforts of John W. Martin than to any other citizen. His work has been most effective in promoting the development and upbuilding of the city as he seems to see far into the possibilities and to work advantageously for public progress. Illinois claims him as a native son, his birth having occurred in Scales Mound, October 9, 1856, his parents being Henry and Keturah (Thomas) Martin, both of whom were natives of England. They came to the United States about 1845, when in young manhood and young womanhood, and the father was engaged in farming and also in lead mining. Mr. Martin passing away in 1900, while his wife died in 1894.

JOHN W. MARTIN.

John W. Martin was reared under the parental roof and supplemented his public-school education by study in the German-English College at Galena, Illinois, and in the State Normal school at Platteville, Wisconsin. Following the completion of his school life he took up the profession of teaching, which he followed for two years. He afterward engaged in farming and in August, 1885, arrived in South Dakota, settling in Watertown. He, today conducts a real-estate and investment business and is a prominent, active and influential business man. He was one of the prime movers in the organization of the Dakota Loan & Trust Company and also of the Watertown National Bank. He was elected a member of the board of directors of both corporations as well as the secretary of the first named and he also served for two years as cashier of the bank. He was one of four who organized time Dakota Mutual insurance Company and has since been active in its conduct and has contributed much to the remarkable growth and success of the business. He is now vice president of the company and is in charge of its loans and real-estate department. Again, he found scope for his industry and enterprise – his dominant qualities – in the organization of the Watertown Commercial Club, of which he is now one of the directors, active in promoting the work of that organization, which has been an effective factor in broadening the business connections of the city and furthering the interests of Watertown along many lines of general and civic improvement. He is likewise the vice president of the First National Bank and indeed has been for a number of years one of the foremost men in the business and financial life of Watertown. He is now heavily interested in South Dakota real estate and as a real-estate and investment broker has an extensive clientage.

The same spirit of activity characterizes his political connections. He is a democrat and has been one of the foremost men of his party in the northeastern section of the state. He served for ten years as a member of the democratic state central committee, was chairman in the year 1904 and in 1912 was chairman of the democratic state executive committee. In 1908 he was made a presidential elector and he has twice been nominated on the democratic ticket for the state legislature, while in 1902 he was the candidate of his party for governor of South Dakota. That his fellow townsmen have the utmost confidence in his business ability and his loyalty to the public good is indicated by the fact that they have seven times elected him to serve as their mayor, during which period he gave the city a most businesslike administration, resulting in public benefit along many lines.

In 1909 Mr. Martin was united in marriage to Mrs. Nellie L. Budd, formerly Miss Hattie Hobart, of Washington, D. C. They hold membership in the Congregational church and are very prominent socially. Mr. Martin holds membership with Kampeska Lodge, No. 13, A. F. & A. M.; Watertown Chapter, No. 12, R. A. M.; Watertown Commandery, No. 7, K. T.; and El Riad Temple, A. A. O. N. M. S., of Sioux Falls. He also belongs to Watertown Lodge, No. 838, B. P. O. E.; to Trishocton Lodge, No. 7, K. P.; to the Ancient Order of United Workmen; and to the Modern Woodmen of America, and he is likewise a member of the Watertown Country Club. In all things he displays an initiative spirit that is an element essential to success. He is not afraid to mark out new paths and where his judgment indicates he does not hesitate to pursue a course that seems to promise success. That his sagacity is keen, his enterprise unfaltering and his progressiveness shrewd is indicated in the high position which he now occupies and the success which has attended his efforts.

WILLIAM H. MARTIN

William H. Martin, chief of police at Sioux Falls, was born at Ashippun, Dodge County, Wisconsin, February 17, 1850, and is descended from Scotch ancestry, his parents being John Duncan and Caroline (Wilks) Martin, both of whom were natives of Dundee, Scotland. In the public schools of his native town William H. Martin pursued his education and remained upon the homestead farm until his fifteenth year, when his patriotic spirit was aroused and he enlisted as a private of Company I, Forty-eighth Wisconsin Volunteer Infantry, continuing in active duty at the front until mustered out on the 24th of June, 1865. following the cessation of hostilities.

Returning to his home in Wisconsin, Mr. Martin became apprenticed to the carpenter's trade, which he followed for several years. When twenty-one years of age he was elected constable in his native town, gaining thus early in life experience in handling those who do not hold themselves amenable to the law. He continued in that position for six years and in 1876 he removed to Waukesha, Wisconsin, where he engaged in business as a contractor and builder until 1882. At that date he was appointed deputy sheriff of the county and made an excellent record during his six years' incumbency in the position. In 1889 he removed to Dakota territory, settling at Sioux Falls, where he again began contracting and building and was thus engaged until May, 1890, but his ability for public service led to his being again called to office. He was appointed a member of the police force and for two years acted as a patrolman, when the eminently satisfactory character of his service made him the logical man for chief of the police department and he was appointed to the office on the 1st of May, 1892. Indorsement of the able manner in which he discharged his duties came to him in his reappointment on the 3d of November, 1895, for a term of two years, and following his retirement from that position he served during 1897-8 as a guard at the state penitentiary. On the 2d of May, 1900, he was again made a member of the police department and appointed chief, in which important position he has continuously served, covering a period of fourteen consecutive years. That Sioux Falls has the reputation of being one of the best policed cities in the west is due in large measure to the executive ability and high sense of official honor of the man who stands at the head of the police system. From July 7, 1905, to October 1, 1911, he was deputy warden of the South Dakota State Penitentiary, and for more than a third of a century he has held office in one capacity or another, a record that is seldom equaled.

On the 13th of December, 1876, Mr. Martin was united in marriage to Miss Mary A. Best, a daughter of John and Margaret Best, of Dousman, Wisconsin, and they have one child, Stella M., now Mrs. E. E. Smith, of Wilmer, Minnesota.

In fraternal circles Mr. Martin is widely and prominently known, as he holds membership in Unity Lodge, No. 130, A. F. & A. M.; has taken the thirty-second degree in the Scottish Rite; belongs to El Riad Temple, A. A. O. N. M. S.; is a member of the Elks Lodge, No. 262; and is identified with Joe Hooker Post, No. 10, G. A. R. The last named enables him to maintain pleasant relations with the boys in blue with whom he was connected through the ties of active military service on the battlefields of the south. His political allegiance is given the republican party and he keeps in close touch with the issues and questions of the day, but at no time have political or personal prejudices or views interfered with the faithful performance of his official duties. His record is indeed most commendable and there is perhaps no other chief of police in all the state whose incumbency in office covers so extended a period.

GEORGE E. MASTERS

G. E. MASTERS, one of the prominent business men and honored citizens of Spencer, McCook County, was born in Steuben County, New York, February 26, 1853, a son of Samuel and Margaret (Farrington) Masters, of whose four children we incorporate the following brief data: Augusta A. is the wife of C. P. Sherwood, state dairy commissioner of South Dakota, and they reside in DeSmet; Jesse F. B. is likewise a resident of that place: Genevieve is the wife of W. G. Renwick, auditor for the zinc syndicate and a resident of the city of Chicago; and George E. is the subject of this review. Samuel Masters was born in New Jersey, in 1822, and when a child accompanied his parents on their removal to Steuben County, New York, where he was reared to the sturdy discipline of the farm, demical education, in Ithaca, New York, being given the advantages of an academy. There he completed a course in civil engineering, and in later years he found his services as a surveyor in much requisition, in connection with his agricultural operations. In 1878 he removed with his family to Minnesota, and three years later came to South Dakota, locating in Kingsbury County, where he took up a quarter section of government land. He rendered efficient service as county surveyor for a number of years and was one of the influential citizens of his section. He was a Democrat in politics and was a man of impregnable integrity and marked mentality. While a resident of Steuben County, New York, he held the office of superintendent of schools for several years, having also been a successful teacher and prominent in educational work. He died in 1893, having passed the psalmist's span of three score years and ten. His widow is still living and resides in the home of her daughter, Mrs. Sherwood, in DeSmet, being seventy-six years of age at the time of this writing, in 1903.

George E. Masters was reared under the gracious influences of a cultured and refined home, and after completing the curriculum of the public schools continued his studies for two years in Corning Academy, at Corning, New York. At the age of twenty-one he took a position as clerk in a drug store in that place, where he was employed for three years. In 1876 he set forth to carve out his career in the west, and for two years was employed in the city of Chicago. In 1878 he located in Walnut Grove, Minnesota, in which locality he was employed at farm work, and there, in 1879, he was married to Miss Margaret Gilmore. In the spring of the following year, he came with his bride to South Dakota, and during the ensuing summer he was employed in the company store of Walls, Harrison & Shute, railroad contractors, who were then engaged in the construction of the line between Tracy and Pierre. In the fall of that year Mr. Masters took a position as brakeman on this road, and in December went to DeSmet, Kingsbury County, in which locality he has filed entry on a tree claim in 1879 and on a homestead in the spring of 1880, his eldest son having been the first white child born in what is now the thriving little city of DeSmet. He continued to reside on his homestead until 1886, duly proving on the property under the homestead laws. Within this interval, in 1881, he accepted a position with the Empire Lumber Company, at DeSmet, and continued in the employ of this concern for ten and one-half years, while for one year he was an employee of the firm of Hanson & Lambert, engaged in the same line of enterprise in DeSmet. In 1893 he associated himself with his brother Jesse in the sheep business, in which he continued a short time. In 1892 he was candidate on the Democratic ticket for the office of state senator, there being three tickets in the field during that campaign. He succeeded in winning sufficient Republican votes to compass the election of the Populist candidate, and though he was himself defeated he gained no little influence in the ranks of his party, and this led to his securing the appointment of postmaster at DeSmet, an office which he held for four years under the administration of President Cleveland. In the winter of 1884, there was organized in DeSmet Company E of the National Guard of the Territory of Dakota, and our subject was made third sergeant of the same, from which position he finally rose to the office of captain. At the outbreak of the Spanish-American war Mr. Masters was senior captain of his regiment, which in 1898 tendered its services to the government, enlisting for service in the Philippines, where it made a brilliant record. Mr. Masters accompanied the regiment to Sioux Falls and there was rejected for service on account of his physical proportions. This was the reason given but he has ever been certain that the real cause of his rejection was one of political nature. He was, however, given the privilege of naming the lieutenants of the company over which he had so long been in command, and his choice fell upon Harry Hubbard and Sidney Morrison for first and second lieutenants, respectively. On bidding the boys farewell the last to grasp his hand were Lieutenant Morrison and Lewis Chase, both of whom met their death in the Philippines while in discharge of their patriotic duties.

In March, 1899, Mr. Masters accepted a position with the John W. Tuttle Lumber Company, as manager of their yards at Spencer, where he has since been located, being one of the honored and popular citizens of the place. He is a stanch advocate of the principles of the Democratic party and has long been an active worker in its cause. While a resident of DeSmet he served for a number of years as a member of the village council and also as a member of the board of education, while at the time of this writing he is president of the board of education in Spencer.

He is affiliated with Spencer Lodge, No. 126, Free and Accepted Masons, to which he transferred his membership from DeSmet Lodge, of which latter he is past master, as is he also of the lodge of the Ancient Order of United Workmen in that place. He and his wife are valued members of the Baptist church. Mention has been made of the fact that Mr. Masters was married in 1879, his nuptials having been solemnized, in July of that year, to Miss Margaret Gilmore, a resident of St. Charles, Minnesota, and a native of that state. They are the parents of nine children: Arthur, who is a resident of Dayton, Washington; Alexander also resides in that place; Vere H. is manager of the State Bank of Farmer; Claude is employed in a printing establishment here; and Juniata, Hazel, Genevieve, Ronald and George. Jr., remain at the parental home.

JAMES E. MATHER

James E. Mather, a member of the well-known law firm of Mather & Stover of Watertown, was born in Frazee, Minnesota, on the 1st of December, 1879, his parents being William H. and Lucy E. Mather. His elementary education was obtained in the public schools of Council Bluffs, Iowa, and later he was a student of Tabor College, Iowa. Deciding to enter the legal profession, he attended the Omaha School of Law, from which he was graduated in 1902. He began the practice of his profession in Omaha, Nebraska, later becoming assistant general attorney of the Cudahy Packing Company, and for two years practiced in that state and in Iowa. At the end of that period, he went to Chicago as general counsel for the A. Booth Packing Company and he made his home there until 1907, which year witnessed his arrival in Watertown. He began practice there as a member of the firm of Louchs & Mather and subsequently Mr. Stover was admitted to partnership. On the retirement of Mr. Louchs, the name was changed to Mather & Stover. The firm is meeting with good success, their clientage being of a representative character.

In 1900 Mr. Mather was united in marriage to Miss Ruby Agnes Bryant, who died in 1909, and two of the three children born to them are also deceased, the only one now living being Margaret, aged ten years. In 1910 Mr. Mather wedded Miss Maude P. Robinson, of Omaha, by whom he has a son, George, aged three years. They are members of the Episcopal church and are quite prominent socially. Mr. Mather belongs to Kampeska Lodge, No. 13, A. F. & A. M., and is a Knight Templar Mason, being an officer of the Grand Commandery of South Dakota. He is also connected with the Modern Woodmen of America and the Benevolent Protective Order of Elks. His political support is given to the republican party. There is a military chapter in his record as he served for ten years in the National Guard. He was a member of the organization at the outbreak of the Spanish-American war and was for two years in the Philippines with the Fifty-first Iowa Volunteer Infantry. When mustered out of the Guards he held the rank of brevet major. He has always been found true to every trust reposed in him and commands the respect and confidence of all with whom he is brought in contact.

RICHARD W. MATHIESON

Richard W. MATHIESON, one of the prominent and honored citizens of Fort Pierre, Stanley County, was born in Colesburg, Delaware county, Iowa, on the 5th of August, 1849, and is a son of Robert and Ann (Wood) Mathieson, the former of whom was born in Scotland, where records extant trace the lineage back through thirty-four generations, while the latter was born in England. The father of the subject was killed in the Indian massacre at Spirit Lake, Iowa, in 1857, his devoted wife surviving him by several years. The subject came with other members of the family, including his widowed mother, to the territory of Dakota in the spring of 1862, settling first in Bon Homme County and removing thence, in the fall of the same year, to Yankton, which was the family home for several years, Mr. Mathieson having completed his early educational training in the public schools of that city. In 1863 he entered upon an apprenticeship at the printer's trade in the office of the Union and Dakotan, a paper published in Yankton, and on the 29th of February of the following year he enlisted in Company B, First Dakota Cavalry, of which William Tripp was captain, and in the same year accompanied his regiment on the expedition to the Yellowstone River, under General Sully. In 1865 he took part in the expedition to Devil's Lake, and was mustered out of the service in November of that year, at Sioux City. Thereafter he was for some time employed at his trade, and also identified with early surveying work in the territory. Thereafter he conducted a wood yard and farmed and freighted four miles below Yankton for about five years. In the spring of 1871 he went to Colorado, where he was engaged in prospecting and mining during the major portion of the next eighteen months. In 1873 he made a trip up the Missouri river with a mule-team and assisted in the erection of Fort Lincoln, and in 1874 had charge of the sutler's teams in General Custer's expedition to the Black Hills. There he panned out about fifty cents, in gold dust, which he brought back with him, the amount being sufficient to prove to others that gold was to be found in that section. In September, 1874, he was associated with another man in the building of a skiff. in which they came down the Missouri river from

Bismarck to Yankton. In March, 1875, Mr. Mathieson went to the Black Hills with a stock of merchandise, and disposed of the same, returning to Yankton in the fall. He then purchased teams and engaged in freighting to the Black Hills, making the enterprise a most profitable one and continuing the same until 1882, when he disposed of his outfit and purchased a stock of general merchandise in Fort Pierre, in company with his brother, George D., while they also purchased a bunch of cattle and engaged in the raising of stock. After two years the partnership was dissolved, the subject taking the cattle while the brother retained the store as his share. In 1887 our subject removed his cattle to the range on the Cheyenne river, and when the reservation of that name was opened up, he took up his residence in Fort Pierre, where he has since maintained his home, while simultaneously he removed his cattle to a ranch at the Bad River, at the mouth of the Grindstone River, where he has since continued to be engaged in stock growing on an extensive scale. Mr. Mathieson has ever taken a deep interest in the civic and material development and progress of the state of which he is a sterling pioneer. He served one term as a member of the board of commissioners of Stanley County and one term as mayor of the city of Fort Pierre.

Fraternally he is affiliated with the following named bodies: Hiram Lodge, No. 123, Ancient Free and Accepted Masons, at Fort Pierre; Pierre Chapter, No. 22, Royal Arch Masons, in the capital city of the state; De Molay Commandery, No. 3, Knights Templar, in Yankton; and Lodge No. 75, Ancient Order of United Workmen, at Fort Pierre.

On the 28th of August, 1884, Mr. Mathieson was united in marriage to Miss Clara B. Pratt, who was the adopted daughter of David Pratt. She was born in Anoka, Minnesota, on the 14th of March, 1862, and is a daughter of Jonathan L. and Emily Nash, who died when she was a child. Of the children of Mr. and Mrs. Mathieson we enter the names, with respective dates of birth: Maud E., July 28, 1886; Kenneth W., June 19, 1890: Donald E., December 19, 1897.

ALBERT D. MAXWELL

Albert D. Maxwell is a pioneer merchant of Arlington and today occupies a prominent place in that community. The A. D. Maxwell Hardware Company owns the largest hardware store in that section of the state, an important business concern. Mr. Maxwell was born in Clinton, Illinois, November 10, 1855, a son of Martin and Mary E. Maxwell. The father was one of the pioneer lumbermen of Wisconsin, going to that state in 1855. He has passed away but his widow survives.

Albert D. Maxwell was educated in the public schools and upon putting aside his textbooks worked in a hardware store at Durant for a time. He then chartered a boat running on the Chippewa and Mississippi rivers and operated that vessel for two years. In 1880 he arrived in Dakota territory and immediately opened a hardware store in Norden, now Arlington. There was then no railroad in that part of the state and everything was hauled from Volga, the nearest railroad point. Although the pioneer conditions prevailing added unusual obstacles to those that always confront the merchant, Mr. Maxwell persevered and as he used good business judgment in all of his transaction's success came to him and the volume of his trade increased from year to year. His business is now housed in two splendid two-story brick buildings, fifty by one hundred and sixty-five feet in dimensions, and he carries the largest hardware stock in his section of the state. He also handles farm implements, autos and a number of other lines and Dick Maxwell, as he is familiarly called, is known to everyone in his part of South Dakota. His store was not only the first established in Arlington, but was the first hardware store in Kingsbury County, and he has added new lines and adapted his policy to the changing conditions of the section from which he derives his patronage. The prestige that he gained as a merchant in the early history of this section he has maintained. In 1880 he homesteaded land in Brookings County and is the owner of considerable farm property.

Mr. Maxwell was married March 2, 1880, to Miss Charlotte C. Gilmore, a daughter of John Gilmore, of Wisconsin, and their children are: Lou, now Mrs. Albert Royhl, of Arlington; John, Martin E. and Neil, all of whom are associated with their father in business; and Hugh, a resident of Mitchell, this state.

Mr. Maxwell is a republican and has held all of the local offices, proving as capable in an official capacity as in business circles. His religious faith is that of the Methodist church and he takes a helpful interest in the work of that organization. He is loyal to the spirit and purposes of the Masonic order, of which he is a member, belonging to the blue lodge, chapter, commandery and Shrine, and the success that he has gained in a material way is equaled by the esteem and respect in which he is generally held. He is the best-known man in Kingsbury County and one of the capitalists of his section of the state. His wealth has been gained, however, by the exercise of foresight, determination and business acumen and not by questionable practices. He takes satisfaction in the knowledge that he has been able to assist greatly in the commercial development of his section of the state and he has great faith in the future of South Dakota.

ERNEST MAY

ERNEST MAY

The development of the Black Hills country largely coincides with that of its wonderful mining resources and in that development, Ernest May has been an important factor. He was for many years prominently connected with the commercial growth of Lead as an active merchant. He still, owns the store, which is conducted under the name of May & Company, but has turned its management over to others. He also owns about eight thousand acres of valuable land in Wyoming. Although he has had many important business interests which have made heavy demands upon his time, he has still found opportunity to take part in public affairs and has served efficiently in both the lower and upper houses of the state legislature.

Mr. May was born November 8, 1847, in Ebertshausen, Saxony, Germany, a son of Adam and Barbara May. His father was by trade a carpenter. Our subject received his education in Germany and while still living in his native land learned the gunsmith's trade. In 1867, when about twenty years of age, he emigrated to the United States, as he did not wish to serve the required term in the German army. He first made his way to St. Louis and was for two years employed in a stove factory there. In 1869 he went up the Missouri river to Helena, Montana, where he engaged in placer mining, but later entered the mercantile field and continued to give his attention to that business until 1876, when he removed to Deadwood, arriving there on the 12th of August. He became one of the owners of the Wheeler claim in Deadwood Gulch and after selling his interest in the same returned to St. Louis, where he remained until the spring of 1877. He then again made his way to the Black Hills, which had been officially opened to white settlement only a short time before. He opened a store in Lead, which was at first conducted under the name of May & Johnson. At length he purchased the interest of his partner and admitted a cousin to membership in the firm, the style becoming E. & L. May. In 1886 our subject bought out L. May and continued to conduct the store alone until 1901, making it one of the leading mercantile establishments of the city. He then sold the business to John Gilroy, but owing to the purchaser's failure Mr. May again became the owner of the store in 1903. He then turned its management over to a relative, Henry E. May, and an old employe, Charles Stevens, but the latter was interested in the business a few years only, and the store is now conducted under the name of May & Company, the firm being composed of Ernest May and Henry May.

At various times Ernest May has been heavily interested in all of the large and successful mining ventures in the district surrounding Lead, among which should be mentioned: Golden Reward, Isadore Mining Company, Double Standard, Plutus, Harmony, Tornado Consolidation, Mark Twain and later Wasp No. 2. He still has investments in many paying mines in the neighborhood of Lead and is a foremost figure in local financial circles. He is also a large stockholder in the First National Bank. His unquestioned business ability, his enterprise and power of initiative, combined with his faith in the possibilities of the Black Hills district, have made him one of the leaders in its development as a mining district, a development which has been little short of marvelous.

Mr. May was married in 1883 to Miss Gertrude Roderig, and they have two sons, Ernest R., who is a graduate mining engineer; and William F., who is a lawyer by profession. Both, however, are now engaged in looking after their father's extensive landed holdings in Wyoming.

Mr. May is a republican and has been a conspicuous figure in public affairs. He has served as alderman for ten years, was mayor of Lead for one term and is one of the trustees of the town site. His influence has extended beyond local circles, as he represented his district in the house of representatives one term and for six terms in the state senate, during which time he was instrumental in securing the passage of much legislation that has proved of value to the state as a whole. He attends the Congregational church, to the support of which he contributes liberally, and he is well known in Masonic circles, belonging to the various bodies of the York Rite and having taken the thirty-second degree in the Scottish Rite. In all fields of human activity with which he is connected he stands out as a leader among men and may justly be termed one of the foremost citizens not only of Lead but of the whole Black Hills district.

HUBERT BERTON MATHEWS

Hubert B. MATHEWS, one of the able and popular members of the faculty of the State Agricultural College of South Dakota, at Brookings, was born at Eagle Corners, Richland County, Wisconsin, on the 10th of April, 1868. His father, Louis A. Mathews, was born in Ohio, a son of Hubert and Mary Mathews, who were born near the famed old city of Strassburg, Germany, which was at that time included in the province of Alsace-Loraine, France. Shortly after his marriage Hubert Mathews emigrated with his wife to America and settled in Ohio, where he was engaged in farming for a number of years, eventually removing thence to Eagle Corners, Wisconsin. He enlisted as a Union soldier in the war of the Rebellion, was wounded in action and taken captive by the enemy, being incarcerated in Andersonville prison and dying after exchange from the effects of captivity, his body being thrown into the Gulf of Mexico while homeward bound. His widow is still living, having attained the venerable age of eighty-one years and residing in Muscoda, Wisconsin. Louis Mathews was reared to maturity in the state of Wisconsin, and there was solemnized his marriage to Miss Mary Newburn, a daughter of Jeremiah and Catherine Newburn, who were numbered among the early settlers of the Badger state, the former having been a native of Pennsylvania and the latter of Maine. After his marriage the father of our subject settled on a farm in

Richland County, Wisconsin, whence he finally removed to the city of Detroit, Michigan, where he remained two years, at the expiration of which he returned to his farm. He there continued in agricultural pursuits until 1882, when he came to what is now South Dakota and secured a tract of land near Willow Lake, Clark County, where he continued to reside until 1889, when he removed to Seattle, Washington, where he has since been identified with mining enterprises. After locating on his homestead in South Dakota his humble sod house served not only as the family domicile, but also as a place of worship, a school house and a place of public meeting for the settlers of this section, the house having been erected two years previously to his bringing his family to the farm. Louis and Mary Mathews became the parents of eleven children, of whom nine are yet living, while of the number five were graduated in the State Agricultural College of South Dakota, while a sixth is now a student in the institution, being a member of the class of 1905. Of the children we enter a brief record, as follows: Hubert B. is the immediate subject of this review; Sarah died at the age of four years; Emma is the wife of Professor Howard H. Hoy, of the State Agricultural College; Alta is the wife of Perry Smith, of Bisbee, Arizona; Alice is a successful teacher in the public schools of Brookings county; Roscoe A. is a resident of Great Falls, Montana, where he is identified with mining enterprises; Harry is a student in the South Dakota Agricultural College and is a leader in its athletics, having been the winner of the pole-vaulting contest in the state in the season of 1903; Leroy is on a farm in Illinois; Arthur is a student in the high school at Brookings; Oscar graduates in the class of 1904 in the same school, and Minnie, who was the sixth in order of birth, died at Willow Lake, at the age of sixteen years.

Professor Mathews entered the district school at Willow Corners, Wisconsin, when but four years of age, and was there enrolled as a pupil until he had attained the age of thirteen, after which he attended the high school at Muscoda for two terms, coming then to South Dakota and continuing his studies for one term in the school at Willow Lake. In October, 1885, he began teaching in Clark County, this state, devoting his attention to pedagogic work during the winter terms, while he was employed on the farm during the intervening summer. In 1889 he was matriculated in the State Agricultural College, where he continued his studies two terms, when he again began teaching during the winter terms at Willow Lake, in order to earn the funds with which to continue his college work during the summers. While in the college he also availed himself of every opportunity to add to his financial resources, never swerving from the course which he had defined and finally being able to realize his ambition, in the completion of the prescribed course, and he was graduated in the college as a member of the class of 1892, receiving the degree of Bachelor of Science. During his college days he was prominent in the athletic sports and in society work, having been a member of the college ball team and an enthusiastic devotee of all manly sports. He was also president of his class and editor of the college paper. During the summer which witnessed his graduation he also worked with a threshing-machine outfit, thus accumulating a reserve fund which enabled him to enter, in the autumn, the Nebraska State University, at Lincoln, and in that institution he continued his studies until the holiday vacation, when he accepted the principalship of the public schools at Clark City, South Dakota, retaining this incumbency until the following March, when he was appointed an instructor in physics and meteorology in the Agricultural College, whose sessions are held during the summer months, and he was thus enabled to do post-graduate work during the winters, availing himself of the advantages afforded in the University of Michigan, at Ann Arbor, and later of those of the University of Wisconsin, at Madison. In 1896 he was made active professor in the department of physics, being given the full professorship in July of that year, and he has ever since retained this important office, in which his effective and indefatigable efforts have justified the wisdom of his being chosen. At the time when he became connected with the department of physics and electrical engineering no laboratories had been provided for said department, and it is gratifying to note that the college now has supplied for this important department one of the best equipped laboratories to be found in the northwest. In 1898 the degree of Master of Science was conferred upon Professor Mathews by the South Dakota Agricultural College.

He is prominently identified with the Masonic fraternity, being a member of the blue lodge, chapter and commandery at Brookings and of El Riad Temple, Ancient Arabic Order of the Nobles of the Mystic Shrine, at Sioux Falls. He is also affiliated with the Ancient Order of United Workmen and the Modern Woodmen of the World. Mrs. Mathews is also a member of the Ladies' Club of Brookings.

On the 12th of November, 1894, Professor Mathews was united in marriage to Miss Eva E. Plocker, who was born near Plainfield, Wisconsin, being a daughter of James and Fannie Plocker, the former of whom was born in the city of Amsterdam, Holland, and the latter in the state of Maine. The paternal grandfather of Mrs. Mathews was Cornelius Plocker, who was a sea captain, identified with the Dutch East India Company. After his marriage James Plocker settled in the southern part of Wisconsin, where he was engaged in farming for several years, eventually removing to Plainfield, that state, where he died in the year 1884. In the same year his widow and her daughter, Eva E., wife of the subject, came to South Dakota, locating in Elkton, in which vicinity the son, Henry, and daughters, Fannie, Anna and Aura, had previously located and taken up tracts of land, which they were then holding preliminary to proving title. Of the other children of Mrs. Plocker, it may be said that her daughter, Olive, was then residing in Nebraska; Edward and Frank at Bancroft, and Lucinda in Arizona. Mrs. Mathews became a student in the State Agricultural College in the autumn of 1887, thus being a classmate of her future husband. She was graduated in 1892, having previously been a successful and popular teacher in the district schools, while after her graduation she taught in the Brookings city schools. In 1894 the degree of Master of Science was conferred upon her by her alma mater, while in 1891 she completed a course in pharmacy. She was for two years in charge of the art department of the college. Professor and Mrs. Mathews have three children, Hubert, who was born on the 4th of January, 1897; Hermine, who was born on the 4th of October, 1901, and Baby, who was. born at St. Petersburg, Florida, February 24, 1904.

WELLINGTON J. MAYTUM, M. D.

Wellington J. MAYTUM, is engaged in the practice of his profession in the city of Alexandria, Hanson County, and is known as an able and successful physician and surgeon. He is a native of the state of New York, having been born in Penn Yan, Cayuga county, on the nth of December, 1864, and being a son of Charles and Emma Maytum. When he was five years of age his parents removed to Wayne County, Iowa, where his father engaged in milling, and there the Doctor secured his early educational discipline in the public schools, being graduated in the high school at Humeston, as a member of the class of 1885. In 1888 he was matriculated in the medical department of the state university of Iowa, at Iowa City, where he completed a thorough technical course and was graduated in 1891, receiving his degree of Doctor of Medicine. Shortly after his graduation the Doctor came to South Dakota and took up his residence in Alexandria, where he has since been actively engaged in the practice of his profession, the marked success and prestige which have attended his efforts standing as the best voucher for his ability and earnest devotion to the exacting duties of his chosen vocation. In 1896 he took a post-graduate course in the Chicago Polyclinic, and in 1900 he again took a course of special study in this well-known institution, from which it is evident that he at all times keeps in touch with the advances made in the sciences of medicine and surgery. The Doctor is a member of the South Dakota State Medical Society, and was for six years secretary and treasurer of the same. In 1894 he was elected to the office of superintendent of schools of Hanson County, and in the connection did much to systematize and vitalize the work of education in his jurisdiction, holding the position for two years and making an enviable record. He is a stanch adherent of the Democratic party and takes a lively interest in public affairs of a local nature.

Fraternally he is identified with the Masonic order, the Independent Order of Odd Fellows, the Ancient Order of United Workmen, the Modern Woodmen of America, the Modern Brotherhood of America and the Yeomen. He is a skilled and successful physician, a loyal citizen and a man who commands unqualified confidence and esteem in the community in which he has lived and labored to so goodly ends. On the 18th of November, 1895, Mr. Maytum was united in marriage to Miss Lillie May Syferd, who was born and reared in Wayne County, Iowa, being a daughter of John and Eliza Syferd, while she was a resident of Warsaw, Iowa, at the time of her marriage. Of this union have been born five children, namely: Charles K., Genevieve, Cecil, Thelma and Crystal.

WILLIAM H. MARTIN

The city of Sioux Falls is signally favored in having at the head of its police department so able an executive as Chief Martin, who has shown the utmost discrimination and force in the discharge of the executive duties of this important branch of the municipal government. Mr. Martin is a native of the state of Wisconsin, having been born in the town of Ashippun, Dodge County, on the 17th of February, 1850, and being a son of John Duncan Martin and Caroline (Wilks) Martin, both of whom were born and reared in Dundee, Scotland. The future chief received his early educational training in the public schools of his native town, and was reared to the sturdy discipline of the homestead farm. When but fifteen years of age he gave significant evidence of his patriotism and youthful valor by going forth in defense of the Union, whose integrity was then jeopardized by armed rebellion. He enlisted as a private in Company 1, Forty-eighth Wisconsin Volunteer Infantry, with which he proceeded to the front, where he proved himself a faithful young soldier, being mustered out on the 24th of June, 1865, and receiving his honorable discharge. He then returned home and soon afterward entered upon an apprenticeship at the carpenter's trade, becoming a skilled artisan in the line and continuing to follow his trade as a vocation for several years. When twenty-one years of age he was elected constable of his native town, in which capacity he gained his first experience in the handling of malefactors, proving himself a capable officer and remaining incumbent of the position for a period of six years. In 1876 he removed to Waukesha County, Wisconsin, where he was engaged in contracting and building until 1882, when he was appointed deputy sheriff of the county, being inducted into this office on the 1st of January and serving until 1888, making an excellent record. He then came to South Dakota and located in Sioux Falls, where he was engaged in building until May 7, 1890, when he was appointed a member of the police force of the city, serving two years as patrolman and being then, on the 1st of May, 1892, appointed to the position of chief of the police department, giving a most able administration of the office and being reappointed on the 3d of November, 1895, for a term of two years. In 1897-8 he was a guard at the state penitentiary, in this city, and on the 2d of May, 1900, there came a distinctive hark of the popular appreciation of his ability and former services, in his reappointment to the position of chief of the police department, of which he has since remained in tenure.

In politics the chief is a stanch Republican, and fraternally is identified with Unity Lodge, No. 130, Ancient Free and Accepted Masons; Sioux Falls Lodge, No. 262, Benevolent and Protective Order of Elks; Joe Hooker Post, No. 10, Grand Army of the Republic; and Jasper Lodge, No. 9, Ancient Order of United Workmen. On the 13th of December, 1876, Mr. Martin was united in marriage to Miss Mary A. Best, daughter of John and Margaret Best, of Dousman, Wisconsin, and they have one child, Stella M., who remains at the parental home, being one of the popular young ladies of the city.

CHARLES A. McARTHUR

Charles A. McARTHUR, dealer in agricultural implements in the city of Aberdeen, is a native of the state of Minnesota, having been born in Plainview, Wabasha County, on the 11th of September, 1871, and being a son of John and Mary (Campbell) McArthur, who now reside in the city of Seattle, Washington. The subject received his elementary educational discipline in the public schools of Minnesota, and was ten years of age at the time of his parents' removal to Ordway, South Dakota, in 1881. Here he continued his educational work, the family removing to Aberdeen in 1886, and in the high school of this city he was graduated as a member of the class of 1891, having completed the scientific course. After leaving school Mr. McArthur became identified with his father in the implement business, being admitted to partnership in 1893, under the firm name of John McArthur & Sons. This association continued until 1894, when the firm of C. A. McArthur & Company was organized. Under this title the enterprise was continued until November, 1901, when the subject became the sole owner, having individually conducted the business since that time. He handles a full line of agricultural implements and machinery, including the McCormick harvesters and mowers, the John Deer plows, the Gaar-Scott threshing machines and engines, windmills, gasoline engines, the United States cream separators, Winona wagons and a select stock of carriages and buggies. In politics Mr. McArthur gives his support to the Republican party, and fraternally he is identified with the Masonic order, in which he has attained the Knights Templar degrees, and with the Ancient Order of United Workmen.

On the 4th of September, 1895, at Wellsburg, West Virginia, was solemnized the marriage of Mr. McArthur to Miss Clara Bracken, daughter of Margaret R. Bracken, of that place. She was well and favorably known in Aberdeen, having here held the position of delivery clerk in the post office for some time prior to her marriage, and both she and her husband are active in the social life of the community. They have two children, Everett and Stuart.

THOMAS McBATH

Thomas McBath, proprietor of a grain elevator and thus actively connected with the business interests of Watertown, was born in St. Lawrence County, New York, December 27, 1857, a son of Samuel and Jane McBath. The mother died in the east but the father afterward came with his son Thomas to South Dakota, arriving in this state in 1880, and still makes his home at Watertown. The son was educated in the public schools of New York and spent his youthful days upon his father's farm in that state, assisting in its cultivation and improvement as the years went on. When he had reached the age of twenty-three, however, he came with his father to the northwest, with Dakota territory as his destination. Arriving in Codington County, he secured a homestead in Rauville township and also a tree claims near Henry. He made improvements thereon and farmed the place for a while, but after three or four years sold both the homestead and tree claim. He then engaged in buying grain at Groton for one year and for the Northwestern Elevator Company at Willow Lake for three years, and in 1894 established an elevator business in Watertown under his own name. He is also proprietor of an elevator at Thomas and at Yahota and Adelaide but maintains general offices in Watertown. His four elevator interests have made him closely connected with the grain trade of his section of the state, his business having assumed extensive and gratifying proportions. He is also the owner of a quarter section of land in Codington County, within the city limits of Watertown.

Mr. McBath was united in marriage to Miss Effie M. Chase, a daughter of A. D. and Tirzah J. Chase, the former a minister of the Methodist denomination and the first pastor of the Methodist church in Watertown. He came to South Dakota in 1878 and established the first Methodist congregation in the state. He has since been actively identified with the further work of the church and his labors have been attended with splendid results, contributing largely to the moral advancement of South Dakota. Rev. A. D. Chase is still living at the age of eighty-three years but his wife is deceased. It was in September, 1890, that their daughter Effie became the wife of Thomas McBath. The children of this marriage are as follows: Earl, Grace, Harry, Roy, and Wilbur, all at home. All are natives of this state. The parents are members of the Methodist church and guide their lives according to its teachings.

Mr. McBath also belongs to the Masonic lodge, the Benevolent Protective Order of Elks and the Ancient Order of United Workmen. In politics he is a progressive republican, believing in advancement along political lines just as much as in other connections. For five years he has served as a member of the city council and for six years has been a member of the school board. His work in behalf of Watertown, both in office and put of it, has been effective for the upbuilding of the city and the promotion of its best interests. He is a self-made man and one whose business career has been founded upon the substantial principles of industry, integrity and progress.

JOHN J. McCAUGHEY

John J. McCAUGHEY, one of the leading business men of Aberdeen, being president and general manager of the Aberdeen Hardware Company, is a native of the state of New Jersey, having been born in the historic old town of New Brunswick, Middlesex county, on the nth of June, 1857, and being a son of Robert and Agnes (Cummings) McCaughey, the former of whom was born in County Antrim, Ireland, about twelve miles distant from the city of Belfast, on the 12th of March, 1833, while his wife was born in the same locality, on the 12th of January, of that year. The paternal grandfather of the subject was a weaver and a designer of shawl patterns, and removed from Paisley, Scotland, in which city he became one of the leading designers of the famous Paisley shawls, to Ireland in the fall of 1832, just prior to Robert McCaughey's birth. The latter and a younger brother were born in Ireland and two older brothers and two sisters in Scotland. From Ireland he immigrated with his family to America and located in the city of Philadelphia, where he was associated with two of his sons, John and William, in the manufacturing of shawls. About 1858 or '9 the grandparents moved to Wisconsin, near Madison, there continuing to reside until the close of their long and useful lives. Robert McCaughey was a child at the time of the family immigration to the United States, and in his youth, he learned the tanner's trade, continuing to follow the same in New Jersey until 1860, when he came west and joined the family near Madison, Wisconsin. He was there engaged in farming until the autumn of 1875, when he removed to Kasson, Dodge County, Minnesota, where he devoted his attention to farming for the ensuing five years, at the expiration of which he came to the present state of South Dakota, being among the first to file claim to government land in township 120, range 62, Spink County, making entry on the 28th of May, 1880, while he did the first plowing in said township, June 11, 1880, he and his son John J. first filed on land in range 63, but this filing was rejected, as the land had not as yet been thrown open, and thus each of them secured claims in range 62. In the spring of 1881, the remainder of the family came to the county from the old home in Minnesota, and the land secured here in the early pioneer epoch is still retained by the family, the same being located in LaPrairie township and being well improved and under effective cultivation.

John J. McCaughey received his educational training in the public schools of Wisconsin, and accompanied his parents on their removal to Minnesota and eventually to South Dakota, as noted. He remained on the farm until the spring of 1884, when he accepted a position as traveling salesman for farming machinery, being thus engaged for one year, at the expiration of which he established himself in the implement and farming machinery business at Northville, Spink County, where he continued operations two years. He then disposed of his interests in that line, and thereafter was engaged in the buying and shipping of grain until the autumn of 1896, when he became traveling representative of the Acme Harvester Company, of Pekin, Illinois, covering a very considerable territory in the northwest and being thus engaged until the spring of 1899, when he and W. G. Wells purchased the hardware business of E. O. Mead, of Aberdeen, which was thereafter continued under the firm name of Wells & McCaughey until the 1st of January, 1902, when the subject effected the purchase of his partner's interests and forthwith organized the Aberdeen Hardware Company, which was duly incorporated under the laws of the state. He became president and general manager of the company and has since remained incumbent of this important dual office, while he is directing the business of the concern with consummate discrimination and ability. The company utilize a store fifty by one hundred and forty-two feet in dimensions, with basement, and also have a large warehouse located on the line of the Chicago, Minneapolis & St. Paul Railroad. They carry a full and comprehensive stock of heavy and shelf hardware, stoves, ranges, paints, oils, glass, etc., while in addition to controlling a large and representative retail business their jobbing trade is one which is far ramifying and constantly expanding.

In politics Mr. McCaughey is stanchly aligned with the Republican party, but has had no ambition for official preferment. He has attained to the thirty-second degree of Scottish Rite Masonry and is also affiliated with the Ancient Arabic Order of the Nobles of the Mystic Shrine, the Ancient Order of United Workmen and the Modern Woodmen of America. On the nth of June, 1884, was solemnized the marriage of Mr. McCaughey to Miss Nettie L. Austin, who was born in Minnesota, being a daughter of Philip B. Austin, who was one of the honored pioneers of LaPrairie township, Spink County, where he located in 1881, there continuing to reside until 1900, when he removed to the city of Aberdeen, where his death occurred August 26, 1903. Mr. and Mrs. McCaughey have one son, Lester, who is employed in the establishment of which his father is the head.

CHARLES E. McCAULEY, M. D.

A history of the medical profession of Aberdeen would be incomplete and unsatisfactory were their failure to make mention of Dr. Charles E. McCauley, one of the leading general practitioners of that city, of which he has been a resident since 1902. He was born in Cass County, Indiana, in 1875 and is a son of W. H. and Mary (Campbell) McCauley. The family moved to Watertown, South Dakota, in the fall of 1879 and in the following spring the father took up government land near Ashton, farming upon this property until 1898. His wife has passed away and he now makes his home at Ashton.

Dr. Charles E. McCauley acquired his early education in the public schools and later spent one year at the Dakota Wesleyan University at Mitchell. He then enrolled in Rush Medical College at Chicago and after three years began the practice of his profession in North Dakota, where he remained from 1899 to

1901. In the latter year he returned to Rush Medical College and was graduated from that institution in 1902. In the same year he located at Aberdeen and there has since engaged in general practice, winning the prominence and success to which his ability entitles him. He is a capable and conscientious physician, careful in his diagnosis of cases and at all times watchful over the interests of his patients. Through his membership in the American Medical Association and the county and state medical societies he keeps in close touch with the advancement in his profession. In 1902 he served as president of the state society and he is an ex-president of the Aberdeen District Medical Society, his ability being widely recognized in professional circles.

In 1899 Dr. McCauley married Miss Edith Boyer, of Ashton, South Dakota, a daughter of John Boyer, a pioneer in this state, who took up his residence here in 1882. Dr. McCauley is a thirty-second degree Mason, and is a member of the Shrine, and he is also affiliated with the Benevolent Protective Order of Elks, the Modern Woodmen of America and the Ancient Order of United Workmen. He is a close and earnest student of his profession, constantly broadening his knowledge through research and investigation until his ability places him today in the foremost ranks of the medical fraternity in his section.

HON. JAMES H. McCOY

The judicial history of South Dakota bears upon its records a name that stands for high professional honor and integrity in that of James H. McCoy, who since the 1st of April, 1909, has been judge of the supreme court for the fifth district. He was born in Decatur, Illinois, in 1855. He was one of a family of six children whose parents were B. F. and Minerva (Helm) McCoy, the former a farmer by occupation and a native of Greenbrier County, West Virginia, while the latter was a native of Baltimore, Maryland. After acquiring a high-school education in his native city James H. McCoy attended the Illinois Wesleyan. University, from which he was graduated with the Bachelor of Arts degree with the class of 1880. Soon afterward he was admitted to the bar, but did not at once enter upon active practice, for he was appointed special examiner in the United States pension service with headquarters at Louisville, Kentucky, where he remained until 1885. In that year Judge McCoy left Kentucky and came to South Dakota, settling in Britton, Marshall County, where he entered upon the practice of law. There his clientage constantly increased until 1893, when he sought a broader field of labor in Webster, where he practiced successfully until 1900, when he located in Aberdeen. From the outset of his professional career, he was noted for the care and thoroughness with which he prepared his cases as well as for the logic which marked their presentation.

In November, 1901, he was elected to the circuit bench of the fifth district, and on the 1st of April, 1909, was appointed judge of the supreme court for the fifth district, in the general election of November, 1910, he was elected to succeed himself as a member of the supreme court, in which position he has since served with honor and credit. He was also at one time county judge of Marshall County. His record upon the bench has been characterized by the qualities which distinguished him as a man and citizen — a marked devotion to duty combined with a masterly grasp of every problem presented for solution. In addition to his judicial, service he was at one time county auditor for two years. Politically Judge McCoy is a republican.

Judge McCoy was married in Decatur, Illinois, in 1883, to Miss Hannah Heath, and they became the parents of two children, Lelah and Carroll. The family attend the Presbyterian church, in which Judge McCoy and his wife hold membership. He belongs to the Phi Delta Phi, and is a member of Coteau Lodge, No. 59, A. F. & A. M., of Webster; Aberdeen Chapter, No. 14, R. A. M., of Aberdeen; Damascus Commandery, No. 10, K. T. of Aberdeen and the Knights of Pythias fraternity. He is spoken of as "a fine man, well-liked by all his associates." His recognition of opportunity and duty has found response in a ready activity that meets every requirement placed upon him and his course has been a credit and honor to the district that has honored him.

PATTISON FRANCIS McCLURE

PATTISON F. McCLURE

Pattison Francis McClure, banker, financier and Dakota pioneer, occupying the presidency of the Pierre National Bank, has been an influential factor in the development and progress of the state not only along material but also along political lines and in other ways. Progress and patriotism might well be termed the keystone of his character. Opportunity has ever beckoned him on and his activity and even-paced energy have carried him forward into important relations.

Born in Laurel, Franklin County, Indiana, August 8, 1853, Mr. McClure is a son of Captain James R. and Hester A. (Pattison) McClure. The father was born in Trenton, Franklin County, Indiana, July 17, 1828, and attended the common schools to the age of fifteen years, while later he spent three years as a student in Miami University. During his college days he ran away from home to offer his services to the government in the Mexican war and enlisted in the Fifth Indiana Regiment, participating in the campaign from Vera Cruz to the city of Mexico under General Winfield Scott. After being mustered out he resumed the study of law and was admitted to practice in 1851. He at once entered upon the active work of the profession and served as prosecuting attorney in his district in Indiana. On the 16th of February, 1851, he was united in marriage to Miss Hester A. Pattison and after three years' residence in Indiana, following their marriage, they went to Kansas in November, 1854, settling at Junction City, where Captain McClure entered upon the practice of law and played a conspicuous part in the public affairs of the young state. He became allied with those who were working so strenuously to make Kansas a free state. As soon as courts were established, he resumed the practice of his profession and he became one of the original incorporators of Junction City. As one of the territory's pioneer lawyers he took a most active and helpful interest in shaping policies and on numerous occasions was called to positions of public trust, which he filled most capably and creditably. At the time of the Civil War, he again tendered his aid to his country and was made captain of Company B, Second Kansas Regiment, with which he participated in the battles of Wilson Creek, Forsythe, Dug Springs and Shelbina. In the last battle he was severely wounded by a cannon shot in the foot. After recovering he again entered the service as quartermaster of the Eleventh Kansas Regiment, but his wound incapacitated him for command of his troops in the field and he was mustered out with his regiment in 1865. The injury sustained at the front seemed no handicap to his career, however, for his strong and well-balanced intellect enabled him to become the master of various situations and to prove a directing force in public affairs. His name is prominently connected with much of the history of the early development of Kansas. He was registrar of the United States land office from 1867 until 1869, but the greater part of his life was spent in the practice of law and his conduct was ever characterized by the highest qualities. He was recognized as a most able advocate and counsel and his position at the bar was an enviable one. Politically he was a democrat and he took an active interest in many concerns of public importance. For twenty-five years he was senior warden of the Episcopal church at Junction City, was also a prominent Knight Templar Mason, a member of the Grand Army of the Republic and a charter member of the Kansas Commandery of the Loyal Legion. He died July 17, 1903. In his family were twelve children, seven of whom grew to years of maturity.

Pattison F. McClure, whose name introduces this record, acquired his early education in the public schools of Junction City, followed by a course at the State Agricultural College at Manhattan, Kansas, and two years study in Cornell University at Ithaca, New York. Upon his return home he began the study of law under the direction of his father but before completing his law course he went to Illinois and, following a natural instinct for mechanics, began working to perfect a self-binding reaper for one of the prominent implement manufacturers of that state. He became one of the early and successful workers in solving the problems which have revolutionized the manufacture of farm machinery and other mechanical appliances. In 1878 he went abroad in the interest of the American harvesting machine manufacturers, traveling throughout Great Britain, France, Belgium and Spain. In 1879-80 he represented an Ohio concern in Minnesota and in the fall of the latter year came to Dakota territory, settling at Pierre, where he entered the hardware business under the firm name of Gleckler & McClure. That enterprise was successfully conducted by the partners until 1889, when Mr. McClure sold his interest and became one of the, organizers of the Pierre National Bank. He was elected its first president and has continuously and ably filled that position since, while to his keen business ability and foresight is largely due the fact that the bank is today in the front rank of the state's large and prosperous financial institutions.

Aside from the prominence which Mr. McClure has gained lit financial circles, he has also come to the front in other connections. Upon the organization of Hughes County in 1880 he was appointed the first county surveyor and in 1882 was elected a member of the board of county commissioners. In 1885 popular suffrage put him in the office of mayor of Pierre and he was reelected at the close of his first term. From 1885 until 1887 inclusive, he served as a member of the committee which was sent to Washington from Dakota territory to urge the opening to settlement of the Sioux Indian reservation, a measure that was finally adopted and had a most salutary effect in attracting large numbers of settlers to the fertile lands and thus planting the seeds of civilization in that district. He was one of the organizers and leading spirits of the old Pierre Board of Trade, the chief mission of which, in addition to fostering the city's general growth and prosperity, was the carrying forward of the spirited contest over the location of the new state capital, a contest that was ultimately won by Pierre, and to Mr. McClure much credit is due for this achievement. Again in 1904, when the removal of the capital was being agitated, he was foremost in the light for its retention at Pierre, and the present magnificent capitol building is in no small way a token of the effectiveness of his work.

In 1887-8 Mr. McClure served as commissioner of immigration for Dakota territory by appointment of Governor L. K. Church and his work in that connection was characteristic of the enthusiasm he has ever displayed regarding the future possibilities of the state. His work was productive of excellent and immediate results, and who can measure the extent and influence of his labors? In 1889 he was made the democratic candidate for governor of South Dakota after the admission of the state to the Union and made a brilliant canvass, but as the state was normally strongly republican, he was unsuccessful. In 1893 he was appointed South Dakota's commissioner to the World's Columbian Exposition at Chicago and proved not only a most dignified representative of the state but a valuable missionary for the cause of its development and settlement. During the long period that the Dakotas were knocking for admission to the sisterhood of states, Mr. McClure was one of the most ardent workers in that connection and was among the leaders who planned the division of the territory into two states. Into still another held of labor has he put forth his energies, for he has always taken a most active interest in agricultural development, being among the first to appreciate the unbounded possibilities for dairying, stock-raising and alfalfa growing in South Dakota.

On the 24th of July, 1893, Mr. McClure was united in marriage to Mrs. Elizabeth Saxton Bowen, nee Bentley, of Cincinnati, Ohio. During an exceptionally busy life he has found time to enjoy out-of-door recreation and his special fad is his love for dogs. He is of a genial nature, generous in purpose, and as a citizen and business man he has proven a distinct asset to the city and state. Public-spirited and progressive, his labors have not yet reached their full fruition in the state's development. There are few residents of South Dakota who have worked so devotedly and unselfishly for her welfare and her upbuilding. He is president of the State Historical Society and is much interested in the preservation of the early historical data, along which line he is doing important work. Mr. McClure is also a member of the Loyal Legion, being affiliated with Leavenworth (Kansas) Commandery. He is a member of the Kansas Society of the Sons of the American Revolution. Fraternally he is identified with the Masons, belonging to Pierre Lodge, No. 27, A. F. & A. M.; Pierre Chapter, No. 22, R. A. M.; Pierre Commandery, No. 21, K. T.; Oriental Consistory, No. I, A. A. S. R.; and El Riad Temple, A. A. O. N. M. S., of Sioux Falls, South Dakota. Mr. McClure also belongs to the Odd Fellows and in point of service he is the oldest living noble grand of the Pierre lodge of that organization. He is a man of generous impulses and broad views, whose signal service to South Dakota has been manifest in the vigor with which he aided in making this region habitable in the pioneer era, in bringing its resources to light and in stamping his intensely practical ideas upon its development. Such careers are too near us now for their significance to be appraised at its true value, but the future will be able to trace the tremendous effect of their labors upon the society and institutions of their times.

JOHN EDMUND McDOUGALL

John E. McDOUGALL, a representative citizen of Britton, Marshall County, as the name implies, comes of stanch Scottish lineage on the paternal side, and he is a native of Prince Edward Island, having been born in the village of Campbellton, on the 24th of February, 1860. He is a son of John and Grace (Mercerau) McDougall, the former of whom was born on Prince Edward Island, while the latter was a native of New Brunswick. The paternal grandparents of the subject were of pure Scotch lineage, being representatives of the sterling clan McDougall. of the highlands of the fair land of hills and heather. Both were born in Scotland, whence they emigrated to America about the year 1820, settling in Malpeque, Prince Edward Island, and there passing the remainder of their lives. The mother of the subject represented the Scotch, Irish and French strains, her father having been a Scotchman. She died when our subject was but thirteen years of age, and his father subsequently married Miss Jennie McLean, five sons and four daughters having been born of the first union and one son to the latter union. The father died in the month of May, 1902.

John E. McDougall was reared on the homestead farm and received his educational discipline in the public schools of his native place. He remained at home until he had attained the age of twenty years, having in the meanwhile learned the carpenter's trade. At the age noted he went to Maine and thence to Massachusetts, being absent about nine months, after which he returned home, where he remained a few months, at the expiration of which, on November 23, 1880, he started for the west, locating in Minneapolis, Minnesota, where he engaged in the work of his trade. In November, 1883, he went to Norton, Massachusetts, where was solemnized his marriage to Miss Isabel R. Munro, and six weeks later he returned, with his bride, to Minneapolis. In August, 1884, a son was born to them, Edward James, who was graduated in June, 1904, from Pittsburg Academy, Minnesota, and is now at home. On the 26th of December, 1884, Mrs. McDougall was summoned into eternal rest, her remains being interred in Maple Hill cemetery, Minneapolis. On the 25th of May, 1886, Mr. McDougall left Minneapolis and came to Britton, Marshall County, South Dakota, where he has ever since maintained his home. During his residence in Minneapolis, he followed his trade, having been for three years foreman for the firm of McCleary & Quigley, and thereafter having been independently engaged in contracting and building, in which line of enterprise he has successfully continued in Britton. many evidences of his skill and ability being found here. He has ever accorded an unwavering allegiance to the Republican party, in whose ranks he has been an active and valued worker, having been a member of the state central committee for two years, and also having served as a member of the county central committee, while in 1896 he was president of the Republican club of Marshall County. In May, 1904, he was nominated by the Republican party for lieutenant governor. In 1900 he was captain of a Roosevelt rough-rider company, which had a membership of seventy-five and which was much in evidence during the campaign of that year. In November, 1900, Mr. McDougall was elected to represent his county in the lower house of the state legislature, having been the first Republican elected to this office in the county in four years. His record was such that a further manifestation of popular appreciation was given in the election of November, 1902, when he was elected senator from the thirty-second district, comprising the counties of Marshall and Day, being thus a member of the upper house during the eighth general assembly, in 1903, and being made chairman of the appropriation committee, while he was also assigned to other important committees, proving an efficient working member of the deliberative body and still farther fortifying himself in popular esteem. On the 14th of October, 1884, Mr. McDougall united with the Andrew Presbyterian church, in Minneapolis, and in 1887 was admitted by letter to the First Presbyterian church of Britton. He organized a Sunday school in the church in January of that year, and continued as its superintendent for the long period of ten years, at the expiration of which he resigned, and during the ensuing four years refused to accept the position again, though urged to do so. In January, 1901, however, he again resumed the duties of the superintendency, and has since continued to fill the office, his earnest and zealous labors being greatly appreciated, while he is also active in the other departments of church work.

In July, 1883, Mr. McDougall became a member of the Independent Order of Odd Fellows, and in January, 1888, he was primarily instrumental in the organizing of Britton Lodge, in Britton, having been its first noble grand and having represented the same in the grand lodge of the state. He is also affiliated with the Ancient Free and Accepted Masons, of which he was worshipful master for two years, while he has also served as treasurer and chaplain of the same. He is identified with the Royal Arch Masons, and also with the local organizations of the Ancient Order of United Workmen and Mutual Benefit Association. On the 3d of August, 1901, he was mustered into the South Dakota National Guard and on the same day was elected captain of Company A, Third Regiment, located in Britton, while on the 1st of April, 1902, he was promoted to the office of major of the First Battalion of this regiment, of which office he remains incumbent at the time of this writing.

On the 13th of June, 1893. Mr. McDougall consummated a second marriage, being then united to Miss Nettie A. Marsh, of Britton. She was born in Kalamazoo, Michigan, and is a daughter of George J. and Amanda Melvina Marsh. Her mother is dead, while her father resides near Kalamazoo, Michigan. Mr. and Mrs. McDougall have two children, Tyrrell Glenn, who was born on the 29th of March, 1894, and Portia Lois, who was born on the 24th of November, 1896.

ROBERT E. McDOWELL

R. E. McDOWELL, who is private secretary of United States Senator Robert J. Gamble, of South Dakota, is a native of the state of Wisconsin, having boon born near Fox Lake, Dodge County on the 1st day of December, 1866. He is the son of Samuel C. and Margaret J. (Gamble) McDowell, the former of whom was born near Downpatrick, County Down, Ireland, on the 12th of July, 1832, while the latter was born in the same county, near Belfast, on the 16th day of May, 1838. The father of the subject came to the United States when seventeen years of age, having received excellent educational advantages in the Emerald Isle, and was successfully engaged in teaching for a number of years in New York and Wisconsin. He served in the war of the Rebellion, enlisting as a private in Company D, Eighth (Eagle Regiment) Wisconsin Volunteer Infantry, and was honorably discharged from the service as first lieutenant, having served some three years and nine months. During two years of his service, he acted as adjutant of the regiment. While serving with his regiment, it took part in over thirty engagements and battles, in which were included a number of the most memorable battles of the war. On return from the war Mr. McDowell located on a farm in the town of Trenton, near Fox Lake, Wisconsin, becoming one of the honored and influential citizens of that section, removing in 1901 to the village of Fox Lake. He served as a member of the Wisconsin legislature, and held a number of local offices at different times. In politics he is a Republican, and fraternally is commander of the Grand Army of the Republic post. His wife mother of the subject, is a sister of United States Senator Gamble, and of the late John R. Gamble, member of congress from South Dakota, and Hugh S. Gamble, all of Yankton, South Dakota. Jennie B., a sister of the subject, born February, 11, 1870, resides with her parents at Fox Lake, Wisconsin.

Robert E. McDowell secured his preliminary educational training in the public schools, and supplemented the same by a course in Wayland Academy at Beaver Dam, Wisconsin, graduating in 1887; afterward continuing his studies at Yankton College, and Bryant & Stratton Business College in Chicago. He took a position in 1889 in the law offices of Gamble Brothers at Yankton, South Dakota territory (the firm consisting of the late John R. Gamble and the present United States Senator Robert J. Gamble), studied law and was admitted to the bar of the state of South Dakota. He acted as secretary to Senator Gamble while the latter was a member of the house of representatives in the fifty-fourth congress, and thereafter he was for two years engaged in the active practice of his profession in Yankton, being associated with Hon. John Holman, under the firm name of Holman & McDowell. He again acted as private secretary to Mr. Gamble during the fifty-sixth congress, and has continued to act as such since the latter's election to the United States senate in 1901.

The subject is a stanch adherent of the Republican party, is actively identified with the Masonic fraternity, in which he has advanced to the thirty-second degree of the Scottish Rite, holding membership in Oriental Consistory, No. I, in Yankton; is a member of El Riad Temple, Nobles of the Mystic Shrine, in Sioux Falls; is a member of Phoenix Lodge, No. 37, Knights of Pythias, and of Yankton Lodge, No. I, Ancient Order of United Workmen, in the same city. He and his wife are members of the Congregational church in Yankton. On June 6, 1900, Mr. McDowell was married in the Zion Reformed church at Hagerstown, Maryland, to Miss Edith Ellen Eyerly, of Hagerstown, she being a daughter of Hon. George W. Eyerly, an old-time resident and prominent merchant of that city, she is also a sister of Prof. Elmer K. Eyerly, a member of the faculty of the State Agricultural College of South Dakota.

College and was ordained in 1882 and next year located in South Dakota. He has occupied his present position since 1890. He served as chaplain of the South Dakota Infantry in the Philippine war and won the gratitude and affection of all of the men. Always public-spirited, he was selected by Governor Sheldon to superintend the distribution of supplies to the destitute homesteaders in the great drought, a work he accomplished at great labor and sacrifice and to the complete satisfaction of every one affected. He is the president of the State Sunday School Association, and a member of the executive committee of the State Historical Society.

JOHN A. McGILLIVRAY

John A. McGillivray is the present able cashier of the Security Bank of Clark, South Dakota, and has fully demonstrated his fitness for the responsible position which he holds. He was born in Moody County, this state, on the 8th of January, 1888, a son of Duncan A. and Phena (Seaton) McGillivray, natives of Canada and Pennsylvania respectively. Their marriage occurred in South Dakota, the father coming to this state in 1879 in early manhood, while the mother accompanied her parents here when a girl. She passed away about 1895, and Mr. McGillivray was again married, his second union being with Miss Mabel Phelps, of Madison, South Dakota. He took up a homestead in Lake County upon his arrival in this state and resided there for a number of years, engaging in farming. He subsequently became prominent in local politics and was elected sheriff of Lake County, residing in Madison during the four years that he served in office. In 1902 he located in Hartford, where he has since been prominently identified with the milling business. He has served for a number of years as postmaster of that city and is influential in local republican circles.

John A. McGillivray was reared at home and acquired his general education in the Madison and Hartford public schools, supplementing the knowledge there gained by a commercial course at the Sioux Falls Business College. After leaving the last-named institution he secured a position in the Garden City State Bank, where was laid the foundation of his banking career. He was first employed as a bookkeeper but his ability and fidelity to the interests of the bank won him promotion and he became cashier. On the 1st of May, 1913, he severed his connection with that bank and went to Clark, where he accepted the cashiership of the Security Bank, which position he has since held. Under his guidance the prosperity that has in the past characterized the bank has continued and its financial condition is excellent.

In 1910 Mr. McGillivray married Miss Maud Scott, of Hartford, this state. He is a member of Clark Lodge, No. 42, A. F. & A. M., and of the Brotherhood of American Yeomen of Garden City. He likewise belongs to the Clark Commercial Club and is thoroughly in sympathy with the work of that organization in promoting the business expansion of the city. He is well known in the banking fraternity of northeastern South Dakota and is highly respected by all who are brought in contact with him.

CHARLES E. McKINNEY

Charles E. McKINNEY, who has been president of the Sioux Falls National Bank from the time of its organization and who has been a resident of the city for nearly a quarter of a century, claims the old Keystone state as the place of his nativity, having been born in Ulster, Bradford County, Pennsylvania, on the 16th of March, 1858, and being a son of Russel and Elizabeth McKinney, the father being a farmer by vocation. The subject worked on the farm during his youth. After completing the limited curriculum of the district schools he was matriculated in Cook Academy, at Havana, that state, which he attended for three years, going from there to Colgate Academy, Hamilton, New York, where he was graduated in 1878. He took one year at Madison University, also one year in the law department of Michigan University, at

Ann Arbor. In 1880 Mr. McKinney located in the city of Detroit, Michigan. In November, 1880, he came to Sioux Falls, which was then but a frontier village. Here he became a member of the firm of Easton, McKinney & Scougel, and they established banks in Sioux Falls, Yankton and Dell Rapids. In December, 1882, Mr. McKinney further showed his sagacity and enterprising spirit by effecting the organization of the Sioux Falls National Bank, one of the early institutions of the sort in the state and one that has had a history of successful operations, and most able and conservative management. He was made president of the bank at the time of its incorporation and has ever since continued as its chief executive, while the prosperity and prestige which mark the institution are due in large measure to his wise counsel and the discriminating business policy which he has enforced in his official capacity. Mr. McKinney was admitted to the bar of the territory of Dakota, in 1889, but has given but little attention to active professional work. A previously published sketch of his career has spoken of him as follows: "Mr. McKinney has always been an active, enterprising, energetic citizen, occasionally taking a hand in local and state politics, but devoting his time principally to financial matters, in which he has the reputation of being coolheaded and successful. He has been a member of the board of education of his home city and was a member of the commission appointed to adjust the financial matters between North and South Dakota when they assumed statehood. In 1891-2 he was one of the railroad commissioners of South Dakota." In 1902 he was appointed by President Roosevelt a member of the United States mint commissioners. It may be further stated that Mr. McKinney is a stanch advocate of the principles and policies of the Republican party, in whose cause he has ever shown a deep interest.

Mr. McKinney was married in December, 1880, to Miss Allie A. Waterman, of Coldwater, Michigan. Fraternally he is a Mason and has attained all the York and Scottish Rite degrees, and he also belongs to the Ancient Order of United Workmen and the Benevolent and Protective Order of Elks.

DENNIS L. McKINNEY

Since 1881 Dennis L. McKinney has been engaged in the real-estate business in Sioux Falls and he has risen to a high place in business circles of the city, founding his success upon industry, ability and enterprise. He was born in Ulster, Pennsylvania, October 14, 1855, and is a son of Russell and Elizabeth (Newman) McKinney. The father, who was born near Athens, Pennsylvania, about the year 1821, enlisted in 1864 in the Forty-ninth New York Volunteer Infantry and served until the close of the Civil war, being mustered out with his regiment at Elmira, New York, in 1865. In the same year he was accidentally drowned. The grandfather of our subject was Henry McKinney and the great-grandfather was the founder of the family in America, coming to this country from Scotland.

Dennis L. McKinney acquired his early education in the public schools of Ulster and later attended the University at Lewisburg, Pennsylvania. In 1878 he was graduated from the medical department of the University of Pennsylvania and located in Oneida county, New York, where he engaged in general practice for three years. At the end of that time, he discontinued professional work and in 1881 came to Sioux Falls, where he and his brother organized the Sioux Falls National Bank, though it was first a private bank, conducted under the name of McKinney & Scougal. In 1882, however, it was changed to a national bank and Mr. McKinney is still actively interested in the business, being now vice president of the bank. In connection with the bank the brothers also carried on business under the name of the McKinney Loan & Insurance Company, with offices in the bank until 1910, when the growth of both the bank and insurance business necessitated larger quarters and the insurance company moved to another building, our subject taking entire charge of that branch. He does a large volume of business and handles a great deal of valuable property, and his opinion on everything relating to land values is considered authoritative. The business is now conducted under the name of the McKinney & Allen, Incorporated, with Mr. McKinney as president. During the long period of his connection with this line of work he has secured a large and representative following and the success he has achieved is due entirely to his own efforts.

Mr. McKinney has been twice married. On the 4th of June, 1883, at Clarion, Iowa, he wedded Miss Jessie Bennett, who died May 14, 1895, leaving two children, Russell Bennett and Charles Leroy. On the 4th of September, 1902, at Pittsburg, Pennsylvania, Mr. McKinney was again married, his second union being with Miss Emma McCoy.

Mr. McKinney attends the Presbyterian church and is prominent in the Country and Dacotah Clubs. He has been initiated into the Masonic order according to both the Scottish and York Rites and holds membership in the Shrine. He has taken an active interest in politics and during the free silver heresy was an active and earnest worker on the side of a stable currency. His allegiance is given to the republican party and for three years he served as a member of the board of aldermen. He is a man of strong character and sterling worth and well merits the high regard in which he is uniformly held.

HON. THOMAS McKINNON

Hon. Thomas McKinnon, a contractor and builder of Sioux Falls, now representing his district in the upper house of the general assembly, is leaving the impress of his individuality upon the political history as well as the material development of his city and state. He was born in Glasgow, Scotland, in 1860, but spent only the first nine years of his life in the land of hills and heather, being brought to America by his father, John McKinnon, who, in 1869, sailed with his family for the new world. Arriving in Chicago, he there engaged in the contracting and building business until the great fire of 1871. In 1878 he became a resident of Sioux Falls, South Dakota, and established the contracting business in that city, which is still conducted by his son. Later he took up a homestead in McCook County. He was successfully identified with building operations until his life's labors were terminated in death in 1909, when he had reached the age of seventy-four years. His wife, who bore the maiden name of Margaret Morton, died in the year 1905. In their family were six children, of whom Thomas McKinnon was the third in order of birth, the others being: Gean, the wife of Charles Bechtel, of Los Angeles, California; Laughlin, a prominent builder of Los Angeles, California; John, a contractor of Los Angeles, California; Donald, who is deceased; and James, a banker and contractor of Canistota, South Dakota.

Aside from his brothers and sister, Mr. McKinnon of this review has no living relatives, his father and mother both being the last survivors of their respective lines. The family home having been established in Evanston, Illinois, he there attended the public schools until 1878, when at the age of eighteen years he came with the family to South Dakota and joined his father in the contracting and building business, with which line of work he has since been prominently identified. In Sioux Falls and in various other sections of the state are seen evidences of his skill and handiwork. Among the many fine public and private buildings which he has erected are the State Normal School at Springfield, South Dakota, the McCook County courthouse, the Salem high school, the Cherokee high school, the Sioux Falls high school, the School for Deaf Mutes at Sioux Palls and a score of the largest business and hotel structures in the state. His business makes extensive and heavy demands upon his time and energies, for aside from his activities as a contractor he is the vice president of the Plumbing Supply Company, of Sioux Falls, president of the

East Side Sewer Company of Sioux Falls and president of the Sioux Falls Contractors Association. He is also a stockholder in the State Bank & Trust Company of Sioux Falls and he has large real-estate interests.

Yet onerous and important as are the business duties and interests of Mr. McKinnon he has always found time to participate in public affairs relative to the welfare and upbuilding of city and state. He is an active republican, interested in all the important and vital questions affecting state and nation, for more than twenty-seven years has been found in some important public office and has the unusual record of never having been defeated in any election in which he was a candidate. In 1888 he was elected a member of the city council of Sioux Falls and occupied that position for seven years, exercising his official prerogatives in support of many progressive public measures. In 1894 popular suffrage sent him to the state legislature as the representative of his district in the lower house. That his public service has been of a highly commendable character is indicated in the fact that he has been again and again called to office and usually each election has meant a step forward. In 1899 he was elected county commissioner of Minnehaha County and served continuously until 1914, during which period he was for ten years chairman of the board. In the latter year he was elected to the state senate and took his seat in the upper house in 1915, proving one of the most useful, helpful and active members of the senate. He served as chairman of the committee on counties and towns and on the committees on cities under commission government; charitable and penal institutions; food and drugs; and corporations. He was the father of the "park bill," one of the most useful pieces of legislation enacted during, that session. He carefully studied each question which came up for settlement and his intelligent advocacy of a measure usually drew to it further support.

On the 16th of April, 1893, Mr. McKinnon was united in marriage to Miss Kate McFarland, daughter of John and Kate McFarland, of Washington, Illinois. Both were born in Scotland and became pioneer residents of Illinois. Our subject and his wife have three children, namely: Grace M., who is a student in the University of Wisconsin; Donald M., who attends the University of South Dakota; and Ralph A., a student in the Sioux Falls high school.

The family attend the Presbyterian church, in which Mr. McKinnon holds membership, and his life is further guided by the beneficent principles that underlie the Masonic fraternity, to which he belongs. He finds his chief sources of recreation in hunting and motoring, and knows how to play well as well as to work well. He is interested in the good road's movement and his stand upon any question looking to the upbuilding and betterment of the city and state is a decidedly progressive one. He is one of South Dakota's most substantial and respected citizens, living up to the traditions of a sterling Scotch ancestry and exemplifying in his life the notable spirit of American progress and enterprise which has enabled this country to far outdistance many of the older European countries along various lines.

In the industrial world William J. McMakin occupies the position of engineer of the Homestake Mining Company and in Masonic circles he is widely known, having held many important state offices in that order. He is efficient and capable, and also popular personally, his affability making him well liked wherever known. He was born near Henry, Marshall County, Illinois, March 26, 1856, a son of William P. and Angelina (Bradford) McMakin. His father was born in Virginia, whence he removed to Kentucky, and in early life was a river man. He subsequently went to Illinois and located in Marshall County, where he farmed until his death, which occurred about 1862. His wife, who was a native of Indiana, passed away the year following.

William J. McMakin was left an orphan at an early age and was cared for by an aunt and uncle, who became his guardians. For a short time, he attended school in Illinois and then accompanied his guardians to St. James, Minnesota, in 1868. He continued his education in the country schools there until 1874 and then went to Minneapolis, where he secured employment in the flouring

WILLIAM J. McMAKIN

mills. He later worked for the Chicago, Milwaukee & St. Paul Railroad and in 1877 removed to the Black Hills, where he followed placer mining for a time. He later became amalgamator in the quartz mills and on the 1st of April, 1878, entered the employ of the Homestake Mining Company. After some time, he was promoted to the position of stationary engineer in the mills and on the 1st of January, 1910, became engineer in the high-pressure air compressor of the Ellison mine of the Homestake Mining Company. He is at present acting in this capacity and his knowledge of the work involved and his fidelity to the interests of the Homestake Mining Company make him one of that company's trusted servants and his efficiency is recognized by all who are familiar with his record. He is interested financially in various mining projects and companies, and his investments are proving very profitable. The Homestake Veterans Association was organized in 1906 and is composed of men who have been twenty-one years in the service of the company. Mr. McMakin is vice president of the association, which indicates his high standing among those with whom his work brings him in contact.

On Christmas day, 1890, Mr. McMakin was married to Miss Elizabeth C. Ryan, a native of Littleton, Massachusetts, and they have become the parents of four children, of whom three survive, Merva J., Catherine V. and Angeline May.

Mr. McMakin is a republican in politics and supports the candidates and measures of that party at the polls. In June, 1882, he became a member of Central City Lodge, No. 22, A. F. & A. M., and is still identified therewith, having held all of the chairs in the lodge. He is also a member of Golden Gate

Chapter, No. 72, O. E. S., and belongs to the Masonic Veterans Association. He holds membership in Dakota Chapter, No. 3, R. A. M., and from 1888 to 1891 inclusive was high priest thereof. In 1889 he was grand king of the Grand Chapter of the Royal Arch Masons of South Dakota. In 1890 he was deputy grand high priest and in 1891 was made grand high priest. Since 1889 he has been a member of the high priesthood. He is also identified with Black Hills Council, No. 3, R. & S. M., and in 1912 and again in 1913 served as thrice illustrious master. He has held all of the offices in Dakota Commandery, No. 1, K. T., and also in the Grand Commandery. He is also a member of Black Hills Consistory, No. 3, of Deadwood, in which he has held several important offices, and of El Riad Temple, A. A. O. N. M. S., of Sioux Falls, South Dakota. He is a charter member of Naja Temple of Deadwood and was its illustrious potentate in the years 1892, 1893 and 1894. In 1908 he was appointed grand pursuivant in the Grand Lodge of South Dakota, in 1909 was made junior grand warden, in 1910 senior grand warden, in 1911 deputy grand master, and was grand master from June, 1912, to June, 1913. As might be inferred from the many honors that have come to him, his character is one of undoubted integrity and sterling worth, his personality is pleasing, and his friendliness is contagious.

ANDREW P. McMILLAN

Andrew P. McMILLAN is one of the leading merchants of Spink County, having a large and well-equipped general store in Conde, and is vice-president of the State Bank of Doland and the owner of a fine landed estate in the county where he has maintained his home since 1887. He is a native of Minnesota, having been born on the homestead farm, in Harmony township, Filmore county, on the 7th of November, 1859, and being a son of Arthur C. and Rebecca (Cheever) McMillan, both of whom were born in Ohio, of Scotch descent. The paternal great-grandfather of our subject came from Scotland to America in the latter part of the eighteenth century, in company with his two brothers, and their descendants are now to be found in divers' sections of the Union. The parents of the subject removed to Fillmore County, Minnesota, where his father became a successful farmer and stock grower. His present residence in Cresco, Iowa, the mother having died in December, 1893. The subject was reared to the sturdy discipline of the farm, and was about ten years of age at the time of his parents' removal to Iowa, where he secured his early educational discipline in the public schools of Cresco. In 1878 he secured a position as clerk in the mercantile establishment of White & Moon, in Cresco, Iowa, and continued to be employed as a salesman until coming to South Dakota, having in the meanwhile given careful attention to acquiring an intimate knowledge of the various details of the business, familiarizing himself with the values of different lines of goods and thus fortifying himself for an independent career as a merchant. In 1887 he came to Conde, South Dakota, and opened a general merchandise store, one of the first in the town. He began operations upon a modest scale, and by good management and fair dealing his business constantly expanded in scope and importance with the settlement and upbuilding of the surrounding districts and the village, and he now has a large and well-appointed establishment. He handles dry goods, groceries, clothing, shoes, millinery, etc., and his store is one which would do credit to a much more populous town. In 1887 he erected his present business block, which is twenty-four by eighty feet in dimensions and two stories in height. In 1892 Mr. McMillan erected his fine modern residence, at a cost of about three thousand five hundred dollars, the same being one of the most attractive homes in the county, and he is the owner of a valuable farm of three hundred and twenty acres, eight miles southwest of Conde, this county, the same being under a high state of cultivation and yielding good returns. He is one of the principal stockholders in the State Bank of Doland, of which he has been vice-president since 1895. In politics Mr. McMillan is a stalwart Garfield and Bryan man, and although he is essentially public spirited and progressive, he has never sought office of any description. He and his wife are prominent and valued members of the Baptist church in their home town, and he has been superintendent of its Sunday school from the time of organization to the present, covering a period of ten years, while Mrs. McMillan is a popular teacher in the same.

Fraternally Mr. McMillan is identified with the Masonic order, in which he has attained to the chapter degrees; with the lodge and encampment of the Independent Order, of Odd Fellows, as well as the Daughters of Rebekah: and with the Knights of Pythias and the Ancient Order of United Workmen. On the 22d of April, 1884, was solemnized the marriage of Mr. McMillan to Miss Stella K. Hard, who was born and reared in Decorah, Winneshiek County, Iowa, being a daughter of John and Jane (Austin) Hard. Mr. and Mrs. McMillan have the following children: Arthur Edwin, Calla Maude, James Wesley, Leone Dunbar and Lloyd Fountain. Arthur finishes his commercial course at Brookings College in June, 1904, when he will enter into business with his father at Conde.

JAMES McNENNY

James McNenny, judge of the circuit court, with jurisdiction over Lawrence, Butte and Meade counties, his home being at Sturgis, has long enjoyed statewide reputation as an able lawyer and jurist. He was born in Chicago, Illinois, December 6, 1874. His paternal grandfather was one of the pioneers of that state, settling in early days upon a homestead near Elgin, where he continued to reside until his life's labors were ended. He was a native of New York and was of Scotch-Irish descent. His son, James McNenny, Sr., lived in Chicago until his death and was engaged in the dairy business. He married Julia Harrington, a native of Ireland but now a resident of Meade County, South Dakota.

Judge McNenny attended the Chicago public schools until nine years of age, when in 1884 his mother with her four children came to South Dakota, settling upon a farm in Meade County. The entire cash capital of the family at that time was less than one hundred dollars. James McNenny attended the only district school available, walking three miles across the prairies in order to receive the instruction therein given. He later had the benefit of two years' study in the schools of Rapid City and in 1899 he began reading law in the offices of Mike McMahon. He afterward entered the Highland Park College at Des Moines, Iowa, where he pursued the study of law and special courses, including oratory. He had previously learned stenography and he made his way through college by doing stenographic work for lawyers in the evenings and on Saturdays. He was graduated with the class of 1901 and then took the Iowa state examination, which won him admission to the bar with the remarkable percentage of ninety-nine and one-half. In July of the same year, he was admitted to the South Dakota bar and located for practice at Sturgis. The following year he joined Charles C. Polk, under the firm name of Polk & McNenny, which association was continued until 1908. He was elected states attorney of Meade County in 1903 and continued in that office until 1907. In February of the latter year, he was appointed county judge by Governor Crawford and was reelected to the office at the following election, continuing upon the bench until January 1, 1911. He made an excellent record in that position and "won golden opinions from all sorts of people" by reason of the fairness and impartiality of his decisions. He acted as city attorney for Sturgis for a period of six years and in January, 1914, he was appointed to the circuit bench by Governor Byrne, so that he is now serving as judge of the circuit which embraces the three counties of Lawrence, Butte and Meade. He has the happy faculty of losing personal prejudices and any peculiarities of disposition in the impartiality of the office to which life, liberty and property must look for protection.

Throughout the period of his residence in South Dakota, James McNenny has been an important factor in public life, contributing in large measure to those movements which have worked for the benefit and upbuilding of city, county and state. For some years he served as clerk of the board of education of Sturgis. He has been for years much interested in state military affairs. Joining the South Dakota National Guard as a private, he has advanced through successive promotions to the rank of major and is now commanding the Third Battalion of the South Dakota National Guard. He was in 1908 a member of the first rifle team sent to the national encampment at Camp Perry. For one year he served as quartermaster and for a time was judge advocate general of the military organization of the state.

On the 11th of February, 1902, Mr. McNenny was united in marriage to Miss Kate Halbert, a daughter of James B. and Margaret (Moore) Halbert and a niece of the late Judge Joseph B. Moore, of Lead, South Dakota. James B. Halbert was a prominent railway builder residing in Apopka, Florida, and both he and his wife came of old southern colonial families. To Mr. and Mrs. McNenny have been born five children, namely: Kate, Harold, Marion, Mabel and Wilbur.

Judge McNenny is a republican in his political views and does all in his power to further the interests of the party and secure the adoption of the principles which he believes are best adapted to good government. He is a Mason and a member of the Ancient Order of United Workmen and his wife has membership with the Daughters of the American Revolution. They occupy an enviable position in the social circles of city and state and Judge McNenny is recognized as an exceptionally able lawyer, with a splendid record as a jurist since his elevation to the bench.

HON. WILLIAM HENRY McVAY

Hon. William Henry McVay devoted his life to the banking business and became recognized as one of the foremost financiers of South Dakota. He was for many years actively identified with the management and conduct of the First National Bank of Yankton and was its president at the time of his death, which occurred in 1907. His life was one of intense and well directed activity, resulting in the attainment of most honorable success.

Mr. McVay was born November 2, 1839, in Allegheny City, Pennsylvania, a son of James Taylor and Catherine (Bidwell) McVay. The father was born in the vicinity of Pittsburgh, Pennsylvania, and resided there throughout his lifetime, being engaged in the wholesale grocery business. His wife was a native of Connecticut and during her childhood went with her parents to Ohio. By her marriage she became the mother of seven children, including William Henry McVay, who was but three years of age at the time of his parents' death in 1842. He was reared by his maternal grandparents on a farm near Warren, Ohio, and was educated in the district schools and in the public schools of Warren. After putting aside his text-books he entered the employ of his uncle, John C. Bidwell, who operated the Pittsburgh Plow Works, and with him remained until the time of his removal to South Dakota, then Dakota territory, in the year 1876. He made his way to Yankton. In this connection one of the local papers said:

"For a number of years Pittsburgh and Yankton were more closely related in a business way than they have been for many years past. Before the advent of railways steamboat lines connected all then Missouri points with Pennsylvania's marvelous manufacturing center and steamers leaving Pittsburgh were freighted with glassware and iron goods for Yankton. Through this medium no doubt Mr. McVay had formed a favorable opinion of the then capital of Dakota, and he concluded to sever his connection with the overcrowded east and identify himself with the young and rapidly growing west. He came to Yankton during one of its prosperous hey-days, and entered actively into the business circles of the city and surrounding country, through his position as cashier of the new First National Bank, of which his brother was president. Yankton was an important steamboat point at that time and the First National was promoting the river business. The city was a busy one and the bank's affairs were active and prosperous. The new cashier very soon grew into the confidence and esteem of the business interests here by the exercise of those qualities of education and temperament which have since characterized his social and business intercourse with his fellow citizens. He not only became popular but retained during his busy life, the implicit confidence and earnest esteem of all who knew him."

On the 18th of October, 1860, at Warren, Ohio, Mr. McVay was united in marriage to Miss Rebecca Rutan, a daughter of Henry and Mary (Guy) Rutan, of that place. The children of this marriage are: Mary Rutan, the wife of George Wilson; William Henry, who married Alice Jones; Chester Bidwell, who married Jennie Gamble; Howard Guy; and Katherine Bidwell. His interests centered in his family and the greatest pleasure which he derived from his success was that it enabled him to provide liberally for his wife and children.

In politics Mr. McVay was a republican, but was never a politician in the sense of office seeking. Again, we quote from the Press and Dakotan, which said: "It was Governor Howard who discerned in Mr. McVay the man to extricate the finances of the Territory from an embarrassing condition and who in 1879 appointed him treasurer of the Territory. He made no mistake. There was improvement in the credit of the Territory from almost the beginning of Mr. McVay's administration, soon the warrants of the Territory were as good as cash and there were none on the market. Improvement continued until the credit of the Territory was restored and on a substantial basis and when Governor Ordway succeeded Howard, fortunately he made no change. Mr. McVay held the office almost seven years, and when he finally relinquished it, the treasury was well equipped with a handsome balance in favor of the Territory. Mr. McVay, while he was a lifelong republican, was never an office seeker. During Governor Pierce's administration he accepted the position of railroad commissioner for this portion of the Territory, and made an excellent official, but aside from that and the treasurership, he held no public position."

It was upon the removal of the capital from Yankton that Mr. McVay resigned his position as treasurer, not wishing to leave the city in which he had so long made his home. He was associated with the Congregational church at Yankton and was thoroughly allied to all the interests and opportunities of the city. Aside from the offices he held, his entire time was given to his duties in the bank and while cashier in name, he was virtually head of the institution long before he was elected to the presidency. The First National of Yankton is recognized as one of the soundest and most ably conducted of the financial institutions of the state, a result achieved largely through the efforts of Mr. McVay, a man highly esteemed for his assiduous attention to duty and the probity of his business career. His position not only in business, but also in social, educational and church circles is one hard to fill. He stood at all times for advancement and improvement and cooperated most heartily in movements for the general good. He was farsighted and ever looked beyond the exigencies of the moment to the opportunities of the future.

He was a Mason and, in his life, exemplified the beneficent spirit of the craft, which recognizes the brotherhood of mankind and the obligations of the individual to his fellows. He had attractive social characteristics as well as splendid business qualifications; true worth always won his high regard and he held friendship inviolable. His life was strong and purposeful and exerted a beneficent influence upon the community in which he lived.

ROBERT J. McVICKER

The general store at Vermillion owned by Robert J. McVicker is considered one of the best in that section of the state. Mr. McVicker is a native of Pennsylvania, born May 4, 1864, of the marriage of Simpson M. and Eliza (Wilson) McVicker. The father was a farmer and in 1865 removed with his family to Illinois, where he resided for six years. A removal was then made to Iowa, where he purchased land and where he also owned what was known as the Hawley stage station, which was soon afterward discontinued. He purchased additional land from time to time and devoted his energies to farming throughout his active life. Both he and his wife died in the Hawkeye state in 1880. They had eight children: Elmer E., a minister of the gospel at Corvallis, Oregon; Robert J.; Ella, the wife of H. C. Tuttle, of Canada; Lizzie J., the wife of Fred Talcot, of Webb City, Iowa, who is principal of the school at Blairsburg, Iowa; Clarence, engaged in the meat business at Clarion, Iowa; Willa, the wife of George Garth, a farmer residing near Webster City; Albert B., who is engaged in farming near Ackley, Iowa; and Ernest A., who lives in Smith Center, Kansas.

Robert J. McVicker was seven years of age when the family removed from Illinois to Iowa and at that early age, he assisted his brother Elmer in driving a team from one state to the other, the journey requiring three weeks. He assisted his father with the work of the farm and after the tatter's death operated the homestead for two years. As he was compelled by circumstances to devote most of his time to work even when a boy, he received but little training in the schools. When but nine years of age he did a man's work upon the farm and when eighteen years old he entered the employ of a merchant of Webster City, receiving a salary of ten dollars per month and his board. He continued in that connection for two years and then went to Blairsburg, where with money that he had earned and saved he opened a grocery store, in partnership with his former employer, under the firm name of R. J. McVicker & Company. The store was conducted for two years by that firm, which then sold out. Mr. McVicker returned to his former position as clerk, but after a year bought a general store which was carried on under the name of McVicker & Christ man for one year. At the end of that time, he bought his partner's interest and continued to conduct the store alone. In the meantime, in order to induce a physician to locate in his little town, he opened a drug store and placed it in charge of him. In 1891 Mr. McVicker commenced a small banking business in his store and after six months organized a stock company which established the Exchange Bank of Blairsburg, of which he was elected cashier. Six months after accepting that position he disposed of his store, exchanging it for a farm. He continued as cashier of the Exchange Bank of Blairsburg until 1893 and then sold his interest in that institution and severed his official connection therewith. He removed to Vermillion, South Dakota, where, on the 9th of March, 1894, he entered business circles as a member of the firm of Grange & McVicker, owners of a general merchandise store, the senior partner being J. W. Grange. In 1910 Mr. McVicker sold out to his partner and for about three years conducted stores in different places but during that time maintained his residence in Vermillion. On the 28th of January, 1912, he purchased a small stock of groceries in Vermillion and also the Anderson building. A few months later he purchased the adjoining building and increased the business considerably, handling a full line of dry goods, boots, shoes, etc. At the beginning of his venture, he hired one clerk but now has eight employed regularly. He owns a fine residence on Main Street in Vermillion, and also holds title to land in North Dakota.

Mr. McVicker was married the first time to Miss Carrie Grange, a native of Dubuque, Iowa, their wedding occurring in 1892. They became the parents of two children: Hazel G., who is teaching English at Platte, South Dakota; and Carrie N., who is attending the University of South Dakota at Vermillion and preparing herself for kindergarten work. In January, 1895, the wife and mother died and later Mr. McVicker married Miss Priseilia Grange, a sister of his first wife. To them was born a daughter, Ethlyn, who is now in high school. Mrs. McVicker died in 1905 and in 1909 Mr. McVicker married Miss Edith Spencer, a native of South Dakota.

Mr. McVicker is a republican and while living in Iowa was township clerk. He has served as city assessor of Vermillion for one year but has never been a seeker for office He is a trustee of the Methodist Episcopal church and is devoted to the work of that organization. Fraternally he is a member of the blue lodge, chapter, commandery and Shrine of the Masons and has taken the thirty-second degree in the Scottish Rite. He is likewise a prominent member of the Independent Order of Odd Fellows, having held all of the chairs in the subordinate lodge and encampment and being a member of the canton. He has gained material prosperity for himself by building up a prosperous general store and in so doing has also contributed to the development and growth of his city along commercial lines. He is esteemed for his upright character as well as for his business ability and is a valued resident of Vermillion.

H. T. MEACHAM

H. T. Meacham, one of the leading merchants of Gettysburg, Potter County, is a native of the beautiful Wolverine state, having been born in Adamsville, Cass County, Michigan, on the 19th of November, 1861, and being a son of G. A. and Helen M. Meacham, natives respectively of New York and Ohio. The father now resides in Adamsville, Michigan, where he has been engaged in farming for many years. The mother died in 1900. The subject was reared in his native town and there completed the curriculum of the public schools, being graduated in the high school at Elkhart, Indiana, as a member of the class of 1881, while he then put his scholastic acquirements to practical test and use by engaging in teaching, to which profession he gave his attention about three years. He then decided to try his fortunes in what is now South Dakota, whither he came in 1883, arriving in Gettysburg on the 29th of August. He entered claim to three hundred and twenty acres of government land seven miles south of the town, and remained on the same for a number of months and then returning to his home in Michigan for the winter. In the spring of 1884, he came once more to his claim, upon which he made improvements, placing a considerable portion of the land under cultivation and in due time perfecting his title. In the fall of 1884, he was elected county treasurer, on the Republican ticket, and the hold which he had gained upon popular confidence and esteem was shown in the fact that he was the only successful candidate on the ticket, while he also had the distinction of being the first county treasurer elected, his predecessor having been appointed at the time of the organization of the county and having served until the first general election provided regular incumbents for the various offices. Mr. Meacham gave a most able and satisfactory administration of the fiscal affairs of the county during the formative period, and was continued in the office for three successive terms, of two years each. Upon retiring from office he engaged in the real-estate business, to which he gave his attention until 1893, when he went to Chicago, Illinois, where he remained about two years, at the expiration of which he returned to Gettysburg and established himself in the general merchandise business, in which he has ever since successfully continued, controlling a large trade and having a select and comprehensive stock in the various departments. Mr. Meacham has taken a particularly active interest in public affairs of a local order and has been prominent in the councils of the Republican party contingent in the state. In 1896 he was a delegate to the national convention, in St. Louis, which nominated the late and lamented William McKinley for the presidency, and since that time he has served as a member of the Republican state central committee.

Fraternally he is identified with Ionia Lodge, No. 83, Ancient Free and Accepted Masons, in Gettysburg, having been the first candidate initiated in the same; with Faulkton Chapter, Royal Arch Masons, and with

Huron Lodge, No. 444, Benevolent and Protective Order of Elks, at Huron, South Dakota. Mr. Meacham is a bachelor.

EARL R. MEADOWS

Earl R. Meadows is the junior partner in the firm of Lattimer & Meadows, general merchants of Thomas, Hamlin County, South Dakota claims him among her native sons, his birth having occurred three miles west of Thomas, on the 23d of January, 1890. His father, Joseph F. Meadows, was a farmer by occupation. He came to South Dakota with his parents in 1879, the grandfather, Francis R. Meadows, having been one of the early settlers and homesteaders of this part of the state. Joseph F. Meadows shared with the family in the usual difficulties, hardships and privations of life upon the frontier. He was reared to the occupation of farming, which he chose as a life work and which he followed until called to his final rest. He wedded Cinderella Cunningham, now Mrs. D. W. Lattimer, of Thomas. The children of Mr. and Mrs. Joseph F. Meadows are: Earl R.; Lyle F., who married Anna Eastlery; Francis R., who is in partnership with Lyle F., in the contracting and building business at Hayti; Arthur F., of Washington, who married Grace Nichols, of Watertown; and J. Alfred, at home.

Earl R. Meadows was educated in the public schools of Hamlin County and received thorough training in the work of the fields, to which he devoted his attention when he was not busy with his studies. He was only sixteen years of age when he began farming on his own account, renting a tract of land. For four years he carried on general agricultural pursuits, during which period he lived frugally and economically and as the result of his industry and economy secured the capital that enabled him to buy an interest in his present business in connection with Mr. Lattimer. They have a well-appointed store and their success is increasing, for their trade is growing month by month.

Mr. Meadows was joined in wedlock June 17, 1914, to Miss Emmaline Axford, a daughter of D. M. Axford, one of the pioneer settlers of this section of the state. Mr. Meadows is a Methodist in his religious faith and is a Mason, belonging to Sioux Valley Lodge of Castlewood. His political views accord with the principles of the republican party and he is interested in all lines for the progress and development of his section of the state. He is yet a young man and few of his years have won a more creditable or enviable position in commercial circles. He is fortunate in that he has character and ability which inspire confidence in others and the simple weight of his character and ability has carried him into important trade relations.

FREEMAN R. MEADOWS

Freeman R. Meadows, one of the successful real-estate and insurance men of Watertown and a director in the Citizens National Bank, was born in Woodstock, Ontario, Canada, on the 9th of January, 1875, a son of Francis and Isabelle (Martin) Meadows. The father was also born in Woodstock, of English parentage, but the mother's birth occurred in England. She came to Ontario with her parents when a child of six years and her marriage occurred in that province. The father engaged in farming and fruit growing and also operated a cheese factory in Canada. In 1879 he came to South Dakota and located in Watertown. He subsequently homesteaded one hundred and sixty acres of land, preempted another quarter section and took up a tree claim in Hamlin County five miles east of Hazel, where he lived until his death, which occurred in 1884. He was known especially for the interest which he took in the planting of trees in Hamlin County. His widow survives at the age of eighty years and is a remarkably well-preserved woman. She makes her home in Watertown.

Freeman R. Meadows was reared at home and acquired his education in the common schools and at the Watertown Business College. His father died when he was but nine years of age and he then became the mainstay of the family. He had an older brother, but, as he was practically an invalid, the care of the farm devolved largely upon Mr. Meadows of this review, although he was then but a child. He bravely shouldered the burdens thus placed upon him and managed the farm successfully until 1900. In the meantime, he was married, Miss Alma J. Cunningham, of Hamlin County, becoming his wife on the 17th of December, 1895. After leaving home he removed to Watertown and established himself in the real-estate and insurance business, in which he has since continued. He possesses unusual self-reliance and initiative and, as he is also thoroughly familiar with realty values in this section of the state, he has met with success. He represents a number of the better insurance companies and in his capacity as agent has written a great many policies. He owns the business block at No. 105 North Oak Street and is a director in the Citizens National Bank. He is one of the substantial men of Watertown and is a force in the business life of the city.

Mr. and Mrs. Meadows have two children, a daughter and son, Clella V. and Robert Clinton. The family belong to the Methodist Episcopal church and Mr. Meadows is a member of the official board. His political adherence is given to the republican party, but he has not cared for public office. Fraternally he is a member of Kampeska Lodge, No. 13, A. F. & A. M.; Watertown Lodge, No. 17, K. P.; Watertown Lodge, No. 838, B. P. O. E.; Order of Eastern Star; and the Modern Woodmen of America. He also belongs to the Watertown Country Club and the Watertown Commercial Club. His life has been one of constant activity and strict adherence to principles of honor, and his reward is the high esteem in which he is held.

C. A. MELGAARD

C. A. Melgaard, who is engaged in the automobile and implement business at Volin, belongs to that class of enterprising men who have been the real builders and promoters of the west. He has been a resident of South Dakota since the spring of 1875 and in every possible way has cooperated in the work of general development and improvement as the years have gone by. He was, however, but a small child at the time of his arrival in this state. His father, G. A. Melgaard, was born at Odalen, Norway, while his mother, who bore the maiden's name of Anna Maria Jensen, was a native of Denmark. They came to America when single and settled in Racine, Wisconsin, where they were married. The father worked in the wagon factory of Fish Brothers at that place but afterward removed to Chicago, where he engaged in clerking in a dry-goods store. In the spring of 1875, he brought his family to Dakota and settled on a claim in Turner County two and a half miles southwest of Viborg, then known as Daneville. Mr. Melgaard and his sister were the only Norwegians in the settlement, all the other residents of the district being of Danish birth.

C. A. Melgaard was born in Chicago and was only about two and a half years old when the family removed to Dakota. He was reared upon the home farm and remembers many incidents of the early days, including the periods when the crops were destroyed by grasshoppers. His father's crops were thus devastated for four or five years. In his youth he aided in fighting prairie fires and vividly recalls one that was nearly fatal to him when he was a little fellow. With his mother he was visiting in Clay County. He and a little girl playmate were out on the prairie when the fire came down, driven before the wind. His mother ran and gathered both children in her arms and escaped to plowed ground but the smoke almost strangled them.

In 1898 Mr. Melgaard married and began farming on his own account, living on rented land for ten years. He then removed to Volin and in 1908 embarked in the implement business. A year later, in connection with W. O. Nelson, he opened a hardware store, the partnership continuing for three years, at the end of which time Mr. Melgaard sold his interest. In 1912, in partnership with T. A. Wright, he engaged in the implement and automobile business and in 1913 his partner sold out to Ira S. Myron, so that the firm is now Melgaard & Myron. They do an extensive business, for they are situated in the midst of a fine agricultural region and there is a demand for farm machinery of all kinds. They also handle the Ford and Overland automobiles and have an excellent sale for those machines and they maintain a garage and sell all kinds of automobile supplies.

It was in Sioux Falls, on the 1st of March, 1898, that Mr. Melgaard was united in marriage to Miss Lily Meberg, who died ten years later, leaving a son, Duane. Mr. Melgaard holds membership in the Methodist Episcopal church and his life is guided by its teachings. His political support is given to the republican party. He is a member of the Masonic lodge and has taken the thirty-second degree in the Scottish Rite, belonging to Oriental Consistory, No. I, at Yankton, and is a most exemplary representative of the craft. He is a good business man and a good citizen, loyal to the interests of his community and thoroughly reliable in all relations of life. Energy and determination are carrying him far on the road to success and the firm of Melgaard & Myron is regarded as one of the strong commercial combinations of Yankton County.

GEORGE C. MIELENZ

George C. Mielenz, the junior partner in the firm of Mielenz & Company, laundry men at Yankton, his native city, was born in 1880 and is a son of August W. Mielenz, who is mentioned above. During the period of his youth the family home was maintained in Mitchell, South Dakota, and there he attended the public schools and also pursued a commercial course. On starting out for himself he became a drug clerk and was thus employed for two years, but at the end of that time resigned to become a bookkeeper in the steam laundry at Mitchell in which his father was interested until 1901. In that year he came to Yankton to enter the employ of the laundry firm of Fish & Mielenz, and in 1904 he purchased the interest of Mr. Fish and thus became his father's partner in the business, which is still continued under the style of Mielenz & Company. He has active charge and management of the business and in connection with his father has made it a large and flourishing industrial undertaking. The patronage has now grown to extensive proportions and, like his father, George C. Mielenz, devotes his entire time and attention to the management, development and improvement of the business. High grade work is turned out and reasonable prices and fair dealing are further features in their success.

In 1905 Mr. Mielenz was married to Miss Ruby Tralle, of Yankton, and they have become the parents of three children: Robert, Lenore and Kathryn. Mr. Mielenz belongs to St. John's Lodge, No. I, A. F. & A. M.; Yankton Chapter; De Molay Commandery, K. T.; the Knights of Pythias; and to the Congregational church — associations which indicate much of the nature of his interests and the rules which govern his conduct. He has never sought to figure prominently in public affairs, nor has there been anything spectacular in his life, but, recognizing the truth of the old Greek admonition, "Earn thy reward; the gods give nought to sloth," he has worked earnestly and persistently to gain success in the business world.

Oliver E. MESICK, one of the leading business men of Gettysburg, is a native of the Badger state, having been born in Princeton, Green Lake County, Wisconsin, on the 30th of June, 1861, and being a son of David S. and Elizabeth Jane (Moore) Mesick, both of whom were born and reared in the state of New York. The Mesick family is of stanch Holland Dutch extraction, and the original progenitors in America, located at Troy, in the state of New York, in the early colonial epoch, while representatives of this sterling Knickerbocker family were numbered among the earliest settlers in the vicinity of the present capital city of Albany. The Moore family, of Scottish extraction, was likewise early established on American soil. The father of the subject removed from New York to Wisconsin in 1856, becoming one of the pioneers of Green Lake County, where he improved a valuable farm, upon which he continued to reside until his death, in October, 1901, at the venerable age of seventy-three years. His wife died in April, 1897, on the home farm. They became the parents of five children, of whom four are living, the subject of this review having been the third in order of birth.

Oliver E. Mesick was reared to the sturdy discipline of the home farm, and was afforded the advantages of the excellent public schools of his native state, having completed a course in the school at Princeton, Wisconsin, in which he was graduated as a member of the class of 1880. In 1893 he was matriculated in the law department of the University of Minnesota, where he completed the prescribed course and was graduated in 1895, with the degree of Bachelor of Laws, while he was admitted to the bars of Minnesota and South Dakota in the same year.

After graduating from the high school Mr. Mesick engaged in teaching in the public schools of Wisconsin, proving successful in his pedagogic efforts and continuing the same until 1883, when he came to South Dakota and located in Potter county, being one of the very first settlers in the county, which was not formally organized at that time, while he was the first to pay taxes in the county, and still holds as a souvenir the first receipt for taxes issued by the county, the same bearing date of January, 1885. He filed on a tract of four hundred and eighty acres of government land five miles southeast of the present village of Forest City, and forthwith instituted the improvement of his claim, while he also engaged in teaching school at irregular intervals until 1893, having been principal of the public schools in Gettysburg during the last three years of his service in this line. In the year mentioned he entered the law department of the University of Minnesota. After leaving the University he returned to Gettysburg and here established himself in the practice of his profession, in which he met with gratifying success, and he served during 1897-98 as state's attorney of the county. Prior to entering the law school, he had become interested in the agricultural implement business in Gettysburg, being associated with August Maas, under the firm name of Mesick & Maas, the enterprise being carried on by Mr. Maas during the subject's absence while in the university.

Upon his return he divided his attention between his professional work and his implement business, and the latter so rapidly increased in scope and importance that he found it expedient to practically withdraw from the practice of law that he might give his entire attention to his business interests. In 1901 he purchased Mr. Maas' interest in the business, which he has since individually continued, carrying a large and complete stock of agricultural implements and machinery, and owning the three commodious warehouses utilized in the connection, while he also owns and operates the large grain elevator near the tracks of the Chicago & Northwestern Railroad, and he also does a large business in the handling of coal, being the leading dealer of the county. His office building, he still owns and utilizes, while he is the owner of other realty in the county in addition to the properties noted. He retains his original pre-emption claim, and also three other quarter sections adjoining, and the family improved ranch is devoted to general farming and stock growing.

In politics Mr. Mesick gives an unwavering allegiance to the Republican party, and fraternally he is affiliated with Gettysburg Lodge, No. 83, Ancient Free and Accepted Masons, of which he is worshipful master at the time of this writing; he is also a member of the Modern Woodman of America. He is a member of the Baptist church and his wife belongs to the Congregational church. On the 17th of September, 1902, Mr. Mesick was united in marriage to Miss Minerva C. Carter, who was born and reared in Wisconsin, being a daughter of Louis and Margaret Carter, who now maintain their residence in Ripon, Wisconsin.

JOHN G. MILES

John G. Miles, a cigar manufacturer of Brookings, was born in Howard County, Iowa, January 8, 1859, a son of John O. and Louise (Taft) Miles, the former a native of Maine and the latter of Wisconsin. The father went to Iowa about 1854, settling in one of the pioneer districts of the state, where he purchased government land at a dollar and a quarter per acre. With resolute energy he began converting the claim into a cultivable and valuable farm and thereon made his home until his death. His widow afterward took up her abode in Cresco, Iowa, where her remaining days were passed.

John G. Miles had good home training, with the benefits to be derived from public school education in Cresco, where he supplemented the work of the lower grades by a high school course. He came to South Dakota in 1881 and took up a preemption in Day County, which he proved up on. In the spring of 1883 he arrived in Brookings, where he entered the employ of B. J. Kelsey, a general merchant. In the fall of 1885, he established himself in the furniture and hardware business in Brookings, but sold out after five years and for some time thereafter gave his attention to the management of his landed properties. His fellow townsmen, appreciative of his worth and ability, however, called him from private life to public office, electing him sheriff of Brookings County in 1906. He made such an excellent record during his first term that he was reelected and thus served for two terms. When he retired from office, he purchased his present cigar manufacturing business, which he has since conducted, his trade being largely confined to the eastern part of the state. He is also the owner of the speedy pacing horse Dad Mix, with which he has been winning many of the best purses at the various fairs throughout the middle west, the horse never receiving a lower mark than 2:12¾. He is very speedy and will undoubtedly later show among the fast representatives of the track. The landed possessions of Mr. Miles aggregate more than a thousand acres of farming property in Brookings County and in Minnesota.

In 1890 Mr. Miles was married to Miss Katie M. Hall, a daughter of A. M. Hall, a large landowner of Brookings County, who served for four years as county treasurer and otherwise was known as a valued citizen but is now deceased. Mr. and Mrs. Miles became the parents of a son, Hall J. In his political views Mr. Miles has always been a stalwart republican since age conferred upon him the right of franchise. He has served as justice of the peace and as town clerk. He belongs to Brookings Lodge, No. 24, A. F. & A. M.; Brookings Chapter, No. 18, R. A. M.; Brookings Commandery, K. T.; the Ancient Order of United Workmen at Elkton; and the Brookings Commercial Club. He advances steadily along the line which he has chosen as a life work, his close application and his judicious investments being salient features in his prosperous career.

EDGARJ. MILLER

Edgar J. Miller holds a position of distinctive precedence in financial circles of Huron as cashier of the First National Bank, with which institution he has been connected since 1881. He is a representative of one of the best-known families in the city and his record is a credit to a name that has long been held in high honor and regard in the community.

Mr. Miller was born in Whitewater, Wisconsin, June 19, 1864, and is a son of John H. and Harriet (Pratt) Miller, the former born in New York, March 4, 1831, and the latter in the same state. Their marriage occurred in Wisconsin, November 14, 1861, and five years later they removed to Iowa. The family came to South Dakota in 1880 and the father homesteaded land one mile west of Huron in the following year. After he had proved up on his claim he moved into the village, where from that time until his death he remained an active and valued citizen. In 1882 he aided in the organization of the First National Bank and he remained a director in that institution for many years. He was at all times active in municipal work and held a number of county offices, serving from 1885 to 1887 as county treasurer and for four terms as county commissioner. It was he who laid out the grounds in the courthouse square at Huron and superintended the planting of the trees. He died June 2, 1912, and his passing was widely and deeply regretted, as it deprived Huron of a man who had been for over a quarter of a century an active factor in development. John H. Miller was a member of the Methodist church, was connected fraternally with the Benevolent Protective Order of Elks and gave his political allegiance to the republican party. He had three children: Edgar J., of this review; Mrs. Amy K. Glenn, of Huron; and Mrs. C. C. Langley, of Santa Ana, California.

After acquiring a public-school education Edgar J. Miller attended the Iowa State College of Agriculture and Mechanic Arts at Ames. He began his independent career as an employee of the Northwestern Railway and the American Express Company and in 1881 became connected with the First National Bank of Huron, South Dakota, with which he has since been identified. About 1898 he was made cashier of that institution and has capably filled that position since that time, displaying in the discharge of his duty's insight, business ability and discrimination.

In 1886 Mr. Miller was united in marriage to Miss Lillian Giehm, of Tracy, Minnesota, and they became the parents of a daughter, Margaret, who died at the age of thirteen years. Mr. Miller belongs to the Knights of Pythias, the Elks and the Eagles and to the Masonic lodge, chapter, commandery and Shrine. He gives his political allegiance to the republican party and is interested and active in public affairs. For six years he served as alderman from his ward and is at present serving a three years' term as a member of the executive council of the American Bankers Association. He has large farming interests in the vicinity of Huron and occupies a leading place in financial circles of the city, being known as an able and discriminating financier.

ALBERT F. MILLIGAN

A. F. MILLIGAN, state agent of the St. Paul Fire and Marine Insurance Company for South Dakota, with headquarters at Aberdeen, was born at St. Thomas, Ontario, Canada, on April 11, 1863. His parents were James and Mary (Hunt) Milligan, both natives of the province of Ontario, where the father resides at the present, living retired at St. Thomas. The mother died in 1897.

Albert F. Milligan attended the public schools, then taught for three years, after which he entered the St. Thomas Collegiate Institute, taking high position in mathematics and languages. In 1884 he came to Aberdeen, South Dakota, and two years later established himself in the local fire insurance. Five years later he was appointed state agent for the St. Paul Fire and Marine Insurance Company, and has since held that important position. Under his management of this field the company has kept pace with the growth and development of the Northwest, and now controls the leading insurance business in South Dakota. Mr. Milligan gives close attention to the upbuilding of his business, and has done much to gain for his company its success and prestige in South Dakota. Mr. Milligan has other important interests, including those of farming and banking. He is a director of the Aberdeen National Bank and of the First National Bank of Webster, South Dakota, and is also identified with the First State Bank of Aberdeen.

He has always been a member of the Republican party, and is a member of the Masonic fraternity, being a member of Damascus Commandery, No. 10, Knights Templar, and of El Riad Temple, Mystic Shrine, the latter of Sioux Falls. In Ellendale, South Dakota, on August 10, 1888, Mr. Milligan was married to Rose Abbott, who was born and reared in Kandiyohi, Minnesota, being a daughter of Burroughs Abbott, now a resident of Aberdeen. Mrs. Milligan was a successful teacher in the Aberdeen public schools for several years prior to her marriage. Three children have been born to this union: Marjorie, Muriel and Tames Abbott.

GEORGE T. MITCHELL

George T. MITCHELL, one of the successful and highly esteemed farmers of Grant County, has the distinction of being a scion of one of the representative pioneer families of Ionia County, Michigan, where he was born on the 20th of May, 1855, being a son of Curtis B. and Martha (Troop) Mitchell, both of whom were born and reared in the state of New York. The father early removed to Michigan and developed a good farm in Ionia County, and there continued to reside until his death, in November, 1889, at which time he was sixty-eight years of age. His father, George Mitchell, a veteran of the war of 1812, settled in Michigan in 1839. The family was founded in New England in the early colonial epoch, being of Scotch-Irish extraction.

George T. Mitchell was reared on the homestead farm, while his educational advantages were those afforded by the public schools and a commercial college in Grand Rapids, Michigan. Thereafter he was for a number of years employed as a commercial traveling salesman, in which connection he met with excellent success and gained a reputation for ability and energy. In 1882 he came to what is now South Dakota and took up his permanent abode in Melrose township, Grant County, having come here the preceding fall and purchased one hundred and sixty acres of land, upon which he located in June of the year mentioned, while later he added another tract of equal area, so that he now has a farm of two hundred and forty acres, improved with good buildings, fences, etc., and devoted to diversified agriculture and to the raising of good livestock. He gives no little attention to dairying, and furnishes a very considerable supply of milk to the co-operative creamery at Milbank, having been one of those actively identified with the establishment of the enterprise, which met with some opposition or apathy on the start, much trouble having been experienced for a time in securing the co-operation of many of those who are now numbered among its principal supporters, though it now has about one hundred and twenty-five patrons. He was elected president of the operating company at the time of its organization, and has ever since continued in tenure of this office, while it is due in no small degree to his energy and progressive ideas that the institution has built up a fine business, having the best creamery plant in the state. About three and a half million pounds of milk are received each year in the plant, and the annual product aggregates about twenty-six thousand to twenty-eight thousand pounds of butter. Mr. Mitchell is also treasurer of the farmers' grain elevator at Milbank having been one of the organizers of the company and having contributed materially to the success of the enterprise, whose financial prosperity has shown how great benefits may be gained by farmers through such co-operation. About two hundred thousand bushels of wheat and thirty thousand bushels of flax are handled annually. The company buys on a close margin and is thus enabled to declare very gratifying dividends to the stockholders. Mr. Mitchell was a member of the board of county commissioners from 1891 for twelve years and was chairman of the same for nine years. The significance of this long tenure of the important office as a Democrat in a strong Republican County is prima facia, as it indicates in an unmistakable way the high degree of confidence and esteem in which he is held in the county and the objective appreciation of his loyalty and business and executive ability. At the time of this writing, he is also supervisor of his township. He manifests at all times a lively interest in public affairs, particularly those of a local nature, and in politics is a stalwart advocate of the principles of the Democratic party.

Fraternally he is identified with Milbank Lodge, Ancient Free and Accepted Masons, which he represented in the grand lodge of the state for three years, and with Milbank Chapter, Royal Arch Masons, in which he is serving his third year as high priest, while he also holds membership in the auxiliary chapter of the Order of the Eastern Star, and is affiliated with the Modern Woodmen of America and the Ancient Order of United Workmen. At Ionia, Michigan, on the 17th of November, 1880, was solemnized the marriage of Mr. Mitchell to Miss Mary Allen, who was born in Allegany County, New York, as were also her parents, Roy and Melissa (Lewis) Allen, representatives of old colonial stock and now residents of Milbank. Mr. and Mrs. Mitchell have four children, Maude E., Curtis P., Clara M. and Leroy.

W. S. MITCHELL

W. S. Mitchell was born in Aberdeen, Scotland, on the 16th of February, 1861, and received his educational discipline in the excellent schools of his native land, where he remained until he had attained the age of twenty-one years, when he severed the home ties and came to America. He landed in New York City and remained in the national metropolis about six months, at the expiration of which he came to the west and located in St. Cloud, Minnesota, where he followed his trade, that of stone cutter, for the ensuing year, at the expiration of which he returned to New York, where he passed the following year and then came again to St. Cloud, where he made his home until he came to South Dakota and took up his residence in Sioux Falls, where he was engaged in the work of his trade until the following year, when he cast in his lot with that of the good people of Dell Rapids, where he organized the Dell Rapids Granite Company, of which he became secretary and treasurer, the company owning and operating valuable quarries in this locality. He continued to be actively concerned in this line of enterprise for a period of twelve years, at the expiration of which he disposed of his interests and engaged in the hotel and restaurant business in Dell Rapids. He has gained to his place a high reputation for the best of service in all departments, and Mitchell's hotel and restaurant enjoy unmistakable popularity with the traveling public. For the past five years he has been manager of the local opera house and in the connection has given the public an excellent class of entertainments. In politics Mr. Mitchell has ever given an unqualified allegiance to the Republican party but has never sought or desired public office.

He is held in high regard in fraternal circles and he is identified with the Masonic order, the Benevolent and Protective Order of Elks, the Knights of Pythias, Knights of the Maccabees, Modern Woodmen of

America and the Dramatic Order of the Knights of Khorassan. Mr. Mitchell was united in marriage to Miss Hattie Love, and they have one child.

THOMAS W. MOFFITT, M. D.

Dr. Thomas W. Moffitt, a well-known follower of the medical profession practicing successfully at Deadwood, was born at Sarahsville, Ohio, May 25, 1870, a son of Samuel and Elizabeth (Young) Moffitt, who were also natives of the Buckeye state. In early life the father was a lawyer and also became a journalist. At Cambridge, Ohio, he edited a paper called the Jeffersonian and on leaving that place removed to Pittsburgh, Pennsylvania, where he was editor of the Pittsburgh Evening News, continuing his residence in that city up to the time of his death, which occurred in 1888. His widow afterward returned to her home in Sarahsville, Ohio, and there passed away in 1907. Mr. Moffitt was a veteran of the Civil war, having served as a private in an Ohio regiment. To him and his wife were born two children, of whom Dr. Moffitt is the younger. Following the death of her first husband Mrs. Moffitt married again and there were four children born of that union.

Dr. Moffitt completed his public-school education as a high-school pupil in Caldwell, Ohio. He afterward attended the Ohio State University and prepared for his professional career as a student in the Starling Medical College at Columbus. He was graduated in medicine when twenty-three years of age, after which he made his way to South Dakota, settling at Hot Springs, where he engaged in active practice from 1893 until July, 1898. He then removed to Lead, where he joined the medical staff of the Homestake Mining Company, with which he was connected for a year. On the expiration of that period, he located in Deadwood, where he has practiced continuously since. He does not engage in general practice, however, but confines his attention to surgery. He has a comprehensive knowledge of anatomy and the component parts of the human body, of the onslaughts made upon it by disease or left to it as a legacy by progenitors and this, combined with skill in handling delicate surgical instruments, has made him one of the skillful surgeons of his part of the state, enjoying the high regard of his professional brethren as well as of the general public. He is a member and president of the District Medical Society and belongs also to the South Dakota State Medical Association and to the American Medical Association.

On the 28th of October, 1896, Dr. Moffitt was united in marriage to Miss Marilla Anderson, who was born in Illinois, a daughter of Colonel A. R. and, Sarah (Woods) Anderson, both of whom were natives of Ohio. The father, who was an attorney at law, removed from Ohio to Illinois and thence to Sidney, Iowa, where, he was active at both the bar and in politics. He served in an Iowa regiment during the Civil war and was commissioned colonel. On several occasions he was wounded but never seriously. He left the impress of his individuality upon the public welfare and the upbuilding of the state and he held various offices, serving for two terms as a member of congress. Both he and his wife have passed away and are survived by two children, of whom Mrs. Moffitt is the younger. To Dr. and Mrs. Moffitt have been born two children, Sarah Marilla and Thomas W.

Dr. Moffitt is well known as an exemplary representative of the Masonic fraternity and as a loyal member of the Benevolent Protective Order of Elks. In politics he has long been a democrat and has served as a member of the city council of Deadwood and as city physician. He was formerly a member of the state board of health, from 1899 until 1904, having been appointed by Governor Lee. He has a wide and favorable acquaintance and the goodwill and confidence of many friends are cordially extended him.

Elmer W. MONFORE, a well-known and highly respected citizen of Springfield, Bon Homme County, was born in the town of Center Lisle, Broome county, New York, on the 18th of November, 1853, being a son of Peter and Diana A. (Howland) Monfore, of whose eight children seven are living, namely: Emerson J., who resides at Waverly, Kansas; Elmer W., who is the subject of this review; Cora A., who is the wife of Clark S. Rowe, of Sioux Falls, South Dakota; Lana H., who is the wife of Alfred Burkholder, of that city; Alice A., who is the wife of Charles McBeth, of Mankato, Minnesota; Luna B., who is the wife of Professor Joseph W. Whiting, a member of the faculty of the normal school in Springfield, South Dakota; and Peter G., who is likewise a resident of this place.

The father of the subject was born in Delaware county, New York, in 1821, and in the old Empire state he learned the trade of miller. In 1865 he came west to Putnam county, Illinois, where he was engaged in farming for the ensuing three years, at the expiration of which he removed to Marion county, Iowa, where he remained about two years and then came to South Dakota, locating in Springfield, and he was thereafter employed for a number of years by the government as miller at the Santee Indian agency and later at the Ponca agency, after which he lived a retired life in Springfield until his death, which occurred in 1895. On coming here, he took up homestead and tree-culture claims, while at the time of his death he had recently disposed of three hundred and twenty acres of excellent land near Springfield. In politics he was a stanch Republican, and he was a man who ever commanded unqualified esteem. His wife was born in Broome County, New York, and is now living with a married daughter at Mankato, Minnesota.

Elmer W. Monfore was about twelve years of age at the time his parents came from New York to Illinois, and his early educational training was secured in the common schools and supplemented by a course in Bryant & Stratton's Business College in Des Moines, Iowa. After coming to South Dakota, he devoted his attention to farm work for about five years, and later he was employed, for varying intervals, in the mercantile establishments of D. W. Currier, M. H. Day and P. M. Liddy, all of Springfield, the last mentioned having succeeded Mr. Day. In 1881 he engaged in business for himself, conducting a drug and grocery store here for two years, at the expiration of which he admitted to partnership in the enterprise his cousin, Edward C. Monfore, the firm title of E. W. Monfore & Company being adopted at that time. This partnership continued until January 1, 1903, when the firm disposed of the business, since which time our subject has had no active business associations. In politics he is a Republican and he has served as a member of the board of aldermen of Springfield and also as treasurer of the town and as a member of the board of education.

He and his wife are valued members of the First Congregational church, and fraternally he is identified with Mount Zion Lodge, No. 6, Free and Accepted Masons; Scotland Chapter, No. 52, Royal Arch Masons; Springfield Lodge, No. 7, Independent Order of Odd Fellows, and Deborah Lodge, No. 52, Daughters of Rebekah; Springfield Lodge, Knights of Pythias, and Springfield Chapter. No. 2, Order of the Eastern Star. On the 16th of October, 1883, Mr. Monfore was united in marriage to Miss Emma R. Seccombe, of Springfield, and they became the parents of four children: Charles E. (died February 6, 1904), Alberta A., Fred H. and Millicent L.

W. L. MONTGOMERY

W. L. MONTGOMERY, cashier of the Bank of Iowa and Dakota, at Chamberlain, and a member of the present state senate, is a native of the state of Illinois, having been born in Rock Island County. He was reared on the home farm and after completing the curriculum of the public schools continued his studies in the Geneseo Academy, at Geneseo, Illinois. Soon after leaving school, he came west to Nebraska, where he established himself in the real-estate, loan and live-stock business, having his headquarters at Fullerton, Nance County. He removed to northwestern Iowa, where he remained about one year, at the expiration of which he came to Chamberlain, South Dakota, where he engaged in the banking and live-stock business, purchasing an interest in the Bank of Iowa and Dakota. Later he and his father purchased the interests of all other stockholders in the institution, of which they have since maintained control. Mr. Montgomery has ever given an unqualified allegiance to the Republican party, and was elected to represent his district in the state senate. He is a member of the Free and Accepted Masons and of the Benevolent and Protective Order of Elks. Mr. Montgomery was united in marriage to Miss Leone King, of Chamberlain, and they have one child.

CHARLES C. MOODY

CHARLES C. MOODY

Charles C. Moody, throughout his active life, devoted his time and energies to newspaper work and for a number of years published the Sturgis Weekly Record. He was a native of Indiana, born November 28, 1858, and was a son of Gideon C. and Helen (Eliot) Moody, both born in the Empire state. The family is of Irish descent. Gideon C. Moody became a lawyer in early manhood and emigrated to Indiana when that state was still largely a pioneer section. In 1866 he came to South Dakota, locating in Yankton, and was appointed to the supreme bench of Dakota territory. After the admission of South Dakota into the Union he was the first United States senator elected. He was for a number of years attorney for the Homestake Mining Company of Lead and in 1879 removed to Deadwood, where he remained until six years previous to his death. His last days were spent in Los Angeles, California, his demise occurring there March 17, 1904. He served throughout the entire Civil War and held the rank of colonel in the Indiana regular troops. His widow is still living in Los Angeles, California. To them were born five children, of whom Charles C. was the second in order of birth.

Charles C. Moody attended school in Indiana and in Yankton, South Dakota, and thus prepared himself for the duties and responsibilities of life. When eleven years of age he was employed on the Press and Dakotan of Yankton and continued with that paper until the family removed to Deadwood in 1879. For a considerable period, he was associated with his father-in-law in newspaper work and then became editor and publisher of the Evening Press in Deadwood. He removed the plant to Sturgis in 1884 and began the publication of the Sturgis Weekly Record, continuing to issue that paper for over two decades, or until his death, which occurred on the 26th of June, 1906. He possessed the journalist's highly developed news sense, had a command of clear, forceful English, understood thoroughly the typographical part of newspaper publication and was as well an able business man. Under his direction the Sturgis Weekly Record built up a large circulation list and gained a reputation as an excellent weekly. Since his demise his widow has continued its publication and has maintained the high standard established by Mr. Moody.

On the 29th of December, 1880, Mr. Moody was united in marriage to Miss Hattie L. Warner, who was born in Chicago, Illinois, a daughter of Porter and Ellen (Davis) Warner, the former born in Birmingham, Massachusetts, March 17, 1836, and the latter in Syracuse, New York, June 5, 1841. At first Mr. Warner engaged in the newspaper business in his native state but later removed to Chicago, where he continued in that line of work. From that city he went to Denver, Colorado, which remained his home for ten years, but in 1876 he came to South Dakota, locating at Deadwood, where he established the Times, which he continued to publish until his death. The paper was eventually consolidated with the Pioneer, more detailed mention of which is made elsewhere in this work. He was the receiver at the land office in Rapid City at the time of his death and also owned land in this state. He served throughout the Civil war as captain in an Illinois regiment and was wounded in the battle of Gettysburg. His widow now makes her home at Pasadena, California. Mrs. Moody is the oldest of her parents' eleven children and has become the mother of five daughters: Nellie, the wife of M. M. Brown, a resident of Sturgis and cashier of the First National Bank, by whom she has two children, Warner Moody and Helen Frances; Charity, who makes her home with her mother; Hattie and Alice, who died in infancy; and Dorothy, who passed away when twenty-one years of age.

Mrs. Moody is not only the owner of the Sturgis Weekly Record but is also a stockholder in the Commercial National Bank of Sturgis and the Sturgis Lumber & Grain Company. She owns considerable farm and city property in this state and in the management of her interests has proved a woman of marked business ability and sound judgment.

Mr. Moody was a republican but never sought public office. Fraternally he was connected with the Masonic order and the Eagles and was popular not only in those organizations but throughout the community in which he lived. His friends still cherish his memory and the Sturgis Weekly Record is a monument to his life of well-directed activity.

GEORGE W. F. MOORE

George W. F. Moore, one of the progressive and active young business men of Sioux Falls, serving as general agent in South Dakota for the Connecticut General Life Insurance Company, was born in Blue Earth, Minnesota, March 14, 1883. He is a son of George D. and Elizabeth (Myers) Moore, the former a native of Green Springs, Ohio, and now a resident of Northfield, Minnesota. The grandfather of our subject, John Moore, was- a native of Virginia.

George W. F. Moore acquired his education in the public schools of Blue Earth, Minnesota, and in business colleges at Fairmont, Minnesota, and Fargo, North Dakota. When he left the latter city he removed to Elmore, Minnesota, and there turned his attention to the life and fire insurance business. In 1908 he came to Sioux Falls and since that time has been a resident of this city, prominently connected with its business life. He has continued his connection with insurance interests and now occupies the responsible position of general agent in South Dakota for the Connecticut General Life Insurance Company. In this position he has done a great deal to promote the interests of the company and is regarded as one of its most reliable and capable representatives.

On the 9th of June, 1909, at Elmore, Minnesota, Mr. Moore married Miss Alice Marian Petters and they have two children, Gerald Louis and Janet Elizabeth. Mr. Moore is a member of the Congregational church and gives his political allegiance to the democratic party. He holds membership in the Elks Club of Sioux Falls, is a blue lodge Mason and connected also with the Independent Order of Odd Fellows, the Knights of Pythias and the Sons of the American Revolution. He is a resourceful, energetic and capable business man, and his actions conform always to the highest standards of business ethics, so that he enjoys the goodwill and respect of all who are in any way associated with him.

THOMAS H. MOORE

THOMAS H. MOORE

Thomas H. Moore is engaged in the collection business and has proved very successful in collecting outstanding accounts that but for his efforts would have remained unpaid. He is also United States commissioner and county commissioner of Lawrence County, dividing his time between his business affairs and his official duties and finding that he has but little leisure. As industry has characterized him through life, he finds pleasure in doing well the task at hand.

Mr. Moore was born in Nashville, Tennessee, on the 4th of April, 1848, a son of James G. and Mary Ewing (Hiter) Moore. The father was born in Strabane, County Tyrone, Ireland, and the mother in Franklin, Williamson County, Tennessee. The former came to the United States when nineteen years of age and for a number of years resided in Pennsylvania but subsequently removed to Nashville. In 1846 he became a naturalized citizen of the United States. He was a manufacturer of harness and saddlery and supplied the Confederate troops with a portion of their equipment. In 1877 he passed away, having survived his wife for many years. The latter's family were well known and her grandfather, Colonel Thomas McCrory, served in the Revolutionary war. He was born in Ireland but emigrated to North Carolina in colonial days. Members of the family participated in all the subsequent wars and were prominent in public affairs.

Thomas H. Moore was reared in Nashville and received his early education there. From 1863 to 1865 he attended Notre Dame University at Notre Dame, Indiana, after which he returned to Nashville and became a clerk in a hardware store when sixteen years of age. He continued with that concern until 1879, in which year he removed to Lead and had charge of the hardware department of the Thomas James store, now the Hearst Mercantile Company, until 1881. In the last-named year, he removed to Terraville, near Lead, and acted in the capacity of timekeeper for the Deadwood Terra Mining Company until 1883. He then became manager of the George Hearst store and so continued until the spring of 1886. The following year he removed to Sundance, Wyoming, and engaged in the grocery business there until 1892. In the intervening years he was chief chairman of the board of county commissioners of Crook County, for two years was county treasurer and for the same period of time deputy county treasurer.

In 1897 Mr. Moore returned to Lead and engaged in the furniture business for two years. At the expiration of that period, he entered the employ of the Homestake Mining Company and was connected with that concern for five years. In 1904 he became associated with the Lead-Deadwood Gas Light & Fuel Company and for a year had charge of their Deadwood office, after which he was manager of the Lead office for two years. In 1907 he was elected police judge of Lead and served until 1910, holding the office during the serious labor troubles that occurred at that time. In 1911 he established his present business, that of a collection agency, in which he has proven very successful. He is persistent and uses excellent judgment in his dealings with people, adapting his methods of procedure to conditions of the case in hand. In 1908 he was appointed United States commissioner for South Dakota and is still serving in that- capacity. In the fall of 1913, he was appointed county commissioner of Lawrence County to fill a vacancy and was later elected to that position.

On the 19th of September, 1873, Mr. Moore was united in marriage to Miss Elizabeth R. Driver, also a native of Nashville, Tennessee, and a daughter of Captain Driver, who named the American flag Old Glory. To Mr. and Mrs. Moore were born three children: Sadie M., the wife of Dr. John H. Graham, of Lincoln, Nebraska; Van Dyk, who was accidentally killed in Colorado in 1910 when thirty years of age; and Elizabeth D., who married Lee B. Dougan, of Terraville, South Dakota, where he is superintendent of the cyanide plant of the Mogul Mining Company.

Mr. Moore is a republican and has always been active in politics. In 1890, during his residence in Wyoming, he was a member of the constitutional convention held at Cheyenne. He is a member of the board of education of Lead, representing independent district No. 6. Fraternally he is a member of Golden Star Lodge, No. 9, A. F. & A.M., of Lead, of which he is secretary; Golden Belt Chapter, No. 35, R. A. M.; Black Hills Council, No. 3, R. & S. M.; Lead Commandery, No. 18, K. T., in which he is recorder; and Naja Temple, A. A. O. N. M. S., of Deadwood; and he also belongs to the South Dakota Masonic Veterans Association. Mr. Moore has gained financial independence and is known as one of the representative business men of his city, being also held in high esteem for his many admirable traits of character.

WILLIAM MOORE

William MOORE, who is one of the owners and operators of the Armour Roller Mills at Armour, Douglas County, is a native of the province of Ontario, Canada, having been born in the town of Athens, on the loth of May, 1857, a son of Mark and Ann Moore. He received his educational discipline in the excellent schools of his native province, where he was engaged in business until the year 1881, when he came to the United States and located in the city of Cleveland, Ohio, where he resided for two years, at the expiration of which, in 1883, he came to Douglas County, South Dakota, where he established himself in the hardware and agricultural-implement business in the town of Grand View, moving to Armour later and becoming one of the early merchants of the place and building up a most successful enterprise, while he secured a firm hold on the confidence and esteem of the community, so that his business increased in scope and importance with the development and growth of the village and county. In the year 1901, Mr. Moore disposed of this business and shortly afterward purchased an interest in the Armour Roller Mills, of which he assumed the active management at the time. The output of the mills finds a ready demand in the market, and its products are sold throughout the state, the special brands of flour manufactured being the Fancy Patent, the White Rose and the Headlight, all of which have attained a high reputation through South Dakota, being held equal to any brands to be found in any section of the Union. The mills have been equipped with the most modern and improved machinery and accessories, and the most scrupulous care is given to every detail of operation, the daily capacity being for the output of fifty barrels. Through the indefatigable efforts and able administrative powers of Mr. Moore the scope of the business has been greatly expanded, and the enterprise is one which is highly appreciated and which contributes largely to the industrial prestige of the attractive town of Armour. Mr. Moore is a stanch advocate of the principles and policies of the Democratic party, and is at the present time a valued member of the village council.

Fraternally he is identified with Arcania Lodge, No. 97, Free and Accepted Masons, of Armour, South Dakota; Mitchell Chapter, No. 16, Royal Arch Masons, and St. Bernard Commandery, No. II, Knights Templar, the latter two affiliations being with the respective bodies in the city of Mitchell. On the 3d of June, 1891, Mr. Moore was united in marriage to Miss Hattie E. Long, of Cleveland, Ohio, and they are the parents of two fine sons, William A. and Lucius Wells, aged ten and seven, respectively.

GEORGE MOREHOUSE

George MOREHOUSE, deceased, late of Brookings, was one of the representative bankers and capitalists of the state and one of its most honored citizens, while the lesson of his career is a valuable one, showing a particular mastering of expedients, a strong mental grasp and a rare power of initiative, through which forces he has attained a high degree of success and won the proud American title of self-made man.

Mr. Morehouse was a native of the old Empire state, having been born in the town of Holley, Orleans County, New York, on the 23d of December, 1839, being a son of Carlton Morehouse, born in Galloway, Saratoga County. New York, on the nth of December, 1797. The latter was a son of Caleb and Abigail Morehouse, the former of whom was born in the western part of Connecticut, whence he removed to Saratoga County, New York, immediately after the war of the Revolution, and there for many years was engaged in agricultural pursuits. His children were as follows: Erastus, Ransom, Carlton, Henry and William. The father of Caleb Morehouse was the original progenitor of the family in America, whither he emigrated from England in the colonial epoch of our national history, taking up his abode in the western part of Connecticut. During the war of the Revolution his live stock was confiscated by the British soldiers, among the animals taken being a yoke of oxen, which, after a few days, returned to the home farm, much to the surprise and gratification of the owners. In 1846 Caleb Morehouse came west to Kane County, Illinois, in company with his son Carlton, father of the subject, and he died at the home of his son Henry, in Plato township, Kane County, Illinois, said son having been a clergyman of the Methodist Episcopal church and a circuit rider in Illinois from 1848 to 1853. The wife of Caleb Morehouse died in Saratoga County, New York, prior to his removal to the west. Each of their sons was married in Saratoga County, and the son Henry, who was a local preacher and a farmer, was the first of the family to locate in the west, having resided for a time in Kane County, Illinois, whence he removed to Janesville, Bremer County, Iowa, where he passed the remainder of his life. He was the father of two children. Bertha and Hattie. Erastus, the eldest of the sons of Caleb Morehouse, passed his entire life in Saratoga County, New York; Ransom died when a young man; and William, the youngest, became a resident of Janesville, Iowa, about 1866, and there he was engaged in the meat-market business during the remainder of his active business life, retaining his home there until his death.

Carlton Morehouse, the father of the subject, was reared and educated in Saratoga County, New York, growing up on the pioneer farm and in his early youth securing employment as clerk in a local mercantile establishment. On the 7th of December, 1825, was solemnized his marriage to Miss Eliza Cornell, who was born on the 12th of March, 1806, and whose death occurred on the 2d of July, 1863, she being a daughter of William Cornell, of Saratoga County, New York, the Cornell family having been of English lineage and the name having long been identified with the annals of American history. William, Sr., had only two children, and his son and namesake removed to Illinois and took up his abode on a farm at Pleasant Ridge, where he passed the remainder of his life. After his marriage Carlton Morehouse removed to Orleans County, New York, about 1838, and there he was engaged in general merchandise business until 1846, when he removed with his family to Plato township, Kane County, Illinois, where he engaged in farming, later becoming a traveling salesman for Ezra Wood & Company, of Chicago, manufacturers of agricultural implements, remaining thus engaged until his death. His health had been somewhat impaired during the winter of 1854-5 but he had recuperated sufficiently so that he felt himself able to resume his work, and he went to Chicago and died very suddenly, of a congestive chill, while in the office of his employers, his demise occurring on the 6th of April, 1855. He was a Democrat in his political proclivities and served as supervisor of his township after his removal to Illinois. He and his wife were members of the Baptist church and were folk of sterling character, ever commanding the respect of air who knew them. Carlton Morehouse was a man of fine intellectual gifts and marked ability, and his early death alone prevented his rising to a position of prominence in connection with the public and civic affairs of the state of Illinois, of which he was an honored pioneer. Carlton and Eliza (Cornell) Morehouse became the parents of six sons, concerning whom we enter the following brief record: Ransom, who was born in Saratoga County, New York, on the 23d of March, 1827, married Margaret Brown, and he died in Denver, Colorado. Frederick D., who was born in Galloway, Saratoga County, on the 5th of June, 1829, died in Orleans County, New York, on the 16th of July, 1845. William Henry, who was born in Galloway, Saratoga County, on the 10th of January, 1832, married Minerva A. McArthur, and devoted his life to farming and merchandising, his death resulting as the result of an operation performed in the city of Chicago, where he passed away on the 17th of June, 1901. Charles, who was born in Saratoga County, March 13, 1835, died the following year. George is the immediate subject of this sketch. Ezra Wilson, who was born in Saratoga County, April 13, 1845, was a soldier in the Union army during the war of the Rebellion and died on the transport "Spread Eagle" on the Mississippi river, near Napoleon, Arkansas, on the 19th of January, 1863, his body being interred with military honors at Milliken's Bend, Mississippi. The subject of this sketch has little knowledge in regard to his maternal grandmother, but after her death her husband, William Cornell, married Katherine Deforrest Fox, of the old Holland stock of the Mohawk valley of New York. He was born December 31, 1788, and died on the 1st of July, 1859.

George Morehouse passed the first twenty years of his life on the home farm, while he attended the district schools until he had attained the age of sixteen years. At the age of nineteen he left the farm and entered the Bryant & Stratton Business College, in the city of Chicago, where he completed a six-months course. In the following autumn he secured a position in the Racine County Bank, at Racine, Wisconsin, and in the following spring, that of 1861, he manifested the intrinsic loyalty and patriotism of his nature by tendering his services in defense of the Union, in response to the first call for volunteers. He enlisted as a member of Company F, Second Wisconsin Volunteer Infantry, but was later rejected on account of physical disability. In order to recuperate his health, he then made a fishing expedition along the coast of the gulf of St. Lawrence, and in the autumn of 1861 returned to Wisconsin and assumed the position of bookkeeper in the office of the Racine Advocate. In the spring of 1863, he was made chief accountant for Captain J. M. Tillapaugh, who had charge of the enumerating of men eligible for military service, superintending the drafting of soldiers, etc., and thus the subject was located in the city of Milwaukee, Wisconsin, until the spring of 1864, when he went to Brazier City, Louisiana, as bookkeeper in the employ of Captain C. H. Upham, a brother of ex-Governor William H. Upham, of Wisconsin, and there he remained until the close of the war, when he returned to the north and located in Janesville, Iowa, where he was employed as bookkeeper in the flouring mill of his brother Ransom until 1872, when he was elected treasurer of Bremer county, retaining this incumbency three terms and having had no opposing candidate on the occasion of his second and third elections, the different parties each placing his name on its ticket. He thus served from 1872 until 1878, and during the last two years of this period he also held the position of cashier of the Bremer County Bank, in Waverly. On the first of January, 1880, he resigned this latter executive office and in the spring of the same year came to Dakota and settled in Brookings, where he took up his abode on the 27th of February, forthwith directing his efforts to the establishing of a private banking institution, in which the interested principals were himself and his brother William H., of Burlington, Iowa. In 1884 the bank was incorporated with a capital of fifty thousand dollars, and of the same, known as the Bank of Brookings, the subject continued as cashier until the 1st of January, 1901, since which time he has served as president. In the meanwhile, in 1883, the two brothers also established a private bank at Estelline, this state, the same being afterward incorporated as the Bank of Estelline, and of this institution the subject was vice-president, while he was also one of the incorporators of the First National Bank of Volga, Brookings County, in the spring of 1902, being president of this institution. Mr. Morehouse was a man of rare business ability, public-spirited, upright and straightforward in all the relations of life, and he not only contributed in a material way to the advancement of the interests of the great state of South Dakota but also held at all times the unequivocal confidence and regard of those with whom he came in contact, being one of the honored and distinctively representative citizens of the state. He served for eight years as a member of the board of regents of the State Agricultural College, in Brookings, and also was a valued member of the board of education for a number of years. He was from the time of its organization a director and treasurer of the Brookings Land and Trust Company and was also financially interested in numerous other corporations in the city, ever lending his aid and influence to furthering all enterprises which make for the progress and wellbeing of the community. His political allegiance was given to the Republican party, and his religious faith was that of the Baptist church, of which he was a zealous member and to which his widow belongs. He held the office of clerk of the local church from the time of its organization, in 1880. His devotion to the work of the church may be better understood when we state that for eighteen years, or until the church debt was liquidated, he gave his services as janitor, sparing no pains in attending to the work which he thus assumed and arising at five o'clock Sunday mornings to attend to the building of fires in the church and otherwise providing for the comfort of the worshipers. He was known as a man of liberality in the support of all good works, but used proper discrimination in the extension of charity and in other benevolences, while he was ever ready to aid all churches, being tolerant and kindly at all times, and believing that Christianity represents the bulwarks of our national prosperity and spiritual welfare. He manifested particular interest in the success of the Baptist college at Sioux Falls, and this interest was timely and helpful.

Fraternally he was a charter member of Lodge No. 21, Free and Accepted Masons, in Brookings. The family residence is the finest in the city and is a center of gracious and refined hospitality. He was the artificer of his own fortunes and his noteworthy success represents the results of industry, integrity and wise economy. He died November 2, 1903, at his home in Brookings, the cause of his death being cancer of the stomach.

On the 26th of August, 1867, was solemnized the marriage of Mr. Morehouse to Miss Anna P., Crosby, who was born in Belvidere, Illinois, on the 23d of January, 1845, a daughter of Henry L. Crosby, who was born in Fredonia, Chautauqua County, New York, on the 29th of October, 1819, while his wife, whose maiden name was Mary E. King, was born in Delphi, Onondaga county, that state, on the 30th of January, 1819, their marriage having occurred at Fairfield, Kane County, Illinois, on the 10th of March, 1842, while the officiating clergyman was Rev. John S. King, father of the bride. Henry L. Crosby was a son of Nathaniel, who was born in Thompson, Connecticut, February 18, 1786, while the latter's wife, whose maiden name was Sallie Merrill Larned, was born in the same place, December 6, 1793. The maternal grandfather of Mrs. Morehouse was born in Arlington, Bennington County, Vermont, January 16, 1787, and his wife, Anna, nee Bristol, was born in Cornwall, Litchfield County, Connecticut, July 23, 1783. John S. King was a clergyman of the Baptist church and was also a physician. Henry L. and Mary E. (King) Crosby became the parents of seven children, concerning whom we offer the following brief record: Sarah L. was born in Boone County, Illinois, April 7, 1843; Anna B. became the wife of the subject of this review: Elsie, who was born September 1, 1846, died in September, 1871: Lucy, who was born May 29, 1848, died in infancy; William H., who was born September 12, 1849, died in March, 1903, at San Antonio, Texas: Ernest, born December 15, 1852, is a resident of Brookings, and Lucia E., who was born September 19, 1857, is a resident of Oakland, California.

Mr. and Mrs. Morehouse became the parents of two children, Mary Eliza, who was born in Janesville, Iowa, on the 25th of September, 1870, died on the 13th of January, 1875. Henry Carlton, who was born in Waverly, Iowa, September 17, 1877, still remains at the parental home. He was graduated in the Brookings high school, as a member of the class of 1896, and thereafter continued his studies for three years in the State Agricultural College, in this place, while later he completed a commercial course in the same institution. After leaving college he made a trip through Europe and through the Pacific coast states of the Union. He is at present engaged in the real-estate business at Willow City, North Dakota, though, as before stated, he makes his home with his mother in Brookings.

ELI MARTIN MOREHOUSE, M.D.

Dr. Eli Martin Morehouse, a physician and surgeon of Yankton, actively and successfully engaged in practice in this city since 1902 and now recognized as one of the leading representatives of the profession in his section of the state, was born in Owatonna, Minnesota, on the 30th of August, 1869. His father, Eli Morehouse, was born March 2, 1835, in Warren, Ohio, and he, too, took up the study, of medicine and engaged in practice. In 1856 he removed to Minnesota, where he followed his profession during his entire active career, his death there occurring on the 23d of May, 1891. He was prominent both as a physician and business man and in every relation of life was esteemed for his thorough reliability, his energy and his many other sterling traits. He was a recognized leader in political circles and various well merited honors were conferred upon him, including election to the state senate. He was also mayor of his city at the time of his death and his administration was characterized by businesslike management of municipal affairs. He was for many years the recognized leader of his party in his congressional district, and at all times was actuated by a public-spirited devotion to the general good. He married Lorinda A. McRostie, who survives and resides at Owatonna, Minnesota. They had four children, of whom Eli Martin is the eldest, the others being: Effie, the wife of John W. Adsit, of Owatonna, Minnesota; Dr. Guel G. Morehouse, a practicing physician and now the mayor of Owatonna; and Timothy N., deceased.

Dr. Martin Morehouse was a pupil in the public schools of his native city and afterward pursued a classical course in Pillsbury Academy there. Subsequently he entered the Bennett Medical College of Chicago and was graduated therefrom with the class of 1901. The following year he located at Yankton, where he has since remained and in the intervening period, he has become established as one of the leading physicians of the city, being accorded an extensive practice. He meets his duties in a most able and conscientious manner, possessing comprehensive knowledge of the principles of scientific medicine and surgery. He is likewise prominent in civic and social affairs of the city and ranks with its prominent residents. He is a member of the State Medical Association, of the Eighth District Medical Association and the American Medical Association and he keeps in touch with the trend of progress along professional lines.

Dr. Morehouse was married on the 28th of January, 1897, to Miss Winnifred L. Hanna, a daughter of James Hanna, of New York. Dr. and Mrs. Morehouse occupy a prominent social position, the hospitality of the best homes being freely accorded them, while the good cheer of their own household is greatly enjoyed by their many friends. Dr. Morehouse has attained high rank in Masonry, being a thirty-second degree Mason of the Yankton consistory and belonging also to Yankton commandery, in which he served during 1912 and 1913 as eminent commander. He is likewise a Knight of Pythias and an Odd Fellow. His political allegiance has always been given to the democratic party and while he keeps well informed on the questions and issues of the day his political service has always been in the path of his profession. He has been superintendent of the county board of health, county physician of the poor and a member of the pension examining board. He is widely known because of his professional activity and his public spirit and his record has ever been such as will bear close investigation and scrutiny, establishing him high in general regard.

CHARLES J. MORRIS

CHARLES J. MORRIS

Since 1899 Charles J. Morris has been engaged in the general practice of law in Sioux Falls and for the past three years has been connected with important litigated interests as a member of the firm of Morris & Caldwell. As a public-spirited citizen he has also taken a prominent part in the political life of his city and state and for four years rendered his district efficient and discriminating service as a member of the legislature, during a portion of which time he served as speaker of the house of representatives.

Mr. Morris was born on a farm at the Black Jack Mine, near Galena, Illinois, January 10, 1871, and is a son of James and Louisa Morris, the former born in Hereford, England, July 4, 1829, and the latter in Zurich, Switzerland, February 26, 1837. The father came to America in 1856 and located near Galena, Illinois, where he engaged in farming for a number of years. He died in Galena, March 4, 1906, having survived his wife since February 18, 1904.

Charles J. Morris acquired his early education in the common schools and afterward attended the German-English College in Galena. Following this he enrolled in the Northern Illinois Normal School at Dixon, graduating in 1896. He read law while engaged in teaching school and completed his law course at the Dixon College of Law, receiving the degree of B. L. in 1898. Some idea of his ambition, energy and enterprise may be gained from the fact that he paid his own tuition during his college career, attending school alternate years and working when not engaged with his books. He acted as a book canvasser at one time, at another as traveling salesman, engaged also in railroad work and at the time of the World's Fair was a reporter for a Chicago newspaper. He was admitted to the bar of Wisconsin in 1898, while located at Hazel Green as principal of the high school. In June, 1899, he came to South Dakota and began the practice of his profession in Sioux Falls, October 2, 1899, of which city he has since remained an honored and respected resident. He engaged in general legal practice alone until 1910 and in that year formed a partnership with Charles V. Caldwell. This firm is recognized today as one of the leading law firms of the city, connected through an extensive and growing clientage with a great deal of important litigation. Mr.

Morris is a strong, forceful and able lawyer, well versed in the underlying principles of his profession and is a conscientious and successful practitioner.

Aside from his profession, Mr. Morris has also taken a prominent and active part in civic and political affairs and has held various positions of public trust and responsibility. He entered the South Dakota legislature for the first time in 1909 and his work received the hearty indorsement of his constituents in his reelection in 1910. He served as chairman of the committee on judiciary in the house in 1909 and his record in this capacity added to his growing prominence as a competent legislator. In the session of 1911, he received a unanimous vote of all parties for speaker of the house and this office he filled creditably and impartially until he left the legislative body. On April 13, 1911, he was appointed assistant United States district attorney for the district of South Dakota, serving in this position until January, 1913, when he was made district attorney in place of E. E. Wagner, who resigned.

Mr. Morris is a stanch republican and stands high in his party's councils. In the 1910 campaign he served his party as secretary of the state central committee, and in the election of that year South Dakota was one of the two states in the Union that showed a republican gain over the vote at the previous election.

While teaching at Hazel Green Mr. Morris became acquainted with Senator La Follette and became convinced that the work he was doing was for the best interest of humanity and that La Follette's program would result in much benefit for the masses. He found in South Dakota, the special interest intrenched in the affairs of government and dictating every political act as La Follette found them intrenched in Wisconsin. When the progressive republicans of South Dakota declared warfare on this condition, Mr. Morris joined their forces and has been one of the aggressive forces in placing in the people's hands the reins of government.

In the legislature, in the office of United States attorney, and in his campaigns before the people, Mr. Morris insisted that the individual citizen be given a hearing and be fully protected in his rights, and he also took the stand that the rich and powerful corporations were well able to take care of themselves and their property and that those of small capital most needed the protection of the strong arm of the government. He accordingly, in the local affairs of his home city, in the legislature and in the office of United States attorney, insisted that every one receive full protection in his rights and that justice be meted out to all — alike to rich and poor, great and small.

Mr. Morris was instrumental in putting through the house in the legislative session of 1909 the electric headlight bill which was backed by the organized trainmen and vigorously opposed by a powerful lobby of the railway companies. He also introduced in and forced through the house at the same session, the bill increasing the supreme judges from three to five. This law has greatly promoted justice by enabling cases to be speedily terminated in that court, while formerly they were often held up for years. He also introduced and backed the bills which resulted in our present juvenile court law. While speaker, the bill which created a third congressional district became a law and it was quite generally thought Mr. Morris was the logical candidate for congressman of the first district. He was strongly urged by leaders of the progressive republican forces to become a candidate. His legislative friend, C. H. Dillon, being a candidate, he decided to stick to his duties in the United States attorney's office and threw his support to Mr. Dillon.

Mr. Morris' work in the various public offices he has held has been approved by the great body of the citizens of the state and there are many in all parts of the state who will gladly back him for any office he may in the future seek. He is a strong, aggressive fighter in life's battles. His predominant characteristics are his straightforwardness, fairness, firmness and honesty in all things. He has always insisted that a candidate for office should let the voters know much of his life's history, the things he stands for, so that the voter may know what candidate will most nearly carry out his principles, if elected. He has also always insisted that a man cannot be made honest by electing him to office. Honesty in a candidate first and then as much of other merits as can be piled on, expresses his views.

In the city of Washington, July 10, 1907, Bishop Frank M. Bristol of the Methodist church officiating, Mr. Morris was united in marriage to Virginia Hazen, daughter of the late A. W. Hazen, for many years naval officer in the United States custom house at Baltimore. She is a niece of General A. Depew Hazen, deceased, who for a long period was third assistant postmaster general, and a grandniece of Senator Chauncey M. Depew. Many of her other relations are prominent in official, professional and social circles in the national capital. Her ancestry can be traced back to Napoleon Bonaparte. Mrs. Morris was a pupil of the late Dr. W. J. Bischoff, of Washington, who was for thirty years the leading teacher and composer of the national capital. Under his masterful instruction, Mrs. Morris became one of the leading soprano soloists of Washington, occupying the position of soloist at the First Congregational church and taking leading solo parts in concert work. She appeared on several musical programs at the White House, while occupied by President McKinley. Mrs. Morris is not only a soloist of high and dramatic quality but is an all-around and thorough musician. Since coming to South Dakota, she has delighted with her singing audiences in her home city, at the state capital and in other cities in the state where she has appeared as soloist for the Eastern Star, Federated Woman's Clubs and other gatherings Mr. Morris has taken an active part in Masonry, being a member of the higher Masonic bodies, and having served as worshipful master of Unity Lodge, No. 130, of his home city. He has also served as patron of Jasper Chapter, No. 8, Order of the Eastern Star, and is also a member of Sioux Falls Lodge, No. 262, B. P. O. E.

Mr. Morris is a man of varied interests, and this, coupled with his wide training and experience, forcefulness, honesty and fairness, has made him an effective force in community advancement and growth, and his official and professional records have placed him in the front rank of progressive and substantial citizens of his city and state.

HENRY S. MORRIS

Henry S. MORRIS, is not only one of the leading business men and representative citizens of Roberts County, but also one of the earliest settlers of this part of the state and, as his father, W. K. Morris, bore an important part in the early history of eastern Dakota and was one of the first white men to locate within the present limits of Roberts County, it is appropriate that a brief review of his life be given in this connection. W. K. Morris was born in Hartford, Connecticut, September 11, 1842, the son of a city missionary who moved to Washington County, New York, when his son was an "infant. In the latter state Mr. Morris grew to maturity and received his education and he moved thence to Minnesota, in 1864, locating in Blue Earth County, where he made his home until 1870. In that year he was selected to take charge of the Good Will Mission in South Dakota, and on December 1st he set forth with two yoke of oxen and a yoke of cows hitched to two wagons containing his family and a modest outfit of household goods. After a journey of fourteen days, he arrived at his destination, seeing no white men after passing the town of New Ulin until reaching the mission. Mr. Morris had never seen any Sioux Indians until he reached his field of labor, and at that time could neither speak nor understand their language. In due time, however, he acquired a thorough knowledge of the same and from the beginning his work among the Indians was blessed with beneficial results. He taught at Good Will Mission under the supervision of Rev. S. R. Reggs until 1873, when he was placed in full charge of the school, holding the position during the ensuing seventeen years. In 1890 he went to the Omaha and Winnebago reservation, where he had charge of a school until 1894, at which time he transferred to the church at Pine Ridge agency, when he was licensed a minister. After preaching at the latter place until July, 1897, he gave up his missionary work and settled at Sisseton, Roberts County, near which town he engaged in farming and stock raising, but is now living a life of retirement. Mr. Morris was married in 1876 to Miss Martha T. Riggs, sister of Thomas Lawrence Riggs, of the South Dakota State Historical Society, the union being blessed with five children, of whom Henry S. of this review is the first in order of birth. Mr. Morris is a man of intelligence and culture, and having devoted much attention to South Dakota, its settlement and various interests, he is considered an authority on all matters relating to the history of the state.

Henry Morris, cashier of the First National Bank of Sisseton and president of the Citizens' Bank at White Rock, was born at Stirling, Minnesota, June 21, 1868. At the age of two years, he was brought to South Dakota and from that time until a youth in his teens lived with his parents at Good Will Mission, where he received his early educational training. Later he entered the State University of Minnesota and after being graduated from the academic department of that institution in 1891, spent one year as special agent of the government, making land allotments to the Indians on the reservation. At the expiration of the time, he was elected clerk of the Roberts County court, which position he held four years, and then came to Sisseton and organized the State Bank, serving as cashier of the same until April, 1900. In the latter year he resigned his position and established the First National Bank of Sisseton, of which he has since been cashier, and is now its vice-president, and in addition thereto he is president of the Citizens' Bank at White Water, an institution he also helped to organize. Politically Mr. Morris is a zealous supporter of the Republican party, and as such has been prominent in its councils and a successful leader in a number of campaigns, He was chairman of the Roberts County central committee in 1896, and rendered valuable service in that capacity.

Mr. Morris is identified with the time-honored Masonic order, and still retains membership with a college fraternity which he joined while pursuing his studies in the State University. On December 20, 1892, he was united in the bonds of wedlock with Miss Mary Strangsway, and is now the father of four children, whose names are Martha D., Wyllys K., Esther F. and Elizabeth R.

WILLIAM A. MORRIS

W. A. Morris, one of the leading members of the legal profession of Spink County, and a prominent citizen of Redfield, was born at Mount Carroll, Carroll County, Illinois, on December 13, 1864, and is the son of J. P. and Jamima Morris, both natives of Ohio. When a youth the father removed to Wisconsin with his parents, and he there grew to manhood, and was there married. From Wisconsin the parents of the subject removed to Carroll County, Illinois, where they resided until 1881, then removed to Fulton, Illinois. In 1896 they came to Redfield. The mother died in 1899, and the father died in July, 1901.

William A. Morris was reared on the home farm in Illinois. He attended the district schools, and then entered the Northern Illinois College at Fulton, where he was graduated in the class of 1883. While a student at college he also read law to some extent. After leaving college he became associated with his brother, S. E. Morris, in the clothing business at Fulton, Illinois. Subsequently they removed their business to Darlington, Wisconsin, and combined the same until S. E. Morris came to South Dakota, at which time the subject resumed his legal studies. In 1888 he came to South Dakota, and the following year was admitted to the bar of the state. In January, 1890, he engaged in the practice at Redfield, where he has since continued with success. In 1894 Mr. Morris was elected state's attorney for Spink County, and was re-elected in 1896. During 1893-4 he also held the office of city attorney for Redfield. At the national meeting of the Sons of Veterans held at Syracuse, New York, in 1901, Mr. Morris was elected by that body to the position of secretary and attorney for the Memorial University, the buildings for which are now in course of erection at Mason City, Iowa. The duties of his dual office requires the presence of Mr. Morris in Mason City a considerable portion of his time.

Mr. Morris is a Republican in politics. He is identified with the Masonic fraternity, belonging to the chapter and commandery of that order. He is also a member of the Knights of Pythias. On December 29, 1892, Mr. Morris was married to Edna Upton, who was born in Illinois, and who came with her parents to South Dakota in 1886. To this union the following children have been born: Marguerite, Helen and Merle, the last named having died at the age of six years.

JAMES W. MORSE

J. W. Morse, the efficient clerk of the courts of Hughes County, comes of stanch old colonial stock in both the paternal and maternal lines, the respective families having been established in New England at an early epoch in our national history, while the genealogical records of the Morse family have been carefully compiled and preserved through the various generations. Professor Samuel F. B. Morse, the distinguished inventor of the electric telegraph, having been a member of the family.

James W. Morse was born in Springfield, the attractive capital city of the state of Illinois, on the 3d of September, 1853, and is a son of James M. and Emma M. (Gregory) Morse, the former of whom was born in Newburyport, Massachusetts, and the latter in Danbury, Connecticut, while they were numbered among the early settlers of Sangamon County, Illinois, the father having been for many years engaged in business in Springfield, where both he and his wife died. The subject secured his early educational discipline in the public schools of his native city, and as a youth learned the art of telegraphy, but shortly afterward learned the watch-making trade to which he devoted his attention for eighteen years. He came to Pierre in 1889 and here engaged in the cigar and tobacco business, and in 1893 was appointed deputy postmaster, in which capacity he continued to serve until November, 1894, when he was elected to his present office of clerk of the courts, having held the same continuously for nearly a decade, through successive re-elections, and having handled the exacting affairs of the office with marked ability and discrimination.

In politics he accords an unwavering support to the Republican party, and is at the present time worshipful master of Pierre Lodge, No. 27, Ancient Free and Accepted Masons, while he is past master of the local lodge of the Ancient Order of United Workmen and past venerable consul of the Pierre Camp of the Modern Woodmen of America. On the 29th of December, 1878, Mr. Morse was united in marriage to Miss Mary J. Schlipf, who was born and reared in Sangamon County, Illinois. They have three children, Bernice W., aged twenty-four years, who holds a clerical position in Pierre post office; Dorothy L., aged twenty-two, who is a stenographer in the office of the secretary of state in her home city; and Kathryn H., at this writing three years of age. The subject's musical abilities are evidenced by the popularity of his productions, among which may be mentioned, "The Soldier's Dream of Home," "Tell my Boy to Meet Me There," "My Boyhood's Home in Sunny Tennessee," and many others of equal merit.

While the Bob and Nels clothing store has for some years passed from the hands of the original proprietors, it has ever remained one of the chief commercial enterprises of the city and the high standard has been in no whit abated since it came under the presidency of Peter J. Morstad, whose name introduces this review. In fact, a spirit of progress has been manifest and the success which has come to the establishment is attributable in large measure to the efforts, close application and sound business judgment of him whose name introduces this record. He was born in Norway, December 27, 1853, his parents being Juul P. and Ingeborg (Lynne) Morstad. The father died in 1877, aged seventy-seven years, while the mother passed away in the year 1907, having survived her husband for three decades. They had two sons and four daughters, of whom two sons and three daughters are living.

Peter J. Morstad, the fifth in order of birth, benefited by a high-school course in Norway and in 1870, when a youth of sixteen years, came to America with a brother aged eighteen years, making his way to Albert Lea, Minnesota, where lived his married sister and a paternal uncle, who had come to the new world in 1848. Mr. Morstad was employed at farm labor for five years in the county of Freeborn, of which Albert Lea is the county seat. He spent that entire time in the employ of Hans Christopherson, whose daughter he afterward married. In 1875 he left the farm and entered the farm implement business as clerk in a store in Albert Lea, being connected therewith for two years, the last year as silent partner of T. L. Torgeson. He afterward spent two years as a clerk in a general store in Albert Lea and in 1881 removed to Miner County, Dakota territory, where he took a preemption claim and also a tree claim, totaling three hundred and twenty acres of land. In October of that year, he located in Grand Forks, where he spent a year as clerk in the general store conducted by M. I. Mandelson. In 1882 he purchased the Star clothing business in connection with A. Christopherson and with his former employer as a silent partner. Three months later, however, the store was destroyed by fire, and as no other location could be secured in that town, Mr. Morstad found it necessary to seek a home elsewhere.

On the 6th of April, 1883, Mr. Morstad located in Sioux Falls and opened the Boston Clothing Store in connection with A. Christopherson under the firm style of Morstad & Christopherson, which association was continued until the 1st of September, 1911, the partnership being dissolved on that date. Mr. Morstad then purchased an interest in the Bob & Nels Clothing Company, Incorporated, and now carries on the business. He is president and general manager with Mrs. Nels Arnston as part owner of the business. This is one of the old established mercantile houses of the city. In fact, it is regarded as one of the landmarks of this part of the state. The store was opened by R. E. Vreeland and Nels Arnston, and following the custom of those days when every man was known to his acquaintances by his first name, these two young merchants named their store after the popular nickname it had been given by the people of the time, calling it the Bob and Nels Store. The name has since been retained, although the original proprietors have both passed away. The business has now been in existence for twenty- four years and many of its old patrons remain with it, showing that the most reliable business methods have ever been employed. An extensive line of clothing and men's furnishings is carried and a liberal patronage is enjoyed, for the firm has ever employed progressive methods and has carried a most up-to-date line of goods. In all business transactions they are thoroughly reliable and trustworthy and the success which has come to the. institution is the merited reward of the energy, close application and business ability of the owners.

On the 10th of January, 1884, at Manchester, Minnesota, Mr. Morstad was united in marriage to Miss Antoinette Christopherson, a daughter of Hans Christopherson, and their children are: Juul Henry, treasurer of the Bob & Nels Clothing Company; Irene Cora Marie; Porter Alfred, of San Francisco; Carl Alfred and Clay Eugene Grant. All the children are at home save Porter Alfred.

The parents hold membership in the Lutheran church and Mr. Morstad belongs also to the Masonic lodge. He is also connected with the Elks and is a member of the Commercial Club. In politics he is a republican and for four terms, or eight years, he served as one of the aldermen of Sioux Falls, during which period his influence was ever on the side of right, progress and improvement. In fact, he stands for all that is commendable in commercial and municipal affairs and has done much to further those interests which are a matter of civic virtue and civic pride.

EDWARD MOSCRIP

Edward MOSCRIP, son of Thomas and Sally (Reynolds) Moscrip, was born in Delaware County, New York, October 14, 1838. His early years were spent in his native state, where he grew to manhood on a farm, and in the subscription schools of Delaware county he received a fair education, his principal training, however, being of an intensely practical nature, obtained by coming in contact with the world in various capacities. Mr. Moscrip followed agricultural pursuits in New York until the year 1857, when he went to Oshkosh, Wisconsin, and engaged in lumbering, continuing that line of business until 1861. In the spring of the latter year he responded to President Lincoln's call for volunteers by enlisting in Company E, Second Wisconsin Infantry, which was part of the celebrated Iron Brigade, the only brigade of western troops in the Army of the Potomac, being the First Brigade of the First Division, First Army Corps, Army of the Potomac, with which he shared all the realities of war in several of the southern campaigns, taking part in some of the bloodiest battles of the Rebellion, among which were the first Bull Run, Gainesville, second Bull Run, Chancellorsville, Fredericksburg, Antietam, Gettysburg, the Wilderness and many others, in all of which his conduct was that of a brave and heroic soldier who never hesitated when duty called and whose record is one of which any veteran might well feel proud. On May 10, 1864, in the battle of Spotsylvania Court House, he was shot in the hip, the injury being such as to render him almost helpless for a year, during which time he received hospital attention at various places, remaining for some time at the Soldiers' Home in the city of New York. Mr. Moscrip was discharged at Providence, Rhode Island, in April, 1865, and immediately thereafter returned to Oshkosh, Wisconsin, where in the spring of the following year he resumed lumbering in the pineries of that state. He was quite fortunate in this business and followed it about seven years, during which time he realized considerable wealth and laid the foundation of his subsequent success as a farmer and stock raiser. In the month of March, 1868, Mr. Moscrip was united in marriage to Miss Margaret Gilmore, of Illinois, and four years later, with his wife and two children, drove from Wisconsin to Lincoln County, South Dakota, and purchased a quarter section of land in La Valley township, which he improved and which he made his home during the ensuing five years. Disposing of his place at the end of that time, he bought the southwest quarter of section 2, La Valley township, which he still owns, converting his land the meanwhile into a finely cultivated and splendidly improved farm, his dwelling and barn, erected in 1900, being among the best buildings of the kind in the community. As a farmer Mr. Moscrip ranks with the most enterprising and successful of Lincoln County agriculturists, and he also has an enviable reputation as a raiser of livestock, his horses, cattle and hogs being carefully selected from the most approved breeds and he seldom fails to realize every year handsome profits from the sale of these animals. Not only as an up-to-date farmer and stock man is Mr. Moscrip known, but he has long been before the people as a leader in various public enterprises, among which may be noted the locating and laying out of highways, the building up of the local school system, also his activity and usefulness as chairman of the town board. He is a Republican in politics, and in 1890 represented Lincoln County in the lower house of the legislature, a position unsought on his part, but filled with credit to himself and to his constituents.

Mr. Moscrip belongs to several secret fraternities and benevolent societies, among which are the Masonic lodge at Sioux Falls, the Union Veterans' Union at the same place, and the Grand Army post, which holds its sessions in Canton. The family of Mr. and Mrs. Moscrip consists of one son and two daughters, whose names in order of birth are, Annie. Elva and William G. The oldest daughter married Joseph Shebal, a farmer and stock raiser of LaValley township; Annie is the wife of Charles Davey and lives on a farm in Wisconsin, and William G., who married Miss Eva, Messner, is a resident of LaValley township and a prosperous tiller of the soil.

HERBERT LEON MOSES

Herbert Leon Moses, a well-known attorney of Rapid City, was born in Lima, Grant County, Wisconsin, on the 4th of July, 1874, a son of Martin L. and Mary G. (Watkins) Moses, the former a native of Trumbull County, Ohio. The paternal grandfather, Luke Moses, was one of the early settlers in the Western Reserve, a section of what is now northern Ohio and which was at that time claimed by Connecticut. He removed to Grant County, Wisconsin, with his family in 1850 and took up a homestead there. The maternal grandparents of our subject were Stephen Decatur and Mary (Hirst) Watkins, the former of whom was one of General Ethan Allen's Green Mountain Boys in the Revolutionary war. Mr. and Mrs. Martin Luke Moses are the parents of six children, of whom the subject of this review is the eldest. They are yet living and reside at Platteville, Wisconsin.

Herbert Leon Moses received his elementary education in the district schools and continued his studies in the high school at Platteville and in the Platteville Normal School. He attended the University of Wisconsin and in 1894 was graduated from the law school there with the degree of Bachelor of Laws. Soon after finishing his legal course, he settled at Lancaster, Wisconsin, for the practice of his profession as a member of the firm of Bushnell, Watkins & Moses. At the time of the excitement due to the discovery of gold in Alaska he went north and spent three years in Alaska and the Klondike country, after which he returned to Lancaster and resumed the practice of law as a member of the above-mentioned firm. In February, 1910, he removed to Rapid City, South Dakota, where he has since remained, and in the five years that he has resided there has built up a gratifying practice. He is well versed in the underlying principles of law, is familiar with precedent and statute, and his care in preparing his cases, combined with his skill in their presentation, enables him to generally win a verdict favorable to his clients.

Mr. Moses was united in marriage on the 8th of September, 1907, to Miss Mabelle Lou Beig, a daughter of John H. and Mary (Wagner) Beig, residents of Lancaster, Wisconsin, and natives of Germany.

Mr. Moses is a progressive democrat in political matters, is a Mason and is a member of the Congregational church. His wife is also a member of that church, is active in the work of the Ladies Aid Society and is also prominent in the Fortnightly Club. Mr. Moses recreation is found chiefly in gardening. He realizes fully the power that rests in the hands of the members of the legal profession and in his practice places the dignity and honor of the law above all other considerations, thus gaining the confidence of his colleagues and of the general public.

ALFRED J. MOXNESS

Alfred J. Moxness, cashier of the State Bank of Andover, was born in Elizabeth, Minnesota, December 4, 1882, and is the eldest in a family of nine children, eight of whom are living. The parents are Nick and Marine Moxness, natives of Norway, born in 1860 and 1861 respectively. They were married in that country and soon afterward crossed the Atlantic, settling in Elizabeth, Minnesota, where the father worked as a laborer. During the pioneer epoch in the history of Day County, South Dakota, they made their way to Bristol and the same year, 1885, the father homesteaded land, after which he bent his energies to the development and improvement of the farm which he occupied and successfully operated until 1909. Since that year he has been engaged in buying grain in Bristol and success in gratifying measure has attended his efforts. He and his wife are consistent Christian people, holding membership in the Lutheran church. His political views accord with republican principle and he has served as county commissioner and otherwise taken part in political activity.

In his youthful days Alfred J. Moxness divided his time between attendance at the district schools and work upon the home farm, giving his father the benefit of his service until he attained his majority. He then turned from agricultural life to become bookkeeper in a bank, where he was employed from 1904 until 1911. In the latter year he removed to Andover, accepting the position as cashier of the State Bank of Andover, which is a growing and reliable institution capitalized for ten thousand dollars, with surplus and undivided profits of forty-five hundred dollars and average deposits of seventy-five thousand dollars.

In 1907 Mr. Moxness was united in marriage to Miss Serena Aadland, a native of Hay County and a daughter of Hans Aadland, who was an early settler of Day County, this state. Our subject and his wife have two children, Harley and Alfred, Jr.

Reared in the faith of the Lutheran church, Mr. Moxness has always adhered to its teachings and is one of the faithful members of that denomination in Bristol. He belongs to the Masons, the Independent Order of Odd Fellows, the Knights of the Maccabees and to the Elks lodge of Aberdeen. In politics a republican, he is now serving as town clerk and was also deputy treasurer of Day County in 1907 but at the end of a year resigned his position and resumed active connection with the banking business, in which he has made a creditable record. He has carefully studied every phase of the business and contributes in large measure to the success of the institution with which he is now connected and which finds in him a most popular and obliging official.

Henry August Muller is widely and favorably known in Sioux Falls, South Dakota, and its surrounding territory as member of the legal firm of Muller & Conway, which has been in existence for many years. He has handled many important cases since he opened an office here and has proven an able lawyer of wide knowledge who readily makes himself master of a situation and who is ever loyal to the interests of his clients. Since May, 1901, he has also acted as United States referee in bankruptcy.

Mr. Muller was born in Cassville, Grant County, Wisconsin, August 4, 1865, and is a son of William and Mary (Grattan) Muller, the father a native of Alsace-Lorraine, then a province of France, and the mother of Queens County, Ireland. William Muller came to America in 1849, at the age of twelve years, and now makes his home in Sioux Falls with his son, Henry A. The paternal grandfather was also named William Muller and was of French birth, while the grandmother was a German. Our subject is one of a family of five sons and three daughters, of whom four sons and two daughters are living.

Henry August Muller began his education in the common schools of Cassville, Wisconsin, at the age of five years, and continued there until 1873, when the family removed to Bon Homme County, Dakota, where the parents had preempted both a homestead and timber claim of one hundred and sixty acres each. Here Mr. Muller continued his education during two winters in a country log schoolhouse two miles from his home, his teacher being Maggie Hogan, who received in remuneration for her services the magnificent salary of fifteen dollars per month. Teachers at that time, however, even if they were not as well qualified as those of the present, gave the best in them to their pupils. In January, 1886, when he was about twenty-one years of age, he entered the Agricultural College at Brookings and after attending for five terms commenced teaching six miles south of Scotland, this state. He made his headquarters in Scotland and every day rode six miles to his school on horseback. At night he recited to Professor Alexander Strachan, of the Scotland Academy, in Latin, algebra, history, composition and rhetoric for two years, and in 1889 entered the State University of South Dakota at Vermillion, where he remained until March, 1891.

In April of that year, while on the home farm, he was kicked in the face by a horse, this unfortunate accident confining him in a hospital for one year. After his recovery he came to Sioux Falls in March, 1892, and entered the law office of Powers & Conway, where he applied himself so diligently to the study of law that in November, 1892, he was admitted to practice before the bar of the state. In the fall of 1893 the firm of Fawcett, Muller & Conway was formed, which lasted eight months and then became the firm of Muller & Conway, as it continues today. His partner, Daniel J. Conway, is an able lawyer of wide reputation. The firm has been one of the strongest in this part of the state and they have handled successfully a number of the more important cases in Sioux Falls.

On January 2, 1900, in Thorntown, Boone County, Indiana, Mr. Muller was united in marriage to Miss Alice E. Bassett, a daughter of Alonzo Bassett, who was an agriculturist by occupation and passed away in the '70s. He served as a sergeant in the Civil war with the Seventh Wisconsin Volunteer Infantry and was twice wounded. Mrs. Muller was born near Fond du Lac, Wisconsin, and after graduation from a normal school at Aurora, Illinois, was for a number of years a successful and popular teacher before her marriage. She later read law and was admitted to the bar of the state, enjoying prestige as an able practitioner. She now conducts a school of stenography and typewriting in Sioux Falls.

In his political views Mr. Muller is independent, indorsing candidates according to their qualifications and not according to their affiliations. He stands high in the Masonic order, being a Knight Templar and Shriner and having reached the thirty-second degree in the Scottish Rite. He is a member of the Dacotah Club. The feature standing out most strongly in Mr. Muller's career is his tenacious purpose in achieving success. All his attainments must be ascribed to his unflagging energy. He pursued his education under adverse circumstances and continued it in spite of handicaps. Yet he succeeded, and he has won for himself a place worthy of his efforts.

JOHN R. MULLER

JOHN R. MULLER

John R. Muller, a well-known farmer of Bon Homme County, was born in Cassville, Wisconsin, January 6, 1869, and is a son of William and Mary (Grattan) Muller. His father was born in Alsace, France, now a part of Germany, May 27, 1837, and was only fourteen years of age when he came to this country in 1851 with his father, William Muller, Sr. The journey was made in a sailing vessel, which was three months in crossing the Atlantic, and after landing in New Orleans they proceeded up the Mississippi river to St. Louis, where the father worked for a year or so. During this time, they were joined by the remainder of the family. Later they removed to Davenport, Iowa, where William Muller, Jr., was employed as a clerk in a general merchandise store. For some years he continued to work in the north during the summer months, returning to St. Louis each winter. Subsequently he located at Cassville, Wisconsin, where he secured a situation in a store and was thus employed for some time but later turned his attention to farming.

In 1873 he came to Dakota territory and deciding to make Bon Homme County his home, he preempted a homestead and also a timber claim, the latter on section 24, township 93, range 62, Hancock precinct. The preemption claim was located five miles west of Perkins and the family residence was the first house built between Choteau creek and Springfield on the main stage line and mail route from Sioux City and Yankton to the Black Hills, by way of Fort Randall and Fort Pierre. It was therefore natural that travelers should stay overnight at the Muller home and they entertained many who were journeying from the eastern part of the state to the west, or were returning to the east. Their first residence was a log house with a dirt roof but in 1876 a better house was built on the timber claim, the lower story being of sod and the upper story of timber. Still later a good frame house was erected, which remained the family residence until the parents retired in March, 1903, and removed to Tyndall, South Dakota. There Mrs. Muller died in 1908. She was a native of Ireland and accompanied her parents on their emigration to the United States. Mr. and Mrs. Grattan first located in St. Louis, Missouri, but afterward removed to Grant County, Wisconsin. Since the death of his wife Mr. Muller has made his home with a son, who resides in Sioux Falls, South Dakota. They were the parents of eight children, six of whom are still living: William G., who is residing on Choteau creek; Henry A., who was educated at the State Agricultural College at Brookings and the

106

State University at Vermillion, and is now an attorney of Sioux Falls and state referee on banking; Mary, the wife of W. G. Treffry, of Treffry, Idaho; John R., of this review; Katherine, now a teacher in the Minneapolis schools, who attended college at Madison, South Dakota, and at Yankton, and was also graduated from the Springfield Normal School; and Gerald, who was a student at the South Dakota Wesleyan University at Mitchell and at the State Normal School of Springfield, and was for several years superintendent of the Bon Homme county schools but is now principal of the schools at Emery, South Dakota.

During the first years of his residence in Dakota territory, the father endured many hardships and had many unpleasant experiences, but the 12th of January, 1888, is always especially vivid in his memory, as he then narrowly escaped death by freezing. He, with two other men, were west of the river, where they had gone to get hay, and, although they started home as soon as the storm broke, by the time they reached the river the wind was so high that it swept the loaded wagons along the smooth ice of the river downstream and it was impossible to make any headway across the river. The teams were at length unhitched and all started for home, but Mr. Muller, who was ahead on foot, became separated from the others and when he learned that they had gone on without him he sought the best shelter obtainable and succeeded in finding a somewhat protected spot in the gulch, where he tramped back and forth among the scrub oaks for twelve hours, or throughout the night. By morning the storm had abated and he found a trail leading to his home. The determination and physical vitality that enabled him to survive such a night have been strong factors in his success and the material prosperity that he has gained is well merited. He is freely accorded the esteem of his fellow citizens, who honor him as a man of ability and integrity.

John R. Muller was about six years of age when he accompanied his parents on their removal to Dakota territory. He was reared chiefly in Bon Homme County, where he attended the public schools, and remained with his father upon the home farm until his marriage, being of great assistance in the operation of the homestead. He now owns the northwest quarter of section 24, township 93, range 61, Hancock precinct, and as his land adjoins the town of Perkins it is especially valuable. It is not only favorably located but is also naturally productive and its fertility has been conserved by wise methods of cultivation. Mr. Muller is progressive and alert and uses the latest improved machinery in his farm work, which insures greater efficiency. His crops are excellent and, as he studies the markets carefully, he is able to sell to advantage. His residence is large and supplied with all conveniences and the barn is commodious and is well arranged. There are two immense silos on the place, while a fine grove and orchards further enhance the value of the property.

Mr. Muller was married on Christmas Day of 1902, to Miss Julia M. Snow, who was born in Beloit, Wisconsin. Her parents, Charles and Mary (Henry) Snow, came to Dakota territory early in March, 1887, and settled in Bon Homme County. Both passed away in 1908 at Perkins. To Mr. and Mrs. Muller have been born three children: Mary, who died at the age of six months; Alice; and Clara. Mr. Muller is a democrat in his political belief and belongs to Mount Zion Lodge, A. F. & A. M., at Springfield.

FRANCIS M. MURPHY

FRANCIS M. MURPHY.

Born and educated on the western verge of Missouri, removing in his youth to southern Colorado, and coming to the Black Hills in the full flush and vigor of his manhood, and having thus been practically a pioneer in three states of the great West, the late Francis M. Murphy, of Pennington County, was the very embodiment of its spirit, the broad sweep of its vision, the prodigious enterprise that drives its activities, and its daring faith which laughs at impossibilities and challenges fate herself into the lists ready to meet her on almost equal terms. His life began on December 22, 1843, in Platte County, Missouri, and he lived there until he reached the age of sixteen years, receiving in the public schools of that county all the book learning he ever got from academic teaching. In 1859, when he was just completing his sixteenth year, he accompanied his parents to Colorado, and with them settled in the southern part of the state.

There he united with his father in extensive farming operations, working for a few years at a salary and then becoming a partner in the business. This relation continued until 1870, when he was married and started a similar enterprise in raising stock and general farming for himself. This he conducted with success until 1879, when he deemed it wise to try his fortunes amid the glowing promises of the Black Hills, and leaving his family at their Colorado home, he came directly to Rapid City, arriving in November, and bringing with him a band of cattle as a basis of operations. He took a squatter's claim on Rapid creek, five miles southeast of the city, and in the following spring, after the government survey had been made, filed on the land he had taken up, and this he made his home until his death. It is still occupied by his widow and children, and shows in its development and the well-disposed and valuable improvements he made on it the character of his enterprise and progressiveness. He remained in this section until the spring of 1880, then returned to Colorado, closed out his interests there, and brought his family to their new abiding place. The cattle he brought with him on his first trip had wintered well and were in good condition for the enlargement of his stock industry, and he at once widened its scope and increased its proportions to more imposing magnitude, at the same time preparing to carry on in connection with it a vigorous general farming business suited to his circumstances. He worked hard to get his land fully irrigated and in good condition, and in all his undertakings in this connection, was very successful, being accounted at his untimely death, on March 26, 1900, one of the leading individual farmers and cattle growers in this part of the state. Being energetic, progressive and public-spirited, his influence in business circles and along industrial lines was felt far and wide, and was always wholesome and elevating in its effect; and his death was universally felt to be a loss to the county and state in which he had cast his lot, as well as a personal bereavement to the admiring friends whom he numbered by the host. He took an active part in public affairs also: and although a Democrat in politics, and a staunch supporter of his party in state and national issues, he was not partisan, but patriotic in local affairs, and clearly saw and ardently worked for the best interests of the community without reference to party or personal considerations. He was buried at Rapid City with many demonstrations of popular esteem, and his last hours were brightened with the reflection that his enterprise and capacity had secured ample provision for the comfort of his family after his decease.

He belonged to the Masonic fraternity, with membership in the lodge at Rapid City. On October 10, 1870, Mr. Murphy was united in marriage with Miss Sarah J. Morris, a native of Missouri, but having at the time in Arapahoe county, Colorado, where the marriage occurred. They became the parents of four children, Isaac M., David R., Mary E. (Mrs. Haas) and Edna. The sons are now, in connection with their mother, carrying on the business. They have taken up land of their own, and with their mother hold everything in common; and although it is high praise, it is but a just meed to merit to say that they are in every way worthy followers of their father.

THOMAS D. MURRIN

Thomas D. Murrin, manager of the Hearst Mercantile Company of Lead, is an able representative of one of the largest commercial concerns of the state and is recognized as a representative business man of the city. He was born in Grafton, West Virginia, in October, 1864, a son of Thomas D. and Delia (Wimsey) Murrin. The father was born in Ireland but in 1856 settled in Ohio, whence he enlisted for service in the Civil War, remaining with his command until discharged in 1865 with the rank of captain of volunteers. After the close of hostilities, he was engaged in various lines of occupation and in 1868 settled in Cheyenne, Wyoming. He later lived for a time in Nebraska but in 1877 removed to the Black Hills, where he engaged in business for a number of years. He passed away in 1892 and in his passing the city lost one of its worthy pioneers. His wife survived for three years, her demise occurring in 1895.

THOMAS D. MURRIN

Thomas D. Murrin received his education in a number of different places as the family removed from one state to another, but the greater part of it was acquired in Central City, South Dakota. He was obliged to put aside his textbooks when fourteen years of age although his educational opportunities had been quite limited. He was first employed as a clerk in a mercantile establishment and in 1888 became an employe in the George Hearst store, now conducted under the style of the Hearst Mercantile Company. He entered the service of that concern in a minor position but his willingness to work, his quick intelligence and his initiative gained him promotion carrying with it increased responsibility. He gained a practical knowledge of all phases of the business and in 1891 was made manager of branch stores at Nemo and Piedmont, this state. After ably serving in that capacity for ten years he was made assistant manager of the Lead store in 1901 and three years later was made manager. He is the present incumbent in that place and is proving an able executive. He has general supervision of all departments, the management of each department being under the care of its manager. During his connection with the Hearst Mercantile Company, he has witnessed its steady and healthy growth and has seen it develop into the largest establishment of the kind in the state. He devotes his whole time to the interests of the company and his initiative and knowledge of the needs of the business have enabled him to inaugurate a number of improvements in its management.

In 1907 Mr. Murrin married Miss Julia Concannon, of Illinois. Politically he is a democrat but has never taken more than a citizen's interest in political affairs. Fraternally he belongs to Olive Branch Lodge, No. 47, A. F. & A. M., of Sturgis; Golden Belt Chapter, No. 35, R. A. M.; Lead Commandery, No. 18, K. T.; Black Hills Council, No. 3, R. & S. M.; and Naja Temple, A. A. O. N. M. S., of Deadwood. He also holds membership in Lead Lodge, No. 747, B. P. O. E. He is thoroughly equipped by training and temperament for his responsible work as manager of the Hearst Mercantile Company and the prosperity of the establishment is assured as long as he remains in control. Personally, he is pleasant, affable, courteous to all and never too busy to spare the time to talk with a friend. He is one of the best liked men in the city and has the respect of all who know him.

IRA SIDNEY MYRON

Ira Sidney Myron is conducting a growing and profitable business as a dealer in farm implements and automobiles at Volin. Not only as a business man, however, does he deserve representation in this volume, but also as a member of one of the honored old pioneer families, his children being of the fourth generation of the family in South Dakota. He was born four miles south of Mechling, November 19, 1877. His grandparents all came to Dakota in 1859. His paternal grandfather was Sivert Myron, whose son, Helge Myron, was born in Drammen, Norway, November 1, 1850. During the latter's infancy his parents left the land of the midnight sun and came to the new world, settling in Wisconsin in 1851. In 1858 Sivert Myron went with his family to Nebraska and thence crossed into Dakota territory as soon as the land was thrown open for entry in 1859. He took up a claim four miles south of Mechling and increased his property by additional purchase from time to time until at his death he was the owner of five hundred acres. He built the first log house occupied by a permanent settler in Dakota and a part of that house is now in the state museum at Pierre. His son, Helge Myron, was a little lad at the time of the arrival of the family in South Dakota and in the work of developing the farm he bore a helpful part, his responsibilities increasing with his increasing age and strength. He married Britta Bottolfson, who was born near Decorah, Iowa, a daughter of Ole Bottolfson, who was born near Bergen, Norway, January 11, 1828, and came to America in 1847, settling in Wisconsin, where he lived until his marriage. Three days afterward he started with his bride for Decorah, Iowa, traveling across the country with an ox team. He took up government land ten miles from that place and there Mrs. Myron, his eldest child, was born in 1856. In 1858 the parents removed to North Bend, Cedar County, Nebraska, and in 1859 crossed the line into Dakota, filing on a homestead four miles west of Vermillion. Mr. Bottolfson filled the office of probate judge in Clay County for seven or eight years, being one of the first incumbents in that position, living on his farm while acting as judge. After her husband's death Mrs. Bottolfson became the wife of Ole I. Hanson and is now living nine miles north of Vermillion at an advanced age.

When the Myron family came to the west Helge Myron and his brother walked all the way from Wisconsin to Nebraska, driving cattle and following the wagons drawn by oxen which conveyed the household effects. They were six weeks upon the way, while it required eight weeks for the Bottolfson family to make their way from Decorah, Iowa, to Nebraska. They made the journey in the spring, at which time the roads were in very bad condition, and it was necessary for the cattle to swim the streams. Mr. and Mrs. Helge Myron became the parents of six children. Olin, a graduate of the Springfield Normal School and also from the normal school at Madison, engaged in teaching for a number of years and afterward, attended law college at Minneapolis, Minnesota. He is now engaged in the practice of his profession in Milaca, Minnesota. Ira Sidney, whose name introduces this review, was the second in order of birth. Emily died in 1910. Amy is a teacher in Fairfax, Gregory County. Anna is also engaged in teaching. Florence attended Springfield Normal and fitted herself for teaching. All of the others attended college at Vermillion and all have been teachers, thus contributing in substantial measure to the educational development of the state, while in other ways the family has done much for South Dakota's advancement and progress. The father passed away April 10, 1905, but the mother is still living and makes her home at Volin.

Ira S. Myron, born upon the old home farm, has, with the exception of a year which the family spent at Chadron, Nebraska, always made his home near the boundary line between Clay and Yankton counties.

About 1900 he began farming on his own account six miles east of Volin and in 1913 took up his abode in the town and purchased an interest in the implement and automobile business of G. A. Melgaard. In the spring of 1915, he bought out his partner and now conducts the business alone. He has a garage, deals in automobile supplies and handles the Ford and Overland cars, for which he has had an excellent sale. He also handles many of the leading kinds of farm implements and his business is steadily growing along substantial lines.

On the 28th of August, 1901, Mr. Myron was married to Miss Inez Marie Bervin, a native of Dakota and a daughter of Ed. O. Bervin, who was born in Norway. The three children of this marriage are: Edward, Inez and Ira Sidney.

Mr. Myron well remembers the flood of March and April, 1881, although he was then but four years of age. He distinctly recalls being in the boat with the waters all around in crossing to St. James, Nebraska, and remembers the mud on the floors of their dwelling upon their return a few weeks later — the deposit of the water which stood in their home. On the 12th of January, 1888, when the blizzard broke, he was at school. The teacher dismissed school about half past two in the afternoon and on his way home Mr. Myron was met by his father, who, fearing that the children might be lost in the storm, had started for them. Mrs. Myron was at school on the same day, but the teacher of that school kept the children with her all night in the schoolhouse. Mr. Myron is a republican in his political views and keeps well informed on the questions and issues of the day.

He holds membership in the Lutheran church, and fraternally he is a thirty-second degree Mason and also connected with the Odd Fellows lodge at Wakanda. He has a wide acquaintance in this part of the state, in which practically his entire life has been passed. The work begun by his grandparents in pioneer times and continued by his father is being yet carried on by him in support of all the plans and projects for the upbuilding and benefit of his district.

NEWMAN C. NASH

Newman C. Nash, well known as the editor and publisher of the Sioux Valley News, at Canton, is a native of the old Empire state, having been born in Orleans County, New York, on the 15th of February, 1848, and being a son of Francis and Catherine V. (Curtis) Nash. His father was born in Genesee County, New York, of English and Holland Dutch descent, and w by vocation a farmer. The mother of our subject was born in Berkshire County, Massachusetts, and in the agnatic line was of Holland Dutch descent, while her mother was a representative of families established in New England in the colonial epoch of our national history. Francis and Catherine V. Nash became the parents of nine children, of whom the subject of this review was the eldest son, while of the number seven are living at the present time.

Newman C. Nash passed his early childhood days on the homestead farm in Orleans County, New York, and was seven years of age at the time of his parents' removal to Rock County, Wisconsin, where his father became a pioneer farmer, and there the parents passed the remainder of their lives, honored by all who knew them. The subject was reared to the sturdy discipline of the home farm, duly availing himself of the advantages afforded by the common schools of the locality and period, and he was still a member of the parental household at the time when the dark cloud of Civil War obscured the national horizon. When but seventeen years of age he enlisted as a private in Company A, Thirteenth Wisconsin Volunteer Infantry, with which he continued in active service for four years and three months, participating in all of the many engagements in which his command was involved, so that the history of his regiment is practically the history of his faithful and valiant career as a soldier of the republic. He received his honorable discharge on the 28th of December, 1865.

As soon as he was mustered out Mr. Nash returned to Rock County, Wisconsin, and was thereafter engaged in agricultural pursuits near the city of Janesville, that county, until 1871, when he came as a pioneer to the territory of Dakota. He arrived in Lincoln County in February of that year and in Canton township took up a homestead claim of one hundred and sixty acres, perfecting his title in due course of time and forthwith instituting the improvement and cultivation of his land. He continued to reside on this ranch until the autumn of 1876, when he removed to the city of Canton, which was then a small frontier village, and in January of the following year he has initiated his career in connection with the "art preservative of all arts," by purchasing a half interest in the plant and business of the Sioux Valley News, of which he became the sole proprietor in the following April. This was one of the first papers published in the territory, and he has presided over its destinies consecutively from the time noted. The paper is a model in the matter of letter press, discrimination is displayed in the news columns and those devoted to miscellaneous reading, while even a cursory glance establishes the fact that the editorial department is under the control of a man who keeps himself well informed regarding matters of public moment and who writes forcibly and with directness in expressing his opinions. The News has a circulation of fourteen hundred copies and is a welcome visitor in the majority of the homes in this section of the state. Mr. Nash is a valued and influential member of the South Dakota Press Association, of which he was president for two years, and politically he is a stanch adherent of the Republican party, whose principles he supports by his franchise and personal influence.

He is an appreciative and most popular member of the Grand Army of the Republic, being affiliated with General Lyon Post, No. 11, while from June, 1893, to June, 1894, he held the office of commander of the order for the department of South Dakota. He is also past grand master of the grand lodge of the Independent Order of Odd Fellows in the state, and is affiliated with the Masonic fraternity and the Modern Woodmen of America. He and his wife are zealous members of the Congregational church in their home city, and he has served as a member of its board of trustees for more than a decade and a half. He was a member of the board of education for several years, and has also rendered effective service in other local offices of public trust, including that of postmaster, of which he was incumbent from April, 1890, to June, 1894.

On the 26th of June, 1865, Mr. Nash was united in marriage to Miss Jennie E. Williston, who was born and reared in Janesville, Wisconsin, and of their five children we incorporate the following brief record: Nina M., is the director of the model school in the Aberdeen Normal; George W. is state superintendent of schools for South Dakota; Clara W., a graduate of Yankton College, is married; Marion is deceased; and Francis F. is also a graduate of Yankton College, and is junior member of the firm of N. C. Nash & Son, publishers of the Sioux Valley News, of Canton, and the Harrisburg News, of Harrisburg.

GEORGE NELSON

George Nelson is the president of the Scandinavian Bank at Viborg and is carefully directing the interests of that institution in a manner that is leading to its substantial development, growth and success. He was born in Mount Carroll, Illinois, January 25, 1872, and is a son of Chris and Margaret Nelson. The family came to South Dakota in the year of his birth and established their home near Viborg, the father securing a homestead in Turner County. For a number of years, he engaged in farming and contributed to the agricultural development and progress of the section in which he lived. He survives but his wife has passed away.

George Nelson was reared in Turner County and after mastering the branches of learning taught in the district schools continued his education in the University of South Dakota at Vermillion, where he made his way by his own efforts, working in order to earn the money to pay his tuition. He spent one year in college and afterward engaged in teaching school, displaying ability to impart clearly and readily to others the knowledge that he had acquired. In early manhood he also worked upon the home farm and became familiar with every phase of life incident to the development of the fields. In 1898 he came to Viborg and assisted in the organization of the Scandinavian Bank, of which he became the first cashier, occupying that position until he was called to the presidency of the institution in 1912. From the beginning the business of the bank has constantly increased. It is capitalized for twenty thousand dollars and its officers are: George Nelson, president; P. C. Madsen, vice president; Joseph Swenson, cashier; and Harold Larson, assistant cashier. Mr. Nelson studies every question bearing upon the banking business and his close application, unremitting energy and broad knowledge of financial affairs have been the strong and salient elements in the success of the institution of which he is the head. He is also interested in South Dakota real estate, in which he has made judicious investments.

On the 24th of June, 1897, Mr. Nelson was united in marriage to Miss Cora Christensen, a daughter of Nels Christensen. Their children are as follows: Everett, Margaret, Merton, Emmett, Louise, Lillian, Joy and Ralph. Mr. Nelson's religious views are in accord with the Protestant faith. In politics he is a republican, recognized as a stalwart supporter of the party but not an office seeker. He has served, however, as city treasurer and in that position, as in every other relation of public trust, he proved himself true, loyal and capable. He belongs to the Danish Brotherhood of America, to the Odd Fellows society and in Masonry has attained the thirty-second degree of the Scottish Rite. South Dakota finds him an enterprising citizen, greatly interested in the welfare of the state and contributing in every possible way toward the advancement of the interests of the commonwealth.

E. C. NELSON

On the roster of efficient and public-spirited officials of Turner County appears the name of E. C. Nelson, who has served two terms as county treasurer. He was born in Denmark, December 11, 1879. His father dying before the son was born, he was reared in the home of his maternal grandparents, Peter and Petranilla Nelson. With them he came to the United States in 1887 and located in Mecosta County, Michigan, whence in the same year they moved to Turner County, South Dakota. Until he was nineteen years of age he remained upon the farm and attended district school, supplementing this by one year at the Baptist College at Sioux Falls. When he began his independent career, he became connected with the grain business and followed this as an employe for nine years. In May, 1908, he was appointed deputy county treasurer and in 1910 was elected treasurer of Turner County, serving by reelection since that time. He has proven capable, conscientious and reliable in the discharge of his duties and his record is a credit to his ability and his public spirit. In 1915 he removed to Wakonda where he is associated with the Wakonda State Bank as vice president.

Mr. Nelson has been twice married. In 1908 he wedded Miss Byrde Hirst, a daughter of W. J. Hirst of Parker. She died in the spring of 1909 and on the 11th of December, 1912, Mr. Nelson married Miss Stella Grieve, a daughter of F. A. Grieve of Parker, South Dakota. Mr. Nelson is connected fraternally with the Masonic lodge of Parker and is noble grand in the Independent Order of Odd Fellows. He gives his political allegiance to the republican party and in addition to his present office has held other positions of trust and responsibility. He has served as city auditor and city assessor of Viborg, and has been a member of the republican county central committee and a delegate to numerous county conventions. He has accomplished a great deal of important work in the public service and his record has been one of straightforward and conscientious endeavor in whatever position he has been found.

OLOF NELSON

Commercial activity in Yankton finds a worthy representative in Olof Nelson, who is engaged in merchandising and is also identified with other business enterprises. He has a high-class grocery establishment, carrying a large and carefully selected line of goods, and his success in that field is the direct result of earnest labor, close application and a ready recognition of opportunity. He was born September 20, 1864, in Sweden, his parents being Nels Olson and Kersten Nelson. The public schools of his native land afforded him his educational advantages and in 1883, when a young man of nineteen years, he crossed the Atlantic to the new world, arriving in that year in Yankton. He was entirely without funds, but he recognized the fact that industry is the basis of success and he was not afraid to work. He began as a laborer, but his ability and trustworthiness won him promotion and three years later he was occupying a clerkship in a general store, in which he remained for four years, gaining his initial experience along mercantile lines. At the same time, he was carefully saving his earnings until the sum was sufficient to enable him to embark in business on his own account.

In 1891 Mr. Nelson established a grocery store, which he has now successfully conducted for twenty-three years and which is the only high-class exclusive grocery in the city. The stock which he carries is large and carefully selected, embracing both staple and fancy groceries, and he is accorded a liberal patronage by those who desire the highest grade of goods. Moreover, he had the foresight to invest in farm property when land could be obtained at a very reasonable figure and he is now the owner of valuable South Dakota farm lands from which he derives a gratifying annual income. He has been identified with the promotion of many enterprises in the community. Energy and determination characterize him in all that he does and, in his vocabulary, there is no such word as fail. He pursues the course that he has marked out with diligence and when obstacles arrive, he overcomes them by determined effort and thoroughly reliable methods.

Mr. Nelson is a member of the Yankton Commercial Club and for several years has served as one of its directors, while for one year he occupied the position of president. His political indorsement has been given to the republican party since he won the right of franchise and he has served acceptably in some local offices, being a member of the city council for two years and treasurer of Yankton County for two terms. He has served for an extended period on the board of education and is much interested in the cause of the public schools, doing everything in his power to raise the standard of instruction.

On the 17th of May, 1892, Mr. Nelson was married to Miss Karolina Carlson, a daughter of C. G. Carlson, and their children are: Albert M., Ernest L., Esther M., Edith A. and Clarence T. Mr. Nelson belongs to the Ancient Order of United Workmen, being one of its most prominent representatives in South Dakota, having served as grand master of the state. He also belongs to St. John's Lodge, No. I, A. F. & A. M.; and has attained the thirty-second degree of the Scottish Rite as a member of Oriental Consistory, No. I, A. A. S. R. His religious belief is that of the Lutheran church, in which he has been a very active worker, and he has served in all of the lay offices of the church. Its teachings constitute his guiding spirit and the motives which make him so honorable and purposeful a man in all life's relations. He stands today as one of the city's prosperous and highly respected citizens, his success due to his sterling integrity in all of his business dealings and an early appreciation of the many advantages afforded by a new and growing country.

HARLEY D. NEWBY, M. D.

Dr. Harley D. Newby is a successful young medical practitioner of Parker, his native town, where he has followed his profession since December, 1912. His birth occurred on the 12th of November, 1885, his parents being Isom H. and Libbie A. Newby, a sketch of whom appears elsewhere in this work.

Harley D. Newby acquired his early education in the public schools and subsequently spent four years as a student in the University of South Dakota at Vermillion. In further preparation for a professional career, he entered Rush Medical College of Chicago, which institution conferred upon him the degree of M. D. at the end of four years or in 1911. He then spent eighteen months as interne in the Cook County Hospital and in December, 1912, opened an office at Parker, where he has since built up a gratifying and remunerative practice, having manifested his skill and ability in the successful treatment of many different cases. With the advanced thought and work of the fraternity he keeps in close touch through his membership in the Yankton District Medical Society, the South Dakota State Medical Society and the American Medical Association.

Since age conferred upon him the right of franchise Dr. Newby has cast his ballot in support of the men and measures of the republican party, believing firmly in its principles. His religious faith is that of the Baptist church, while fraternally he is identified with the Masons and the Independent Order of Odd Fellows. His interest in the development of his native state is deep and helpful and he well deserves a place among its representative citizens and rising young physicians.

HON. ISOM H. NEWBY

HON. ISOM H. NEWBY

Activity along public lines has won for Hon. Isom H. Newby the high reputation which he bears as a public-spirited citizen and one whose efforts have been of far-reaching effect and benefit. Moreover, in business circles he has achieved success, accomplishing what he has undertaken by reason of his well formulated plans and his force of character. He was born at Fort Madison, Lee County, Iowa, June 10, 1853, and is a son of I. H. and Catharine (Hoskins) Newby, the former a native of Indiana and the latter of Ohio. The paternal grandfather, G. A. Newby, arrived in Lee County, Iowa, in 1835, removing to that state from Indiana. He was of English lineage, while his wife was of Scotch descent, representing a family that removed from Ohio to Iowa in pioneer times. I. H. Newby, Sr., engaged in general merchandising in Iowa and both he and his wife spent their remaining days in Lee County, with the interests of which he was closely identified from pioneer times, contributing much to the work of general development and progress as the years passed. In the family were three children: Rebecca J., the deceased wife of Luther McNeil; Albert G., who removed to Finley, Turner County, South Dakota, a year prior to his brother, Isom, and passed away here; and Isom, of this review.

In taking up the personal history of our subject we present to our readers one who is widely and favorably known. His boyhood and youth were spent in Iowa unmarked by any event of special importance but after he attained his majority he started out in the world on his own account, making his way to Turner County, South Dakota, in March, 1874. He has since resided in this part of the state. He first homesteaded land near Parker, his place being about four miles southeast of the town and there he tilled and developed the soil until he took up his abode in Parker in February, 1882. For twenty-seven years he has engaged in the live-stock business, buying and shipping stock and also feeding to some extent. For the past sixteen years he has shipped over one hundred carloads of stock annually and he pays out more than ten thousand dollars per month for stock. In 1912 he shipped seventy-seven carloads of hogs and enough cattle and sheep to make more than one hundred carloads. His business has thus been conducted on an extensive scale and he has reaped the rich results of his labor. In business affairs his judgment is sound, his industry unfaltering and his enterprise is of an aggressive character productive of good results.

In politics Mr. Newby is widely known. He was active in democratic circles until 1805 and since that time has been a progressive republican. It is well known that he stands fearlessly by his honest convictions and never deviates from a course which he believes to be right, he was elected sheriff of Turner County in

November, 1882, on the democratic ticket, although there was a normal republican majority in the county of fourteen hundred. He was reelected in 1885 and again in 1887, serving in all for six years. He was elected county commissioner on the republican ticket, filling the office for one term of three years and was chairman of the board for two years. In 1891 he was elected to the state senate and while serving in the general assembly gave careful consideration to each question which came up lor settlement. He has been for four terms, or eight years, mayor of Parker and has given to the city a businesslike and progressive administration, characterized by many needed reforms and improvements. He has also been a member of the school board for eleven years and the cause of education has found in him a stalwart champion. In 1914 he was elected treasurer of Turner County in which office he is now serving. Thus, along many lines of public service his loyalty has been demonstrated and his ability proven.

On the 27th of December, 1877, Mr. Newby was united in marriage to Miss Libbie A. Harrington, who was born in Lee County, Iowa, in 1857 and attended the same district school with her husband. She is a daughter of John and Elizabeth (McNeill) Harrington, early settlers of Iowa, to which state they removed from Ohio. The father was a native of New York. Both the parents spent their last days in Lee County, Iowa, and it was to that county that Mr. Newby returned for his bride. To them has been born one son, Harley D., whose birth occurred November 12, 1885. He is a graduate of the high school of Parker, won the Bachelor of Arts degree upon graduation from the State University of South Dakota and afterward entered Rush Medical College of Chicago, from which he was graduated in June, 1911. He spent eighteen months as interne in the Cook County Hospital and has since practiced in Parker. He stood first in a competitive class of seventy, in the medical college, who took the examination for interne in the Cook County Hospital and he was number three in the entire competing class of one hundred and forty, representing the different medical schools of the state.

Mr. and Mrs. Newby hold membership in the Baptist church in the work of which they take an active and helpful part. He is chairman of the board of trustees, has assisted largely in all departments of church work and was superintendent of the Sunday-school during six years of his service as county sheriff, during which period he was absent only three times. He served altogether as Sunday-school superintendent for many years and has been a most active factor in promoting the religious education of the young.

Fraternally he is a Royal Arch Mason and he is connected with various fraternal insurance orders. His has indeed been a busy and useful life and he is a prominent factor in business circles, in political activity and moral progress in his community.

ALFRED NEWTON

ALFRED NEWTON

Alfred Newton was one of the prominent and well-known agriculturists of Clay County, residing on section 9, Riverside township. He was born in Rochester, New York, in 1847, a son of John and Ann (South) Newton, natives of England and Scotland respectively. He lost his father when but two years of age and his mother subsequently married John Newton and our subject assumed the surname, Newton. He has a sister, Mrs. T. S. Stanley, residing near Portland, Oregon, and a stepbrother, Henry, who is a resident of Spokane, Washington. The parents emigrated to the new world in early life and the father died in New York state, as did his stepfather. The mother afterward removed to South Dakota and made her home with her son Alfred until her death in 1882, being buried in Vermillion.

Alfred Newton first attended the schools of Littleville, New York, and subsequently was a student in an academy at Avon, Livingston County, that state. As a boy he ran a bootblack stand and drove a bus and while in the former business had among his patrons Judge Reed, of Philadelphia, Horace Greeley and a number of other well-known men. On the 2d of November, 1870, he came to South Dakota and settled on section 9, Clay County, taking up a quarter section as a homestead. The country at that time was very sparsely settled and much of the land was still uncultivated. He devoted many years to the development of his farm and as his resources increased invested in additional land until his holdings aggregated thirteen hundred acres. Of this eleven hundred and sixty acres were in Clay County and two hundred and forty acres in Stanley County. He carried on general farming and raised considerable stock, deriving therefrom a good income. He continued to reside upon his original homestead until his death, which occurred on the 28th of February, 1915.

Mr. Newton was married in Rochester, New York, August 15, 1869, to Miss Julia McGovern, Bishop McQuade performing the ceremony. Mrs. Newton was born in Ireland but was only two years of age when she accompanied her parents on their removal to America, the family locating in New York state, where both parents died. Her father was killed in an accident. Mrs. Newton survived her husband only a short time passing away on the 3d of March, 1915. To them were born a son and daughter, namely: Ann, the wife of Dan McLarkley, a resident of Iowa; and Charles J., who now operates the home farm.

By his ballot Mr. Newton supported the men and measures of the republican party and for fourteen years acceptably served as postmaster of Riverside. Fraternally he was a Mason and his daily life was the embodiment of the spirit of fraternity that underlies that great order. Both Mr. and Mrs. Newton were among the early settlers of this locality and in their passing Clay County lost two of its prominent and highly respected pioneers.

IRA L. NICHOLS

I. L. NICHOLS, of Elk Point, Union County, has the distinction of being a native of the old Buckeye state, having been born in Belmont County, Ohio, on the 12th of June, 1853, and being a son of Balaam and Abigail (Hatcher) Nichols, the former a farmer by vocation. After duly availing himself of the advantage of the common schools of his native state Mr. Nichols continued his studies for some time in Washington and Jefferson College, at Washington, Pennsylvania, and later entered Franklin College, at New Athens, Ohio, where he was graduated in 1879, with the degree of Bachelor of Arts. For about three years he was successfully engaged in teaching in the public schools of Ohio, and then took up the study of the law at St. Clairsville, Belmont County, under the preceptorship of the well-known firm of A. H. and W. Mitchell. In 1882 he came to the present state of South Dakota and took up his residence in Elk Point, where he was admitted to the bar, becoming one of the early practitioners in the county and having soon gained distinctive precedence as an able and discriminating trial lawyer and counselor. He has remained continuously in practice, and has had to do with much important litigation during the intervening years. He has ever accorded a stanch allegiance to the Republican party, and on its ticket, in 1884, he was elected state's attorney of Union County, while the same preferment came to him again in 1888, 1900 and 1902, so that he is incumbent of this important office at the time of this writing. Fraternally he is identified with the Masonic order, being affiliated with the lodge and chapter of the same in his home town. On the 2d of July, 1881, Mr. Nichols was united in marriage to Miss Mary Emma Hewetson, of St. Clairsville, Ohio, and they have three children. — Charles B., Albert H. and Nellie C.

HENRY NOBLE

Henry NOBLE, was born January 26, 1852, at Garnadilla, Iowa, and there grew to maturity on a farm. During his boyhood and youth, he attended the public schools of his neighborhood, and until his twenty-fifth year remained under the parental roof, assisting his father in running the home place and contributing his full share to the support of the family. In 1877 Mr. Noble severed home ties and engaged with the Chicago, Milwaukee & St. Paul Railroad as fire-man, the duties of which position he discharged until 1879, when he was promoted engineer, with headquarters in the town of McGregor. In 1883 he was transferred to Mitchell, South Dakota, and after remaining ten years at that place, removed to Aberdeen, where he has since resided, being on the run between these two points. Mr. Noble's run is one of the most important on the Chicago, Milwaukee & St. Paul system in the west and his responsibilities are therefore very great. During his long period of service, he has rarely been absent from duty, and his efficiency and faithful service have been such as to gain the unbounded confidence of his superiors.

Fraternally Mr. Noble is a Knight Templar and a thirty-second-degree Scottish Rite Mason, being one of the leading members of the order in the city of his residence and honored at different times with important official station. He is also an influential factor in the Brotherhood of Locomotive Engineers, and as a citizen enjoys in a marked degree the confidence and esteem of the community. Blessed with a strong physique and endowed with an ardent nature, he is exceedingly fond of field sports and out-of-door amusements, and during his vacations finds his greatest enjoyment with the rod and gun. In 1872, while residing in his native state of Iowa, Mr. Noble was united in marriage with Miss Phila Pickett, a union which has been blessed with two children, Lila, a teacher in the public schools, and a son by the name of Field.

WILLIAM I. NOBLE

William I. Noble, who is successfully established in the real-estate and loan business at Clear Lake, and is one of the representative citizens of Deuel County, was born in the beautiful little city of St. Thomas, province of Ontario, Canada, on the 1st of March, 1865, and is a son of Elnathan and Mary (McBride) Noble, both of whom were likewise born and reared in Ontario, while the latter met her death in a railway accident at St. Thomas, in 1884. The father of the subject was born near St. Thomas and was there identified with the great, basic art of agriculture until 1886, when he came to Clear Lake, South Dakota, where his death occurred in 1888, his remains being laid to rest beside those of his loved and devoted wife, at St. Thomas, Ontario. Isband Noble, the grandfather of the subject, emigrated when a young man from Massachusetts to Canada, in company with the other members of the family, which was early established in New England and which was loyal to the British crown at the time of the Revolution, the lineage being traced back to Scotch derivation. The mother of the subject was a daughter of Malcolm and Catherine (Campbell) McBride, who emigrated to Canada in early days from Campbellford, Argyleshire, Scotland, settling nine miles south of London, Ontario, in Middlesex County, where they passed the residue of their days.

William I. Noble received his early educational discipline in the public schools of Elgin County, Ontario, and then attended the collegiate institute in St. Thomas, where he completed the classical course and then took up the matriculation-work of the University of Toronto, where he gave his attention to different courses, making a specialty of mathematics. After the completion of his university work, he decided to come to South Dakota, the principal reason for taking this action being that his health had become somewhat impaired. He came to this state in March, 1886, and located in Deuel County, where he gave his attention to farming for the first four years, and thus fully recuperated his physical energies. Thereafter he served two years as deputy county treasurer, and since that time has been engaged in the real-estate and loan business in Clear Lake, having a wide circle of loyal friends in this section of the state and being known as a progressive young business man.

In politics Mr. Noble maintains an independent attitude, and his fraternal relations are here noted in somewhat of detail: Phoenix Lodge, No. 129, Ancient Free and Accepted Masons, at Clear Lake; Watertown Chapter, Royal Arch Masons: Clear Lake Lodge, No. 97, Ancient Order of United Workmen, and its auxiliary, Hiawath Lodge, No. 83, Degree of Honor; charter member of Clear Lake Lodge, No. 144, Independent Order of Odd Fellows, of which he is past noble grand; Encampment No. 14, Independent Order of Odd Fellows, at Watertown; charter member of the Patriarchs Militant, No. 1, at Gary; and New Century Lodge, No. 81, Daughters of Rebekah. On the 16th of February, 1886, Mr. Noble was united in marriage to Miss Josephine Cook, of St. Thomas, Ontario, who died on the 20th of December, 1897, of pulmonary tuberculosis, being survived by one son, Roy, who is eleven years of age at the time of this writing, in 1904. She was a daughter of Ebenezer and Mary Cook, of Springfield, Ontario. On the 26th of July, 1899, Mr. Noble married Miss Etta M. Liscomb, daughter of I. P. Liscomb, a prominent citizen of Clear Lake, and of this union has been born one son, Perry, who is now three years of age.

Charles L. Norton, one of the prominent and influential citizens and leading business men of the city of Sioux Falls, holding at the present time the office of cashier of the Sioux Falls National Bank, and also of the Security Savings Bank, claims the old Empire state as the place of his nativity, having been born in Warren County, New York, on the 26th of May, 1852, and being a son of Lindsey D. and Electa S. (Squiers) Norton, both of whom were born and reared in that state, where they remained until about 1860, when they removed to Wisconsin and located in the village of Edgerton, Rock County, where the father engaged in farming.

The subject received his elementary educational training in the schools of his native county, and was about eight years of age at the time of the family removal to Edgerton, Wisconsin, where he continued to attend the public schools until he had attained the age of fourteen years, when he started to learn the art of telegraphy, in which he became an expert. From 1869 to 1878 he served as station agent at various points on the St. Paul & Sioux City Railroad in Iowa and Minnesota, from which latter state, in August, 1878, he came to South Dakota and located in Sioux Falls, as representative of the St. Paul & Sioux City Railroad, retaining this office until 1880, when he resigned the same. In the meanwhile, in 1880, Mr. Norton was chosen assistant cashier of the First National Bank of Sioux Falls, and in the following year was elected cashier of the Sioux Falls National Bank, of which position he has ever since remained in tenure, having gained a high reputation as a conservative financier and able executive officer. In December, 1902, he was one of the organizers of the Security Savings Bank of Sioux Falls, of which he was chosen cashier at the time of its incorporation, while he still holds this office and is a member of the directorates of each of these important and popular institutions. He is a loyal and progressive citizen and has ever shown a deep interest in local affairs of a public nature, and has lent his aid and influence in support of all worthy objects for the general good. In politics he has been a stanch supporter of the Republican party from the time of attaining his majority, and he has served four terms as treasurer of Minnehaha County. He was elected in April, 1904, treasurer of the city of Sioux Falls. He represented the second ward on the board of aldermen for one term, and was for two years a member of the board of education.

Fraternally he is an appreciative and popular member of the Masonic order, being affiliated with Minnehaha Lodge, No. 5, Ancient Free and Accepted Masons; Sioux Falls Chapter, No. 2, Royal Arch Masons; and Cyrene Commandery, Knights Templar. In September, 1874, Mr. Norton was united in marriage to Miss Abigail S. Frost, a daughter of Hon. James C. Frost, at that time resident of Minnesota. Mr. and Mrs. Norton have three children, James L., Edith B. and Maxfield W.

THOMAS HENRY NULL

Thomas Henry Null is a lawyer of Huron, where he has engaged in practice for more than a quarter of a century. He was born in Warren County, Ohio, February 10, 1862. His father, Benjamin Null, was a son of Henry Null and a grandson of Charles Null, who with a brother came to America from Germany before the Revolutionary war, both settling in Virginia and participating in the struggle for independence. In 1796, following Wayne's treaty with the Indians, Charles Null made his way to the Miami valley of Ohio and was among the earliest of its permanent settlers, taking up his abode about forty miles from Cincinnati. In 1800 he returned to Virginia and removed his family to the new wilderness home, after which the Nulls were there represented through several generations. The mother of our subject bore the maiden name of Mary J. Stevens and was also a native of Ohio and a member of one of the earliest pioneer families. Both Mr. and Mrs. Benjamin Null are now deceased.

Thomas Henry Null was the second in a family of three children. He attended school in Warren County, Ohio, and at the age of seventeen years began reading law, carefully mastering the principles of jurisprudence until he was qualified for the bar. In 1883 he was admitted to practice in Dakota territory soon after his arrival here in the same year. He settled first in Jerauld County, where he took up a. claim, and in 1884 he entered law practice at Waterbury, while in 1886 he located at Wessington Springs. He served as state's attorney there from 1886 until 1888 inclusive and proved a capable official in that position. In 1889 he removed to Huron and afterward joined John M. Davis under the firm name of Davis & Null. In 1910 he was joined by Mr. Royhl under the firm style of Null & Royhl, and that relation has since continued. From 1897 until 1901 he served as special counsel to the state railway commission in the celebrated freight rate cases. He has been connected with other important litigation and has proven his ability to successfully solve intricate and involved legal problems.

On the 25th of May, 1887, Mr. Null was united in marriage to Miss Innis Burton, a daughter of James and Caroline Burton, of Jefferson, Iowa, and they have two children, Gertrude and Fern. Mr. Null finds recreation in the study of geology, in which he has always been deeply interested. He is an enthusiastic hunter of big game and is an expert trap shot. Independent in politics, he leaves office seeking to others. However, he is well known in fraternal circles as a Mason, an Elk and an Eagle, and he holds membership in the German Reformed church. Mr. Null is a self-educated as well as self-made man, making his own way in life unaided from his eleventh year. In his youthful days he worked on farms, sold papers, blacked shoes, and also served an apprenticeship to the blacksmith's trade. While working in the blacksmith shop, he boarded with students and teachers, and this it was that aroused his ambition for an education. Once he set his face in that direction, he never faltered, and steadily he has advanced step by step until he is now one of the leading lawyers and citizens, not only of Huron, but of the state.

Oscar W. Nystuen, manager for South Dakota for the Union Central Life Insurance Company of Cincinnati, Ohio, was born in Valders, Norway, September 14, 1880. He is a son of K. K. and Marian (Wangenstein) Nystuen, both of whom were also born in Norway. With his parents, brothers and sister he came to the United States in 1882. The family settled in Worth County, Iowa, where they remained until 1891. His father then purchased land in Freeborn County, Minnesota, within a mile of Albert Lea, and upon this property he still resides. He has survived his wife since March, 1903.

Oscar W. Nystuen acquired his early education in the public schools of Albert Lea, Minnesota, and later attended Luther Academy in that city. He turned his attention first to the newspaper business, acting as a reporter and rising from this position to be editor of the Times-Enterprise at Albert Lea. Following this he spent eighteen months as confidential agent for a large wholesale house in Chicago and then in April, 1910, came to Sioux Falls, South Dakota, as general agent for the South Dakota branch of the Scandia Life Insurance Company. He held that position for three years and then on the 19th of March, 1913, was made state manager for the Union Central Life Insurance Company of Cincinnati. He has accomplished a great deal of capable work in this responsible position and is regarded as one of the leading and successful business men of Sioux Falls.

On the 21st of June, 1905, at Albert Lea, Minnesota, Mr. Nystuen was united in marriage to Miss Alice Lillian White, the ceremony being performed by the bride's father, Rev. F. E. White, assisted by Rev. G. H. Patterson. Mr. and Mrs. Nystuen have become the parents of three daughters, Dorothy Marian, Harriett Annabel and Lois Lillian. Mrs. Nystuen is regarded by critics — as criticisms from authorities and newspapers from Boston to Los Angeles, Spokane to Minneapolis disclose — as the possessor of one of the most wonderfully beautiful voices in the country.

Mr. Nystuen is a member of the Lutheran church and gives his political allegiance to the republican party. He is a Scottish Rite Mason, belonging to the Shrine, and holds membership also in the Knights of Pythias and the Elks Club of Sioux Falls. The duties of his position with the Union Central Life Insurance Company have always been discharged in a capable, far-sighted and progressive way, and in both business and social life he occupies an enviable position.

Important and extensive are the business connections of Martin P. Ohlman, who since 1870 has been continuously connected with the commercial and industrial development and financial interests of Yankton. Notably energetic, prompt and reliable, he possesses in large measure that quality of common sense which is too often lacking in the business world and which has enabled him to correctly judge of his opportunities and advantages. A native of Germany, he was born in Schleswig-Holstein, on the 12th of September, 1846, a son of Peter M. Ohlman, who spent his entire life in Germany, his birth having there occurred in 1797 and his death in 1847. He was proprietor of a tannery and also engaged in the manufacture of gloves. He married Marie Krimling, who has also long since passed away, her death occurring in 1853. They had a family of six children, three sons and three daughters. All of the sisters came to America and two are yet living, but the brothers of our subject have passed away.

Martin P. Ohlman was educated in the Hadersleben Academy and the desire for broader experience and wide business opportunities led him to bid adieu to the fatherland when in his twentieth year and come to the United States. He made his way direct to Yankton, where he arrived on the 7th of July, 1866, being a guest of the old Ash Hotel. He had no capital, but was willing to work at anything that would yield him an honest living. He was employed at various occupations during the three months of his stay there, after which he went to Sioux City, where he secured a clerkship in the Northwestern Hotel, spending a year there. He next took a position in the wholesale grocery house of Tootle & Charles in the capacity of salesman and buyer. In those days that house was the great shipping and forwarding house for the upper Missouri river, handling all supplies for the government and Indian agencies. Their business reached mammoth proportions, for they loaded many boats daily. Mr. Ohlman occupied that position of responsibility for three years and then, in 1870, returned to Yankton, where he established the wholesale house of Adler & Ohlman. From the beginning the enterprise proved a profitable one and was successfully conducted for twenty years, or until 1890. At that date Mr. Adler removed to Chicago and the business was closed out, Mr. Ohlman turning his attention to other things. On the 1st of July, 1890, he incorporated the American State Bank and became its first president. He has since continued in that position and has helped to make the bank one of the strong financial institutions of the northwest. It is capitalized for twenty-five thousand dollars, has a surplus of twelve thousand five hundred dollars and undivided profits of ten thousand dollars and is the third in size of the Yankton banks. The scope of his business activities and investments, however, is a broad one, for he is a director and treasurer of the Yankton Gas Company, a director of the Yankton Telephone Company, a director and treasurer of the Yankton Bridge & Ferry Company, a stockholder in the Yankton Brick & Tile Company, and a director of the United States Annuity Life Insurance Company, Chicago. He also has large real-estate holdings, having made extensive purchases of property in Yankton, and he likewise has various investments outside of the city.

It would be but to give a one-sided view of Mr. Ohlman, however, to mention him only as a business man, for he has been active along other lines, especially in matters of public concern. His political indorsement has long been given to the republican party and he has ever kept well informed on the questions and issues before the people. For four terms he served as county commissioner and for three terms filled the office of alderman. He was likewise city treasurer of Yankton for one term and for twelve years was a member of the board of education, doing much to further the interests of public instruction in this city. He has stood for its moral development as an active member of the Episcopal church, in which he served as vestryman for a number of years.

Since early in the year 1885 he has been a member of the Masonic fraternity and upon him has been conferred the honorary thirty-third degree. He has held high office in the Royal Arch chapter and in the commandery and is the present grand treasurer of the grand commandery of South Dakota, which position he has filled with credit and honor to the organization for the past ten years. He holds membership in St. John's Lodge, No. I, A. F. & A. M.; Yankton Chapter, No. I, R. A. M.; De Molay Commandery, No. 3, K. T.; Oriental Consistory, No. I, and in 1907 was made inspector general honorary of the thirty-third degree at Washington, D. C. Since 1868 he has been affiliated with the Independent Order of Odd Fellows, which he joined in Sioux City, afterward transferring his membership to the Yankton lodge, in which he has filled all of the chairs. He has likewise served as grand treasurer of the grand lodge of Dakota Territory for six years.

On the 7th of November, 1871, Mr. Ohlman was united in marriage to Miss Emilie Oesterling, a native of Fort Wayne, Indiana, and a daughter of Joachim and Marie Oesterling. They were married in Dakota City, Nebraska. The family home was established in Sioux City in 1856 and there Mr. Oesterling opened the old Des Moines House, the first hotel of that place. Mr. and Mrs. Ohlman have become parents of three daughters and two sons: Maud E., the wife of Dr. D. R. Rudgers, of San Diego, California; Wilfred Julius, who is a druggist and chemist at Sioux City, Iowa; Amy, the wife of C. H. Ross, president of the Ross Lumber Company of Minneapolis, Minnesota; Martin P., Jr., who is engaged in the insurance business in Yankton; and Marie Augusta, at home.

Mr. Ohlman is interested in the support of the Sacred Heart Hospital, of which he is one of the trustees, and he is taking a most helpful and active part in the construction of the new hospital building. He has traveled extensively over America and Europe, finding in this a pleasurable source of recreation, and he also enjoys motoring. Persistency and hard work have been potent factors in bringing him his success and his has been a creditable record inasmuch as he started out in life in the new world empty-handed and without influential friends to aid him. The period of struggle of the early years has given way now to the comfort enjoyed through the competence which he has acquired. He was never afraid of hard work and as he advanced step by step in his business career there came to him broader opportunities and better advantages until he has long been accounted one of the foremost business men of Yankton, in which city he has resided since pioneer times.

EDGAR C. OLSON

In all of his business career, progressive and successful as it has been, his has never been the command of the tyrant to go, but always the call of the leader to come, and thus Edgar C. Olson today occupies a conspicuous and enviable position in the commercial circles, not only of Sioux Falls, but of the northwest, being at the head of a company which owns a chain of clothing stores throughout this part of the country.

He is a native of Oconomowoc, Wisconsin, born April 6, 1874, his parents being Gabriel and Martha (Nelson) Olson. He was the seventh in order of birth in a family of three sons and five daughters, all of whom are yet living with the exception of the eldest son, John G., who died in 1904. The removal of the family in 1875 to Kasson, Minnesota, enabled Edgar C. Olson to their pursue his education in the public schools. He also attended high school at St. Paul, Minnesota, and spent three years as a student in a night school in that city in order to overcome what he regarded as a lack of early educational opportunities. He has ever been a student of life and in the school of experience he has learned many valuable lessons which he has put to good use.

Mr. Olson became a clerk in a clothing store in St. Paul in 1890, and there remained until 1900, when he went to Marshall, Minnesota, and in partnership with a brother, established a clothing store under the firm name of Olson Brothers. This was successfully conducted for two years. In 1902 the firm of Olson Brothers opened a branch store at Brookings, South Dakota, which is still in operation and Edgar C. Olson continued in charge there until 1912, when he came to Sioux Falls, where the previous year he had been instrumental in organizing the firm of Olson, Delaney & Berdahl. This firm continued until July 15, 1913, at which time the business was taken over by the present E. C. Olson Company. Theirs is one of the leading clothing establishments, not only of the city, but also of this section of the country, and their store presents a most attractive appearance. The fixtures are of late design done in fumed oak. The big suit rack will accommodate twelve hundred men's and boys' suits and overcoats, and the stock includes clothing, hats, haberdashery and men's furnishings.

As the years have passed Edgar C. Olson has established business in various sections until he now has a chain of nine stores. The one at Watertown, South Dakota, established in 1907, which was conducted under the name of Olson-McCosham Company, is now under the name of The Olson-Lee Company. The business at Rapid City was started in 1909 and has always been conducted under the firm style of Olson & Company. M. G. Olson, brother of E. C. Olson, established stores at Montevideo, Minnesota; Wheaton, Minnesota; Sisseton, South Dakota, and Grand Forks, North Dakota. These are all owned by the E. C. Olson Company, together with the stores at Rapid City, at Brookings and at Sioux Falls. The business today is extensive, being one of the important commercial enterprises of the northwest and the capability, progressiveness and laudable ambition of E. C. Olson and his brother have constituted a substantial foundation upon which their success has been built.

On the 8th of January, 1905, at Brookings, South Dakota, Mr. Olson was united in marriage to Miss Callie T. Williams, a daughter of Edward Williams, and they have one son, Lyle Williams, born July 31, 1907. The parents are members of the Baptist church, while Mr. Olson belongs also to the Masonic fraternity, having taken the degrees of the York Rite and the Mystic Shrine. He is likewise connected with the Benevolent Protective Order of Elks and with the Commercial Club and his political allegiance is given to the republican party. While he is never neglectful of the duties of citizenship and in fact stands many times as a leader in support of public projects, he has never sought political preferment, giving to his business affairs that close attention which is largely the secret of success. He keeps in touch with the most modern commercial methods and conforms his interests to the highest requirements of commercial ethics.

JUDGE ALPHA F. ORR

Judge Alpha F. Orr, occupying the municipal court bench in Sioux Falls, in the performance of his judicial duties adds to his comprehensive knowledge of the law the excellent trait of executing the business of the courts with fairness and dispatch. He was born in Jersey City, New Jersey, April 28, 1860, and is a son of James and Susannah (Royle) Orr, the former a native of Belfast County, Ireland.

Judge Orr acquired his education in the Whitestown (N. Y.) Seminary and at Hamilton College, Clinton, New York. Following this he taught school for six or seven years in New York state and then, having determined upon a legal career, studied law. He was admitted to the bar on the 6th of October, 1882, and in 1889 he located in Sioux Falls, of which he has since been a resident. Gradually he has advanced in his profession to a foremost place in the ranks of the legal fraternity, possessing the ability which enables him to cope with intricate legal problems and bring them to a successful solution. With a mind naturally logical and analytical in its reasoning Judge Orr has never feared the labor so necessary in the preparation of cases for the courts, while in his presentation of his cause he has displayed the soundest reasoning and the utmost accuracy. He became well known at the South Dakota bar and at length was elected city attorney of Sioux Falls, serving one year. He was later elected states attorney for four years and in 1912 was made judge of the municipal court for a term of four years. Since his elevation to the bench Judge Orr has allowed no personal feeling or opinion to sway him in the fair and faithful administration of justice and he dispatches the business of the court in the same prompt and able manner with which he cared for the interests of his clients as a practitioner.

In April, 1886, Judge Orr was united in marriage to Miss Eva E. Green and both are well and favorably known in social circles of Sioux Falls. Judge Orr belongs to the Elks, the Dacotah Club, the Masonic blue lodge and the Knights of Pythias and gives his political allegiance to the republican party. He has won prominence on the bench of the municipal court and has gained equal success as a practicing attorney, his analytical mind, untiring energy and strong purpose being important elements in his progress.

COLONEL THOMAS G. ORR

Colonel Thomas G. Orr, the efficient superintendent of the South Dakota State Soldiers' Home at Hot Springs, was born in Martinsburg, Knox County, Ohio, June 22, 1848, a son of Dr. Thomas and Lavinia (Thompson) Orr. The father was born in Pennsylvania and the mother was a native of Newell County, Ohio. Both have gone to their final rest, the father's death occurring in 1855 at New Cumberland, West Virginia, and the mother passing away in 1853 at Martinsburg, Ohio. For forty-five years Dr. Orr was actively engaged in the practice of medicine. To him and his wife were born five sons and two daughters, Colonel Thomas Orr being the youngest.

The last named had but meager opportunities for schooling in his boyhood days and acquired the greater part of his education after the Civil war. He was left an orphan when about seven years of age and went to Volney, Allamakee County, Iowa, where he made his home with a brother. While still a child he found employment with a dry-goods firm and continued with that house for three years, after which he went to Lansing, where he entered the employ of the Lansing Mirror as printer's devil. His connection with that paper, was maintained until July, 1861, when he put aside all private considerations and enlisted in the Union army, becoming a member of Company C, Fifth Iowa Volunteer Infantry. He was but thirteen years and fifteen days old when he stood on the box to be sworn in and because of the United States rules he was not accepted at first. Later his captain interceded for him and explained to the mustering officer that he had no parents and no home and the officer in charge sent an account of the case to headquarters in Washington. In the meantime, Colonel Orr was made captain's clerk and served in that capacity for three months, at the end of which time authority came from Washington to muster him into the army as a drummer boy. In 1864, after three years of service, he was transferred to Company G, Fifth Iowa Cavalry, at Atlanta, Georgia, as a veteran volunteer. Until the 8th of November, 1865, he held the rank of orderly to the colonel of the regiment and on that date was mustered out at Nashville, Tennessee, after which he returned to Clinton, Iowa, where he received his pay and then went to Lansing, where he spent a few weeks in visiting. He felt the need of a more thorough education and attended a select private school at Waukon, Iowa, for three months and in 1864 went to Chicago and accepted a position as express messenger for the Merchants' Union Express Company, which operated between Chicago and Burlington, Iowa. During that time, he took a night course in a commercial school in Chicago, from which he was graduated in the course of time. In the fall of 1866, the company with which he was connected failed and he returned to Lansing, Iowa, where for a time he acted as clerk in a clothing and hardware store. He then became bookkeeper for a large grain firm, holding that position for five years. Upon the dissolution of the firm in 1873 he entered into a co-partnership for the conduct of a grain business at De Soto, Victory and Badax City, Wisconsin, and he was a resident of Victory until 1877, when he became a partner in and general manager of a large company buying grain at twenty-six different stations. He devoted his time and energies to his duties in that connection until 1883, when he resigned and came to Dakota territory, filing a claim near Aberdeen on the 9th of November, 1883. He then went to Viroqua, Wisconsin, which remained his home until April 2, 1884, at which date he located on his claim in Dakota territory, his family arriving a few days before Christmas, which anniversary was spent at Bayles' ranch.

In the fall of 1884 Colonel Orr was asked by a committee of citizens to become a candidate for register of deeds of Walworth County, which he did, being elected and serving for four years. It is interesting to note that his campaign cost him only five dollars. While he served as register of deeds his wife and family continued to reside upon the claim. At the end of his term, he was made chief of the enrolling and engineering force appointed by the territorial legislature of 1888 and 1889. He served in that capacity for sixty days and then opened a real-estate office at Bangor, Walworth County. In 1892 the family removed to Brookings in order that the children might have the educational advantages afforded there but the Colonel did not join them until some time afterward. In 1893 he accepted a position as collector for the Walter Atwood Company of Hoosick, New York, his territory being Dakota and the southern half of the state of Minnesota. He continued with that company until 1895, his residence remaining in Brookings, and then became field manager for a fire insurance company, whose headquarters were in Madison, Wisconsin. After a year spent in the employ of that concern, he resigned to accept a position with the Chicago, Milwaukee & St. Paul Railroad and was made townsite agent at Evarts and he was engaged in selling town lots there until the town of Mobridge was platted and he was made townsite agent for a year under the municipality. He sold the first lots recorded there for one hundred and ninety-five dollars apiece. A few weeks later he was taken sick and returned to his family at Brookings. It was necessary for him to undergo an operation for cancer of the bowels and he went to a hospital at Rochester, Minnesota, conducted by the celebrated Mayo Brothers. The operation proved successful and he is now one of the two patients who have recovered from that disease.

In 1897 Colonel Orr returned to Brookings and was made deputy food and dairy commissioner under Professor A. H. Wheaton. When Mr. Cook became head of the service the Colonel was reappointed and continued to act as commissioner until he resigned in 1900 because of impaired health. Seven years later he was appointed a member of the board of the State Soldiers' Home under Governor Herried and a year and a half later was reappointed, serving for two years under Governor Vessey. In January, 1911, he was elected by the board as superintendent of the State Soldiers' Home and assumed office on the 1st of April of that year. He has since had charge of the affairs of the institution and has been ably assisted by his wife, who serves as matron. She has had much experience in that line of work, having been for about five years matron in the State Agricultural College at Brookings.

Colonel Orr is a republican but his interest in public affairs has never taken the form of a desire to hold office. He is a member of the blue lodge, chapter and council in Masonry and has held a number of offices in that order. He is president of the Home-Coming Association and believes firmly in the value of gatherings that bring together all those interested in any way in this section of the state. Colonel Orr has invariably manifested the same spirit of devotion to the public good that led him as a boy of little more than thirteen to offer his services to his country as a soldier, being the youngest enrolled soldier from Iowa. His record was one of hard service as he took part in from sixty-one to sixty-five engagements, was twice wounded and yet was with his regiment every day of the time that elapsed from his enlistment until his discharge at the close of the war. His experience as a soldier and his understanding of the veterans of the war, coupled with his wide business knowledge, make him an excellent man for the post of superintendent of the South Dakota State Soldiers' Home and his administration is proving not only satisfactory to the board of directors but also meets the approval of the soldiers who live therein.

ALBERT H. ORVIS

Many elements figure in the success of one who gains prominence at the bar. He must possess not only accurate and comprehensive knowledge of the law, but discrimination in applying its principles and ability to clearly and cogently present his case. Oratory as well as logic frequently constitutes a feature in winning favorable verdicts and, added to this, there must be a recognition and observation of a high standard of professional ethics. Lacking in none of these qualities, Albert H. Orvis is now a well-known and successful attorney of Yankton. He was born in Jefferson County, New York, May 19, 1857. His father, Chester Orvis, who was born in 1823, devoted his life to general farming and passed away in 1896, in the seventy-third year of his age. His wife, who in her maidenhood was Esther A. Ware, was born in July, 1831, and had reached the age of sixty-four years when death called her in April, 1896. The Orvis and Ware families both came of old colonial stock, the Orvis family tracing its ancestry back to Farmington, Connecticut, to which place George Orvis came from the old world in 1658 or earlier. The Ware family was established in Boston as early as 1642 and both families were represented in the war of the Revolution.

Mr. and Mrs. Chester Orvis had four sons who reached adult age, of whom Albert H., is the second in order of birth. The country schools afforded him his early educational opportunities and he afterward attended the high school at Watertown, New York. The year 1875 witnessed his arrival in the middle west. He made his way to Iowa, where he taught school and farmed. Six years were spent in that state and in May, 1881, he came to the territory of Dakota, settling near Mitchell, where he engaged in farming. He afterward removed to Buffalo County, where he proved up a preemption claim, and his ability and worth were readily recognized, as is indicated in his appointment to the office of register of deeds. Later he was elected to the same position, in which he served for three years and four months. He then resigned and went to Chamberlain, where he spent several months, after which he became a resident of Scotland, South Dakota. In 1892 he arrived in Yankton and here entered into partnership in the practice of law with Levi B. French under the firm style of French & Orvis. He began studying law several years before and in 1886 was admitted to the bar. While advancement in the law is proverbially slow, he possessed persistency of purpose and knew that ability must ultimately win its reward. He, therefore, studied broadly and prepared his cases with great precision and care, preparing for defense as well as for attack. Today he is accorded a large clientage, that connects him with much important litigation. In the year 1897 he was chosen city attorney and in 1898 was reelected and on the expiration of his second term was elected state's attorney, in which office he served for a term of two years. He continues in general law practice and his work before the courts indicates him to be one well versed in the basic principles of the profession. He holds membership in the South Dakota State Bar Association.

On the 24th of October, 1878, Mr. Orvis was united in marriage to Miss Linnie P. Hall, a daughter of Hiram and Katherine (Groff) Hall, residents of Shell Rock, Iowa. They have become parents of three children, who are yet living: Caroline, who is a graduate of Yankton College; Harriet, who is a graduate of the University of Nebraska and of the College of Medicine of that institution and who entered the Mary Thompson Hospital for Women and Children in Chicago as interne in the fall of 1915; and Herbert C, at home.

Mr. Orvis is a republican where national issues are involved. He does not feel that politics, however, should enter into local elections, where the capability of the candidate is the only point to consider, and, therefore, he casts an independent local ballot. In Masonry he has attained the degree of the Royal Arch chapter. Since 1903 he has been a member of the board of education and has served as its president for seven years, doing effective and earnest work to promote the interests of the schools and giving to the city a system of public instruction of which it has every reason to be proud. He enjoys outdoor sports and in these finds his recreation. In an analyzation of his life work it is found that reliability and integrity have featured largely in his success, as well as close adherence to the ethics of his profession.

GABRIEL J. OSTROOT

Gabriel J. Ostroot, one of the enterprising and promising young business men of Kingsbury County and South Dakota, is the secretary and treasurer of the Lake Preston Milling Company. His birth occurred in Cherokee county, Iowa, on the 8th of October, 1880, his parents being Jonas and Carrie Ostroot. The father came to this state in 1882, settling on a tree claim and carrying on agricultural pursuits for some time. Subsequently he turned his attention to general merchandising and still conducts a store, being accorded a liberal patronage and being widely recognized as a prosperous and esteemed citizen of his community.

Gabriel J. Ostroot, who was but two years of age when brought to South Dakota by his parents, acquired his early education in the public schools of Brookings and later entered Brookings College, completing the commercial course in that institution in 1900. After putting aside his textbooks he was identified with his father in business until 1907, when he came to Lake Preston and became connected with the Ostroot Elevator Company, which owned a number of elevators. Later he purchased an interest in the Lake Preston Milling Company and assumed the position of secretary and treasurer, in which dual capacity he has served to the present time. The company supplies light and power to Lake Preston, De Smet, Hetland and Erwin and is an incorporated concern the stock of which is held by Lake Preston people. Mr. Ostroot has contributed in no uncertain degree to the success of the company and enjoys an enviable reputation as a progressive and substantial young business man.

On the 10th of June, 1913, Mr. Ostroot was united in marriage to Miss Ida T. Larson, a daughter of Sievert H. Larson. They now have one child, Geraldine. Mr. Ostroot gives his political allegiance to the republican party and is a Lutheran in religious faith, while fraternally he is identified with the Masons and the Independent Order of Odd Fellows, He has resided in this state throughout almost his entire life, or for about a third of a century, and has made a host of friends who esteem him highly for his many good traits of character and genuine personal worth.

Matthew Owens, who has charge of the business of the Tuttle Lumber Company at Humboldt, Minnehaha County, claims as the place of his nativity the old Pine Tree state, having been born in Franklin County, Maine, on the 5th of June, 1832, and being a son of Thomas and Abigail (Tarr) Owens, the former of whom was born in County Wicklow, Ireland, while the latter was born in Maine. The father of the subject was reared and educated in the Emerald Isle, where he remained until he had attained the age of twenty-three years, when he emigrated to America, where he believed better opportunities were afforded for the attaining of success through individual effort. He located in the state of Maine, where his marriage occurred, and in 1852 he removed thence with his family to Wisconsin, becoming one of the pioneers of Lafayette County, that state, where he continued to reside until 1864, when he located in Wabasha County, Minnesota, where he continued to be identified with agricultural pursuits until his death, his wife also passing the closing years of her life in said county. Of their twelve children five are yet living, the subject of this sketch having been the ninth in order of birth.

Matthew Owens passed his boyhood days in Wisconsin and Minnesota, where he secured such educational advantages as were afforded in the public schools, in the meanwhile assisting his father in the work of the farm. At the age of twenty-one years, he secured employment in a hardware store at Plain View, Minnesota, and there learned the tinner's trade, to which he gave his attention until 1879, when he came to the present state of South Dakota and cast in his lot with its pioneers. He arrived at his destination on the 22d of July and shortly afterward filed entry upon a homestead claim in Buffalo township, Minnehaha County, retaining the property in his possession for two years and then exchanging the same for a farm about a mile distant from the same. There he continued to be engaged in farming and stock growing for the ensuing two years, at the expiration of which he removed to Madison, Lake County, where he followed the work of his trade for the following four years, within which time he assisted in the erection of the normal school building and other large structures. He thereafter devoted his attention to the cultivation of his farm until 1891, when he took up his residence in Montrose, McCook County, and there engaged in the hardware business. In the following year he sold his farm, and in December, 1893, his hardware establishment was destroyed by fire, entailing practically a total loss, with no insurance indemnity, and under these adverse conditions he found it expedient to again resume work at his trade, which he there followed for two years. In 1898 Mr. Owens came to Humbolt and accepted his present position in charge of the local interest of the Tuttle Lumber Company, in which connection he has accomplished an excellent work in extending the scope of the business, while he is also a stockholder in the Farmers' Bank and the owner of good town property. In politics Mr. Owens is arrayed in support of the principles of the Populist party, and he has shown a deep interest in public affairs and in the furthering of the cause of his party. He has held various township and school offices, and in 1890 was candidate in the independent ticket for representative of his district, making a spirited canvass, but meeting defeat with the remainder of the ticket. He is identified in a fraternal way with the local lodge of the Ancient Free and Accepted Masons, and also with that of the Ancient Order of United Workmen.

On the 13th of October, 1875, in Minnesota. Mr. Owens was united in marriage to Miss Augusta Fricke, who was born in the state of New York, of stanch German lineage, and of their children we enter the following brief record: Earl G. died at the age of nine years; Mabel I. completed her education in a normal school at Winona, Minnesota, and is now a successful teacher in the public schools of Minneapolis, Minnesota; Alfred E., who was born in the original sod house built by his father on section 3, Buffalo township, on the 30th of December, 1880, a winter memorable in the annals of the state by reason of its extreme severity, was a young man of fine character and marked ability, and a most promising life was cut short by his death, at Lead, in the Black Hills, on the 22d of March, 1904: Mattie was graduated in the state normal school in Madison, as a member of the class of 1904, and remains at the parental home, as do also the younger daughters, Annie and Minnie.

HARLAN P. PACKARD

Harlan P. Packard, secretary and general manager of the Merchants Mutual Insurance Association, is one of the most distinguished and prominent residents of Redfield, South Dakota. He has been a resident of this state since 1881, but his early home was in the east, for he was born in Madrid, St. Lawrence County, New York, on the 2d of June, 1845, and comes of a very old and prominent family of English origin. The first to locate in this country was Hiram Packard, who crossed the Atlantic in 1638, on the ship Vigilant, and settled in New England. Our subject is a direct descendant of John and Priscilla (Mullens) Alden, and his grandfathers on both sides were identified with the Revolutionary war. He is today a member of the Sons of the Revolution and also the Mayflower Descendants. His parents were Hiram and Caroline (Dimick) Packard, who spent their entire lives in New York and at their death were laid to rest in the cemetery at Madrid. The father was a farmer by occupation and died when our subject was only two years old.

Harlan P. Packard was reared and educated in the Empire state and was graduated from the Potsdam Academy in 1863. Feeling that his country needed his services, he immediately enlisted after leaving school as an engineer in the Fiftieth New York Engineer Corps, with which he served until honorably discharged when hostilities ceased. Returning to his home, he engaged in clerking in a dry-goods store in Canton, New York, and then in Ogdensburg, New York, where he remained until 1868, when he started west and located in Janesville, Minnesota. There he embarked in the dry-goods business on his own account and conducted a store there until removing to Redfield, South Dakota, in 1881. There he carried on the same business for some years, having established the first general store in that section of the state. The lumber used in the erection of his store building had to be hauled from Huron with ox teams. Success attended his efforts as a merchant and he continued in the dry-goods business until 1895, when he disposed of the name and organized the Merchants Mutual Insurance Association, to which he has since devoted his entire time, making it one of the safest and most reliable institutions of the kind in the state. He is a man of exceptional business ability and sound judgment and has been able to carry forward to successful completion whatever he has undertaken. He today the owner of considerable property in Redfield, having erected the present Central hotel and two store buildings, besides the building now occupied by the Watkins Hardware Company.

At Janesville, Minnesota, on the 29th of March, 1876, Mr. Packard was united in marriage to Miss Mary E. Wentworth, a daughter of Mrs. Virginia Wentworth and a preservative of a very prominent family of that state. To them have been born five children, namely: Harlan, who is now treasurer of the Merchants Mutual Insurance Association; Franklin H., a druggist of Redfield; Lillian, the wife of C. L. Holton, an electrician Minneapolis; Hazel, a graduate of the Cumnock School of Oratory, at Evanston, Illinois, and now teaching dramatic art in Minneapolis, Minnesota; and Clayton, attending the University of Minnesota.

His fellow citizens, recognizing his worth and ability, have called Mr. Packard to public office and for four years he most acceptably served as mayor of Redfield. He has also represented his district three times in the state legislature and for four years served as a member of the state board of charities and correction.

While a member of the legislature he was instrumental in securing the location of the Home for the Feeble Minded at Redfield. He has always done everything in his power to promote the interests of the city and is justly regarded as one of its representative and most influential citizens. He is one of the most prominent members of the Grand Army of the Republic of South Dakota and served as department commander. He belongs to the Masonic fraternity and is a member of the Mystic Shrine and the Benevolent Protective Order of Elks.

MARTIN L. PARISH

Martin L. Parish, a young attorney of Fairfax with a growing practice, was born in New York, December 6, 1881, a son of Hart and Mary A. (Ikler) Parish. The father devoted his life to the occupation of farming and in 1883 brought the family to Dakota territory, settling in Charles Mix County, at Chandler, where he homesteaded. For a quarter of a century, he there engaged in farming and he and his wife now reside upon a farm at Dixon. His efforts have been a valuable factor in advancing agricultural progress.

Brought to this state when in his second year, Martin L. Parish attended the public schools and afterward entered Yankton College. He was graduated from the academy and later followed the profession of teaching for six years. In the meantime, in 1904, he homesteaded a tract of land in Gregory County. In 1906 he was elected to the office of clerk of the courts and subsequently entered the office of Edwin M. Starcher at Fairfax, who was engaged in the practice of law and in the abstract business, later succeeding to the business. Devoting his leisure time to the study of law, he was admitted to the bar on the 26th of October, 1912, and although one of the younger attorneys of the county, has won a fair share of the public practice and it is well known that he is most devoted to the interests of his clients, doing everything in his power to win success along the lines of legitimate practice. He also continues president of the Starcher Abstract Company and is doing a good business in that connection.

On the 19th of August, 1912, Mr. Parish was united in marriage to Miss Lydia Morach, a native of Nebraska and a daughter of the Rev. Jacob Morach, a Congregational minister. They now have two children, Elizabeth G. and Mary Doris.

Mr. and Mrs. Parish hold membership in the Congregational church and are accorded cordial welcome in the best homes of the city, occupying an enviable social position. Mr. Parish exercises his right of franchise in support of the men and measures of the republican party and for six years was clerk of the courts. He belongs to the Masonic lodge of Bonesteel and to the Commercial Club of Fairfax, and he is fond of motoring and enjoys outdoor life, thus gaining his recreation. His entire life has conformed to high standards, making him a respected citizen of Gregory County, while his unfeigned cordiality and goodwill toward all have won for him well deserved popularity.

Herbert E. Parker was well known as a valued resident of Sioux Falls. He saw the possibilities for advancement and improvement in the city and ever labored to make these a reality. It was not so much the success he achieved that gave him high standing in business circles, as the progressive methods which he followed and the honorable policy which he pursued. He was born in Sparta, Wisconsin, July 22, 1863, and spent his boyhood days upon the farm there, early becoming familiar with the best methods of tilling the soil and caring for the crops. After mastering the branches of learning taught in the district schools he became a student in the high school at Boscobel, where he was graduated. In 1882 he came to Sioux Falls, where he worked as a journeyman carpenter. He afterward found an opening in the restaurant business and turned his attention to that pursuit. Subsequently he became a guard at the South Dakota penitentiary, where he remained for three years. He then entered the coal and wood business and later he engaged in the ice business with his brother, John, the association being maintained until 1906, when our subject withdrew, his brother continuing the business. Herbert E. Parker remained in the coal, wood and feed business, was the first man to engage in the wholesale seed business in South Dakota and at one time was for six years in the employ of the Standard Oil Company. He was industrious and energetic and was also straightforward and reliable with firm belief in the golden rule, which he ever endeavored to follow in the conduct of his business interests. People who gave him their support knew that his word was to be depended upon and that his promises would be kept and his obligations met. He therefore gained an enviable reputation and his business record constituted an example well worthy of emulation.

In 1883 Mr. Parker was united in marriage to Miss Nellie Clark, a native of Minnesota. They became the parents of seven children, who are yet living, Nellie A., Harry E., Bessie H., Erne R., Burton L., Margaret K. and Teddy Hugh.

Mr. Parker was prominent in Masonic circles, holding membership in Unity Lodge. No. 103, A. F. & A. M., of which he became a charter member. He served as junior warden for a number of years and refused higher positions on account of the pressure of business duties. He was also connected with the Ancient Order of United Workmen, the Knights of Labor and the Benevolent Protective Order of Elks and in his life exemplified the sterling principles of those organizations. In his political views he was independent, voting for men and measures rather than party, while his religious connection was with the Congregational church, which found in him a consistent and faithful member. He was a public-spirited man, withholding his indorsement and support from no measure that he deemed would prove of public value and benefit. A fitting epitaph for him would be the words of the philosopher that "an honest man is the noblest work of God."

RALPH WINFIELD PARLIMAN

The name of Parliman has figured prominently in connection with the history of the legal profession in South Dakota for many years and has always been a synonym for professional honor, enterprise and progress. He whose name introduces this review is now successfully practicing in Sioux Falls in partnership with his son and namesake, and the firm is regarded as one of the strongest at the bar of South Dakota. He was born at Newton Falls, Ohio, January 25, 1860, a son of Edwin and Jerusha Isabel (North) Parliman, who became residents of Sioux Falls in the summer of 1877. The paternal grandfather, Dr. William Parliman, was also a native of Ohio and for sixty years practiced medicine in Decorah, Iowa, where he passed away. He came of Holland Dutch ancestry.

Edwin Parliman, the father, was born in Stark County, Ohio, December 12, 1832, and completed his education in Allegheny College at Meadville, Pennsylvania, where he was graduated with the class of 1850, when he was eighteen years of age. He was twenty-one years of age when he removed to Decorah, Iowa, where he learned the watchmaker's trade, and in 1857 he became a resident of Austin, Minnesota, where he continued until his removal to Hastings in the same state. Wishing to turn from commercial to professional pursuits, he took up the study of law and in 1860 was admitted to the bar, entering upon active practice in Hastings, where he remained until 1862. Being unable to longer content himself to remain at home while the preservation of the Union was at stake, he offered his services to the government and was instrumental in raising Company F, of the Second Minnesota Cavalry in 1862. On the 31st of December, 1863, he was commissioned first lieutenant of his company and on the 15th of May, 1865, was promoted to the rank of captain, with which he served until mustered out on the 2d of December, 1865, when he was brevetted major. His was a most creditable military record, involving active duty against the Indians in the west — a most arduous warfare because of the spirit and military methods of his wily foes.

After the close of the war Edwin Parliman resumed the practice of law in Hastings and for four years he served as county attorney of Dakota county, Minnesota. He remained in active practice in Hastings until 1877, when he came to Sioux Falls, opened an office and prepared a home for his family who followed in March, 1878. There he was appointed county attorney for Minnehaha County by the county board and served for three years. He likewise was made city attorney of Sioux Falls, and was the first incumbent in that office. He continued in the active practice of his profession until 1890, when he was elected county judge of Minnehaha County and remained upon the bench until January 1, 1898, having been elected upon the republican ticket at each election after the creation of South Dakota as a state until 1896, when he was defeated. He then resumed the practice of law in partnership with Harry R. Carleton but later was alone in his profession. When the new bankruptcy law went into effect, he was appointed referee in bankruptcy, which position he held until a short time prior to his death, when the condition of his health forced him to resign and he was succeeded by his son, Ralph W. Parliman, through appointment of Judge Garland of the federal court. On the 1st of March, 1899, he had been joined in a law partnership by his son, Ralph, under the firm style of Parliman & Parliman. He was the first chief of the fire department of Sioux Falls and on the occasion of his death the firemen of the city, as well as the members of the bar, attended his funeral in a body. He passed away June 5, 1899, and his wife died June 3, 1905.

In 1852 Judge Parliman was united in marriage to Miss Jerusha Isabel North and they became parents of four children: Mrs. Emma Donaldson, of Lakeville, Minnesota; R. W., of this review; Mrs. Percy Scofield, of Lakeville, Minnesota; and Mrs. Mate Brickner, of West St. Paul.

Ralph W. Parliman acquired his education in the public schools of Hastings, Minnesota, being graduated with the class of 1877. In that year he went with his parents to Lincoln County, South Dakota, and for five years was upon a farm. In 1884 he entered his father's law office at Egan, South Dakota, where he continued his studies until June, 1887. At that time, he opened a law office in Britton, South Dakota, and the following year was elected district attorney of Marshall County, in which position he served until January 1, 1890. He then removed to Webster, South Dakota, where he continued in active practice until March 1, 1899, when he returned to Sioux Falls and joined his father in a partnership that continued until the latter's death on the 5th of June of that year. R. W. Parliman afterward practiced alone until October 4, 1905, when he admitted his son, Ralph W. Jr., to a partnership that still continues. The offices he has held have been largely in the strict path of his profession. He was district attorney of Marshall County and in June, 1899, was made United States referee in bankruptcy, in which position he served for two years. He was also a member of the school board at Webster, South Dakota, for some years and in 1894 was appointed postmaster at that place by President Cleveland, continuing in the office until July, 1898. His military record is that of quartermaster of Colonel Grigsby's Cowboy Regiment, the Third United States Volunteer Cavalry, with which he served until the command was mustered out at the close of the Spanish-American war. In politics he has always been a republican, earnest and stalwart in support of the party.

At Claremont, South Dakota, on the 16th of March, 1888, Mr. Parliman was united in marriage to Miss Mattie A. Chamberlain and they have become the parents of six children: Ralph W.; Marie L.; James C; John E.; Beatrice I.; Joseph W.; and Mercedes, who died when one year old. James and John are students in the law department of the University of South Dakota and the oldest son, Ralph Winfield, Jr., is one of the younger representatives of the South Dakota bar. He was born in Britton, this state, September 20, 1889. In his early youth the family removed to Sioux Falls and he continued his education in the public schools until graduated from the high school. He later had the advantage of two years' instruction in the University of South Dakota at Vermillion, where he pursued the law course. He was then admitted to the bar and joined his father in practice, being now a member of the law firm of Parliman & Parliman and representing the third generation of the law firm founded by his grandfather in 1877.

The Parliman family attend the Congregational church and Mr. Parliman is well known in fraternal and social circles. He belongs to the Masons and also holds membership with the Independent Order of Odd Fellows, the Ancient Order of United Workmen, the Modern Woodmen of America, the Benevolent Protective Order of Elks and the Dacotah Club. His interest in all is sincere and abiding and his loyalty to their principles is marked. The greater part of his life has been spent in this state and he has a wide acquaintance, warm friendship being accorded him in recognition of his sterling professional and personal worth.

ALBERTIS E. PARMENTER

Albertis E. Parmenter, commonly known as "Bert," is now engaged in the abstract business in Scotland, South Dakota. He was a pioneer miller of Hutchinson County and was connected with that business until 1900. He was born in Erie County, New York, April 28, 1851, a son of Stillman and Catherine (Van Camp) Parmenter, likewise natives of the Empire state. The father was descended from one of the old Dutch families that early settled in the Mohawk valley.

Bert Parmenter remained at home until he reached the age of eighteen years and then went to Springville, on Cattaraugus creek, which forms the southern boundary of his native county, and for five years applied himself to learning the miller's, trade. At the end of that time, he left New York and came west. He arrived in Dakota in 1874, reaching Yankton on Saturday, June 13th of that year. He anticipated the development of the great northwest into one of the most important grain-producing regions of the world and was looking for a suitable site for a grist mill. The week following his arrival in Yankton he traveled up the Jim River and selected a site in the southern part of Hutchinson County, where he built a dam and erected the first mill between Yankton and the mountains. It was a small affair, having only two run of burrs, but it was sufficient for the time. It was completed in the fall of 1875 and was used to grind the crop of that year. It subsequently became too small and a new structure was erected in 1885 that was much larger. The roller process was adopted and the capacity increased to one hundred and twenty-five barrels per day. The business was later incorporated as the Maxwell & Parmenter Milling Company, Mr. Parmenter's partner being his brother-in-law. In 1893 Mr. Parmenter bought out Mr. Maxwell and conducted the business as the A. E. Parmenter Mill until he sold it to the Mennonites on the 1st of April, 1900. In 1883 Mr. Parmenter moved into Scotland and has since resided in the same house. On the 12th of January, 1901, he entered upon his duties as registrar of deeds for Bon Homme County and at the same time took up the abstract business, in which he has continued to the present time. He has an excellent set of abstract books and prepares most of the abstracts made in the county.

Mr. Parmenter was married in Yankton, on the 2d of September, 1879, to Miss Annie C. Maxwell, who came to this state with her parents from Dubuque, Iowa. Her father, John Maxwell, was a native of Montreal, Canada, while her mother, who bore the maiden name of Susan C. Languedoc, was a native of Quebec. The three surviving children of Mr. and Mrs. Parmenter are: John C, who married Miss Frances Walker and is manager of the Farmer's Elevator and agent for the Chicago, Milwaukee & St. Paul Railway at Blaha, this state; Eugenia, the wife of J. L. Meighen, judge of the county court of Bon Homme County; and Donald C, who was graduated from the Scotland high school with the class of 1915.

Mr. Parmenter achieved success as a miller but he had to endure many of the hardships of pioneer life. The spring floods of 1881, coming at the close of the "winter of the deep snow," were unusually high and did much damage to the mill. The floating ice formed a gorge below Yankton and the high waters overflowed for many miles upstream. Jim River received its share and the waters backed up so that for twenty-four hours the current ran up stream from the top of the eight-foot dam. Later when the deep drifts of the Jim River valley melted in a warm spring sun a flood swept down upon the mill and carried away the Hume, the wheelhouse and the wheel, depositing them six miles downstream. Anticipating the rising waters, Mr. Parmenter had removed all flour and wheat from the mill to a safe place and thus minimized his loss. In the fall of 1878, a prairie fire swept through the valley and burned stacks of wheat and hay in the mill yard and the mill itself was saved only by great effort. Mr. Parmenter's first experience with a real South Dakota blizzard was on January 12, 1888, one of the memorable days in the history of the state. His brother-in-law, who had been longer on the plains, had often spoken of them but Mr. Parmenter rather fancied that they were but myths. This morning his brother-in-law remarked as the two walked down to the office that it was typical blizzard weather, although it was a warm sunny day. They had been in the office but a few minutes when their vision was limited to the glass of the windows and their hands were invisible at arm's length. The blizzard was on in earnest and it was with great difficulty that they were able to grope their way back to the house at nightfall.

Mr. Parmenter is a democrat in politics and has taken an active part in public affairs. Fraternally he belongs to the blue lodge and chapter of the Masonic order at Scotland. He has witnessed the great development of the state from the time that it was an unbroken prairie to the present when it is a highly developed agricultural region dotted with thriving villages, towns and cities. His reminiscences cover nearly the entire period of the existence of the state and territory and his accounts of the early days are of great value in enabling the younger generation to realize to some extent the lives which their fathers lived in South Dakota in its pioneer epoch. Not only has he been an interested observer of the growth and development of the state but he has aided materially therein.

JOSEPH W. PARMLEY

JOSEPH W. PARMLEY

Joseph W. Parmley is an exponent of the spirit of progress which is dominating the development of South Dakota and the northwest. He makes his home at Ipswich, Edmunds County, and has been closely associated with its development along educational, agricultural and commercial lines. His interests, however, have even wider significance and effect, for he is concerned in the good roads' movement and in various other plans and projects which have to do with the development and upbuilding of the state, not only for the immediate present but also for the future. Mr. Parmley is a native of Iowa county, Wisconsin, born January 12, 1861, and is a son of Joseph and Jane (Ashton) Parmley. After completing a common-school course he attended the State Normal School of Platteville and the Lawrence University at Appleton, Wisconsin.

His residence in Dakota territory dates from 1883. After looking over the northwest he concluded that it would eventually be a great agricultural empire. The railroads had reached Aberdeen and already extensions were being considered. Mr. Parmley studied the map and said that Borne day the Chicago, Milwaukee & St. Paul Railway Company would build west to the Pacific and felt that there was no more feasible route than from Aberdeen straight to the coast. He started out on foot and when forty miles west stopped on the present town site of Roscoe and looked around him for miles, the meeting of sky and prairie constituting his horizon. He secured a part of the present town site of Roscoe as his preemption, then returned to Aberdeen, purchased lumber for a shanty and drove back to his claim. In connection with Charles P. Morgan of Chicago he named the "town" Roscoe, in honor of

Roscoe Conklin, who was then at the zenith of his career. Other settlers soon came and in connection with Henry Huck, Mr. Parmley in September of that year began the publication of the Roscoe Herald, of which he afterward became sole owner. He continued to publish that paper until 1910, when he purchased the South Dakota Tribune and merged the two journals under the name of the Ipswich Tribune. All this time he was working earnestly for the development of the district in which he had located and his efforts extended beneficially along many lines.

When Edmunds County was organized in August, 1883, Mr. Parmley was appointed superintendent of schools and was elected to that office in the fall of 1884. He was instrumental in organizing the educational system of the county, and when he retired from the position of county superintendent the educational work had been placed upon an excellent basis, leading to its continued growth and development. When he left the position of county superintendent, he was elected register of deeds and county clerk. In 1887 he studied law and was admitted to the bar but has never engaged in active practice. His knowledge of the law, however, has been of the utmost value to him in conducting his private business interests and in promoting public projects. Moreover, he served as county judge for a number of terms both by election and by appointment of the governor, and he has also been numbered among the lawmakers of the state, having for two terms been a member of the state legislature. He has been urged by a large constituency on several occasions to become a candidate for congress, for governor and for the United States senate but has always declined. He has ever regarded the pursuits of private life as in themselves abundantly worthy of his best efforts and has preferred that his public service should be done as a private citizen. Those who know aught of his career recognize, too, that his efforts have been far-reaching and effective and that many public movements owe much to his indorsement and active support.

Mr. Parmley is intensely interested in better farming methods and was a pioneer in introducing Durum wheat, better varieties of corn, alfalfa and drought resistant forage crops. He has also introduced and bred herds of registered cattle and at the present time has the largest herd of Shetland ponies in the northwest. Moreover, he is the owner of the business conducted under the name of the Edmunds County Abstract Company and is half owner of the McPherson County Abstract Company at Leola. His resourceful business ability has not been exhausted even through these connections and into other fields he has extended his efforts, being at the head of the Aberdeen Pressed Brick Company and active in developing an industry that promises much for the northwest.

Moreover, Mr. Parmley is known as the father of the good roads movement in the state and is president of the South Dakota Good Roads Association. He was the originator of a plan to build an improved public highway from Aberdeen to Mobridge, which against his protest was named the Parmley Highway. Later he led the movement for the extension of the road to the falls of St. Anthony east and to the falls of the Yellowstone west, thus making a great road from the Twin Cities to the Yellowstone National Park. This has developed into a great cross-country road and is now extending east as far as Chicago and west to Seattle, while the plan is to continue east to Plymouth Rock, making a great transcontinental highway. Mr. Parmley has been at the head of this undertaking and for the past two years has been president of the organization known as the Yellowstone Trail Association. The value of such a project cannot be overestimated and the promoters of such an undertaking deserve the gratitude of their fellowmen.

Mr. Parmley is also intensely interested in the world peace movement and is in demand as a lecturer on the subject of the settlement of disputes between nations by arbitration or a world court. He is now president of the South Dakota Peace Society. He has traveled extensively in the United States, Canada and Mexico and his writings descriptive of his journeys, as well as of subjects of general discussion, are in demand by many magazines. Beside the honorary positions above mentioned that he fills, he is a trustee of the Dakota Wesley University and is a member of the National Scientific and other societies. It would be tautological in this connection to enter into any series of statements showing him to be a man of broad culture, of liberal knowledge and wide public spirit, for these have been shadowed forth between the lines of this review. He looks at life from a wide standpoint, recognizes the opportunities for national and world progress and attacks everything with a contagious enthusiasm. Mr. Parmley is a member of a number of secret societies, including the Modern Woodmen of America and the United Workmen. He is also a thirty-second degree Mason and a member of the Mystic Shrine.

In 1886 Mr. Parmley was united in marriage to Miss Lissie E. Baker, of Dodgeville, Wisconsin, a daughter of Francis and Mary (Dony) Baker. Two children have been born of this union: Loren, now twenty years of age, who is attending the State University of South Dakota; and Irene, who is attending high school in Ipswich.

RUSSELL G. PARMLEY

Russell G. PARMLEY, senior member of the well-known firm of R. G. Parmley & Brother, dealers in coal, coke, fire brick, clay, lime and cement, sewer pipe, pressed brick, etc., in the city of Sioux Falls, with headquarters at 201 Second avenue south, is one of the representative business men of the city, where he has maintained his home for a quarter of a century, his business career having closely followed the Industrial development of the town, of which he may consistently be termed a pioneer, while he commands the confidence and regard which are the invariable concomitants of sterling integrity and straightforward business methods.

Mr. Parmley was born on a farm in Rock County, Wisconsin, on the 13th of March, 1851, being a son of Ira and Aurora E. (Austin) Parmley, both of whom are now deceased, while of their seven children five are living. The subject was reared to the wholesome discipline of the farm and received his early educational training in the common schools of his native county, including a course in the high school in Janesville. He continued to be associated with the management of the old homestead farm until he had attained the age of twenty-five years, when he established himself in the grain business in Footville, Wisconsin, where he continued operations until 1878, when he came to the territory of Dakota and located in what was then the village of Sioux Falls, where he engaged in the coal and wood business. His energy and good management made the venture a successful one from the time of its initiation, and three years later he admitted his brother Harry to partnership. Since that time the enterprise has been consecutively conducted under the firm name of R. G. Parmley & Brother, while its scope has been expanded materially and the business controlled has become a large and important one in the various lines of products handled, while special attention has been given to the building of cement walks, in which line they are numbered among the leading contractors in the city. Mr. Parmley was one of the organizers of the Union National Bank, of which he was vice-president until the time of its closing business. He was elected president of the old Commercial Club, which accomplished excellent work in exploiting the attractions and resources of the city and state, and he is at the present time president of the Dakota Club, a strong and valued business and social organization. He is a stanch advocate of the principles and policies of the Republican party, and while not ambitious for public office his loyalty to his home city has been such that he has consented to serve as a member of the city council and also of the board of education.

Fraternally he is identified with the Masonic order, in which he has attained the chivalric degrees, being affiliated with Cyrene Commandery, Knights Templar. On the 25th of December, 1872, Mr. Parmley was united in marriage to Miss Fannie A. Dann. of Center. Rock county, Wisconsin, and they have two sons. Arthur L. and Frank G.

ASHER K. PAY

ASHER K. PAY

The value of industry, enterprise and ability is well illustrated in the career of Asher K. Pay, who, starting in business with a capital of ninety-six dollars, has so intelligently and capably managed his interests that he is today the proprietor of the finest art store in Sioux Falls and the builder, owner and manager of the Colonial Theater, which is the finest and most modern house of entertainment in the state. He was born in Washington, Iowa, November 13, 1866, and is a son of Thomas L. and Jennie (Wagner) Pay. The father was born in Dover, England, and was twelve years of age when he accompanied his parents on their removal to America. After coming to South Dakota, he took up a homestead in Brookings County, in 1881, and there lived for many years.

Asher K. Pay spent his early life upon the home farm in Brookings County and acquired only a limited common-school education. For some time, he spent his summers learning the trade of a painter and paper hanger and attended school during the winter months. In 1858 he came to Sioux Falls and after working for one year at his trade determined to engage in business on his own account. With a capital of only ninety-six dollars, he established a small art store and from this humble beginning has developed his present large and profitable enterprise. He understands the business in principle and detail, is industrious, ambitious and energetic and has therefore met with excellent success, controlling today a large and representative patronage. On the 13th of June, 1914, he opened the Colonial Theater to the public. A fire had swept away the wholesale drug house that stood on the site where the theater is now located and Mr. Pay purchased the ruins and erected there the finest moving picture house in the state.

On the 3d of June, 1891, at Sioux Falls, Mr. Pay was united in marriage to Miss Dora Gremmels, and they have three children, Howard H., Milton A. and Clifford T. They have a beautiful summer home on Lake Okoboji, Iowa. It is equipped with waterworks and all modern conveniences and here the family spend the summer months each year.

Mr. Pay belongs to the Elks Club and is a York Rite Mason, holding membership in the Shrine. His political support is given the men and measures of the republican party. He has an extensive circle of friends in Sioux Falls, where he has resided for over a quarter of a century, and he merits the confidence and trust which are uniformly accorded him.

LEWIS VICTOR PEEK

Lewis V. Peek, of Wilmot, was born near Portage City, Columbia County, Wisconsin, September 26, 1862, being one of a family of four children, whose father, William H. Peek, a native of New York, was an early settler of Wisconsin, and by occupation a tiller of the soil. Lewis V. was reared to agricultural pursuits, acquired a strong physique under the rugged but wholesome discipline of the farm and grew to young manhood in Minnesota, to which state his parents removed when he was but a child. Later, in 1882, he accompanied the family to South Dakota and subsequently began clerking in a store at Milbank, but after spending a short time in that town he accepted a similar position in Wilmot, where he sold goods for one year.

In 1887 Mr. Peek was appointed deputy county treasurer and two years later succeeded to the office of treasurer to fill out the unexpired term of William McKissick, discharging the duties of the position until 1893, having been elected for a full term in 1891. Retiring from the office at the expiration of his period of service, he took a claim in the northern part of the county, where the name Victor was given to a township in compliment to him, and a little later he secured the post office at Vernon, to accommodate people of that locality. After residing on his claim until the fall of 1894, Mr. Peek was elected cashier of the First State Bank of Wilmot, accordingly he returned to the town and entered upon his duties, discharging the same to the satisfaction of all concerned until January, 1902, when he resigned. He is still interested in the bank, however, being a stockholder and a member of the board of directors, in addition to which he is secretary and treasurer of the Wilmot Land and Loan Company, the organization of which was brought about mainly through his agency and influence. He is also interested in agriculture and stock raising, and owns considerable valuable farm land in Roberts County, which he personally manages, also a fine residence in Wilmot and other city property, his various enterprises having succeeded so well that he is now numbered with the financially strong and reliable men of the community honored by his citizenship.

Mr. Peek has been and is still one of the leading men of Wilmot and since locating in the city he has been very closely identified with its history and development. He served several terms as trustee and mayor under the original municipal government and after a city charter was secured, he was also honored with official station, being mayor at the present time.

Like the majority of enterprising men, Mr. Peek is a Mason and stands high in the order, belonging to the blue lodge at Wilmot, the chapter at Milbank, the commandery at Watertown, the Scottish Rite at Aberdeen and the Mystic Shrine, which holds its session in the city of Sioux Falls. He is also a member of the Independent Order of Odd Fellows and the Knights of Pythias, and their several auxiliaries, and an active worker in the local lodge of the Modern Woodmen of America, with which he is connected.

Mr. Peek, on February 17, 1887, was married to Miss Ida C. Bailly, daughter of Alexander P. Bailly, of Minnesota, and is the father of one child, Stewart Irving Peek, whose birth occurred on April 18, 1896. As already indicated, Mr. Peek is one of Wilmot's valued and highly esteemed citizens. He has borne well his part in life and is now conducting a flourishing business and meeting with the success that is justly deserved.

OLIVER S. PENDAR

Oliver S. Pendar, the virtual founder of the town of Salem, McCook County, which he named in honor of his native place, and one of the popular and well-known citizens of Sioux Falls, where he holds the responsible office of clerk of both the United States circuit and district courts, was born in the historic old city of Salem, Massachusetts, on the 29th of September, 1857, and comes of stanch old colonial stock. He secured his early education in the public schools and was graduated in the Salem high school, where he was reared to manhood. In 1877, at the age of twenty years, he started for the west, believing that better opportunities were here afforded for advancement through personal effort. He was located in the city of Minneapolis for one year, at the expiration of which, in 1878, he cast in his lot with the pioneers of what is now the state of South Dakota, taking up his residence in McCook County, where he took up a timber and a pre-emption claim, in due time perfecting his title to the property, to whose improvement he gave his attention. In 1879 a post office was established at the point now occupied by the flourishing little city of Salem and the subject was appointed the first postmaster, while he gave the name of Salem to the same in grateful memory of his home town, while the title was retained by the village which eventually grew up on the site. In connection with his official duties as postmaster he established a general store, in 1879, and continued to conduct the same until 1886, having been the first merchant of Salem and having built up an excellent trade. In the year last mentioned he turned his attention to the real-estate and loan business, in which line he successfully conducted operations until 1890, when he was appointed clerk of the United States district court and removed to the city of Sioux Falls, having received this appointment on the 30th of January, at the hands of Judge Edgerton, who was then presiding on the bench of the district court for the district comprising the state. On the 17th of the following June, Mr. Pendar received from Judge Caldwell the appointment of clerk of the United States circuit court for the same district, which office he still holds. The district clerkship he retained until October, 1891, when he retired from the same, but on the 26th of December, 1896, Judge Garland reappointed him to the office and he has since been in tenure of both, giving a service which has been satisfactory to all concerned. As has been said of him in another published article he is "a genial good fellow, well-liked by everybody, and is a competent official." In politics he has ever been an uncompromising Republican, and up to 1888 he took an active part in the political affairs of the territory, having served as a delegate to several territorial and state conventions.

He is a Knight Templar Mason and is also identified with the auxiliary organization, the Ancient Arabic Order of the Nobles of the Mystic Shrine. In 1883 Mr. Pendar was united in marriage to Miss Mary E. Flint, who was born and reared in his native town of Salem, Massachusetts, the date of the marriage having been November 1st of the year mentioned. She died in July of the following year (1884.)

DR. EDWIN L. PERKINS

Dr. Edwin L. Perkins has devoted his attention to the practice of medicine and surgery in Sioux Falls for the past ten years, and in his life-work has won an enviable reputation as an able and exemplary representative of the profession.

Dr. Perkins was born in Prairie du Sac, Wisconsin, November 8, 1870, the son of Loring A. and Julia Morrill Perkins. The family dates its origin historically from early English ancestors of the period of Elizabeth. Men of science and invention are numbered among its members, and the name of Perkins is prominent in the early history of the New England colonies and among the makers of history during the Revolutionary period.

Dr. Perkins has been a resident of Sioux Falls since May 4, 1889. Beginning his education in the public schools at Montello, Wisconsin, he subsequently entered the Sioux Falls College from which institution he was graduated in 1892. After teaching in the Sioux Falls High School a number of years, he prepared for the practice of medicine, graduating from the Northwestern University Medical School of Chicago in 1904, and the following year he completed the course in the Chicago Post-Graduate Hospital. He immediately began practice in Sioux Falls, and has remained there continuously since. He is a member of several medical societies, and a progressive student in the realm of his profession. It was largely through the influence of Dr. Perkins that the McKennan Hospital at Sioux Falls was founded.

On the 21st of June, 1906, at Excelsior, Minnesota, Dr. Perkins was united in marriage to Miss Sena Marie Swenson, by whom he has three children, namely: Mary Elizabeth, Edwin Morrill and Ralph Hiram.

In politics Dr. Perkins is a democrat, while in his religious faith he is associated with the Congregational church. Fraternally he is identified with the Masons, belonging to the Consistory and the Shrine. He is also a member of the South Dakota Chapter of the Sons of the American Revolution. Dr. Perkins' professional labors are all in the direction of the general uplift of the community in which he lives, and he enjoys the respect of his brethren of the medical fraternity by reason of his strict conformity to a high standard of professional ethics.

HENRY AMOS PERRITON

Henry A. Perriton, a representative and esteemed citizen of Huron, there opened a drug store in July, 1907, and has since conducted the same with gratifying and well merited success his birth occurred in Illinois in 1877, his parents being J. S. and Jean Scott (Lindsay) Perriton, who came to South Dakota in 1882 and located at Ashton. The father took up a tract of government land and three years later embarked in the butchering business. He is now living retired at Huron, enjoying the fruits of his former labor in well-earned ease. His wife was called to her final rest on the 28th of August, 1905.

Henry A. Perriton, who was a little lad of five years when he came to this state with his parents, acquired his early education in the public schools and subsequently attended the University of South Dakota at Vermillion for four years, while in 1902 he was graduated from the Highland Park College of Pharmacy at Des Moines, Iowa. In 1903 he removed to Huron and there identified himself with the drug business, working in various capacities. In July, 1907, he opened a drug store on his own account and has thus remained in business throughout the intervening eight years. He carries a complete and attractively arranged stock of drugs and druggists' sundries and well merits the liberal patronage which is accorded him. On the 1st of July, 1905, Mr. Perriton was united in marriage to Miss Elizabeth Lee Halk, of Lexington, Virginia, her parents being Alexander E. and Virginia Halk. The father is deceased, but the mother survives and now lives with Mr. and Mrs. Perriton.

In his political views Mr. Perriton is a republican, strongly advocating and supporting the principles of that party. In Masonry he is identified with the blue lodge, the chapter, the commandery and the Shrine. He is a past commander of La Co Tah Commandery, No. 6, and now acts as grand sword bearer of the grand commandery, while his other fraternal connections are with the Benevolent and Protective Order of Elks and the Knights of Pythias. Mr. Perriton possesses a genial, courteous manner that has won him many friends among those whom he has met in his business capacity, while those whom he meets in social and fraternal circles have retained for him warm regard.

GEORGE S. PERRY

G. S. PERRY was born in Berkshire, England, on the 12th of January, 1853, and is a son of William and Charlotte (Hobbs) Perry, the father dying in Cleveland, Ohio, in April, 1880, aged about sixty years, and the mother at Mitchell, South Dakota, on December 24, 1889, aged seventy-three years, six months and thirteen days. The subject received his early educational training in his native land, and was twelve years of age at the time of his parents' emigration to America. The family located in the city of Cleveland, Ohio, and here Mr. Perry soon gave distinctive evidence of his predilection for mechanical pursuits, since when he was but fourteen years of age he was not only acting as engineer in a manufacturing establishment, but also had the general charge of the factory during the illness of the owner. At the age of seventeen he secured a position as fireman on the Cleveland & Wheeling Railroad, and two and one-half years later had been promoted to the position of engineer. He thus continued in the service of the road noted for another year and then entered the employ of the Baltimore & Ohio Railroad Company, with headquarters in the city of Pittsburg. He remained with this company until the great strike of 1877, at which time he entered the employ of the Canada Southern. When the Vanderbilts secured control of the Chicago, Milwaukee & St. Paul Railroad, in 1879, Mr. Perry was assigned an engine and operated the same in connection with the building of the road westward from Glencoe, Minnesota, to Ortonville, South Dakota, his conductors at the time being Andrew W. Glenn and Charles Dean, with whom he has ever since been associated in the same relative capacity, their official alliance, if so it may be termed, having thus continued for nearly, a quarter of a century. They continued with the extension of the road to Bristol, and reached Aberdeen, South Dakota, in 1881. Mr. Perry also worked on construction to Ashton and Ellendale and was then given the passenger run to Milbank. In June, 1883, he was the driver of the engine on the construction of the track southward to Woonsocket, where the extension from the south was met. He was given the first passenger run on this branch, between Aberdeen and Mitchell, and for twenty-one years he has continued to thus traverse this branch. In thirty years of service Mr. Perry has never had a serious wreck and has never personally been injured in any accident. He has confined his attention exclusively to the demands placed upon him as an engineer, taking pride in his work, knowing its responsibilities and realizing that it is worthy of his best efforts. He is a veteran and trusted employe of the company and has the high regard of all who know him.

He is identified with the Brotherhood of Locomotive Engineers and also with the Masonic fraternity, in which he has attained to the Knights Templar degrees, being a member of the various bodies of the order in Aberdeen, where he has a pleasant home and is well and favorably known. He is a stanch Republican in politics. At Saint Thomas, Ontario, Canada, on the 6th of July, 1878, Mr. Perry was united in marriage to Miss Leila Whitcomb, daughter of S. W. Whitcomb, who was for many years an engineer on the New York Central Railroad. Mr. and Mrs. Perry have five children, namely: George W., Cora, Dean, Floyd N. and Leila M. The first named was educated in the Goldie College, Wilmington, Delaware.

Among the residents of Sioux Falls to whom the state pays a merited tribute of respect and honor is Dr. George Atwood Pettigrew, who for a long period was a successful physician and surgeon and attained high rank in that field of labor. Later he became a prominent figure in banking circles of the state. It is not alone his professional and business career, however, that entitle him to mention in this volume, for he is one of the leading Masons of South Dakota, upon whom the craft has bestowed high honors. He has held some of the most important offices within the gift of the fraternity and is now most worthy grand patron of the Eastern Star, thus filling the position of highest distinction in that branch of Masonry in the world.

Dr. Pettigrew is one of New England's native sons, his birth having occurred in Ludlow, Vermont, April 6, 1858, his parents being Josiah Walker and Susan Ann (Atwood) Pettigrew, the former a native of Ludlow and the latter of Londonderry, Vermont. He spent his youthful days under the parental roof and supplemented his early public-school education by a course of study in the Black River Academy of Ludlow and in the Colby Academy of New London, New Hampshire. Upon the foundation of a broad classical course, he built the superstructure of his professional knowledge. Entering Dartmouth College at Hanover, New Hampshire, he was graduated from the medical department with the class of 1882 and then sought the opportunities for professional advancement offered by the west, making his way to South Dakota, then a part of the territory of Dakota. He entered upon active practice at Flandreau on the 2d of February, 1883, and in June, 1884, formed a partnership with Dr. F. A. Spafford, which continued until February, 1891. He then retired from active practice and turned his attention to the real-estate, loan and banking business. He was surgeon of the Chicago, Milwaukee & St. Paul Railroad Company for eight years, was government physician to the Indians for a similar period and was surgeon of the Second Regiment of Territorial Guards and their successors from 1885 until 1898. He also acted as surgeon general of South Dakota for four years under Governor Sheldon and in 1884 was made a member of the United States pension examining board, in which position he continued until 1901 with the exception of one year. He also acted as surgeon of the First and Second Regiments of the South Dakota National Guard from their organization until their departure for the Philippines. He won professional prominence and honor and had the high regard and esteem of his fellow members of the medical fraternity.

DR. GEORGE A. PETTIGREW

At length, however, Dr. Pettigrew determined to retire from the practice of medicine and in May, 1891, became one of the organizers of the Flandreau State Bank, of which he was chosen president, and so continued for twelve years, or until July, 1903. At that date he resigned and on the 3d of September following removed to Sioux Falls. He has since been prominently identified with financial interests of this city. In 1896 he became an officer of the Union Savings Association of Sioux Falls and so continued until 1913. His opinions have carried weight in financial as well as professional circles, and his enterprise, sound judgment and determination have been important factors in the successful conduct of two of South Dakota's strong banking institutions.

On the 19th of October, 1887, Dr. Pettigrew was married, in Troy, New York, to Miss Eudora Zulette Stearns, who was born at Felchville, Vermont, July 28, 1858. To them was born a daughter, Addie Stearns, whose birth occurred September 7, 1890. In July, 1912, they adopted a two-and-a-half-year-old girl, Madeleine. The family are prominent socially and have an extensive circle of warm friends, not only in Sioux Falls, hut also in other sections of the state.

As previously stated, Dr. Pettigrew is one of the prominent Masons of South Dakota, having attained the thirty-third degree of the Scottish Rite and the Royal Order of Scotland. Many Masonic honors have been conferred upon him. He was called to the office of grand secretary of the Grand Chapter of Royal Arch Masons of South Dakota in 1889 and still continues in that position, covering a period of a quarter of a century. In 1895 he was elected grand secretary of the Grand Lodge of Masons and in 1894 was chosen grand recorder of the Grand Commandery of Knights Templar, while in 1896 he was made grand recorder of the Grand High Priesthood. He was also grand commander of the Knights Templar in 1907. He became a member of the Eastern Star, was grand patron in the local chapter in 1891, 1892 and 1893, and on the 30th of September, 1913, at the fourteenth triennial meeting of the General Grand Chapter of the World at Chicago, he was elected most worthy grand patron over a constituency of over seven hundred thousand members, thus receiving the highest office within the gift of that organization in the entire world. He, is a member of the Order of Red Cross of Constantine, to which none but thirty-third degree Masons can belong, and he is a past potentate of El Riad Temple of the Mystic Shrine. He likewise holds membership with the Odd Fellows, the Modern Woodmen of America and the Knights of Pythias, and while in active practice was a member of the Association of Military Surgeons of America, but is not now connected with that organization. His entire life has been an exemplification of the basic principles of brotherhood and mutual helpfulness upon which Masonry is founded, and thus he has reached out along constantly broadening lines of usefulness. He possesses the executive ability necessary for leadership, the social qualities which are equally essential and the high moral purpose without which honors and admiration are never won. He was a member and president of the school board of Sioux Falls for three years and in April, 1913, was reelected for a term of five years.

HARRY ELMER PHELPS

Harry E. Phelps, the present able and popular incumbent of the office of state's attorney of Marshall County, was born in Hillsdale, Mills County, Iowa, on the 23d of June, 1876, and is a son of Phineas and Fanny V. (Fogg) Phelps, the former of whom was born in New Hampshire and the latter in Maine, while the ancestry is of mingled English, Scotch and Welsh strains. When the subject was a child his parents removed to Minneapolis, Minnesota, and in the public schools of that fair city he received his early educational training, being graduated in the South high school in June, 1895, after which he was matriculated in the law department of the University of Minnesota, in the same city, completing the prescribed technical course and being graduated on the 2d of June, 1898, with the degree of Bachelor of Laws, and being duly admitted to the bar of the state. He initiated the active work of his profession in Minneapolis, where he was engaged in practice one year, at the expiration of which, in March, 1900, he came to Britton, South Dakota, where he has since won recognition and distinctive prestige in his profession, while he has proved a very discriminating and capable public prosecutor, having been elected state's attorney of Marshall County in November, 1902.

In politics he accords an uncompromising allegiance to the Republican party and is an active worker in its behalf in the various campaigns. Fraternally he is identified with the local lodges of the Ancient Free and Accepted Masons and the Independent Order of Odd Fellows. On the 13th of June, 1901, was solemnized the marriage of Mr. Phelps to Miss Vivian E. Furber, who was born in Owatonna, Minnesota, on the 31st of January, 1875, being a daughter of Charles M. Furber, of Britton, South Dakota.

JOHN A. PHELPS

John A. PHELPS, one of the interested principals in the Plartford Milling Company, at Hartford, Minnehaha County, is a native of the state of Minnesota, having been born in Shelton, Houston County, on the 1st of February, 1863, a son of John and Julia (Lyon) Phelps. The father died in 1899, and the mother is living at Richville, Washington. The subject attended the public schools of his native town until he had completed a course in the high school, and at the age of eighteen years he identified himself with the milling business there, working in various mills in Minnesota and gaining a thorough knowledge of the business in all its details. In 1886 he came to Madison, South Dakota, and there held the position of head miller in the Madison roller mills until April, 1902, when he came to Hartford and associated himself with Duncan A. McGillidray in the erection of the finely equipped roller-process mill which is now operated by them under the title of the Hartford Milling Company, our subject having the supervision of the operation of the mill, which is one of the best in this section, having a capacity for the output of one hundred barrels of flour per day. while the various brands manufactured, have gained a high reputation, so that the business of the company is constantly increasing in scope and importance. Mr. Phelps is a stanch advocate of the principles and policies of the Republican party, in whose cause he takes an active interest, though he has never desired the honors or emoluments of public office.

Fraternally he is affiliated with Hartford Lodge, Free and Accepted Masons, at Hartford, and with the chapter, Royal Arch Masons, at Madison, South Dakota. On the 25th of August, 1887, was solemnized the marriage of Mr. Phelps to Miss Elva Berry, of Money Creek, Minnesota, and she was summoned into eternal rest on the 25th of October, 1892, being survived by her only child. Hazel May, who was born on the 16th of March, 1891.

JAMES PHILIP

JAMES PHILIP

The history of South Dakota is still in the making, but there are those who wrote its early chapters whose names deserve to be honored and their memory perpetuated throughout all the years to come while this commonwealth endures. They are those who penetrated into the frontier regions, met the hardships, difficulties and privations of pioneer life and aided in planting the seeds of civilization which are now coming into rich fruition. Among this number was James Philip, usually known as Scotty Philip. There was a time when almost every stockman, from the owner of large herds down to the humblest cowboy of the northwest, knew him, and he went through every experience of life on the plains from the period of early settlement here to the present age of advanced civilization. At all times his efforts and his influence counted for progress and the capability and resourcefulness which he manifested in business brought to him substantial success.

Mr. Philip was born in Morayshire, Scotland, in March, 1858, a son of George and Catherine Philip. The father was a farmer, living at Auchness, Dallas, Morayshire, and it was upon the home farm that James Philip spent his youth and received the initial training that enabled him to become a successful agriculturist and stock-raiser in later life. He acquired his education in the common schools of his native village of Dallas and in 1875, when seventeen years of age, he came to the United States, wishing to enjoy the benefits and opportunities offered by the great and growing western country. He made his way to Wyoming and to western Nebraska and, going to Cheyenne, in the former state, there entered upon an engagement to act as cattle herder. After a year he went to the Black Hills, where he spent a winter among the pioneer prospectors and miners, meeting the usual difficulties and hardships of life in the mining camps. Subsequently he returned to Fort Laramie, Wyoming, where he secured employment as a teamster in the government service, being thus engaged until 1877. He next went to Fort Robinson, where he became an army scout, acting in that capacity during the Indian troubles of that period. In the meantime, he had been employed as a cowboy with the first cattle outfit that utilized the range on Running Water, remaining there until the fall of 1878-9. Subsequently he freighted with a bull team from Chadron, Nebraska, to the Black Hills and from Fort Pierre to Deadwood over the old Black Hills trail, being thus engaged until 1882. About that time, he located on Bad River, near where the town of Philip now stands, and turned his attention to the cattle business, in which he was always afterward extensively engaged until the time of his death on the 23d of July, 1911. In 1896 he effected the organization of the Minnesota & Dakota Cattle Company, with headquarters at Fort Pierre, and was made general manager, so continuing until January, 1900, when he disposed of his interests. He afterward engaged in cattle raising on his own account and the business was conducted most successfully. He was widely recognized as one of the leading stockmen of the northwest. The Capital Journal of July 24, 1911, said of him:

"He was known from Mexico to Canada and in all the stock yards of the country as Scotty Philip. His herds of cattle at times numbered many thousands and no roundup from the Black Hills to the Missouri river for more than a quarter of a century was complete without the presence of this cattle king, and at every shipping season his business was eagerly sought by the railroad companies. Mr. Philip a few years ago purchased the famous Du Pree buffalo herd and by an act of congress he fenced in about twenty thousand acres of land on the Missouri river above Fort Pierre, where this famous herd is kept."

150

The buffaloes on the Philip ranch now number about four hundred and twenty-five and are valued at two hundred and fifty dollars each, although the hide with the head attached frequently sells at from six to eight hundred dollars, while specimens of the head mounted bring all the way up to five hundred dollars.

Mr. Philip was not alone deeply and extensively interested in the stock business, for after the building of railroads west of the Missouri river he became unusually active in support of the commercial and industrial development of that section and cooperated in every movement for the upbuilding of the business interests of Fort Pierre. For many years he made his home in that city and was interested in everything of a financial nature throughout the entire community. He was not only associated with the Minnesota & Dakota Cattle Company but was for many years a director in the Stock Growers Bank at Fort Pierre, in the Missouri River Transportation Company and various similar concerns. He had extensive landed interests in Stanley County as well as many business investments and he was among the leaders of his section of the state who believed in the efficacy of irrigation as the means of developing central and western South Dakota. He had the confidence of thousands of business men as well as plainsmen and nowhere that he went was he without friends and acquaintances. Physically he was a man large of stature and in any gathering of people he was a conspicuous and prominent figure.

Aside from business connections for profit or for the benefit of the town Mr. Philip was active in public affairs and was chairman of the first board of county commissioners in Stanley County following its organization in 1890. Nine years later he was elected a member of the state senate from the district comprising Stanley and Lyman counties, but his ambition was not in the line of office holding and, while he did not hesitate to support the principles in which he believed, he was willing that others should fill the offices. He ever voted with the democratic party and did all in his power to further its interests and promote its success.

In 1879, at Pine Ridge Agency, South Dakota, Mr. Philip was married to Sarah Larvie, daughter of Joseph Larvie, who was a French-Canadian voyageur and came to what afterward was the territory of Dakota in the employ of the Hudson's Bay Fur Company. Her mother was a Cheyenne Indian, who was afterward with the Sioux and became adopted as one of them. Ten children were born unto Mr. and Mrs. Philip, five of whom are living: Olive, now the wife of Hugh M. Schultz, of Fort Pierre, South Dakota; and Hazel, Clara, Stanley and Roderick, all of whom live at Fort Pierre, as does his widow. Their home is on the Buffalo ranch, about six miles north of the city, and they are widely and favorably known in this section of the state. Aside from his immediate family Mr. Philip had but one relative in South Dakota, this being George Philip, a well-known attorney of Fort Pierre.

Mr. Philip was a prominent Mason, holding membership in the various branches of that fraternity. He attained the Knight Templar degree of the York Rite, the thirty-second degree of the Scottish Rite and was a member of El Riad Temple of the Mystic Shrine at Sioux Falls. He became a charter member of Capital City Commandery, K. T. In the gallery of the Historical Society in the state capitol at Pierre hangs an oil painting of Scotty Philip. The above record of an eventful, useful, and busy life will in a degree perpetuate his memory, which is enshrined in the hearts of all who knew him. He was one of the typical pioneers of the northwest — resolute, determined and purposeful — meeting uncomplainingly the hardships of frontier life and contributing in substantial measure to the work of general improvement and development, so that his name is inseparably interwoven with the history of the northwest.

HON. KIRK GUNBY PHILLIPS

Hon. Kirk Gunby Phillips, deceased, was one of the pioneer settlers of the Black Hills and took an active and helpful part in promoting its substantial development and improvement, so that his history has become an integral chapter in the record of that section of the state. A native of Maryland, he was born in Wicomico County, November 25, 1851, a son of Levin and Mary (Gunby) Phillips, who were also natives of Maryland. The mother died in the year 1857 and the father survived until 1863. He was an extensive landowner and farmer and to his business interests devoted his entire attention, never caring for public office. He was twice married and by the first union had one child, while five were born of the second marriage.

Kirk G. Phillips was the third child and at the place of his nativity in Maryland he attended the public schools. He went alone to Montana in 1867, when a youth of but sixteen years, traveling overland from Omaha and settling near Helena, where he engaged in mining on his own account and in the employ of others. In 1876 he removed to Deadwood, journeying by stage to Ogden, thence by rail to Sidney and on by stage to the Black Hills, where he arrived in 1876. Establishing his home in Deadwood, he engaged in the drug business for a short time, after which he obtained a contract for building the Boulder ditch. When he had completed the contract, he again engaged in the drug business, in which he continued throughout the remainder of his life, being one of the well-known, enterprising and representative merchants of his city. About 1900 he extended the scope of his activities to include the sale of mining and milling supplies. His business was conducted along both retail and wholesale lines and a liberal patronage was accorded him. He was also a large stockholder and director of the mine known as Wasp No. 2 and was connected with various other mining projects and enterprises. He was also a landowner and had considerable city realty. His investments were judiciously made and success attended his intelligently directed efforts and crowned his industry and determination with prosperity.

On the 30th of June, 1887, Mr. Phillips was united in marriage to Miss Annie I. Cooper, who was born near Morristown, New Jersey. In 1913 she was called upon to mourn the loss of her husband, who passed away on the 7th of August of that year. Since his death she has continued the drug business as before and also managed the other interests and investments left her.

Mr. Phillips was well known in Masonic circles, holding membership in Deadwood Lodge, No. 7, F. & A. M.; Royal Arch Chapter; Dakota Commandry, No. I, K. T.; Deadwood Consistory, S. P. R. S.; and Naja Temple of the Mystic Shrine. He was also connected with the Benevolent Protective Order of Elks and the Ancient Order of United Workmen and in religious faith was an Episcopalian. Mr. Phillips gave his political allegiance to the republican party, being one of its most stalwart supporters, and on several occasions, he was called to public office. He was the first mayor of Deadwood after the granting of the city charter and filled that position for two years. He was also county treasurer for six years and then higher honors were conferred upon him in his election to the office of state treasurer, in which he served for four years. Mr. Phillips entered upon the duties of this office under the most trying circumstances. The treasury had been swept clean by his predecessor and warrants were selling at ninety cents on the dollar. Within thirty days, so strong was his personal credit and the faith the moneyed men had in him, he raised three hundred and twenty-five thousand dollars and sent the money changers and usurers flying to their holes. His subsequent administration of the financial affairs of the state was a source of pride to every citizen. He immediately made good a loss of twenty-five thousand, five hundred and forty-five dollars of the state funds sustained by the failure of the Dakota National Bank of Sioux Falls, borrowing the money at a high rate of interest on his own personal security. And two months later, when Governor Lee demanded that the state's money be brought to Pierre in actual cash for the legislature to count, Mr. Phillips complied and at a heavy personal expense expressed to Pierre every dollar of the state's cash. In 1898 he was his party's candidate for governor but the fever heat of populism was yet too hot in the laud and he was defeated by the small majority of three hundred and eighty-five votes. Probably no state ever elected a governor by so small a majority. Realizing his strength, the whole force of the campaign by the opposition had been waged against him. His opinions long carried weight in the councils of his party and none questioned his devotion to the best interests of the state. Nature qualified him for leadership. He never regarded lightly the duties and obligations which devolved upon him but on the contrary did full justice to every task of a public or private nature and was ever working toward higher ideals in manhood and in citizenship.

MAJOR JOHN A. PICKLER

MAJ. JOHN A. PICKLER   MRS. ALICE M. A. PICKLER

Major J. A. PICKLER, is a native of Washington County, Indiana, where he was born on the 24th of January, 1844, being a son of George and Emily (Martin) Pickler, the former of whom was born in Indiana and the latter in Kentucky, while both families early settled in the Hoosier state, in the pioneer epoch. The father of the subject was for many years engaged in agricultural pursuits, finally removing to Davis County, Iowa, where he engaged in merchandising, as did he later in Kirkville, Missouri, where both he and his wife passed the closing years of their earnest and useful lives. Major Pickler passed his boyhood days on the old Indiana homestead and secured his preliminary educational discipline in the district schools, after which he completed a course of study in the high school at Bloomfield, Iowa, where his parents had taken up their abode. He was later matriculated in the Iowa State University, where he was graduated as a member of the class of 1870, with the degree of Bachelor of Philosophy. Shortly afterwards he entered the law department of the celebrated University of Michigan, at Ann Arbor, where he completed the prescribed course and was graduated in 1872, receiving the degree of Bachelor of Laws. Alter thus fortifying himself for the work of his exacting profession he engaged in the practice of law in Kirksville, Missouri, whence, in 1875, he removed to Muscatine, Iowa, where he entered into a professional alliance as a member of the law firm of Hoffman, Pickler & Brown, which held high prestige at the bar of the Hawkeye state, and he continued to be thus associated until coming to South Dakota, in

153

1882, since which year he has retained his home in Faulk County. He possesses one of the largest and best selected libraries in the state.

Prompted by intrinsic loyalty and patriotism. Major Pickler early offered his services in defense of the Union when "grim-visaged war reared its horrid front." In 1862 he enlisted in Company D, Third Iowa Volunteer Cavalry, in which he became a non-commissioned officer. During his period of service with this command he was granted a furlough of thirty days in order that he might attend, in Philadelphia, a military training school for applicants for command in colored troops. He was later examined, in the city of St. Louis, and passed for captaincy, and there rejoining his regiment to await developments. He continued in active service with the Third Iowa Cavalry until 1864, when he veteranized and rejoined the same company and regiment, being promoted to second lieutenant, first lieutenant and finally captain of Company D, in the meanwhile having declined to be mustered in as captain in the One Hundred and Twenty-second Regiment in the United States Colored Infantry. Upon being mustered out of the Third Cavalry he was made major of the One Hundred and Thirty-eighth Regiment of United States Colored Infantry, at the age of twenty-one years, and commanded this regiment for several months at Atlanta, Georgia. This regiment was mustered out in January, 1866, and Major Tickler then received his honorable discharge. He participated in a number of the notable engagements of the great internecine conflict and made an enviable record as a faithful and valiant soldier and able commanding officer. He retains a deep interest in his did comrades in arms and is an honored member of the Grand Army of the Republic.

In September, 1882, Major Tickler came from Iowa by railroad to Mitchell, South Dakota, and thence by stage to Huron, at which point he joined a party of gentlemen who were going to the center of Faulk County to locate a town, which they hoped to make the county seat. The party proceeded by rail to Miller, Hand County, where the subject and others of the company procured lumber for claim shanties, the material being loaded with other lumber belonging to others of the party and designed for the construction of a hotel in the new town. In the procession that finally proceeded northward over the untrampled prairies there were thirteen wagons, each being well loaded. For eight miles out of Miller they followed a somewhat beaten track, but thereafter proceeded across the prairies without a trail, placing lath on various high points as they traveled, in order that they might find their way back by the same route. On sun fall of the second day they arrived on the present site of Faulkton, locating that town on the south back of the Nixon River. The next day Major Pickler settled upon a preemption claim adjoining the town, and his pleasant home is located on this property, a considerable portion of which is now platted into town lots. He was active in assisting in the organization and development of Faulk County, being one of the pioneers of this part of the state, and one of the most prominent members of the bar of this section.

In politics he has ever given an uncompromising allegiance to the Republican party and has long been known as one of its leaders in the state. He served as state's attorney of Adair County, Missouri, and while engaged in practice in Iowa was a Garfield elector from the second district of that state. He served as a member of the legislature of Iowa, and in 1885 was elected to the territorial legislature of South Dakota. By his old colonel of the Third Iowa Cavalry, General John W. Noble, secretary of the interior under President Harrison, he was appointed an inspector in the public-land service, in which capacity he served until his election to congress in 1889. Upon the admission of South Dakota to the Union Major Pickler was elected at large as one of the first members of congress from the state, the fifty-first congress. He was reelected at large to the fifty-second, fifty-third and fifty-fourth congresses, and thus was a representative of his state in the lower house of the federal legislature for four successive congresses, within which he accomplished much for the furtherance of the best interests of South Dakota. He served as a member of the committees of public land, Indian affairs, invalid pensions, irrigation of arid lands, alcoholic-liquor traffic and that of claims. He was chairman of the committee on invalid pensions in the fifty-fourth congress. He was not a candidate for re-election to the fifty-fifth congress, but was a candidate for nomination for the United States senate. He received the Republican legislative caucus nomination and the unanimous vote of the caucus for more than thirty days, but the Republicans were lacking five votes of a majority and as it was deemed improbable that a Republican could be elected, the representatives of the party, with one exception, voted for Hon. James H. Kyle to succeed himself as senator, and he was duly elected. The senate succeeding President McKinley's first election was known to be very equally divided between the Republicans and the opposition, and the national Republican committee was very desirous, and so expressed itself to Major Pickler, that in case it became apparent that a Republican could not be elected, the Republican strength in South Dakota he thrown to a man who would, if necessary, vote for the tariff and financial policies of the Republican party. In accordance with this expressed desire of the national leaders, and after protracted support by the caucus, Major Pickler advised the change of vote from himself to Senator Kyle, who could be relied upon to support the measures desired.

The Major is identified with the Ancient Free and Accepted Masons, the Knights of Pythias and the Ancient Order of United Workmen. He and his wife are prominent and valued members of the Methodist Episcopal church in their home city. On the 16th of November, 1870, was solemnized the marriage of Major Pickler to Miss Alice M. Alt, who was born in Johnson County, Iowa, in 1848, being a daughter of Joseph A. Alt, one of the sterling pioneers of that state. They have four children. Lulu A., Madge E., Alfred A. and Dale Alice.

JOSEPH E. PILCHER

Joseph E. Pilcher, proprietor of the largest drug house in Custer, was born in Racine, Ohio, on August 18, 1851. He attended the public schools of his native county until about sixteen years of age, when he went to Indiana, and for some time thereafter worked on a farm in Jefferson County, that state, later taking a commercial course in an Indianapolis business college. In 1878 Mr. Pilcher went to Colorado, where he entered the employ of the Santa Fe Railroad Company, which was then constructing one of its lines through that country, and after working there for some time he assisted in building branches of the same system in New Mexico and Arizona, remaining with the company in different capacities until 1880. In the latter year he made a business trip to Europe, returning in the fall of 1881, and immediately thereafter came to the Black Hills, locating at Deadwood, where he engaged in the hotel business, conducting the same until the spring of 1883, when he disposed of his interests in that place and changed his abode to Custer City. After devoting his attention for the greater part of a year to mica and gold mining, Mr. Pilcher, in the spring of 1884, accepted a position with the Adams Express Company, being appointed to a local agency in Nebraska, but later he was promoted traveling auditor of the company, and in that capacity visited various parts of New Mexico, and other western states and territories, discharging his duties in an able and business-like manner until his resignation, in August, 1886. After severing his connection with the above company, Mr. Pilcher returned to Custer City and, entering politics, was elected the same year register of deeds for Custer County, which position he held until 1891, proving an exceedingly efficient and popular official; meanwhile, in the fall of 1890, he was appointed assistant secretary of the state senate, in which capacity he served two terms, and in 1893 was sent to Chicago in charge of the Black Hills mineral exhibit at the World's Fair. Returning to Custer City, he resumed mining in various parts of the Hills, but not meeting with the results anticipated, he discontinued that line of work three years later and purchased a drug store, to which business he has since devoted his attention, building up a large and lucrative patronage.

Mr. Pilcher is still interested in mining and owns considerable mineral property in the Black Hills, some of which is quite valuable and from which he reasonably hopes to realize a fortune. As an authority in all matters relating to the mining industry, he is frequently consulted by experts and others, and in 1898 he had charge of the large mineral exhibit of the Black Hills at Omaha. He has devoted much study to mining in all of its phases, has made many valuable researches and original investigations, being a scientific assayer, as well as a graduate of the School of Mines at Rapid City, one of the most thorough institutions of the kind in the world. Mr. Pilcher is a Republican in politics, and for a number of years has been an active party worker and an influential factor in the public affairs of his city and county. He is now second vice-president of the Black Hills Mining Men's Association, and he is also interested in various other local enterprises for the promotion of the material welfare of his adopted state.

Fraternally he is a Mason, in which order he has held various official positions, and he also holds membership with the Modern Brotherhood of America and the Knights of Pythias. Mr. Pilcher, on April 10, 1886, entered the marriage, relation with Miss Jennie Thornby, of New York, and is now the father of two sons, Rufus T. and Warren T. Pilcher.

CHARLES FRANKLIN PIERCE

C. F. Pierce, superintendent of the Riggs Institute, at Flandreau, Moody County, was born in the town of Ware, Hampshire County, Massachusetts, on the 17th of January, 1858, and secured his early educational training in the public schools of his native state and at times assisted his father in the machine shops. In 1873 he accompanied his parents on their removal to Nebraska, and they settled on a farm near Creighton, Knox County, where his father took up government land and became numbered among the pioneers of that section. In 1876 the subject taught his first term of school and with money earned by teaching during the winter terms he was enabled to continue his own educational discipline, entering Boone Seminary, at Boone, Nebraska, where he prosecuted his studies for two years, after which he was engaged in teaching in the public schools of that state for several years. In 1887 Mr. Pierce entered the Indian school service as a teacher at the Santee Agency, Nebraska, where he soon received a promotion to superintendent of the school. In 1892 he was transferred to Oneida, Wisconsin, where he was detailed to erect buildings and organize a school among the Oneida Indians. In 1895 he was again promoted, being made disbursing officer at that place, while in 1900 he was transferred to his present important office as superintendent of the Riggs Institute at Flandreau.

Mr. Pierce is a Republican, and has been frequently a delegate to county and state conventions in the different states in which he has resided. In 1884 he was elected superintendent of schools for Knox County, Nebraska, and thereafter he became editor and publisher of the Transcript, at Creighton, that county. He is a member of the Masonic fraternity, the order of the Eastern Star, the Knights of the Maccabees, and Ancient Order of United Workmen. His religious faith is that of the Methodist Episcopal church. Mr. Pierce was married to Miss Laura A. Jasmer and they have had five children.

Isaac Piles is a retired merchant of Yankton and president of the Yankton Gas Company. His name long stood as a synonym for business integrity and enterprise in the city in which he resides, for his energy and determination made him ready to meet any emergency and his laudable ambition, guided by honorable principles, carried him forward to success. Every state in the Union has contributed to the citizenship of South Dakota, and Isaac Piles is among those whom Ohio has given to the northwest. He was born in Noble County, on the 15th of January, 1848. He represents an old family of Maryland, his father, James Piles, and his grandfather, Nathaniel Piles, having both been born in that state. James Piles devoted his life to various business pursuits, engaging in farming, merchandising and hotel keeping, continuing active in business up to the time of his death, which occurred in 1855. His mother, Margaret (English) Piles — with her family of ten children — then removed to the middle west, settling in Pottawattamie County, Iowa, where her eldest son, William H. Piles, had entered a large tract of land in 1855.

Isaac Piles was a lad of eight summers when the family arrived in Iowa. He was the youngest in a family of ten children, of whom three are yet living, and largely reared in Iowa, he attended the public schools of Council Bluffs and when his school days were over secured a clerkship in a general store, being afterward employed in a similar capacity in a shoe store. Previous to this time he had had other interesting experiences, for in his fifteenth year he crossed the plains to Denver and the mining country, driving a team both to and from Colorado. The year 1873 witnessed his arrival in Yankton and, believing this a good field for commercial activity, he opened a shoe store. Time proved the wisdom of his opinion, for as the years passed his trade grew and his business returned to him a gratifying income. For thirty-eight years he was thus actively connected with commercial interests in Yankton, retiring from business in 1911, with a competency, which he had acquired entirely through his close application and able management. He was one of those who reorganized the Yankton Gas Company, of which he has since been the president and is one of the directors.

On the 21st of September, 1873, Mr. Piles was joined in marriage to Miss Florence A. King, a daughter of Robert and Mary Ellen (Gier) King, of Pittsburgh, Pennsylvania. Robert King was a soldier in the Civil war and lost his life on the battlefield. Mr. and Mrs. Piles now have an attractive home in Yankton and its good cheer and hospitality have been greatly enjoyed by their many friends. Close application and strict integrity in the conduct of his business affairs were important factors in his continued success, but in more recent years, when there have been periods of recreation, Mr. Piles has spent some time in fishing and in travel, both of which are sources of delight to him. He votes with the democratic party, while not a politician in the usually accepted sense of the term. He has served for two terms as a member of the city council, exercising his official prerogatives in support of various movements for the public good.

In Masonry Mr. Piles has attained high rank, belonging to St. John's Lodge, No. I, A. F. & A. M.; Yankton Chapter, No. I, R. A. M.; De Molay Commandery, No. 3, K. T.; Oriental Consistory, No. I, in which he has taken the thirty-second degree; and the K. C. C. H. He is now a past eminent commander of the commandery and has held various other offices in the organization, and in his life exemplifies the beneficent spirit of the craft. For many years he has belonged to the Independent Order of Odd Fellows, and likewise has membership with the Elks. He served for some years as president of the Commercial Club and made it an effective organization for improving conditions along business and civic lines in Yankton. He is widely known as one of the honored pioneer merchants of southeastern Dakota and one of its most highly esteemed citizens.

JAMES ERNEST PLATT

James E. PLATT, cashier of the Security Bank of Clark, was born in Decatur, New York, on the nth of March, 1866, and is a son of Rev. James Nelson Piatt and Laura (Sibley) Piatt, both of whom were likewise born in the old Empire state. The father of the subject, who is now president of the Security Bank of Clark, which was organized in 1888, came to South Dakota in 1884, having been for twenty years previously a member of the Upper Iowa Methodist Episcopal conference. The subject of this sketch was graduated in the high school at Manchester, Iowa, as a member of the class of 1881, under Superintendent C. D. Clark, now United States senator from Wyoming. Thereafter he continued his studies in Cornell College, at Mount Vernon, Iowa: The Upper Iowa University, at Fayette; and in 1884 he was graduated in Epworth Seminary, at Epworth, Iowa, having taken a three-years classical course. During his vacations in his early youth, he worked on various farms, but early manifested a desire to secure a position in a bank. After his graduation, when seventeen years of age, he came to Clark, South Dakota, in 1884, and secured a clerical position in the banking establishment of D. Wayne & Company, who later disposed of their interests in the line to G. C. Griffin, who organized the bank of Clark, Mr. Piatt remaining with the new institution about a year, at the expiration of which he engaged in the real-estate and loan business in partnership with his father, and in September, 1888, they organized the Security Bank of Clark, of which he has since been cashier, showing distinctive ability in the handling of the affairs of the institution, which is one of the solid and popular banking concerns of the state. He has large real-estate holdings in the town and county; is treasurer of the Fraternity Gold Mining and Milling Company, operating in the Black Hills, with headquarters at Hill City, and he has been treasurer of the Clark Co-Operative Creamery Company since its organization, in 1898. He was elected cashier of the Security Bank when but twenty years of age, and has been prominently concerned in banking in Clark for a full score of years. In politics Mr. Piatt is a stalwart Republican, taking an active interest in forwarding the party cause and having been a delegate to nearly all the state conventions of his party since the admission of South Dakota to the Union. He was for five years incumbent of the dual office of clerk and treasurer of the city of Clark, and for two years gave effective service as its mayor, his administration being marked by a progressive and business-like policy. In 1902 he was appointed major and paymaster of the South Dakota National Guard, his commission to extend over a period of five years. In 1895 he was elected treasurer of the state board of agriculture, of which office he has since remained in tenure.

Fraternally he is identified with Clark Lodge, No. 42, Ancient Free and Accepted Masons, of which he is past worshipful master and present secretary; Olivet Chapter, No. 14, Royal Arch Masons; Watertown Commandery, No. 7, Knights Templar; Aberdeen Consistory, Ancient Accepted Scottish Rite, in which he attained to the thirty-second degree in January, 1902; El Riad Temple, Ancient Arabic Order of the Nobles of the Mystic Shrine, at Sioux Falls; Huron Lodge, No. 144, Benevolent and Protective Order of Elks; El Kim Ran Temple, Dramatic Order of the Knights of Khorassan, at Watertown; and Myrtle Lodge, No. 43, Knights of Pythias, at Clark. In 1899-1900 he was grand chancellor of the state grand lodge of the last-mentioned order, and in 1903 he was elected supreme representative of the order for South Dakota, being a delegate to the general assembly of the same in Louisville, Kentucky, in August, 1904. On the 19th of June, in the First Methodist Episcopal church of the city of Chicago, was solemnized the marriage of Mr. Piatt to Miss Katharine A. Boyle, formerly of Jamestown, North Dakota, but a teacher in the public schools of Clark for a few years prior to her marriage.

J. T. Potter, of Keystone, is a native of Boston, Massachusetts, where he was born on September 14, 1847. He is the son of William E. and Elizabeth (Lewis) Potter, the former also a native of Boston, and the latter of historic Plymouth, in the same state. They were descendants of old colonial families, active and prominent in the early history of New England, the members of which bore their parts creditably in the affairs of that section in peace and war. The father's American ancestors came to this country and settled at Concord, Massachusetts, in 1635 and the mothers to Plymouth in 1630. The paternal great-grandfather was a soldier in the Revolution, participating in the siege of Boston and many other important engagements, and in subsequent wars members of both families have served their country with efficiency and manly courage. Both families have maintained their homes in Massachusetts from the time of their first arrival on American soil. Mr. Potter's father was a bookkeeper and accountant in Boston, and there the son grew to the age of twenty years and was educated for mercantile life. In 1877 he came west to Earlville, Iowa, and during the next two years was engaged in merchandising there. In 1879 he returned to Boston and entered the service of a large wholesale house, first in the establishment and later as traveling salesman. In 1880 he came to Fort Meade to take a position in the post trader's store, and he remained there employed in the store until the post tradership was abolished in 1883, when he came to Sturgis and opened a dry-goods and gents' furnishing store of his own. The town had then only a village organization, and soon after his arrival there he was elected chairman of the board of trustees. When the place was incorporated as a city, he became its first mayor. In the fall of 1890, he was elected to the state senate on the Republican ticket, thus becoming a member of the second state legislative assembly. In the ensuing sessions of the body, he demonstrated that he had legislative capacity of a high order, shrewdness in the management of public business and a wide knowledge of the needs of the state and his section in particular. He has always been prominent in public and social affairs at Sturgis, and is recognized on all sides as one of the leading and most useful citizens of the community. He has long been active in Freemasonry, and while living at Fort Meade organized a Masonic lodge at Sturgis, which he served four years and a half as its worshipful master. He was successful in trade at Sturgis and conducted a large business. In 1891 he sold out and went to Chicago, where he secured employment with Carson, Pirie, Scott & Company, wholesale dry-goods merchants, with whom he remained until 1901. He then returned to this state and locating at Keystone, taking charge of the Keystone Trading Company as manager. This company was formed by the consolidation of the Bee Hive, owned by J. C. Haines, and the Stone-Finney Company's store, which had been doing business at Keystone for a number of years. By the consolidation and necessary enlargement of the stock the Keystone Trading Company became the largest general merchandising establishment in this part of the Hills. It is incorporated, with J. O. Haines, of Rapid City, as president and Mr. Potter as secretary, treasurer and manager, the latter being also one of the principal stockholders. He is enterprising and progressive, makes a study of the needs of his trade and is diligent in providing for them, and always enforces the upmost integrity and fair dealing on the part of his employes toward his patrons.

In fraternal relations he is an enthusiastic Freemason, belonging to lodge, chapter, council and commandery in the fraternity, and taking a leading part in the work of each. On September 5, 1865, Mr. Potter was married at Boston, Massachusetts, to Miss Fannie F. Trott, a native of that city. By virtue of his ancestry and through his own desire Mr. Potter is an honored member of the Sons of the Revolution at Boston, Massachusetts.

CHARLES E. PRENTIS

CHARLES E. PRENTIS

C. E. Prentis, one of the pioneer merchants of South Dakota, actively identified with the business interests of Vermillion, was born September 30, 1847, in Dane County, Wisconsin, a son of John and Catherine P. (Williams) Prentis, who were natives of Massachusetts and Vermont respectively and descendants of early New England families. The father was a farmer by occupation and about 1830 made the overland trip to Wisconsin, where he engaged in general agricultural pursuits until his death.

C. E. Prentis attended the public schools of his native county to the age of eighteen years and then went east to Poughkeepsie, New York, where he pursued a course in Eastman's Commercial College. Later he returned to Madison, Wisconsin, where he secured a position as bookkeeper, acting in that capacity for about one and a half years. Consideration of the opportunities offered in the west led him to the belief that he would find it profitable to try his fortune in Dakota and in company with a friend and associate, A. E. Lee, he determined to engage in general merchandising at Vermillion. It was about the middle of the year 1869 that Mr. Lee reached that place and selected a site in what is now known as the bottoms. A small building was erected and a few months later Mr. Prentis removed to Vermillion, arriving in September, 1869. Both then went to Chicago, where they purchased a stock of general merchandise and the firm of Lee & Prentis was thus formed and launched into business. From the beginning their enterprise prospered, reliable business methods, unfaltering energy and perseverance winning for them a growing trade. Later a two-story brick building was erected, which they occupied until 1881, the year of the big flood. The little village grew apace and with the increase in its population their trade became larger and larger, for straightforward business methods commended them to public support. With the growth of Vermillion, the business center of the city was removed from the bottoms to the present site of the town and in 1881 Lee & Prentis erected their present building, in which they have continued successfully to the present time. Their house is not only widely known throughout Clay County but also over the greater part of South Dakota and is the largest establishment of its kind in the county. Moreover, in point of continuous existence theirs is the oldest business house in North or South Dakota and has become one of the most important. It meant much in pioneer times when trade facilities were few in their section of the state and it has ever kept abreast with modern progress.

Mr. Prentis, however, has not confined his activities to merchandising alone. He recognized the future value of farm lands throughout the west and began making investments, being at one time the owner of over seven thousand acres in Clay County. In 1914, when prices had greatly advanced, he sold practically all his holdings in Clay County, although he still has property in other sections of the state. He and his partner, Mr. Lee, own and operate a fine ranch of sixteen thousand acres in Nebraska and Mr. Prentis is a stockholder in and vice president of the Citizens Bank & Trust Company of Vermillion.

On the 7th of November, 1872, Mr. Prentis was united in marriage to Miss Mary F. Stanley, who died September 14, 1906, leaving a daughter, Kathryn, the wife of Robert Howe Munger, of Sioux City. On the 2d of September, 1909, Mr. Prentis wedded Mrs. Belle (Stanley) Bell, a sister of his first wife.

In his political views Mr. Prentis has long been a stalwart republican and has filled a number of local offices, to which he has been called by the vote of his fellow townsmen, serving at the present time as mayor of Vermillion. He also became the first charter member of the Congregational church, in the work of which he has ever taken an active and helpful interest. He is likewise a member and vice president of the Vermillion Commercial Club and he is a Mason, belonging to the blue lodge, chapter and commandery of Vermillion, and to El Riad Temple of the Mystic Shrine at Sioux Falls. He is a lover of outdoor life and enjoys traveling. In nature he is quiet and unassuming but is most kind hearted and public spirited. His business life has not been void of the trials and tribulations that constitute the struggle of pioneer days and many residents of this part of the state are grateful for the credit and favors extended them in the period of financial depression caused by the grasshopper scourge and other incidents of pioneer life. The record of Mr. Prentis is a most creditable one. There have been no esoteric chapters in his life history but a manifestation of indefatigable industry and unswerving integrity in all his business dealings.

WALTHALL WOOLDRIDGE PRICE, D. D. S.

Dr. Walthall Wooldridge Price, the pioneer dentist of Centerville, where he has been engaged in practice continuously since the spring of 1898, is well known in professional circles throughout the state. His birth occurred at Dillons Mills, Virginia, on the 3d of December, 1871, his parents being Ferdinand and Lucinda Catherine Price, both of whom have passed away. The paternal grandfather of our subject held the rank of major in the Revolutionary army under Lafayette, and the famous general called on him when visiting the United States in 1824. Ferdinand Price, who was an agriculturist by occupation, served as a lieutenant in the Confederate army during the Civil War.

Walthall W. Price acquired his early education in an old log schoolhouse in the south and later spent a year in an academy. Subsequently he followed the profession of teaching for a few years and then entered the Baltimore College of Dental Surgery, from which institution he was graduated in 1897. He first practiced in Virginia for a year and in the spring of 1898 removed to Centerville, South Dakota, opening his office on the 11th of March.

He was then the only representative of the profession in the town and has there remained continuously since, his practice growing with the population of the district. His ability has won him enviable recognition among the representatives of the dental fraternity throughout the state and he is a popular member of the South Dakota State Dental Association, attending all of its meetings and having served as its secretary and treasurer He has invested largely in real estate and is now the owner of considerable property.

On the 16th of May, 1900, Dr. Price was united in marriage to Miss Elia Newsome, of North Carolina, by whom he has two children, Virginia Carolina and Mary Kathryn. He gives his political allegiance to the democratic party and has ably served his fellow townsmen in the capacity of alderman. Fraternally he is identified with the Masons and the Ancient Order of United Workmen, while his religious faith is that of the Baptist church. He is a man of easy dignity, frank and cordial in address and possessing that confidence and courage which rightly come from conscious personal ability, a correct conception of things and a habitual regard for what is best in the exercise of human activities.

ORVILLE U. PRYCE

Orville U. PRYCE, of Deadwood, where he holds the position of manager of the Deadwood-Colorado Investment Company, is a native of the Badger state, having been born in Albany, Green County, Wisconsin, on the 9th of January, 1867, and being a son of Evan and Sarah Pryce, both of whom were born in Newtown, Wales, being representatives of old and honored families. They are now residing at Boulder, Colorado. The subject received his preliminary educational training in the public schools and thereafter continued his studies in the seminary at Evansville, Wisconsin, and the Northwestern Business College, in Madison, that state, in which institution he completed a thorough commercial course. In 1890 he came to South Dakota and secured a position as bookkeeper and stenographer in the Citizens National Bank at Madison, Lake County, retaining this incumbency until 1901. In 1895 he went to Cripple Creek, Colorado, and remained about three years in that state, where he devoted his attention to mining, becoming interested in the development of good properties. He then returned to South Dakota and resumed his residence in the Black Hills district, where he had been located for some time prior to going to Colorado, and here he is now one of the successful and representative mining brokers and operators of the district.

In politics he gives his allegiance to the Republican party, and fraternally is affiliated with Deadwood Lodge, No. 7, Ancient Free and Accepted Masons, and Deadwood Lodge. No. 51, Ancient Order of United Workmen. On the 19th of June, 1902, Mr. Pryce was united in marriage to Miss Maryella Ellis, who was born in the city of Utica, New York, on the 18th of September, 1870, being a daughter of David and Elizabeth Ellis.

CYRUS C. PUCKETT

Cyrus C. Puckett is one of the representative men of Tyndall, South Dakota, where he is engaged in the practice of law and is also editor of an up-to-date and reliable weekly newspaper. His great-grandfather, Daniel Puckett, was a Quaker, who, hating slavery, removed from South Carolina to southeastern Indiana about 1800. His son, the grandfather of our subject, was Cyrus Puckett, who married Bettie Thomas, and they became the parents of Cyrus J. Puckett, who was born in Fountain County, Indiana, December 26, 1840. In 1848 the last named was taken by his parents from Indiana to Jo Daviess County, Illinois, the trip being made by team, as there were then no railroads in that part of the country. Although he was but eight years old at the time, he remembers a deer which was running about the yard of the hotel in Chicago at which they stopped, and he also remembers that a guest of the hotel placed him upon the deer's back and that the deer allowed him to ride there. An uncle of C. J. Puckett, Levi Coffin by name, kept one of the stations of the underground railway in Indiana, thus helping many escaping slaves to reach Canada and freedom. It was he who gave shelter to the original of the character of Eliza in Mrs. Stowe's "Uncle Tom's Cabin." The young woman in question actually made her escape across the Ohio river much as described in the famous novel and Mr. Coffin assisted her on her way north.

Cyrus J. Puckett married Elizabeth Deetz, a daughter of William and Mary (Kleese) Deetz and a native of Sullivan County, Pennsylvania. The Deetz family was early established in this country and all of its men proved their patriotism by active participation in the war of the Revolution. C. J. Puckett removed from Jo Daviess County, Illinois, to Hutchinson County, South Dakota, in 1884, buying three hundred and twenty acres of land situated two miles north of Scotland. He at once became recognized as a leader in progressive farming in the state and was the first to demonstrate that corn could be profitably grown here. He also set out the first orchard in the region and sowed the first meadow of timothy and clover. He was likewise interested in educational advancement and was one of the founders of Scotland Academy, serving also as trustee of the institution. In 1901 he took up his abode in Vermillion and there still makes his home. C. J. Puckett was twice married and by his first wife had three sons, namely: Frank, a banker of Hosmer, South Dakota; Walter, an agriculturist of Roundup, Montana; and Willard, who follows farming at Stillwater, North Dakota. To Mr. Puckett and his second wife were born two sons: Cyrus C, of this review; and Owen, a civil engineer of Edmonton, Alberta, Canada.

Cyrus C. Puckett was born in Jo Daviess County, Illinois, January 25, 1882, and was but two years of age when brought by his parents to Hutchinson County, this state. He received his elementary education in the common schools of the neighborhood and was later for two years a student in Scotland Academy and for one year in Warren Academy, Jo Daviess County, Illinois. His collegiate and professional work was done at the State University of South Dakota, located at Vermillion, where he studied for four years, being graduated with the Bachelor of Arts degree in 1905. While still a student in the university he spent the summers from 1903 to 1905 on a claim in Edmunds County, South Dakota, thus securing valuable experience and making enough money to partially pay his college expenses. After 1905 he entered the postal service at Vermillion and was identified there-with until 1909. He took up the study of law after 1907 and received the LL. B. degree upon the completion of his course in 1910. Upon his admission to the bar in that year he opened an office in Tyndall, where he has since been building up a growing law practice. In 1911 he formed a partnership with Dr. Klima and W. W. French in purchasing the Tyndall Tribune, which paper they have since published together. Mr. Puckett has charge of the editorial work, Dr. Klima the operating department and Mr. French the business management of the paper. It is a well edited and well conducted country weekly, giving to its subscribers not only a full account of local happenings but also keeping them informed as to the great events occurring in the world at large. Its editorials are potent forces in promoting many worthy enterprises and always seek the advancement of Bon Homme County and the state of South Dakota. As it has a wide circulation and is recognized as one of the best advertising mediums of the county, it is accorded a liberal patronage by local merchants.

Mr. Puckett is a republican in politics and his religious allegiance is given to the Congregational church. Fraternally he belongs to the Masonic order, being a member and master of Tyndall Lodge, A. F. & A. M., and likewise a member of the chapter at Vermillion. He also belongs to the well-known college fraternity, Beta Theta Pi. He recalls the fearful blizzard which occurred January 12, 1888. He and his mother and two brothers were at home and were not exposed to danger, but a girl living with the family, who was at school, was obliged to remain there throughout the night, as it would have been tempting death to endeavor to return home. The stock was left unfed that night, as it was altogether unsafe to go out into the storm even to the barn. Mr. Puckett has proved himself worthy of his pioneer ancestors, and as a lawyer and editor is doing much to further the welfare of his county and state.

R

EDWIN T. RAMSEY, M. D.

Dr. Edwin T. Ramsey is one of the most widely known and successful physicians of Clark County and is thoroughly progressive and up-to-date in all matters pertaining to his profession. He was born in London, Ontario, on the 29th of April, 1877, a son of Edwin and Isabella (Henderson) Ramsey. The father was a native of Hull, England, and the mother of County Durham, that country. The former went to Canada with his parents as a child and the latter emigrated to the Dominion as a young woman. They were married in London, Ontario, where Mr. Ramsey, Sr., was for many years prominently identified with contracting and building. He died in 1912, having for almost a quarter of a century survived his wife, who passed away in 1888.

Dr. Edwin T. Ramsey was reared under the parental roof and attended the public schools of London, Ontario, in the acquirement of his early education. He completed his high-school work in 1896 and then began his professional study, entering the medical department of the Western University of London, from which he was graduated with the class of 1900. He spent a short time in practice in Loomis, Nebraska, and then came to South Dakota in the fall of 1901, locating in Clark, where he has since remained. He is one of the foremost practitioners of northeastern South Dakota and his position of leadership in his profession is due to a large extent to his constant study. For some years past he has spent a month or more in Chicago or Philadelphia every fall, attending the clinics of those medical centers and familiarizing himself with the most approved methods of procedure and the latest discoveries in the field of medical science. He is a member of the Watertown District Medical Society, of which he was the first president; and also holds membership in the Sioux Valley Medical Society; the South Dakota State Medical Society, of which he served as president in 1905; and the American Medical Association. For the past eight years he has been superintendent of the county board of health and for the same length of time has been county coroner. His practice is large and representative, and he has the unqualified respect of his colleagues, who often call him in consultation.

Dr. Ramsey was married in 1910 to Miss Harriett Bennett, of Clark, who is a daughter of Eugene and Emma L. Bennett and a granddaughter of Judge John Bennett, one of the first supreme court judges of South Dakota. Her father is deceased, having been buried on New Year's Day, 1906, but her mother is still living and continues to make her home in Clark.

The Doctor gives his political support to the men and measures of the republican party. Fraternally he belongs to Clark Lodge, No. 46, A. F. & A. M., of which he is now worthy master, and is also connected with Olivet Chapter, No. 28, R. A. M., at Clark, of which he is high priest; Watertown Commandery, No. 7, K. T.; Aberdeen Consistory, No. 4, A. & A. S. R.; and Yelduz Temple, A. A. O. N. M. S., of Aberdeen. Dr. Ramsey is as highly esteemed as a man and citizen as he is as a physician and surgeon and his many admirable qualities have gained him a host of warm personal friends.

W. Norman Rapalee is proprietor of an extensive and growing marble and monument business at Yankton, which he established in 1908 and has since successfully conducted. He is a product of the northwest and possesses the enterprising spirit that has ever dominated this section of the country. His birth occurred in Bon Homme County, South Dakota, October 15, 1878. His father, Daniel W. Rapalee, a native of the state of New York, served as a soldier in the Union army, enlisting when but fourteen years of age as a member of the Eighty-fourth Illinois Volunteer Infantry, with which he was connected for about two years. In 1874 he arrived in Dakota territory, establishing his home in Bon Homme County, where he became owner of a farm, having four hundred and eighty acres, which he homesteaded and preempted. Not a furrow had been turned nor an improvement made upon his place at the time when the land came into his possession, but with resolute spirit he undertook the task of transforming the prairie into productive fields and for twenty years successfully devoted his attention to general agricultural pursuits. In 1894, however, he retired from farming and entered the marble and monument business, later settling in Sioux City, where he still makes his home. His wife, who bore the maiden name of Fannie Crenshaw Prior, is now deceased.

After mastering the elementary branches of learning taught in the district school near the old home farm upon which he was reared, W. Norman Rapalee became a student in the Tyndall high school, from which he was graduated with the class of 1897. Later he pursued a business course in Sioux City and his practical training along business lines was received under the direction of his father, whom he assisted in the monument and marble business. After acquainting himself with the trade through actual experience in the work of marble cutting, he went upon the road, representing the business as a traveling salesman, and thus he gained further valuable knowledge and experience. In 1908 he came to Yankton, where he embarked in a similar business on his own account, and such has been the growth of the undertaking that he is now at the head of the largest enterprise of the kind in the state. His patronage covers a wide territory and the excellence and attractiveness of the output insures a continued and gratifying patronage.

On the 17th of August, 1910, Mr. Rapalee was married to Miss Jennie M. Scace, a daughter of Frank and Lillian M. (Buser) Scace, of Primghar, Iowa. Mrs. Rapalee is a graduate of the Cedar Falls Normal College and for a short time was a teacher in the Yankton schools. By her marriage she has become the mother of one child, Norma Olivette. Mr. and Mrs. Rapalee attend the Congregational church and he belongs to several fraternal organizations, including the Masonic, Odd Fellows and Elks lodges. He votes independently when casting a ballot at local elections, but when national issues are involved supports the principles of the republican party. He is a member of the Commercial Club and is in hearty sympathy with the purposes of that organization. He enjoys hunting and motoring, but never allows recreation to interfere with the performance of his business duties. His success is due to fair dealing and close application, and he ranks today among the most prominent of the city's younger generation of business men.

ALFRED E. RAYNES

Alfred E. Raynes is the editor and proprietor of the Gazette, published at Andover, and is one of the well-known and popular newspaper men of Day County. He was born in Greenwich, England, January 28, 1856, and his parents, John G. and Sarah (Newman) Raynes, were also natives of that country. They brought their family to America when their son Alfred was two years of age, the family home being established near Fond du Lac, Wisconsin, whence a removal was afterward made to Danville, Dodge County. It was there that Alfred E. Raynes learned the printer's trade in the office of the Columbus Republican and still later he was employed on various dailies in Chicago. He became identified with newspaper publication in the Dakota territory when in 1884 he purchased the Andover Gazette, which he has since conducted with growing and gratifying success. He has kept in touch with the trend of progress along journalistic lines, publishes a neat and attractive sheet and in the dissemination of local and general news meets the wishes of his readers and has thereby gained a liberal patronage. He is also the owner of one hundred and sixty acres of land near Andover.

Aside from his activity in business he has done much to further public progress. He was the first president of the board of trustees following the incorporation of the town of Andover and he has likewise filled the position of postmaster. A stalwart republican, he has been chairman of the county republican central committee and for a long time was secretary. During President Harrison's administration he was a member of the republican state central committee and was by him appointed postmaster. No movement relating to the welfare of the community fails to elicit his interest and when his judgment sanctions a plan, he gives to it hearty cooperation.

In June, 1885, Mr. Raynes was united in marriage to Miss Bessie S. Swan, a native of Canada and a daughter of William and Tressa Swan. To them have been born five children, two sons and three daughters, as follows: Marjorie, the wife of Glenn Hoffman, who operates a fruit ranch in the state of Washington; Rex, who is a student in a dental college of Denver, Colorado; Harry, a registered pharmacist residing in Aberdeen; Marie, a high school graduate who is now engaged in teaching; and Kathleen, who is attending school.

Mr. Raynes belongs to the Ancient Order of United Workmen and to the Masonic fraternity and the Eastern Star and erected the first story of the Masonic Hall, which was finished by the Masons. His is a well-rounded development, manifest in active interest in all those things which have to do with the life of a community, and in personal connections as well as in editorial avenues he has contributed much to public progress.

Harvey J. Rice, receiver of the United States land office at Huron, and grand secretary of the Odd Fellows in South Dakota, was born at Freeport, Illinois, April 23, 1849, the son of John and Milvira (Williams) Rice. In his childhood his parents removed to Nauvoo, where Harvey attended the common schools, and later graduated from the University of Carlinsville, in 1865. It was at this time his intention to become a lawyer and to that end he became a student in the law office of George Scoville, in Chicago, but developing taste along commercial lines he took the business course in the Bryant & Stratton College of Chicago and in 1869, in company with his brother John, engaged in the dry goods business in Chicago, in which he continued until the fire in 1871. Soon after they engaged in general merchandise at Austin, Illinois, disposing of the same in 1875 to enter the employ of the Chicago & Northwestern Railway. Wilen the Dakota divisions were under construction he was made storekeeper in charge of all material and in that capacity came to Dakota and established company headquarters in Huron in 1880. He continued with the railway company until 1887, when he resigned to become teller in the Huron National Bank and continued in this position until appointed railway commissioner for Dakota territory by Governor Mellette in the spring of 1889. This position he held through two terms, until March, 1893, when he engaged in the mercantile business in Huron, which he still conducts. In 1884 he was elected mayor of Huron and re-elected for five terms. In 1902 he was appointed receiver of the land office and continues in the position. He is an ardent Republican and is one of the party's safest councilors.

Mr. Rice is a thirty-second-degree Mason, a Knight Templar, and is a past grand master of the order in the state. He is also a prominent Odd Fellow and for four years represented the state in the sovereign grand lodge. He has been the grand secretary of the order for the past ten years. Mr. Rice was married, December 25, 1873, to Miss Elizabeth Kimes. Two sons have been born to them, John A., who was drowned in the James River at Huron, and George H., who is engaged in business in Huron. South Dakota has no more competent, reliable, and useful citizen than Harvey J. Rice.

J. A. RICKERT

J. A. RICKERT, a financier of more than local reputation, is a native of Trumbull County, Ohio, and the oldest in a family of twelve children, whose father and mother were of German and Irish descent respectively. Mr. Rickert was born September 21, 1852, and four years later, with his parents, emigrated to Olmsted County, Minnesota, where he grew to manhood on a farm, meanwhile receiving his preliminary education in the district schools of that county. In 1871 he entered St. Vincent's College, Wheeling, West Virginia, where he pursued his studies for two years, meanwhile attending night school at the Bryant & Stratton Business College, of that city, completing the full commercial course at that institution. For the six years following Mr. Rickert was engaged as clerk, timekeeper and bookkeeper, in Wheeling, West Virginia, and in towns in Minnesota. In 1879 he came to South Dakota and took up a homestead in Grant County, near Milbank. In 1881 he disposed of his claim and with the proceeds engaged in the general merchandise business two years later at Corona, this state, where he carried on a very successful business during the ensuing sixteen years, all of which time he served as postmaster of the town, besides holding various township and municipal offices.

In 1896 Mr. Rickert was elected treasurer of Roberts County, and upon taking charge of the office moved to Wilmot, where he resided until the seat of justice was changed to Sisseton, when he took up his abode at the latter place and has since made it his home. He was re-elected in 1898 and served both terms in an able and satisfactory manner, proving a painstaking, obliging and popular public servant. During his last term he built an elevator at Sisseton and engaged in the grain business, and about the same time associated himself with H. S. Morris and Howard Babcock and organized the First National Bank of Sisseton, becoming president of the institution, which position he still holds. Still later he became one of the organizers, stockholders and officers of three new banks, known as the Citizens' State Bank of White Rock, the First State Bank of Summit, and the Roberts County State Bank, of Corona, and is a stockholder in the Sisseton Loan and Title Company and the Roberts County Land and Loan Company. Mr. Rickert owns a fine business property at Corona and a nice residence in Sisseton. He has charge and the management of the extensive farm properties of the Sisseton Loan and Title Company, of which they own about thirty farms in Roberts and neighboring counties. Mr. Rickert was married in December, 1882, the union being blessed with one child, a son, Paul M., who is now pursuing his studies in Pillsbury Academy at Owatonna, Minnesota.

Mr. Rickert is a Mason and a member of the Ancient Order of United Workmen. In politics he has always been an enthusiastic Republican. The distinction which he has achieved in financial and business circles has given him considerable reputation, and as a public-spirited citizen he is deeply interested in all that tends to the material development and general prosperity of his city, county and state.

GEORGE H. RICHARDS, M. D.

Dr. George H. Richards, engaged in the practice of medicine and surgery at Clear Lake, was born on the 29th of April, 1879, at Melbourne, Ontario, Canada, his parents being Wilson and Emma Richards, the former a farmer by occupation. Both are still living.

In the public schools of his native country Dr. George H. Richards pursued his early education and afterward attended the Collegiate Institute of London, Ontario, from which he was graduated with the class of 1900. He pursued his professional course in Trinity University, the medical department of which was amalgamated with Toronto University during Dr. Richards' work there and immediately after completing his course in 1904 he entered upon the practice of medicine. He spent two years as an interne in a hospital and then took up the private practice of medicine at Wessington Springs, South Dakota, where he remained for two years. At the end of that time, he secured a claim at Underwood, Pennington County, where he practiced for two years and then removed to Chamberlain, where he remained for a year and a half. In 1912 he took up his residence in Clear Lake, purchased property and is now permanently located there. He has been accorded a liberal share of the public patronage along the line of his profession and is well known as a capable physician and surgeon. He reads broadly, keeping in touch with the trend of modern thought and action in the line of his profession, and is a member of the Watertown District Medical Society, the South Dakota State Medical Society and the American Medical Association.

On the 29th of April, 1908, Dr. Richards was united in marriage to Miss Florence Moulton, a daughter of David and Nellie Moulton, representatives of old-time families of South Dakota, and they have one son, George, who was born November 19, 1913. Mrs. Richards is of the Catholic faith.

Fraternally Dr. Richards is a Mason, belonging to Phoenix Lodge, No. 129, A. F. & A. M., of Clear Lake, and he also has membership with the Modern Woodmen of America. His political allegiance is given to the republican party and he is a public-spirited citizen, devoted to every movement that tends to promote the substantial upbuilding of the community. He enjoys spending a leisure hour in fishing or in his motor car, but his professional duties are his first interest and are ever performed with a conscientious recognition of the obligations that devolve upon him in that connection.

ZINA RICHEY

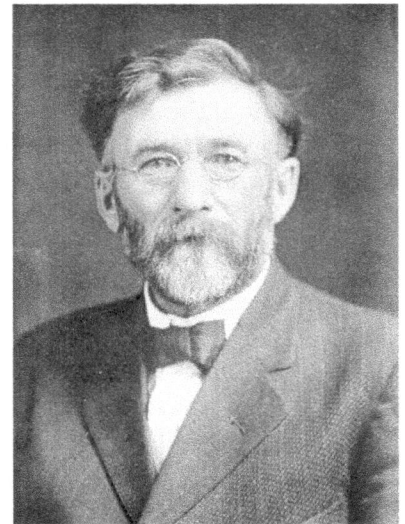

Zina Richey is proprietor of one of the leading hardware establishments of Yankton, having throughout a long period been identified with the business interests of the city. He is a native of Orleans County, New York, born February 25, 1849. His father, John Richey, a native of Belfast, Ireland, came to America when a young man and engaged in farming in the Empire state. He was married there to Miss Mary Sturgis, who was also born in New York, and they became the parents of five children as follows: Zina, of this review; Sarah, who became the wife of William H, Cady, of Ponca, Nebraska; William H., who died May 16, 1914, in Orleans County, New York; John W., who also died in Orleans County on Christmas day of 1910; and Nora, who departed this life in 1881. The father passed away in Ponca, Nebraska, when he had reached the ripe old age of eighty-five years, and the mother died a few years previously.

Zina Richey was reared on the homestead farm, assisting his father in the work of the fields during the spring and summer months, while in the winter season he pursued his studies in the common schools to the age of fifteen years. After putting aside his text-books he continued on the farm one year and subsequently became an apprentice to the tinsmith's trade, being thus engaged for three years. He then followed his trade as a journeyman until 1870, when he decided to make a permanent location in Yankton, South Dakota. In that year he found employment with the well-known firm of Wynn, Buckwalter & Company, with whom he remained three years, and then opened a hardware establishment of his own on Third street, near Broadway. Soon thereafter he admitted J. H. Dix to a partnership and business was conducted under the firm style of Richey & Dix for about three years, when the partnership was dissolved and Mr. Richey continued in business alone during the subsequent two years. At the end of that period, he admitted E. C. Dudley to a partnership and for two years business was conducted under the firm name of Dudley & Richey. D. M. Gross then became a member of the firm, which assumed the title of Dudley, Richey & Gross. Business was so conducted for three years, when Mr. Dudley retired and the name was then changed to Richey & Gross. Mr. Gross died in 1889 and his son then assumed the father's interest, the business being carried on under the same style until 1891, at which date Mr. Richey disposed of his interest to D. D. Gross and was not engaged in any business for a few months. He then again embarked in the hardware business and has continued to the present time. His long experience has given him a thorough understanding of the trade and his is today one of the leading concerns of its kind in the city. He carries a large and well selected line of shelf and heavy hardware and has a liberal patronage which he well merits, owing to his honorable dealing and enterprising methods.

Although Mr. Richey gives strict attention to business, he yet finds time to cooperate in all movements and measures for the good of the city, taking an active part in matters of public moment. He has always given his political support to the republican party and was a member of the first board of charities and corrections of South Dakota and during territorial days was a member of the board of trustees of the Territorial Hospital for the Insane. He was also for two or three years a member of the board of aldermen of Yankton and since 1898 has served as justice of the peace. He has always discharged his official duties in the same capable manner that he conducts his private affairs, so that he fully merits the confidence of his constituents. He is very prominent in fraternal circles as a member of Dakota Lodge, No. I, I. O. O. F., in which he has occupied all the chairs. He has likewise filled all the offices in the Grand Lodge of the state and is past grand master of the Grand Lodge of South Dakota. He was a member of the committee appointed to organize this lodge, was a member of its first session and has been a member of every session of that body since its inception. He is also a member of Yankton Encampment, No. 2, I. O. O. F., in which he has filled all the chairs, and is past grand patriarch of the Grand Encampment of South Dakota. He was for eight years a member of the Sovereign Grand Lodge of Odd Fellows and is a past grand representative. He is perhaps the best known and most able exponent of Odd fellowship in the state. Mr. Richey is equally prominent in Masonic circles, being a member of St. John Lodge, No. I, A. F. & A. M., and Oriental Consistory, No. I, at Yankton. He also holds membership with the Ancient Order of United Workmen.

It was on the 24th of February, 1874, that Mr. Richey was united in marriage to Miss Ernie E. Russell, a native of Trumbull County, Ohio, who presides with gracious hospitality over their pleasant home. Mr. Richey has long been connected with the business interests of his city and has lived a life such as to give him high standing in the eyes of his community. He is generally recognized as a man whose long years of earnest labor in Yankton have not only contributed to his own prosperity but have also influenced general growth and advancement.

HON. AMUND O. RINGSRUD

The name of Hon. Amund O. Ringsrud is written large on the pages of South Dakota's history because of his prominent and helpful connection with public offices and his activity in the field of commerce, which constitutes the basis of the material development and greatness of the state. While he is now widely known as the proprietor of an establishment conducted under the name of the Ringsrud Mercantile Company at Elk Point, he is equally widely known as having had the honor of serving as the first secretary of state of South Dakota.

He was born in Norway on the 13th of September, 1854, a son of Ole O. and Karen (Amundson) Ringsrud, who came to the United States in 1867. They were among the first residents of Union County, Dakota, and the work of development, improvement and civilization seemed scarcely begun in that district. Much of the land was still in possession of the government and Ole O. Ringsrud homesteaded a quarter section of land in Brule township, on which he lived to the time of his death in 1876, devoting his energies to the cultivation and improvement of his farm. His widow survived him for thirty-eight years and passed away at the advanced age of ninety-one years. She was born November 17, 1822, and death called her on the 2d of April, 1914.

Amund O. Ringsrud was a little lad in his thirteenth year at the time the family made the long voyage across the Atlantic to the new world. For a brief period after the establishment of the home in South Dakota he attended public school and then worked upon his father's farm until he reached his sixteenth year. He then received his initial training along mercantile lines in a clerkship in a general store at Elk Point. He spent eight and a half years in that way, gaining broad, practical experience, which constituted the foundation for his present success in mercantile lines. After that period spent in a clerkship, however, he became an active factor in political circles and the recognition of his worth and ability on the part of his fellow citizens led to his election to the office of registrar of deeds of Union County in 1878. Reelection continued him in the position for three terms, or six years, and he retired from office as he had entered it — with the confidence and goodwill of all concerned. When his third term as registrar had expired, he was elected county treasurer of Union County and continued as the custodian of the public funds through two terms, or for a period of four years. Still higher political honors awaited him, however, for in 1889 he was elected secretary of state of South Dakota, having the honor of being the first man chosen to that position in the newly organized commonwealth. As in the positions which he had previously held, he discharged his duties with such promptness, faithfulness and capability that he was reelected and remained for two terms as one of the state officers.

In the meantime, Mr. Ringsrud had become actively and prominently identified with the business life of Elk Point, having established a mercantile enterprise in 1885, which he incorporated under the name of the Ringsrud Mercantile Company in 1896. In that year he was candidate on the republican ticket for governor of South Dakota but in the election met defeat when Bryan and free silver swept the state, the party losing in the election the congressman, the governor and the presidential electors. He now represents his county as a committeeman of the republican party and is still deeply interested in the political situation of the country, although not seeking office at the present time. He now devotes the greater part of his energies to the conduct of his growing commercial interests and is today at the head of one of the most important mercantile establishments of his part of the state. He carries a very large and carefully selected line of goods and is thus ready to meet the varied wants and needs of a diverse patronage. His store is attractive in its arrangements, his prices are reasonable and in the conduct of his business he displays unfaltering energy and progressiveness. He is also a member of the board of directors of the Union County Bank.

In 1876 Mr. Ringsrud was married to Miss Emma F. Snyder, of New Hampton, Iowa, and to them have been born two daughters and a son: Grace Ellen, now the wife of F. W. Ford, of Elk Point; Stella May, at home; and Alfred H., who is engaged in the automobile business in Elk Point. Mr. Ringsrud is a leader in Masonic circles, holding membership in Elk Point Lodge, No. 3, F. & A. M.; Vermillion Chapter, No. 21, R. A. M.; De Molay Commandery, K. T., of Yankton; Oriental Consistory, No. I, A. & A. S. R. of Yankton; and El Riad Temple A. A. O. N. M. S., of Sioux Falls. He is now president of the Elk Point Commercial Club and displays in marked measure the spirit of initiative in promoting and fostering the interests whereby the club is doing such splendid work in advancing the commercial connections of the city and in furthering all interests which are a matter of civic virtue and civic pride. From early manhood

Mr. Ringsrud has been a leading figure in South Dakota and is widely known throughout the state as one whose record is of signal usefulness and honor.

G. C. REDFIELD, D. O.

Dr. G. C. Redfield is one of the younger members of the medical profession of Rapid City, but has already built up an enviable reputation for ability and conscientiousness. He was born in Canton, South Dakota, on the 29th of February, 1880, and was the third in order of birth in a family of four children whose parents were Leonard L. and Margaret (Scarborough) Redfield. The father, who was a native of Pennsylvania, became a pioneer settler and farmer of Lincoln County, South Dakota, but he and his wife are now living in Denver, Colorado.

Dr. Redfield entered the public schools of Canton at the usual age and after finishing the course offered therein entered the Augustana College, also of Canton, and subsequently matriculated in the State University of South Dakota, where he pursued a three-year course. After leaving that institution he entered the American School of Osteopathy at Kirksville, Missouri, from which he was graduated with honors in the class of 1900. He first located for practice at Wabash, Indiana, where he remained for two years, after which he removed to Parker, South Dakota, which remained his home for seven years. In 1909 he arrived in Rapid City and in the seven years that have since intervened he has met with unusual success. Professionally he has a high standing among his colleagues and has gained the confidence of the general public with the result that his practice has grown steadily and rapidly.

On the 9th of February, 1903, Dr. Redfield was united in marriage with Miss May Walrod, a daughter of Charles M. and Dora (Murphy) Walrod, of Le Mars, Iowa. The Doctor takes an active part in state politics and is one of the leaders in the republican party. He is now serving as a member of the state board of charities and corrections under appointment by Governor Byrne. During the years 1911 and 1912 he was on the Rapid City board of commissioners. He gives to his public duties the same close application and energy that he does to his private affairs and has proved a very capable official. Fraternally he is connected with the Masonic order and has held all of the chairs in the blue lodge and chapter. He is also a member of the Knights of Pythias and the Elks. While in college he was quite prominent in athletics and was captain of the first team that represented the State University of South Dakota in inter-collegiate football. He was also on his college baseball team. He still retains a love for sports and outdoor life and finds his chief recreation in hunting and fishing. His professional success is founded upon a thorough knowledge of the principles of osteopathy and skill in their application and upon a personality that gives his patients confidence that he will do all in his power to effect a cure. He has a high conception of a doctor's duties and privileges and no one is more scrupulous in the observance of the strictest code of professional ethics. Although he gives most of his time to the practice of his profession, he realizes that every citizen has civic duties the performance of which cannot be delegated to anyone else, and is always ready to aid in securing the advancement and progress of his community.

EUGENE REILEY

One of the representative and able citizens of Sioux Falls and one of the most popular men in public life who ever held office in Minnehaha County is Eugene Reiley, who on December 31, 1914, ended the second term of his efficient and conscientious service in the office of sheriff. He was born in Burlington, Iowa, February 11, 1864, and is a son of Michael and Sarah N. (Ingraham) Reiley. The grandfather, Deocis D. Reiley, came to America from Scotland in 1848 and in 1849 went overland with ox teams to California, where he was murdered for his gold.

Eugene Reiley acquired his education in the public schools of Burlington and in Elliott's Business College in that city. At the age of seventeen he entered a wholesale shoe house and remained in this connection until 1888, when he came to Sioux Falls. Here he established himself in the retail shoe business, conducting this enterprise until 1895. Two years later he was appointed deputy circuit court clerk and served two years, after which he was appointed clerk to fill a vacancy caused by a resignation. Upon the close of his term, he engaged in the real-estate business until 1907, when he was made deputy sheriff of Minnehaha County, serving in that position for four years. In 1910 he was elected sheriff by a majority of fourteen hundred and nineteen, taking the office January 1, 1911, and so remarkable a record did he make that at the expiration of his term he was reelected to that position. This is the more noteworthy from the fact that Mr. Reiley ran on the democratic ticket in a county which normally showed a republican majority of twenty-five hundred.

On the 16th of June, 1885, at Brighton, Iowa, Mr. Reiley was united in marriage to Miss Molly Swisher, a daughter of Benedict Swisher, and they have become the parents of six children: Ethel Fern, the wife of P. I. Neister; Ruth Eva, who married Ray F. Manary; Michael Eugene; Sarah Eliza; Floyd Benedict; and Florentine Molly.

Mr. Reiley is a member of the Presbyterian church, is a blue lodge Mason and is connected also with the Knights of Pythias and the Elks. He is probably one of the most popular men in public life in Minnehaha County. His election as a democrat in a strong republican county, the first time by a large majority and the second time without opposition, proves this assertion to the fullest extent. He is pronounced by attorneys generally as the most efficient, most courteous and most absolutely impartial sheriff who ever held office and his friends and opponents alike speak in the highest terms of his accomplishments and of the qualities in his character which made them possible. Mr. Reiley is a gentleman at all times and as such holds the trust, confidence and high regard of all who are in any way associated with him.

JACOB P. RESNER

Jacob P. RESNER, cashier of the bank of Scotland, Bon Homme County, was born in Plotzk, South Russia, on the 14th of March. 1863, being a son of Andrew and Anna M. (Lyer) Resner, of whose two children he is the elder, the other being Dr. Andrew K., who is a successful practicing physician at Planning, Iowa. The father of the subject was a native of Wurtemberg, Germany, where he was reared to the life of a farmer, continuing to there devote his attention to this great basic industry until 1877, when he emigrated with his family to the United States, spending a short interval in the state of Iowa and thence coming directly to the territory of Dakota, locating in Hutchinson county, where he entered claim to three quarter sections of land, under the homestead, pre-emption and tree-culture acts, respectively, and here he has ever since continued to make his home, having improved his land and placed it under a high state of cultivation and having thus contributed to the development of the resources of the great state of South Dakota. He has been successful in his labors and is now one of the representative and substantial citizens of Hutchinson County. He is a Republican in politics and has held various local offices of public trust, ever retaining the confidence of his fellow men. His devoted and cherished wife died in the fatherland, in

1869, and he later married Miss Caroline Stortz, and they are the parents of four children, Daniel and John, who reside in Scotland, Bon Homme County: Emanuel, who remains at the parental home; and Mary, who is the wife of L. W. Hoffman, of the village of Scotland.

Jacob P. Resner, to whom this sketch is dedicated, was about eight years of age at the time of his father's emigration from Germany to America, and he received his education in both German and English, having prosecuted his studies in the public schools of South Dakota after the family here took up their abode. That he made good use of the advantages thus accorded is shown in the fact that he was for three years successfully engaged in teaching in the district schools of Hutchinson County prior to his marriage, which occurred in 1885. After his marriage he settled on a quarter section of land in that county, having secured the same as a preemption claim, proving up on the property after attaining his legal majority. He made good improvements on his farm and devoted his attention to its cultivation for four years, at the expiration of which he removed to Scotland, in the adjoining county of Bon Homme, to accept the position of treasurer and manager of the Farmers' Elevator Company. He retained this incumbency two years and then purchased the elevator of the company, continuing its proprietor for the ensuing seven years, when he disposed of the property and became manager of the elevators here owned by the Spencer Grain Company, in important corporation engaged in the handling of grain throughout this section. He remained with this concern three years, during which time he was also individually engaged in the real-estate business, having his office on Main Street in the village of Scotland. He continued in the real-estate business after severing his connection with the company mentioned and also accepted a position as manager of the local interests of Shannerd Brothers, extensive grain buyers of Bridgewater, this state. In August, 1902, Mr. Resner accepted the position of cashier of the Bank of Scotland, one of the solid and popular monetary institutions of this section, and he has since continued to give most discriminating service in this important executive office, gaining to the bank new prestige and handling its affairs with marked ability and to the entire satisfaction of its stockholders. Shannerd Brothers were most reluctant to dispense with his services and finally prevailed upon Mr. Resner to continue in their employ as manager of their interests in this section, and the details of the business he now assigns principally to a deputy, though maintaining a general supervision of all transactions. The political support of the subject is given in an unqualified way to the Republican party, of whose principles he is a stanch advocate, having been prominent in political affairs in a local way for a number of years past. He served four years as a member of the village council and for the past six years has been a valued member of the board of education, while for three years he was incumbent of the office of village assessor and is in tenure of this office at the time of this writing.

His religious faith is that of the German Congregational church, of which both he and his wife are zealous members, and he is prominently identified with the Masonic fraternity, being affiliated with Scotland Lodge, No. 52, Free and Accepted Masons; Scotland Chapter, No. 31, Royal Arch Masons: Yankton Commandery, Knights Templar; and Yankton Consistory, No. I, of the Ancient Accepted Scottish Rite, at Yankton. He also holds membership in Security Lodge, No. 48, Knights of Pythias, and Scotland Camp, No. 977. Modern Woodmen of America. On the 14th of December, 1885, Mr. Resner was united in marriage to Miss Christina Redmann, of Yankton County, whither her parents emigrated from Russia in 1873. Of this union have been born seven children, namely: Edward, William, Julius, Amerlia, Lydia, Bertha and Arthur.

The record of Andy C. Ricketts in public service is well known and is a most creditable one, for capability and fidelity to duty have ever marked his public activities. He is one of the adopted sons of South Dakota, his birth having occurred in Charleston, Coles County, Illinois, September 29, 1875, his parents being Joshua T. and Louisa Anna (Bensley) Ricketts. He attended the schools of Fort Pierre, the family having come to this state during his early boyhood. After his textbooks were put aside, he became actively connected with the meat market and thus received his initial business training. He has held various public offices to which he has been called by his fellow townsmen, who recognize in him the qualities of progressive citizenship. He filled the office of city treasurer, was also chosen city auditor and was elected to represent the first ward in the city council. He has been school treasurer of Fort Pierre and was first elected clerk of the courts of Stanley County in November, 1908, to which office he was reelected in November, 1910, 1912, and 1914. He is discharging the duties devolving upon him with promptness and efficiency. He is also treasurer of the Fort Pierre volunteer fire department. In his political views he is a republican, having supported the party since attaining his majority. He is in thorough sympathy with its principles and purposes and therefore gives to it unwavering allegiance.

On the 9th of November, 1904, Mr. Ricketts was married at Fort Pierre to Miss Mable E. Barkley, daughter of John M. Barkley. They have many warm friends in the city where they reside and their home is a hospitable one, its good cheer being greatly enjoyed by their many friends. Fraternally Mr. Ricketts is connected with Hiram Lodge, No. 123, A. F. & A. M. of Fort Pierre; Pierre Chapter, No. 22, R. A. M., of Pierre and the Elks Lodge, No. 444, of Huron, South Dakota. Almost his entire life has been spent in the northwest and its spirit of enterprise and progress finds an exponent in him.

FRANK H. RIPLEY

Frank H. Ripley, county auditor of Brookings County and one of its native sons, was born June 11, 1881, his parents being Charles S. and Sarah M. (Armstrong) Ripley, who in the year 1878 came to South Dakota from Fond du Lac, Wisconsin. Following his arrival, the father homesteaded the northeast quarter of section 34, Trenton township, Brookings County, and subsequently acquired various other farms, of which he has disposed at different times, now retaining possession of only a half section, which includes the original homestead and a quarter section adjoining it on the east. He figured for an extended period as one of the leading agriculturists of the county but in 1907 retired from active farm work and removed to Aurora, where he has since lived, giving his attention to his real-estate holdings, and he has leisure to enjoy those things which are to him a matter of interest and recreation. In politics he is a republican but, while he has served as a delegate to county and state conventions, he has never been an aspirant for public office. He and his wife hold membership in the Methodist Episcopal church.

Frank H. Ripley was reared upon the old homestead farm, with the usual experiences that fall to the lot of the farm lad upon the frontier. After acquiring his preliminary education in the public schools, he attended the State College at Brookings and when his studies were completed, he taught school through one term — the winter term of 1898-9. He then turned his attention to the grain business at Elkton and Aurora, buying grain for two different firms. In 1909, in company with his brother, Charles A., he embarked in the mercantile business at Aurora, in which he still retains his interest. He was actively associated therewith up to the time when he assumed the duties of his present office on the 1st of March,

1913. It was in November, 1912, that he was elected to the position of county auditor and he was renominated in the spring primary of 1914, being reelected without opposition, a fact which attests strongly his personal popularity and the capability with which he discharges his duties.

On the 23d of January, 1907, Mr. Ripley was united in marriage to Miss Goldie Lombard, of Aurora, also a native of Brookings County. Her father, Colmar D. Lombard, came to Brookings County in 1878 from Chatfield, Minnesota. Both Mr. and Mrs. Ripley are widely and favorably known in this part of the state and the hospitality of the best homes is freely accorded them. Mr. Ripley belongs to Elkton Lodge, No. 57, A. F. & A. M., and to Brookings Chapter, No. 18, R. A. M., and is also a member of the Brookings Commercial Club. He has always resided in the county which has honored him with office and the fact that some of his staunchest friends are those who have known him from his boyhood to the present is an indication of the fact that his has been a well spent life.

AUGUST J. RISKE

August J. Riske is proprietor of a hardware and furniture store at Doland and although he entered upon this connection only in January, 1915, he has already built up a business of large and gratifying proportions which indicates his enterprising spirit and progressive methods. The year 1881 witnessed his arrival in South Dakota, for in the spring of that year he removed from Dodge County, Wisconsin, to this state, which was then under territorial rule. He was born at Duberphal, Prussia, on the 8th of June, 1860, his parents being Frederick and Wilhelmina (Siedschlag) Riske. The father became a pioneer farmer of Wisconsin, in which state both he and his wife passed away, and their remains were interred at Beaver Dam, that state.

At the usual age August J. Riske became a pupil in the public schools of Wisconsin, pursuing his studies through the winter months, while the summer seasons were devoted to work upon the home farm. About the time he attained his majority he left home and came to South Dakota, settling at Arlington, where he embarked in the lumber business. In 1885 he removed to Doland, where he continued in that business for twenty years. Eventually he turned his attention to real-estate dealing, in which he won success. In October, 1913, he went into the general merchandizing business but in January, 1915, he made a change to his present lines, hardware and furniture. He also maintains undertaking parlors in connection with his store. He has erected a very fine business block containing store rooms and offices, the building being fifty by eighty feet. He has otherwise contributed to the material development and progress of Spink County, where he now owns about two thousand acres of land, and he has improved fifteen different farms with suitable buildings. The spirit of enterprise and progress has actuated him throughout his entire life and his energy has enabled him to overcome all the difficulties and obstacles that seemed to bar his path to success.

On the 6th of February, 1889, at Doland, South Dakota, Mr. Riske was united in marriage to Miss Lela Warner, a daughter of Benjamin and Orisa Warner. The father, a pioneer agriculturist of South Dakota, died in April, 1915, and the mother passed away in 1912, their remains being interred in the Doland cemetery. Mr. and Mrs. Riske have three children, namely: Bernice, who gave her hand in marriage to H. G. Skogmo, formerly a grocer of Minneapolis, Minnesota, but now with Mr. Riske at Doland; Orisa, who is a graduate of the Northwestern Conservatory of Music, and is now teaching music at Doland; and Berwyn, who is eight years of age.

Mr. Riske is a blue lodge Mason and also holds membership with the Modern Woodmen of America. In politics he is a stalwart republican and his fellow townsmen, appreciating his worth and ability, have frequently called him to office. He has served as town clerk for fifteen years and has been mayor of the city, to which he gave a businesslike administration. His methods, whether in connection with public or private affairs, have at all times been practical, his enterprise unfaltering and his honor unfailing. To indefatigable industry and close application may be attributed the success which today places him among the men of affluence in Spink County.

JAMES ROANE, M. D.

Dr. James Roane, whose student habits of college days have remained with him in all the years of his practice, making him an able physician, with liberal patronage in Yankton, was born in Washington, D. C, January 28, 1860, a son of Archibald and Ruth (Allen) Roane, the former a prominent attorney of the capital city and a native of Tennessee, and a member of one of the most distinguished old Virginia families, the ancestry having been there established in colonial days.

Dr. Roane had especially good educational advantages and after completing a preparatory course entered the Georgetown University, where he devoted seven years to the mastery of classical branches. He then began the study of medicine in the medical department of the same university and won his professional degree as a member of the class of 1882. Immediately after his graduation he was appointed acting assistant surgeon in the United States army, department of the Rio Grande, with headquarters at Fort Ringgold, Texas, and after filling that position for a year returned to Washington.

In 1883 Dr. Roane arrived in Yankton, where he opened an office and began the practice of medicine, remaining here continuously since save for several years spent in European travel and the pursuit of post-graduate and research work in the famous clinics on the continent and in Great Britain. Study under and investigation of the methods of some of the most eminent practitioners of the old world have greatly augmented his knowledge and promoted his efficiency and today he is recognized in his section of South Dakota as a practitioner of broad learning — capable, resourceful and conscientious in his practice. He is a member of the South Dakota State Medical Association, the Eighth District Medical Association and the American Medical Association. Since his college days he has remained a constant student, keeping in touch with the advanced thought and scientific researches of the day, and he has contributed numerous articles to the leading American medical journals.

In April, 1894, was celebrated the marriage of Dr. Roane and Miss Maude Hayden Bush, a daughter of William C. and Frances Josephine (Hayden) Bush, both of Rochester, New York. In his political views Dr. Roane is a democrat, but, while well versed on the questions land issues of the day, has no political aspirations. He is prominent in Masonry, holding membership in Oriental Consistory, No. I, and El Riad Temple, A. A. O. N. M. S., and in 1914 he was honored by election to the office of senior grand warden, grand lodge A. F. & A. M. of South Dakota. He is also identified with the Elks and he has membership in the Episcopal church. Today, as the result of his laudable ambition, his close application and his earnest study, he is prosperous and prominent both in the profession and socially.

A. C. ROBERTS

A. C. Roberts, one of the prominent citizens of Day County, is a native of the old Buckeye state, having been born in the city of Oberlin, Ohio. When the subject was a child his parents removed to Livingston County, Illinois, where he was reared to maturity, having grown up on a farm and having duly availed himself of the advantages of the public schools, including the completion of a high-school course. After leaving school he devoted two years to the study of law, and was admitted to practice in all of the courts of the state of Illinois, and he has a license to practice in all the courts of South Dakota.

In 1876 Mr. Roberts engaged in the active practice of law in Illinois, continuing to follow the work of his profession for two years, and thereafter being engaged in farming in that state, while he was later engaged in the mercantile business for one year. Later he came to South Dakota and took up land in Homer township, Day County, which he improved and placed under effective cultivation, having one of the valuable landed estates of the county. He continued to be actively and successfully engaged in farming and stock growing until 1900, when he took up his residence in Pierpont. where he has since carried on a prosperous enterprise in the handling of grain, coal and lumber. In politics Mr. Roberts maintains an independent attitude. In 1893 he was a member of the state senate, having been elected on the ticket of the People's party. He and his wife are valued and zealous members of the Presbyterian church in Pierpont, and he is an elder in the same at the present time.

Fraternally he is affiliated with the Masonic order, the Modern Woodmen of America and the Ancient Order of United Workmen. Mr. Roberts was married to Miss Rachel Frances Chambers, who was born in Lowell, Lasalle County, Illinois, and they have three children.

E. D. ROBERTS

Although he is the owner of an excellent farm E. D. Roberts gives the greater part of his time to his work as manager of the Eagle Elevator at Turton. He was born at Hamilton, Butler County, Ohio, October 18, 1862, and is a son of John T. and Ellen (Davis) Roberts. The father was called to his reward in May, 1907, and is buried at Ashton, South Dakota. The mother resides with her sons who are living at Ashton. She has now reached the age of seventy-nine years and is accorded the honor that is due to all who have lived long and useful lives. The parents removed to Spink County, this state, in 1881, settling at Ashton, and our subject came to the state a year later.

E. D. Roberts attended the schools of Illinois in the pursuit of his education but when twenty years of age turned his attention to other interests, taking up a preemption claim in Spink County, South Dakota, which he sold to the Town Site Company of Turton. The town of that name now stands upon the land which he entered from the government. Upon disposing of his agricultural interests, he formed a partnership with Frank Coleman under the style of Coleman & Roberts for the conduct of a general store. After about four years he bought one hundred and sixty acres of land and by unremitting labor was enabled to purchase additional land from time to time, bringing his total acreage up to four hundred and eighty acres. He operated his farm until 1901 but in that year rented it to others and assumed charge of the Eagle Elevator at Turton. He still holds that position and gives the greater part of his time to his work in that connection, although he has accumulated more than a competence and could retire if he were so minded.

Mr. Roberts was married in 1885 at Ashton to Miss Hattie West, a daughter of William B. and Ellen (Esterbrook) West. Her father died June 30, 1914, and was buried in the cemetery in Clifton township, Spink County. Her mother is still living in that township. They came to South Dakota in 1879, settling on the Jim River in Spink County. They performed well the work that fell to their lot as pioneers and had many experiences typical of life on the frontier, such as grinding wheat in a coffee mill in order to secure flour. To Mr. and Mrs. Roberts were born two children: Otto, who died in February, 1888, and was laid to rest in Sunnyside cemetery at Turton; and Bertha, at home. They have adopted another son, Paul, who is also at home.

Mr. Roberts is a republican and has held a number of township offices. As a member of the Congregational church, he takes an active part in the work of that organization and contributes to its support. Fraternally he belongs to the Masonic order and has attained the thirty-second degree in the Scottish Rite. He is also past master of the Conde Lodge and a member of the Eastern Star and he likewise holds membership in the Modern Woodmen of America. His has been a life of constant activity that has resulted in the attainment of individual success and the furthering of community advancement.

WILLIAM PENN ROBERTS, M. D.

Sioux Falls claims a number of capable and eminent representatives of the medical profession and in this class ranks Dr. William Penn Roberts, who since 1905 has here made his home. He was born on a farm in Tazewell County, Illinois, January 23, 1869, his parents being Joseph T. and Mary C. (Bosserman) Roberts. The family is of Welsh lineage, the immigrant ancestor locating in New Jersey, and it was in that state that Robert Roberts, grandfather of Dr. Roberts, was born.

Reared in Illinois, Dr. Roberts attended the country schools and also spent two years in a seminary at Westfield, that state, thus laying the foundation for his professional knowledge. Having determined upon the practice of medicine as a life work, he entered the College of Physicians and Surgeons of Chicago and was graduated therefrom in 1894. He then located for practice in Cleghorn, Iowa, where he remained for eleven years, or until 1905, when he came to Sioux Falls. In the intervening period of ten years, he has made continuous progress along professional lines, keeping in touch with the best thinking men of the age and with the most progressive methods.

On the 25th of December, 1893, in Proctor, Illinois, Dr. Roberts was united in marriage to Miss Ida B. Proctor, a daughter of Captain Willard Proctor, of the One Hundred and Fourth Illinois Volunteer Infantry, who served for four years in the Civil War. Dr. and Mrs. Roberts have a son and a daughter: William Proctor, born May 18, 1901; and Florence Charlotte, born January 23, 1914.

The parents attend the Congregational church and Dr. Roberts is well known as a valued member of the Masonic lodge and the Independent Order of Odd Fellows. His political allegiance is given to the republican party. He served for four years as mayor of Cleghorn, Iowa, and was also a member of the school board there. He is interested in all that pertains to the public welfare and his cooperation can be counted upon to further any movement for the general good. Those who know him esteem him highly for his personal qualities, and he has gained many friends during his residence in South Dakota.

DAVID ROBERTSON

David Robertson, an able member of the bar of the state, who has served several terms as a representative of Spink County in the state legislature, comes of stanch Scottish lineage and inherits the sterling characteristics of the canny Scotchman — sterling integrity, marked pragmatic ability and tenacity of purpose, with strong mentality and mature judgment. He is a native of the state of Wisconsin, having been born in Rock County, on the 21st of August, 1855, and being a son of Peter and Helen Robertson, both of whom were born and reared in Scotland, the father having been a native of Glasgow and the mother of Edinburgh. They were married in their native land and shortly afterward, in 1854, immigrated to the United States and settled on a farm in Rock County, Wisconsin, where they remained until 1863, when they removed to Freeborn County, Minnesota, becoming pioneers of that section, where the father improved a good farm, and there both passed the remainder of their lives, secure in the respect and esteem of all who knew them. Of their five children all are yet living. They were consistent members of the Baptist church, and in politics Mr. Robertson espoused the cause of the Republican party.

David Robertson, the immediate subject of this sketch, completed the curriculum of the public schools at Mitchell, Iowa, and was reared to the sturdy discipline of the home farm. In 1881 he was matriculated in Carleton College, in Northfield, Minnesota, where he completed the scientific course and was graduated as a member of the class of 1885, with the degree of Bachelor of Science. He had in the meanwhile been reading law, and after his graduation continued his technical studies in the office of Hon. Calvin L. Brown, of Morris, Minnesota, this able preceptor being now one of the associate justices of the supreme court of that state. Mr. Robertson read law under the direction of Judge Brown for one year, and was then admitted to the bar of Minnesota, in July, 1886. In January of the following year, he came to South Dakota and took up his residence in Conde, where he engaged in the practice of his profession, and in the real-estate business, in which he has since continued. In politics he is a stanch advocate of the principles and policies of the Republican party, in whose ranks he has been an active and valued worker. In 1890 he was elected to the legislature, making an excellent record. Mr. Robertson also takes an active interest in school work and is president of the board of education of Conde.

He is an appreciative and popular member of the Masonic fraternity, being affiliated with the following named bodies of the same: Conde Lodge, No. 134, Ancient Free and Accepted Masons; and South Dakota Consistory, No. 4, Ancient Accepted Scottish Rite, at Aberdeen, having attained to fourteen degrees in this branch of the order at the time of this writing. On the 21st of February, 1887, Mr. Robertson was united in marriage to Miss Priscilla A. Herman, who was born in Glenville, Freeborn County, Minnesota, on the 3d of November, 1857, being a daughter of Philip and Augusta Herman, who are now living at Glenville, Minnesota, her father having been a farmer by vocation. Mr. and Mrs. Robertson have three children living, namely: Len D., who was born on the 17th of December, 1887; George V., who was born on the 14th of February, 1893; and Erskine H., who was born on the 14th of July, 1894. Their only daughter, Vida P., was born October 24, 1890, and died of scarlet fever at the age of fifteen months. Mrs. Robertson is a member of the Methodist Episcopal church and takes special interest in Sunday school work.

It has ever been the endeavor of the public on the whole to place in office those men whose capabilities and qualifications fit them for responsible duties. On various occasions Franklin C. Robinson has been chosen for public office, and as chairman of the South Dakota state railway commission he is proving most efficient. His position necessitates his residence in Pierre, and he dates his connection with the state since 1881, at which time Dakota was still under territorial rule.

Mr. Robinson was born in Salem, Maine, a son of Sullivan and Emily (Clarke) Robinson. His great-grandfather emigrated from England to Nova Scotia before the period of the Revolutionary war and at the close of hostilities between the colonies and the mother country he removed to Maine, since which time representatives of the family have resided on this side of the border. The mother, Mrs. Emily (Clarke) Robinson, was born in this country of Scotch parentage.

It was in the year 1850 that the family came west, settling in Wisconsin, and Franklin C. Robinson acquired his education in the public schools of that state and in Brockway College at Ripon. In 1867 he removed to Minnesota, where he resided until 1881, and during that period he attained to a position of leadership in relation to public affairs. He served in the Minnesota general assembly and was the author of the first legislation regulating railways in that state in connection with freight and passenger rates.

As previously stated, Mr. Robinson arrived in Dakota territory in 1881, settling at Clark, where through the succeeding six years he engaged in the grain business. He then removed to Groton, Brown County, where he continued for some time in the same business. He is still largely interested in the Robinson line of grain elevators in North Dakota, and has become an extensive operator in that branch of commercial activity, his carefully directed efforts bringing to him a gratifying measure of success and his well formulated plans finding tangible expression in prosperity. He also has large investments in ranch and farm lands, wherefrom he derives a most gratifying annual income.

Along political and official lines, too, his activity has been pronounced and resultant. Since age conferred upon him the right of franchise, he has been a republican, casting his first presidential vote for Abraham Lincoln. He was called to office in 1907, when he was named a member of the state board of agriculture, on which he served for two years. In 1908 he was elected a member of the state railway commission, assuming the duties of the office in January, 1909, and serving continuously since. His fellow members of the commission elected him chairman of the board for the years 1913 and 1914. He has studied thoroughly the grave problems of railway control in relation to the public. For over thirty years he has given much attention to the investigation of railway rates and service and their relation to the general good, particularly as affecting a rapidly developing country. His broad knowledge makes him peculiarly fitted for the responsibilities of the important position which he now fills.

Mr. Robinson has been married twice. In 1863 he wedded Miss Rebecca J. Smith, who passed away in 1899, leaving four children. In 1901 Mr. Robinson was again married, his second union being with Zada M. Amsden.

Fraternally he is a Mason, belonging to the lodge, chapter, commandery and Shrine, and the basic principles of the organization which recognizes the brotherhood of mankind find expression in his life. He is today a man of wealth, resulting from his judicious investment and capable direction of his business affairs; he is a man of prominence as the result of his capability and devotion to the public welfare; and his public spirit has made him a valuable and efficient member of the board of railway commissioners.

WILLIAM E. ROBINSON, M. D.

Dr. William E. Robinson, a successful medical practitioner and the mayor of Rapid City, his efforts along various lines constituting a source of the city's upbuilding and progress, was born in South Bend, Indiana, October 28, 1872, a son of John and Mary (Shipley) Robinson, the former a native of the state of New York and the latter of Indiana. The father is deceased but the mother still makes her home in South Bend.

In the public schools of his native city William E. Robinson pursued his studies until graduated from the high school and then entered the College of Physicians and Surgeons at Chicago, where he spent one year. He afterward became a student in the Louisville Medical College of Louisville, Kentucky, from which he was graduated with the class of 1894, winning the M. D. degree. He served during the years 1893 and 1894 as interne in the Louisville City Hospital and also received the M. D. degree from the Kentucky School of Medicine. He spent three years in active practice in Louisville and in 1897 came to South Dakota, settling at Big Stone, where he remained until 1900 and then returned to Louisville, where he did one year's post-graduate work. In 1901 he returned to South Dakota, settling at Spearfish, where he remained until 1907, when he removed to Rapid City, where a very extensive practice has been accorded him. Outside his private practice he is surgeon for the Chicago, Milwaukee & St. Paul Railroad. He has ever kept in close touch with the advanced thought of the profession, its latest discoveries and researches and his ability has gained him distinction in his chosen professional field. His energies have also found considerable scope outside strict professional paths, for he is one of the owners and vice president of the Warren Lumber Company and owns a valuable ranch near Farmingdale.

Dr. Robinson has always been a republican, active in local councils of the party and in state affairs. In May, 1914, he was chosen mayor of Rapid City and is serving as the city's first mayor under the three-commissioner plan, being elected for a five years' term. His policies are of the most thoroughly progressive type and his administration promises to be one of unusual advancement and benefit for the city. If he has a hobby in this connection, it is good streets and roads and he has worked tirelessly to further the improvement of both. Probably, however, his most notable achievement has been the harmonizing of discordant interests and the development of the "pull together" spirit so essential to real municipal progress.

On the 14th of September, 1905, Dr. Robinson was united in marriage to Miss Creta G. Daggett, a daughter of David and Julia (Lepla) Daggett and a representative of one of the pioneer families, of Spearfish. Her father was the first druggist of that place, where he settled in 1885. Dr. and Mrs. Robinson have one son, True William.

Fraternally Dr. Robinson is a Mason, an Elk and a Modern Woodman. He has served for several terms as county coroner and he is a member of the county, state and national medical societies. He is widely recognized as among the most prominently successful young physicians of South Dakota and at the same time his public service has been of the utmost value and benefit to the community in which he makes his home and in which his fellow citizens entertain for him the highest respect and regard.

ROY B. ROCKWELL

An excellent record of public service is that which Roy B. Rockwell has made in the position of clerk of the courts of Hyde County, in which capacity he is now serving for the fifth term. He was born at Morris, Illinois, March 4, 1876, a son of Eugene and Sarah (Sawyer) Rockwell. The father's birth occurred in

Cortland County, New York, while the mother was born in Putnam, Connecticut. In early life Eugene Rockwell engaged in merchandising, removing from Wisconsin to Morris, Illinois, and his wife there conducted a millinery business for a number of years. They were married in Morris and Mr. Rockwell carried on merchandising there for some time and also in other Illinois towns. His wife died in 1883, while his death occurred in 1885. In the family were three sons: Curtis E., who is engaged in ranching near Highmore; Roy B.; and Frank C, who was born but a short time before his mother's death and was adopted by a Mr. and Mrs. Palmer. He is now a farmer and resides at Brookings, South Dakota.

Roy B. Rockwell pursued his education in the public schools of Chebanse and Maroa, Illinois, and in the district schools of Nebraska, to which state he removed when about ten years of age. He worked as a ranch boy near Alliance for about four years, after which he returned to Chicago, Illinois, where he attended school for a year and a half, at the same time taking treatment for defective hearing. He then went to Chebanse, Illinois, where he learned the printing trade, after which he removed to Maroa, Illinois, where he worked for the Illinois Central for a number of months. He next went to Onarga, Illinois, where he attended Grand Prairie Seminary for about two years, pursuing a commercial course. He has always been ambitious to advance his education and broad reading and a retentive memory have made him a well-informed man. He has also learned many lessons in the school of experience. When he had completed his commercial course he secured a position as a bookkeeper in Chicago, where he remained for about two years, when he returned to Chebanse, there working at the printer's trade for three years. In the meantime, he had spent about six months in traveling through the west on a bicycle. After abandoning the printer's trade, he engaged in selling machinery and in bookkeeping for about six months and in August, 1900, he went to Rock Rapids, Iowa, where he met his brother, Curtis E. Rockwell. Together they came to South Dakota and filed on a claim in Hyde County, since which time they have been residents of the county. Roy Rockwell took charge of the Highmore Herald, managing the paper for about three years, and during that time he also proved up on his claim. He afterward took up his abode on the claim, where he engaged in raising stock and also cultivated some crops, remaining upon that place until January, 1907, when he assumed the duties of clerk of the courts in Hyde County. In May, 1912, he purchased the Hyde County Bulletin from H. C. Shober, who had established the paper in 1885. This he issues weekly and does all the writing for the paper, employing two people to attend to the mechanical part of the business, while he has entire charge of the office work. He is still connected with Curtis Rockwell under the style of Rockwell Brothers. They are operating a ranch of six hundred and forty acres, raising both grain and stock.

In his political views Mr. Rockwell has always been an earnest republican and since called to the office of county clerk in 1907 he has continuously filled the position, being now the incumbent for the fifth term, his reflections being incontrovertible proof of the confidence reposed in him by his fellow townsmen and of the efficiency with which he has discharged his duties. He has also held some township offices. Fraternally he is connected with Ree Valley Lodge, No. 70, F. & A. M., and with the Elks lodge at Huron and is loyal to the teachings and purposes of those organizations, which are based upon a recognition of the brotherhood of mankind. From the age of ten years Roy B. Rockwell has largely depended upon his own resources and has been both the architect and the builder of his own fortunes. He has overcome obstacles and difficulties which would have utterly discouraged others, but by determined effort he has worked his way upward, constantly learning new and valuable lessons from experience and gaining a place among those who are recognized as forceful factors in advancing the welfare of the community in which they live.

ELMER E. RODABAUGH

E. E. Rodabaugh, junior member of the well-known law firm of Orr & Rodabaugh, of Sioux Falls, who likewise maintains an office in Garretson, comes of stanch old Pennsylvania German stock, and the name which he bears has been for several generations identified with the annals of the old Keystone state of the Union. He was born on a farm in Lycoming County, that state, on the 18th of September, 1862, and is a son of Benjamin F. and Martha W. Rodabaugh, both of whom were likewise born and reared in that county, where the father is engaged in agricultural pursuits, being one of the representative citizens of this section. Our subject received his more rudimentary educational discipline in the public schools of his native county, and thereafter continued his studies in the Central State Normal School, at Lockhaven, while in 1883 he was matriculated in the University of Pennsylvania, where he followed the scientific course, being a student in that well-known institution for a period of three years. In 1882 he began teaching in the schools of Pennsylvania, and thereafter continued to follow the pedagogic profession at intervals during a period of eighteen years, meeting with marked success in the educational field. In 1890 he came to South Dakota and took up his residence in Sioux Falls, and here engaged in reading law under the preceptorship of Alpha F. Orr, making rapid advancement in his studies, and being admitted to the bar of the state in 1895, since which time he has been successfully established in practice in Sioux Falls, having been associated with Mr. Orr, under the firm name of Orr & Rodabaugh, since 1895, while the firm controls a large and representative business, both as advocates and counselors, maintaining also an office in Garretson, this county, as previously noted. Mr. Rodabaugh is an uncompromising Republican in his political proclivities, and takes an active part in party work in a local sense.

Fraternally he is identified with the Masonic order, in which he is affiliated with Unity Lodge, No. 130, Ancient Free and Accepted Masons, while he also holds membership in Garretson Lodge, No. 74, Ancient Order of United Workmen. Though not a member of any religious body he has a deep reverence for the spiritual verities and his views are perhaps most nearly in harmony with the tenets of the faith of the Methodist Episcopal church. It should be noted in passing that the subject tendered his services to the government at the time of the Spanish-American war, but was rejected by reason of overweight. On the 12th of November, 1898, at Sioux Falls, South Dakota, was solemnized the marriage of Mr. Rodabaugh to Miss Lydia Bailey, who was born in Lancaster, New York, on the 28th of October, 1862, being a daughter of Samuel and Julia Bailey, who are now deceased. Mr. and Mrs. Rodabaugh have no children.

William H. RODDLE, one of the pioneer settlers of what is now the attractive city of Brookings, is a native of the Badger state, which has made many contributions to the personnel of the best citizenship of South Dakota. He was born on a farm in Kenosha County, Wisconsin, on the 28th of December, 1850, being a son of William and Mary Roddle, the former of whom was born in England and the latter in New York City. For many generations the Roddle family has been identified with agricultural pursuits in the south of England, while the ancestors of the subject's mother were among the first to settle in what is now New York City, the lineage being of Holland Dutch extraction. The parents of the subject removed in 1860 from Wisconsin to Wilton, Waseca County, Minnesota, residing there until the time of their deaths, and were numbered among the sterling pioneers of that state.

WILLIAM H. RODDLE.

William H. Roddle received his rudimentary education in the district schools and passed his boyhood days on the homestead farm, later continuing his studies in the public schools. In 1869, at the age of nineteen years, he secured a position as apprentice in a hardware establishment in Waseca, Minnesota, where he remained for the ensuing decade, during the last three years a member of the firm of J. M. Robertson & Company, at the expiration of which, in 1879, he came as a pioneer to the territory of Dakota and took up his residence in the little village of Medary, the then county seat of Brookings County. In October, 1879, he established himself in the hardware business in Brookings, South Dakota, meeting with success in the prosecution of the enterprise, with which he continued to be actively identified until 1896, when he disposed of his interests in this line. He took up the study of law a number of years ago and finally determined to complete a thorough course of technical reading, the result being that he thoroughly informed himself in the science of jurisprudence and was admitted to the bar of the state in 1901, since which time he has been successfully engaged in the practice in the city in which he has for so many years maintained his home, being a member of the well-known and representative law firm of Hall, Lawrence & Roddle.

In politics Mr. Roddle has ever been found stanchly arrayed in support of the principles and policies of the Republican party, in whose ranks he has been an active and efficient worker in South Dakota, both under the territorial and state regimes. In 1892 he was elected treasurer of Brookings County and was chosen as his own successor in 1894, thus serving four consecutive years. In 1896 he was the candidate of his party for the office of secretary of state, being victorious at the polls, where he secured a gratifying majority, and giving a most able and discriminating administration of the affairs of the important office. The popular appreciation of his services in this capacity was significantly manifested in 1898, when he was elected to succeed himself.

Mr. Roddle is one of the prominent and appreciative members of the ancient and honored Masonic fraternity, and has the distinction of being past grand master of Masons of the state. His affiliations are with Brookings Lodge, No. 24, Ancient Free and Accepted Masons; Brookings Chapter, No. 18, Royal Arch Masons; Brookings Commandery, No. 14, Knights Templar; El Riad Temple of the Ancient Arabic Order of the Nobles of the Mystic Shrine, in Sioux Falls, and Brookings Chapter, No. 15, Order of the Eastern Star, while he is also identified with Brookings Lodge, No. 40, Independent Order of Odd Fellows, in his home city, being one of its charter members.

On the 1st of January, 1876, Mr. Roddle was united in marriage to Miss Fannie R. Stevens, who was born in Waushara County, Wisconsin, on the 21st of June, 1856, being a daughter of Royce F. and Lucinda M. Stevens. Of this union have been born two daughters, Mary E., wife of F. J. Alton, of Sioux Falls, South Dakota, and Anna F., who died in infancy.

BURT ROGERS

Burt Rogers holds an important position in financial circles in Deadwood as treasurer of the Black Hills Trust & Savings Bank, one of the leading institutions of its kind in southwestern South Dakota. He understands banking thoroughly not only in its broader aspects but also in the small matters of detail and he directs its affairs so wisely that its assets are steadily increasing.

Mr. Rogers was born in Watertown, New York, on the 12th of May, 1870, a son of Orlo and Louisa (Walts) Rogers, both of whom were also born in that town. The father was a farmer and followed that occupation until his death, which occurred in 1897. The mother survived until June, 1912, when she, too, was called to her final rest. They were the parents of five children, of whom the subject of this review is the third in order of birth. He received his education in the schools of Waterloo and Oswego, New York, and in 1889, when nineteen years of age, he left home and arrived in Sioux Falls, South Dakota, in June of that year. He was employed as court reporter there until 1895 and in the meantime engaged in the real-estate business for several years. In 1895 he went to Pactola, a town in the southern hills, and there engaged in mining for two years. He then removed to Deadwood and for five years did assaying independently. At the end of that time, he assisted in organizing the Black Hills Trust & Savings Bank and for two years was a director in that institution. He was then for a time vice president and he subsequently became cashier of the bank, being the present incumbent of that position. The Black Hills Trust & Savings Bank is one of the largest and most reliable financial institutions in Deadwood and the practical management of its affairs is no small task. Mr. Rogers devotes the greater part of his time to his work at the bank and is demonstrating that he is a financier of no mean ability, as the affairs of the bank are in excellent condition and as its prosperity increases from year to year. He is also interested in a number of mines in the locality of Deadwood and his investments therein add appreciably to his income.

Mr. Rogers was united in marriage on the 2d of June, 1913, to Miss Lulu Shrayer, a native of Norwalk, Connecticut, and a daughter of R. Shrayer. Her father was foreman and manager in a large cotton mill in Norwalk, where he still resides.

Mr. Rogers is a member of the Methodist Episcopal church and gives his political support to the republican party. Fraternally he belongs to the Masonic order and is a member of the Mystic Shrine. He likewise holds membership in the Elks, in the local lodge of which he is past exalted ruler. Since coming to Deadwood, he has identified himself thoroughly with the welfare of the community and has not only won for himself a prominent place in financial circles but has done much in an unostentatious way to advance the public good.

FRANK M. ROOD

High honors have come to Frank M. Rood in connection with the official direction of the interests of the commonwealth. He is now filling the position of secretary of state, having entered upon the duties of this position in January, 1915. Accordingly, he makes his home in Pierre but has business interests elsewhere. He was born at Lenoxville, Susquehanna County, Pennsylvania, October 13, 1856. His father, John T. Rood, who was born in Massachusetts and was a representative of one of the old colonial families of that state, was a teacher and farmer. The mother, who bore the maiden name of Ruby Rogers, was a native of Pennsylvania and both parents are now deceased.

In their family were six children, of whom Frank M. Rood was the second in order of birth. He acquired a public-school education and afterward attended Wyoming Seminary, while subsequently he pursued a business course in a commercial college at Kingston, Pennsylvania. When his school days were over, he turned his attention to the lumber business at Lenoxville, Pennsylvania, and continued therein for two years but the opportunities of the northwest attracted him and in 1877 he settled in Deadwood, Dakota territory. There through the succeeding year he conducted a lumber business and the following year he removed to Whitewood, where he took up a claim, remaining in that locality for a year. He next went to Fort Meade, where he became owner of a ranch and engaged in the raising of livestock. In 1893 he removed to Stanley County, where he continued in the stock business until 1906, when he disposed of his interests in stock and land there. It was in that year that he was elected to represent his district, comprising Stanley and Lyman counties in the state legislature. He afterwards spent a year in Canada and on the Pacific coast and in 1908 he returned to South Dakota, settling at Philip, where he became interested in the mercantile business and in real-estate. He still has his holdings of that character and the capable supervision of his business interests is manifest in the success which is attending him. He has placed his business upon a safe basis and is deriving therefrom a gratifying annual income. In addition to his other interests, he is a director of the Bank of Philip.

Mr. Rood was married May 28, 1886, to Miss Eva J. Voorhees, a daughter of Abraham and Jane (Elliott) Voorhees, the former a native of New York state, and the latter a native of Paisley, Scotland. Mrs. Voorhees came to America in her girlhood days and was reared and educated at Irvington, New Jersey. Mrs. Rood was born in Newark, New Jersey. By her marriage she has become the mother of one daughter, Hazel W.

Mr. Rood is a member of Philip Lodge, No. 150, A. F. & A. M.; Oriental Consistory, No. I, A. A. S. R. of Yankton; and Naja Temple, A. A. O. N. M. S., of Deadwood.

In his political views he has always been a republican since age conferred upon him the right of franchise. He was born in the year in which the party became a national organization and he has never wavered in his allegiance thereto since he cast his first presidential ballot. He could not be said to be a politician in the usual sense of office seeking but in 1914 his fitness for office and his well-known fidelity in citizenship led to his selection for the position of secretary of state. He assumed the duties of the office in January, 1915. He is now directing the important affairs of that position and capably meeting the duties and responsibilities that devolve upon him and he ranks with the state's successful and prominent pioneer citizens and capable public officials.

CHARLES HEMBREY ROSS

The steps in the orderly progression of Charles Hembrey Ross are easily discernible. He has learned to correctly judge of those things which go to make up life's contacts and experiences and he is capable of mature judgment of his own capacities and powers. He is eminently a man of business sense and easily avoids the mistakes and disasters that come to those who, though possessing remarkable faculties in some respects, are liable to erratic movements that result in unwarranted risk and failure. He is recognized as a well-balanced man, of even temper and conservative habit, and possessing that kind of enterprise which leads to great accomplishments. He is today president of the H. W. Ross Lumber Company, the pioneer enterprise of this character in Sioux Falls.

Charles H. Ross was born in Milwaukee, Wisconsin, August 23, 1870, a son of Hiram William and Sarah Ann (Flowers) Ross. His grandfather, Hiram J. Ross, owned and operated a sawmill in Milwaukee, Wisconsin, as early as 1837, having located there in 1835, when the place was first settled. Hiram W. Ross, father of our subject, was a prominent lumberman of the northwest, operating a sawmill at Colby, Wisconsin, for some years, afterward becoming president of the H. W. Ross Lumber Company, operating a line of thirty yards in Minnesota and South Dakota. He maintained the presidency of the company until his death, which robbed the northwest of one of the most prominent figures in lumber circles.

The early education of Charles H. Ross was acquired in the public schools of Milwaukee and he afterward attended the public schools of Sioux Falls, being graduated from the high school with the class of 1888. He then entered the University of South Dakota and completed his course in 1890. It was in 1879 that the family came to this state, settling at Canton. After two years there spent the father regarded Sioux Falls as the most promising town of the territory and removed with his family to this city. With the completion of his collegiate course Charles H. Ross accepted a position in his father's lumber yard and for four years did the work of a day laborer, that he might thoroughly learn the business in every detail. He was not afraid of the hard work involved and knew that only through practical experience and thoroughness could he become absolutely master of the business to which he expected to devote his life. It was not parental authority but personal ability that secured his advancement. As he was qualified for larger responsibilities, they were given him and thus gradually he worked his way upward. In 1893 he was made secretary of the company and after two years was promoted to the position of buyer, continuing to act in that capacity until 1900, when his brother, Hiram E. Ross, became buyer and Charles H. Ross assumed the management of the outside yards, with his residence in Sioux Falls. The company has drawn about it, men of capability, insight and enterprise and this is one of the features of the success which has attended the business. Good wages have always been paid and an employe recognizes the fact that fidelity means promotion as opportunity offers.

Charles H. Ross has not only studied the business immediately under his control but has been a student of trade conditions and of everything affecting the lumber interests of the country. He believes firmly in organization among business men for the further development of their respective lines and he has, therefore, always been connected with associations of lumbermen. In 1901, when in Florida, he received a telegram announcing his election as vice president of the Northwestern Lumbermen's Association and in January, 1902, at the annual meeting held in Minneapolis, he was elected to the presidency. His election as vice president came as a total surprise to him, as he had never sought the office nor dreamed that it was to be given him. For seven years he has been a member of the executive committee of the board of directors of the Northwestern Lumbermen's Association and his sound judgment, keen sagacity and thorough understanding of the trade have done much to further the interests of lumbermen throughout this section of the country. Aside from being president of the H. W. Ross Lumber Company he is vice president of the Sioux Falls Savings Bank and is a director of the Minnehaha Springs Company.

Mr. Ross is pleasantly situated in his home life. He has been married twice. On the 24th of October, 1900, at State Center, Iowa, he wedded Miss Ellen Mae Goodrich, of that place, and they became the parents of two children, Hiram Goodrich and Marjorie. The wife and mother passed away November 24, 1908, and on the 3d of September, 1910, Mr. Ross was united in marriage to Miss Amy Ohlman, a daughter of M. P. Ohlman, president of the American State Bank at Yankton, South Dakota. Mr. and Mrs. Ross occupy one of the attractive homes of Sioux Falls and its hospitality is enjoyed by their friends.

Mr. Ross votes with the republican party but has never been a politician in the sense of office seeking. However, he is never neglectful of the duties of citizenship but on the contrary cooperates in many movements which have direct bearing upon the welfare and progress of city and state. He was made a trustee of the board of education of Sioux Falls and in 1910 was reelected for five years without opposition. He is a member of the Congregational church, in the work of which he is also actively interested, serving as chairman of its board of trustees. He is a prominent Mason, joining the consistory and the Mystic Shrine in 1905. He is also connected with the Knights of Pythias and the Hoo Hoos, the latter an organization of lumbermen. He belongs to the Minnehaha Country and the Dacotah Clubs and he greatly enjoys hunting and fishing. He has made recreation an even balance to his intense business activity and he is an enthusiast with the rod and gun. He has traveled abroad, delighting in the art of Europe and in the scenes of modern and historic interest. The most envious cannot grudge him his success — so worthily has it been won and so honorably used, and his life record stands as incontrovertible proof of the fact that prosperity and an honored name may be won simultaneously.

ADAM ROYHE

A. Royhe is of foreign birth, being a native of Hesse Darmstadt, Germany. He spent his childhood and youth in Hesse Darmstadt, and received a good education in the schools of his native state. He accompanied his parents to the United States and attended school in Wisconsin, where he learned to read and write the English language, having previously obtained a sufficient knowledge of the same to converse fluently. The following summer he worked on the farm and at the age of nineteen left home and began earning his own livelihood, spending some time in the lumber regions of Wisconsin. In company with a friend he came to South Dakota, walking from Marshall, Minnesota, to Kingsbury County, his original destination having been the city of Yankton. On the way they stopped in Brookings County, where they were informed that better land could be obtained in the county of Kingsbury than in the section of country for which they were bound. Accordingly, Mr. Royhe took up a claim, and after spending the summer on the same and reducing about fifteen acres to cultivation, returned to Wisconsin, where he remained until the following spring, purchasing the meanwhile a team of horses, a wagon and various agricultural implements to be used on his western homestead. With the advent of spring, he returned to his claim and broke a considerable portion of ground, spending the succeeding winter in the pioneer section of Wisconsin, and in this way, he divided the time during the ensuing three years. Mr. Royhe took to himself a wife and helpmeet in the person of Miss Minnie Deetman, of Columbia County, Wisconsin, and in the spring of the following year settled permanently in Kingsbury County, South Dakota, remaining on his own claim until 1890, when he took up his residence in Arlington. He still owns the above farm, which is in a high state of cultivation, and in addition thereto has a half section of fine land, which is also well improved and successfully tilled. Mr. Royhe opened a meat market in Arlington, which he operated with encouraging success for two years, and then began handling grain for the Van Dusen firm, continuing with them until erecting an elevator of his own. Since then, he has carried on an extensive grain business, being one of the largest buyers and shippers in the county, and in connection therewith he also deals quite extensively in real estate.

He has been influential in political circles ever since becoming a resident of South Dakota, has held a number of township and county offices and for a number of years has been a delegate to nearly every Republican convention held in his county, district and state. He served with marked ability as state senator, during which time he was on some of the most important committees of the upper house, including among others the committees on banking, insurance, cities and municipal corporations and railroads. He is identified with several local enterprises, being a director of the First National Bank and a stockholder in the same.

He stands high in the Masonic order, and is also identified with the Ancient Order of United Workmen, and with his wife belongs to the Eastern Star lodge. In his religious belief Mr. Royhe subscribes to the German Lutheran faith, his wife being a member of the Episcopal church. They are the parents of four children.

SAMUEL S. RUBLE

SAMUEL S. RUBLE

Samuel S. Ruble is successfully engaged in the undertaking business in Pierre and for ten years was president of the state board of embalmers. He is a native of Pennsylvania, born on the 11th of November, 1863, a son of Michael and Mary (Longacre) Ruble, both of whom are deceased. In the acquirement of his education, he attended the Indiana State Normal School at Indiana, Pennsylvania, and the Huntington (Pa.) Normal School, thus receiving liberal training that qualified him for the practical and responsible duties of later life. He started in the undertaking business in 1886 and has since devoted his life to that pursuit. He began business at Lewistown, Pennsylvania, and in 1900 removed io Pierre, where he has since remained. He now has well-appointed undertaking parlors, carries a full and select line of undertaking supplies and receives a liberal patronage, to which his straightforward business methods well entitle him. That he stands high in the profession is indicated by the fact that he held the office of president of the South Dakota state board of embalmers for ten years, beginning April 6, 1903. The term covers five years and having been reappointed, he continued in the position until April 6, 1913, when he retired. He is a graduate of three colleges of embalming and is therefore thoroughly familiar with the best and most progressive methods of caring for the dead.

Mr. Ruble was married at Mifflintown, Pennsylvania, June 28, 1892, to Miss Laura A. Reynolds, a daughter of Ruben Reynolds of Mifflintown and a niece of General Reynolds who was killed in the memorable battle at Gettysburg, Pennsylvania. Both Mr. and Mrs. Ruble are well known in Pierre, for their many good qualities have gained for them warm regard. In 1891 Mr. Ruble joined the Westminster Presbyterian church at Mifflintown, but on their removal to the west he and his wife transferred their membership to the Congregational church of Pierre in 1900. In politics he has always been a republican and has never known a member of the family that did not support the same party. For two years he was a member of the board of education of Pierre, but he has never sought nor desired political office, preferring to concentrate his energies upon his business affairs which have been of growing importance. Fraternally he is well known, holding membership with the Masons, Odd Fellows, the Knights of Pythias, the Knights of Malta, the Ancient Order of United Workmen, the Red Men, the Junior Order United American Mechanics, the Degree of Honor Fraternity and with the Eastern Star and the Rebekah Lodge, the ladies' auxiliary organizations of the Masons and Odd Fellows orders respectively. He is likewise a member of the Pierre Commercial Club in which connection he does everything to further the interests of the city along material lines. He ever stands for progress and improvement and his influence and efforts count for good in those directions.

JOHN L. RUCKMAN

John L. Ruck man is the present representative of his district in the state legislature and is serving in a progressive and capable manner as a member of that body. In addition to this he is well known in Aberdeen as a successful and prominent lawyer and holds rank with the leading representatives of his profession in this section of the state. He was born in Knoxville, Iowa, January 25, 1868, and is a son of E. B. and Charity (Walker) Ruckman, natives of Kentucky. They removed to Iowa in 1852 and the father engaged in farming and stock-raising in that state.

Mr. Ruckman acquired his early education in the public schools of his native city, and afterward entered the Central University at Pella, Iowa, graduating from that institution with the degree of B. A. in 1893. He then enrolled in Drake University and studied law, receiving his degree in 1902. Following this he practiced for two years in Knoxville and then in 1904 came to Aberdeen, of which city he has since been a resident. His ability has drawn to him a large and representative patronage and he has been connected with the conduct of a great deal of important litigation. In 1908 and 1909 he served as city attorney of Aberdeen and in 1912 was elected a member of the state legislature for a term of two years, at the end of which time he was reelected. He is now a member of that body and his record is one of intelligent and capable work in the public service. A great deal of important legislation bears the stamp of his interest and approval.

Mr. Ruckman is a republican in his political beliefs and well known in fraternal circles, being past master of Oriental Lodge, No. 61, A. F. & A. MM of Knoxville, and belonging also to the Knights of Pythias and the Benevolent Protective Order of Elks. In official, professional and social circles alike he is well and favorably known and he holds a place among the men of marked ability and substantial worth in the community.

FRED H. RUGG *

Business enterprise finds exemplification in the record of Fred H. Rugg, of Rapid City, who is president of the Rugg Lumber & Coal Company. He has made his home there since 1891, and has been closely connected with the development of that section of the state and with events which have shaped its history. Each step in his career has been a forward one and his powers have developed through the exercise of effort. He was born in Claremont, New Hampshire, June 2, 1856, a son of John H. Rugg, also a native of New Hampshire and a descendant of one of New England's earliest families. The original ancestor came to America in 1654, and was one of the first settlers of Lancaster, Massachusetts. His wife and children were victims of the Indian massacre which occurred in 1696. Daniel Rugg, the great-grandfather of Fred H. Rugg, was a soldier of the Revolutionary war. He enlisted on three different occasions, first becoming a member of the Middlesex Regiment under Colonel Samuel Bullard, afterward serving with Colonel Dikes' command during 1776 and 1777, and later under Colonel Ebner Perry in 1780. John H. Rugg, the father of Fred H. Rugg, was a soldier of the Civil war. He enlisted in the Ninth New Hampshire Volunteer Infantry, participated in the hotly contested battle of Antietam and was soon afterward honorably discharged because of physical disability. When he regained his health, however, he reenlisted in the Veterans Reserve Corps and served until the close of the war. His wife, who bore the maiden name of Abigail Blanchard, was descended from early Scotch settlers of New England.

Fred H. Rugg was educated in the public schools of Garemont, New Hampshire, and also pursued an advanced course in the high school. In 1876 he came to the west and followed the profession of civil engineering in connection with various railways west of the Mississippi river, and was for a time located at Shoshone, Idaho. In 1883 he returned to the middle west, settling at Cedar Rapids, Nebraska, where he was employed as a bookkeeper in the office of a flour milling company and later in a bank conducted by his employers. In 1891 he came to Rapid City, where he was engaged in the survey of the Black Hills division of the Northwestern Railway. Six months later he entered the office of the Hulst & Price Lumber Company in the capacity of bookkeeper and was afterward advanced to the position of manager. In 1905 he purchased all other interests and incorporated the business under the name of the Rugg Lumber & Coal Company. He is now managing his interests under that name and is at the head of one of the important commercial enterprises of the city. He is also a director of the First National Life & Accident Insurance Company.

On the 15th of February, 1882, Mr. Rugg was united in marriage to Miss Susan M. Perkins, of Lynn, Massachusetts, a daughter of Captain A. N. Perkins, who for many years was the captain of whaling ships out of Nantucket. To Mr. and Mrs. Rugg have been born two children, but Fred C, the elder, is now deceased. The younger, Harold H., is a student of electrical engineering in the South Dakota State School of Mines.

In politics Mr. Rugg is a republican of the progressive type. He served for four years as a member of the school board of Rapid City and during two years of the time was its president and for one year, he was mayor of Rapid City. In 1912 he was the presidential elector on the progressive ticket. Fraternally he is a Mason. He has attained the Knight Templar degree in the York Rite, the thirty-second degree in the Scottish Rite and is a member of the Mystic Shrine. In 1914 he became grand junior warden of South Dakota. He has always been true to the beneficent spirit of the craft and the high standards of manhood and citizenship which it inculcates. There are indeed few features in his life which could awaken condemnation and the understanding he has displayed in the management of his business interests and his unremitting energy are features which any might well emulate.

Holding always to the highest ideals concerning medical and surgical practice, Dr. David L. Rundlett is today occupying a conspicuous and honorable position as one of the eminent physicians of South Dakota, practicing at Sioux Falls. He was born at Groveland, Massachusetts, on the 25th of March, 1873, and is a son of John Pearson and Sarah Lucy (Hale) Rundlett. The family comes of English origin and the first representative in America arrived in Plymouth, Massachusetts, about 1650. The father of Dr. Rundlett served in the Civil War as a corporal of Company A, Thirty-third Massachusetts Volunteer Infantry, from May, 1862, until the 25th of July, 1865. He participated in the three days' battle at Gettysburg, in the engagements at Chattanooga, Missionary Ridge and Lookout Mountain, and went with Sherman on the celebrated march to the sea, proving his valor and his loyalty on many a hotly contested battlefield.

DR. DAVID L. RUNDLETT

Dr. Rundlett, whose name introduces this review, spent his youthful days in his native city, passed through consecutive grades in its public schools and was graduated from the high school. He afterward entered the Massachusetts College of Pharmacy in Boston, from which he was graduated with the class of 1894. He regarded this, however, as but an initial step to other professional training and entered the medical department of Tufts College of Boston, in which he completed the course in 1901. He then located at New Haven, Connecticut. He was a drug clerk in Boston, Massachusetts, for ten years and after qualifying for medical practice followed his profession in the east until July, 1907, when he sought the growing opportunities of the middle west and came to Sioux Falls, where he has since successfully practiced. He was not long in demonstrating his ability, which brought to him a liberal patronage. The profession and the public recognize the fact that he is a close and discriminating student of the science of medicine and has widely improved his opportunities.

Dr. Rundlett belongs to the Sioux Falls District Medical Society; to the South Dakota State Medical Society; the American Medical Association; and the Sioux Valley Medical Association. Since 1913 he has been one of the censors of the Sioux Falls District Medical Society and is now (1915) chairman of the board of censors. He was also formerly a member of the New Haven County (Conn.) Medical Society and of the Connecticut State Medical Society. His early service as interne in the Boston City Hospital from July, 1899, until July, 1901, gave him the broad experience which only hospital practice can give, and the knowledge there gained proved one of the strongest elements in his later success.

On the 30th of May, 1908, at Sioux Falls, Dr. Rundlett was united in marriage to Evelyn Bevis, a daughter of John and Emma Drexel. They attend the Congregational church and Dr. Rundlett gives his political allegiance to the republican party. He has had an interesting military experience and has done important public service. On the 9th of January, 1906, he enlisted in the Governor's Foot Guards, Second Company, of New Haven, Connecticut, from which he was honorably discharged September 27, 1907. He was also fire department surgeon for New Haven from November 30, 1904, until July, 1907, and was superintendent of the New Haven Emergency Hospital from 1901 until 1904. In Masonry he has attained high rank. He has taken the degrees of the lodge, chapter, council and commandery, has attained the thirty-second degree of the Scottish Rite and is a Noble of the Mystic Shrine. He is also connected with the Knights of Pythias, with the Sons of the American Revolution, the Sons of Veterans, the Dacotah Club, the Country Club, and also of the Commercial Club, all of Sioux Falls. He is also a member of the American Association for the Advancement of Science and of the National Geographic Society. His social qualities render him popular, while his professional attainments have gained for him the high position which he now fills as a representative of the medical fraternity.

SAMUEL WAGNER RUSSELL

Samuel W. Russell, is a native of Pennsylvania, and paternally is descended from one of the oldest families of New England, tracing his ancestry in an unbroken line to Hon. William Russell, who came to America in 1632 with Lord Seal, and who was one of the founders of Connecticut, as well as one of the first judges of the colony. Later, when the colonies revolted, the Russell's espoused the American cause, and a number of the family served with distinction during the Revolution; subsequently they demonstrated their loyalty to the government in the war of 1812, and in the various Indian wars; indeed, the Russell's have been represented in every war in which the United States has been engaged, patriotism and love of country being prominent characteristics of the family.

Benjamin S. Russell, father of the subject, was born in Pennsylvania and is living now in Jamestown, North Dakota, being still active in business. Mary Gaskill, wife of Benjamin S. and mother of Samuel W. Russell, and also a native of the Keystone state, departed this life in the year 1891. Samuel Wagner Russell was born September 27, 1857, in Towanda, Bradford County, and received his early education in the schools of his native town, subsequently, in 1871, entering Shattuck School at Faribault, Minnesota. By reason of failing health, however, he was not able to finish his studies; accordingly, in 1873, he quit school and returned home, remaining with his parents until 1877. In that and the following year he took special courses in civil and mining engineering at Lehigh University, Bethlehem, Pennsylvania, but his health again becoming impaired, he laid aside his studies and during the winter of 1878-9 taught school at Chelton Hills, in his native state. The following summer he went to East St. Louis, Illinois, as bookkeeper for the National Stock Yard Bank, of that place, which position he held for three years, resigning at the expiration of that time to go on the cattle range in Nebraska and Montana.

Mr. Russell enjoyed the free out-of-door life on the range until 1887, when he went to El Paso, Texas, where, in partnership with a Mr. Newman, under the firm name of Newman & Russell, he was engaged for five years in the real-estate and brokerage business. Leaving the latter place in 1892, he located at Eddy, New Mexico, where he dealt in real estate, loaned money, etc., until 1896, when he returned to East St. Louis and accepted a position with the National Stock Yard Company, holding the same until the spring of the year following. Severing his connections with the above concern at the time noted, he went to Miles City, Montana, in connection with one of the largest of the live-stock commission firms, and after remaining at that place until December, 1898, came to Dead wood, South Dakota, where, in partnership with certain gentlemen from Montana, he bought the Uncle Sam Mine, on Elk creek in Lawrence County. Mr. Russell, in 1899, with his partners, organized the Clover Leaf Gold Mining Company, of which he was made vice-president and treasurer, and he still holds these positions, contributing greatly to the success of the enterprise by his energy, executive ability and correct business management. In 1900 he was elected vice-president of the Black Hills Mining Men's Association, of which he was also one of the original organizers, and in December of the same year he took a leading part in organizing the Black Hills Business Men's Club, being chosen its vice-president, which position he has since filled. In addition to the official relations referred to, Mr. Russell at the present time holds the office of first vice-president of the American Mining Congress, a national organization composed of the leading miners and representatives of the largest mining properties in the United States; this high honor, coming to him unsought, is a recognition of his distinguished abilities as a business and a mining man, also a graceful compliment to him as an enterprising, public-spirited man of affairs and accomplished gentleman. Mr. Russell is a master of the profession to which he has devoted so much of his time and attention, and as a practical miner, familiar with all the varied details of the great mining industry, has few equals and no superiors in South Dakota. By his energy and straightforward business course, he has done much in the way of organizing companies and developing valuable mineral properties, and while advancing his own interests in the prosecution of these various enterprises, he has also been instrumental in promoting the prosperity of his association.

Mr. Russell, at the request of the Black Hills Mining Men's Association, accepted the appointment of commissioner to the Louisiana Purchase Exposition from Governor Herreid and when the commissioners organized, in July, 1903, he was elected president and devoted his energies and best abilities to winning success for the state at the St. Louis Exposition. Mr. Russell is a Republican, but has never entered the arena of partisan politics as an office seeker, having no ambition whatever in that direction, although by nature and training well qualified to fill any public position within the power of the people to bestow.

Fraternally he is a thirty-second-degree Mason and in religious matters subscribes to the Episcopal creed, being, with his wife, a consistent member of the church of that name in the city of Deadwood. Mr. Russell has a pleasant and attractive home in Deadwood, his family consisting of himself and wife only. The latter before her marriage, on the 20th of August, 1896, was Miss Mary Logan, of St. Louis, Missouri. Mrs. Russell was born and reared in the latter city and is the daughter of C. C. and Elizabeth (Finigan) Logan, also of St. Louis.

WILLIAM L. RYBURN

W. L. RYBURN, cashier and general manager of the business of the First National Bank of Alexandria, was born in Rockford, Illinois, May 10, 1872, a son of William and Mary (Legge) Ryburn, to whom were born six children, namely: Anna, who resides in Alexandria; George, who is engaged in the real-estate business in this place; John, of Alexandria; Minnie, who is the wife of G. H. Montgomery, engaged in the furniture business in the same place; William L., who figures as the immediate subject of this sketch, and Maud, who is the wife of Dr. E. E. King, of Mitchell, this state. Both the father and mother of the subject were born in Aberdeenshire, Scotland, the former in 1836 and the latter in 1835. The parents of each died when they were children and they were reared in the homes of relatives, and after attaining maturity each came to America in company with relatives. Both located in the city of Rockford, Illinois, where the father learned the trade of blacksmith, in which he was there engaged for nearly thirty years. In 1883 he came with his family to South Dakota and purchased a pre-emption claim in Hanson County, where he continued to be engaged in agricultural pursuits and stock growing up to the time of his death, which occurred in 1898, his devoted wife having been summoned into eternal rest in 1893. Both were worthy members of the Presbyterian church and were folk of sterling character, honored lay all who knew them.

The subject of this review was about ten years of age at the time of his parents' removal to South Dakota, and his early educational training had previously been secured in the public schools of his native city, to which he later returned for the purpose of taking a course in the Rockford Business College, in which he was graduated in 1891, having completed a thorough commercial course. He then returned to his home in South Dakota and was given a position in the Hanson County Bank, in Alexandria, proving himself a capable and faithful executive and being made assistant cashier of the institution in 1894, while in 1899 he was chosen cashier. In 1901 the bank was reorganized and incorporated as the First National Bank of Alexandria, with a capital stock and surplus of fifty thousand dollars, and Mr. Ryburn was forthwith placed in executive charge of the affairs of the institution, which has gained a leading position through his able and well-directed efforts. In 1899 he was sent to Elk Point, Union County, to superintend the business of the Citizens Bank, which was practically a branch of the bank at Alexandria, and there he remained about eighteen months, within which time the institution was reorganized as the First National Bank of Elk Point.

Mr. Ryburn is one of the leaders in the local ranks of the Republican party and is secretary of its county organization. He is a member of Celestial Lodge, No. 37, Free and Accepted Masons, and Mitchell Chapter, Royal Arch Masons, of Alexandria; St. Bernard Commandery, Knights Templar, at Mitchell; Oriental Consistory, No. I, Ancient Accepted Scottish Rite, in Yankton, and El Riad Temple, Ancient Arabic Order of the Nobles of the Mystic Shrine, in Sioux Falls, being an appreciative and enthusiastic affiliate of these various bodies of the time-honored order of Freemasonry. He has held the office of worshipful master of his lodge for the past three years. He and his wife hold membership in the Presbyterian church.

On the 28th of April, 1898. Mr. Ryburn was united in marriage to Miss Edith Peckham, of Alexandria, and they are the parents of two children, Leota and Helen.

EUGENE SAENGER

Among those who have contributed in substantial measure to the commercial development of Sioux Falls is numbered Eugene Saenger, whose energy, enterprise and aggressiveness have been powerful factors in the building up of the bindery and office supply business controlled by the firm of Brown & Saenger, Incorporated. He was born in Freeport, Illinois, February 13, 1860, and is a son of Louis and Marie (Rach) Saenger, natives of Germany. The father fled from that country in 1848 and emigrated to America, where he remained only a short time. He then returned to Europe, going to Switzerland near the German border line, where he met his future wife, who crossed the border to meet him. They were married in Switzerland and went from there to America, locating at Freeport, Illinois, where both passed away on the same day.

Eugene Saenger acquired his education in the public schools of Freeport and in 1874 entered the office of the Freeport Journal, a daily and weekly newspaper. There he learned the bookbinder's trade and followed it afterward in Freeport until the fall of 1881, when he moved to Cedar Rapids, where he was for eight years connected with the Republican Printing Company. On the 1st of May, 1889, Mr. Saenger moved to Sioux Falls, South Dakota, and, in association with Colonel Thomas G. Brown, established a bindery and an office supply business under the name of Brown & Saenger. This continued as a co-partnership until February 14, 1908, when Colonel Brown retired, the business being incorporated as Brown & Saenger, Incorporated. At this time Joseph L. Elliott entered the firm as secretary and treasurer. Brown & Saenger, Incorporated, control a large and growing business in office supplies and their bindery is one of the largest in the city. The concern is conducted along modern business lines and has had a rapid and steady growth. Mr. Saenger has given practically his entire time and attention to its development and his success has placed him among the leading business men of Sioux Falls.

On the 30th of September, 1891, in Sioux Falls, Mr. Saenger was united in marriage to Miss Alice M. Richardson, a daughter of the late Benjamin W. and Mary C. Richardson, the former a captain of Company C, Eighty-first New York Volunteers, during the Civil War. Mr. and Mrs. Saenger have become the parents of a son, Ben, born March 20, 1893. Mr. Saenger gives his political allegiance to the republican party. He holds membership in the Dacotah and Country Clubs and is prominent in Masonry, having taken the thirty-second degree in the Scottish Rite. His course has at all times conformed to the highest business principles and his integrity, honesty and ability have gained him an enviable position in business circles.

JOHN H. SANFORD

John H. Sanford is the owner of a fine ranch of six hundred and forty acres in Bon Homme County, while he maintains his business headquarters and residence in the attractive town of Tyndall, the county seat.

The state of Illinois figures as the place of his nativity, since he was born in Ogle County, on the 12th of December, 1847, a son of Tared W. and Henrietta (Sturgis) Sanford, of whose eight children only three are living at the present time — James W., who is a resident of Santa Clara County, California; Sarah, who is the wife of Arron Rood, of Pueblo, Colorado; and John H., who is the subject of this sketch. Jared Sanford was born in the state of Connecticut, where he was reared to the sturdy discipline of the farm and where his marriage was solemnized. Some time after thus assuming connubial responsibilities he removed to Ogle County, Illinois, where he was engaged in farming until about 1870, when he removed to Missouri and later to Dickinson County, Kansas, where he passed the remainder of his life, his death occurring in 1876, at which time he was seventy-one years of age. While his vocation in life was farming, he had distinctive mechanical ability, and for a number of years he did much work along this line, in connection with his agricultural operations, while he was also a successful stock grower, our subject having gained his initial experience in the breeding of stock under the effective direction of his father. Jared Sanford was a stanch Republican in his political proclivities and he and his wife were zealous members of the Congregational church, the latter having entered into eternal rest in 1854, at the age of forty-five years.

John H. Sanford was reared to farm life and secured his early educational discipline in the public schools, supplementing the same by a course in F. E. Arnold's business college, at Rockford, Illinois. On attaining his legal majority he came into possession of a valuable farm, of one hundred acres, the same having been a part of his father's old homestead in Ogle county, Illinois, and he devoted his attention to the cultivation of the same until the time of his marriage, which occurred on the 30th of December, 1869, when he led to the hymeneal altar Miss Louisa E. Stone, the only daughter of Joseph and Mary Stone, of Ogle county, Illinois, and thereafter he was associated with his father-in-law in the management of the latter's farm until 1880, while for a number of years he was extensively engaged in the buying and shipping of livestock, in which line of enterprise he was very successful, gaining a knowledge which has made him one of the best judges of stock to be found in South Dakota. In 1880 he came to South Dakota and secured a quarter section of land in Bon Homme County. He has since added to his landed estate in the county until he is now the owner of an entire section, as previously stated, and though the tract is valuable farming land he devotes his attention more specially to the cattle industry, being an extensive feeder of stock and a breeder of registered cattle and hogs. He has done much to improve the grade of stock raised in this section and his finely improved farm shows some of the finest specimens of cattle and hogs to be found in the confines of the state. He is progressive and discriminating in his methods and has been very successful in his operations since coming to South Dakota. In politics he gives his support to the Republican party, but he has never been an aspirant for public office.

Fraternally he is identified with Bon Homme Lodge, No. 101, Free and Accepted Masons. He and his wife are the parents of one child, Harry Otis, who is a veterinary surgeon, being successfully established in the practice of his profession at Tyndall.

Walter B. Saunders was well known in Milbank as a foremost citizen to whose enterprise and public spirit the substantial growth and development of the community were largely due. It was not only his activity in the field of banking that gave him preeminence among his fellow townsmen, but a kindly spirit, a helping hand and a generous readiness to assist others. His personal traits and characteristics were such as endeared him to all with whom he came in contact and make his memory a more cherished possession than any material gift could be. He was born in Cattaraugus County, New York, May 13, 1859, and was one of the two children of Nelson and Maria (McCoy) Saunders, who were also natives of that state. The father was a distinguished physician and surgeon of western New York for many years and he passed away in 1896, having for more than two decades survived his wife, who died in 1875. The daughter, Grace, became the wife of A. D. Hapgood and died in 1885, leaving two children, Karl and Chester.

Walter B. Saunders was reared in his native state and supplemented his public-school education by study in the Chamberlain Institute at Randolph, New York, from which he was graduated with the class of 1876. He began business life as a clerk in a bank at Randolph and soon afterward was made assistant cashier, there remaining until 1882. In July of that year, he made his way to Milbank, South Dakota, and in partnership with A. C. Dodge established a private bank of which he became the cashier and so continued until his death, acting all the time as resident manager of the institution. In 1891 the bank was reorganized as a state bank and has existed as such since that date. Throughout his entire business career Mr. Saunders was connected with banking and had intimate knowledge of the great financial problems and of everything bearing directly upon his chosen line of business. In addition to his interest in the bank he was the owner of a large amount of real estate, having made extensive investments in property, and he was also the owner of much live stock in Grant County, making a specialty of the handling of Durham cattle. He likewise owned property in New York and in all of his business affairs his judgment was sound and his sagacity was manifest in the success which attended his efforts.

On the 25th of May, 1884, Mr. Saunders was united in marriage to Miss Kate Crowley, a native of New York and a daughter of Addison Crowley, who was a pioneer citizen and for many years a leading business man of Cattaraugus County. He dealt in lumber and real estate and also engaged in merchandising for a number of years. He likewise served as county sheriff for one term and took a most active and helpful part in the public life of the community. To Mr. and Mrs. Saunders were born four children: Phil C, Corinne, Lewis and Earl M.

The parents were members of the Episcopal church and Mr. Saunders continued a faithful adherent thereof to the time of his death. From his arrival in Milbank, he was actively interested in the public welfare and his labors were ofttimes an effective element in advancing the general good. He ever stood for those things which are a matter of civic virtue and of civic pride. He served for four years as mayor and for thirteen years as a member of the city council and always exercised his official prerogatives on the side of advancement and improvement. He was made one of the three South Dakota commissioners to the Louisiana Purchase Exposition and acted as treasurer of the commission. So thoroughly and conscientiously were his duties performed that at the close of the exposition, instead of there being a deficiency in the public accounts, he was able to turn back into the state treasury over one thousand dollars.

One of the local papers said of him: "Mr. Saunders during his whole life in this city was known as a man of the strictest business integrity. His yea was yea, and his nay was nay, and he enjoyed to the fullest the confidence and respect of all his fellow citizens. While conservative and careful in all business matters, he was nevertheless public-spirited and progressive in all that tended to the advancement of the community, and his many kindly acts of individual benevolence are treasured by numbers who were the recipients of his bounty and helpfulness."

Mr. Saunders was a prominent Knight Templar Mason and when he passed away was laid to rest with Masonic honors. He had truly exemplified in his life the beneficent spirit of the craft. He recognized the brotherhood of mankind and was constantly extending a helping hand to assist others on life's journey who were less fortunate. The board of directors of the Merchants Bank at the time of his death prepared a resolution in which it was said: "His devoted attention to the duties of his office, his strict integrity, his honorable business methods, his upright character as a man and a citizen of this community, have done more to make this banking institution safe and sound in a financial way, and to make it one that the people of this community had confidence in, than any other one connected with its management. The association of the board of directors with Mr. Saunders has been most pleasant and agreeable, and we feel that his untimely death has left vacant a place which cannot be filled by any other person with the same degree of efficiency and success."

Mr. Saunders died on the 9th of May, 1906. Since then, the Merchants Bank has been converted into the Merchants National Bank, with the son, Phil C. Saunders, as its vice president. He was educated in the schools of Milbank and soon after his textbooks were put aside, he entered the bank in which he has worked upward to the position of vice president, acting in that capacity since 1908. He is one of Milbank's native sons, his birth having there occurred October 18, 1885. He is very prominent in Masonry and was made master of Milbank Lodge, No. 20, at the early age of twenty-four years, serving in that capacity two terms. He is also a Royal Arch Mason and has served for six years as king of the chapter. He likewise belongs to the Knight Templar commandery and the Mystic Shrine. He is identified with various business concerns of Milbank, is interested in a lumberyard, is the owner of considerable town property and has large farming interests. He is also one of the leaders in the Commercial Club and there is no phase of public life demanding recognition and support to which he does not give immediate and generous aid. He is following the example of his honored father and the life work of both has been such as to commend them to the highest respect and goodwill of all who have known them.

JACOB SCHAETZEL, Jr.

J. Schaetzel, Jr. one of the best known citizens of Sioux Falls, and who has the distinction of having been the first mayor of the city after its incorporation as such, is a native of the state of Wisconsin, having been born on a farm in Washington County, on the 16th of May, 1850, and being a son of Jacob and Katharine (Kissinger) Schaetzel, both of whom were born in Darmstadt, Germany, the father having been a farmer by vocation and having passed the closing years of his life in Freeport, Illinois, where he died in 1899, his devoted wife passing away in 1885, while all of their eight children are living at the present time. After completing the curriculum of the district schools, the subject continued his studies in the Lawrence University, at Appleton, Wisconsin. At the age of nineteen years, he secured employment as clerk in a store at Freeport, Illinois, where he remained for a period of six years, gaining practical knowledge, which proved of great value to him in his later and independent business operations. Mr. Schaetzel became one of the pioneers of Minnehaha County, South Dakota, where he took up his residence on the 22d of February, 1876, settling in Sioux Falls, which was at the time a straggling little village of about two hundred and fifty population. In the intervening years he has left an indelible impress upon the civic, industrial and business affairs of the city, county and state, while to him has come a due measure of success as the result of his well-directed endeavors along legitimate lines of enterprise. For the first few years after his arrival in the state Mr. Schaetzel gave his attention principally to the real-estate and insurance business and to the shipping in of horses, for which he found a ready demand as the tide of immigration set in. For two years he conducted a livery and sales stable in Sioux Falls, and since that time his name has been associated with a large number of important and varied business enterprises, while he has accumulated a competence. He is the owner of valuable property in the city and county and is a stockholder in various industrial and financial concerns, having been at one time a stockholder in the German Bank, and a member of its directorate. As has been well said of him, "There are no negative elements in his makeup; he is energetic and enterprising, and is a good citizen."

In politics Mr. Schaetzel accords an uncompromising allegiance to the Republican party, in whose cause he has been an active worker, being one of the wheelhorses of the party in Minnehaha County. In 1881, upon the death of Thomas T. Cochran, who has been incumbent of the office, he was elected president of the village council of Sioux Falls, and forthwith showed his progressive ideas and strong power of initiative by vigorously agitating the question of securing to the place a charter as a city, its population and commercial prestige at the time entitling its incorporation as such. He called a meeting of the citizens for the consideration of the matter, and within the autumn of that year definite steps were taken toward the accomplishment of the desired end a city charter being drafted and other necessary preliminary work accomplished. The president of the village then went to the territorial capital and presented the claims of Sioux Falls to the legislature, which duly passed the bill authorizing the incorporation as a city. At the first general election under the new charter, in 1882, Mr. Schaetzel was further honored by his fellow citizens by being elected the first mayor of the city, receiving a most gratifying support and continuing in tenure of the office for a term of two years, while he gave a most able, careful and business-like administration, the burdens imposed upon him in the connection being heavy, as his term of office was one marked by reorganization and readjustment in municipal affairs, but his vigorous policy was such that harmony and wise administration marked the course of his official career. He was county commissioner for the fifth district during the years 1893-4-5, and was a very active and influential member of the board, while his aid and influence have at all times been loyally given in support of all measures and undertakings for the advancement of the best interests of the city and state.

On the 7th of September, 1871, Mr. Schaetzel was united in marriage to Miss Catharine Brenner, who was born and reared in Washington county, Wisconsin, being a daughter of Peter and Christina (Kissinger) Brenner, both of whom died in Polk, Washington County, Wisconsin. Mr. and Mrs. Schaetzel have two children, Marie, who is the wife of Ernest D. Skillman, of Irene, this state, and William A., who is engaged in business at Elk Point. The subject is a member of the Masonic fraternity, in which he has passed the degrees of lodge and chapter.

ADOLPH G. SCHMIDT

Adolph G. Schmidt, who is successfully engaged in the real estate and loan business at Madison, has been a resident of Lake County for the past twenty-eight years and has taken an active part in the public life of his community. His birth occurred in Wisconsin on the 19th of January, 1859, his parents being John C. and Christina Schmidt. The father, a carpenter, farmer and merchant, is still living.

In the acquirement of an education Adolph G. Schmidt attended the public schools and Way land Academy at Beaver Dam, Wisconsin. Subsequently he devoted his attention to general agricultural pursuits in the Badger state for a number of years or until 1886, when he came to South Dakota. Here he purchased land and followed farming for about seven years. On the expiration of that period, in 1892, he was elected registrar of deeds for Lake County and two years later won reelection, making a highly creditable and commendable record in that connection. At the end of his second term, he embarked in the real-estate business at Madison and has been engaged therein continuously to the present time. He keeps thoroughly informed on realty values and his advice is frequently sought to good advantage. From 1896 until 1910 he was alone in business but in the latter year formed a partnership with Mr. Robeck, the firm style being Schmidt & Robeck. That firm has been the greatest factor in bringing to Lake County the substantial farmers that now make up the greater part of its population and who have proved such desirable citizens. The firm also engages in the loan business.

On the 24th of December, 1881, Mr. Schmidt was joined in wedlock to Miss Mary A. Ablard, a daughter of James and Mary Ablard. Their children, all of whom are living, are five in number, namely: William, a resident of Redfield; Winnie, the wife of Harry Curtis, of Redfield; Elmer, of Redfield; Goldy; and Ada. The wife and mother died at Madison in May, 1914.

Mr. Schmidt gives his political allegiance to the republican party and is widely recognized as a progressive and public-spirited citizen who does all in his power to promote the general welfare and to advance the interests of his home community. He held the office of mayor for one term and served as alderman for a period of sixteen years, proving a public official of ability and worth. The cause of education has ever found in him a stanch champion and he has served as a member of the school board for many years. His religious faith is that of the English Baptist church, while fraternally he is identified with the Masons and the Independent Order of Odd Fellows. In hunting and motoring he finds both recreation and pleasure. He is a man of undoubted integrity in business, of progressive spirit and marked enterprise, whose popularity and prosperity have been won through his many good qualities and his well-directed effort.

FREDERICK B. SCHNEERER, M. D.

Dr. Frederick B. Schneerer, actively engaged in the practice of medicine and surgery in Deadwood, was born in Norwalk, Ohio, January 8, 1877, a son of Frederick W. and Abbie (Cahoon) Schneerer, the former a native of Cleveland and the latter of Elyria, Ohio. The paternal grandfather was among the first homesteaders at Cleveland and the maternal grandfather was one of the early settlers at North Avon, Ohio. Dr. Frederick W. Schneerer, the father, engaged in the practice of medicine in early life at Norwalk, Ohio, and has continuously followed his chosen profession since 1874. Success has attended his efforts and he is today an extensive landowner in his native state. He has likewise held various local offices and is an influential citizen in the community in which he makes his home, his activities having done much to promote the welfare and progress of his section of the state, while along professional lines he has ever held to the highest standards and made his work of great worth to his fellowmen. To him and his wife were born four children, of whom Frederick B. is the eldest. Karl E. is now a practicing physician and surgeon of Norwalk, Ohio. Mary C. is the wife of Herbert E. Parker, secretary of the Young Men's Christian Association at Plainfield, New Jersey. Theodore Cahoon is an active representative of the medical fraternity at Los Angeles, California.

Dr. Frederick B. Schneerer attended the public schools of Norwalk, Ohio, until he had completed the high-school course, after which he entered Kenyon College at Gambier, Ohio, and then spent a year at Cincinnati in 1900. He won the Ph. G. degree upon the completion of a course of study in the normal school at Valparaiso, Indiana. He completed his course in medicine at the Bennett Medical College of Chicago with the class of 1902 and thus completed his preparation for his profession. During his schooldays he had worked at intervals through vacations and he practiced medicine for one year before reaching the age of twenty-five. He came west to Deadwood, arriving in August, 1903, and there he has since remained, an able and active member of the medical profession. Reading and research have kept him in touch with the advanced thought of the day and have brought him understanding of the most modern scientific methods of medical and surgical practice. He is also a landowner in Ohio and in Montana. In April, 1898, he enlisted in the Hospital Corps of the Sixteenth Ohio Regiment, which was changed to the Sixth Ohio Volunteer Infantry, and had charge of the hospital department. He served for two years in the army, spending eight months of that time in Cuba. He suffered an attack of typhoid fever at Chickamauga Park, where he remained for three months before going to Cuba. He is a member of the South Dakota Eclectic Medical Society, the National Eclectic Medical Association, the Ninth District Medical Society and the American Medical Association.

On the 6th of July, 1904, Dr. Schneerer was united in marriage to Miss Verda Mary Phillips, who was born in Montreal, Canada, a daughter of Harry and Matilda (Barr) Phillips, natives of England and Edgewood, Iowa, respectively. The father is now a contractor at Deadwood. To Dr. and Mrs. Schneerer have been born two children, Verda Louise and Helen Mary.

Dr. Schneerer is a member of the Masonic fraternity, in which he has attained high rank. He belongs to the blue lodge at Deadwood, in which he served as master in 1906 and 1907. He is a consistory Mason, having attained the thirty-second degree in the Scottish Rite, he also belongs to the York Rite bodies and he is a member of the Mystic Shrine. He is also exalted ruler of the Elks. His religious faith is that of the Methodist Episcopal church and his political belief that of the republican party, but the only offices which he has held have been along the strict path of his profession. He has served as city physician, as county physician, as pension examiner and as a member of the board of health. He holds to high professional ideals and utilizes every opportunity for advancing to the high standards which he has set up.

LEWIS V. SCHNEIDER

L. V. Schneider, one of the most prominent and highly honored business men of Salem, McCook County, was born in La Crosse, Wisconsin, on the 28th of December, 1860, being a son of Joseph and Frances (Ringl) Schneider, of whose children eight are living at the present time. The father of the subject was born in Austria, where he was reared to maturity, there learning the trade of cabinetmaking. As a young man he emigrated to the United States, and passed a number of years in the state of New York, where he followed the vocation of carpenter and builder. About 1855 he came west to La Crosse, Wisconsin, as one of the pioneers of the place, and there he followed contracting and building for some time, also devoting no little attention to work as a millwright, through which association he was finally led to engage in the milling business. In 1890 he sold his milling interests in Sheldon, Minnesota, where he had resided for a number of years, and came to South Dakota to pass his declining days with his sons. He died in October, 1897, at the age of sixty-seven years. His widow now resides with her daughter, Mrs. Frances Roop, of Salem, this state. Joseph Schneider was a Democrat in politics, but was not deflected from its original principles by the heresy of free silver. He was a member of the Lutheran church, as is also his widow, who was born in Austria.

The subject of this review secured his early educational raining in the common schools of the pioneer epoch in Wisconsin, having attended school in a little log building of the most primitive type. At the age of thirteen years, he secured a position in a general store at La Crosse, Wisconsin, working the first year for his board and clothing and being thereafter advanced in salary from year to year, as his value increased. He retained this clerical position seven years and then, in the spring of 1881, came to the territory of Dakota, being one-week enroute. His financial resources were represented in the sum of about five hundred dollars, which he had saved from his earnings, and after returning to La Crosse to make a final settlement of his affairs preliminary to taking up his permanent abode in what is now South Dakota, he returned to Sioux Falls, in May, 1881, driving through from Valley Springs, where the railway train had been compelled to stop, by reason of the damage done to the roadbed by heavy storms. He finally reached his destination, having been compelled to ford numerous swollen streams and to encounter other annoying obstacles. Upon his arrival he entered the employ of Frank Kunerth, a prominent general merchant of Sioux Falls and one who stands high in Masonic circles. In December, 1881, Mr. Schneider engaged in business on his own responsibility, entering into partnership with P. L. Runkel, and coming to Salem. Here they erected a store building and on the 27th of the following March formally opened the same for business, having a stock of general merchandise. The enterprise prospered and in June, 1889, Mr. Schneider purchased his partner's interest and soon afterward admitted his brother Henry to partnership, while in 1890 his brother Joseph also became a member of the firm. On the 2d of March, 1899, to meet the exigencies of the constantly increasing business, the firm was incorporated as the Schneider Brothers' Company, under which title the business has since been continued, the establishment of the company being one of the best equipped department stores in this section of the state and commanding a large and widely extended trade throughout the surrounding country. In addition to a full and select line of general merchandise the company also conduct an extensive trade in the handling of farming implements and machinery, this department having been an adjunct of the business since 1882, while in the connection it may be noted that our subject sold the first binder ever sold in the county. In 1892 Mr. Schneider was prominently concerned in the organization of the McCook State Bank, of Salem, of which he was chosen president, retaining this office until 1897, when he disposed of his interest in the institution. In 1895, in company with his two brothers, he purchased the Salem flouring mill, and in 1892 they established in connection with the same a modern heating and electric-lighting plant, supplying public facilities in these lines, and at that time they effected the organization of a stock company, known as the Salem Milling, Lighting and Heating Company, under which corporate title the enterprise has since been successfully conducted. Since its organization Mr. Schneider has served as its president.

Since 1896 Mr. Schneider has been aligned with the Republican party, while prior to that time he was a sound-money Democrat. In 1896 he was persuaded to accept the nomination of the Republican party for state senator from his district, but met defeat in the Democratic landslide which prevailed in this section in that campaign. In 1888 he was chairman of the Democratic central committee of his county, and later served as councilman and mayor of Salem. He and his wife are members of the Presbyterian church.

He is a prominent and valued member of the Masonic fraternity in the state, and was a member of the building committee which had the supervision of the erection of the fine Masonic temple in Yankton, being also a member of the board of trustees, as is he at the present time. His Masonic affiliations are briefly noted as follows: Fortitude Lodge, No. 73, Ancient Free and Accepted Masons; Chapter No. 34, Royal Arch Masons; Constantine Commandery, No. II, Knights Templar; Oriental Consistory, No. I, Ancient Accepted Scottish Rite, in which he has attained the thirty-second degree; and EI Riad Temple, Ancient Arabic Order of the Nobles of the Mystic Shrine. He also holds membership in Salem Lodge, No. 106, Independent Order of Odd Fellows; the Knights of the Maccabees and the Ancient Order of United Workmen. On the 28th of August, 1883. Mr. Schneider was united in marriage to Miss Emma Jehlen, of La Crosse, Wisconsin, and they have one child, Mae.

J. HENRY SCHNITZEL

J. HENRY SCHNITZEL

J. Henry Schnitzel, the general manager of the Golden Reward Consolidated Gold Mining & Milling Company, has headquarters at Deadwood and is well known as a mining expert and an administrative officer of ability. He was born in Gernsheim, Bavaria, Germany, on the 20th of September, 1860, a son of Phillip and Fredericka (Kobler) Schnitzel. The father was a native of the same locality and an officer in the German army, as were all of his brothers. He was connected with military affairs until his death, which occurred in 1864. The mother came of a long-established family who were also prominent in the army. She died in the same year as did her husband, in 1864.

J. Henry Schnitzel was an only child and was left an orphan when but four years of age. His grandmother and uncle became his guardians and he was given excellent educational opportunities. From five to ten years, he attended a military school and then attended Latin school and later college. He specialized in the study of chemistry as applied to manufacturing and received his degree as a pharmacist when twenty years of age. In the meantime, he had gained considerable experience as a druggist and after gaining his degree he worked for one year for the Merk Chemical Company at Darmstadt and then came to the United States on a visit to relatives living in Monmouth, Illinois. At that time, he had no idea of making his home in this country, but he entered the employ of his uncle, who conducted a packing house at that place, and was given charge of the plant and office, in that way securing a thorough business training. At the same time, he kept informed as to the advancement in chemistry.

In 1886 Mr. Schnitzel came to Deadwood, where he was employed in a butcher shop for about a year, and at the same time worked for the carbonate camp in the Bald Mountain district, remaining with them until 1890. He was then employed as a chemist and assayer in the Deadwood & Delaware smelter until 1894, and in the meantime developed some mining properties of his own in Wyoming and Montana, which he still owns. During that period, he was also executive for George W. Perkins, president of the Chicago, Burlington & Quincy Railroad in his mining operations. In 1894 Mr. Schnitzel established an assay and chemical office in Lead and incidentally engaged in mining on his own account by leasing and working property belonging to him. He continued as an assayer and chemist until 1904 and his business in that line became very extensive, affording employment at times for one hundred men. He also continued the development of his mining properties and realized large returns from his ventures. In the fall of 1905, he was made general manager of the Golden Reward Consolidated Gold Mining & Milling Company, whose property was located in the Bald Mountain district in 1895 by Harris Franklin, who was actively identified with it for many years but finally sold his interest. It is the largest mine in the district and outside of the Homestake the largest in the Black Hills. The work of Mr. Schnitzel as general manager has been very satisfactory to the directors, as he has instituted many new and improved processes and has been very progressive in all phases of operation. In developing the property, he seeks always to avoid waste of time, labor or ore, and by his efficient methods secures the largest return with the least expenditure of money and energy.

Mr. Schnitzel was for many years interested in the cattle business in Wyoming on an extensive scale but sold out in 1912. He is a director in the Consolidated Power & Light Company of Deadwood and in a number of mining corporations. He is now devoting practically his entire time and thought to the Golden Reward Company and his successful record as its general manager is the natural result of the concentration of his abilities upon his work in that capacity.

On the 12th of May, 1895, Mr. Schnitzel was united in marriage to Miss Lena Scheuble, of Lienheim, Baden, Germany. To their union have been born three children: Phillip, Frederick and Henry.

Mr. Schnitzel is well known fraternally, being a member of the Golden Star Lodge, No. 9, F. & A. M., of Lead; Golden Belt Chapter, No. 35, R. A. M., of Lead; Lead Commandery, No. 18, K. T.; Black Hills Council, No. 3, R. & S. M.; Black Hills Consistory, No. 3, A. & A. S. R., of Deadwood; and of Naja Temple, A. A. O. N. M. S., of Deadwood. His political allegiance is given to the republican party, but he has never been active in politics, as his business interests have demanded his undivided attention. He is one of the representative and respected mining men of the Black Hills and has gained not only financial independence but also the esteem of those who come in contact with him.

FRANCIS H. SCHOONMAKER, M. D.

Francis H. Schoonmaker, M. D., of Arlington, was born in Gardner, Illinois, September 24, 1858, being the oldest in a family of four children, whose parents were W. H. and M. E. (Hall) Schoonmaker. The father, a native of New York and of German-English descent, went to Illinois when a young man and engaged in merchandising in the town of Gardner, to which line of business he devoted the greater part of his life. He spent some twelve or fifteen years in Joliet, Illinois, where he also conducted a mercantile establishment and finished his life work in that city, dying about 1891. Mrs. Schoonmaker still makes her home in the above place, and of her four children there are still living Francis H., Charles F. and Lorise AL, the deceased member of the family dying in infancy.

Doctor Schoonmaker was reared to manhood in his native state, attended the schools of Gardner and other places until the age of seventeen, spending his vacations the meantime on a farm, where he early learned the lessons of industry, which had so much to do in shaping his future course of life. Having decided to enter the medical profession, he spent one and a half years in preliminary study under the direction of Dr. C. B. Alford, of Odell, Illinois, now of Huron, South Dakota, and in 1884, at the age of twenty-six, entered the Chicago Medical College of Northwestern University, from which he was graduated three years later. In the spring of 1887 Doctor Schoonmaker located in Beloit, Kansas, but not finding a favorable opening at that place, he returned to Illinois in September of the same year and the following

December came to Arlington, South Dakota, where he has since been actively engaged in the practice of his profession.

Doctor Schoonmaker, in 1892, entered the marriage relation with Miss Frances A, Searles, of Joliet, Illinois, daughter of M. E. and J. M. Searles, the father for many years a leading grocer of that city, also deputy postmaster. One child has been born to this union, a son who answers to the name of William F.

The Doctor is a member of the Masonic fraternity, belonging to the blue lodge and chapter at Arlington, and the commandery at Brookings. He is also identified with the Ancient Order of United Woodmen, the Woodmen and the Degree of Honor, being at this time grand medical examiner of the first named order. He acts in the capacity of medical examiner for the leading life insurance companies represented in this part of the state, and for some time past has been serving as coroner of Kingsbury County, to which office he was elected by the Republican party. Although a Republican in principle, he generally votes as his judgment dictates, especially in local affairs, where politics should cut but little figure. Mrs. Schoonmaker is a member of the Baptist church of Arlington; she is also a member of the Eastern Star and Degree of Honor. While not subscribing to any creed or statement of faith, the Doctor has a profound regard for religion and the church, being a liberal contributor to the congregation with which his wife is identified.

CHARLES T. SCHROYER, M. D.

Dr. Charles T. Schroyer, a practicing physician of Sioux Falls, was born in Adamsville, Ohio, on the 27th of July, 1876, a son of Peter C. and Emma Schroyer. The father has always followed farming and stock-raising, thus providing for the support of his family. He sent his son Charles to the public schools and in mastering his studies the boy displayed special aptitude, so that he taught one term of school when but thirteen years of age. The succeeding year he entered the Ohio State University, from which he was graduated in 1898, having completed the medical course. He located for practice in Adams Mills, Ohio, where he remained for about one year, when, thinking that better opportunities might be enjoyed in the new and growing northwest, he came to South Dakota, settling at Baltic, where he remained for ten years. On the expiration of that decade, he removed to Chester, where for four years he successfully engaged in practice, his professional duties becoming more and more extensive and important and thus making heavier demands upon his time. He likewise became a stockholder in the Farmers State Bank while having his abode in Chester. In January, 1915, he removed to Sioux Falls and opened an office in the Minnehaha building. For many years he has been making a specialty of the treatment of cancer and he has met with such marked success therein that of late years he has devoted his time exclusively to the treatment of that disease.

On the 2d of October, 1900, Dr. Schroyer was united in marriage to Mite Hilda Holmes, a daughter of George Holmes. They have four children, namely: Doxie, Maurice, Denver and Chester. The religious faith of Dr. and Mrs. Schroyer is that of the Methodist church and they manifest a helpful interest in its work. He is prominently known in fraternal circles, holding membership with the Masons at Colton, the Elks at Sioux Falls and the Knights of Pythias, the Modern Woodmen and the Modern Brotherhood of America, all at Chester. In the Elks lodge at Sioux Falls he is a charter member. His political allegiance is given to the democratic party but he does not seek nor desire public office, preferring to concentrate his energies upon his professional duties. He enjoys the automobile and other forms of outdoor sport and thus he maintains that even balance in physical and mental development and power that means so much to every professional man. He is conscientious in the performance of all his professional duties, never regarding lightly the work that he has undertaken, and his ready sympathy and intuition as well as his scientific knowledge have been factors in his growing success.

JOHN W. SCHULTZ

John W. Schultz, one of the leading merchants and representative citizens of Wessington, Beadle County, is a native of Germany, where he was born on the 23d of February, 1835. After his father's death the widow came with her two sons and two daughters to America, the family locating in Cincinnati, Ohio, where she passed the remainder of her life, while of the children our subject is now the only survivor. The early educational discipline of Mr. Schultz was secured in the excellent schools of his fatherland, and he was about fourteen years of age at the time of the family emigration to America. He thereafter attended the common schools in Cincinnati, Ohio, and effectively supplemented the training he had previously received. After attaining years of maturity he devoted his attention to farming in the old Buckeye state until 1855, when he came west as a pioneer of the state of Iowa, locating in Dubuque, Dubuque county, where he was engaged in the mercantile business until 1882, in which year he came to what is now the state of South Dakota and became one of the early settlers of Wessington, where he was engaged in the general merchandise business until 1885, when he removed to Hand County, which lies contiguous on the west of Beadle county, and there successfully continued farming until 1897, when he returned to Wessington, where he now controls the most extensive mercantile business in this section, drawing his trade from a wide radius of country and having the confidence and esteem of the people of this locality, where he has made his home for so many years. He is a straightforward and reliable business man, urbane and courteous at all times and his name is a synonym of honor and integrity wherever he is known. He has ever been a stalwart advocate of the principles and policies for which the Republican party stands sponsor, and has been an active worker in its cause. In 1894 he represented Hand County in the state senate, where he made a most creditable record. Though he was candidate on the Republican ticket in the preceding election his personal popularity was such as to enable him to overcome the large Populist majority which was normally given in Hand County at that period, and his election was a merited tribute of popular esteem and good will. He also served one term as a member of the board of commissioners of Hand County. He is identified with the Masonic fraternity and the Ancient Order of United Workmen.

PETER H. SCHULTZ

Peter H. Schultz, a leading, influential and prosperous citizen of Kingsbury County, has made his home in South Dakota for more than a quarter of a century and during the past sixteen years has successfully conducted business as a member of the firm of Richards & Schultz, general merchants of Iroquois. His birth occurred in Germany on the 26th of August, 1869, his parents being John H. and Anna M. Schultz, the former a cooper and farmer by occupation. He began his education in the schools of the fatherland and subsequently pursued a high-school course in Denmark. After putting aside his textbooks he worked on a farm until the time of his emigration to the United States, in 1888. He made his way direct to South Dakota and on the 5th of June of that year arrived in Iroquois. During the following three years he was engaged in farm work and then embarked in the butchering business at Iroquois, there conducting an enterprise of that character for seven and a half years. On the expiration of that period, in 1898, in association with Frank A. Richards, he opened a general merchandising establishment, beginning business on a modest scale. The firm has since been conducted under the style of Richards & Schultz and has been accorded a constantly growing and gratifying patronage until the business is now a very profitable one. The proprietors study the wishes of their patrons and especially cater to the needs and demands of the farmer. Mr. Schultz is a stockholder in the Farmers Elevator Company and also in the Bank of Bancroft and enjoys an enviable reputation as one of the substantial, enterprising and public-spirited citizens of his community.

On the 21st of January, 1899, Mr. Schultz was united in marriage to Miss Ella M. Brown, a daughter of James P. Brown, who took up a homestead claim in South Dakota in 1882. To them have been born two children, Philo H. and Leo M.

Mr. Schultz is a republican in politics and in 1912 was chosen as the representative of the twenty-third district in the state legislature, making such a creditable record that he was again nominated by his party for reelection. He has also served as a member of the township board and has ever been a most public-spirited and loyal citizen who has done everything in his power to promote the general welfare and advance the best interests of the community. Fraternally he is identified with the Masons, belonging to the consistory at Yankton and also to the Mystic Shrine at Sioux Falls. He is likewise affiliated with the Independent Order of Odd Fellows, the Benevolent Protective Order of Elks, the Ancient Order of United Workmen, the Modern Woodmen of America and the Danish Brotherhood. He delights in fishing, hunting and motoring and in social circles has made many friends who appreciate his character worth and enjoy his companionship.

KNUTE E. SEIM

Knute E. Seim, vice president of the Bank of Vienna, is one of the popular and prominent young business men of Clark County. His birth occurred in Norway on the 29th of November, 1884, his parents being Elling and Ragnilda Seim, who emigrated to the United States and established their home at Willow Lakes, Clark County, South Dakota, in 1890. The father here purchased six hundred acres of land and still cultivates the property, having met with a gratifying measure of success in his undertakings as an agriculturist. Both Mr. and Mrs. Elling Seim are well known and highly esteemed throughout the community which has now been their home for a quarter of a century.

Knute E. Seim, who was a lad of six years when brought to this state by his parents, attended the public schools in the acquirement of an education, and after putting aside his text-books assisted his father in the operation of the home farm. Subsequently he was employed in a store at Vienna, Clark County, for three years, and afterward was engaged in the grain business at that place for a similar period. In 1910 he was elected county treasurer on the republican ticket, took office on the 1st of January, 1911, and was reelected in 1912, serving two terms in that position. He made a most creditable and highly commendable record in that capacity, discharging the important duties devolving upon him in a prompt and efficient manner. He is vice president of the Bank of Vienna and is known as an able and progressive business man.

On the 24th of November, 1908, he was united in marriage to Miss Emma Knadle, a daughter of John and Mary Knadle, of Vienna. They have two children: Kenneth, born in 1909; and Eileen, born in 1914. In politics Mr. Seim is a stanch republican, while his religious faith is that of the Lutheran church. His fraternal relations are with the Masons, the Independent Order of Odd Fellows and the Knights of Pythias, and fishing and hunting afford him recreation. A man of genial, cordial nature, he has gained the goodwill and friendship of all with whom he has been associated in public, fraternal and social relations.

THOMAS J. SHANARD

Thomas J. Shanard is well known in financial circles of South Dakota as president of the Dolton State Bank and as cashier of the First National Bank of Bridgewater, having served in the latter capacity during the past two decades. His birth occurred in Brownsville, Minnesota, on the 6th of January, 1869, his parents being J. H. and Mary A. Shanard, the latter of whom is still living. In 1872 the family came to South Dakota, locating at Elk Point, where the father conducted a hotel on the present site of the First National Bank. Subsequently he removed to Yankton and there embarked in the lumber business, conducting an enterprise of that character in association with Harry Wynn. His demise occurred in 1911, after he had resided in this state for a period covering nearly four decades, and in his passing the community lost one of its prosperous business men as well as respected and public-spirited citizens.

Thomas J. Shanard, who was but three years of age when brought to this state by his parents, pursued his early education in the public schools and afterward attended the University of South Dakota, being graduated from that institution with the class of 1891. Subsequently he was identified with his father in the lumber business for three years and on the expiration of that period came to Bridgewater to take the position of cashier of the First National Bank of that place, E. L. Abel being president of the institution. In this capacity he has served continuously during the past twenty years and has won and maintained an enviable reputation as a courteous, obliging and able official, his efforts contributing in no small degree to the continued growth and success of the bank. He is likewise president of the Dolton State Bank. He is also extensively interested in real estate and has gained recognition among the substantial and representative citizens of McCook County.

On the 4th of June, 1913, Mr. Shanard was united in marriage to Miss Clara Morgan, a daughter of John C. and Clara (Wilson) Morgan, of Canonsburg, Pennsylvania. Mr. and Mrs. Shanard have one child, John Morgan. Mr. Shanard gives his political allegiance to the republican party, while fraternally he is identified with the Masons, the Independent Order of Odd Fellows and the Benevolent Protective Order of Elks. He is fond of motoring, baseball and other outdoor sports, finding therein needed recreation. The period of his residence in South Dakota covers more than four decades and he is therefore largely familiar with its annals from pioneer times down to the present, while in the work of development and progress he has done his share.

LEWIS J. SHAW

Lewis J. Shaw, a member of the Shaw Company, funeral directors at Watertown, was born in Cresco, Iowa, on the 27th of November, 1869, his parents being James J. and Ella Shaw. The family arrived in South Dakota in 1880, settling at Milbank, where the father engaged in the grocery business and also conducted a general store until 1883, when he left that place and went to Cresco, Iowa, where he spent one year farming. He afterward took up his abode in Madison, South Dakota, where he conducted a grocery store, but he was living retired at the time of his death on Thanksgiving Day, 1914, having through his well-directed business affairs won a handsome competence that enabled him to rest from further labor.

His wife survives and makes her home at Madison. The father had a military record of which he might well have been proud. He was with Grant's army at Vicksburg and served all through the south, Florida, Mobile, New Orleans, etc., four years in all.

L. J. Shaw completed his common-school education when fourteen years of age. Having decided upon newspaper work as a vocation he became associated with the Sentinel at Madison, where he worked for five or six years and then went to the Clay County Freeman at Vermillion and from there to Hawarden, Iowa, where he formed a partnership and published the Hawarden Republican. Desiring then to supplement his earlier common-school education he entered the Madison Normal School and was graduated with the class of 1896, having completed the four years' course in two and one-half years. Before he had had an opportunity to locate, he was urged to accept the position of principal of the Hurley (S. D.) schools and remained there three years. He then turned his attention to the furniture and undertaking business in Mitchell, where he remained for three years, and on the expiration of that period came to Watertown in 1903. Here he opened a furniture store in partnership with F. L. Bramble but in the spring of 1908, he became the organizer of the Cozey Home Furniture Company. After five years in this connection, he withdrew and founded his present undertaking establishment. He has met with a fair measure of success since embarking in that business and now has a well-appointed store, carrying a well selected line of goods to meet the varied tastes of the general public.

In July, 1897, Mr. Shaw was united in marriage to Miss Dora Noble, a daughter of Harvey Noble, of Mitchell, and they have become the parents of four children: Verne, aged fourteen; Lorese, aged twelve; Harvey J., six; and Lois Alyne, in her fourth year. The parents hold membership in the Methodist church and are highly esteemed residents of Watertown.

Mr. Shaw is a republican and keeps well informed on the questions and issues of the day but is not a politician in the sense of office seeking. Fraternally he is a Mason and has attained the Knight Templar degree of the York Rite. He also has membership with the Elks, the Modern Woodmen of America, the Workmen, the Eagles and the Owls and he is also a member of the Watertown Country Club. His enthusiasm in lines of recreation is for the automobile and with his machine he enjoys his leisure hours. He realizes, however, that industry and close application are the basis of success and in the use of those qualities he is winning prosperity.

JACOB SCHAETZEL, JR.

By his life's labors Jacob Schaetzel, Jr., has contributed much toward the development of Sioux Falls, serving as its first mayor in 1882-3-4. He is today president of the Irene State Bank, of Irene, Clay County, South Dakota, an institution of safe and sound principle.

Mr. Schaetzel was born on a farm in Washington County, Wisconsin, May 16, 1850, a son of Jacob and Katherine (Kissinger) Schaetzel, both of whom were born in Hesse Darmstadt, Germany. The father's birth occurred in 1825 and he came with his parents in 1840 to America, the family making their way to Washington county, Wisconsin, soon after their arrival. In 1868 he located in Freeport, Illinois, where he passed away October 29, 1900, lacking only six days of being seventy-six years of age. His wife passed away in Freeport, November 14, 1886. The father, who was an agriculturist and miller by occupation, attained prosperity by close application and thorough methods, and was well and favorably known in the neighborhood in which he resided. In his family were eight children.

Jacob Schaetzel, Jr., attended country school in Washington county and rounded out his education with a course at Lawrence University in Appleton, Wisconsin. He left that institution in June, 1868, joining his parents, who then lived near Freeport, Illinois, and he remained upon the farm for five months. He then secured employment as a clerk in a general merchandise store in Freeport, where he remained for a period of six years, gaining practical and valuable knowledge along commercial lines. In September, 1875, he came to Sioux Falls, South Dakota, but shortly afterward returned to his home in Illinois. However, he was favorably impressed with the opportunities which the young village of two hundred and fifty people offered, and in March, 1876, returned to make his permanent residence here. He is therefore one of the early pioneers of Sioux Falls and his active career is closely intertwined with its history of advancement. For a few years Mr. Schaetzel gave attention to the real-estate and insurance business and also engaged in shipping horses. For a time, he conducted a livery and sale stable in Sioux Falls and has gradually become connected with a number of important business enterprises. He also owns valuable property and is a stockholder in a number of industries and financial concerns. Among other interests with which he is connected is the Irene State Bank, of Irene, South Dakota, of which he is president. He has shown himself able in all situations and impeccable in all business deals. While he has made his way to the fore, he has always been considerate of the interests of others and has been a real builder of success, whose path to fortune has not been strewn with the wreck of others. He has not only built for himself but for the greatness of this state and for generations which now enjoy such prosperous conditions as he has helped to make possible.

The political history of Mr. Schaetzel is a chapter by itself. He is a republican — and that a republican Simon-pure. He does not belong to any of the fringes of the republican party but as a straight republican has always supported the principles and candidates of his party. He has done much toward raising the prestige of that organization in Minnehaha County. It was in 1881, upon the death of Thomas Cochran, who had been the incumbent of the office, that Mr. Schaetzel was elected president of the village council of Sioux Falls and instanter gave evidence of his progressive ideas and his initiative by vigorously agitating the question of securing a charter for the city. He called a meeting of the citizens and in the autumn of that year definite steps were taken toward the accomplishment of the desired end. A city charter was drafted and other preliminary work was accomplished. The president of the village board then presented his claims to the legislature and a bill authorizing the incorporation was duly passed. At the first general election in 1882 Mr. Schaetzel was chosen the first mayor of the city, receiving a most gratifying support and continuing in office for two years. Many initiatory laws had to be passed and Mr. Schaetzel had much to do in forming them. It may be said that his administration made the life of the young city prosperous from the beginning. He carefully brought together antagonizing interests and succeeded in his effort to make the beginning of the new city a period auguring well for the future. The salary attached to his office was one dollar a year and the warrant for his first year's remuneration has never been cashed, it being confiscated by his friends who had it framed that he might keep it as a memento of his first year of successful city government. The warrant for the second year's salary, one dollar, was suitably engraved and is now in Mr. Schaetzel's possession. In the next year, 1884, his constituents presented him with a handsome gold watch, chain and charm, suitably engraved, as being a gift from "the boys." Mr. Schaetzel served as county commissioner from the fifth district during 1893-4-5, and was an influential member of the board. He was for four years a member of the penitentiary board and did valuable work in that connection. In fact, he has ever been loyal in his support of measures and undertakings to promote the best interests of the state and city.

On September 7, 1871, in Washington County, Wisconsin, Mr. Schaetzel wedded Miss Catharine Brenner, who was born and grew to womanhood in that county. She is a daughter of Peter and Christina (Kissinger) Brenner. Mr. and Mrs. Schaetzel are the parents of two children: Marie E., who is the wife of

E. D. Skillman, cashier of The State Bank of Irene, South Dakota; and William A., the president of the Union County Bank, at Elk Point, South Dakota.

Mr. and Mrs. Schaetzel attend the Evangelical Lutheran church. Fraternally he is affiliated with the Masonic order, being a member of the lodge and chapter. For over thirty-eight years Mr. Schaetzel has been a resident of Sioux Falls and has proven himself in those long years a man of truly public spirit. He has given as much effort toward promoting the general welfare as he has to securing a competence, and there are few residents living today who have more disinterestedly rendered their service. In the history of Minnehaha County and Sioux Falls he should be given a place of honor, and the respect, confidence and veneration which he enjoys are but a slight token of the appreciation of a man of unselfish citizenship — a man of the west who has worked for the growing prosperity of the west unselfishly and with results that show themselves in comfortable and far-advanced conditions of civilization.

GEORGE SCHLOSSER

In newspaper circles the name of George Schlosser is widely known, for through an extended period he was connected with newspaper publication and news service. At the present time, however, he has retired from that field and is concentrating his efforts upon the management of his private business affairs and upon the furtherance of public activities and benevolent work, which make a strong appeal to him. He was born in Lodi, Wisconsin, September 3, 1857. His father, Henry Schlosser, a native of Germany, came to the United States in the early '50s. He was by trade a wagon maker and blacksmith and became identified with industrial interests at Lodi, where he conducted business until after the outbreak of the Civil War. He enlisted in the United States army during the latter part of that struggle and came to Dakota territory with General Sully, serving with the frontier forces for about fifteen months. He spent the later years of his life in Sioux Falls, passing away at the home of his son George in 1907, when he had reached the ripe old age of seventy-six years. His wife, who was Mrs. Frederica Schlosser, died during the early boyhood of their son George, who was the eldest of a family of six children.

In the public schools of Lodi, Wisconsin, George Schlosser was educated and later began learning the printer's trade in his home city. He was eager to master the business and continued in the house where he was originally employed, winning promotion from one position to another until 1883, when he came to Dakota territory. He settled first at Blunt, where he remained for five years, there establishing and conducting the Blunt Advocate. He afterward became a resident of Aberdeen, where he owned and published the Aberdeen Daily News. In 1896 he removed to Sioux Falls, where he established the ready print service, conducting business under the name of the South Dakota Newspaper Union. This undertaking, carefully managed by Mr. Schlosser, became a distinct success and advanced him far on the high road to fortune. In 1911 he disposed of the business and since that time has devoted his energies to his private business affairs and investments and to the many public undertakings in which he is deeply interested and which have constituted a vital force in pushing forward the wheels of progress in this section of the state. He served for some time as the efficient and popular secretary of the Commercial Club, his efforts in that direction being highly resultant and beneficial. He resigned in July, 1914, to take up the promotion of the Sioux Falls & Western Railway, which project is destined to make tributary to Sioux Falls an important section of the state with large natural resources needing a market outlet. He was the promoter of the Carpenter Hotel and has been largely instrumental in bringing various business enterprises and valuable commercial projects to the city. He is one of the directors and stockholders of the Queen City Fire Insurance Company and his private investments have been of an important and gratifying character.

Mr. Schlosser is free from partisan bias in his efforts for the public good and thus casts an independent local ballot, but where national issues are involved votes with the republican party. He was postmaster of the city and is president of the Sioux Falls public library and along lines which tend to ameliorate the hard conditions of life for the unfortunate he has done important and helpful work. He is president of the South Dakota Children's Home Society and has been deeply interested in this most worthy charity since its foundation. His religious faith is that of the Congregational church, which finds in him a worthy, loyal and helpful member and one of its generous supporters. He is now serving on its board of trustees. In Masonry he has reached the thirty-second degree of the Scottish Rite and his own life shows his appreciation of the teachings of the craft, which recognizes the brotherhood of mankind. He also belongs to the Independent Order of Odd Fellows and the Benevolent Protective Order of Elks.

On the 3d of March, 1877, Mr. Schlosser was married to Miss Ellen Louise Chandler, a daughter of Norman V. and Matilda Jane (Fox) Chandler, of Reedsburg, Wisconsin. They are the parents of seven children: Harry C., now living in Los Angeles, California; Arthur R., who is superintendent of the state training school at Plankinton, South Dakota; Nellie, a member of the faculty of the State Normal School at River Falls, Wisconsin; Hazel, assistant librarian of the Sioux Falls public library; Bertine, at home; and Ralph and Phillip, who are conducting their father's ranch in Montana.

Mr. Schlosser is a splendid type of a useful citizen. Some one has said he might be described as a general utility man because of the extent, importance and value of his public work. Few projects looking to the city's advancement have failed to elicit and receive his hearty cooperation and in many instances such a movement has been instituted by him and personally supervised to a successful completion. He is indeed one of the most worthy residents of Sioux Falls and he enjoys in unqualified measure the confidence, goodwill and honor of his fellowmen.

FRED ANDREW SEAMAN

F. A. SEAMAN, secretary of the Big Four Land and Cattle Company, incorporated, of Faulkton, was born at Arcade, Wyoming County, New York, on March 11, 1857. His parents were Andrew and Mary A. (Jackman) Seaman, the former a native of Holland, who came to America when he was seventeen years old with his people. The mother was born in Sardinia, Erie County, New York. The father died in 1882, and the mother has made her home in Faulkton, being now in her seventieth year. Her mother resides at Oshkosh, Wisconsin, and is in her ninety-first year.

Fred A. Seaman resided in Arcade, New York, until he was twenty-five years of age. He received a common-school and academic education. He then took a four-years course at reading law in the office of the district attorney's office of Wyoming county, and was admitted to practice both in New York and South Dakota. He came to South Dakota in 1883, and located at La Foon, which afterwards became the first county seat of Faulk County. He organized the Faulk County Bank in La Foon in 1885, of which he became cashier. He removed to Faulkton in the fall of 1886, moving the bank from La Foon. The bank was closed in 1890. He was on a ranch for five years, which ranch he still owns, it being seven miles southeast of Faulkton, and containing six hundred and forty acres.

Mr. Seaman was married December 2, 1886, to Miss Julia E. Smith, of La Foon, the daughter of Hon. D. S. Smith, who served in the South Dakota state senate. To the union two sons and five daughters have been born, of whom only the sons are living, Leonard A. and Paul S.

Mr. Seaman is a Mason, being a member of the blue lodge and chapter. Modern Woodmen of America, the Ancient Order of United Workmen and the Royal Arcanum. He is a member of the Congregational church, and is superintendent of the Sunday school for the past three years. For the last three years he has been secretary of the Big Four Land and Cattle Company. For seven years he was district collector for the Deering and McCormick Harvester Companies.

HERMAN V. SEARS

H. V. SEARS, of Plankinton, Aurora County, was born in Rock County, Wisconsin, on the 23d of October, 1848, being a son of Thomas W. and Elizabeth K. (Stone) Sears, of whose four children three are living: Herman V., subject of this sketch; Edgar P., engaged in the real-estate business in Salt Lake City; and Minnie, wife of J. F. Anderson, a lumber merchant of Mitchell, South Dakota. Thomas W. Sears was born in Southampton, England, and was ten years of age at the time of his parents' emigration to America, the family settling on a farm in New York state, where he was reared and educated. He came west about 1845 and settled in Rock County, Wisconsin, as a pioneer farmer, purchasing government land and there continuing to follow agricultural pursuits until 1867, when he removed to West Union, Iowa, where he engaged in mercantile business and was also interested in farming. In 1882 he came to Chamberlain, South Dakota, and here made wise investments in connection with various enterprises, having likewise been in advance of the tide of immigration in this state, as had he been in Wisconsin and Iowa. He here lived practically retired until his death, in 1887. He was a Republican in politics and both he and his wife were active members of the Congregational church, her death occurring in 1888.

Herman V. Sears secured his rudimentary education in the public schools and thereafter attended the Allen's Hill Seminary, at Allen's Hill, Wisconsin. He continued to be identified with farming until 1873, when he engaged in the livery and live-stock business in West Union, Iowa. In 1881 he came as a pioneer to Chamberlain, South Dakota, and here, on the 1st of January of that year, was associated with George Wright in opening to the public the popular hotel then known as the Wright House and now as the Mussman House. One year later he sold his interest to his partner and engaged in the livery and live-stock business, disposing of his livery a few years later and then becoming extensively engaged in the ranching business in Jackson County, being associated in this enterprise with his eldest son. In 1900 Mr. Sears, in company with J. W. Sanford and W. L. Montgomery, organized the Commercial Bank at Plankinton, and he was chosen cashier of the same, in which capacity he has since served, the bank having gained a high reputation for stability and capable management. In the spring of 1903, the subject purchased the interest of Mr. Sanford and the institution is now owned by him and Mr. Montgomery. Mr. Sears is a progressive and public-spirited citizen, is a stalwart Republican in politics and served as a member of the council and the school board while a resident of Chamberlain.

He is a member of West Union Lodge, Independent Order of Odd Fellows, in West Union, Iowa, and also of the Iowa Legion of Honor, while he is identified with the various bodies of the Masonic fraternity in Chamberlain and with the consistory of the Scottish Rite in Yankton, having attained to the thirty-second degree in the same. On the 5th of March, 1869, Mr. Sears was united in marriage to Miss Libbie Wade, of Sumner, Iowa, who died June 14, 1882, and of their four children three are living, namely: Fred H., who has charge of the ranching business in which he is associated with his father; Nellie W., who has charge of the books in the lumber yards of J. F. Anderson at the headquarters in Mitchell, this state; and Charles W., who is in the marine service at Yokohama, Japan, having participated in the Chinese campaign and also in the military maneuvers in the Philippines. On August 8, 1884, Mr. Sears was married to Miss Belle Drury, of Mason, Illinois, and they have one child. Lulu M. Sears, born September 20, 1889.

ROBERT T. SEDAM

Robert T. Sedam was born in Uniontown, Pennsylvania, on the 15th of February, 1839, being a son of Robert and Eve Sedam, representatives of early settled families in that section of our national domain. He received most meager educational advantages in his youth, his actual schooling being confined to six months, but his alert mentality and determination have enabled him to overcome this preliminary handicap, and through self-application, observation and active association with men and affairs he has gained a broad fund of practical knowledge and is recognized as a man of strong intellectuality. In May, 1839, at the age of six weeks, Mr. Sedam accompanied his parents on their removal to Freeport, Stephenson County, Illinois, where he was reared to manhood, the family having located on a farm in Stephenson County, as pioneers of that section.

Mr. Sedam continued to be identified with agricultural pursuits in Illinois until there came the call to higher duty, as the integrity of the nation was imperiled through armed rebellion. On the 19th of April, 1861, he tendered his services in defense of the Union, enlisting as a private in Company C, Fifteenth Illinois Volunteer Infantry, with which he proceeded to the front, his regiment being assigned to the Army of the Tennessee. He continued in active service for four years, six months and twelve days, receiving his honorable discharge, at Springfield, in July, 1865, after having made a record as a valiant and faithful soldier and having participated in many of the most notable battles of the great conflict. In October, 1864, at Acworth, Georgia, Mr. Sedam was captured by the Confederate forces under General Hood, and was held a prisoner in Andersonville for seven months and twelve days, enduring to the full the horrors and privations of that ill-famed prison pen. After the close of the war Mr. Sedam returned to Ogle County, Illinois, where he continued to be identified with agricultural pursuits until 1881, in October of which year he came to what is now the state of South Dakota, and took up the first claim in the present township of St. Lawrence, Hand County, filing a homestead entry. He continued to be actively engaged in farming and stock growing until October, 1895, when he took up his residence in the village of St. Lawrence, where he is now in the employ of F. A. Altenow, who is here engaged in the general merchandise business.

In politics Mr. Sedam has ever given a stanch support to the Republican party, and in 1893 he was elected to represent his district in the state legislature, serving one term, during the third general assembly. He is now chairman of the board of education of his home town and chairman of the Hand County Republican committee. He is a prominent and honored member of the Masonic fraternity, being identified with Lodge No. 39, Ancient Free and Accepted Masons; and St. Lawrence Chapter, No. 24, Royal Arch Masons, in each of which he has passed the official chairs. He is high priest of his chapter at the time of this writing, and in 1894 he had the distinction of serving as grand high priest of the grand chapter of the state. He also holds membership in St. Lawrence Lodge, No. 29, Ancient Order of United Workmen, in which he has held the office of master three years, while in 1895 he was grand foreman of the grand lodge of the order in the state. He manifests his deep interest in his old comrades in arms by affiliating with Colonel Ellis Post, No. 53, Grand Army of the Republic. His wife is a zealous and active member of the Methodist Episcopal church.

On the 1st of October, 1865, in Beloit. Wisconsin, Mr. Sedam was united in marriage to Miss Emeret M. Buckley, who was born in Genesee County, New York, and who was reared and educated in Illinois, being a daughter of Ebenezer and Emily Buckley. Mr. and Mrs. Sedam have eleven children, whose names, in order of birth, are as follows: Robert, John, Edward, Howard, Fred, Almeda, Jennie, Fannie, Ralph, James and Eva.

GENERAL MARK WENTWORTH SHEAFE

GENERAL MARK W. SHEAFE

A distinguished and honored citizen of South Dakota is General Mark Wentworth Sheafe, of Watertown, who was identified with the pioneer development of the territory and has as well been a factor in the upbuilding of the state. He was born May 18, 1844, in Brooklyn, New York, and in the paternal line is descended from one of the oldest English families, the name of Wentworth being not unknown in English history and at the same time appearing frequently on the pages of America's annals. The lineage can be traced back to the year 1066, before the time of the Norman conquest. The records have been carefully preserved and proven and many men of distinction in England have borne the name of Wentworth, which is still known there. The name of Sheafe originated in Cranebroke, Kent, England, in 1520, and the family history has been preserved from that time to the present. John Wentworth, an ancestor of General Sheafe, was the last royal governor of New Hampshire in 1775. His father, Governor Benning Wentworth, was mentioned by Longfellow in his poem entitled "Tales of a Wayside Inn." The son of Governor Wentworth was one of the signers of the original Articles of Confederation in 1778, representing the colony of New Hampshire.

In the maternal line General Sheafe is also descended from good old colonial stock, having emigrated from England to Massachusetts in 1646. The family during the Revolutionary war owned Bunker Hill at Charlestown, where, but for a mistake, the battle of that name would have been fought. In that battle were two great-grandfathers of General Sheafe and the records show that the family have participated in every war waged by this country from the first Indian war — King Philip's — down to the Spanish-American war.

General Sheafe passed his boyhood and youth in Boston, acquiring a liberal education for those days, and at the age of seventeen was examined for and prepared to enter Harvard College. However, the Civil War had just begun and, fired with enthusiasm, he, with a number of his fellow students and friends, enlisted in the Forty-fourth Regiment of Massachusetts Volunteers, becoming members of Company H, with which he went to the front. On the expiration of his term of service he accompanied his father to Janesville, Wisconsin, where he entered the First National Bank. While there residing, he was married in 1866 to Miss Cassa A. Hall, by whom he had three children.

In 1871 General Sheafe was desirous of going to the frontier and Dakota territory seemed to him a promising field for endeavor and energy. Accordingly in the fall of that year he removed to Elk Point, Union County, where he became extensively engaged in a lumber business and also in milling. It is a strange coincidence that he should have been the first to ship freight by rail into the territory, and in connection with his large flouring mills he was the first in the territory to adopt the roller process, discarding the old-time millstones. While conducting private business interests he was always more or less prominently connected with public interests and activities and thus aided in shaping the history of county and state along various lines. In 1877 he was selected by Governor Pennington to accompany Colonel, later General, F. D. Grant on a trip into the Indian country with a view of establishing a trail between the Missouri river at Fort Pierre and the Black Hills.

The Indians were restive and somewhat hostile but the trip was made in company with four other parties and its object successfully accomplished, the old Black Hills trail being adopted. In 1881 General Sheafe witnessed the great flood of the Missouri river bottom when the city of Vermillion was completely wiped out and the fertile river valley was ten feet under water. At that time, he lent his endeavors to saving the lives of settlers and was himself reported drowned. In fact, he had the doubtful pleasure of reading his own obituary as printed in the Sioux City Journal, but apologies were duly made to the public.

In 1882 General Sheafe married Miss Agnes Spark, a native of Edinburgh, Scotland, and to them two children were born, Mark Wentworth and Mary Agnes. The former is a prominent lawyer of Codington County and has been twice elected as state's attorney.

In 1885 General Sheafe was appointed register of the United States land office at Watertown under President Cleveland and removed to the city which is now his home. In that year he also received at the hands of Governor G. A. Pierce the commission as colonel of the Second Regiment, Dakota National Guard, with instructions to perfect the organization of the regiment, which he did, serving as colonel commanding for fifteen years with great success. In 1893 he was again appointed register of the United States land office at Watertown, which position he filled until April, 1897.

In the meantime, he continued the successful management of his business affairs and broadened the scope of his activities. In 1890 he was elected president of the Dakota Loan & Trust Company, a financial institution for making loans on real estate, the stock of which was owned in New England. Crop failures and a low ebb in financial matters throughout the west compelled the liquidation of this corporation, with but slight loss, however, to its stockholders and clients.

In 1898, at the time the war was declared against Spain by the United States, Colonel Sheafe prepared his regiment for active service and it was one of the first ready for the front. The First South Dakota Regiment made a record second to none. At this time Colonel Sheafe was appointed brigadier general of the United States volunteers by President McKinley and was ordered to report for duty with his brigade, which consisted of the Third New York, Twenty-second Kansas and One Hundred and Fifty-ninth Indiana Regiments. In command of his brigade, he gained great credit and the love of his officers and men. The war ending, he asked to be relieved of his command and returned to civil life, assuming again the management of his business affairs. He was for many years largely engaged in handling range cattle on the then uninhabited plains west of the Missouri river and looks back upon the free life with the cowboys, among the wild Texas steer and the bronchos with great pleasure, especially so from the fact that they have both been legislated out of existence in the northwest.

General Sheafe was six times elected mayor of Elk Point and was also elected to the territorial senate in 1874, being today almost the only survivor of that body. In 1890 he was elected to the second state legislative assembly as senator from Codington County and served with credit to himself and honor to his constituents. In 1876 he was selected as territorial delegate to the democratic national convention at St. Louis. In 1897 General Sheafe represented the state of South Dakota at the inauguration of William McKinley to the presidency and was assigned for duty with a mounted troop, acting as bodyguard to the president. In 1913 he was selected to represent the state at the inauguration of President Wilson and on that occasion acted as aid to the grand marshal.

In politics General Sheafe is an old-time Jeffersonian-Jacksonian democrat, with all the honor that the name implies. His religious creed is that of the Protestant Episcopal church, of which his forefathers had been adherents for over four hundred years. He is connected with the Masonic fraternity, having had the higher degrees conferred upon him. He is also a member of the Benevolent Protective Order of Elks and regards that organization as one doing much good in the world. He likewise holds membership with the Sons of the American Revolution and the Military Order of Foreign Wars of the United States. General Sheafe has had a varied experience. Descended from an old distinguished family of Massachusetts and New Hampshire, distinguished both in civil and military connections, he yearned for the freedom and simple life of the far west. As a soldier in the Civil and Spanish American wars be received praise and as a government official, he has done his full duty; as a lawmaker his record is good and as a business man he has ever been known for his probity. He has seen the territory which he loved and which contained a total of twenty thousand white inhabitants in 1871, blossom and bring forth two noble states. He has witnessed the passing of the buffalo, the antelope and the cowboy. He has seen his own beloved state, South Dakota, spring up from a few organized counties on the Missouri river and become a grand sovereign commonwealth, rich in soil and resources and equally rich in its acquired advantages. He has lent the best endeavors of his best days to helping bring about this result, and when the last call is made and "taps" are sounded over his body, his wish is that it may rest in the bosom of this state — his home.

JOSIAH SHELDON

For a number of years, the subject of this review has been very closely identified with the history of Lincoln County, South Dakota, being one of the early settlers and substantial citizens of this part of the state and the founder of the thriving town of Lennox, in which he now resides. Josiah Sheldon embodies many of the sturdy elements of New England manhood and traces his genealogy to an early period in the history of Vermont, of which state his parents, Samuel and Lavina (Ballard) Sheldon, were natives, both born, reared and married in the old county of Franklin. About the year 1850 Samuel Sheldon migrated to Dane County, Wisconsin, of which he was an early settler, and there took up a tract of government land which he cleared and converted into one of the most productive farms in that part of the state. He was a successful agriculturist, a worthy citizen and lived on the place he originally located until his death, which occurred in 1876, his second wife, the subject's mother, departing this life in 1858. By a previous marriage with Permelia Martin, who died in Vermont, he had one child, a son, by the name of Nelson, and to his union with Lavina Ballard four children were born, namely: Harmon, who, with the subject, laid out the town of Lennox, South Dakota, but who is now living a retired life in Wright County, Minnesota; Polly, wife of Sebastian Basford, of Clear Lake, Iowa; Josiah, of this review, and Desire, twins, the latter, who married William Dunlap, dying in the year 1887. By his third wife, Emma Ross, Mr. Sheldon was the father of one child that died in infancy.

Josiah Sheldon is a native of Franklin County, Vermont, where his birth occurred in the year 1842. He enjoyed but limited educational advantages, never attending school after his sixteenth year, and when old enough to work he took his place in the fields, where he labored early and late, helping to run the farm and contributing to the support of the family. After remaining at home until attaining his majority he started out to make his own way and from 1850 to 1876 followed agricultural pursuits in Minnesota, removing the latter year to South Dakota and taking up a claim in the northern part of Lincoln County, where the village of Lennox now stands, this thriving town being a part of the original quarter section which he purchased from the government. In addition to this land, he also entered one hundred and sixty acres about one and a half miles west of Lennox and in 1890, in partnership with his brother, laid out the town and began a series of improvements which in due time attracted a thrifty class of people to the locality, many of whom purchased lots and became permanent residents.

Mr. Sheldon moved to the present site of the village before the advent of the Chicago, Milwaukee & St. Paul Railroad in 1879 and donated about forty acres of his land for town purposes, selling all the rest except two lots which he reserved for his own use. He was a member of the first board of trustees of Lennox and in that capacity did much to advance the interests of the town and promote its growth, lending his influence to every enterprise calculated to stimulate business and industry, at the same time giving an earnest and whole-hearted support to measures having for their object the social, intellectual and moral well-being of the community.

In his political affiliations Mr. Palmer is a Republican and he has long been a factor of considerable importance in local party circles, besides manifesting an active interest in district and state affairs, laboring diligently during campaigns and contributing not a little to the success of the ticket as an organizer and worker. His fraternal relations are represented by the Masonic order, belonging to Lodge No. 35, at Lennox, and the Grand Army of the Republic Post, No. 21, which meets at Elsworth, his right to membership in the latter organization depending upon the three years which he gave to the service of his country during the dark and troublous period of the Civil War. Mr. Palmer, on October 18, 1864, enlisted at Mt. Pleasant, Iowa, in Company C, Fourth Iowa Cavalry, which was assigned to duty in the Army of the Southwest, where he took part in several noted battles, including, among others, the siege of Vicksburg, and many minor engagements, to say nothing of the long, tiresome marches in which he took part and the numerous vicissitudes and hardships endured while defending the flag and upholding the integrity of the Republic. He was discharged December 5, 1864, at Memphis, Tennessee, with an honorable record, and since leaving the army he has been as earnest and loyal to the government as when fighting in its behalf on Southern battlefields. Mr. Palmer is one of the well-known and widely respected men of Lincoln County, who has dignified every station to which called and whose influence has ever been exercised on the right side of every moral issue. Those who know him best speak in complimentary terms of his many excellent characteristics and his record in the past may be taken as an earnest of continued usefulness and prosperity in years to come.

CARL G. SHERWOOD

C. G. SHERWOOD, was born on a farm on Connecticut hill, Broome County, New York, near Whitney Point, on the 18th of January, 1855, being a son of George and Mary A. (Jeffords) Sherwood. His father was a fanner by vocation and was a man of no little influence in his section of the Empire state. He was a member of the New York legislature in 1873-4, as a representative of the Binghamton district; was a stanch abolitionist during the crucial epoch leading up to the war of the Rebellion, and supported the Republican party from the time of its organization until his death. He was of English and French extraction, and his ancestors were numbered among the early settlers near Greene, Chenango County. New York. The paternal grandmother of the subject bore the maiden name of Budlong, and her family resided near Utica, New York. The maternal ancestors, the Jefords, came to Chenango County, New York, from Connecticut and were of English and Irish lineage.

The subject was a farmer's boy, and it was with extraordinary difficulty and under discouraging circumstances that he obtained an ordinary common-school education. He was reared on a rough and stony farm, near Binghamton, New York, and the work of cultivating the land was more than ordinarily arduous. The land was new and he aided in reclaiming quite a portion of the farm from the native forest. His parents were poor, and the members of the family had to work hard and live closely in order to make ends meet. Thus, the early educational advantages afforded our subject were very limited, but his alert mentality and his appreciation of the values of life early quickened his ambition to action, his first fixed purpose being to prepare himself for the profession of law. His parents were very devout in their religious life and it was their earnest wish that he should enter the ministry, and it was by reason of their insistency in this regard that he left the high school at Binghamton and came to the west to carve out his own fortunes. Through his personal efforts he had paid the expenses of carrying forward his studies in the high school through the tenth grade. In 1879 he came west, and when he first crossed the Mississippi river his cash capital was represented in the sum of ten cents. He taught in the district schools on the Illinois side of the river for two years, and in the meanwhile borrowed technical books of A. R. McCoy, of Clinton, Iowa, just across the river, and devoted his evenings and other leisure moments to the reading of law, while his vacations were likewise devoted to this work. He continued to live in Whiteside County, Illinois, and in Clinton, Iowa, at intervals, until June, 1881, when he was admitted to the bar of Iowa, in the city mentioned. In the following month he secured admission to the Minnesota bar, at Laverne, while he became a member of the bar of Codington County, Dakota, in 1882. He came to Watertown, this county, in July, 1881, and on the 7th of the following month took up his residence in the village of Clark, where he has ever since maintained his home and been actively and successfully engaged in the practice of his chosen profession. He has been employed by the county in most of its important litigations, including the prosecution of Christ Christianson, who was convicted of murder and sentenced to the penitentiary for life, this being the only murder trial ever held in the county. Mr. Sherwood has been signally prospered in his efforts and the tangible results are seen in his valuable property interests. He is the owner of a well-improved farm of twelve hundred acres and also of considerable other real estate, including his attractive home in Clark. He has one of the best libraries in this section of the state, the same being valued at twenty-five hundred dollars.

Mr. Sherwood has been active in public affairs from the time of taking up his residence here. He served from 1882 until 1887 as register of deeds of the county, and was a member of the constitutional conventions, in Sioux Falls, in 1883 and 1889, while he was a delegate to the national Republican convention which nominated McKinley for the presidency in 1896. He was state senator from the twenty-ninth senatorial district of South Dakota in the first state senate convened, and was temporary and permanent chairman of the first Republican state convention held after the admission of South Dakota into the Union and chairman of the Republican state convention held at Sioux Falls, May 23, 1900, the largest convention ever held in the state. He has been a delegate from his county to every state convention of his party, with one exception, served for nearly a decade as chairman of the county central committee and is at the present time a member of the Republican state central committee. He has been intimately identified with the industrial, political and civic development of Clark County, having been thus associated with its interests from the time of its organization, while his was the distinction of being elected its first register of deeds.

Mr. Sherwood has been affiliated with the Masonic fraternity since 1883, being a member of the lodge and chapter in Clark and the commandery of Knights Templar in Watertown. He was initiated in the Independent Order of Odd Fellows in 1884, and is a member of the lodge in Clark. He is also identified with the Knights of Pythias, the Modern Woodmen of America, the Ancient Order of United Workmen and the Modern Brotherhood of America, while in 1902 he became a member of the Benevolent and Protective Order of Elks at Watertown. Both he and his wife were reared in the faith of the Baptist church, but they now attend and give support to the Methodist Episcopal church.

On the loth of February, 1885, at Clark, this state, was solemnized the marriage of Mr. Sherwood to Miss Nellie C. Fountain, a daughter of George H. and Dollie A. Fountain, who were pioneers in Nashua, Iowa, whence they later removed to Minneapolis, Minnesota, and from that city to Clark, South Dakota, in 1879, being among the first to settle in the vicinity of this now thriving city, the site being unmarked by a single building at the time of their arrival, while their nearest neighbors were six miles distant. Of the four children born to Mr. and Mrs. Sherwood we enter brief record, the date of birth being given in each respective connection, and the three living still remain at the parental home: George F., May 5, 1887; Harry A., September 15, 1888, died December 1, 1892; Mary Carlton, June 3, 1892; and Dollie Viola, July 2, 1897.

LEONARD M. SIMONS

Leonard M. Simons is not only a successful lawyer of Belle Fourche but is also connected with the financial interests of that town as vice president of the First National Bank. He has been connected with state politics in an important capacity, as he served for three terms as secretary of the state senate. He is a native of Fulton, New York, born January 22, 1874, a son of Perry M. and Helen (Loyale) Simons. The father was born near Rome, New York, in 1834. and the mother near the boundary line between Canada and New York in 1838. Perry M. Simons was in early manhood a farmer but later became a general contractor and constructed many public works. Neither he nor his wife ever removed west and both are deceased. They were the parents of four children, of whom Leonard M. Simons is the third in order of birth.

The last named acquired his elementary education in the schools of New York and after removing west attended Redfield College and the University of South Dakota at Vermillion. He began supporting himself when very young, paying his own way by selling papers when but ten years of age, and one year later he became printer's devil in a newspaper office at Fulton, New York. He learned the printer's trade there and was connected with the newspaper business until 1890, although he was employed during that time in other towns. In that year he removed to South Dakota, where he worked at various occupations and also attended school. A part of the time he was employed in a law office and devoted his spare time to the study of law, finding it so much to his liking that, in 1900, he definitely began preparation for a legal career, becoming a law student in the office of Sterling & Morris. In 1904 he was admitted to the bar and located at Mitchell, where he practiced until 1905, in which year he removed to Belle Fourche. In the seven years that he has lived there he has secured a large and profitable clientage and possesses the respect of his professional brethren and the general public. He is also a stockholder, director and the vice president of the First National Bank, and owns considerable farming land in South Dakota.

Mr. Simons was married March 17, 1908, to Miss Florence L. Dickson, a native of Flandreau, South Dakota. Her parents are Frank and Rose (Gridley) Dickson, the latter a native of Wauwatosa, Wisconsin. The family moved from Wisconsin to Flandreau, South Dakota, in pioneer days and the father engaged in the hardware business at that place. Subsequent removals were made to Armour and to Mitchell, where

Mr. Dickson organized the Mitchell Wholesale Fruit and Grocery Company, of which he is now president. Mr. and Mrs. Simons have two daughters, Helen Roseltha and Charlotte Louise.

Mr. Simons is a republican and for three terms was secretary of the state senate. His religious allegiance is given to the Congregational church and its tenets are the guiding principles of his life. He has attained high rank in the Masonic order, having taken all of the degrees in the Scottish Rite up to and including the thirty-second, and also in the York Rite. He is a member of the Mystic Shrine. He is an officer in the Rose Croix at Deadwood and belongs to Black Hills Consistory, No. 3. He likewise holds membership in Mitchell Lodge, No. 1059, B. P. O. E. He takes an active interest in public affairs and has participated in a number of movements looking toward the advancement of the community. He was one of those responsible for issuing the first blue book of the state and edited three, editions of same. He has left the impress of his individuality upon the development of Belle Fourche and it is safe to predict that in the years to come he will accomplish yet more.

JOHN CURTIS SIMMONS

J. C. SIMMONS, the able and popular cashier of the Bank of Frederick, at Frederick, Brown County, was born in Grangeville, Saratoga County, New York, in the year 1857, and is a son of William Simmons, who was born and reared in Ireland, whence he emigrated to the United States and took up his residence in Saratoga County, New York, where he died when our subject was but eighteen months of age, so that the latter has very meager data in regard to his family genealogy. The subject was reared in his native county, in whose public schools he secured excellent educational advantages, so that he became eligible for pedagogic honors, having there been successfully engaged in teaching for about three years. In 1882 he came as a pioneer to the present state of South Dakota and located in Aberdeen, in which place he arrived on the 18th of May. He entered the employ of C. A. Bliss, merchant and banker, with whom he remained until 1886, when he came to Frederick and, with others, purchased the Dow Brothers' Bank, organizing then the Bank of Frederick, in which institution he has ever since been incumbent of the office of cashier, handling his executive duties with marked discrimination and ability and having thus done much to maintain the bank on a firm foundation and to gain to it high popularity. The institution controls a large and successful business, being capitalized for fifteen thousand dollars and having a surplus fund of half that amount. During the financial depression of 1893-4 the bank was one of the few which, through careful and conservative management, successfully weathered the storm and added to its prestige and solidity, no assessment having been levied on its stockholders during that critical period. In addition to his banking interests Mr. Simmons is the owner of a large amount of valuable real estate in the county and also has important interests in livestock.

In politics he gives his allegiance to the Republican party, and fraternally has attained to the thirty-second degree of Ancient Accepted Scottish Rite Masonry, being also affiliated with the Ancient Arabic Order of the Nobles of the Mystic Shrine. He has shown much interest in public affairs and in the promotion of all objects tending to conserve the general welfare and progress. He was a member of the first legislature of the state, having been elected to represent his district in 1889. On the 3d of December, 1891, Mr. Simmons was united in marriage to Miss Emma Burton, who was born in Wisconsin, being a daughter of William Burton, who came to South Dakota in 1882, becoming one of the honored and influential pioneers of Brown County. Mr. and Mrs. Simmons have one child, Ruth.

JAMES SIMPSON

In Sioux Falls the name of James Simpson is an honored one, for his work as an educator stamped him not only as a man of ability in that profession but as one guided by broad humanitarian purposes. His life work proved a blessing to those who came under his instruction, for he devoted his time to teaching the deaf and dumb and his sympathy proved an interpretative force in understanding those who came under his guidance, enabling him to assist them in the largest possible measure.

Mr. Simpson was born January 21, 1854, in Oakland County, Michigan. His parents died when he was but three years of age and he afterward lived among relatives there until he reached the age of thirteen or fourteen years. Being deaf, he then entered the State School for the Deaf at Flint, Michigan, where he remained for four years, after which he went to New York City and attended the Fanwood School for the Deaf, continuing in that institution for three years. Later he was employed for three years at the jewelry trade in the northern part of New York, after which he returned to Michigan and worked on a farm until he reached the age of twenty-five. He was then appointed to teach the school for the deaf at Council Bluffs, Iowa, spending three years at that place, after which he went to Sioux Falls in 1881 to visit E. G. Wright and was asked to establish a school for the deaf in that city. The land for the school was donated by several wealthy people and he opened the school in 1881 with five pupils. The attendance gradually grew, however, until it is now a large and prosperous institution. Mr. Simpson continued the work of teaching until 1903, when his health failed. He then resigned and went to the Black Hills, hoping to be benefited by the change, but the trip proved unavailing and he returned to Sioux Falls, where he passed away October 16, 1903.

Mr. Simpson had been married in 1880, in Council Bluffs, to Miss Anna Laura Wright, a pupil of the Council Bluffs school, and they became the parents of three children, Howard W., Grant M. and Laurence A. The two youngest are now connected with the Orpheum circuit and live in Kansas City. The mother is still living in Sioux Falls.

Upon the death of Mr. Simpson, the school was conducted by Miss Donald from 1903 until 1907 and in the latter year J. D. McLaughlin took charge, so continuing for three years. In 1910 the eldest son, Howard W. Simpson, was appointed to the position of superintendent. He was born in the school in Sioux Falls, February 7, 1882. His father and mother both being deaf, he was acquainted with the sign language from his birth. He attended the city schools in Sioux Falls and the State College at Brookings, South Dakota, and in 1898 he joined the First South Dakota Infantry and went to the Philippines, where he was engaged in military duty for one year and five months. For several years thereafter he was employed on a ranch in Jerauld County and still later went upon the road as a traveling salesman, while subsequently he became connected with the Bradstreet Company at Sioux Falls. He was likewise for a year and a half engaged in the improvement of a homestead claim in Meade County.

On the 20th of June, 1906, Mr. Simpson was married to Miss Stella Irene Ridby, of Peshtigo, Wisconsin, and they have one child, Virginia, who was born January 28, 1911. In religious faith Mr. and Mrs. Simpson are Congregationalists and fraternally he is a Mason, belonging to Unity Lodge, No. 130, F. & A. M., while in both the York and Scottish Rites he has attained high rank, being now a Knight Templar and a thirty-second degree Mason. He was called to become his father's successor in 1910 and under his guidance the School for the Deaf at Sioux Falls is in a prosperous condition and is doing splendid work.

Dell Rapids has never been called upon to mourn the loss of a citizen whose death has been more deeply and widely regretted than that of Ritchie Simpson. He was a very popular man and his popularity lay in his sterling worth, as manifest in every relation of life, in his social, genial nature and kindly spirit, which were constantly manifest in friendly, generous act. As the owner of the Dell Rapids Granite Quarries, he was at the head of one of the important industrial enterprises of Minnehaha County and was regarded as one of the alert, energetic business men of his section of the state. He also had other commercial connections and at the same time he was active and progressive in matters of citizenship relating to the public welfare. He was born in Aberdeenshire, Scotland, on the 3d of February, 1856, and was a son of Andrew and Annabel Simpson, the former a stone-cutter.

Ritchie Simpson acquired his education in the public schools of his native country but when twelve years of age he left school and was apprenticed to the stone-cutter's trade. Even at that early age he manifested marked industry and energy and had completed his apprenticeship when he reached the age of fifteen. He then left the land of hills and heather for the new world and settled at Pigeon Cove, Massachusetts, on Cape Ann. He afterward worked in various states throughout the east, spending about eleven years in that way, and on the expiration of that period removed westward to Missouri. Later he spent some time in Virginia and afterward went to Wisconsin and subsequently he returned on a visit to his native land. In the spring of 1883 he arrived in South Dakota, settling at Dell Rapids, where he formed a company to quarry stone in 1885. This enterprise proved successful for a few years and then met financial difficulties. At that time Mr. Simpson, in connection with W. S. Mitchell, leased the property from the bank and in three years had become the owner of the quarries, which he subsequently operated alone. He owned all the property of the original company and about seventy acres additional, and something of the extent and importance of his undertakings is indicated in the fact that he employed about thirty-five men through the winter seasons and a larger number in the summer. The stone quarries are recognized as among the best to be found in the United States. There is very little iron in the granite, hence there are no stains on the buildings from which it is constructed. It is also notable because of its uniformity of color and the product of the quarries is in great demand in Kansas City, Omaha and Chicago. Many of the buildings throughout South Dakota have been erected from granite from his quarries, including the State Normal at Madison, the state building at Plankinton and the post office at Yankton. Much of the stone was also used in the construction of the insane asylum at Yankton. In the operation of the quarries the work is done most systematically, the latest improved machinery is utilized and the careful management of the owner resulted in the attainment of a most gratifying success. In developing his quarries, he employed a large number of men and his pay roll was a substantial help to the general business conditions of the growing city.

In 1884 Mr. Simpson was married to Miss Cora Williams, a daughter of Horatio A. and Carrie Williams. Her father went to Dell Rapids in 1876 as miller for William Van Eps of Sioux Falls and operated the old mill at that place. Soon after he sent for his family, who remained in Cherokee, Iowa, and they came with ox teams across a wild country of one hundred miles or more, it requiring seven days to make the trip. The maternal grandfather of Mrs. Simpson was Jens Nelson, a pioneer of Lake County, South Dakota, who was among the first to take up land there. The father and mother of Mrs. Simpson both died in Dell Rapids. Twin daughters were born of the marriage of Mr. and Mrs. Simpson — Nellie and Mary, who are graduates of the State University and both were teachers in the schools of Scotland, South Dakota, until after the father's death, when Mary returned to live with her mother, who since the death of the husband and father has ably conducted the business which he left and with her daughter Mary occupies the old home.

Mr. Simpson's political allegiance was given to the republican party. He was for some years an active and influential worker in political circles and in 1907 was representative from this district in the state legislature, where he gave earnest consideration to the various vital questions which came up for settlement. For twenty-five years he was a member of the board of education and the public schools ever found in him a stalwart champion and one whose efforts in their behalf were most effective. He belonged to Dell Rapids Lodge, No. 40, A. F. & A. M.; to Marion Chapter, No. 31, O. E. S.; and to the Odd Fellows lodge and was in hearty sympathy with the beneficent spirit which underlies those organizations. He never had occasion to regret his determination to come to America that he might try his fortune on this side of the Atlantic, for here he found the opportunities which he sought and which are always open to energetic and ambitious young men. In their improvement he worked his way steadily upward and his position as a substantial, reliable business man was an invincible one. He was ever alert to the best interests of Dell Rapids and cooperated heartily in many measures which have been of immense benefit to the town. When he died on the 3d of October, 1914, the news of his death was everywhere received with genuine regret and his funeral was the largest ever held in Dell Rapids. For twenty-five years he had been a victim of asthma and hay fever. Each year, with regularity, the months of August and September found him ill, but the coming of cooler days brought relief. However, the constant recurrence of his trouble had been insidiously undermining his strength. For twenty-six years he had never been able to go down town in September, but in the fall of 1914, he seemed better and attended the ceremonies of the laying of the corner stone of the new hospital and a few days later attended a meeting of the school board. Whether the strain was too much in his weakened condition is not known, but he soon afterward passed to his final sleep. He was buried with full Masonic honors and a vast concourse of people gathered to pay their last tribute of respect. Everywhere he is spoken of in terms of high regard, of warm friendship and of brotherly love. His life was indeed fruitful of good deeds and characterized by the highest honor and his memory will ever remain a cherished possession to those who knew him.

ROBERT LINCOLN SLAGLE

South Dakota has every reason to be proud of her State University at Vermillion, as since its founding it has grown steadily and rapidly in excellence and in influence and has had much to do in developing the mind and spirit that must always keep pace with material progress if the commonwealth is in the end to occupy a place of honor in the world. It has been fortunate in its administrators as its presidents have from its establishment been men possessing the virility of character that is only associated with the west and also men who have combined fine intellectual training and broad culture in the best sense of that word with business and executive ability of a high order.

The present head of the institution, Robert Lincoln Slagle, was born in Hanover, York County, Pennsylvania, March 17, 1865, a son of William

Augustus and Margaret Elizabeth (Stine) Slagle. After receiving a thorough elementary and secondary education he entered Lafayette College at Easton, Pennsylvania, and there took his undergraduate work, receiving the degree of Bachelor of Arts in 1887. At the completion of a further course of study he was given the degree of Master of Arts in 1890 by his alma mater and four years later Johns Hopkins University of Baltimore, Maryland, conferred upon him the degree of Doctor of Philosophy. For one year he was an analyst and food investigator in New York City, being an associate of Professor W. O. Atwater, the first pure' food expert of the federal government.

Since 1895 Mr. Slagle has been a teacher and educational administrator. In that year he became professor of chemistry in the South Dakota State College and held that chair until 1897, when he became professor of chemistry in the South Dakota State School of Mines, and in 1899 was elected president of that institution. In 1906 he returned to the South Dakota State College as chief executive and held that position until 1914. On the 1st of February, 1914, he was installed as president of the State University of South Dakota at Vermillion. All of the above-named institutions are under the control of the same governing board. His ability to plan wisely, to direct efficiently the labors of others and secure the cooperation of the governing board, faculty and students has grown from year to year and as his responsibilities have increased his power as an executive has increased in like proportion. He makes a careful study not only of educational conditions, educational developments and the trend of educational movements throughout the country at large, but he also seeks to understand fully the conditions peculiar to South Dakota and the lines along which her greatest development will probably lie. Only by so doing can he so direct the State University that it shall prove of the greatest service to the people of the state and so be in truth a state university. The institution maintains a high standard of scholarship and at the same time all forms of student activity are encouraged, as it is believed that they in their proper place form an essential part of the best. and most efficient college training. The University of South Dakota has already gained an honorable place among the state universities of the west and a continuance of the present wise policy of administration will without doubt, gain it more prestige and influence in the future.

Dr. Slagle was married May 28, 1896, at St. Paul, Minnesota, to Miss Gertrude Anna Riemann, a daughter of Paul Riemann. Dr. Slagle is a communicant of the Protestant Episcopal church and does all in his power to further moral development and the application to life of the principles of Christianity. He is a member of the Sons of the American Revolution a Fellow in the American Association for the Advancement of Science and a member of the Phi Beta Kappa. Fraternally he is a Knights Templar Mason. In all that he does he manifests not only the aggressiveness and willingness to take the initiative that is characteristic of the American people, but also that patience and thoroughness which goes to the root of a matter even though to do so requires a painstaking and laborious investigation, this latter characteristic being his heritage from his German forbears. The family, however, has been in the United States for many generations, his ancestors being numbered among the first German settlers in the province of Pennsylvania in colonial times. He has been associated with the state of South Dakota for more than two decades and has thoroughly identified himself with her interests and by so doing has gained honor not only among those immediately connected with him in educational work but also among the people at large.

ALBERT SMITH

Albert SMITH was born in the village of Laharpe, Hancock County, Illinois. He was granted the advantages of the common schools in his youth and thereafter took a course of study in Knox College, at

Galesburg, Illinois. In 1872 he removed to Minnesota, where he remained until 1875, when he returned home, by reason of the impaired health of his father, who died shortly afterward. The subject again went to Minnesota, and established himself in the hardware business in Wright County, where he continued operations about six years, meeting with fair success. His health finally became delicate and this led to his removing to South Dakota, whither he came in 1883. He located on a farm eight miles north of Britton, in Day County, the place being now in Marshall County, and shortly afterward he returned to Howard, Minnesota. In the spring of 1884, he came once more to Day County, South Dakota, and became one of the organizers of the first bank in Webster, while he served as cashier of the same until 1888, when the institution was closed, owing to depressed financial conditions, though the promoters of the enterprise allowed none of their patrons to lose by reason of the suspension. In the autumn of that year Mr. Smith was elected county auditor, of which office he continued incumbent for the long period of six years, after which he served in various other offices of public trust and responsibility, ever proving himself a discriminating and faithful executive. In 1900 he was elected clerk of the courts, and has since served as such. He is also representative of a number of the leading fire-insurance companies and does a very considerable business as underwriter for the same.

Fraternally he is identified with the Masonic order, and also with the Independent Order of Odd Fellows and the Knights of Pythias. Mr. Smith was united in marriage to Miss Hannah J. Alley, who was born in West Virginia, and they have two sons.

DANIEL HOWARD SMITH

Daniel H. Smith, who is incumbent of the office of railroad commissioner for the northern district of South Dakota, is a native of the state of Wisconsin, having been born in Marquette County, on the 18th of December, 1864, and being a son of Rev. William and Elizabeth H. (Chambers) Smith, both natives of the state of Pennsylvania. The father of the subject was a clergyman of the United Presbyterian church, in whose work he continued to be zealously engaged until his death, which occurred in July, 1873. His devoted wife survived him many years, being summoned into eternal rest in April, 1898. They became the parents of eight children, of whom four are living.

The subject of this review received his early education in the public schools of his native county, and continued to reside in Wisconsin until he had attained the age of eighteen years, having been there engaged in farming until 1883, when, in company with his mother, he came to South Dakota and located in the village of Blunt. In the following year he entered the employ of the Van Dusen Grain Company, and in 1885 was made agent of this concern at Harrold, Hughes County, where he remained until December, 1886, when he went to southern California, where he passed one year. Upon his return to South Dakota, in 1888, Mr. Smith located in the village of Miller, where he re-entered the employ of the Van Dusen Grain Company, to whose interests he continued to devote his attention until 1890, when he established himself in the retail grocery business in Miller, under the firm name of D. H. Smith & Company. In December, 1894, he disposed of his interests in this line and on the 1st of the following January he accepted a position in the office of the state commissioner of schools and public lands, taking up his residence in the capital city of the state at that time and continuing to serve in the capacity noted until January 1, 1903, when he returned to Miller.

On the 4th of November, 1902, he was elected to his present office as railroad commissioner of the northern district of the state, and in this position, he has given most able and efficient service, justifying the confidence reposed in him and indicated in his unanimous election. Mr. Smith has served as township treasurer, as a member of the board of education and as city assessor of Miller. He is an active and earnest worker in the upbuilding of his city.

Fraternally he is identified with the Masonic order and the Knights of Pythias. When a young man he became a member of the Presbyterian church and is an active and zealous church worker. On Christmas day, 1888, Mr. Smith was united in marriage to Miss Eva R. Dunn, of Millersburg, Illinois, and she entered into the life eternal on the 19th of March, 1890, being survived by her only child, C. Everett. On the 28th of November, 1892, Mr. Smith wedded Miss Georgiana Clayton, of Ludington, Michigan, and they have two children, Harry A. and Fred C.

HON. ELLISON GRIFFITH SMITH

Hon. Ellison Griffith Smith, judge of the supreme court from the fourth district, has been a member of the bar of South Dakota for over a third of a century and has won distinction as a lawyer, legislator and jurist. His birth occurred in Cincinnati, Ohio, December 5, 1851, and he is a son of Amos G. and Mary (Ellison) Smith, the former born on the 14th of April, 1813, in Bucks County, Pennsylvania, and the latter a native of Trenton, New Jersey. As a child the father was taken by his parents, George and Elizabeth (Thornton) Smith, to Noble County, Ohio. George Smith was a native of Germany and accompanied his parents on their emigration to the United States, the family settling in Pennsylvania. There his marriage occurred and he continued to reside there until his removal to Ohio. The American progenitor of the Thornton family removed from England to the new world many years ago and settled in New England.

Amos G. Smith grew to manhood in the Buckeye state and was married in 1851. For a number of years, he followed merchandising in Noble County, Ohio, but in 1858 abandoned that occupation on account of impaired health and removed to Delaware County, Iowa, where he engaged extensively in farming and stock raising for a number of years. He was prominent in his locality and was highly respected by all who knew him. He passed away in 1908. To him and his wife were born seven children, of whom our subject is the oldest. Another son, Jason T. Smith, is also a resident of South Dakota. For a time, he practiced law in Yankton but is now director of agencies for the First National Life Insurance Company of South Dakota.

Judge Ellison G. Smith, who was but a child when the family removed to Delaware County, Iowa, received his elementary education in the public schools there. Subsequently he attended Lenox College of Hopkinton, Delaware County, which institution conferred upon him the degree of Bachelor of Arts in 1871. He prepared for the legal profession in the College of Law of the Iowa State University and in 1874 received the degree of LL. B. In that year he was elected principal of the Mechanicsville high school and held that position for one year. He then reviewed his law course preparatory to engaging in the practice of his profession and in 1876 he made his way to Yankton, South Dakota, where he became a partner of Hon. G. C. Moody, who became successively judge of the territorial federal court and United States senator. Mr. Smith then took charge of the entire law business of the firm, which was extensive and important and which included that of the office of register in bankruptcy. He proved equal to the splendid opportunity thus afforded him and soon gained recognition as an attorney of unusual ability. He practiced for a number of years in Yankton and appeared as counsel in most of the important litigation held in the courts of that district.

From 1878 to 1882 he served as territorial district attorney and he was for some time the associate of the Hon. Hugh Campbell as special assistant United States district attorney. For several years he held the position of reporter for the territorial supreme court of Dakota and in 1889, while the incumbent in that office, was elected judge of the first judicial circuit. By reelection he served in that capacity for twenty years, or until the 1st of April, 1909, when he was appointed judge of the supreme court of South Dakota from the fourth district. In the general election held in November, 1910, he was elected to that office for a term of six years. He possesses the faculty of going surely and directly to the vital point of a matter and has the poise and impartiality which are so essential to the judge. As he also has a thorough understanding of the basic principles of jurisprudence and a wide knowledge of statute and precedent his decisions are sound interpretations of the law. Although the greater part of his public service has been in connection with the courts, he was at one time identified with the legislative branch of government, being from 1886 to 1889 the representative of Yankton County in the territorial legislature. He has always given his political allegiance to the republican party.

Judge Smith was married, in Delaware County, Iowa, in 1877, to Miss Anna Kirkwood, a native of the province of Ontario, Canada, who passed away in July, 1909, leaving three children: Ellison G., a graduate of the Columbian University of Washington, D. C, who is now practicing in Sioux City, Iowa; Agnes G., at home; and Amos Campbell, a civil engineer connected with the Chicago, Milwaukee & St. Paul Railroad at Aberdeen, South Dakota.

Judge Smith is a York Rite Mason, belonging to St. John's Lodge, No. I, A. F. & A. M., at Yankton; the Royal Arch chapter at Yankton; and De Molay Commandery No. I, K. T., at Yankton. He likewise holds membership in the Modern Woodmen of America, the Ancient Order of United Workmen and the Independent Order of Odd Fellows. He is an honored member of the South Dakota State Bar Association and the American Bar Association and cooperates in the efforts of those organizations to increase the efficiency of the courts. He was for many years a member of the Yankton school board and has always taken the deepest interest in the welfare of the public schools, recognizing their paramount importance. He belongs to the Congregational church and in all relations of life has measured up to high standards of manhood. He is held in high esteem not only because of his ability but also because of his broad-mindedness, fairness and integrity.

RICHARD L. SMITH

R. L. Smith, is a native of Jennings County, Indiana, where he was born on the 26th of April, 1833, being one of the eleven children born to James P. and Eliza A. (Beecham) Smith. His father was a farmer and each of the eight sons assisted in the work of the homestead place, while during the winter terms they were able to attend the district schools. At the age of eighteen Mr. Smith proved himself eligible for pedagogic honors, securing a license to teach school. He proved successful in his work as a teacher and devoted his attention to this profession for three successive years, while during this time he relegated the work of the farm to his younger brothers and worked at the carpenter's trade during the summer vacation periods. During this time, he was giving as much attention as possible to the study of medicine, first carrying on his studies under the direction of his older brother, a successful practicing physician, and then passing two years under the effective preceptorship of Dr. William F. Riley, of Omega, Indiana, who took a great interest in the young man and aided him in more ways than one. The subject, during this time, made his home with his preceptor and in the fall of 1835, he obtained from Dr. Riley a certificate of qualification which enabled him to practice medicine under the laws of Indiana. After a short time, he removed to Illinois, being engaged in practice at Decatur for two years and then taking up his residence in Salem, that state, while in the following year he entered the office of Dr. Stephen F. Mercer, of that place, and devoted two years to a systematic review of his professional studies.

At the outbreak of the Rebellion Dr. Smith was among the first to tender his services in defense of the Union. On May 9, 1861, he enlisted as a private in Company G, Twenty-first Illinois Volunteer Infantry, and for the ensuing four years and nine months the history of his regiment is coincident with his personal career as a valiant and loyal soldier. He participated in many of the most important battles incident to the progress of the great fratricidal conflict, his regiment being for the greater portion of the time a part of the Army of the Cumberland, and it was his good fortune to escape wounds and sickness, while he never asked for or received a furlough or a leave of absence. He was always present for active duty or for detached service and his fidelity and zeal never wavered during the long and arduous service which he rendered in behalf of the nation's honor and integrity. He was made first lieutenant of his company in October, 1862, prior to the battle of Stone River, in which he was an active participant. He was promoted to captain after the capture of Atlanta in 1864 and received his honorable discharge, at Springfield, Illinois, on the 6th of February, 1866.

After the close of his military service Dr. Smith returned to his former home, in Marion County, Illinois, for the purpose of securing a much-needed rest, and there he purchased a farm, which he operated by proxy. In 1868 he made a vigorous campaign for the office of clerk of the circuit court, and he states that in the connection he was "defeated by a respectable majority." In June, 1869, he was appointed by President Grant as superintendent of Indian schools for the northwest, Nez Perce's, of Idaho; Shoshones, of Wyoming; and Red Clouds, of South Dakota, resigning in February, 1872. In October, 1872, Dr. Smith entered the employ of the great publishing house of Lippincott & Company, of Philadelphia, and was assigned the management of their educational department for the northwest. In the following year he was appointed steward of the Illinois state prison, at Joliet, retaining this office until 1874, after which he devoted his attention to his profession until 1882, when he came to South Dakota and took up a claim in township 113, range 70, Hand County, where he has ever since maintained his home and where he has developed and improved a valuable farm of six hundred and forty acres. Five acres of his ranch are under cultivation and the remainder is devoted to the raising of hay and to grazing purposes. He raises an excellent grade of livestock, giving special attention to the breeding of horses, in which he has met with marked success. He has not been actively engaged in the practice of his profession for a number of years, but still takes a deep interest in the science and keeps in touch with the advances made in the same.

Dr. Smith has been an active factor in public affairs ever since coming to the territory and the state of South Dakota can find no one more loyal to its interests than is he. He has been a stanch supporter of the principles of the Republican party from the time of its organization. He was the first superintendent of schools for Hand County and a member of the first state constitutional convention, and in 1891 he was elected a member of the board of county commissioners of Hand County, serving three years, during the last of which he was chairman of the board. In 1892 he was the nominee of his party for the state senate, but met the defeat which attended the ticket in general throughout the state. In 1902 he was elected to represent his district in the lower house of the legislature, serving during the ensuing general assembly with marked ability and to the satisfaction of his constituents who had honored him by their preferment. He was chairman of the committee on public health and also a member of the important committees on ways and means and education. In March, 1902, the Doctor was made the recipient of a beautiful gold-headed cane, which was presented by the Aberdeen District Medical Society, in recognition of his valuable services as chairman of the house committee first mentioned.

The Doctor is a member of Masonic fraternity and of the State Historical Society. In religious matters he is liberal and tolerant, having the deepest respect for the essential spiritual verities. On the 15th of July,

1872, Dr. Smith was united in marriage to Miss Emma D. White, of Iuka, Illinois. She was born in Bond County, Illinois, and is a daughter of Robert F. White, who was an honored pioneer of Illinois. Dr. and Mrs. Smith have two sons, Lawrence N. W., born in prison, Joliet, Illinois, April 6, 1874, and who is now on the home farm, and Clarence I. W., who was born in Marion County, Illinois, December 7, 1876, and is also on the home farm.

HOMER S. SMYTHE

Homer S. SMYTHE, one of the highly honored citizens of Sanborn County, where he is at present serving as deputy county treasurer, is a native of the old Keystone state of the Union, having been born in Genter County, Pennsylvania, on the 11th of February, 1843, and being a son of William and Margaret (Watson) Smythe, the former of whom was born in Dauphin County,

Pennsylvania, in 1799, while the latter was born in Glinton County, that state, in 1804. The father of the subject received a collegiate education and was a man of marked ability, having been a surveyor by profession and having also been identified with agricultural pursuits. He removed with his family to Illinois in 1863, and there passed the remainder of his long and useful life, his death occurring in the city of Freeport, in 1880, while he had there lived retired for a number of years. His devoted wife passed away in 1856, and he remarried in 1858, his second wife dying in Freeport in 1887. Of their seven children four are living, the subject of this sketch being the only representative of the family in South Dakota. William Smythe was in early life a supporter of the Whig party, but transferred his allegiance to the Republican party at the time of its organization and ever afterward was a stalwart advocate of its principles. He and his wife were devoted members of the Presbyterian church, in which he served as elder for a half century. Fraternally he was identified with the Independent Order of Odd Fellows.

Homer S. Smythe, the immediate subject of this sketch, received his preliminary educational discipline in the common schools of Pennsylvania. He enlisted as a private in Company E, Forty-ninth Pennsylvania Infantry Volunteers, on August 14, 1861, and was discharged December 21, 1864, by reason of expiration of time of service. Was wounded at Spottsylvania Court House, Virginia, May 10, 1864. He was twenty years of age at the time of the family removal to Illinois, and there continued to maintain his home, devoting his attention to the machinist's trade, until 1883, when he came to Sanborn County, South Dakota, where he took up a half section of government land, which he still owns, having made good improvements on the place, of which fifty-seven acres are under cultivation, while the remainder is used in connection with the raising of livestock. Mr. Smythe has been a prominent figure in local affairs of a public nature since coming to this county, and has held official preferment much of the time, having served four years as register of deeds, while for the past five years he has been deputy county treasurer.

He is a member of the Presbyterian church, as is also Mrs. Smythe, and fraternally is identified with the Masonic order. In politics he gives an unswerving support to the Republican party and its principles. On the 21st of December, 1880, Mr. Smythe was married to Mrs. Julia (Rodman) Smythe, widow of W. R. Smythe, of Tiffin, Ohio, and a daughter of Samuel and Mary (Madden) Rodman, of Center County, Pennsylvania, in which state she was born January 1, 1843. No children have been born of this union, but Mrs. Smythe has two children by her first marriage: William R. who is a civil engineer at Canon City, Colorado, and Leon L., who is a clergyman of the Presbyterian church and now pastor of the church at Volga, Brookings County, this state.

When George W. Snow, a successful real-estate and insurance man of Springfield, South Dakota, first came to the territory, on the 24th of November, 1869, all that there was of Springfield was one family who were living in a dugout. Although he did not remain long on that visit, he returned the following year and settled permanently in the state, so that he is one of the earliest pioneers who are yet living.

Mr. Snow was born in Posey County, Indiana, on the 13th of December, 1842, and is a son of Augustus Frank and Catherine M. (Feit) Snow, the former born in Pittsburgh, Pennsylvania, on the 21st of March, 1816, and the latter in Baltimore, Maryland, on the 25th of July, 1819. Their marriage occurred in Posey County, Indiana, on the 4th of April, 1837, and they remained there until December, 1848, when they removed to Monfort, Grant County, Wisconsin. Their son, George W., enlisted in August, 1862, in Company F. Twentieth Wisconsin Volunteer Infantry, and served in the Union army until the close of the Civil war. He participated in the battle of Prairie Grove, Arkansas, on December 7, 1862; sieges of Vicksburg, Mississippi, and Mobile, Spanish Fort and Fort Morgan, Alabama, and other engagements. He was at Spanish Fort when the news came of Lee's surrender and Lincoln's assassination. Later his regiment was sent to Galveston to quell border disturbances and he saw service even in Mexico, the United States troops crossing the border to make peace between the insurrectors and the established authorities during the Maximilian regime. He was mustered out July 14, 1865, at Galveston, and was two weeks on his way home. In 1866 Mr. Snow attended the Patch Grove Academy in Grant County, Wisconsin, conducted by a graduate from Harvard, and subsequently took a course in a commercial college at Madison, Wisconsin. About this time his old captain opened a store in Dodgeville, and Mr. Snow entered his employ as a clerk, remaining in that capacity until he came west in the spring of 1870.

Upon his first visit to Springfield Mr. Snow remained only long enough to file upon a claim a mile and a half from the present town site and then returned to Wisconsin. In May, 1870, together with five companions, he drove through Iowa by wagon, camping by the wayside and reaching Springfield, this state, in seventeen days. On his first trip he had no horse and was compelled to pay four dollars per day for a pony, and this experience taught him a lesson. Accordingly, the party brought their own horses and wagons, driving through in 1870. Some of the young men established a sawmill on the flats near Springfield and Mr. Snow purchased an interest in the enterprise. As the nearby timber was cut off, the mill was moved up the river from time to time until all the big timber upon its banks was manufactured into lumber. After proving up on his preemption claim Mr. Snow filed on a timber claim west of Tyndall, but later sold the relinquishment for one hundred dollars, which would not buy an acre of the place now. Later he filed on a homestead claim near the site of the present Springfield railroad station and in two years secured title to the same, his three years' service in the army shortening the length of residence required.

In 1876, with several companions, Mr. Snow went to the Black Hills and located a placer claim near Hill City in Palmer's Gulch, where they found enough gold to pay them fairly well, but, hearing of the fabulous strikes at Deadwood, they pulled up stakes and migrated to the new diggings. Their hopes were not realized, however, and they returned without the fortune that they set out to find. Provisions were very high in the Hills and the boys sold some of theirs, so much in fact that they subsequently did not have enough for themselves. Mr. Snow and one other returned to Yankton and with oxen took back two loads of provisions, returning by way of Fort Pierre. The Indians about that time became hostile and killed four men, one of these men being a man to whom Mr. Snow had been talking but a few hours before he was killed and scalped. The Indian uprising was so disquieting that the party left the Hills in October and went home, having been absent since the preceding April.

After his return Mr. Snow clerked for a time and then secured the nomination for treasurer of Bon Homme County on the republican ticket, while his employer, M. H. Day, ran for the legislature as a democrat. They campaigned together and both were elected. After serving for two terms, or four years, as county treasurer, Mr. Snow, in partnership with an uncle, Reuben Groot, opened a bank in Springfield, and for twenty years the institution was one of the prosperous and solid financial institutions of South Dakota. The partners experienced an old-time bank robbery, in which the safe was dynamited and five thousand dollars in money was stolen. The perpetrators of the crime were apprehended and some of them are still serving out their sentence. At the end of twenty years of successful banking Mr. Snow and his partner sold out. He then turned his attention to real estate and insurance and is still engaged in that business, in which he has met with signal success. At one time or another he has owned nearly every tract of land in the township in which Springfield is located, besides many farms in surrounding townships and counties, and he still holds title to several thousand acres of fine farming and grazing lands.

Mr. Snow has been twice married. On the 19th of April, 1874, he was united in marriage to Miss Sylvia L. Tyler, the well-known pioneer preacher, Rev. Ward, performing the ceremony. Mrs. Snow passed away in May, 1878, leaving a son, Harry, who died in August of the same year. In February, 1882, Mr. Snow married Mrs. Alberta M. Davison, nee Mead, by whom he has two sons: George G., who is associated with his father in the real-estate business and who attended the law school of the University of Michigan at Ann Arbor two years and the law department of Yale University for two years, graduating from the latter institution with the class of 1907; and Frank M., who graduated from the Springfield high school, attended an institution of higher learning at Colorado Springs for one year and was a student for a like length of time in the University of Washington and the University of Nebraska. He has since written for various journals in the west. Mrs. Snow died April 28, 1912.

Mr. Snow has been a factor in the making of his adopted state, having served as a delegate to the Sioux Falls Constitutional Convention in 1889 and as a member of the first state legislature. He has been a member of both branches of the legislature and used his vote and influence in that body to secure appropriation for the State Normal School at Springfield. He was also twice called to the lieutenant governor's chair and during both terms was able to further advance the interests of the school. His political belief is that of the republican party. Since 1867 he has been an Odd Fellow and has served in the state grand lodge as grand master and treasurer. In 1881 he became a Mason and has now taken the thirty-second degree in that order. He affiliates with the blue lodge at Springfield, the consistory at Yankton and El Riad Temple of the Mystic Shrine at Sioux Falls, in all of which branches of Masonry he has filled some of the chairs. He is a comrade of General Steedman Post, G. A. R., at Springfield, and in 1901 and 1902 served as department commander. There are few living today who have known Dakota earlier or more intimately than Mr. Snow and few have done more in shaping its affairs, not only in his home locality but in the state at large.

HALVOR C. SOLBERG

Halvor C. Solberg, one of the representative educators of the state, being a member of the faculty of the State Agricultural College, at Brookings, was born in Norway, on the 5th of March, 1861, a son of Christian and Anna Solberg, both of whom were born and reared in Norway, where the latter died when the subject of this sketch was a child of but five years. About the year 1867 Christian Solberg bade adieu to the fair land of his birth and set forth to seek his fortunes in America. He proceeded to Minnesota and settled in the town of Spring Grove, where he followed the trade of carpenter for some time, while he is at the present time a prosperous farmer in Minnesota, having consummated a second marriage a few years after his emigration to the United States.

After the death of his mother the subject of this review was reared to the age of seventeen years in the same home of his aunt, Mrs. Arne Sortaasen, who was a resident of Brottum, Norway. There he received his early educational training under excellent auspices, and at the age noted he came to America and joined his father in Minnesota. There he worked on the farm during the summer months, availing himself of the advantages afforded by the district schools during the winter terms, thus continuing his studies for a period of three years and sparing no effort in augmenting his fund of knowledge. In 1881 he came westward to Fargo, North Dakota, where he remained about two years, devoting his attention principally to the work of carpentry and cabinetmaking. He then came to what is now South Dakota and entered claim to a half section of land in what is now Marshall County, the tract being at the time thirty miles distant from any settlement. He held the land for a time, in the meanwhile finding employment in a furniture store at Columbia. At the expiration of three years Professor Solberg disposed of his land and shortly afterward was matriculated as a student in the State Agricultural College, where he continued his studies for four years, completing the prescribed course and in the meanwhile being employed in the institution as a teacher of carpentry, wood turning, etc., having marked skill in these lines. He was graduated in the college as a member of the class of 1891, receiving the degree of Bachelor of Science, and thereafter continued to devote his entire attention to teaching the practical art mentioned, while in 1892 he was chosen full professor of the mechanical engineering department of the college, having simultaneously been called to a similar position in the North Dakota Agricultural College, a preferment which he resigned soon after his appointment and before assuming the duties of the office. He has since continued at the head of the mechanical department of his alma mater and has brought the same up to a high standard, making it one of the most popular and valuable departments in the institution. Owing to the specific nature of the course of study in the agricultural college and the practical work exemplified, the sessions are held during the summer months, while the students have their longest vacation during the winter. This fact enabled Professor Solberg to attend during such vacation periods Purdue University, at Lafayette, Indiana, and he was there graduated as a member of the class of 1895, receiving the degree of Bachelor of Mechanical Engineering, and the following year he received the degree of Mechanical Engineer.

At the time when Professor Solberg entered upon his executive duties in the agricultural college the mechanical department was maintained on a very modest basis, its functions comprising only an elemental form of shop work, while the facilities were meagre. Under his enthusiastic and able direction, a steady growth was had and the department rapidly increased in popularity, so that it became necessary to provide new and adequate quarters and modern mechanical accessories. The advance that has been made under his direction is best indicated in the statement that during the present year, 1903, more than two hundred and fifty students are availing themselves of the advantages of the department, of which Professor Solberg has just reason to be proud, not alone on the score noted, but also by reason of the fact that the equipment throughout is one of the best to be found in any similar institution in the northwest. So far as can be learned he was the first to introduce the short course in practical steam engineering, and the value of the same has been appreciated not only by the students, but also by other institutions which have followed his initiative, the course having proved a distinctive drawing card for the college.

In politics the Professor gives his support to the Republican party and fraternally he is identified with the lodge, chapter and commandery of the Masonic order, as well as with the auxiliary organization, the Order of the Eastern Star, of which Mrs. Solberg also is a member. He is likewise chief of engineering and ordnance of the National Guard, holding the rank of colonel. He is a member of the Modern Woodmen of America and of the National Society for the Promotion of Engineering Education. He and his wife are members of the Lutheran church, in whose work they take an active interest, while their pleasant home is a center of gracious and refined hospitality.

On the 27th of May, 1887, was solemnized the marriage of Professor Solberg to Miss Bolletta Egeberg, who was born in Norway, being a daughter of Halvor and Olena Egeberg, who emigrated to the United States in 1867, residing for a few years in Minnesota and thence removing to Brookings County, South Dakota, where Mr. Egeberg took up a large tract of land, being now one of the prominent and influential farmers of the county. His wife passed away in 1893. Mrs. Solberg secured her early educational training in the district schools and then entered the State Agricultural College, where she formed the acquaintance of her future husband, who was a student in the institution at the time. They are the parents of three children, Harry, Ada Elizabeth and Ruby.

JAMES SOLBERG

J. SOLBERG, president of the Merchants' Exchange Bank of Lake Preston, is a native of Norway, where his birth occurred on February 17, 1852. His parents, Peter and Georgiana Solberg, also of Norwegian birth, came to America in 1853, and located at Buffalo, New York, moving from there to London, Ontario, and later to Winona, Minnesota, where the father followed his trade of shoemaking until 1876, when he moved to Le Seuer County, Minnesota, and engaged in farming. He departed this life in the latter state, July 2, 1903, leaving to mourn his loss a widow and six children, the former still on the home farm in the county of Le Seuer.

Until thirteen years of age the subject of this review spent the greater part of his life in London, Canada, and received his preliminary education in the schools of that place. He remained with his parents until about the age of twenty-two and then went to Chicago, Illinois, where he spent two years as clerk in a boot and shoe house. Resigning his position at the expiration of the time noted, he went to St. Paul, Minnesota, and during the ensuing two years represented the interests of the Schaffer & Rossum Saddlery Hardware Company, of that city, as a traveling salesman. Severing his connection with this firm, Mr. Solberg embarked in merchandising at Lake Crystal, Minnesota, and after spending nine prosperous years m that town, disposed of his business and in the spring of 1893 came to South Dakota and purchased an interest in the Merchants' Exchange Bank of Lake Preston, with the career of which institution he has since been identified. Mr. Solberg served the bank several years as vice-president, but in 1900 was elected president and in the latter capacity he still continues, filling the position in an able and satisfactory manner and by his energy and progressive business methods adding greatly to the prestige and influence of the institution. As a financier he is familiar with monetary questions, and their relation to commercial and industrial life, and occupies a prominent place among his compeers. In connection with banking, he deals quite extensively in real estate, and now owns a large body of fine land in Kingsbury County, also a beautiful residence property in the town of Lake Preston, in addition to his financial interests represented by the bank of which he is chief executive.

On January 16, 1879, Mr. Solberg was united in marriage with Miss Carrie I. Gutterson, of Winona County, Minnesota, the daughter of Egel and Magla Gutterson, natives of Norway, the union being terminated by the death of the loving and faithful wife on the 17th day of March, 1901.

Fraternally Mr. Solberg is a member of the Masonic brotherhood, belonging to the blue lodge at Lake Preston, the chapter at Arlington and the commandery at Brookings. He is also identified with the Eastern Star lodge, of which his wife was a charter member and the first matron, and his name has long adorned the records of the Ancient Order of United Workmen in the place where he resides. In politics he always has been stanchly Republican, and stood firmly, by the party during all of its trials, caused by the wave of Populism, which a few years ago spread throughout the entire west.

OSCAR LUDWICK SOLIE

As president of the Cataract Book and Stationery Company Oscar Ludwick Solie is at the head of one of the leading commercial enterprises of Sioux Falls. He is a man of marked enterprise and progressiveness, who throughout his business career has brooked no obstacles that could be overcome by persistent, earnest and honorable effort. Sioux Falls is proud to number him among her native sons. His birth here occurred August 10, 1872, his parents being Christian and Thina (Ovren) Solie. The father was born in Holmstrom, Norway, and in early manhood came to the United States, being at that time about eighteen or nineteen years of age. He first settled at Sioux City, Iowa, where he was engaged in the grocery business but later, he removed by wagon to Sioux Falls, where he again established a grocery store which he conducted for several years. Subsequently he was engaged in the grain business until burned out. For an extended period, he was classed among the representative business men of the city, being among those whose efforts were an important element in the upbuilding of the northwest. He died in November, 1895.

In the public schools of Sioux Falls Oscar Ludwick Solie pursued his education and later spent a year in school at Yankton, South Dakota, after which he became a student in the Sioux Falls Business College. Throughout his commercial career he has been connected with the book and stationery business, his initial step being made as clerk in a stationery and book business in Sioux Falls. In 1892 he went to Aspen, Colorado, and became manager of the Ovren Book & Stationery Company at that place, the senior partner of the firm being his maternal uncle. He was there employed for six years and in 1899 returned to Sioux Falls, where he took charge of the stationery department of Brown & Saenger, with whom he continued for sixteen months. On the expiration of that period, he purchased the Cataract Book Store and formed a corporation under the name of the Cataract Book and Stationery Company, of which he was secretary and treasurer during the first three years, while since 1912 he has been the president. The company conducts a retail business in books and stationery, office supplies, filing cabinets and loose-leaf ledgers and binders. Mr. Solie's first partner was I. H. Dokken and the business was incorporated for eight thousand dollars, but the capital has since been increased to fifteen thousand dollars, indicating something of the rapid and substantial growth of the business. In 1908 the company purchased the Sioux Falls Trunk Factory, whereby larger and more commodious quarters were secured at No. 121 North Phillips Avenue. Here they have one of the largest single store rooms in the city, but it was soon found necessary to build an addition to take care of the growing business in the trunk factory. This department supplies everything necessary for the traveler in up-to-date luggage and theirs is the only trunk factory in the state. In 1910 a wholesale school department was added in connection which occupies the entire second floor. This school department is one of the most complete in the northwest and handles everything for the school room. The Cataract Book & Stationery Company is also interested in the rebuilding and repairing of typewriters and supplies all makes of typewriters. The business today is one of the most important commercial enterprises, not only of Sioux Falls, but of the state and at its head are men of marked enterprise and keen discernment, who keep in close touch with every phase of the business and conduct their interests along most progressive lines.

Mr. Solie has an interesting military record, inasmuch as he served for three years as a member of Company B, of the South Dakota National Guard. In politics he is a republican and in religious faith a

Lutheran. He has attained high rank in Masonry, being a member of the Consistory and of the Shrine, and he is also prominent and popular in club circles, holding membership with the Elks Club, the Sioux Athletic Club and the City Temple Club. What he has accomplished has been the result of the utilization of the opportunities which have come to him and the innate talents which are his. He has steadily worked his way upward step by step and while his life has not been actuated by any vaulting ambition, he has never failed to follow the lead of his opportunities which have carried him into important commercial relations.

R. H. SOMERS

R. H. SOMERS, who holds the responsible office of government agent for the Lower Brule Indian agency, is a native of New Brunswick, Canada, where he was born October 23, 1857, being a son of Lafayette and Elizabeth A. (Chapman) Somers, and the eldest of their nine surviving children, the others being as follows: Amelia, the wife of L. W. Lewis, who lives at Madison, Wisconsin; Lowell, a resident of Lafayette, Indiana; Clifford M., a farmer on the Lower Brule reservation; Lafayette, a resident of Chamberlain, this state; and Le Baron B., Peolia L., Fred D. and Eliza M., who remain at the parental home. The father of our subject was born in New Brunswick, Canada, in 1826, and when a young man he removed to Robertstown, Maine, where he served an apprenticeship at the trade of blacksmith, after which he returned to his home in Canada, where he continued to follow his trade until 1878, when he emigrated with his family to the territory of Dakota, locating in Brule City, the prospective terminal of the Chicago, Milwaukee & St. Paul Railroad, though by a later dispensation Chamberlain was made the terminus. He engaged in farming and stock growing and continued to reside in Brule City until 1898, when he removed to Chamberlain, where he is now living retired. His wife was likewise a native of Canada, and is one of the honored pioneer women of the state.

Major R. H. Somers, the immediate subject of this sketch, acquired his early education in the schools of his native province, and before attaining the age of sixteen he entered upon an apprenticeship at the blacksmith trade, under the effective direction of his father. After the removal of the family to Dakota he bought an ax and began chopping wood for the steamboats plying the Missouri River, and after being thus occupied for one year he was tendered and accepted the position of blacksmith at Fort Hale, where he served four years. In 1883 he left this position and removed to Chamberlain, and devoted the following three years to farming and stock raising. In July, 1886, he married Miss Helena F. Archer, of Brule County, and as a severe drought the following year caused an entire loss of his crops he removed from his ranch to the village of Chamberlain and here opened a blacksmith shop, which he conducted until the spring of 1888, when he sold the same and returned to his farm. The droughts continued, however, and in 1891 he was forced to again abandon his agricultural operations and to re-engage in the blacksmith business in Chamberlain, where he continued at his trade until 1898, having also engaged in the livery business in 1894, making a success of both enterprises. In October, 1897, Major Somers was appointed deputy United States marshal, in which capacity he served until May, 1901, when he resigned to assume the duties of his present office as agent at the Lower Brule Indian agency, his appointment having been conferred on the 15th of May.

He is a stanch Republican in his political proclivities, and fraternally is identified with Chamberlain Lodge, No. 56, Free and Accepted Masons; Pilgrim Chapter, Royal Arch Masons; Castle Lodge, No. 10, Knights of Pythias, of which he is a charter member; and Chamberlain Lodge, No. 88, Ancient Order of United Workmen. Our subject and his wife are the parents of five children, all of whom are still beneath the home roof, namely: Robert E., Frances E., Evelyn, Lucky H. and Thomas M.

Dr. F. A. Spafford, active as a representative of the medical profession in Flandreau, is today the oldest physician of that city, inasmuch as others who were located there at the time of his arrival have all passed away or gone to other scenes of activity. His success from the beginning was assured because of the thoroughness of his preparatory work and because of his wide reading in later years, keeping him in touch with the advanced thought of the profession. He was born in Ludlow, Vermont, on the 13th of October, 1855, and is a son of Alva M. and Mary (Angier) Spafford, the former a contractor and builder, but both now deceased.

Dr. Spafford supplemented his public-school and academic education by a medical course at Dartmouth College and was graduated with the class of 1879. He has since taken post graduate courses in New York, Berlin and Edinburgh. Before his graduation from Dartmouth, however, he went to Raleigh, North Carolina, in 1877 and there spent three years teaching Latin and Greek in Shaw University. He then resumed the study of medicine but was later made lecturer in the medical department of Shaw University, serving in that capacity for one year. For a time, he was also professor of anatomy and chemistry in the Leonard Medical College at Raleigh, North Carolina.

Dr. Spafford arrived in South Dakota in 1884 and opened an office for practice in Flandreau, where he has since remained, covering a period of three decades. He is most widely and favorably known throughout the state, ranking very high in his profession. His wide study and broad experience have gained him knowledge that makes his opinions largely accepted as standard by other representatives of the profession here. His standing is furthermore attested in the fact that he was twice honored with election to the presidency of the state medical society in 1898 and 1914. He is a fellow of the American College of Surgeons; is likewise a member of the Sioux Valley Medical Association, the Sioux Falls District Medical Association; and is a fellow of the American Medical Association and the Anglo-American Medical Society, of Berlin.

In 1881 Dr. Spafford was married to Miss Hattie E. A. Davis, of Boston, Massachusetts, a daughter of Thomas P. Davis, and they have one daughter, Lillian W., now Mrs. W. L. Rolfe. Dr. Spafford is of the Baptist faith, while his wife holds membership in the Episcopal church. He indorses the democratic principles in exercising his right of franchise and his fraternal relations are with the Masons, the Elks and the Odd Fellows. He is now past grand commander of the state in Masonry and holds high rank in that order.

Many public projects have benefited by his cooperation and public spirit. He has been president of the board of regents of the State University and has been a member of that board for twelve years. At present he is lecturer on medical jurisprudence at the South Dakota State University College of Law. He has probably the finest library, both medical and otherwise, in the state. He has acted as president of the Flandreau school board for twenty-seven years and the present excellent school system of the city is attributable in no small measure to his efforts. He has also been a member of the local board of health for a number of years and he stands for advancement and progress along all lines. He finds rest and recreation in travel and in fishing. He is a map of high purpose and lofty ideals, who has used his talents wisely and well and improved his opportunities to the benefit and betterment of his fellowmen and of his city and state.

JOHN E. SPARLING

J. E. Sparling, of Gettysburg, Potter County, being a member of the general merchandise firm of Clark & Sparling, is a native of "merrie old England," having been born in the town of Barwick-in-Elmet, Yorkshire, on the 27th of October, 1870, and being a son of George and Sarah (Dyson) Sparling, who were born and reared in the same locality. The father and the subject came to America in 1883, and reached Spink County, South Dakota, in April of the same year, where they remained about two years and then removed to Potter County, where the father of the subject was engaged in fanning until 188-9, when he removed to Gettysburg and engaged in the hardware business. In 1894 he removed to Bowdle, Edmunds County, South Dakota, and in 1899 he took up his abode in Marshall, Minnesota, where he has since devoted his attention to the implement business. The subject received his early educational training in his native town and after coming to the United States continued his studies in the public schools of South Dakota, as opportunity permitted. He was associated with his father in the general merchandise and implement business until the spring of 1899, and thereafter he was engaged in the implement business in Bowdle, Edmunds County, this state, until the spring of 1903, when he became associated with his father-in-law, Mr. Clark, in the mercantile business in Gettysburg, as noted in the initial paragraph of this article.

He is independent in politics and has attained the thirty-second degree in Scottish Rite Masonry, being identified with the consistory at Aberdeen, and with the temple of the Ancient Arabic Order of the Nobles of the Mystic Shrine at Sioux Falls, while he also holds membership in the Knights of Pythias, the Ancient Order of United Workmen and the Modern Woodmen of America. On the 6th of May, 1896, Mr. Sparling wedded Miss Maud C. Clark, daughter of James B. Clark, of Gettysburg, and they are prominent ill the social circles of their home town, enjoying marked popularity in the community.

JUSTIN LEVI SPAULDING

Justin L. SPAULDING, was born in Mooretown, Vermont, June 17, 1841. He was educated at the state normal school at Bloomington, Illinois, entering this institution at the age of sixteen. He pursued his studies here until the outbreak of the Civil War in 1861, when he enlisted in the Thirty-third Illinois Infantry, under Colonel Oglesby. He served in the army until his health became broken, when he was discharged, and returning to Bloomington, he re-entered the normal school, from which he soon graduated with high honors. After leaving the normal school he was elected city surveyor of Bloomington and county surveyor of McLean County, Illinois. Following this he was elected city clerk of Bloomington, which position he retained until 1865. In May, 1863, he was married to Miss Adra A. Stiles, also a graduate from the State Normal, in Rochelle, Illinois. Soon after his marriage he removed to Chicago where for two years or more Mr. Spaulding did court reporting in the criminal courts and gained a wide reputation as an expert stenographer, being second in speed in the United States. In 1882 Mr. Spaulding came to Huron, South Dakota, and took a position in the United States land office; this he filled for seven years or more, during which time he was elected a member of the board of county commissioners, serving as its chairman for two years. Meanwhile he was admitted to the South Dakota bar. In 1889 he was elected county clerk of Beadle County, and two years later he was re-elected to the same office. The following spring he was taken seriously sick, and on May 22, 1891, he passed away. He was survived by his wife and one daughter. Rose Blanche, who still reside in Huron. His daughter in later years has become quite prominent in the work of several of the state lodges and has been honored with the position of department secretary of the state Woman's Relief Corps, and with various offices in the Rebekah state assembly, and is at present the warden of that body. She is also a member of the local Order of the Eastern Star. At the time of his death, Mr. Spaulding was a prominent Odd Fellow, an influential Mason, and a leading member of the Grand Army of the Republic. Mr. Spaulding was prominent in the political affairs of both Illinois and South Dakota during his life time, and was universally esteemed by all who were privileged to know him.

JOHN A. STANLEY

JOHN A. STANLEY

John A. Stanley has recently become a resident of Lead, having taken possession of the Lead Daily Call as owner and editor New Year's Day, 1915. Previous to removing to Lead he was for a number of years a resident of Hot Springs, where he was widely and most favorably known. He was born at West Salem, Wisconsin, on the 24th of October, 1862, a son of William H. and Rebecca (Aiken) Stanley, who were born at Adams near Watertown, New York, July 8, 1817, and in Tioga County, Pennsylvania, January 1, 1841, respectively. The father, who was a practicing physician, removed to West Salem, Wisconsin, about 1857 and there he resided until about 1879, when he came to Deuel County, this state, locating at Gary, which was then the terminus of the Northwestern Railroad, therefore a town of considerable importance. He remained there until 1887, when he removed to Hot Springs, which remained his home until his death in 1891. He gained a lucrative practice in Hot Springs and won also the respect and confidence of the general public and his professional brethren. In 1849, he, like so many others, made the long, wearisome and dangerous trip to the Pacific coast in search of gold and was for a short time connected with mining in California, though he also practiced medicine. He was a prominent Mason and, in his thoughts, and deeds exemplified the brotherly spirit that is the foundation of the craft. His widow survives and is still a resident of Hot Springs, South Dakota.

John A. Stanley, who was the second in order of birth in a family of nine children, attended the public schools of West Salem, Wisconsin, and there acquired a knowledge of the branches usually taught. When twenty years of age he entered the printing office of the Interstate at Gary, South Dakota, and the following year went to Watertown, this state, where he was employed by General S. J. Conklin, the first president of the South Dakota Press Association and for many years a leading newspaper man of the territory and state. In 1886 he severed his connection with that gentleman and went to Hermosa, Custer County, where he established a newspaper known as the Pilot, which he conducted successfully until February, 1892. At that time, he removed to Hot Springs and purchased the Hot Springs Star, which he edited and published until the winter of 1909, when he disposed of it. In the meantime, he had become interested in an irrigation project which was being developed by a concern known as the Hot Springs Irrigation & Live Stock Company. He has since disposed of his interest in that company but he owns extensive land in the Cheyenne valley, a part of which he is irrigating and using as a stock ranch, together with his son Ward. He is also interested in an irrigated ranch in the Elk Mountain country in the western part of the Black Hills and is president of the company operating the same. He likewise holds title to a number of tracts of land in Fall River County and is vice president of the Stockmen's Bank of Hot Springs. As previously stated, he assumed charge of the Lead Daily Call, January 1, 1915, having purchased the paper a short time previously. He is giving the publication of that journal his personal attention and his general business knowledge and ability, combined with his years of experience as a newspaper man, ensure its success.

Mr. Stanley was married on the 6th of April, 1887, to Miss Alice Wood, a native of Corry, Pennsylvania, and a daughter of S. H. and Sarah (Jones) Wood. Both of her parents were born in the state of New York. On coming westward, they first located in Michigan, the father being for a number of years a warden in the state penitentiary at Jackson. In 1884 the family removed to Dakota territory but after about a year returned to Michigan. The father, however, became an extensive landowner in Deuel County, South Dakota. He died in the Wolverine state in 1885. His widow survives and now makes her home with our subject. To Mr. and Mrs. Stanley have been born two children. Ward Allen, whose natal day was the 11th of April, 1888, is a resident of Hot Springs, where he is assistant postmaster. In September, 1910, he was united in marriage to Miss Mae Randall, of Rapid City. Elton Wood, born April 9, 1890, was graduated from the George Washington University at Washington, D. C, in June, 1915.

Mr. Stanley is a republican and for more than sixteen years served efficiently as postmaster of Hot Springs, taking office March 1, 1898, and severing his connection therewith in June, 1914. He is a leader in all movements looking toward the moral betterment of his community and is a consistent member of the Methodist Episcopal church. The rules which govern his life are further indicated in his membership in the Masonic order, belonging to the blue lodge, the chapter and commandery. He is held in high esteem among his Masonic brethren and is a past master of the blue lodge. He is also affiliated with the Modern Woodmen of America and the Yeomen. In 1913 he was president of the Commercial Club of Hot Springs and under his direction the organization was able to accomplish much for the commercial expansion of its city.

TOM STAPLETON

Tom Stapleton, who holds a prominent position in the affairs, of Minnehaha County, is president of the Farmers Elevator Company of Ellis, and one of the most extensive landowners in this section of the state. His birth occurred in St. Stephens, Cornwall, England, on the 24th of July, 1849, and his parents were William and Mary Ann (Pengelley) Stapleton, both natives of the same county, where their entire lives were spent. The father was a blacksmith and taught his son the trade. The latter was reared under the parental roof and acquired a limited education in the common schools.

In 1871, when a young man of about twenty-two, Mr. Stapleton crossed the Atlantic to Canada, where, however, he spent only about three months. Upon leaving Cobourg, Ontario, he came to the States, locating in Shullsburg, Wisconsin, where he opened a blacksmith shop and followed his trade for ten years. In 1881 he removed to South Dakota, settling in Minnehaha County and engaging in farming. He had purchased a farm in Split Rock township as far back as 1874, when he drove through from Le Mars, Iowa, being favorably impressed with the opportunities offered in that county. However, he never resided upon that farm and subsequently sold it. Upon settling in Minnehaha County, he first located in Benton township, where he resided until 1906, and then removed to Sioux Falls, where he has since made his home. He proved a most successful farmer and as his resources increased, he invested in more land until he is now the owner of twelve hundred and eighty acres of land, all situated in Benton township with the exception of a quarter section in Wayne township. He is also a business man of no mean ability and organized the Farmers Elevator Company of Ellis, serving as its president since its organization in 1903.

Mr. Stapleton was married in 1877 at Galena, Illinois, to Miss Elizabeth Ann Tothill, of Shullsburg, Wisconsin, and they have become the parents of five children, four of whom survive, as follows: William M., who is engaged in farming on the old homestead; Benjamin T., a contractor and builder of Portland, Oregon; Glen T., a resident of Gaston, Oregon where he is engaged in banking; and Orra Belle, at home, librarian of Carnegie Library at Sioux Falls. Mrs. Stapleton is a consistent member of the Methodist Episcopal church and takes an active part in the work of that organization.

Mr. Stapleton is a stanch republican in politics. While living in Benton township he served as clerk of the school board for twenty-two years, and as township treasurer for twenty years. He is a member of Minnehaha Lodge, A. F. & A. M.; and of Sioux Falls Lodge, No. 262, B. P. O. E. He has done much to further the agricultural development of the county and in a business, way has been a force in the commercial life of Sioux Falls, while his unswerving integrity has commended him to the respect of all who know him.

SOLOMON STAR

SOLOMON STAR

Solomon Star, was born in the kingdom of Bavaria, Germany, on the 20th of December, 1840, a son of Marcus and Minnie (Friedlander) Star, also natives of that country. Early in life the father embarked in mercantile business in Bavaria and so continued until his death, which occurred on the 7th of October, 1884. He had survived his wife for ten years, as she passed away on the 1st of July, 1874.

Mr. Star of this review is the fifth in order of birth in a family of ten children. In 1850, before he was ten years of age, he came with an uncle, Joseph Friedlander, to the United States. They located at Cincinnati, Ohio, where the subject of this review attended school but after about a year he removed to Circleville, Ohio, where he continued his education in the schools of that city for about six years, or from 1851 to 1857. In the latter year to begin clerking in a general store and was so employed until 1862. He then went to Missouri and engaged in business for himself at Marshall, remaining there until 1865, in which

he moved his stock to St. Joseph, Missouri, where for three months he conducted a store. At the end of that time, he took his stock to Virginia City, Montana, and continued in business there until 1876, when he came to South Dakota and located in Deadwood. He opened a hardware store, which he conducted until 1893, when he sold his interests in that line and engaged in the flour-milling business. In 1896, however, he disposed of that interest as well and for three years lived practically retired, but in 1899 he was elected clerk of the courts, which office he has held ever since. During the fifteen years in which he has been the incumbent in the office he has devoted his time to his duties and as he is punctual and systematic in all that he does the affairs of the office are kept in good condition. His length of service is in itself ample testimony to the efficiency and conscientiousness with which he discharges his duties.

Mr. Star is a republican in his political belief and fraternally belongs to the Masonic lodge, in which he has attained the thirty-third degree and is past grand master of Masons in Montana. He also belongs to the Ancient Order of United Workmen. He has been a resident of South Dakota since pioneer days and has seen the marvelous development that has taken place in the almost forty years that have elapsed since his arrival in 1876. When he came to Deadwood, he moved his goods with a team of oxen and although he crossed the Sioux reservation was unmolested by the Indians. A few years previously when he had moved his goods from Missouri to Montana, he also made the journey by ox team. On his arrival in the Black Hills there were still many buffalo, deer and elk and everywhere were evidences of primitive conditions. He has not only witnessed the change that has transformed this region to a settled and prosperous section but has done his full share in bringing this about and deserves the honor and respect that are paid to those who by their labors have made possible the development of today. His reminiscences of pioneer life do much toward giving the present generation some idea of life in the early days of the state.

EDWIN M. STARCHER

Edwin M. STARCHER, president of the Gregory County State Bank, at Fairfax, Gregory County, is a native of West Virginia, having been born in Ripley, Jackson county, on Christmas day of the year 1863, and being a son of Jacob L. and Marian G. (Webb) Starcher, the former of whom was likewise born in Jackson County, that state, in 1832, while the latter was born in the city of Charleston, West Virginia, at that time having been still an integral portion of the Old Dominion state. The father of the subject was reared and educated in his native state and is a man of high intellectuality and marked business acumen. In his earlier years he was a successful teacher, having been thus engaged in different places, while he also followed mercantile pursuits as a young man, being now identified with this line of enterprise in Ripley, West Virginia, where he was also engaged in the banking business for some time. He has accumulated an estate of four hundred thousand dollars, the same representing the results of his own efforts since the close of the Civil War. He was a stanch Union man during that crucial epoch and was sheriff of his county at the time, and he is a stanch Democrat in politics. He visited various portions of the great northwest in a very early day, having been with a government surveying party which made its way up the Red River through what is the present state of South Dakota, the same being then on the very frontier of civilization. He is a member of the Masonic fraternity, and both he and his devoted wife are communicants of the Protestant Episcopal church. They have only two children, the elder of whom, Floyd, is now a resident of the city of Richmond, Virginia.

When the subject was a child of six years his parents removed to the state of Minnesota, and located in Hastings, in whose public schools he secured his early educational training. In 1880 he entered the Northwestern Ohio Normal University, at Ada, where he continued his studies for one year. He then entered the law department of Washington and Lee University, at Lexington, Virginia, and was there graduated in June, 1888, coming forth well equipped for the practice of his chosen profession. Shortly after his graduation Mr. Starcher came to South Dakota and located in the town of Wheeler, Charles Mix County, where he established himself in the practice of law, and that he soon gained popularity and professional prestige is evident when we revert to the fact that within the first year of his residence here, he was elected state's attorney of his county, of which office he remained incumbent for two years, proving an able and discriminating prosecutor. This was before the admission of the state, and he served as the last district attorney and first state's attorney in that county, being in office at the time of the admission of the state to the Union. He continued in the active practice of his profession in that county for a period of ten years, at the expiration of which, in 1898, he took up his residence in Fairfax, where he has since maintained his home. In his youthful days he was employed in a drug store and gained a thorough knowledge of the business, being now a registered pharmacist. He has been consecutively engaged in the drug business ever since he came to South Dakota, and thus it may be seen that he is distinctively a man of affairs, having a great capacity for work and that of a successful order, both in professional and business lines. When he took up his residence in the present thriving little city of Fairfax, in 1898, the county had not yet been organized, and he was prominently identified with public affairs here from the start. He is a stanch advocate of the principles of the Democratic party, and as a candidate of the same he was elected the first county judge of Gregory County, to which dignified position he has since been three times re-elected, being incumbent of the office at the present time and having made an enviable record on the bench, as has he also in the active practice of his profession. He has also served for four years as city attorney, having been the first and only occupant of the position in this city. He is the owner of the only drug store here, is president of the Gregory State Bank and is the owner of valuable realty in the village and county. As if all these interests were not sufficient to tax his powers of supervision, Judge Starcher is also engaged in the abstract business, having an excellent system of records and being the pioneer in this line in the county.

He and his wife are communicants of the Episcopal church, and fraternally he is affiliated with the Masons, the Independent Order of Odd Fellows, the Knights of Pythias and the Modern Woodmen of America. On the 11th of November, 1901, was solemnized the marriage of Judge Starcher to Miss Marian B. Helenbolt, who was born in Minnesota, being a daughter of Harry and Mary E. (Blake) Helenbolt, who removed to Nebraska when she was a child, her father being now one of the successful farmers of that state.

ROYAL B. STEARNS

(This biographical sketch had no beginning in the original document. A decision was made to include this bio for its Masonic significance.)

Royal B. STEARNS - native town and secured his early educational training in its public schools, after which he completed a course of study in St. Lawrence University, in Canton, that state, where he was graduated as a member of the class of 1880. He then took up the study of law. in the office of Hon. Leslie W. Russell, of that place, one of the most eminent members of the bar of the state. He served as attorney general of the state, was a member of congress for several terms, while in 1884 he was defeated for the United States senate by a few votes, his opponent being the Hon. William M. Evarts. He later became an associate justice of the supreme court of the state, resigning this office a short time before his death. Under this able and honored preceptor Judge Stearns prosecuted his legal studies, continuing in the office of Judge Russell until 1884, when he accompanied his preceptor to Albany, being one of his clerks while he was serving as attorney general. During the winter of 1884 the subject took a course of lectures in the Albany Law School, having been admitted to the bar of the state in November of the preceding year. Judge Stearns was graduated in the law department of Union University, in Albany, on the 22d of May, 1884, having completed the prescribed two-years course in one year, and from this institution he received the degree of Bachelor of Law, after his graduation he entered upon the active practice of his profession in Canton, New York, where he remained one year. In April, 1885, he came west on business, and became so impressed with the attractions of this division of our national domain that he located in Wadena, Minnesota, where he was associated in practice with Frank Wilson until 1887, meeting with excellent success. In 1889 his father died and he returned to his old home in New York to assist in the settlement of the estate. He had previously, in 1887, visited South Dakota on business, remaining several months, and upon returning to the west he located in Fort Pierre, this state, in 1890. Here he has since been engaged in active practice, retaining at the present time a large and representative clientage and holding high prestige at the bar of the state. He served three terms as state's attorney for Stanley County, and one term as judge of the county court, making an excellent record in each of these offices. He was one of those prominently concerned in bringing about the abolishment of the grand-jury system in South Dakota, and he drew the first information for murder after the law of 1896 went into effect, said information having been drawn on the 3d of July of that year, while the law went into effect only two days previously. During his first term as county attorney, he was prosecutor in three murder trials, and while serving on the county bench he settled the estate of Frederick Dupree, amounting to one hundred and eighty thousand dollars. The Judge has been an ardent and effective worker in the cause of the Republican party, and in 1892-3 was secretary of the Republican League of the state. Early in the year 1893 Gov. Charles H. Sheldon selected Mr. Stearns for one of his staff and commissioned him a colonel. He held this appointment for four years, and did his full share of the honors and entertaining at the South Dakota building at the World's Fair in Chicago during the season of 1893. He was also appointed and commissioned by Governor Sheldon to represent this state as a delegate to the World's Real Estate Congress, held in Chicago during the week commencing October 12, 1893.

He was a charter member of Hiram Lodge, No. 123, Ancient Free and Accepted Masons, at Fort Pierre, and the charter for the same was secured largely through his efforts, as there was no little opposition on the part of other lodges. Owing to the danger entailed in crossing the Missouri river at certain seasons of the year he finally secured the required dispensation from the grand lodge. He has been a strong advocate of the project of building a railroad from Pierre to the Black Hills, and his opinions and written articles on the subject have been freely quoted and republished.

From the time of locating in the state Judge Stearns has been more or less interested in real estate and stock raising enterprises, and in 1900 he effected the organization of the St. Paul & Fort Pierre Cattle Company, of which he has been vice-president and general manager from the time of its inception. J. B. Little, of St. Paul, Minnesota, is president, and H. A. Knight, of Minneapolis, is secretary and treasurer. The company is capitalized for one hundred thousand dollars, and is engaged in the grazing and maturing of beef cattle, having one of the finest stock ranches west of the Missouri river, the same being located on the Bad River, two and one-half miles south of Fort Pierre, where they have a large ranch and fine ranch buildings. They make a specialty of buying Texas cattle, shipping them to their ranch and here maturing them for the Chicago market, while the company are rapidly increasing the number of stock fed on the ranch, conducting operations on a constantly increasing scale.

On the 24th of November, 1893, Judge Stearns was united in marriage to Mrs. Mary A. Miar, who was born and reared in Williamsport, Pennsylvania, being a daughter of John Heyler, a prominent farmer of Tioga County. No children have been born of this union.

W. F. STEARNS

W. F. STEARNS, treasurer of Douglas County, was born on a farm in Seneca County, Ohio, on the 15th of September, 1850, being the eldest of the four surviving children of John B. and Adaline H. (Kelly) Stearns. His brother Alden W. is a broker of mining stock, residing in Garden Grove, Iowa; Clara is the wife of J. D. Bartow, of Plankinton, South Dakota: and Grace is the wife of J. E. Vail, of Garden Grove, Iowa. The father of the subject was born in the state of New York, and when he was five years of age his parents emigrated thence to Ohio, becoming pioneers of that commonwealth, and there he was reared to maturity on a farm, securing a common-school education. He continued to be engaged in agricultural pursuits in Seneca county until 1883, when he rented his fine farm, comprising three hundred and sixty acres, and came west, taking up a homestead claim in what is Beadle County, South Dakota. After proving up on his claim he returned to Ohio, where he remained one year, at the expiration of which he returned to South Dakota and located in the village of Plankinton, where he became prominently identified with the grain and live-stock business, continuing operations in the line until his death, which there occurred in 1890, at which time he was sixty-six years of age. He was a stanch Republican in politics, and though he never sought office he was an important factor in the councils of his party while a resident of Ohio, having been a close personal friend of ex-Governor Charles Foster, whose home was in Seneca county, and having been one of his able lieutenants in various campaigns. He was a member of the Methodist church and was a man of marked business acumen and sterling character, commanding the respect of all who knew him. His wife, who was likewise born in Ohio, is now living at Garden Grove, Iowa.

W. F. Stearns was reared on the homestead farm and secured his educational discipline in the public schools of his native county. Upon attaining maturity, he assumed charge of the home farm, to whose management he continued to give his attention until 1877, when he came to the west, locating in Wilson County, Kansas, where he secured a tract of land and was engaged in farming about eight years. In the spring of 1885, he came to what is now the state of South Dakota and located in Plankinton, where he was engaged in the buying and shipping of grain until 1893, having built up a large and profitable enterprise in the line. In the year mentioned he removed to Armour, where he has since maintained his home. Here he established a general mercantile business, becoming one of the pioneer business men of the town and one of its leading citizens, and he continued this business until the autumn of 1902, when he disposed of the same, since which time he has given his entire attention to his official duties and to the supervision of his private interests.

Mr. Stearns is one of the wheelhorses of the Democratic party in this section, having been an efficient worker in its cause. In July 1898, he was appointed to the office of county treasurer, to fill the vacancy caused by the death of the regular incumbent, the late J. F. James, and in the election of November, 1900, he was returned to the office by popular vote, giving so able an administration as to lead to his re-election as his own successor in the autumn of 1902, so that he is now serving his third consecutive term as county treasurer. He was for a number of years a member of the board of education and at all times manifests a lively interest in all that concerns the welfare and advancement of his home town and county.

Fraternally he is identified with Arcania Lodge, No. 18, Free and Accepted Masons; with Armour Tent, No. 18, Knights of the Maccabees, and with Plankinton Lodge, No. 77, Ancient Order of United Workmen. On the 21st of October, 1875, was solemnized the marriage of Mr. Stearns to Miss Alice C. Her, who was born and reared in Seneca county, Ohio, being a daughter of Conrad and Julia Her, and the subject and his wife are the parents of four children: Pearl H., Lloyd A., Grace and Walter, all of whom remain beneath the parental rooftree.

ALBERT STEELE

A. STEELE, who holds the responsible and exacting position of day foreman of the great stamp mills of the Homestake Mining Company, at Lead, is of Scottish extraction in the paternal line, though the name, in the form of Stahl, has been identified with the annals of Norway since the fourteenth century, when the original representatives in the far Norseland immigrated thither from Scotland. The subject was born in Trondhjem, Norway, on the 6th of April, 1838, being a son of Roald and Kjersten Olsen. After coming to the United States, the subject reverted to the English spelling of the name and the one which was undoubtedly the original orthography in Scotland. His father passed his entire life in Norway, engaged in agricultural pursuits, and our subject was thus reared as a farmer lad. At the age of fifteen years, he accompanied a Lutheran clergyman to the northern part of Norway, where he passed four years, and he then penetrated still farther north, making three trips to Spitsbergen with Captain Carlson, whose stanch little vessel went forth for the hunting of walruses, seals and polar bears. Later Mr. Steele made a trip in a brig to Hammerfest, the most northerly civilized town in the world, and thence returned with a load of fish to Gothenburg, Sweden, where the vessel was laden with lumber and proceeded to Hull, England, where our subject left the ship and went on a Russian brig, bound for Riga, Russia, and loaded with flaxseed for the market at Belfast, Ireland. The vessel was wrecked on the west coast of Scotland, and the members of the crew were picked up and brought into Glasgow, whence Mr. Steele shipped on the American vessel "Cornelia," of Portland, Maine, the same being bound for Brazil. When three weeks out from Glasgow the vessel was wrecked and went to the bottom of the sea, the crew and passengers taking to the boats and being picked up within twenty-four hours by a Welsh brig, and they were landed on Silly Island, whence Mr. Steele embarked on a steamboat for Penzance, Cornwall, England, thence to Red Ruth and finally to Falmouth, where he and his companions appealed to the American consul, who sent them on to Liverpool, via Dublin, where they were looked after by the same consul. There the subject sailed finally on a ship named "Henry Brigham," bound for San Francisco, and the voyage was an exceedingly rough one, necessitating the throwing overboard of one hundred tons of the cargo, while the vessel was greatly disabled, but finally dropped anchor in San Francisco in September, 1861. The vessel was here seized by the government, as it was owned in the south, then in rebellion against the Union. After being identified with the coasting trade for one year Mr. Steele went on the stampede of gold seekers to Alaska, but he immediately returned to San Francisco, where he remained until 1864, when he came to Idaho, where he was engaged in quartz mining for the ensuing three years. He then returned to California where he followed the same vocation until 1878, when he set forth for the Black Hills, arriving in February. On the 2d of the following month he entered the employ of the Homestake Mining Company as a miner, and was soon afterward made foreman of the Highland mine, retaining this position two years, at the expiration of which the company gave further evidence of appreciation of his ability and fidelity by promoting him to the present office as foreman of the stamp mills, the capacity of the mills having been increased from three hundred and sixty to six hundred and forty stamps since he assumed his position as foreman. He has a pleasant home in Lead and is held in high esteem in the community. In politics Mr. Steele gives his support to the Republican party, and fraternally he is identified with the lodge, chapter and commandery of the Masonic order, and also with the auxiliary organization, the Order of the Eastern Star.

In January, 1880, Mr. Steele was united in marriage to Miss Theresa Hienish, who was born in Germany, and who died in 1881, leaving one child, Theresa Marie, who is now a stenographer in the state auditor's office, at Lincoln, Nebraska. In February, 1884, Mr. Steele wedded Miss Mary Ann Leonard, who was born and reared in Pennsylvania, and they became the parents of six children, namely: Ellen, Caroline, Albert J., Agnes Catherine, John Leonard and Mary Cecelia. While out hunting September 5, 1903, Albert

J. was accidentally shot by one of his companions and died a few hours later. He was a bright boy sixteen years old.

EDWARD STENGER

Edward STENGER was born June 5, 158, in Douglas County, Oregon, and there spent his childhood and early youth, beginning life for himself when but sixteen years of age. Leaving the parental roof in the spring of 1874, he began trailing cattle through eastern Oregon, and after two years at that kind of work settled in Grant County, where he engaged in stock raising upon his own responsibility, in addition to which he also bought and shipped cattle and in due time built up a large and flourishing business. In 1882 he disposed of his interests in Oregon and trailed horses into Montana, going as far as Bozeman, where he located, later turning his attention to horses and sheep, in the raising of which his efforts were crowned with a large measure of success.

Mr. Stenger, in the early part of 1884, started for the Black Hills, arriving at Spearfish on the 3d day of July following, but not being able to find a favorable location on Battle Creek, he took up a pre-emption about eighteen miles from Rapid City, to which he brought a large number of horses the same year. The following spring he bought a ranch on Battle creek and for two years thereafter raised horses on quite an extensive scale, adding cattle in 1886, both of which lines of industry he still pursues. In 1887 he began sheep raising in connection with his other business and with characteristic energy has gradually extended the scope of his operations until he is now regarded the leading livestock man in his part of the country. He purchased from time-to-time extensive tracts of land adjoining his ranch, and at this writing owns on Battle creek about seven thousand acres, two thousand of which are irrigated, a large part of the latter being in cultivation. In addition to his live-stock interests, he devotes considerable attention to farming, raising large crops of grain and hay which he feeds to his cattle, besides marketing each year the vegetable crops which his land produces in abundance. Mr. Stenger's ranch is not only the largest on Battle creek, but is also one of the best improved and most valuable; he spends the summer months on the place, giving personal attention to its management, but of winter seasons lives in Hermosa, where he owns a beautiful and well-appointed residence, one of the finest homes in the city.

In 1886 Mr. Stenger, at the urgent solicitation of many of his friends, erected a hotel in Hermosa, which he ran for some time, under the name of the Battle River House, but which is now known as the Glendale Hotel. After acting for some time in the capacity of "mine host," he retired from the hotel business and rented the property, later disposing of it at a liberal margin on the investment. Since then, he has given all of his time and attention to his live-stock business. In matters of business, Mr. Stenger is energetic, wide-awake and progressive, and he occupies no small place in public esteem.

He holds membership with the Masonic fraternity, Modern Woodmen of America and Ancient Order of United Workmen, and in politics supports the Democratic party. Mr. Stenger, on April 17, 1887, contracted a matrimonial alliance with Miss Amanda Thomas, of Missouri, the marriage being blessed with two daughters. Eva and Edna.

THOMAS STERLING

Thomas STERLING, is a lawyer practicing his profession at Redfield, S. D.. Mr. Sterling was born in Fairfield County, Ohio, February 21, 1851. His parents belonged to the agricultural class, and were a sturdy, hard-working, independent people. Charles Sterling, his father, is a progressive fanner and in good circumstances. He removed from Ohio in 1855 and located at LeRoy, McLean County, Ill., where he now resides. He is of Scotch-Irish descent. His wife, Anna Kesler, is of German descent. Though Thomas had only the meager educational facilities afforded by the district school, and was compelled to work on the farm during the spring and summer months, his teachers were for the most part of a splendid type and from them the lad received an inspiration to go beyond the limited training of a county school. When nineteen years of age, he entered the Illinois Wesleyan University at Bloomington, Ill., and in order to earn the means with which to complete the course he taught for three terms in the district school. During his term at college, he was the winner of the sophomore prize essay, and was class orator on his graduation in 1875. He was a member of the Munsellian Literary Society of that institution. The two years following his graduation he was principal of schools at Bement, Ill., and devoted his leisure hours to reading law. In June, 1877, he entered the law office of Hay, Greene & Littler, at Springfield, Ill., for the purpose of taking up the study of the legal profession in earnest, and was admitted to the bar in June of the following year. He immediately began to practice at Springfield in partnership with Joseph M. Grout, a fellow-student in the same office, and was city attorney of Springfield in 1881-2. The healthful climate and the prospective settlement and rapid development of the then Territory of Dakota attracted the young lawyer, and in October, 1882, he located at Northville, Spink County, S. D., where he at once engaged in the practice of law and in the real estate business. In 1886 he was elected district attorney of Spink County and in 1887 removed to Redfield, where he has since resided.

In January, 1891, he formed a law partnership with Mr. W. A. Morris, under the firm name of Sterling & Morris, which continued until January, 1901. Mr. Sterling has succeeded in building up an extensive law practice, and is regarded as one of the leading lawyers of South Dakota. He has been engaged in a number of important civil cases affecting public interests, and relating to questions of procedure in the new state. He was made president of the South Dakota Bar Association at its meeting in February, 1901. In politics he has always been a Republican. He was a member of the constitutional conventions of 1883 and 1889, and was chairman of the judiciary committee in the latter convention. He was also a member of the first state senate in 1889-90, and served as chairman of the judiciary committee in that body. In the following year he was a candidate before the legislature, though not previously, for the United States senate. He was defeated by the combined Populist and Democratic votes which were given to Senator Kyle.

He is a member of the Masonic and A. O. U. W. fraternities. His church connections are with the Congregational body. In 1887, he was married to Anna Dunn, at Bement, Ill. She died in 1881. In 1883, he was again married, to Mrs. Emma R. Thayer, of Northville, S. D. He has one child, Cloyd Dunn Sterling.

THOMAS A. STEVENS

T. A. Stevens, the popular postmaster at Chamberlain, was born in the city of Elgin, Illinois, on the 26th of January, 1840, being a son of Josiah and Sarah (Rowley) Stevens, of whose eight children he is the younger of the two surviving, his sister, Caroline, being now the wife of Jacob Ebersole, of Fredericktown,

Ohio. The parents of the subject were both born in the village of Painted Post, New York, and the genealogy in the paternal line is traced back to ancestors who came from Liverpool, England, to America, in 1654, and the subject has in his possession a valued heirloom in the form of a cane which was brought over to the new world by the founder of his family, the name and date being carved on the cane, while he himself bears the full patronymic of his colonial ancestor, while the cane has been handed down from generation to generation to persons thus bearing the name of their first American progenitor. The maternal ancestry is of Irish extraction, and the name has likewise been identified with the annals of our national history from the colonial epoch.

In 1834 Josiah Stevens emigrated from New York to Illinois, making the long overland trip with wagons, and he took up a claim of government land lying within the present corporate limits of the great city of Chicago. A year later he traded this land for a team of horses and removed to Elgin, that state, being one of its early settlers, and thereafter he was engaged in railroad work for several years. About 1853 he removed to Rockford, and later to Pecatonica, Illinois, where he was railroad station agent up to the time of his retirement from active work, about the year 1860, while his death there occurred in 1872, at the age of seventy years. He was a Democrat up to the time of the formation of the Republican party, when his anti-slavery views led him to espouse the cause of the new party, of whose principles he ever afterward continued a stanch advocate, while he was one of the early members of the Masonic fraternity in Illinois and active in its work.

Thomas A. Stevens received a common-school education in his native slate. On the outbreak of the Civil War, he was among the first to tender his services in defense of the Union. On April 17, 1861, the day after President Lincoln issued his first call for volunteers, he enlisted as a private in the Rockford Zouaves, being the first person in the town of Pecatonica to enter the service. The zouaves were mustered in as Company D, Eleventh Illinois Volunteer Infantry, on the 1st of May, and the command was one of the first to pass through Chicago enroute to the front. He served with this regiment during his three-months term of enlistment and after being mustered out assisted in raising a company which became Company K, First Illinois Cavalry, and of which he was made first lieutenant, in which capacity he served until January 1, 1864. In July of that year he enlisted in Company C, One Hundred and Forty-sixth Illinois Volunteer Infantry, with which he served as first lieutenant until August 1, 1865, when he was mustered out, receiving his honorable discharge.

After the close of the war Mr. Stevens, in May, 1866, started from Illinois for the west, making the trip overland with team and wagon. Upon reaching Fort Riley, Kansas, he found that there was an uprising of Indians, and he returned to Omaha, whence he proceeded by steamboat up the Missouri river to Fort Benton, Montana, whence he proceeded by stage to Helena, now the capital of that great state. In that locality he engaged in prospecting for gold and in general contracting, in which he continued until the fall of 1868, when he returned to his home town in Illinois, where he established himself in the grocery business. In the spring of 1872, just after the great fire in that city, he went to Chicago, where he entered the employ of the Adams Express Company, in whose service he there continued until March 1, 1882, when he started for Chamberlain, South Dakota, his brother Erastus C., having come to this territory in 1878, as a pioneer settler, and having come to Chamberlain in 1881, as a contractor and builder, his arrival here being simultaneous with that of the railroad. He erected a number of the first buildings in the town. After the subject's advent in the town, he became associated with his brother in the contracting business, to which he devoted his attention about three years. In 1885 he was appointed deputy register of deeds, serving about four years. In 1889 he was elected register of deeds, serving one term and being defeated in the ensuing election by reason of the Populistic wave which swept over the west in that campaign. In 1892, under the administration of President Harrison, he was appointed clerk at the Crow Creek Indian agency, in which capacity he served until June 1, 1804, when he was removed by President Cleveland, by reason of his political views. He then came to Chamberlain and established himself in the abstract business and also became a prominent figure in political affairs, being made chairman of the Republican County central committee. On the 6th of March, 1898, Mr. Stevens was appointed postmaster at Chamberlin, under President McKinley, and on the 6th of March, 1902, he was reappointed, under President Roosevelt. Both appointments came as the result of popular endorsement in the community.

Mr. Stevens has been an uncompromising Republican from the time of attaining his majority, having cast his first presidential vote for Lincoln, as did he also his second, having been at that time a soldier in the field and making the trip from New Orleans to his home in Illinois for the purpose of thus exercising his franchise.

He is one of the charter members of McKinzie Post, No. 340, Grand Army of the Republic, and is also affiliated with Chamberlain Lodge, No. 56, Free and Accepted Masons. On the 23d of August, 1865, Mr. Stevens was united in marriage to Miss Emily Elliott, of Pecatonica, Illinois, and her death occurred, at Crow Creek agency, in April, 1893. Of the five children of this union four are living; Lucy, who remains at the paternal home; Elizabeth, who is the wife of Ray Gooder, of Iona, this state; Harry, who is at the paternal home: and Erastus C, who is deputy postmaster under his father.

HON. FRED B. STILES

Hon. Fred B. Stiles, a member of the state senate and a well-known banker of Owanka, had the distinction during the legislative session of 1915 of being the youngest member of the general assembly in either house. He was born in Cherokee, Iowa, March 4, 1887, and was the third of the four children born of the marriage of Charles A. and Frances (Bailey) Stiles. The father is a native of Iowa and of English parentage, while the mother was born in Connecticut. Spending his youthful days under the parental roof at Cherokee, Fred B. Stiles attended the public schools and later spent a year as a student in the University of Iowa and two years in the University of Wisconsin. When his college days were over, he entered the employ of a railway and telephone company and in 1909 removed to South Dakota, settling at Owanka, where he became identified with financial interests, a connection which has since been maintained. He is a stockholder in several telephone enterprises and his investments have been judiciously made. He seems to readily recognize the possibilities of any business situation and his sound judgment and energy are important factors in his success.

On the 10th of February, 1910, Mr. Stiles wedded Frances Kenney, of Cherokee, Iowa, and they have one child, Frances. Fraternally Mr. Stiles is connected with the Odd Fellows, the Elks, the Modern Woodmen of America and the Masons and in the last named he has taken the degrees of lodge and chapter and of the Scottish Rite to the thirty-second. He also belongs to the Kappa Sigma, a college fraternity. His political allegiance is stanchly given to the republican party and in 1914 he was elected on its ticket to the office of state senator, becoming the youngest member of either branch of the legislature, in which he took a prominent part, both in debates on the floor and in committee service. He has studied closely the vital questions and issues of the day and his opinions show comprehensive understanding of the questions under discussion. His recreation comes to him through outdoor sports and motoring constitutes a favorite source of pleasure. He is an enthusiastic advocate of the good roads movement and at all times stands for progress and improvement where the general interests of society will be conserved. In business he has prospered, in public life has steadily progressed and in social circles he displays the cordiality and geniality which render him popular.

Business and political interests of Sioux Falls have been influenced in an important way by the activities of Albert H. Stites, whose interests have extended to both fields, in each of which he has won for himself an important position and an honored name. He is regarded as one of the leading druggists of Sioux Falls and, having been connected with this business since the beginning of his active career, has won the success which comes from practical experience and thorough knowledge.

He was born in Millerstown, Pennsylvania, March 2, 1858, and attended the public schools in that locality, graduating from the high school in 1875. Following this he went to Philadelphia and entered a drug store as clerk. He was graduated from the Philadelphia College of Pharmacy in 1879 and afterward continued in the drug business in that city until 1881. In June of that year, he came to Sioux Falls and opened a drug store in the old Land Office building, which in 1883 was removed and the Peck building erected on the same site. During this removal Mr. Stites had to conduct business elsewhere, but on the completion of the new building he returned to his first location, where he remained until October, 1914, when he established his present store in more commodious and modern quarters in the new Carpenter Hotel building. From 1885 to 1889 Frank S. Kimball was associated with Mr. Stites in the drug business but since that time he has carried on the enterprise alone. He has been very successful and has built up a large and representative patronage, for his store is considered one of the finest and most modern in the city. Mr. Stites was president of the territorial and state pharmaceutical societies for six years and is very well known among the druggists of South Dakota.

Mr. Stites was married April 14, 1884, to Miss Lizzie M. Law, a daughter of John Law of Chicago, Illinois, and they have a son, Samuel L. Stites, who was born July 7, 1885. A daughter, Eda G., died in 1907 at the age of seventeen. On the 14th of April, 1908, Samuel L. Stites married Miss Florence Harrison, a daughter of Charles M. Harrison, and they have two children, Ruth E. and Frances Ann.

Mr. Stites of this review is a member of Minnehaha Lodge, No. 5, A. F. & A. M., and in 1896 was master of the same. He is also a member of the Country, the Elks and the Dacotah Clubs and is well known in social circles of Sioux Falls. He gives his political allegiance to the republican party and is prominent and active in public affairs. In 1895 he was elected county commissioner and assumed the duties of that office in the following January. He was elected mayor of the city of Sioux Falls in April, 1896, and filled that position until 1898, when he was elected to the state senate, in which he served for two terms, leaving the impress of his ability and energy upon a great deal of important legislation. From 1906 to July 1, 1910, Mr. Stites was postmaster of Sioux Falls under appointment by President Roosevelt. He is a man whose business reputation is beyond question and whose official record has been varied in service and faultless in honor.

JAMES H. STEPHENS

J. H. Stephens, of Springfield, Bon Homme County, is a native of the state of Illinois, having been born in Jo Daviess County, on the 16th of September, 1850. He passed his boyhood days in his native county, where he attended the common schools, and he was about ten years of age at the time when the family removed to Wisconsin, where he continued to attend school until the age of fifteen years, when he entered upon an apprenticeship at the trade of harness making, becoming a skilled workman. He thereafter worked as a journeyman in various towns and subsequently came west to Sioux City, Iowa, remaining about one year and then returning east to the city of Chicago. In 1872 he came to Yankton, Dakota, where he remained one year, at the expiration of which he took up his residence in Springfield, where he opened a harness shop and also a furniture and undertaking establishment, becoming one of the pioneer merchants of the town, and he successfully continued his operations in the lines noted until 1897, when he disposed of his interests and has since lived practically retired, giving a general supervision to his capitalistic investments. His political support is given to the Republican party, and in 1878-9 he served as a member of the lower house of the territorial assembly, while in 1894 he was elected to represent his district in the state senate, being chosen as his own successor in 1896.

Fraternally he holds membership in the Free and Accepted Masons; Yankton Chapter, No. 2, Royal Arch Masons, and Independent Order of Odd Fellows. Mr. Stephens was married to Miss Emily A. Place, of Yankton, who died, being survived by three children, and subsequently Mr. Stephens consummated a second marriage, being then united to Miss Henrietta Hyatt, of Illinois, and they are the parents of three children.

E. F. STEVENS

E. F. Stevens, who has a fine farm north of the town of Woonsocket, Sanborn County, is a native of the Badger state, having been born in Rock County, Wisconsin. He was reared on the homestead farm in Wisconsin, where he received a good common-school education, having been a successful teacher for one year while a young man. He continued to assist in, the work and management of the home farm until he had attained his legal majority, and thereafter was engaged in farming on his own responsibility in Wisconsin until he took up his residence in Sanborn County, South Dakota, locating upon a farm which is an integral portion of his present fine place. He has made excellent improvements of a permanent nature, having good buildings, windmills, fences, etc. He raises a fine grade of cattle and feeds each year a great many sheep and hogs, his dealings in livestock being quite extensive. He is one of the leaders of the Republican party in his county, being a member of the county central committee and having served for eight years as clerk of his township.

He is a member of the Masonic fraternity and also of the Modern Woodmen of America. Mr. Stevens was united in marriage to Miss Amanda E. Hopkins, and they have two children.

Charles Griffin St. John, residing at Clear Lake, is the county superintendent of schools of Deuel County and is allied with that progressive element which is seeking the continued advancement and improvement of the school system of the state. He was born in Lafayette, near Sparta, Wisconsin, on the 6th of February, 1873, and is a son of Levi and Jane (Jones) St. John, the former a native of St. Johnsbury, Vermont, while the latter was born near Cardiff, Wales, and came to America when a child of seven years with an uncle and aunt, who settled in Columbus, Wisconsin, where Jane Jones grew to womanhood and was married. In 1883 Levi St. John brought his family to South Dakota and secured a homestead a mile and a half southeast of Clear Lake, in Deuel County, on which he resided until the time of his death, transforming a wild tract of land into richly cultivated fields. He was busily engaged in farming until 1891, when his life's labors were ended. His widow afterward removed to Clear Lake, where she now resides at the advanced age of eighty-eight years.

Charles G. St. John spent his youthful days under the parental roof and acquired his education in the public schools of his native state and of South Dakota, ultimately becoming a student in the South Dakota State Normal, from which he was graduated with the class of 1901. Prior to this time, he had taught two terms in the district schools of Deuel County and before his college course was ended he remained away from the normal for one year to act as principal of the Clear Lake school. In the fall of 1901 he went to Toronto, South Dakota, being principal of the school of that city for three years, and later he was out of educational work for two years, during which period he operated the home farm and in the winter of 1906-7 engaged in the grain business in North Dakota. He then resumed his work in the educational field and in the fall of 1907 again went to Toronto as principal of the school there. In the fall of 1909, he went to Clear Lake to accept the position of principal of the school of that place, in which position he continued for three years, and for two years of that time the school won first prize in the state exhibit of education at the state fair, carrying off first honors in 1911 and 1912, while in 1913 the county prize was won. In November, 1912, Professor St. John was elected county superintendent of schools and so satisfactory was his administration that he was reelected in 1914 without opposition. It is a recognized fact that his interest in the work inspires teachers and pupils under him, that his methods are at once practical and progressive and that his efforts are resultant.

On the 27th of December, 1907, Mr. St. John was married to Miss Pearl Ida Borne, of Clear Lake, and to them has been born a daughter, Nina Marie. Mrs. St. John is a daughter of August and Matilda (Burfield) Borne, now residents of Minneapolis, and a granddaughter of Colonel Burfield of Minnesota. The family attend the Baptist church, of which Mrs. St John is a member.

Professor St. John belongs to Phoenix Lodge, No. 129, A. F. & A. M., of Clear Lake. In politics he is a republican, and his interest in the political questions of the day is that of the student who delves deep into the real reason of things. Beside his professional activity he is president of the Clear Lake Farmers Elevator Company and president of the Clear Lake Electric Light & Telephone Company. He owns two hundred acres of valuable farm land two miles southwest of Clear Lake but after all his chief interest is in his work in the educational field, where his labors are of far-reaching influence and benefit. He was a delegate to the state convention of the graded school's department in 1910 and was elected president of the common graded department and now holds the office of vice president of the superintendent's department of education. He is also a member of the State Reading Circle board. His sagacity is keen and his vision is broad and his labors are producing splendid results for the public-school system of the state.

JAMES A. STEWART

James A. STEWART, postmaster of Edgemont and president of the Citizens' Bank, at the same place, is a native of Newton County, Indiana, born May 18, 1863. His father was a tiller of the soil, and to this kind of labor young Stewart was reared, his early experience on the farm being instrumental in forming industrious habits and teaching him the important lessons of independence and self-reliance. At the proper age he entered the district school and attended the same of winter seasons until the age of seventeen. While still a youth he left home and went with a brother to Furnas County, Nebraska, where the two took up land, and later he spent two years teaching in the public schools of that state. Discontinuing educational work, he served a two-years apprenticeship at the printer's trade in Arrapahoe, and after becoming an efficient workman followed his chosen calling in various parts of the west, traveling over a number of states and territories and finding employment in Denver, San Francisco and other cities and towns.

In the spring of 1895 Mr. Stewart came to South Dakota and, in partnership with Harvey Goddard, purchased the Edgemont Express, a weekly paper which had been established a number of years before under the name of the Dudley Reporter. This paper was originally started in a settlement across the river, known as Dudley, but later was moved to Edgemont, where it has since been published, being the oldest paper in the town, abo one of the best edited and most influential local sheets in the county of Fall River. Mr. Stewart was identified with this publication until October, 1897, when he disposed of his interests in the office to Mr. Goddard and the same month was appointed post master of Edgemont, which position he still holds. In 1899 he embarked in the sheep business on the Cheyenne river, and is now regarded as one of the leaders of this important industry in western Dakota. He keeps a number of men employed to look after his extensive live-stock interests, owns large tracts of fine grazing land in various parts of the country and from this business alone derives a liberal income. In June, 1903, Mr. Stewart and George Forbes organized the Citizens' Bank, of Edgemont, the former being made president and the latter cashier. The enterprise thus far has more than realized the high expectations of the proprietors, the bank being one of the solid and popular monetary institutions of the state, and the business already is rapidly increasing. Mr. Stewart is careful and conservative as a financier and possesses executive ability of a high order. The confidence reposed in him by business men and the people in general is attested by the steady growth of the bank in public favor and although of brief duration his experience in monetary affairs has already won him an enviable reputation in financial circles. In politics he has always been an ardent Republican, and an influential member of the party. Since becoming a resident of Fall River County he has taken a prominent part in politics, serving as a delegate to nearly every county, district and state convention during the interim, and in April, 1902, he was honored by being elected mayor of Edgemont, which office he has since held: he also served several years as a member of the local school board.

Mr. Stewart has filled worthily important public trusts, and in every relation of life has been true and faithful in the discharge of his duties. He belongs to the Masonic fraternity, has held various official positions in the order and endeavors to exemplify the precepts and teachings of the same in his various relations with his fellow men. Mr. Stewart's domestic life began in 1888, on June 19th of which year was solemnized his marriage with Miss Ada N. Witherow, of Illinois, the ceremony taking place in Afton, Iowa. Mr. and Mrs. Stewart are the parents of four children, viz: Lloyd, Fern, Albert and Ada.

FRANK M. STEWART

Frank M. Stewart, of Buffalo Gap, is a well-known representative of the live-stock interests of South Dakota and as a director of the American National Live Stock Company exercises a great deal of influence in the management of the affairs of that powerful corporation. He is also connected in important capacities with many other concerns in the state and is one of its leading citizens. He is not only known for his business ability and important connections but also because of his marked public spirit and his capacity for friendship and his warm-hearted hospitality.

Mr. Stewart was born in Livermore, Indiana county, Pennsylvania, on the 11th of February, 1860, a son of Thomas G. and Josephine (McFarland) Stewart, both natives of Westmoreland County, Pennsylvania. In his early manhood the father engaged in the retail mercantile business at Livermore, but later became a wholesale grocer of Johnstown, Pennsylvania, and Baltimore, Maryland. He was connected with the business life of Baltimore from 1868 until 1886, when he retired from active life. He passed away in that city in the spring of 1890 after surviving his wife for many years, her demise occurring in 1869.

Frank M. Stewart, the only child born to his parents, attended school in Johnstown, Pennsylvania; Winchester, Virginia; and Baltimore, Maryland. When seventeen years of age he became associated with his father in business and was given charge of the books. He remained in the employ of his father until he was twenty-six years of age, when he moved westward and settled at Buffalo Gap, South Dakota. He homesteaded land and immediately engaged in ranching. Success has attended his labors from the first and he is now interested in a ranch of six thousand acres in Custer County. He also owns, a tract of land in Fall River County and in 1893 began breeding Hereford cattle. He believes in raising full blooded stock and now has about two hundred head of pure-bred Herefords, as fine a herd as any in his part of the state. He also has sixty pure bred Percheron horses, having begun to raise that breed in 1910. He devotes about five hundred acres of land to raising alfalfa and is enthusiastic over the possibilities of that crop in South Dakota. Since its organization in 1896 he has been a director of the American National Live Stock Company and for eight sessions represented the live-stock interests in the state legislature. He is vice president of the Dakota Power Company, of Rapid City; ex-vice president of the First National Life Insurance Company, of Pierre; and is now serving on the board of directors of that institution; secretary and third owner of the Evans Hotel at Hot Springs; and president of the Hot Springs Gypsum Products Company.

On the 22d of January, 1884, Mr. Stewart married Miss Rose B. Taylor, a daughter of Mortimer and Sarah Jean (Burns) Taylor. The father was born in Loudoun County, Virginia, and the mother in Towson, Maryland. In early life Mr. Taylor engaged in the mercantile business in Baltimore but later turned his attention to railroading. He served for a time as captain of the Home Guards and his military record was a creditable one. He passed away on the 17th of April, 1897, and his wife died about 1873. To their union were born nine children, of whom Mrs. Stewart is the youngest. Mrs. Stewart attended school in Loudoun County, Virginia, and Baltimore, Maryland, but the greater part of her education was acquired under private tutors. She has become the mother of two daughters. Sara Jean graduated from the All Saints Episcopal Boarding School at Sioux Falls with the class of 1904, was for four years a student in the Peabody Conservatory of Music of Baltimore, Maryland, and for one year attended the American Conservatory of

Music of Chicago. In 1910 she studied under William Shakespeare, of London, England, and is a thoroughly trained musician. She has an exceptionally fine voice and has gained a considerable reputation as a singer. Belle also graduated from the All Saints Episcopal School at Sioux Falls and in 1910 graduated from the Hannah Moore Academy, of Baltimore. In that year she and her sister were given a trip abroad as a graduation present from their parents and for four months visited the places of greatest interest in Europe. The family are noted for their delightful hospitality and are welcomed in the best social circles of the state. They are sincerely interested in all projects that have as their object the betterment of civic conditions and no good cause appeals to them in vain.

Mr. Stewart is a democrat and has served upon a number of the state committees. For four years he was a member of the state brand committee under appointment of Governor Lee and for a similar length of time served on the state livestock committee, being appointed by Governor Elrod. Governor Vessey made him a member of the state livestock sanitary board and he was an influential factor in the work of all of the committees on which he served. Since its organization in 1892 he has been secretary-treasurer of the Western South Dakota Stock Growers Association and for one year had the honor of serving as vice president of the American National Live Stock Association. He was the first president of the Buffalo Gap Fair Association and although he has many interests of state or national scope, he has always found time to aid in the management of the affairs of his home locality and Buffalo Gap has profited in many ways from his experience and practical wisdom.

Fraternally Mr. Stewart is widely known, belonging to Washington Lodge, No. 3, A. F. & A. M., of Baltimore, Maryland, which was instituted in 1770; Hot Springs Chapter, No. 33, R. A. M.; Battle Mountain Commandery, No. 15, K. T., of Hot Springs; Black Hills Consistory, No. 3, A. & A. S. R., of Deadwood; and Naja Temple, A. A. O. N. M. S., of Deadwood. He also holds membership with Martha Chapter, No. 22, O. E. S., of Hot Springs, of which he was patron for four years, and likewise is identified with the Modern Woodmen of America of Hot Springs. His wife and daughters belong to the Eastern Star and also to the Royal Neighbors.

When Mr. Stewart removed to the Black Hills he was in very ill health, having suffered from asthma for years, and he was not expected to live very long. He found the climate very beneficial and after proving up upon his homestead removed his family to Buffalo Gap, where he erected his present beautiful residence, the finest in the town. While living upon his ranch he had a number of exciting experiences, due to the unsettled condition of the country and the resentment of the Indians toward the white men. From pioneer times Mr. Stewart has taken a prominent part in promoting the welfare and advancement of not only his section but the whole state of South Dakota and has left the impress of his individuality upon its history. He believes enthusiastically in the great future in store for the northwest and finds his greatest pleasure in doing something to promote the welfare of the state which he has served so ably for many years.

CHARLES H. STILWILL

C. H. Stilwill, he able and popular incumbent of the office of postmaster at Tyndall, is a native of the old Empire state of the Union, having been born in Genesee County, New York, on the 7th of February, 1843, a son of Hiram R. and Melinda (Drake) Stilwill, of whose four children three survive, namely: Kesiah, who is the wife of John P. Dickey, of Cherokee, Iowa; Charles H., subject of this sketch; and John G., who is superintendent of the Emma mines, at Alta City, Utah. Hiram R. Stilwill was likewise born in

Genesee County, of stanch Holland ancestry, and in his native county he received a good English education, having been for a number of years a successful teacher in the district schools, while later he gave his attention to the nursery business. He died of typhus fever, in 1853, at the age of thirty-seven years, our subject having been a lad of ten years at the time. His widow subsequently contracted a second marriage, becoming the wife of Joseph B. Craft, and of this union was born one child, George H., who is now a resident of Oakfield, New York, The mother was summoned into eternal rest in 1871. Her father, John Drake, was an active participant in the war of 1812. William Stilwill, the paternal grandfather of our subject, was born in Cattaraugus County, New York, whither his parents immigrated from Holland, and there he took up a tract of land in what was commonly known as the Holland Purchase, Charles H. Stillwill, whose name introduces this sketch, was reared in his native county and received his early educational training in the common schools.

In 1865 he severed the home ties and set forth to seek his fortunes in the west. He came to Iowa, arriving in Dubuque the day following the assassination of President Lincoln, and he thence carried the news of this lamentable tragedy into Delaware County, that state, where he devoted his attention to farm work for the ensuing three years. He was married in 1868 and shortly afterward engaged in the manufacture of fanning mills, at Hopkinton, Iowa, and one year later he removed to a farm which he had previously purchased, in Delaware County, and there he continued to be engaged in agricultural pursuits until the spring of 1879, when he disposed of his farm and came to the territory of Dakota, passing the first summer in Yankton, and arriving in Bon Homme County, on the 7th of September, 1879. For about sixteen months thereafter he served as deputy register of deeds of the county, and in 1881 he was appointed clerk of the courts, which incumbency he retained for the long period of eleven years, giving most capable and satisfactory service. Within this time, he also gave his attention to the real-estate business, becoming one of the leading representatives of this line of enterprise in this section. He associated himself with G. W. Roberts, of Yankton, and Thomas Thorson, of Canton, in the organization of the Corn Belt Real Estate Association, which has accomplished so great a work in furthering the settlement of the state and the development of its industrial resources, Mr. Stilwill has been called to other offices of public trust, having served as deputy sheriff and as deputy county treasurer, and in all positions, he has held the implicit confidence of the people of the county. In 1897 he was appointed postmaster at Tyndall, and in 1902 he received a reappointment under President Roosevelt. He is still largely interested in real estate, owning valuable property in Tyndall and extensive tracts of farming land in the county, and he has done much to promote the general welfare and material progress of this favored section of our great commonwealth.

In politics Mr. Stilwill gives an unequivocal allegiance to the Republican party, and fraternally he is affiliated with Bon Homme Lodge, No. 101, Free and Accepted Masons; Scotland Chapter, Royal Arch Masons; Springfield Lodge, Independent Order of Odd Fellows; and Tyndall Lodge, Knights of Pythias. He is a member of the Congregational church, as was also his devoted and cherished wife.

On the 11th of February, 1868, was solemnized the marriage of Mr. Stilwill to Miss Marian Kirkwood, of Hopkinton, Iowa, who proved to him a true helpmeet until her death, which occurred on the 12th of March, 1903. She was held in affectionate regard by all who knew her, being a woman of gracious and noble character, and she is survived by her four children, namely: Agnes, who is the wife of James D. Elliott, United States district attorney, residing in Tyndall; Dr. Hiram R., who is a practicing physician in Denver, Colorado: Charles M., who is a well-known attorney of Tyndall, being individually mentioned on another page of this work, and Hayes K., who is bookkeeper in the Security Bank, of Tyndall.

CHARLES M. STILWILL

Charles M. STILWILL, one of the able and successful young members of the bar of the state, established in the practice of his profession at Tyndall, Bon Homme County, was born in Hopkinton, Delaware county, Iowa, on the 8th of November, 1875, being a son of Charles H. and Marion (Kirkwood) Stilwill. His father is now postmaster of Tyndall and is individually mentioned on other pages of this work, so that a recapitulation of the family history is not demanded at this juncture. The subject has passed practically his entire life in South Dakota, since he was a child of about five years at the time when his parents removed here from Iowa, and here his early education was received in the public schools, after which he continued his studies in Yankton College. In 1892 he began reading law under the preceptorship of James D. Elliott, of Tyndall, United States district attorney at this time, and in 1894 he was matriculated in the law department of the Iowa State University, at Iowa City, where he was graduated in the spring of 1896. After his graduation Mr. Stilwill associated himself with the law firm of Shull & Farnsworth, of Sioux City, Iowa, remaining with this concern until April 1, 1897, when his former preceptor, J. D. Elliott, was appointed United States district attorney and the subject accepted a partnership with him, and here he has since remained as a partner to Mr. Elliott, while through his ability and discrimination he has gained distinctive prestige in his chosen profession, to which he gives his undivided attention. In politics he gives an inflexible allegiance to the Republican party and has been an active worker in its cause. For the past four years he has been secretary of the Republican committee at Tyndall. He is a member of the Congregational church at Tyndall, and is treasurer of the church at the time of this writing, taking a zealous interest in all departments of its work.

Fraternally he is a member of Bon Homme Lodge, No. 101, Free and Accepted Masons, of which he is secretary; and he is also identified with the Ancient Order of United Workmen and the Modern Woodmen of America. On the 27th of December, 1899, was solemnized the marriage of Mr. Stilwill to Miss Mary A. McAuley, of Tyndall, and they are the parents of three children, Helen C. Ruth M. and Charles Frederick.

GEORGE H. STODDART

George H. Stoddart, city auditor of Brookings, was born in Shullsburg, Wisconsin, on the 29th of July, 1854, his parents being William and Sophia (Hatt) Stoddart, the former a native of Glasgow, Scotland, and the latter probably of, New York City. William Stoddart was but a young lad at the time his parents died and he and his four brothers were reared by their grandparents. In his young manhood he and two of his brothers came to the United States and William Stoddart settled at West Point, New York, where he pursued a seven years' medical course under one of the government surgeons at that place, eventually winning his M. D. degree. At that time Lee, McClellan and Burnside were all at the West Point Military Academy and Mr. Stoddart knew them well. Following his graduation, he went to Shullsburg, Wisconsin, where he practiced for several years, and subsequently removed to Minersville, afterward to Jamestown and still later to Boscobel, Wisconsin. In the meantime, he had entered upon the work of the ministry of the Congregational church and gave his later life to Christian service. He passed away at Black Earth, Wisconsin, where he was occupying a pulpit at the time.

George H. Stoddart spent his youth in Wisconsin and was educated in the public schools. He left the parental roof at the age of nineteen years and in 1873 made his way to Yankton, South Dakota, where he became identified with the government survey work, with which he was connected for five years. In the spring of 1878, he removed to Codington County and took up a homestead on the shores of Lake Kampeska. In 1880 he proved up on the land, for which he paid a dollar and a quarter per acre, and that year he went to work in the engineering department of the Chicago & Northwestern Railroad Company, working with the surveying force of that road for eight years, during which period he gradually advanced and in 1888 became roadmaster of that division, in which important capacity he served for ten years. During that time, or in 1891, he transferred his headquarters to Brookings, where he has since resided, and in 1898 he resigned his position, but the following year ran the transit for the surveying gang on the location of the road from Tyler to Astoria and subsequently did special work for the road at different times. In 1903 he was elected city clerk of Brookings, which was then acting under a special charter. After the city came under the general laws he continued his work, but the name of the office was changed to that of city auditor, in which position he has continued to serve. From the fact that the city owns its electric light, heat and power plant, heating the business section of the city, and also owns its telephone line, the position is one of importance and Mr. Stoddart has been most faithful and efficient in the discharge of his duties.

In 1891 Mr. Stoddart was united in marriage to Miss Marie Marrow, of Redfield, South Dakota, and they became the parents of three children, of whom two are yet living: Mattie, who is attending the South Dakota State College at Brookings; and Harriett.

Mr. Stoddart is a member of Brookings Lodge, No. 24, A. F. & A. M.; Brookings Chapter, No. 18, R. A. M.; Brookings Commandery, No. 14, K. T.; and he and his wife are members of Brookings Chapter, No. 15, 0. E. S. He also belongs to the Modern Woodmen of America and the Ancient Order of United Workmen and he has membership in the Brookings Commercial Club, while his wife and daughters are members of the First Presbyterian church. He is one of the representative citizens of Brookings and in an analyzation of his life work it will be found that loyalty to duty has been one of his strong characteristics. If study and work can make for efficiency — and it always does — there is no doubt that he has displayed efficiency in every position to which he has been called. Another proof of this is found in the fact that he has been continuously promoted and that his life work has been of constantly increasing responsibility and value.

D. G. STOKES

D. G. STOKES, one of the Kading farmers and stock growers of Marshall County, was born in Wright County, Minnesota, on the 8th of January, 1859, and is a son of Frederick and Mary (Hogue) Stokes, both of whom were born and reared in England. The father of the subject came to America in the early fifties and remained for some time in the state of New York, whence he came to the west and settled thirty miles north of the city of Minneapolis, Minnesota, where both he and his wife still reside. They became the parents of twelve children, of whom the subject was the sixth in order of birth.

D. G. Stokes secured his early educational training in the public schools of Minnesota, duly availing himself of the advantages thus afforded and thus laying the foundation for a successful career in connection with the active duties and responsibilities of life. He was identified with the saw milling business in Minnesota until 1888, when he came to the present state of South Dakota, which was admitted to the Union about two years later, and he joined his brother, H. L., at Burch, Marshall County, the latter having located here in 1886. They continued to be associated in the carrying on of a general merchandise business in Burch until 1896, when they removed their stock of goods to Britton, where the enterprise has since been continued and where the firm have built up a large and representative business, having a well-appointed store and carrying a select and comprehensive stock. They are also the owners of sixteen hundred acres of fine farming and grazing land in the county the homestead ranch being located four miles northwest of Britton. The subject resides on the farm and has direct supervision of its operation, while his brother has charge of the mercantile business and is also president of the Marshall County Bank, in Britton. The ranch is chiefly devoted to the raising of high-grade live stock upon an extensive scale, and on the same is to be found one of the finest herds of registered Galloway cattle in this section of the state. The subject also buys and ships grain upon a large scale, having his headquarters at Burch and controlling an important business in the line. The ranch is supplied with an abundance of pure water, a fine artesian well of six-inch piping having been sunk to a depth of nine hundred and thirty-five feet, and having a flow which affords a twenty-five horse power, said power being utilized in the grinding of feed and also for other purposes.

In his political proclivities Mr. Stokes is an uncompromising advocate of the principles of the Republican party, and he has taken a lively interest in the promotion of its cause, while he has held various county and township offices, and in 1902 was elected to represent his county in the state legislature, where he made an excellent record as a zealous working member of the lower house.

He is identified with the Masonic fraternity and also with the Independent Order of Odd Fellows, in which latter he has served as noble grand of his lodge. On the 28th of November, 1882, Mr. Stokes was united in marriage to Miss Rosamond Eastor, who was born and reared in Minnesota, and they have two sons. Guy L. and Max G.

WILLIAM HENRY STOKES

W. H. STOKES, was born in the town of Porter, Rock County, Wisconsin, on the 16th of May, 1845, being the son of Charles and Anna E. (Kimble) Stokes, the former of whom was born in Ambridge, Somersetshire, England, in 1812, while the latter was a native of Saugerties, New York, being of English and Dutch lineage. He was educated in the district schools in Wisconsin until the age of nineteen, finishing with one term in a select school at Mitchell, Mitchell County, Iowa. His early life was spent on the farm. His business life began May 16, 1866. He was associated with his brothers in the sawmill and lumber business until the spring of 1872. From 1872 until the present time, 1904, he has been interested with various parties in the milling business, ten years in Janesville, Waseca County, Minnesota, and the remainder of the time up to the present date in the milling and grain business at Watertown, South Dakota. At present he is president and manager of the W. H. Stokes Milling Company, while his son-in-law, F. E. Hawley, is the secretary and treasurer.

The old milling plant, built in 1882 at Watertown, South Dakota, was destroyed by fire March 13, 1901, and the summer following the fire the present substantial mill and elevator plant was erected on the same site, business being resumed on December 19, 1901. The W. H. Stokes Milling Company's mill and elevator are decidedly the largest and most modern in the state. The brick elevator and steel tanks have a capacity of one hundred and forty thousand bushels and are practically fireproof. The subject of this sketch has also been largely interested in farming, now owning and controlling something over five thousand acres of land, most of which is in Codington County, South Dakota. W. H. Stokes is recognized as one of the leading business men of the state and at the present time is found worthy of having his name enrolled in the Financial Red Book of America for 1903.

Mr. Stokes was married to Miss Elsie Minerva Grout on December 23, 1872. She was born at York, Wisconsin, September 18, 1853, being the daughter of Leroy and Cordelia (Flower) Grout, the former of whom was born at Vermont and the latter in the state of New York. Nine children were born to Mr. and Mrs. Stokes. Their names are: Ella Glencora, wife of F. E. Hawley; Gladys May, Maud Leonore, Alice Wilhelmena, Elsie Minerva, William Henry, Jr., Louisa Alcott, Anna Kimble and Philip Douglas, all of whom are now living. Mr. and Mrs. Stokes and six of their children are members of the Congregational church.

Mr. Stokes is a member of the Masonic fraternity, being affiliated with the Kampeska Lodge, No. 13, Ancient Free and Accepted Masons; Watertown Chapter, No. 12, Royal Arch Masons, and Watertown Commandery, No. 7, Knights Templar. He served as eminent commander of the commandery for two years. Politically Mr. Stokes has always been a Republican, although he has never aspired to any political office or influence.

JOHN C. STOUGHTON

JOHN C. STOUGHTON

John C. Stoughton, the popular postmaster of the thriving little village of Geddes, was born in Ionia County, Michigan, on the 13th of July, 1844, and is a scion of a family which has been identified with the history of the United States from the time of the Revolutionary epoch. His parents, Samuel E. and Emily H. (Park) Stoughton, were both born in the state of New York, and of their ten children only two survive, the subject of this sketch and his brother, Charles J., who is a resident of Howard City, Michigan. The father of the subject was born on the 17th of April, 1814, and his devoted wife was born on the 20th of February, 1816, and both were children at the time when their respective parents removed from the old Empire state and became pioneers of Michigan, settling in the vicinity of the present beautiful city of Detroit, and in that state, both were reared to maturity, their marriage being solemnized May 21, 1835. After he had attained manhood Samuel E. Stoughton purchased a tract of government land in Ionia County, Michigan, where he developed a farm from the virgin forest, becoming one of the substantial citizens of that section and ever retaining the high regard of all who knew him. On the old homestead farm which he had reclaimed for the wilderness he continued to reside until his death, which occurred in 1872, while his wife passed away in 1883. Mr. Stoughton identified himself with the Republican party at the time of its organization and ever afterward remained a stanch advocate of its principles, and while he was never ambitious for political preferment, he was called upon to serve in various offices of local trust. His father, Dellucine Stoughton, was a veteran of the war of 1812, and his grandchildren recall that in his later years he found pleasure in entertaining them by singing the old army songs. He was a son of Amaziah Stoughton, who came with his parents from England to the United States about the time of the Revolution, the family settling in the state of New York, with whose annals the name has long been identified, and thus the subject of this sketch is of the fifth generation of the family in America.

John C. Stoughton, whose name initiates this review, was reared to the discipline of the old homestead farm in Ionia County, Michigan, and after availing himself of the advantages of the common schools he entered, in 1865, Kalamazoo College, in Kalamazoo, that state, where he continued his studies for two years. His financial resources then reached a low ebb, and he accordingly left college and devoted the following year to teaching in the schools of his native state. He then removed to Kansas, where he continued his pedagogic labors, in Atchison and Leavenworth counties, for the ensuing four years. His father's death occurred in 1872, as before noted, and he was appointed administrator of the estate, returning home to settle up the affairs of the same. He was married the following year and decided to remain in Michigan, where for a number of years he devoted his attention to teaching during the winter terms, while farming constituted his vocation during the remaining months of the year. In 1883, in company with four others, Mr. Stoughton came on a prospecting trip to South Dakota, with a view of selecting a permanent place of residence. The party came by railroad as far as Plankinton, where they purchased a mule-team and wagon and set forth to look over the country to the west of that point, and three of the number, of whom our subject was one, finally filed claims to a quarter section each of land in Charles Mix County, Mr. Stoughton securing an excellent claim seven miles northwest of the present village of Geddes, whose site was unmarked by any habitation at that time. He settled on his claim and in September of the following year his wife joined him in the new home. He later purchased an adjoining quarter section, and during the intervening years he has brought his fine farm of three hundred and twenty acres under most effective cultivation, has made excellent improvements on the same and has been successful in his efforts. In the spring of 1900 Mr. Stoughton was appointed postmaster of the new town of Geddes, to which he forthwith removed with his family, taking charge of the office in June of that year, and having since remained incumbent. He is a stalwart advocate of the principles of the Republican party and has taken a lively interest in the promotion of its cause. In the autumn of 1883, he was elected a member of the board of county commissioners, in which capacity he gave most efficient service, retaining the office three years. It may be said that the post office at Geddes was established in June, 1900, in which month our subject assumed control, and further data in the connection will indicate the rapid upbuilding and substantial increase in population of the town. In April, 1902, only one year and nine months after the establishing of the office, it was placed on the list of presidential offices, the salary of the postmaster being at the time raised to eleven hundred dollars a year, while three months later it was raised to twelve hundred, in accordance with the increase of business, while in July of the present year (1903) a further increase to fourteen hundred dollars was made. Mr. and Mrs. Stoughton are members of the Congregational church, and he was one of those prominently concerned in effecting the erection of the church of this denomination in the village of Jasper, the property being later sold to the Methodist Episcopal society, who now own and occupy the edifice.

Mr. Stoughton was initiated in the Masonic fraternity in 1869 and has been a charter member of two lodges in Charles Mix County, this state, being now affiliated with Geddes Lodge, Free and Accepted Masons. On the 4th of March, 1873, was solemnized the marriage of Mr. Stoughton to Miss Selena V. Bovee, of Greenville, Michigan. She was born in Lenawee County, Michigan, being a daughter of M. and JuHa Bovee, and of her marriage has been born one son, Elmer B., who was assistant postmaster at Geddes. He was born in Greenville, Michigan, on the 14th of April, 1879, and after attending the public schools entered Ward Academy, in Charles Mix County, where he was graduated as a member of the class of 1898, after which he was for one term a student in Yankton College, having later been engaged in teaching for a short time. He has recently (1904) resigned his position in the post office and has removed to Lyman County, South Dakota, where he has taken up a homestead, on which he expects to make his future home.

The spirit of enterprise and progress which has been the dominant factor in the upbuilding of the northwest find's expression in the life of Oscar E. Stuart, who is now filling the position of treasurer of Stanley County. He has been a lifelong resident of this state and is a representative of one of the pioneer families. His birth occurred at Swan Lake, South Dakota, September 12, 1879, his parents being O. C. and Elsie M. Stuart. The father homesteaded a tract of land in Turner County and there engaged in farming. He belonged to that class of diligent progressive men who have been the upbuilders of the great west, bringing about its rapid and substantial development. He was ambitious that his children should have good educational opportunities as a preparation for life's practical and responsible duties and after mastering the elementary branches of learning, Oscar E. Stuart entered the high school at Chamberlain, South Dakota, in which he completed the full course and was graduated. His more specifically literary course was pursued in the University of South Dakota, where he won his Bachelor of Arts degree as a member of the class of 1900. Immediately afterward he made his entrance into business life and was connected at different periods with the abstract business and with banking. His developing powers and his recognized worth led later to his selection for public office and on the 5th of November, 1912, and again in November, 1914, he was elected treasurer of Stanley County, in which capacity he is now serving.

On the 18th of February, 1907, at Vermillion, South Dakota, Mr. Stuart was united in marriage to Miss Grace Wildman, a daughter of W. H. Wildman, a Civil war veteran. In religious faith Mr. Stuart is a Presbyterian and his fraternal relations are with Mt. Moriah Lodge, A. F. & A. M. of Kadoka, South Dakota, of which he was secretary in 1912. His political allegiance has always been given to the republican party and of its principles he is an earnest and stalwart advocate. He keeps well informed on the questions and issues of the day and is thus able to support his position by intelligent argument. He is proving a capable public official, carefully guarding the interests of the county as the custodian of its public funds and his record is winning for him the high regard and the indorsement of many who hold opposite political views.

JAMES F. SUMMERS

There are certain rules which must be followed if success in business is attained and these rules are as inflexible as the laws of the Medes and Persians. Advancement in any line of legitimate business can only be won through close application, intelligently directed energy and thorough reliability, all of which Mr. Summers has included in his daily business life, which has at length brought him to a prominent place in financial circles in the western part of the state, for he is now president of The Bank of Spearfish. He was born in Bedford County, Virginia, September 15, 1850, a son of Castlereigh and Agnes J. (Tinsley) Summers, both of whom were natives of Virginia. The father, who was born in 1816, died in 1911 and the mother passed away in 1861, when less than thirty years of age. The father was in early life a wagon maker and blacksmith but later engaged in the general contracting business and subsequently became a farmer. He emigrated to Kansas in 1868, settling in Atchison County, and about 1871 he removed to Sedgwick County, locating near Wichita, where he spent his remaining days to the last two years of his life, which he passed with a daughter in Oklahoma. He served for two years as a soldier in the Confederate army during the Civil war.

In his father's family of five children James F. Summers was the second in order of birth. He attended school in Newcastle, Virginia, and after completing the high-school course matriculated in a college at Roanoke, that state. He pursued a course in law in his native state and was admitted to practice in Kansas. In the meantime, however, other business interests had occupied his attention. He engaged in railroad work in Kansas during the years 1868 and 1869, being employed on the Missouri River Railroad from Atchison. He afterward rented land and engaged in farming in Atchison County, Kansas, until 1870, when he went to the southwestern part of that state, where he took a claim before he had attained his majority. After reaching the age of twenty-one he filed and proved up the claim and continued there until 1876. He engaged in ranching and in driving cattle from Texas but at length he disposed of his holdings in the Sunflower state and made his way to the Black Hills country, going by way of Denver and Cheyenne, traveling on foot most of the way. He proceeded to Custer and on the 7th of March, 1877, arrived in Deadwood. He first worked in the Aurora, an underground mine, for a short time and afterward spent a few months in speculating in Deadwood real estate. He next turned his attention to the boot and shoe business, in which he continued for about two months, when he engaged in prospecting. In the fall of 1877, he was employed as a copyist in the office of the register of deeds and there remained until January 26, 1878, when he went to Denver by stage to assist his sister, whose husband had died, in the settlement of her real-estate interests.

On the 12th of April of the same year Mr. Summers returned to Deadwood and purchased an interest in a cigar and tobacco business, continuing therein until the 26th of September, 1879, when his establishment was destroyed by fire. He then disposed of his interests along that line and entered the Merchants' National Bank as general bookkeeper, continuing there until November, 1882.

He then removed to Spearfish and established a bank under the firm name of Stebbius, Fox & Company for the conduct of a general banking business. The institution existed as a private bank until 1887, when it was incorporated under the state laws. Three years later it was reincorporated under the laws enacted in 1890. Mr. Summers was cashier and manager of the institution from its establishment until 1904, when he was elected to the presidency of The Bank of Spearfish. In 1883 he erected the building occupied by the bank, it being the first brick building in Spearfish and the first bank building. In addition to his large holdings in the bank Mr. Summers is the owner of a mercantile establishment at Clearmont, Wyoming, and is the owner of considerable land in South Dakota and other states. He operates a ranch of four hundred and eighty acres as a stock farm, breeding first class stock, making a specialty of Percheron horses arid Polled Hereford cattle. His various business interests have been carefully conducted. He displays sound judgment and keen discrimination and allows no obstacles to block his path if they can be overcome by determined and honorable effort.

On the 30th of October, 1878, Mr. Summers was married to Mrs. Elizabeth J. (Murray) Fisher. She was born of English parentage, and her father, mother and sister were all lost on the steamer Atlantic while enroute to the United States.

In politics Mr. Summers is a stalwart democrat and when but twenty-one years of age he served as justice of the peace in Kansas, being well qualified for this position owing to the fact that he had previously studied law in Virginia and had been admitted to the bar in Kansas. He was the first mayor of Spearfish and has filled that position for a number of terms since, giving to the city a businesslike and progressive administration characterized by various needed reforms and substantial improvements. He was one of the first members of the state normal school board and did much toward securing the building of the school. He holds the oldest continuous notarial commission in Lawrence County, his papers dating from 1879.

Fraternally he is a Mason and has attained the thirty-second degree of the Scottish Rite and the Knights Templar degree in the York Rite. He has been in business continuously in Spearfish for a longer period than any other man, having been identified with the commercial and financial interests of the city for thirty-two years. He has contributed much to its material upbuilding and progress and his well-directed life work has brought to him a very substantial measure of success which is the merited reward of his energy and his ability. What he has done for Spearfish places him among its foremost citizens and men of prominence and his worth is widely acknowledged by all.

JOHN WILLIAM SUMMERS

JOHN W. SUMMERS

John William Summers, filling the office of city auditor at Yankton, was born in Kent, England, May 21, 1845. His father, John William Summers, was a native of the county of Essex, England, born July 18, 1821, but at an early age accompanied his parents on their removal to Kent County, the family settling in the town of Dartford, where John William Summers, Sr., was reared and spent his remaining days. His life was devoted to general agricultural pursuits. He reached the very advanced age of ninety years, passing away in 1909. In early manhood he had wedded Jane Allchin, a native of Horton Kirby, Kent County, England, born in 1828. She is still living at Dartford at the age of eighty-seven years.

John William Summers, whose name introduces this review, is the eldest in a family of eight children and was born, reared and educated in the town of Dartford. He left school at the age of sixteen years and for some time thereafter assisted his father in farm work but turned from agricultural pursuits to industrial interests and while yet a young man became a foreman with the Isaac Charles Cement Manufacturing Company. As time passed on, he rose in the esteem and confidence of his employers, as he demonstrated his worth, his industry, energy and reliability, and was made manager of the branch plant at West Dreyton, Middlesex, where he continued for three and a half years. He next erected a lime manufacturing plant near Dunstavale, in the county of Middlesex, and managed that business until 1889, when he decided to come to the United States. He was commissioned by William Plankington to come to Yankton, South Dakota, to build the Yankton Portland cement plant and after this was completed, he was made superintendent and continued to act in that capacity until March, 1909, when a change was affected in ownership, the plant passing into other hands after the death of Mr. Plankington. Mr. Summers continued as an employe but not as superintendent until May, 1910, when he was elected city auditor for a five years' term under the commission form of government. His work in this connection is highly efficient and satisfactory to all concerned. He devotes his time to the duties of the office and is making a most creditable record therein.

In 1867 Mr. Summers was united in marriage to Miss Julia Elizabeth Tolhurst, a native of Dartford, Kent County, England, and they have become parents of the following children: two who died in infancy; Mary Louise, who passed away while pursuing her education in Yankton; Elsie Kate, who died at the age of eighteen years; Florence, the wife of Charles Gaughran, a resident of Omaha, Nebraska; Maud Mary, also living in Omaha; Grace, the wife of Guy Livingston, of Yankton; Christina Julia, who is engaged in teaching kindergarten in Yankton; Dorothy, at home; John William, now of Arlington, Minnesota; and Ruth, who is also under the parental roof.

Mr. Summers has a military chapter in his life record, inasmuch as he served as a member of the Twelfth Kent Volunteers while in England. Following his arrival in the new world he began studying political situations and questions and has since given his vote to the republican party. He is a member of St. John's Lodge, No. I, A. F. & A. M.; Yankton Chapter, No. I, R. A. M.; Robert De Molay Commandery, No. 3, K. T.; and Oriental Consistory, No. I, S. P. R. S. He has thus advanced far in Masonry and is in thorough sympathy with the purposes and teachings of the craft. He likewise has membership with the Knights of the Maccabees and with the Elks, while his religious faith is that of the Episcopal church. High and honorable principles have actuated him in all of his relations and have won for him the high regard of those with whom he has been brought in contact. Starting out in life for himself empty-handed at the age of sixteen years, he can truly be called a self-made man, for he has been both the architect and builder of his own fortune. He has worked earnestly and untiringly and, advancing step by step, his course has brought him to a creditable place.

B. S. SUMMERWILL

B. S. Summerwill, although one of the younger business men of Canton, is one of the most prosperous. He is a lumber merchant and is thoroughly awake to the changes in conditions which have occurred in the last few years and which demand new methods on the part of the man who is conducting a business enterprise. His progressiveness and his ability to adapt himself to these changed conditions are the salient factors in his success. He was born near Sioux City, Iowa, on the 17th of March, 1886, a son of W. J. and Florence (Slemmons) Summerwill, natives of England and of Ohio respectively. His father died when he was eleven years of age and his mother survived but four years, so that he was thrown upon his own resources when only a lad in his teens. He secured a good education, however, attending Shattuck Military Academy, and upon finishing school identified himself with the lumber business, beginning as yardman. In 1905, when but nineteen years of age, he purchased a small yard at Brunswick, Nebraska, and was subsequently in the lumber business in Sioux City, Iowa. In 1909 he located in South Dakota and bought the nucleus of the large business which he now controls and which is one of the most important of its kind in the southeastern part of the state. He understands thoroughly the details as well as the broader phases of the trade and is systematic in his methods, all of which make it but natural that his business should grow and prosper. He recognizes the fact that cooperation is the keynote of modern commercial life and he is one of the most active members of the Canton Commercial Club, serving as president thereof for two years. He is also president of the Canton Racing Association.

Mr. Summerwill was married in 1907 to Miss Edna Wengert, a daughter of H. G. and Anna (Johnson) Wengert, of Mapleton, Iowa. To Mr. and Mrs. Summerwill have been born two children, William and Edna, who represent the fourth generation, as not only the grandparents on the mother's side, but also the great-grandparents are still living and enjoying excellent health. The father is a republican in his political allegiance and stanchly supports that party at the polls. Fraternally he is a member of Silver Star Lodge, No. 4, A. F. & A. M., of Canton, and of both the Commandery and Shrine of Sioux City, Iowa. He also belongs to the Atheneum Debating Society. He finds physical recreation in hunting and motoring, is an enthusiastic sportsman and has an exceptionally fine collection of guns, while his interest in motoring has led him to take an active part in the good-roads movement in the state. The fact that he has attained his present success through his own labors without the aid of influential friends is a matter of justifiable pride and is proof of his ability and aggressiveness.

EDWARD WILLIAM SWAFFORD, M. D.

Dr. Edward William Swafford has entered upon the active work of a profession which many regard as the most important to which an individual can turn his attention, and recognizing the fact that advancement must depend upon individual merit, he has made every effort to promote his knowledge and thus enhance his efficiency in ministering to his patients. He practices in Sturgis, where he is now widely and favorably known. He was born in St. Louis, Missouri, July 7, 1878, a son of Lorenzo D. and Josephine (Cox) Swafford. The father's birth occurred in St. Joseph, Missouri, October 9, 1846, and the mother was born at Collinsville, Illinois, April 6, 1847. In early life Lorenzo D. Swafford learned the trade of an iron molder and was engaged in that line of business until 1862, when he enlisted for service in the Civil war as a private in Company H, Fortieth Missouri Volunteer Infantry. He remained at the front throughout the period of hostilities and was wounded by a gunshot in the left knee. After leaving the army he returned to St. Louis, where he engaged in teaming and acted as a street-car driver in the days when horses were the motive power. He continued in that business until his death, which occurred in 1899, his wife surviving him until 1905.

Dr. Swafford is the eldest of four children. He attended the public schools of St. Louis and in 1900 went to Chicago, where he attended night school, becoming a student in Armour Institute. In 1903 he matriculated in the Bennett Medical College, from which he was graduated with the class of 1905. Long before this, however, he had known the stress and strain of business activity and responsibility. When but ten years of age he assisted in the support of his mother in St. Louis, beginning work as a cash boy in Nugent's department store, where he was employed for nine years, during which time he constantly worked his way upward. At the end of that period, he entered the shops of the St. Louis, Iron Mountain & Southern Railroad Company to learn the machinist's trade and was employed at that work until 1900, when he went to Chicago, where he entered a preparatory school, becoming, as stated, a student in Armour Institute, which he attended during the night sessions while working for the R. T. Crane Company through the day and in vacation periods. He advanced in that connection and was given charge of the tool room. Following his graduation from the Bennett Medical College, which marked the fulfillment of the hope that he had long cherished, he became an interne in the Cook County Hospital, where he remained for eighteen months, gaining that broad practical experience which only hospital practice can bring. He then opened an office in Chicago, where he remained until December, 1908, when he removed to Sturgis and established a private hospital under his own name. Since that time, he has practiced continuously in Sturgis, not only in the hospital but also as a general physician and surgeon. He is also a landowner in South Dakota and has city property.

On the 29th of September, 1909, Dr. Swafford was married to Miss Ellen Tomlinson, who was born at Alton, Illinois, a daughter of David George and Mary Elizabeth (Levick) Tomlinson. Her father was born in Staffordshire, England, August 14, 1847, and when twelve years of age came with his parents to the new world, the family home being established at Alton, Illinois, where in early life he learned the blacksmith's trade. He there resided until 1905, when he removed with his family to Dallas, Texas. He is now traveling salesman for a house engaged in the manufacture of horse nails, traveling out of St. Louis. At one time he was mayor of Alton yet he has never been very active in politics. His wife passed away March 30, 1896. Their daughter, Mrs. Swafford, was the third in a family of nine children. She attended school at East

Alton, also Shurtleff College at Upper Alton and was graduated in nursing in Chicago. Dr. Swafford has but one child, George Harry, born of a former marriage. His first wife died in 1905, leaving this little son, then but three years of age, his birth having occurred January 5, 1902.

Dr. Swafford is a Mason and has taken the degrees of the blue lodge and of the Scottish Rite up to and including the thirty-second degree. In politics he is a republican and has served as one of the commissioners of the county board of insanity for a number of years. He is medical examiner for various insurance companies and is local surgeon for the Chicago & Northwestern Railroad Company. In professional circles he has been accorded high honors. He belongs to the Ninth District Medical Society, of which he was secretary in 1911 and 1912, while through the following year he was its president. He is also a member of the state and national medical associations and thus keeps in touch with the advanced thought and methods of the profession.

HARRY E. SWANDER

A large grocery and bakery business in Rapid City — one of the largest of its kind in the state — is incontrovertible proof of the ability and energy of its owner, Harry E. Swander. He was born in Tiffin, Ohio, on the 8th of July, 1863, and is a son of Harrison and Alice (Farley) Swander, natives of the Buckeye state and of Missouri respectively. The father, who was a merchant and farmer by occupation, removed to Iowa in 1859 and was there married. He subsequently returned to Ohio with his wife and there she resided during the Civil war. He bore arms during the entire conflict, serving in all for four years and eight months, or through three enlistments, as a member of Missouri volunteer cavalry. In 1868 he returned to Iowa with his family and first located in Decatur County, but subsequently removed to Taylor County and is now living retired at Gravity, that county. His wife passed away when the subject of this review was but five years old. She was the mother of two children, the other being Edward H., a resident of Missouri.

Harry E. Swander attended district school for a short time and made the best of his rather limited opportunities for securing an education. When but twelve years of age he left home and began work upon a farm. In 1879 he became an apprentice to the baker's trade at Bedford, Iowa, but after serving in that capacity for one and a half years he worked in various places as a journeyman baker. In 1885 he began business on his own account at Clarinda, Iowa, in partnership with another ambitious man who, like himself, possessed little capital but a great deal of determination and business ability. They began their enterprise with less than one hundred dollars to invest, Mr. Swander's share being thirty-seven dollars. The venture, however, proved a success and the bakery was sold a year later at a good profit. Mr. Swander then went to the Black Hills but remained for only a short time, after which he returned to Bedford, Iowa. A year later he went to southwestern Nebraska but the hard times of 1887 proved disastrous to him and he lost all that he had accumulated. In 1888 he removed to Alliance, Nebraska, where he found employment as a lineman, and be worked into the Black Hills while connected with the Burlington Railway line. He returned to Alliance, however, and opened a restaurant there which he conducted for a year. In 1890 Mr. Swander arrived in Rapid City and established a fancy grocery, confectionery and bakery business upon a small scale but so well did he understand his trade and so efficiently were his business interests managed that the enterprise grew rapidly. In 1900 he sold out and turned his attention to the stock business but after two years he abandoned that line of endeavor, as he lost heavily owing to the fact that large numbers of his stock had been killed by severe winter storms. In 1902 he again engaged in the grocery and bakery business and has since continued therein, as it has proved an unqualified success. His trade is constantly increasing in volume and importance and his establishment is one of the best and largest of its kind in South Dakota. He is interested in other enterprises, being one of the companies which is operating the New Harney Hotel of Rapid City, a stockholder in the Dakota Power Company and in the Dakota Plaster Company. He has also invested to some extent in mining property.

Mr. Swander was married in 1884 and had four children by his first wife, as follows: Edward H., a traveling salesman; Geraldine; Charles; and Harry A., who lost his life by drowning when seven years old. Mr. Swander was married January 30, 1915, to Mrs. Clara I. Patton, the widow of John D. Patton. Mrs. Swander is well and favorably known by the traveling public as the owner of the Patton Hotel.

Fraternally Mr. Swander is a member of the Knights of Pythias, the Elks and the Masons and in all of those organizations is highly esteemed and popular. He has at various times met with discouragement and financial reverses but his determination has never wavered and his faith in the value of industry, coupled with sound judgment, has been justified, as he is now one of the leading business men in his line in the Black Hills. In striving for and gaining material success he has never forgotten that to deal justly and live uprightly is to most truly succeed and the respect which all who know him entertain for him is proof of his integrity.

ORLANDO P. SWARTZ

O. P. Swartz, one of the prominent and highly honored business men of Hutchinson county, is a native of the state of Illinois, having been born in Jo Daviess County, on the 21st of April, 1864, and being a son of Elias M. and Susan (Rudy) Swartz, of whose eight children we incorporate the following brief record: Martins H., is a resident of Gillette, Wyoming; Edith is the wife of James Brown, of Menno, South Dakota; Sarah is the wife of Schuyler C. Freeburg, of Sunnyside, California; George is engaged in the drug business in Parkston, South Dakota; Maud is the wife of Nelson C. Davis, of Crook County, Wyoming; Frederick is likewise a resident of that county, as is also Grover; and Orlando P., is the immediate subject of this sketch. Elias M. Swartz was born in Center County, Pennsylvania, being a representative of one of the sterling pioneer families of the old Keystone state and coming of stanch German lineage. As a young man he removed to Illinois, settling in Stephenson County, engaging in agricultural pursuits, this being the vocation to which he had been reared. He later removed to Jo Daviess County, where he continued to reside until 1882, when he came to South Dakota, remaining for a short interval in the village of Scotland and then entering claim to land in Charles Mix County, where he engaged in the breeding and raising of cattle and horses, becoming one of the prominent and influential citizens of that section and commanding the most unqualified esteem of those who knew him and had cognizance of his sterling qualities of mind and heart. He died in 1901, having been a member of the Methodist Episcopal church, while his political allegiance was given to the Democratic party. His widow now makes her home with her children in Wyoming, she likewise being a member of the Methodist Episcopal church.

The subject of this sketch remained at the parental home until he had attained the age of twelve years, having in the meanwhile attended the public schools and assisted in the work of the farm, and he then went to the city of Freeport, Illinois, where he resided in the home of his uncle about five years, during which period he continued his educational work in the schools of that place. In 1879, he returned home, remaining one year, at the expiration of which he went to Iowa Falls, Iowa, where he was employed in the drug establishment of his uncle, John L. Swartz, for the ensuing three years. In July, 1883, he came to Scotland, Bon Homme County, South Dakota, where he secured a clerical position in the drug store of another uncle, William P. Swartz, and in 1884 he went to Springfield, Bon Homme County, where he was employed for two years in the drug store of Bonesteel & Turner, having in the meanwhile become an expert pharmacist. In September, 1886, in which year the town of Parkston was founded, he took up his residence here and engaged in the drug business on his own responsibility. In 1888 he entered into partnership with Frank Wiedman, who was here engaged in the hardware business at the time, and thereafter until 1898 the firm of Wiedman & Swartz here conducted a most prosperous business in the handling of hardware, implements and drugs. In the year mentioned they disposed of the drug department of their enterprise and added a general line of merchandise, building up one of the most important and extensive trades of the sort in this section of the state. In 1901 they also purchased a general stove business at Milltown, and they now conduct the same as a branch of their Parkston establishment. In 1901, Mr. Swartz was appointed postmaster of Milltown, and he is still incumbent of this office, in which he is serving by proxy.

In politics he is found arrayed as a stanch advocate of the principles of the Republican party, while fraternally he has attained the thirty-second degree in Scottish Rite Masonry, being identified with Oriental Consistory, No. I, at Yankton. His ancient-craft membership is in Resurgam Lodge, No. 31, Free and Accepted Masons, at Mitchell, and he belongs to El Riad Temple, Mystic Shrine, at Sioux Falls, while he is also a member of Milltown Camp, No. 6153, Modern Woodmen of America. On the 25th of September, 1885, Mr. Swartz was united in marriage to Miss Margie W. Robinson, of Iowa Falls, Iowa, she having been born in Concord County, New Hampshire, daughter of Horace Robinson, deceased. Of this union have been born two children, Mabel C., who is attending All Saints' Academy in Sioux Falls, and William R., who remains at the parental home. Mrs. Swartz is a member of the Congregational church of Iowa Falls, Iowa.

OLE S. SWEXSON

Ole S. Swenson, serving in a creditable manner as warden of the South Dakota state penitentiary at Sioux Falls, was born in Halingdal, Norway, November 9, 1845, and is a son of Swen and Julia (Sanderson) Swenson, also natives of that locality. The family is descended from a Scottish nobleman of the Clement clan, who fled from his native country in 1604 for political reasons and settled in Halingdal. In the course of years, the name became changed to its present form.

Ole S. Swenson began his education in the country schools of Nicollet County, Minnesota, where his parents had settled on a farm in 1857. He later attended public school at St. Peter, Minnesota, and, laying aside his books at the age of eighteen, began clerking in a store in that city. In 1876 he established a hardware store there, but business being poor on account of the plague of grasshoppers he moved his stock to Grand Meadow, where he controlled an important patronage for four years. At the end of that time, he came to Sioux Falls, where from 1880 until 1892 he was a well-known hardware merchant. In the latter year he disposed of his interest in that business and turned his attention to flour milling, engaging in that occupation until 1902. He is a director in the Queen City Fire Insurance Company of South Dakota, also in the Albert Lea Gas Company of Albert Lea, Minnesota; in the Union Insurance Association of

Sioux Falls and a member of the executive committee of that company. He is a man whose business ability is known and recognized.

In 1872, at St. Peter, Minnesota, Mr. Swenson married Miss Celia Thompson, a daughter of Stone and Julia (Roan) Thompson. Mrs. Swenson passed away in 1879, leaving two children, Arthur W. and Josephine G. In 1880, at Grand Meadow, Minnesota, Mr. Swenson was again married, his second union being with Miss Eliza Susan Ranney, by whom he has three children, William L., Norma M. and Ernest S.

Mr. Swenson was reared a Lutheran and holds membership in the Elks Club of Sioux Falls. He is a thirty-second degree Scottish Rite Mason and is affiliated also with the Woodmen of the World. He is a republican in his political beliefs and stands high in the party's councils, taking an intelligent and active interest in public affairs. From 1898 until 1902 he was chairman of the republican central committee of Minnehaha County and he has been at all times a loyal supporter of the party's principles and candidates. His fellow citizens, recognizing his worth and ability, have called upon him to fill positions of honor and trust. In 1886 he was elected county treasurer and so acceptably did he fill that office that he was reelected in 1888, serving in all four years. He then declined to become a candidate for reelection. In 1901 he was first appointed warden of the South Dakota penitentiary and after serving two years was reappointed for a similar period of time. He was then out of office until 1909, when he was again given that position, in which he has since served by reappointment. He has made many improvements in the institution. When he took charge in 1901 there was no work for the prisoners except in the quarry and on the farm, which was not enough to give employment to all of them, but Mr. Swenson went before the legislature and was instrumental in getting a bill passed to establish a shirt factory and twine plant. The former has now been in operation since 1905 and the latter since 1909. There are now two hundred and twenty spindles in use in the twine factory, manufacturing about seven million pounds of twine annually, which is one-half of what the state uses. The prison is now up-to-date in all its appointments, having a good dining room, chapel, laundry, hospital, solitary apartments, deputies' offices, measurement rooms, music room, carpenter shops, bath rooms, etc.. There are a total of two hundred and eleven prisoners and the honor system, which has recently been recommended or put in operation in different states, has been tried here for some years. There is an evening school with studies up to the eighth grade and fifty-five prisoners in voluntary attendance. The teachers are also prisoners. There is also a moving-picture machine and exhibitions are given once or twice each week. Besides this, there is an orchestra and a quartette to lead the singing, all composed of prisoners. In 1901 the lockstep was abolished and the prisoners are now dressed in cadet gray, the stripes being used only temporarily as a punishment. The farm consists of five hundred and eighty acres and all of the buildings thereon have been erected by prison labor, with no foreman.

In Sioux Falls Mr. Swenson is known as a refined and courteous gentleman, progressive in his views, and straightforward and honorable in all relations of life, and he holds the esteem and confidence of all who are in any way associated with him.

T

HENRY TAMMEN

Henry Tammen is one of the alert, energetic and wide-awake business men and merchants of Yankton and his name is well known in financial circles. He is a native of Germany, born May 5, 1859, and is the third in order of birth in a family of five children whose parents were Heinrich G. and Marie (Kirchoff) Tammen, both of whom are deceased. The father followed teaching throughout his entire business career in his native land.

Henry Tammen received his education in Germany and there remained to the age of nineteen years, when, venturing where opportunity led the way, he emigrated to America and for four years was engaged in the manufacture of confectionery at Washington, D. C.. In 1883 he arrived in Yankton, South Dakota, and his first business venture here was in the same line of trade but later he engaged in the grocery and dry-goods business, in which he has continued to the present time, with growing success. He carries a well selected line of goods, studies the needs and demands of the trade, and at all times gives fair and courteous treatment to his patrons. His is today one of the important concerns of this character in the city.

In 1888 Mr. Tammen chose a companion for the journey of life through his marriage to Miss Lizzie Weber, a native of Wisconsin. Their home has been blessed with one son and two daughters: Henry, Jr., who is manager of the Yankton Opera House; Laura; and Marguerite.

Where national issues are involved Mr. Tammen gives his political support to the democratic party but at local elections he votes independently. His fraternal relations connect him with the Masons, the Benevolent Protective Order of Elks and the Knights of Pythias. He finds his chief recreation and delight in motoring. He has ever led a busy, active and useful life which has won him the confidence and goodwill of his fellowmen by reason of the honorable and straightforward policy which he has ever followed, and today he is accounted one of the city's most prosperous and most substantial German citizens.

Between the ages of nine and eleven years — boy that he was — Frank L. Van Tassel was teaching writing and, in that way, partially earned the money that paid for his later education. Today he stands as one of the foremost business men in the state of South Dakota. He has made his home since 1868 in Yankton, where he is secretary and manager of the Excelsior Mill Company, president of the First National Bank of Yankton and a partner in the ownership and control of many other important business enterprises which have been chief factors in the growth and development of city and state.

Mr. Van Tassel was born in Conneautville, Crawford County, Pennsylvania, January 29, 1851. His father, E. B. Van Tassel, was a practicing attorney, very prominent in the locality in which he made his home. He was born in Mayfield, Chautauqua County, New York, and was a representative of an old American family. He wedded Rachel Litchfield, who was born in Massachusetts and belonged to one of the old and prominent New England families. Both are now deceased. Their son, Frank L. Van Tassel, was the third in order of birth in a family of ten children, of whom six are yet living, namely: Mrs. Anna Adella Brown, the widow of Dr. W. H. H. Brown, who was a dentist of Los Angeles, California; Mina, the wife of Dr. Alva Johnston, of Meadville, Pennsylvania; William, a resident of Prescott, Arizona; Harry, who makes his home at Moosejaw, Saskatchewan; and Nettie, the wife of James Van Summers, of Bath, England.

Frank L. Van Tassel, who is the oldest of the surviving members of the family, was reared in his native town and when a very young lad took writing lessons of Spencer, the originator of the Spencerian system. This was during the period of the Civil War. So proficient did he become that between the ages of nine and eleven years he taught the Spencerian system of penmanship and, saving his money, was thus enabled to attend the Meadville Commercial College at Meadville, Pennsylvania, for about a year. His fame as a writer had spread and he soon received a call from Hummiston's (Cleveland) Institute at Cleveland, Ohio, where he was to teach writing in exchange for tuition, board, clothing, etc.. He there remained from 1866 until June, 1868, when the school was sold and Mr. Van Tassel then came to the territory of Dakota, where his uncle, Laban H. Litchfield, was filling the position of United States marshal. He made his way direct to Yankton, arriving on the 26th of June, and soon found employment as a bookkeeper in the pioneer general merchandise store owned by the firm of Bramble & Miner. He applied himself earnestly to the mastery of the business and proved so efficient and capable as a salesman, that he was admitted to a partnership in 1876, remaining active in the management and control of the store until the firm passed out of existence in 1883, owing to the cessation of river traffic.

In the meantime, Mr. Van Tassel had become interested in other enterprises. In 1872, in connection with William Bordens, the firm of Bramble & Miner built the Excelsior Mill and in 1875 Mr. Van Tassel was made secretary of the company, at which time the business was incorporated. This mill from its inception has done a splendid business and has been enlarged from time to time to meet the growing demands of the trade, becoming one of the foremost productive industries of the state. Mr. Van Tassel has been identified with the business since 1872 and throughout the entire period to the present time has bent his energies largely to the further development and upbuilding of the trade. He is now a heavy stockholder in the company, of which he is secretary and general manager, and in these connections, he bends his energies to administrative direction and executive control. The capacity of the mill is one hundred and seventy-five barrels per day, and he was one of the pioneers in advertising and introducing its products, making this a means of outfitting concerns for the Black Hill country. His recognition of opportunities, his unfaltering energy, his unflagging determination and his reliable business methods have been the salient features in the upbuilding of a most extensive and successful milling enterprise.

Not alone, however, has his attention been confined to this line, for other interests have felt the stimulus of his activity, have profited by his insight and benefited by his control. He has been a director of the First National Bank of Yankton for many years and in 1907 was elected to its presidency, so that he now has important voice in its management. In the spring of 1873, he was made the first agent of the first railroad in South Dakota — the Dakota Southern — serving in that capacity for a short period. In 1906 he became a director in the Schwenk-Barth Brewing Company of Yankton, and he is secretary of the Yankton Telephone Company, being the promoter of the first company that built lines into Sioux Falls, Pierre, Mitchell, Huron, Watertown and Yankton. Eventually he sold out the business at a great profit to himself and his associates. In 1904 he and his associates organized the present Yankton Telephone Company. He was also a director in the first artesian well company in the state, and indeed has been a pioneer and promoter in many lines of activity which have led to the present development, growth and prosperity of South Dakota.

Not alone along individual lines has Mr. Van Tassel put forth his efforts, for his labors have been a salient feature in advancing the welfare of the state in directions from which he has derived no individual profit. For example, he was a member of the board of trustees of the State Hospital for the Insane at Yankton, serving under Governors Pierce and Church. In politics he has always been a democrat, but his interest is merely that pf a progressive citizen and not of one who seeks office.

On the 19th of October, 1875, Mr. Van Tassel was united in marriage to Mrs. Sarah Bordens, of Yankton, and they have one daughter, Frances, the wife of B. F. Dudley, of Yankton. Mr. Van Tassel and his family occupy a prominent social position and he ranks high in Masonry, belonging, to St. John's Lodge, No. I, F. & A. M.; Yankton Chapter, No. I, R. A. M., of which he is a past high priest; De Molay Commandery, No. 3, K. T., of which he is a past eminent commander; and Oriental Consistory, No. I, A. A. S. R., of which he is the present master of Kadosh. He is likewise a member of El Riad Temple of the Nobles of the Mystic Shrine at Sioux Falls, and he belongs to the Elks Lodge, No. 994. He is temperate in all things and there is an even balance in his life which has been one of the strong features in his success. He is conservative, yet not to the point of blocking progress, and attention to business has been one of the strong features in his advancement. He has always been willing to assist young men to get a start in life and has done real philanthropic work along that line. His efforts have been an element in the growth of city, county and state, his influence has been far-reaching and beneficial, and the worth of his example is widely recognized, for it indicates what may be accomplished when determination and laudable ambition lead the way.

EDWARD TENGE *

Edward Tenge, a retired merchant of Yankton, who for a long period occupied a most creditable position in commercial circles of the city as a dealer in furniture, was born at Hildersheim, Hanover, Germany, on the 27th of November, 1849. His father, Franz Tenge, was for many years an officer in the German cavalry and his father was a man of prominence in that country. The mother of Edward Tenge bore the maiden name of Charlotte Lohse and was a woman of unusual intellectual force and ability. She lived to the remarkable old age of ninety-three years and by her marriage became the mother of three children, of whom Edward is the second in order of birth. His brother, Fred Tenge, is now a resident of Milwaukee, Wisconsin.

In the public schools of his native country while spending his boyhood days under the parental roof Edward Tenge pursued his education and afterward entered the employ of the North German Lloyd Steamship Company, with which he was connected for a year and a half. In 1869 he came to America, settling in New York City, where he found employment in a grocery store, while later he was with a sugar-refining establishment, there continuing until April, 1876. Hearing and heeding the call of the west, he arrived in that month in Yankton and secured a position with J. R. Sanborn in the furniture business. His capability, energy and trustworthiness won him the goodwill and confidence of his employer, who admitted him to a partnership in 1892. Their relation continued with mutual pleasure and profit until 1900, when Mr. Tenge became sole proprietor of the furniture and undertaking business, which he conducted with growing success until 1910, when he sold out to his son, William S. Tenge, who still continues the business. In the meantime, he had built up a patronage of substantial proportions and derived therefrom a good annual profit. He enjoyed an unassailable reputation for business integrity as well as enterprise and thus he had no difficulty in retaining patrons.

On the 26th of June, 1873, Mr. Tenge was united in marriage to Miss Bertha Eckert, a native of Germany, and they became the parents of five children, of whom four are yet living: Tessie, now the wife of George A. Pardoe, of Fargo, North Dakota; Carrie, the deceased wife of Clarence Hall, of Wagner, South Dakota; Emily, the wife of S. C. Hicks, of St. Paul, Minnesota; and William S., living in Yankton and now at the head of the business established by his father.

The religious faith of the family is that of the Lutheran church, to which Mr. and Mrs. Tenge belong. His political indorsement is given to the republican party where national issues are involved, but he casts an independent local ballot, on such occasions considering only the capability of the candidate for the duties of the office without regard to party affiliations. He is the secretary, treasurer and superintendent of the Yankton Cemetery Association and has been connected with other projects of a public and semi-public character.

Fraternally he is a Mason of high rank and has been a member of that order for twenty years. He has taken the thirty-second degree in the Scottish Rite, has crossed the sands of the desert with the Nobles of the Mystic Shrine and has held many offices, including that of grand master of the grand lodge of South Dakota in 1902 and 1903 and that of master of St. John's Lodge, No. I, two terms. His is a creditable record in the various walks of life in which he has been active. He has never had occasion to regret his determination to seek a home in the new world, for here he found favorable business conditions which he has improved. It was soon recognized that he was straightforward in all of his dealings and that his word was to be thoroughly relied upon. Men knew that they could trust him to do what he promised and his close application, strict attention to business and laudable ambition brought him to the place which he occupies today as one of the prosperous and highly respected citizens of Yankton. While connected with its mercantile interests he worked incessantly without a vacation and now his friends rejoice that he has leisure to participate in those interests which are a matter of enjoyment and recreation to him. Everywhere he is spoken of in terms of high esteem and that his life has been used to good advantage finds tangible evidence in the real-estate in Yankton which he owns and in the warm regard entertained for him by those who know him.

HORACE EUGENE THAYER

Horace E. THAYER, mayor of Canton, Lincoln County, was born at Blissfield, Lenawee County, Michigan, on the 28th of February, 1859, being a son of Andrew J. and Phoebe A. (Hill) Thayer. His father is of the ninth generation of the family in America, being a lineal descendant of Thomas Thayer, who settled in Braintree, Massachusetts, in 1630, as one of its original colonists, having come to the new world from Braintree, Essex County, England. Andrew J. Thayer was born in Cameron, Steuben County, New York, on the 12th of February, 1829, and his vocation in life has been that of farming. He is a veteran of the war of the Rebellion, having enlisted on the 27th of February, 1863, as a member of Company K, Eleventh Michigan Volunteer Infantry, which was attached to the Second Brigade of the First Division of the Fourteenth Army Corps, and he served until the close of the war, when he received his honorable discharge. He is now a resident of Hampton, Iowa, and his cherished and devoted wife is also living. She was born on the 8th of April, 1839, at Petersburg, Lenawee County, Michigan, her parents having been numbered among the earliest settlers of that county, whither they emigrated from Vermont, in the year 1830, nearly a decade before Michigan was admitted to statehood.

Horace E. Thayer received his early educational training in the public schools of Allamakee County, Iowa, and when seventeen years of age he began teaching in that county, being thus successfully employed for eight terms. He then entered the telegraph office of the Iowa Central Railroad at Mason City, Iowa, in 1883, and there he devoted a period of six months to learning the art of telegraphy. In August of thit year his marriage was solemnized, and immediately thereafter he removed to Mason City, Iowa, where he was given the position of night operator in the station of the Iowa Central Railroad, retaining this incumbency until the autumn of the following year, when he received promotion from the hands of the company, being made railway billing clerk at Hampton, Iowa. This office he filled until the autumn of 1886, when he resigned from the employ of the Iowa Central Company and returned to Mason City, where for six months he held the position of night agent in the general offices of the Chicago, Milwaukee & St. Paul Railroad, being then promoted to the position of billing agent and two weeks later to that of cashier, in tenure of which responsible office he there continued for the ensuing five years, at the expiration of which, in 1891, he received the promotion, over several older employes, to the position of agent for the company at Canton, South Dakota, where he entered upon his executive duties on the 2d of July of that year. He retained this position for the long period of eight years, his service being most acceptable to the company and gaining him still further commendation, but his health had in the meanwhile become somewhat impaired and this fact, coupled with a desire for a change of occupation, led him to resign his position on the 1st of May, 1899. He then entered into partnership with his brother-in-law, Thomas S. Stinson, and engaged in the general merchandise business in Canton, the firm securing most eligible and attractive quarters in the two-story stone building known as the Post Office block, while to the new store was given the name of the Enterprise, a designation which is most consistently applied. The concern has taken a foremost position by reason of the progressive ideas and correct methods brought to bear, and the business controlled at the present time is second to none of similar character in the county, while both of the interested principals command the unqualified confidence and regard of all who know them. The entire business and stock of the Enterprise was purchased, February 8, 1904, by Horace E. Thayer, the enterprise being now conducted under the firm name of Horace E. Thayer.

In politics Mr. Thayer has ever given a stanch allegiance to the principles of the Republican party and he has shown a deep interest in all that concerns the welfare and progress of his home city and county. He has served three terms as a member of the board of aldermen of Canton, having been first elected in 1893, while he was chosen as his own successor in the following year, being again elected to the office in 1900.

In 1902 he was elected to the mayoralty of the city, for a term of two years, and he has given a most able and business-like administration of the municipal government and has gained unequivocal endorsement as a progressive and public-spirited executive.

Fraternally, he is identified with the Knights of Pythias and the Masonic order. He became affiliated with the lodge of the former in Mason City, Iowa, in 1890, and in 1892 transferred his membership to Canton Lodge, No. 52, in Canton, of which he is past chancellor commander. In June, 1902, he was initiated as entered apprentice in Silver Star Lodge. No. 4, Free and Accepted Masons, in which he was duly raised to the master's degree.

At Eldora, Iowa, on the 8th of August, 1883, Mr. Thayer was united in marriage to Miss Minnie Bell Young, of Ackley, that state, she being a daughter of Joseph H. Young, who was a valiant soldier in the Civil war, in which he served as a member of Company H, One Hundred and Eighty-ninth Pennsylvania Volunteer Infantry, enlisting in 1863 and receiving an honorable discharge at the close of the great conflict which determined the integrity of the Union. Mr. and Mrs. Thayer have three daughters: Neva Bell, who was born in Mason City, Iowa, on the 1st of April, 1884; Vera Luella, who was born in Canton, South Dakota, July 31, 1894, and Nila May, who was born in Canton. May 26, 1897.

ELIAS MASON THOMAS

Elias Mason Thomas, a representative of one of the oldest families in the United States, a veteran of the Civil war and today one of the valued and prominent residents of Huron, has made his record an honor and a credit to a name that is held in high esteem and regard in the communities where it is known. He has been a resident of Huron since 1883, and during the greater part of that time has engaged in the real estate business, taking also a prominent, and active part in public affairs. He is now doing efficient and creditable work as clerk of the courts.

Mr. Thomas was born in McHenry County, Illinois, August 3, 1847, a son of Elias A. and Hester A. (Snow) Thomas, the former born August 11, 1811, and the latter April 28, 1819. The Thomas family was founded in America by John Alden, who came over to the United States in the Mayflower and whose great-great-great-granddaughter married Noah Thomas, of Middleboro, Massachusetts. The name Elias has been repeated in the Thomas family through many generations and was borne by the Thomas who served in the Revolutionary war and witnessed Burgoyne's surrender to General Gates. The old musket which he carried is still in existence and in the possession of the subject of this review. Elias A. Thomas moved from Vermont to Illinois in 1843, driving overland with teams and he settled in pioneer times in McHenry County, taking up government land, upon which he lived until his death. From the time of the foundation of the republican party he was a stanch supporter of its principles and he took an intelligent interest in public affairs. The mother of the subject of this review was a daughter of Eben Snow, of Vermont, who served in the War of 1812. She was married to Elias A. Thomas December 17, 1840, and they became the parents of the following children: Adelia, who was born July 29, 1842, and who died January 10, 1899; Emma H., who was born August 5, 1844, and who died November 23, 1880; Elias Mason, of this review; Eben Snow, who was born November 11, 1849, and who died April 8, 1852; Clara Maria, who was born April 30, 1852, and who died June 8, 1875; and Hester Ann, who was born November 26, 1854, and who died October 19, 1872.

Elias Mason Thomas acquired his early education in the public schools of McHenry County and in 1864 enlisted for service in the Civil War, joining Company G, Fifty-second Illinois Volunteer Infantry. He participated in many important engagements and took part in Sherman's march to the sea. Following his honorable discharge, he engaged in farming in Illinois for some time and then went to Chicago, where he held a position as bookkeeper. In 1883 he came to South Dakota, locating in Huron, and he has since been a resident of that city where he has become widely and favorably known. He has been engaged in the real-estate business for many years and has been very successful in that Held, being regarded as an expert judge of land values. His integrity is beyond question and his ability of a high order and he has, therefore, won an enviable place in business circles.

On the 8th of December, 1868, Mr. Thomas was united in marriage to Miss Ruth R, Henion, of Michigan, and they have become the parents of three daughters, all of whom are married. Mr. Thomas is connected fraternally with the Masonic lodge, the Knights of Pythias and the Benevolent Protective Order of Elks and is well known in the affairs of Kilpatrick Post, No. 4, G. A. R. He gives his political allegiance to the republican party and during the period of his residence in Huron has taken an active interest in public affairs, cooperating in all measures and projects for the general good. For six years he served as deputy treasurer and he was for one term police justice. In 1912 he was elected clerk of courts in Huron and has since done creditable and able work in this office to which he was reelected in 1914. Aside from this he has taken part in various progressive public movements, having been one of the organizers of the Central South Dakota Fair and for two years its secretary. He is a member of the State Soldiers' Home Board and was instrumental in securing the cannon for the courtyard which was presented to the Grand Army of the Republic. He is a man of high standards, progressive views and loyal public spirit and has been a factor in the accomplishment of a great deal of important work along lines of community development.

ORVILLE W. THOMPSON

O. W. THOMPSON, cashier of the First National Bank of Vermillion, Clay County, was born in the town of Vermillion, which is still his home, on the 13th of November, 1871, so that his boyhood days were passed under the territorial regime. He is a son of that honored pioneer, Myron D. Thompson, to whom specific reference is made on another page of this volume, so that it is not necessary to recapitulate the family history at this point. The subject secured his fundamental educational training in the public schools of his native town, having been graduated in the Vermillion high school as a member of the class of 1887, while later he was matriculated in the State University of South Dakota, at Vermillion, where he completed the classical course and was graduated in 1893, receiving the degree of Bachelor of Arts. Shortly afterward he became associated with his father in the grain and lumber business, the latter having at the time been a member of the firm of Thompson & Lewis. In 1896 the title was changed to the Thompson-Lewis Company, and two years later the business was incorporated under the style of the Thompson Lumber Company, the subject having been vice-president of this company from the time of its organization. In 1896 he was elected cashier of the First National Bank of Vermilion, and he has ever since retained this incumbency, proving himself one of the discriminating and able young financiers of the state and evincing an executive power which has done much to further the prestige of the institution mentioned. Mr. Thompson and his brother, Martin L., organized the Thompson Brothers Cattle Company, of which he is president, and they control an extensive business, having a fine stock ranch of sixty-five thousand acres, in Potter County.

In politics Mr. Thompson has been a stanch advocate of the principles of the Republican party from the time of attaining his legal majority, and he is one of the active and zealous workers in its cause, being a member of the Republican state central committee at the time of this writing. He is a member of the

Baptist Church, and fraternally has attained the Knights Templar degree in the Masonic order, being also identified with the Ancient Arabic Order of the Nobles of the Mystic Shrine and the Benevolent and Protective Order of Elks.

M. D. THOMPSON

M. D. THOMPSON

No matter in how much fantastic theorizing one may indulge as to the cause of success, it is invariably found on careful analysis that the successful men owe their position to industry, enterprise and persistency of purpose. Such is the record of M. D. Thompson, who has been continuously connected with business affairs for a longer period than any other resident of North or South Dakota. Residing at Vermillion, he is engaged in banking, in the grain business and in dealing in farm machinery. He was born in Saratoga County, New York, in 1847, a son of Orville Thompson, who followed fanning in Washington County, New York, until his death.

The son acquired his early education in the public schools and afterward attended the Fort Edward Institute of New York, from which he was graduated with the class of 1863. Subsequently he made his way westward to Wisconsin, where he engaged in clerking for about two years, and in June, 1869, he went to Clay County, Dakota territory, where he purchased an interest in the general store of James McHenry. At the same time Martin J. Lewis became a partner and later Mr. Thompson and Mr. Lewis purchased Mr. McHenry's interest. The nature of the business has been somewhat changed, for the Thompson-Lewis Company now deals in farm implements, grain and lumber, and its trade has grown to extensive and gratifying proportions. Mr. Lewis passed away in 1896, continuing active in the business until his demise, but the name of the Thompson-Lewis Company has been retained. Mr. Thompson is an extensive owner of well improved farm lands in Clay County and also of valuable properties in Vermillion. He was one of the organizers of the private bank conducted under the name of D. M. Inman & Company at Vermillion in 1872. This was the second bank of Vermillion and was conducted under the original plan of organization until 1889, when it was converted into the First National Bank, which is capitalized for fifty thousand dollars and of which Mr. Thompson is one of the principal stockholders. For a considerable period, he served as vice president of the institution and in 1912 was elected to the presidency, in which position he has active voice in the management of the bank and in formulating its policy.

On January 6, 1870, occurred the marriage of Mr. Thompson and Miss Anna E. Lewis, a daughter of William L. Lewis, of Columbus, Wisconsin, and to them have been born two sons. Orville W., a graduate of the State University of South Dakota, was cashier of the First National Bank of Vermillion for ten years and while living in Clay County was elected state senator for a two years' term. He is now a resident of Chicago, where he is secretary and treasurer of the James P. Marsh Manufacturing Company. Martin L., also a graduate of the State University, is a partner in the Thompson-Lewis Company of Vermillion.

Mr. Thompson is a stalwart republican, but not an aspirant for office. He and his family hold membership in the Baptist church. Fraternally he is a Mason and an Odd Fellow and, in the former has attained the Knight Templar degree and is also a member of the Mystic Shrine. For forty-six years he has been continuously connected with business affairs in Clay County and has steadily advanced in the scope and importance of his interests and activities. His success is the direct outcome of earnest, persistent effort intelligently directed and he stands in the foremost rank among those who have been most active and efficient in furthering the upbuilding of his part of the state.

T. J. THOMPSON

T. J. Thompson was born and reared in Winterport, Maine, where he received his educational training in the common school. As a youth he sailed before the mast for one year, and then served an apprenticeship at the art of telegraphing, becoming an expert operator. Finally, he came to the west and located in Iowa, where he was engaged as operator and station agent at various points for a number of years. He then moved to Hastings, Nebraska, in which city he established himself in the hardware business, there continuing to be successfully identified with this line of enterprise for about fifteen years, at the expiration of which he came to South Dakota, and took up his residence in the thriving and progressive little town of Fairfax, where he engaged in the same line of business, having the only hardware establishment in the town, and having built up a large and prosperous business. He still retains the ownership of a valuable tract of land in Sheridan County, Nebraska. For one year the subject also conducted a branch hardware store in Bonesteel, but he now centers his interests in Fairfax.

In politics he is a stanch advocate of the principles of the Republican party, and fraternally he is identified with the Masonic fraternity. Mr. Thompson was married to Miss Mary Abbott, who was born and reared in the same town as was himself, and they have three children.

COLONEL WILLIAM J. THORNBY

Colonel William J. Thornby, who is connected with the government assaying office at Deadwood, was born in Greenwich, Washington County, New York, April 27, 1856, a son of James H. and Catharine (Couron) Thornby. The father was born in Armagh, Ireland, and as a young man came to the United States, settling in Syracuse, New York. For years he was upon the road as a traveling salesman, continuing in that business until his death in 1870. Following his demise the mother removed to Troy, New York, and in that city, Colonel Thornby pursued his education. He was one of five children, four of whom yet survive.

After his school days were over Colonel Thornby was employed in a foundry in Troy during the summer and in Griswold's Opera House during the winter until 1876, when he went to the Centennial Exposition in Philadelphia. He was there employed at a soda fountain in Machinery Hall for three months and afterward engaged in selling cider in the Agricultural building. While there he became acquainted with Dr. Nichols, from the Black Hills, who had an exhibition of placer dirt from the gold regions and showed the visitors how gold was extracted by placer miners. Colonel Thornby became interested in this and in the fall returned to Troy, New York, and from there went to Chicago, on to Omaha and to Cheyenne, Wyoming, by train and arranged to proceed from the last-named place by Wade's freight, which was drawn by horses and mules. They left Cheyenne on the 27th of March, 1877, and arrived in Deadwood on the 19th of April. Although he had paid to ride in one of the wagons Colonel Thornby had to walk all of the way, a distance of three hundred miles, as the roads were very bad. After reaching his destination he worked for a newspaper called The Pioneer until January, 1879, acting as solicitor for the paper and also having charge of some of the delivery routes. He afterward went to Custer with Professor Walter P. Jenney, a government geologist, and through him received valuable instruction in geology and mineralogy. They were to investigate certain mining claims six miles south of Custer but failed to find anything valuable. Colonel Thornby became interested in the Grand Junction mine, three miles north of Custer, and during that time helped lay out and organize Junction City Subsequently he went to where Hot Springs is now situated and was the first to locate Minnehaha Springs. He there took one hundred and sixty acres of government land, after which he returned to Hill City and induced several men to come to the springs. Dr. Jennings, of Deadwood, organized a company to improve the springs, which are now famous. With the development and growth of the district Colonel Thornby became closely associated. He was elected the first county assessor of Custer County and was long retained in that position, being re-elected a number of times. He was also chosen the first county judge and the first justice of the peace of Custer City acting in that capacity in 1880. Still higher political honors awaited him, however, for in 1892 he was elected state senator from the district comprising Custer and Fall River counties. He continued farming and mining and also purchased a ranch near Hermosa, which he still owns. He afterward established an assaying office at Ragged Top and was employed in the government assaying office at Deadwood in 1898. There he has since remained and is one of the most valued and experienced men in that connection, his labors being of the utmost worth. He is also a member of the school board of Deadwood and for three years he was a trustee of the School of Mines.

In 1894 Colonel Thornby was married to Miss Bertha Youmans, a teacher in the Spearfish Normal School, who was born at Winona, Minnesota. They have become the parents of two children: Mary Youmans, now a student in Brookings College; and Catherine Moore, attending the public schools. The religious faith of the family is that of the Episcopal church and the political belief of Colonel Thornby is that of the republican party. He belongs to the Deadwood lodge of Elks and is a prominent Mason, holding membership in the blue lodge and chapter, in Dakota Commandery, No. I, K, T., of which he is a past eminent commander, and in Naja Temple of the Mystic Shrine, of which he is chief rabban. He is most highly respected and his worth as a man and citizen is widely acknowledged. In 1887 Governor Church made him a member of his staff, with the rank of colonel, he being the first to whom this title has been accorded west of the Missouri river.

ALBION THORNE

Albion THORNE, who maintains his home in the pleasant little city of Hartford, Minnehaha County, is a native of the old Pine Tree state, having been born in Canton, Oxford County, Maine, on the 19th of October, 1836, and being a son of John Owen Thorne, a farmer by vocation, who was born at Lisbon, Maine, in 1804, and who died in Dell Rapids, South Dakota, in 1874. His wife, whose maiden name was Mary Hall Billings, was born at Temple, New Hampshire, on the 24th of September, 1810, and died in Sioux Falls, South Dakota, on the 6th of April, 1901, both of these sterling pioneers having been numbered among the earliest permanent settlers in Minnehaha County. Both families were established in New England in the colonial era, and Thomas Thorne, grandfather of our subject, was an active participant in the war of 1812, and a pioneer settler in the state of Maine. Albion Thorne, to whom this sketch is dedicated, completed the curriculum of the common schools in his native county, and thereafter continued his educational discipline in Westbrook Seminary and the Maine State Seminary, now known as Bates College, while in September, 1858, he was matriculated in Tufts College, at Somerville, Massachusetts, where he pursued a classical and scientific course of study.

On the 9th of September, 1862, he enlisted as a member of Company C, Twenty-third Maine Volunteer Infantry, in which he was made first lieutenant, remaining in the service for ten months and then receiving his honorable discharge. Thereafter he was engaged in the mercantile business for one year at Canton, Maine, in the meanwhile taking up the study of law and making such progress that he secured admission to the bar of Oxford County in 1866, and began the practice of his profession after closing out his mercantile interests. In 1864-5 he served as superintendent of schools in his native county, and was also justice of the peace for a time. In 1868 he removed to Waterloo, Iowa, where he held the superintendency of the East Side school from 1869 to 1871, in which latter year he came to the territory of Dakota and located in Dell Rapids, and he was superintendent of schools for Minnehaha County from 1872 to 1874, inclusive, while from 1872 to 1878 he also served as district attorney for the county. From 1881 to 1891 he was secretary of the board of education of Dell Rapids, and thereafter was clerk of the county courts, with residence in Sioux Falls, until 1895. In 1881 he represented his county in the territorial legislature, and he has been otherwise prominent in public and civic affairs, while he has attained precedence as an able lawyer. He has maintained his home in Hartford. In politics Mr. Thorne gave his allegiance to the Democratic party up to the time when the Confederacy fired upon the Walls of old Fort Sumter, and thereafter he supported the Republican party until he became convinced that it was bowing down to false gods, and he has since opposed its policies in the upholding of trusts, expansion of territory, etc., while he holds himself aloof from any political affiliation at the present time.

On the 7th of September, 1862, Mr. Thorne was initiated in Oriental Star Lodge, No. 21, Ancient Free and Accepted Masons, at Livermore, Maine, and was master of the same in 1868. He became a member of Dell Rapids Lodge, No. 8, Independent Order of Odd Fellows, in 1876, and has held all the principal offices, including that of chief patriarch of Occidental Encampment, Patriarchs Militant. He attended the Universalist church and one of its colleges in Maine, and is favorably inclined to the same, but is tolerant in his attitude. On the 18th of July, 1868, at Canton, Maine, Mr. Thorne was united in marriage to Miss Clara Maria Bolster, of Dixfield, that state, and of their children we here enter the names and respective dates of birth; Bina May, February 19, 1870: Alice Cynthia, July 15, 1873; Mabel Marth, July 7, 1875; Otis Albion, May 1, 1879; Arthur Albion, May 7, 1883; Grace Clara, August 29, 1886; and William Bolster, January 27, 1886

THOMAS THORSON

Thomas THORSON, one of the leading citizens of Canton, Lincoln County, where he is engaged in the real-estate business and where he holds the office of president of the First National Bank, was born in Norway, on the 14th of November, 1848, and was there reared to the age of six years, when, in 1854, he accompanied his parents on their immigration to the United States, the family settling in northeastern Iowa, where his father became numbered among the pioneer farmers, taking up government land near the town of McGregor. There our subject availed himself of the advantages of the public schools, continuing to assist his father in the work and management of the home farm until 1869, when he secured a position as clerk in a hardware establishment in Sioux City, Iowa. In 1871 he removed to Beloit, Lyon County, that state, where he opened the first store in the county, building up a successful general-merchandise business and becoming one of the influential citizens of that section. In the autumn of 1871, he was elected the first recorder of file county, and in 1874 was elected county auditor. After the expiration of his term in this office, in 1873, he accepted a position as traveling representative of the Sioux City Journal, and continued in this line of work for the ensuing six years, at the expiration of which, in 1881, he located in Canton, South Dakota, and here engaged in the real-estate business, doing much to further the development and settlement of this section and having ever since continued to be here prominently identified with this important line of enterprise, in which connection he has become the owner of much valuable city realty and farming and grazing land. He at once identified himself intimately and helpfully with public affairs, and he served two terms as mayor of Canton, while he was elected to represent his county in the provisional legislature of 1885. He has been at all times an uncompromising advocate of the principles of the Republican party and an active worker in its cause, and in 1892 he was shown further distinction at the hands of his party and the voters of the state in being chosen secretary of state, giving an able administration and being chosen as his own successor in 1894, on which occasion he received the largest plurality ever given to any candidate on the state ticket — a significant evidence of popular confidence and esteem. After his retirement from office, he again turned his attention to his real-estate business, which he has continued with marked success. He became one of the stockholders of the First National Bank of Canton at the time of its organization, was a member of its directorate for many years and in January, 1903, was elected to the presidency of the institution, which is one of the solid and prosperous banks of the state.

On July 12, 1882, Mr. Thorson married Miss Jessie Hunt, of Dodge County, Minnesota. Fraternally, he is a Knight of Pythias and in the Masonic order he has attained all the degrees of the York and Scottish rites, up to and including the thirty-second, and is also affiliated with the Mystic Shrine. His religious connection is with the Lutheran church.

CHARLES D. TIDRICK

Charles D. TIDRICK, one of the representatives and highly esteemed citizens of Chamberlain, is a native of Winterset, Iowa, where he was born on the 24th of May, 1863, being a son of Levi M. and Martha (Bell) Tidrick, of whose eleven children seven are living, namely: Lee, a resident of Winterset, Iowa; Addie, wife of O. M. White, of that place; Grace, wife of E. W. Geiger, of Ottawa, Kansas; Hoyt, Joseph and George, all residents of Winterset, and Charles D., the immediate subject of this sketch. Levi Tidrick was born in Guernsey County, Ohio, in 1827, and when twenty years of age he removed thence to St. Louis, Missouri, where his brother, Robert L., a prominent attorney and receiver of the land office, was then residing, and in 1848 they both went to Winterset, Iowa, where the father of our subject took up his permanent abode, his brother eventually removing to the city of Des Moines. Levi Tidrick was married at Winterset, and took up the study of medicine, being enabled to defray nearly the entire expense of his course in the St. Louis Medical College, and receiving some financial assistance from his brother Robert. After his graduation in this institution Dr. Tidrick continued in the active practice of his profession in Winterset until his death, in 1896, at the age of sixty-nine years. His death was the result of exposure in Florida, where he passed the winter of that year on his orange farm, the season being one in which the severe frosts did so great damage to the Florida fruit crops. The Doctor was widely known and much loved in his section of Iowa, and his death was deeply lamented in his home town. His widow still resides in Winterset.

Charles D. Tidrick acquired his early educational discipline in the public schools of his home village, being graduated in the Winterset high school and then entering the Normal School at Ladoga, Indiana, later continuing his studies at the State University of Iowa, at Iowa City, where he was a student for four years. After leaving school he passed a short interval in Indian Territory, and in the spring of 1884 came to Beresford, South Dakota, where he secured a position as auditor for F. M. Slagle & Company, lumber dealers. He retained this responsible office about five years, being located at the firm's yards in Alton, Iowa. In 1888 he was elected recorder of Sioux county, that state, on the Democratic ticket, his victory at the polls being the more noteworthy by reason of the fact that the county had a normal Republican party of about one thousand at the time. He was re-elected in 1890, thus serving two terms.

In 1893 Mr. Tidrick effected the organization of the German Savings Bank in Alton, disposing of his interests in the same in the fall of that year, when he came to Chamberlain. Here, in the spring of 1894, in company with G. W. Pitts, he organized the Bank of Iowa & Dakota, of which he became president. In 1896 they sold the bank and purchased the electric-lighting and gas plants of Chamberlain, which they have since owned and operated. Mr. Tidrick is the owner of twenty-five hundred acres of valuable land in Brule County, and fifteen hundred acres in contiguous counties, while he conducts a large business in the real-estate line, and in the extending of financial loans, as well as in the insurance and abstracting department of his business. Mr. Tidrick built and now owns the gas plant at Chamberlain. He is a stalwart Democrat in politics, and is now a member of the board of aldermen of his town. In 1897 he was appointed United States commissioner for this district, and is strictly serving in this capacity.

Fraternally he is identified with Chamberlain Lodge, No. 56, Free and Accepted Masons; Chamberlain Lodge, No. 88, Ancient Order of United Workmen; Sioux Falls Lodge, No. 262, Benevolent and Protective Order of Elks; Castle Lodge, No. 10, Knights of Pythias, and Sioux Tent, Knights of the Maccabees. In 1893, Mr. Tidrick was married to Aliss Lillian Love, of Albion, Indiana, and they have three daughters, Eugenia, Mary and Frances.

FRED LEWIS TIFFANY

Fred L. Tiffany, one of the able and popular young members of the bar of Walworth County, and now incumbent of the office of United States court commissioner for the northern district of the state, was born in Mason City, Cerro Gordo County, Iowa, on the 20th of May, 1877, and is a son of David M. and Addie R. Tiffany, the former of whom was born in the state of New York and the latter in that of New Hampshire, while they are now residents of Mitchell, South Dakota, the father being a merchant by vocation. The subject passed his boyhood days in his native town, where he completed the curriculum of the public schools, having been graduated in the high school as a member of the class of 1896. He then entered the University of Minnesota in the city of Minneapolis, where he continued his studies in the academic department for two years and later completed the prescribed course in the law department, in which he was graduated in June, 1901, with the degree of Bachelor of Laws, being simultaneously admitted to the bar of the state, as was he to that of South Dakota a short time afterward. In June of the same year he came to Mitchell, this state, and there initiated the active practice of his profession, remaining there until March, 1902, when he located in Selby, Walworth County, where he was engaged in practice until June 16, 1903, when he was appointed to his present office, by Judge J. H. Garland, of the United States district court, and then removed to Everts, where he has since given his attention to his official duties, while he also continues the practice of the law, in the minutiae of which he is thoroughly well informed. In politics Mr. Tiffany gives his allegiance to the Republican party, and he takes a lively interest in the questions and issues of the hour.

Fraternally he is identified with the Masonic order, while he is also affiliated with two college fraternities, the Phi Kappa Psi and Phi Delta Phi. On the 20th of May, 1902, was consummated the marriage of Mr. Tiffany to Miss Florence Gregory, who was born in Racine, Wisconsin, on the loth of December, 1877, being a daughter of William H. and Ellen R. Gregory, now residents of Mitchell, South Dakota. Of this union has been born a fine little son, Lewis Gregory Tiffany, who was ushered into the world on the loth of April, 1903.

ISAAC J. TODD

Isaac J. TODD, a member of the firm of Todd Brothers, of Salem, Hanson County, was born in the city of Elgin, Illinois, which was then a small village, on the 25th of September, 1854, being a son of James and Eliza (Boyce) Todd, to whom were born five sons and five daughters, all of whom are yet living. James Todd was born in the county of Armagh, Ireland, where he was reared and educated and where he learned the trade of weaver. At the age of twenty-six years he emigrated from the fair Emerald Isle to America, locating in Ohio, where his marriage was solemnized, shortly after which event he removed to Elgin, Illinois, where he learned the molder's trade, to which he there continued to devote his attention until about 1856, when he removed with his family to Winneshiek County, Iowa, where he took up government land and turned his attention to agricultural pursuits, eventually becoming the owner of a valuable landed estate of four hundred acres and being one of the honored and influential citizens of the county. He was the architect of his own fortunes, having come to America without financial reinforcement or influential friends and having won prosperity by hard work and good management. He was a man of inflexible integrity and most generous and kindly impulses, and after coming to the United States he aided in bringing his brothers here. In politics he was a Republican, and while in his native land was a communicant of the church of England, but became a member of the Methodist Episcopal church after coming to America. His devoted and cherished wife passed to her reward in 1900, and his death occurred in 1887.

The subject of this sketch was a child of but two years at the time when his parents removed to the pioneer farm in Iowa, and there he was reared under sturdy and invigorating discipline, his educational advantages being such as were afforded in the common schools of the locality and period. He continued to be associated in the management of the home farm until he had attained the age of twenty-five years, when, in 1879, he came to South Dakota and located in McCook County, entering claim to a homestead of one hundred and sixty acres, near Montrose. There he developed a valuable farm, and for five years he was also engaged in the buying and shipping of grain, in which line of enterprise he was very successful. In 1886 Mr. Todd was elected register of deeds of McCook County, serving one term, and in 1888, upon retiring from office, he engaged in the real-estate business, in which he has been particularly successful, being associated with his brother since 1894. The firm handle principally their own properties, being at the present time the owners of more than three thousand acres of valuable farming land in McCook and adjoining counties.

Mr. Todd is a stanch adherent of the Republican party, and for a number of years was a member of its state central committee. He is affiliated with Montrose Lodge, No. 48, Free and Accepted Masons; Chapter No. 73, Royal Arch Masons: Commandery No. 17, Knights Templar; the Scottish Rite consistory at Yankton, and the Ancient Order of United Workmen. Mr. Todd was married September 29, 1885, to Miss Ida McCooke, of Montrose, South Dakota, and there have been born to this union six children, two boys, now dead, and four girls living, viz: Adah M., Geneva E., Elva and Nauva.

FREDERICK TREON, M. D.

Frederick Treon, M. D., one of the representative physicians and surgeons of the state, established in the practice of his profession in Chamberlain, was born in Shelby County, Indiana, on the 12th of August, 1857, and is a son of Dr. Andrew and Lydia (Steinberger) Treon, of whose five children three are living, namely: Rebecca, the wife of Edward Gabbert, of Bloomington, Illinois; Frederick, the subject of this sketch, and Elizabeth, the wife of Robert Lytle, of Michigan City, Indiana. The father of our subject was born in Lebanon county, Pennsylvania, where he was reared and educated. As a young man he removed thence to Miamisburg, Ohio, where he read medicine under the preceptorage of his uncle. Dr. John Treon, being graduated in his chosen profession and then locating in Shelby County, Indiana, in the thirties, when that locality was practically unreclaimed from the wilderness. He was one of the pioneer physicians of the county, and there he continued in practice until his death, in 1865, at the age of sixty-two years. He was twice married, the maiden name of his first wife having been Coffman, and of their children five are living, namely: Samuel, who is a resident of Mattoon, Illinois, was a valiant soldier in the war of the Rebellion, being severely wounded in the siege of Vicksburg and re-enlisting after recovering from the effects of this injury; Jackson, who was likewise a soldier in the Civil War, is now a resident of Washington, Indiana: Sarah is the wife of John Heck, of Bartholomew County, that state: Sabill is the wife of H. C. Williamson, of Michigan City, Indiana, and Charlotte is the wife of William Collins, of Bartholomew County. Michael Treon, grandfather of the Doctor, was born in France, and he also was a physician, the family name having thus been long and prominently identified with the medical profession, the subject and two of his cousins, his father and grandfather, his uncle Michael and his great-uncle, John Treon, all having adopted the profession as a vocation.

After availing himself of the advantages afforded in the public schools of his native county Dr. Treon continued his studies in the academy at Franklin, Indiana, and when about eight years of age he secured a position in the machine shops of Haskill & Barker, in Michigan City, where he completed a special course in geometry and trigonometry and civil and mechanical engineering. He was not yet satisfied with his mental attainments, however, and thus entered upon a careful study of anatomy under the personal direction of Dr. J. Sadler, of Edinburg, Indiana, with a view of preparing himself for the practice of medicine. He thus continued his technical studies for two years, in the meanwhile clerking in a drug store and by this means supplemented his knowledge of materia medica and therapeutics. In the fall of 1876 he went to Aurora, Indiana, and began the systematic study of medicine under the preceptorship of Drs. James and L. K. Lamb, remaining in their office until the latter part of the following year, when he was matriculated in the Ohio Medical College, in Cincinnati, where he continued his studies two years, being then graduated and receiving his degree of Doctor of Medicine. He at once entered upon the active practice of his profession, forming a partnership with his father-in-law. Dr. James Lamb, with whom he continued to be associated for six years. In 1886 Dr. Treon was appointed physician in the government Indian service, being assigned to service at the Crow Creek Indian reservation, in South Dakota. His commission expired four years later and he then went to the city of Chicago, where he took a post-graduate course in Rush Medical College and then opened an office in Hyde Park, that city, where he was in practice about three months, being then reappointed to the Indian service and assigned to the San Carlos agency, in Arizona, where he remained six months, being then transferred to the Crow Creek agency, where he had previously served with so much acceptability. In 1893 the Doctor was appointed Indian agent for this reservation and also for the Lower Brule agency, retaining this incumbency four years and seven months and making an excellent record as an executive. In the spring of 1898 he came to Chamberlain, and soon afterward was appointed medical examiner, under General Andrew E. Lee, in the Spanish-American war service, being located at Sioux Falls. Later he was offered a commission as assistant surgeon under Colonel

Grigsby, but did not accept the office. In the fall of 1898, the Doctor located in Chamberlain, where he has since been actively engaged in practice. In the fall of 1900, he became associated with R. F. Terpenning in the drug business and under the firm name of Terpenning & Treon they now conduct one of the leading pharmacies of the city, Mr. Terpenning being a graduate in pharmacy and a skilled chemist. The Doctor is a member of the South Dakota State Medical Society, of the Mitchell District Medical Society, and of the American Medical Association. In politics he is a stanch advocate of the principles of the Democratic party, and both he and his wife are members of the Presbyterian church.

Fraternally he is identified with Chamberlain Lodge, No. 56, Free and Accepted Masons; Pilgrim Chapter. No. 32, Royal Arch Masons: St. Bernard Commandery, No. II, Knights Templar, at Mitchell; Sioux Falls Lodge, No. 262, Benevolent and Protective Order of Elks: Castle Lodge. No. 10, Knights of Pythias, and also with the local organizations of the Ancient Order of United Workmen, the Mutual Benefit Association and the Knights of the Maccabees, being medical examiner for these three lodges, as well as for numerous old-time insurance companies. On the 29th of March, 1879, Dr. Treon was united in marriage to Miss Rella L. Lamb, daughter of Dr. James Lamb, of Aurora, Indiana, and their only child. Dr. James F. Lamb, is a graduate of the Ohio Medical College, in Cincinnati, and is engaged in the practice of his profession in Aurora, Indiana.

PHILETUS CLARK TRUMAN

Philetus C. TRUMAN, who died at his home in Volga, on the 27th of October, 1901, as the result of an attack of pneumonia, was born in Preston, Chenango County, New York, on the 20th of December, 1841, being a son of Clark and Clarissa Truman. His father was born on Long Island, New York, and his ancestors were numbered among the early settlers in Connecticut, whether they came from England in the colonial era of our national history. Representatives of the name later removed to Long Island, New York, locating at Little Falls, and thence the father of the subject removed to Chenango County, New York, where they remained for a number of years, finally coming west to Magnolia, Iowa, where the parents passed the remainder of their lives.

Mr. Truman received his rudimentary education in the district schools of his native county where he was reared on the home farm, and later he continued his studies in the institution at DeRuyter, New York. He effectually supplemented this early discipline during later years, being a close observer and student and becoming a man of broad and liberal information and distinctive intellectuality. In 1856 he left the parental home and went to Wisconsin, where he devoted several years to teaching, in the schools of Rock, Dane and Green County, while he simultaneously gave special attention to the reading of law. In July, 1862, he went to Magnolia, Iowa, where he married Miss Eunice Truman, whose death occurred in November, 1873. She is survived by one daughter, Alice M., who is now the wife of John C. Jenkins, of Brookings, this state. After his marriage Mr. Truman continued his residence in Iowa, where he was engaged in teaching school for several terms, while for several years he served as superintendent of schools in Shelby County and also as county surveyor. In 1873 he was admitted to the bar of that state, and thereafter was successfully engaged in the practice of his profession at Harlan, Iowa, until 1881, when he came to Brookings County, South Dakota, and took up a pre-emption claim in Lake, Sinai township, upon which he resided until he had perfected his title. He then located in the village of Volga, where he resumed the practice of his profession, entering into partnership with Arthur S. Mitchell, with whom he continued in practice until 1891, from which time forward until his death he conducted an individual and independent practice of general order, gaining marked prestige. In 1893-4 he served as county judge, and in the fall of the latter year was elected to represent Brookings County in the state legislature, in which he proved a valuable and conscientious working member. In politics he gave an unwavering allegiance to the Republican party, of whose principles he was an able and effective advocate, taking an active part in forwarding the party cause. He was reared in die faith of the Seventh-day Baptist church, but upon coming to Volga enrolled himself as a member of the Presbyterian church, ordering his life in harmony with the faith which he professed.

He was one of the prominent members of the Masonic fraternity in this county, having been identified with Mystic Lodge, No. 89, Ancient Free and Accepted Masons, of which he was past master; Chapter No. 17, Royal Arch Masons, at Arlington; and Golden Rod Chapter. No. 58, Order of the Eastern Star, of which his widow is also a valued member. At the time of his death Mr. Truman was the owner of sixteen hundred and forty acres of farming; land, in Brookings and Kingsbury counties, and also of a considerable amount of property in Volga. He was a naturalist of marked ability and enthusiasm, and in this line held a high reputation for his intimate and comprehensive knowledge, while he had the finest collection of lepidoptera and coleoptera in the northwest, and having given much of his time in the later years of his life to study and investigation along this line and to the perfecting of his fine collection. He retired from the active practice of his profession in 1900, and thereafter gave his attention to his capitalistic and landed interests.

On the 12th of January, 1892. Mr. Truman was united in marriage to Miss Mary E. Dickerson, who was born in Jordan, Minnesota, being a daughter of David D. and Emeline (Edgerton) Dickerson, natives of Oneida and Madison County, New York, respectively. The mother of Mrs. Truman was summoned into eternal rest on the 27th of December, 1900, at the age of seventh-three years, and Mr. Dickerson made his home with his daughter, Mrs. Truman, having attained the venerable age of seventy-nine years at the time of his death, December 25, 1903.

Mrs. Truman is a lady of culture and gracious personality, and is prominent in the social life of the community, while her beautiful home is a center of refined hospitality. She was educated in the seminary at Whitestown, New York, and in the Agricultural College, at Brookings, South Dakota, and was a popular teacher in the public schools of this state for several years prior to her marriage. She is a musician and also possesses much literary ability, while she and her husband passed many grateful hours in their fine library and in the arranging of his collection of specimens to which reference has been made, and which she still retains. She is an active worker in the local chapter of the Order of the Eastern Star, of which she is past worthy matron, while she has also served as grand conductress in the grand chapter of this state. She is a member of the Presbyterian church, and active in forwarding the work in its different departments. She was made administratrix of her husband's estate, and still retains a personal supervision of her various properties.

JACOB TSCHETTER

Jacob Tschetter, hails from far-away Russia, in the southern part of which country his birth occurred on October 27, 1857. His parents were Joseph and Mary (Wipf) Tschetter, both natives of Russia, the father for a number of years a farmer of considerable means and a man of much more than ordinary influence and social standing. In 1875 he immigrated to the United States and settled at Elkhart, Indiana, but after living there until the spring of the following year, moved his family to South Dakota, locating in Hutchinson County, where he took up a homestead and pre-empted a claim, both of which he at once proceeded to improve. He was an industrious man, developed a good farm and spent the remainder of his life on the same, dying in the year 1884. His wife who is still living, resides on the home place in Hutchinson County.

Jacob Tschetter spent his childhood and youth in the land of his nativity, and at the age of eighteen accompanied the family to the United States, receiving his first knowledge of the English language and of American manners and customs at Elkhart, Indiana. He attended school there a part of one year, and in 1876 removed with his parents to South Dakota, where he assisted his father in improving the farm, remaining at home until 1877, in the fall of which year he entered the marriage relation with Miss Anna Mendel, a native of Russia, and purchasing land near the family homestead engaged in the pursuit of agriculture. Meeting with encouraging success as a farmer, he subsequently purchased other lands, until in due time he found himself the owner of five hundred and twenty acres, the greater part of which he reduced to cultivation and otherwise improved and upon which he continued to live and prosper until 1884. In that year he abandoned agriculture and, moving to the town of Bridgewater, engaged in merchandising, in connection with which he also did a thriving business for some time buying and shipping cattle. Mr. Tschetter embarked in the latter line of trade with a partner in whom he reposed great confidence, but the latter, becoming financially embarrassed, so involved the entire business that at the end of two years the firm was obliged to close its doors and go to the wall. During the two years following this disaster the subject was variously employed, working for some time in a machine shop until elected city marshal, the duties of which position he discharged in an eminently satisfactory manner for several years. At the expiration of his official term, he was appointed deputy sheriff of McCook County, and after leaving that office served as deputy United States marshal for six years, during which time he became widely known as a faithful and efficient public servant. In the course of his business career, especially in that part immediately following his financial reverses, Mr., Tschetter became involved in a number of law suits, growing out of the collecting of outstanding accounts, several of which he carried to the circuit court, thence to the supreme court, where verdicts were rendered in his favor. Considering his limited experience in litigation in this country and his indifferent knowledge of the English language, having attended school no more than six weeks in America, his success in pushing his cases to final issue and winning verdicts was little less than remarkable, as nearly everybody acquainted with the matter predicted his certain defeat. Realizing the justice of his cause, however, he refused to abide by the adverse decisions of lower courts and, appealing from the same to higher tribunals, obtained the victory to which in law as well as equity he was so clearly entitled.

For some years past Mr. Tschetter has been dealing in real estate, and his reputation as a clear-headed, far-seeing man has won him a large and lucrative patronage. He has made a number of important sales in different parts of the state, one of which, including the transfer of farm property in Beadle county, amounting to ninety-six thousand dollars, being the largest landed deal effected in South Dakota during the year 1902, Mr. and Mrs. Tschetter are the parents of six children, namely: Jacob, a clothing merchant at Bridgewater; Joseph, a teacher in the public schools; Susan and Anna are also engaged in educational work, while David and Mary are still at home. Susan, the older daughter, was the first young lady of Russian parentage to teach in the schools of Hutchinson County, and one of the first of her nationality to engage in educational work in the state. She and her sister Anna are fine vocalists and leading members of the choir of the Mennonite church, to which the family belong. Joseph is also an accomplished musician; he organized the Lutheran College Band of Sioux Falls, was a member of the First Regimental Band for some years, and at this time is leader and instructor of the Goodrich Band, one of the finest organizations of the kind in South Dakota.

In politics Mr. Tschetter was a Democrat until 1896, since which time he has become an ardent supporter of the Republican party, his change of views being caused by the free silver fallacy, which he could in no wise endorse, having always been an advocate of a sound and stable currency based upon the gold standard. For a number of years prior to 1896 he served on the Democratic state central committee, and since abandoning his former position he has been equally as active in his efforts to advance the interests of the party with which he is now identified, being one of the Republican leaders in McCook County, and an influential factor in district and state, as well as in local politics.

Fraternally he is a Mason, belonging to Sioux Falls Lodge, No. 262, and he is also an active worker in the Ancient Order of United Workmen and the Modern Woodmen of America, holding important official positions in both. Religiously he was born and reared in the Mennonite faith, and is still a loyal member of the church of that time, as are also his wife and the other members of the family, being among the leaders and liberal supporters of the congregation worshiping in Bridgewater. Mr. Tschetter is a man of strong intellectuality, great personal force, and occupies a conspicuous position among the representative citizens of McCook County.

NEWTON S. TUBES

N. S. Tubes, of Custer City, is a native of Oneida County, New York, and dates his birth from November 22, 1853, having first seen the light of day in the town of Weston, near which the parental homestead is situated. His youthful years were spent on his father's farm, where he early learned the lessons of industry, thrift and self-reliance, which have so materially influenced his subsequent life, and in the public schools he received a modest educational training. When a mere lad he began working for himself and so assiduously did he apply himself that at the age of sixteen he found himself the possessor of several hundred dollars, which he judiciously invested in land, thus early in life becoming a tiller of the soil upon his own responsibility. A hard worker and good manager, he took advantage of every opportunity to improve his condition, and it was not long until he was regarded one of the most energetic and successful agriculturists of the community in which he resided. He continued to cultivate his farm and prosper until 1879, when he disposed of his interests in York state and started west, arriving at Cheyenne, Wyoming, on March 24th of that year. Shortly after reaching his destination Mr. Tubbs engaged in dairying near Cheyenne, in connection with which he also bought cattle, meeting with encouraging success in both lines of business. Later he discontinued his operations in Wyoming and in the fall of 1879 drove through with an ox-team to the Black Hills and took up land adjoining Custer City which place, at that time, was an insignificant hamlet, consisting of a few log shacks and occupied by a transient population, attracted thither by the prospect of gold. Having faith in the future growth and ultimate prosperity of the town, Mr. Tubbs decided to make it his permanent place of abode; accordingly, he began improving his land, and in a short time started a dairy, which he operated for several years with profitable results, also established a cheese factory, which in like manner proved the source of a handsome income. While prosecuting these enterprises he turned his attention to stock raising, beginning on a small scale, but gradually enlarging the business until within a comparatively short time he had it established upon a firm basis with every prospect of continued success. In the fall of 1882, he went to Cheyenne and bought one thousand head of sheep, which he drove through to the Hills and herded on a large tract of fine grazing land near Red Canon, about ten miles from the Cheyenne river. This was the first attempt at sheep raising in the Black Hills country and to Mr. Tubbs belongs the honor of being the father of the industry in southwestern Dakota. From that time to the present his business has steadily grown in magnitude and importance until he is now the largest and most successful sheep raiser in the state, owning extensive tracts of land in various parts of the country and running from sixteen to twenty-five thousand head every year.

In addition to his large live-stock interests Mr. Tubbs is identified with various other enterprises, notable among which is the Edgemont Irrigation and Improvement Company, an undertaking inaugurated in 1895 to carry water from the Cheyenne river to a large area of surrounding country for the purpose of reclaiming and reducing to cultivation lands which up to that time were little better than dry, sterile wastes. This laudable object, however, failed of accomplishment by reason of the financial embarrassment of the company, after which Mr. Tubbs secured the entire canal and lands to the amount of ten thousand acres, taking possession of the property in January, 1903. He is now rapidly pushing the enterprise to completion and when finished it will doubtless make him one of the wealthiest men in the west, as the canal is the largest artificial waterway in the state, and the land when properly irrigated will be among the richest and most productive in Dakota.

Mr. Tubbs has manifested commendable zeal in all of his undertakings and possesses the ability, judgment and fertility of resource essential to the prosecution of large and important enterprises. He is not only a broad-minded, public spirited man of affairs but tactful, shrewd and a natural leader who in business knows no such word as fail and who labors for the public good while advancing his own interests. His home, adjoining the corporate limits of Custer City, is perhaps the finest and most costly private residence in this part of the state, and he has been exceedingly liberal in surrounding himself and those dependent upon him with the conveniences and comforts of life and all the luxuries which large wealth and refined taste suggest. He was married in Custer City, August 3, 1883, to Miss Jennie Page, of Illinois, the union being terminated by the death of the loving and faithful companion, after a happy wedded experience of nearly nine years' duration. Mrs. Tubbs departed this life on the 22d day of March, 1902, leaving besides a husband three children to mourn her untimely loss, namely: George, Page and Alice.

Mr. Tubbs holds membership with several secret fraternal organizations, belonging to the Masonic lodge at Custer City, also to the Independent Order of Odd Fellows, Modern Woodmen of America, Knights of the Maccabees and Ancient Order of United Workmen, at the same place, being an active worker in the different orders.

HENRY C. TUCKER

Henry C. TUCKER, of Geddes, editor and publisher of the Charles Mix County News, was born in New York, on the 30th of October, 1854, being a son of Samuel and Martha (Crumb) Tucker, of whose seven children four are yet living. The father of the subject was born in Madison County, New York, whither his father removed from Massachusetts, while the father of the latter was a soldier under General Putnam in the war of the Revolution. In one of the battles in which he took part his hat was almost shot to pieces, and General Putnam presented him with a new hat, recognizing the bravery which he had displayed in thus becoming a mark for so many bullets. Upon attaining manhood, the father of our subject engaged in farming and hop growing in his native county, having planted the first field of hops in that section of the state, and in connection with this line of enterprise he became very successful, being one of the substantial fanners and honored citizens of Madison County at the time of his death, which occurred in 1888, at which time he was sixty years of age. His widow still survives him and resides on the old homestead farm. He was a Democrat in politics and ever took a deep interest in public affairs, though he never sought official preferment.

Henry C. Tucker was reared on the homestead farm and early began to lend his aid in connection with its cultivation. After attending the public schools of the locality, he continued his studies in the DeRuyter

Institute and the New York Central Conference Seminary, an institution conducted under the auspices of the Methodist Episcopal church. In 1875 he came to the west and located in Shelby County, Iowa, where he bought a tract of land and engaged in agricultural pursuits, while he also invested in a ditching machine, which he operated throughout that locality for several years, being one of the pioneers in the locality and finding his machine in much demand. In 1883 he disposed of his interests in Iowa and came to Charles Mix County, South Dakota, being numbered among the first settlers in the county. He filed on a claim in Jackson township, but after one year sold his relinquishment to the same, and in July, 1884, in company with Charles W. Pratt, he purchased the Charles Mix County News, a weekly paper, which was at that time published in the village of Darlington, its founding dating back only to the preceding November. In October, 1884, they removed the plant to Edgerton and shortly afterward our subject purchased his partner's interest in the enterprise and thereafter continued the publication of the paper in Darlington until I goo, when he removed his plant to the new town of Geddes, his office building having been the third building erected in the town and his paper the first to be published in the town. The office of the News is well equipped with modern machinery and other accessories, the old hand presses originally utilized having been replaced by those of modern design, while the paper has an excellent circulation through the county. Mr. Tucker is one of the town's most enthusiastic and loyal citizens and is at the present time president of the village council, and while a resident of Edgerton he acted as postmaster of the place. He is a stanch Republican in his political adherency and has made his paper an effective exponent of the party cause.

Fraternally, he is identified with Geddes Lodge, Free and Accepted Masons, and Signal Camp, No. 444, Modern Woodmen of America, of which latter he is venerable consul. Mr. Tucker was united in marriage to Miss Victoria Ashby, of Shelby County, Iowa, and they are the parents of four children, Maud, who is the wife of William Fowler, who is engaged in the lumber business in Geddes; Roy, who is in the office with his father; Bert, who remains at the parental home, and Ella, who is the wife of Charles Zink, of this county.

ARTHUR HENRY TUFTS, M. D.

An eminent physician and surgeon and able educator in the field of his profession and a man of broad humanitarian principles, Dr. Arthur Henry Tufts has throughout the period of his residence in Sioux Falls occupied a central place on the stage of public activity. His professional interests indicate but one line of his broad usefulness, for aside from that his efforts have been a forceful and beneficial influence in promoting the intellectual and moral progress of Sioux Falls.

A native of Vermont, Dr. Tufts was born in Wardsboro on the 14th of January, 1856, a son of John and Desdemona Sophia (Barber) Tufts. The family comes of Scotch-Irish and English lineage and the ancestral record dates back to the eleventh century. The progenitor of the Tufts family on American soil was John Tufts, who came from County Down, Ireland, and arrived in the new world in the early part of the eighteenth century and settled at West Brookfield, Massachusetts, where the home which he erected in 1734 is still standing. During the early childhood of Arthur Henry Tufts his parents removed westward to Geneseo, Illinois, where he pursued a high-school course and afterward continued his studies in Grinnell College at Grinnell, Iowa. Having determined upon the practice of medicine as a life work, he entered the College of Physicians and Surgeons at Baltimore, Maryland, and afterward matriculated in the medical department of the College of the city of New York, from which he was graduated with the class of 1883. In that year he located for practice in Sioux Falls, South Dakota, where he has since continuously remained, covering a period of more than three decades, enjoying well merited success as an active representative of his profession and winning high reputation as one of the most able and skilled physicians of the state. In 1887 he entered into partnership with Dr. S. A. Brown, of Sioux Falls, in a connection that has since been maintained uninterruptedly — a partnership wholly congenial and of mutual benefit. The firm is one of the most prominent in the state, their high standing being attested by the regard entertained for them by their professional brethren. Dr. Tufts has been chosen for both city health officer and county health officer, ably serving in the former position for eight years. An extensive practice has been accorded him and he is regarded as the most careful and conscientious physician, seldom, if ever, at fault in the diagnosis of his cases or in anticipating the outcome of disease. Broad reading and investigation have kept him in touch with the most modern scientific ideas and methods and he manifests intense interest in anything that tends to bring to man the key to the complex mystery which we call life. His broad humanitarianism, too, is an element in his constantly growing success, for his interest in his fellowmen is deep and sincere and along various lines he is continuously reaching out a helping hand.

At Grafton, Vermont, Dr. Tufts was united in marriage to Miss Harriet Lemira Deane, a daughter of Benjamin F. Deane. Their children are: Marion D., a teacher in the public schools of Sioux Falls; and Helen A., a teacher in the All Saints School. Both are graduates of the University of Wisconsin.

Dr. Tufts gives his political allegiance to the republican party and always keeps well informed on the significant problems and questions of the day, yet the only offices he has filled have been in the strict path of his profession. For twenty years he served as secretary of the board of pension examiners, being first appointed as the republican representative on the board by President Grover Cleveland. He continued in that position until the Wilson administration, when his connection with the board ceased. His work was most efficient and his services highly satisfactory.

In Masonic circles, too, Dr. Tufts is a man of influence, his activities constituting a strong element in the upbuilding of the organization in his section of the state. He holds membership in Unity Lodge, No. 130, A. F. & A. M., of which he was the first secretary. This was the last created of the Masonic lodges in Sioux Falls, but is now the largest in point of membership in the state. His partner, Dr. Brown, was really the prime factor in organizing this lodge and both he and Dr. Tufts have been most active in advancing its interests. The latter was senior warden for one term, was master for one term and for one term was treasurer. With the exception of the period spent in those offices, he has continuously served as secretary since the lodge was created. He has attained the Knights Templar degree in the commandery, the thirty-second degree in the Scottish Rite and has crossed the sands of the desert with the Nobles of the Mystic Shrine. His social nature finds expression in his connection with the Country Club, of which he is a popular member. Among his chief activities should be mentioned his work for the advancement of the cause of temperance and the upbuilding of the church. He is a stalwart advocate of temperance both by precept and example, for he has never tasted liquor of any kind nor has he ever used tobacco. A member of the Congregational church, he has been a cooperant factor in every effort for moral progress and social uplift in his community. He has held all of the offices in the church, including that of deacon, and was chairman of the board of trustees when the present house of worship was erected. In the Young Men's Christian Association of Sioux Falls he has long been an earnest worker. The first meeting called to organize the association was held in his office and he was chosen its first president. When the Sioux Falls College, a Baptist school, was organized in 1883 Dr. Tufts became professor of physiology and natural history of that institution and so continued until 1886, when his growing general practice forced him to withdraw from college work. His life has indeed been one of widespread usefulness. He has studied existing conditions and the signs of the times, has recognized the opportunities for progress and has employed most practical methods in working toward high ideals. Association with Dr. Tufts means expansion and elevation.

J. F. TURNER, M. D.

Dr. J. F. Turner, who is a prominent and well-known physician and surgeon in Canton, South Dakota, was born in Butler County, Pennsylvania, on the 16th of October, 1866, his parents being George B. and Sarah J. F. Turner, who spent their entire lives in that county. The father followed farming in early manhood but during the last decade of his life resided in West Sunbury, Butler County, where he was variously engaged. He was one of the well-known citizens of his section and served for several years as justice of the peace at West Sunbury.

J. F. Turner acquired his education in the West Sunbury Academy and subsequently prepared for the practice of his chosen profession as a student in the Baltimore Medical College, from which institution he was graduated with the class of 1893. He then took a civil service examination in Washington, D. C, and spent about seventeen years in field service under the government, his work being in the Indian department. For seven years prior to his resignation in 1909 he acted as physician and assistant superintendent of the Asylum for Insane Indians at Canton, South Dakota. In 1909 he tendered his resignation and entered into private practice at Canton, where he has remained to the present time, and the success and reputation which he now enjoys have come in recognition of his ability to cope with the intricate problems testing the powers of the physician.

In June, 1902, Dr. Turner was united in marriage to Miss Anna Chambers, of Toledo, Oregon, in which state he was stationed for about three years. He is identified fraternally with the following organizations: Silver Star Lodge, No. 4, A. F. & A. M.; Siroc Chapter, No. 4, R. A. M.; and Sioux Falls Lodge, No. 262, B. P. O. E.. He is also a valued member of the Canton Commercial Club and is held in high esteem by those with whom he comes in contact in the varied relations of life. In matters of citizenship, he is progressive, desiring the welfare and upbuilding of the community to the extent not only of indorsing beneficial public measures but also of cooperating in all movements for the general good.

JAMES P. TURNER

James P. Turner is conducting a general blacksmithing and woodworking establishment and general repair shop at Faulkton and is thus closely associated with industrial activity there. He was born in Elgin County, Ontario, Canada, December 1, 1858, a son of James and Mary (Jardine) Turner, natives of Scotland, the mother being but a young girl when the family removed to Canada. The father was about twenty-five years of age when he became a resident of that country. In the land of hills and heather he had previously learned the carpenter's trade and in the new world he carried on contracting and building until his death, which occurred in March, 1864, when his son James was about five years of age. In the fall of 1893, the mother came to the United States and now resides with her son in Faulkton.

The family numbered five children, of whom James P. Turner is the third in order of birth. He attended the public schools of Canada and at the age of nineteen years began learning the blacksmith's trade, at which he served a four years' apprenticeship. In 1883 he came to Dakota territory and worked in Watertown for a year, removing thence in the spring of 1884 to Faulk County. He opened a shop at La Foon, then the county seat, and he was one of the first to establish a blacksmithing business in Faulkton when the county seat was removed to that place. He has continuously engaged in blacksmithing there save while he served as postmaster, and he is now operating a general repair shop and doing both blacksmithing and woodworking, having a well-equipped plant. He is likewise proprietor of the leading drug store in Faulkton, which is being managed by his son, Hugh A., while the father devotes his entire attention to industrial pursuits.

On the 3d of February, 1887, Mr. Turner was united in marriage to Miss Belle K. Puntine, a native of Ontario, Canada, and a daughter of John and Margaret (McDonald) Puntine, who have passed away. To Mr. and Mrs. Turner were born five children, as follows: Jessie A., who is the wife of E. E. Aaron, a ranchman residing at Billings, Montana; Hugh A., who is engaged in the drug business at Faulkton; Frank A., who resides at home and has pursued a course in civil engineering at the South Dakota State School of Mines at Rapid City; and Muriel B. and Charles J., both of whom are attending school and are still at home. The wife and mother passed away December 15, 1900, and her death was deeply regretted by her many friends.

Mr. Turner is well known in Masonic circles, holding membership in the lodge and chapter of Faulkton, being a past master of the former, while in the latter he has served as high priest. He has attained the Knight Templar degree in Redfield Commandery and he is ever most loyal to the teachings of the craft. At the present writing he is serving as secretary of both the lodge and chapter. He also belongs to the Ancient Order of United Workmen, the Modern Brotherhood of America and the Modern Woodmen of America. In his religious belief he is a Baptist, while his political faith is that of the republican party. He is recognized as one of its prominent representatives in Faulk County and he served as postmaster of Faulkton under the administration of President Taft. He was also called to the office of mayor and then after being out of the position for a time was reelected and is serving for the second year as chief executive of the city, to which he gives a businesslike and progressive administration. He has been a member of the board of education for a number of years, is a director of the Providence Hospital and lends hearty aid and cooperation to all movements that are of value and worth to the city.

JOHN L. TURNER

John L. Turner, in point of consecutive identification the oldest merchant in the state of South Dakota save for one exception, retaining his residence and business headquarters in the attractive town of Springfield, Bon Homme County, is a scion of a family which has been identified with the annals of American history from the early colonial epoch, and is himself a native of Geneseo, Livingston county, New York, where he was born on the 26th of August, 1843, being a son of Lyman and Martha (Lewis) Turner, of whose five children he is the eldest of the three surviving, his sisters being Mary H., a maiden lady, residing in New York City, and Isabella L., the wife of Charles S. Pease, of Albany, New York. The father of the subject was born in Connecticut, in 1809, his ancestors in the agnatic line having emigrated from England to America in 1648, taking up their abode in the colony of Massachusetts, whence representatives later went into Connecticut, where the name became one of prominence, as representative of the highest order of citizenship. Members of the family rendered valiant service as Continental soldiers during the war of the Revolution, and patriotism and loyalty have been distinguishing family traits in successive generations. As a young man Lyman Turner removed with his father. Matthe Turner, who was born in 1777, to New York City, whither an older brother had preceded them, and after remaining for a short time in the national metropolis he removed to Geneseo, that state, where he established himself in the mercantile business. In later years he became extensively engaged in the cattle business in that section of the Empire state, and was a member of the company which imported the first shorthorn cattle into that district. He eventually retired from mercantile pursuits and devoted his entire attention to the breeding of blooded livestock, in which connection he gained a high reputation, being very successful in his efforts and becoming an extensive land owner. He died at the age of fifty-five years, in the very prime of his honorable and useful manhood, his demise occurring in 1864. He was originally an old-line Whig in his political adherency, and espoused the cause of the Republican party at the time of its organization, ever afterward remaining a radical advocate of its principles, though he never sought official preferment. He and his wife were communicants of the Protestant Episcopal church and were persons of sterling character, retaining the high regard of all who knew them. The mother of the subject entered into the eternal life in 1861, at the age of forty-two years.

John L. Turner remained at the parental home until he had attained the age of twenty-two years and after completing a course of study in the high school at Geneseo he entered a private boarding school conducted by Dr. Reed, at Geneva, New York, and later continued his studies in a commercial college at Rochester, that state. After thus completing his educational discipline, he became actively associated with his father in the cattle business, which he continued after the death of his father until 1867, when he removed to Ann Arbor, Michigan, where he resided until 1870, giving his attention to property interests of the estate in that locality. In the year last mentioned he cast in his lot with what is now the state of South Dakota, coming to Springfield and here establishing himself in the general merchandise business. About three years later he became associated with Henry E. Bonesteel in the prosecution of the enterprise, under the firm name of Bonesteel & Turner, and this partnership obtained for a quarter of a century, being dissolved in 1898, after which John W. Turner, the son of our subject, became associated with him in the business, proving an able coadjutor, and the enterprise has since been continued under the firm name of J. L. Turner & Son. The business has grown to extensive proportions, drawing its trade from a wide radius of contiguous country, while the stock carried is select and comprehensive and the firm is one whose reputation for reliability and fair dealing is of the highest. Mr. Turner is also the owner and operator of the Artesian roller mills in Springfield, and for many years he also conducted a drug store in the town, having recently disposed of this branch of his business.

In 1864 Mr. Turner enlisted as a member of the Fifty-eighth New York National Guards, in which he was made sergeant major, and during his term of service he was on guard duty at Elmira, New York, receiving his honorable discharge in December, 1864. Mr. Turner has ever been a stanch adherent of the Republican party and has taken an active interest in promoting the party cause. Soon after coming to Springfield, he was appointed postmaster of the town, being the first incumbent of this office, which he continued to hold for a number of years, while his also was the distinction of being the first mayor of the town, of which position he was likewise incumbent for several years. He may well be mentioned as one of the founders and builders of Springfield, to whose interests he has ever been most loyal, doing all in his power to promote its advancement and material upbuilding. In 1896 he was candidate of his party for presidential elector, and in 1892 he was an alternate delegate to the national Republican convention, in Minneapolis.

He has been a member of the Masonic fraternity since 1865 and is a charter member of Mount Zion Lodge, No. 6, of Springfield; he was a delegate at the organization of the grand lodge of the territory of Dakota, being senior grand warden of this body in 1879. He is also a charter member of the Masonic Veterans' Association and is identified with DeMolay Commandery, No. 3, Knights Templar, at Yankton, and with El Riad Temple, Ancient Arabic Order of the Nobles of the Mystic Shrine, in Sioux Falls. He is one of the prominent members and a communicant of Ascension church, Protestant Episcopal in whose organization he took an active part, and he has been a member of its vestry from that time to the present. He was for several years a member of the board of education of Springfield, and in 1883 he was a member of the state constitutional convention, which assembled in Sioux Falls. On the 17th of May, 1865, was solemnized the marriage of Mr. Turner to Miss Mary A. Finley, of Geneseo, New York, and they became the parents of one son, John W., who was born on the 8th of October, 1866, and who is now associated with his father in business, being one of the able and popular young men of the county, Mrs. Turner entered into eternal rest on the 8th of March, 1884, having been a devoted communicant of the Episcopal church, and on the 2d of February, 1888, Mr. Turner was united in marriage to Miss Fanny E. Howes, of Springfield, who presides with gracious dignity over their attractive home, no children having been born of this union.

JOHN WILLARD TUTHILL

JOHN W. TUTHILL

The rapid growth of Sioux Falls is attributable to the efforts, sound judgment and public spirit of such citizens and business men as John Willard Tuthill, who is now conducting an extensive wholesale and retail business under the name of the John W. Tuthill Lumber Company. He was born in Chenango County, New York, July 6, 1846, a son of George and Hannah (Davis) Tuthill, both of whom were also natives of the Empire state. The paternal grandfather, Jeremiah Tuthill, was likewise born in that state, of English descent, the ancestral line being traced back to the decade of the '20s in the seventeenth century, when an immigrant ancestor located at Southold, on Long Island, being one of the original settlers.

At Norwich, New York, John W. Tuthill acquired his early education. It was in 1856 that his father removed with his family to Clinton, Iowa, and there he resumed his studies, mastering such branches of learning as were taught in the public schools. In 1863 he went to Chicago to obtain business training there. He secured a position with Coolbaugh & Brooks, private bankers, and while thus engaged devoted himself to the task of thoroughly mastering business principles and methods and thus gaining an accurate business education. He would advise young men to early secure a place in a bank if they wish thorough training, as bank duties promote quick thinking, punctuality and other traits which are indispensable in the attainment of success. Mr. Tuthill remained in Chicago until 1866 and then returned to Clinton, Iowa, where he entered the employ of C. Lamb & Sons, with whom he remained until 1869, when at the age of twenty-three years he went to State Center, Iowa, where he purchased a lumberyard, conducting business at that point until March, 1882. He next removed to Sioux Falls with his family and throughout the intervening period of more than thirty-two years he has engaged in the lumber trade there. He purchased a lumberyard on East Eighth street from Edwin Sharp & Company and conducted it independently until August, 1884, when the business was incorporated, John W. Tuthill becoming president; S. G. Tuthill, a brother who is now engaged in the lumber business in Minneapolis, vice president; and George L. Irvine, secretary and treasurer. At that time the present name of the John W. Tuthill Lumber Company was assumed. In addition to the yard at Sioux Falls the company then owned and conducted yards at Valley Springs, Hartford, Montrose and Salem, the last named being at that time the terminus of the Northwestern Railroad. In 1904 a reorganization was effected with John W. Tuthill as president; Peter Mintenef, of Minneapolis, vice president; A. W. Tuthill, secretary and treasurer; George B. Tuthill, general manager; and C. L. Tuthill, assistant secretary and treasurer. The business is now largely conducted under the management of the sons. The first wholesale interests of the Tuthill Lumber Company covered a trade in sash and doors, there being a large demand for such an output. The excellence of their product has won for them an enviable reputation and they largely concentrate their energies on dealing in sash and doors as wholesalers and retailers.

The organization of the Tuthill Company served as the nucleus around which gathered other business enterprises, the Tuthill concern being directly responsible for bringing to Sioux Falls other important business interests which have contributed largely to the upbuilding of the city. Since his arrival in Sioux Falls, J. W. Tuthill has been a most important factor in advancing the growth and development of the business, which is now one of the most extensive of the kind in the state. Today the company owns and operates thirty-two lumber yards, twenty-five of which are in South Dakota, six in Minnesota and one in Iowa. In supplying the yards with material and through selling to other concerns a wholesale business was gradually developed and in 1896 a warehouse was built, since which time a wholesale business has been continuously conducted with growing success. While it is owned by the John W. Tuthill Lumber Company, it is operated as a distinct and separate concern and its trade covers three states, its patrons including many of the largest line yard concerns in the northwest. The retail yard takes care of the city business, selling all kinds of building materials, coal and coke. The transfer yard, likewise under separate management, purchases and distributes to the Tuthill yards all their material which come from the four corners of the earth. Promptness in filling orders, reliability in all transactions and progressive methods have been factors in the success of the enterprise throughout the period of its existence and its moving spirit has been John W. Tuthill, today one of the most prominent, honored and prosperous business men of Sioux Falls. The Tuthill Lumber Company has a capital stock of four hundred and fifty thousand dollars and undivided profits of ninety thousand. The office and wholesale buildings include forty thousand feet of floor space.

On the 22d of September, 1868, at Columbus, Ohio, Mr. Tuthill was united in marriage to Miss Jennie M. Buck, a daughter of Solomon and Sarah Buck, and they have three sons: Arthur W., who is secretary-treasurer; George B., general manager; and Chauncey L., assistant secretary and treasurer of the company. All three are married. The last-named wedded Miss Amelia Steenson and they have one son, John Steenson Tuthill.

The religious faith of the family is that of the Congregational church. Mr. Tuthill is a Knight Templar Mason and a member of the Mystic Shrine, while his political allegiance is given to the republican party. Honored and respected by all, there is no man who occupies a more enviable position in trade circles of the city, not alone by reason of the success he has achieved, but also owing to the straightforward business policy which he has ever followed. His record, too, shows that success is not a matter of genius, as held by some, but is rather the outcome of clear judgment, experience and enterprise. Industry, persistent and unremitting, has characterized his business career. Unceasing energy and close application have constituted the keynote of his success.

LAWRENCE S. TYLER

L. S. TYLER, president of the First National Bank of Salem, McCook County, is one of the influential and honored citizens of this section of the state, and his character and prominence are such as to eminently entitle him to recognition in this history. Mr. Tyler was born in the village of Compton, province of Ontario, Canada, on the 19th of August, 1854, a son of Damon Y. and Maria (Taylor) Tyler, to whom were born four children, namely: Lewis, who is engaged in the hardware business in Salem, this state: Leonora, who is the wife of E. E. Quiggle, of Rapid City, South Dakota; Lydia, who is the wife of Henry

Seavers, of Duluth, Minnesota: and Lawrence S., who is the subject of this sketch. Damon Y. Tyler was born in the state of New Hampshire, where he was reared to maturity. As a young man he secured a position in the employ of the well-known firm of Fairbanks, Morse & Company, manufacturers of scales, in the city of Philadelphia, and while there he was married. His father had in the meanwhile removed to the province of Ontario, Canada, and he also took up his residence there, remaining but a short time and finally removing to Columbia County, Wisconsin, where he purchased a tract of railroad land and engaged in farming, to which he there continued to give his attention about ten years, at the expiration of which he took up his abode in the town of Big Spring, that county, in which vicinity he purchased a large farm. In 1867 he located in Merrimac, Sauk county, that state, where he established himself in the mercantile business, also serving as postmaster of the town for the long period of fourteen years. In 1882 he retired from active business, and he is still residing in that place, one of the honored pioneers of the state. He is a Republican in politics and both he and his wife are members of the Baptist church. The subject of this review attended the common schools until he had attained the age of fourteen years, when he began to depend upon his own resources, securing work on a farm and receiving the princely stipend of ten dollars a month for his services.

At the age of eighteen he became identified with the construction of bridges on the line of the Chicago & Northwestern Railroad, in the employ of which he continued about three years. Upon attaining his majority, he removed to Rock County, Minnesota, where he purchased a quarter section of land, in Magnolia township, where he was engaged in farming for the ensuing four years. In the spring of 1880 Mr. Tyler accepted a position with the firm of Peter Thompson & Company, prominent dealers in agricultural machinery and implements at Adrian, Minnesota, serving as their bookkeeper and general office manager until 1883, when he came to Salem, South Dakota, here erecting a substantial block and engaging in the hardware business, building up a large and prosperous enterprise and continuing the same about eighteen years. In 1888 he became associated with others in the organization of the McCook County State Bank, and in 1892, after failure of the Salem Bank, the fine building of the defunct institution was purchased of the receiver and the McCook County State Bank forthwith took possession of this newly acquired property, which is still utilized for the counting rooms of its successor, the First National Bank.

In 1899 Mr. Tyler and Mr. S. W. Appleton, now of Sioux City, acquired the entire ownership of the state bank, of which our subject had served consecutively as president from the year 1896 up to that time. In 1901 Mr. Appleton sold his stock in the institution, which was then reorganized as the First National Bank of Salem, of which Mr. Tyler was chosen president, a position he had held with the state bank up to the reorganization, while the interested principals in the new bank include the subject and C. J. Ives, F. H. Putnam and Thomas Brown, of Sioux Falls, and Thomas Bishop, of Salem. After the reorganization Mr. Tyler disposed of his hardware business, and the banking enterprise has grown to such proportions as to demand the major portion of his time and attention in his chief executive capacity. Mr. Tyler is the owner of one hundred and sixty acres of farming land in this county, seven hundred acres in Hand County, one hundred and sixty acres in Buffalo County and also a half interest in a fine farm of four hundred and eighty acres in the last-mentioned county. He owns a controlling interest in the creamery at Salem, being manager, secretary and treasurer of the Salem Creamery Association. He is treasurer of the Salem Mill and Lighting Company, treasurer of the South Dakota Dairy and Buttermaker's Association, treasurer of the school district, and secretary of the Salem Cemetery Association, in the organization of which he was associated with George Sanderson and L. V. Schneider.

He is held in the highest confidence and esteem in the county and has been called upon to serve as guardian and as administrator of important estates. Mr. Tyler is a stanch advocate of the principles of the Republican party, and has ever shown a deep interest in public affairs. He has served for more than a decade and a half as member of the village council, being incumbent of this position at the present time.

He and his wife are prominent and zealous members of the Methodist Episcopal church, of whose board of trustees he is secretary, being also incumbent of the office of steward.

Mr. Tyler has completed the circle of York Rite Masonry, being affiliated with the following bodies: Fortitude Lodge, No. 73, Ancient Free and Accepted Masons; Salem Chapter, No. 34, Royal Arch Masons; Constantine Council, No. 2, Royal and Select Masters; and Constantine Commandery, No. 17, Knights Templar, while he has also become a member of the auxiliary organization, the Ancient Arabic Order of the Nobles of the Mystic Shrine, holding membership in El Riad Temple, in Sioux Falls. He is identified with Salem Lodge, No. 28, Ancient Order of United Workmen, of which he is financier. On the 24th of January, 1877, Mr. Tyler was united in marriage to Miss Hattie Blackman, of Merrimack, Wisconsin, and to them were born three children, two of whom survive, Nellie L., the wife of Roy Palmer, of Chamberlain, South Dakota, and Grace L., who remains at the parental home.

HERBERT B. TYSELL

Herbert B. Tysell, who since September, 1902, has been editor and owner of the Marshall County Journal, published at Britton, was born at Hawley, Minnesota, June 27, 1880, a son of C. G. and Angeline (Burgess) Tysell. The father was born in Sweden in 1846 a son of Karl John Tysell, who was a member of the crack regiment of the King's Guards, stationed at the king's palace in Stockholm, Sweden. He was a very large man, straight as an arrow and of fine physique. Coming to the United States, he died at Hawley, Minnesota, at the advanced age of eighty-five years. His son, C. G. Tysell, became a resident of Hawley in 1872 and worked with a construction crew during the building of the railway to that place. He afterward homesteaded, proved up his claim and is still owner of that land. He turned from agricultural pursuits to engage in the hardware business, in which he continued successfully until a few years ago, when he retired with a substantial competence earned through his close and careful connection with business. In Hawley he married Angeline Burgess, who was born in Fayette, Maine, in 1849, a daughter of Benjamin Burgess, who was likewise a native of the Pine Tree state and there lived until 1860, when he removed to Missouri, settling near Chillicothe. He followed farming there for several years and in the early '70s went to Hawley, Minnesota, where he passed away. To Mr. and Mrs. C. G. Tysell were born six children, three of whom survive, as follows: Herbert B., of this review; John C, who is employed by the government in the agricultural experiment station at Dickinson, North Dakota; and Albion, who follows farming in North Dakota. The parents are members of the Congregational church and are people of the highest respectability, their many good traits of character winning for them wide confidence and warm regard. In his fraternal connections Mr. Tysell is an Odd Fellow, while in political belief he is a republican.

Herbert B. Tysell attended the high school of his native town and for one term was a student in the Carleton College at Northfield, Minnesota. He was afterward employed in his father's store until 1896, when he began learning the printer's trade. He worked at Moorhead, Hawley and Waseca, Minnesota, and to some extent in Wisconsin and Iowa. In February, 1902, he removed to Britton, where in September of the same year he purchased the Marshall County Journal, which now has a circulation of one thousand. In connection with the publication of the paper he conducts a good job printing office and has secured a liberal patronage in that connection. He devotes the greater part of his time to his newspaper work and has made the Journal an interesting sheet, classed with the best country papers of its part of the state.

On the 19th of April, 1905, Mr. Tysell was united in marriage to Miss Lucy Jones, a daughter of E. O. Jones, who took up his abode among the early settlers of Marshall County in 1883. He held the office of county auditor and is now living retired in Britton, having devoted his attention to agricultural pursuits throughout his active business career with excellent success. Our subject and his wife have two children: Eleanor, who is attending school; and John, who is four years of age.

Mr. Tysell belongs to the Masonic fraternity, has passed through all of the chairs of the local lodge and for seven years was secretary of the Royal Arch chapter to which he belongs. He is also identified with the consistory and with the Mystic Shrine at Aberdeen and he is likewise a member of the Modern Woodmen. In politics he is a republican and for four years filled the office of postmaster at Britton. The guiding principle of his life is found in the teachings of the Methodist Episcopal church, of which he is an attendant. His entire career has been in harmony with noble purposes and he ever endeavors to follow closely in those paths which lead to loyalty and fidelity in citizenship, to integrity and reliability in business life and to trustworthiness in every relation.

⍨

EVERETT M. VALENTINE, D. D. S.

Dentistry is unique among the professions in that it demands a threefold qualification — mechanical skill and ingenuity, a practical working knowledge of the science and the business ability which can manage the financial end. All these Dr. Everett M. Valentine possesses and he has gained a prominent place in the ranks of his profession in Yankton. He was born in Bay City, Michigan, September 14, 1866. His father, William B. Valentine, was a native of Buffalo, New York, and removed with his family to Yankton in 1870, there conducting business as a contractor and builder. He erected various churches in the town and other buildings in nearby sections and continued active in the business to the time of his death, which occurred February 12, 1906. He was also recognized as a local political leader, giving stalwart support to the republican party, but, although he served as county commissioner, he was never a politician in the usually accepted sense of office-seeking. He married Elfreda Mathias, a native of England, born at or near Greenwich near London. On coming to the new world, she lived first in Quebec, Canada, and afterward removed to Buffalo, New York, where she was married. She survives her husband and is now a resident of Chicago. To them were born four children: Florence, living in Chicago; Elfreda, the wife of L. J. Potter, also of that city; Everett M.; and Charles, who is conducting business as a contractor in Phoenix, Arizona.

Dr. Valentine was brought to Yankton when about three years of age and was reared in the city which is still his home. He passed through consecutive grades in its public schools, pursuing the high-school course, and afterward attended Yankton College, in which he was one of the first students. After his college days were over, he was employed in various ways until he decided upon a professional career, determining to take up the study of dentistry. At the age of twenty-five he entered the Missouri Dental College of St. Louis and was graduated therefrom with the D. D. S. degree in 1894. He then began practice in California, Missouri, where he remained for two years. He had an excellent practice there, but in 1896 removed to Yankton where he has since remained. He is today the oldest dentist in Yankton in years of continuous connection with the profession and he has a large practice. His office is supplied with the latest improved appliances for dental surgery and the work which he does is satisfactory to his many patrons, as is indicated by his growing success. He is a member of the South Dakota Dental Association, of which he was at one time vice president. He also belongs to the First District Dental Association and has been honored with its presidency.

In November, 1901, in California, Missouri, Dr. Valentine was united in marriage to Miss Jess Gordon, and their two children are Everett and Lucretia. The parents are members of the Congregational church, of which Dr. Valentine was formerly treasurer. His political allegiance is given to the republican party and his fraternal relations are with the Masons. He holds membership in St. John's Lodge, No. I, A. F. & A. M.; Oriental Consistory, No. I, S. P. R. S.; and El Riad Temple of the Mystic Shrine at Sioux Falls. He was at one time president of the Yankton Dramatic Club, continuing in that position for many years, and he has attained an enviable reputation as an amateur producer of plays and is an amateur actor, possessing natural dramatic talent. However, he concentrates his energies most largely upon his profession and it finds in him a prominent and worthy representative, who enjoys the confidence and respect of his colleagues and the goodwill of the general public.

JOHN S. VETTER

John S. Vetter has the distinction of being a native of the great western metropolis, the city of Chicago, where he was born on the 4th of March, 1857, being a son of George and Ursula (Knecht) Vetter, both of whom were born in the kingdom of Wurtemberg, Germany. There also was born the paternal grandfather, George Vetter, who is a land owner and a man of influence in his community, having lived a retired life in Wurtemberg for a number of years prior to his death. The maternal grandfather of our subject was a merchant tailor by vocation. George Vetter, Jr., father of him whose name initiates this review, came to America before attaining his legal majority, arriving in 1849, remaining a resident of Canada until 1851, when he removed to the city of Chicago, which then gave slight evidence of becoming a great metropolis. There he was for a time employed in the old Gage foundry and later became a minister in the German Evangelical church. He continued to be identified with the Illinois conference of this church until his death, and was assigned to various pastoral charges under its jurisdiction. In 1866 he was sent to Germany by the general conference of the church in the United States, passing two years in his fatherland and one year in Switzerland, and being accompanied by his family. He had previously served one year in the Union army during the war of the Rebellion, having enlisted as a member of the Seventy-sixth Illinois Volunteer Infantry and having been in the command of General Grant a portion of the time, while he was incumbent of the office of sergeant of his company at the time of his discharge, on account of physical disability. The father died in Aberdeen March 14, 1903. They became the parents of three children, of whom the subject is the youngest.

John S. Vetter was reared in Illinois, and after attending the public schools in various towns and cities in which his father was established as pastor, he entered Northwestern College, at Naperville, that state, where he continued his studies for two years. He then took up his abode in Kankakee, that state, where he became bookkeeper in the clothing establishment conducted by his uncle, John G. Knecht, with whom he remained five years, at the expiration of which he returned to Chicago, where he was for some time identified with the men's furnishing-goods business. In 1882 Mr. Vetter came to what is now the state of South Dakota and took up homestead, pre-emption and tree claim in Brown County, twelve miles northwest of Aberdeen. He at once began the work of developing and improving his property and still owns the same, while he has since added to his landed possessions until he now has a fine estate comprising two entire sections, while the same is devoted to diversified agriculture and to the raising of livestock. The permanent improvements on the place are of excellent order, and include a fine artesian well, sunk to a depth of eleven hundred feet. He raises principally wheat and corn, having had ninety acres of the latter in 1903, while he gives special attention to the growing of the shorthorn type of cattle and the raising of hogs.

In politics Mr. Vetter is a stanch advocate of the principles of the Republican party, and has been an active worker in its cause. In 1891 he was chosen clerk of the courts of Brown County, in which capacity he served four years, and in 1885-6 he was deputy sheriff, this being in the formative period of the history of the county, when lawlessness was often in evidence, making the office no sinecure. On the 1st of February, 1898, Mr. Vetter was appointed register of the United States land office in Aberdeen, and on the 1st of March, 1902, was reappointed, by President Roosevelt, being the present incumbent of this responsible position and having given a most able administration of the affairs of the office. He has passed the degrees of York Rite Masonry and is also identified with the Ancient Order of United Workmen, the Modern Woodmen of America and the Royal Arcanum, while he and his wife are zealous members of the Presbyterian church.

On the 12th of September, 1889, was solemnized the marriage of Mr. Vetter to Miss Elizabeth Cole, who was born in New Jersey, being a daughter of James Cole, who came to South Dakota in 1883, and resided in Edmunds County on their removal to the state of Nebraska. Mr. and Mrs. Vetter have two children, James H. and Crsula E.

FRED LESLIE VILAS

Fred Leslie Vilas, a leading and progressive merchant of Pierre, has there been engaged in the drug business for the past six years and is now the proprietor of one of the most modern and handsomely equipped establishments of the kind in the state. His birth occurred in Lake City, Minnesota, on the 27th of October, 1881, his parents being Elbert E. and Amanda (Jones) Vilas, the former a native of Michigan and the latter of Pennsylvania. He was the younger of two sons and was but two years of age when in 1883 the family home was established at Clark, South Dakota, where he attended the grammar and high schools. When a youth of fifteen he began work in a drug store and at the age of nineteen, having passed the state board examination, he enjoyed the distinction of being the youngest registered pharmacist in South Dakota. Soon afterward he embarked in the drug business on his own account at Erwin with a total capital of but twenty-seven dollars, there remaining for two years. Subsequently he spent two and a half years in business at Bryant and then removed to Brookings, where he successfully conducted a drug store for three years. In 1909 he located at Pierre, purchasing the old pioneer drug business known as the Black Hawk Medicine Company, the first drug store in that section of South Dakota. Of this establishment he has since remained the proprietor and has made it one of the most up-to-date and splendidly equipped stores in the state. He carries a complete line of drugs and druggists' sundries and has attracted and retained an extensive and gratifying patronage.

On the 27th of October, 1903, at Plankinton, South Dakota, Mr. Vilas was united in marriage to Miss Adelaide Samuels, a daughter of John Samuels. They have two children, Loraine and Fred Leslie, Jr. At the polls Mr. Vilas supports the men and measures of the democracy but is not otherwise active in politics. Fraternally he is identified with the Benevolent Protective Order of Elks and the Masons, belonging to the commandery and the Mystic Shrine. He is likewise a valued member of the Commercial Club, deeply interested in all movements tending toward the development and upbuilding of the city. In outdoor sports he finds needed recreation as well as pleasure. Mr. Vilas is a self-educated, self-made man who has builded the superstructure of his success on the sure foundation of character, ability and worth, and he has long been numbered among the representative and substantial citizens of the state in which practically his entire life has been spent.

A. W. VOEDISCH

A. W. Voedisch, the only manufacturing jeweler in South Dakota, is prominently connected with business interests of Aberdeen as proprietor of the business controlled by the Voedisch Jewelry Company, which he organized in 1894. He is also well known among the music lovers in the city and highly esteemed as the originator of the Aberdeen May Musical Festival which under his direction has become one of the important annual events in musical circles of the state. Mr. Voedisch was born in Watertown, Wisconsin, in 1872 and is a son of Frederick and Catherine Voedisch, who removed to Minnesota in 1882, taking up government land near the South Dakota line. One year and a half later they removed to North Dakota, where the father died.

A. W. Voedisch acquired a grammar and high school education and following the completion of his studies became connected with the jewelry business, in which he has since continued. In 1894, when he was twenty-two years of age, he came to Aberdeen and established the Voedisch Jewelry Company, locating his enterprise in the building now occupied by the Firey drug store. He later established himself in the Bowles building and in 1905 removed to his present location, where he has a fine store twenty-five by seventy feet in dimensions. Mr. Voedisch is the only manufacturing jeweler in South Dakota and he manufactures all kinds of solid gold goods and fills a number of special orders, doing the manufacturing for over one hundred and twenty jewelers in various parts of the northwest. He employs ten men in his manufacturing department and he has besides, a modern retail store which his able management has made a profitable business institution.

In 1899 Mr. Voedisch was united in marriage to Miss Ethel Kelly of Aberdeen and they have become the parents of two sons. Mr. Voedisch is a thirty-second degree Mason, holding membership in the lodge, chapter, commandery and Shrine, and he belongs also to the Knights of Pythias, the Benevolent Protective Order of Elks and the Ancient Order of United Workmen. His political allegiance is given to the republican party.

Mr. Voedisch is well known as the founder of the Aberdeen May Musical Festival, of which he has been director since its organization in 1901. This festival is held for three days every May and is supported by the best musical talent in the country, attracting music lovers from all parts of the northwest. Mr. Voedisch as a leading spirit in the promotion of this enterprise has been warmly commended by those of Aberdeen for the service which he has rendered the city in bringing into it each year about five thousand people of the finest type of citizenship. He is prominent in both business and musical circles and his sterling worth is manifest in the appreciation of a large circle of friends.

JOHN HOWARD VOORHEES

John Howard Voorhees, one of the prominent representatives of the bar in Sioux Falls, is connected with important business and litigated interests as a member of the well-known firm of Bailey & Voorhees. He was born in South Branch, New Jersey, February 20, 1867, and is a son of Samuel G. and Jane (Brokaw) Voorhees. The paternal branch of the family is of Holland extraction and was established on Long Island in 1660. The maternal branch is of Huguenot ancestry. In 1869 his parents removed to Middlebush, New Jersey, where he resided until he came to Sioux Falls.

John H. Voorhees, as his name is generally written, received his college preparatory education at the Rutgers grammar school at New Brunswick, New Jersey, and took his college course at Rutgers College, which is also located at New Brunswick. He graduated from that college in 1888 with the degree of A. B. In his freshman year in college, he became a member of the Zeta Psi fraternity and during his senior year he was elected to membership in the Phi Beta Kappa society. In 1891 he received from his alma mater the degree of A. M.

In October, 1888, Mr. Voorhees came to Sioux Falls and entered the law office of Charles O. Bailey. He was admitted to the bar of the territory of Dakota in 1889 and to the bar of the supreme court of the state of South Dakota shortly after statehood, and was later admitted to the bar of the supreme court of the United States. In 1891 he entered into partnership with Mr. Bailey under the firm name of Bailey & Voorhees. This relationship has continued since its formation and at the time of the writing of this sketch this firm is one of the oldest, possibly the oldest, law firms in South Dakota. It is now composed of Charles O. Bailey, John H. Voorhees, Peter G. Honegger, who became connected with it in 1904, and Theodore M. Bailey, who entered the firm in 1912. Bailey & Voorhees have been the attorneys in South Dakota for the Illinois Central Railroad Company since 1891 and they have also for the past twenty years been the counsel in South Dakota for the Western Union Telegraph Company. They are attorneys also for the Chicago, Milwaukee & St. Paul Railway Company, the American and Wells Fargo & Company Express Companies and various insurance companies. In addition, they are retained by many local and non-resident corporations and also carry on an extensive commercial law business. In their offices is a law library of over ten thousand volumes, one of the largest private law libraries west of the Mississippi river.

On the 5th of June, 1894, at Sioux Falls, Mr. Voorhees was united in marriage to Miss Bessie A. Tabor, a daughter of Holmes Tabor. Two children have been born to this marriage, Lorraine Brokaw and Mildred Tabor. The former was married October 29, 1914, to Neil Loynachan, of Manchester, New Hampshire.

Mr. Voorhees affiliates with the Episcopal church and gives his political allegiance to the republican party. He is a thirty-second degree Mason, a member of the Ancient Arabic Order of the Nobles of the Mystic Shrine and a member and a past eminent commander of Supreme Commandery, No. 2, Knights Templar, of Sioux Falls. He was a charter member of Sioux Falls Lodge, No. 262, of the Benevolent and Protective Order of Elks, and is No. 4 on the roll of membership of that lodge and is one of its past exalted rulers. He holds memberships in the Elks, the Dacotah and the Minnehaha Country Clubs of Sioux Falls.

Mr. Voorhees has been secretary of the Minnehaha County Bar Association since its organization in February, 1897, and has also been secretary of the South Dakota Bar Association since its organization in December, 1897. He is a member of the American Bar Association, has six times been a member of the general council of that association and has served on various of its committees. In 1912 he was elected a member of the executive committee of that association and was reelected to that committee in 1913 and 1914.

Mr. Voorhees has won prominence and. distinct ion in his profession and his ability and experience have been contributing factors in making the firm of Bailey & Voorhees one of the leading law firms of South Dakota and the northwest.

N. M. WADE, M. D.

N. M. Wade, is a native of Virginia and springs from one of the old families of that historic commonwealth, his ancestors for three generations having been American in all the term implies. He attended the common schools and when a young man took up the study of medicine, which he prosecuted with great assiduity, first under private instruction and later in the Chicago Medical College. He was graduated therefrom in 1880, and three years later came to South Dakota and engaged actively in the practice of his profession. Subsequently he sought a wider field in the Black Hills and since 1895 has been located at Lead City, where he enjoys a large and lucrative practice. For a while he was connected with the medical department of the United States army in the department of the Platte and at this time, he is official physician of Lead City, besides holding the position of grand medical examiner for the Ancient Order of United Workmen of South Dakota. Dr. Wade has read and studied extensively and kept himself fully abreast the times in all matters relating to his profession. He is a politician of considerable prominence, a leader of the Democratic party in Lead City and Lawrence County, and at the present time is chairman of the county central committee.

He is identified with several secret fraternal organizations, being a Knight Templar in the Masonic order, a member of the Independent Order of Odd Fellows and the Benevolent and Protective Order of Elks. Dr. Wade married Miss Anna Stanley, who was born in Wisconsin, and they are the parents of three children.

EDWARD E. WAGNER

Edward E. Wagner, one of the leading members of the South Dakota bar, practicing successfully in Sioux Falls, was born on a farm in Lyon County, Iowa, October 22, 1874. He is a son of James H. and Louisa E. (Conklin) Wagner, the former a native of Pennsylvania and the latter of Ohio. The father passed away in 1884. The family is of German origin but was founded in this country at an early day, as the grandfather of our subject was born in Pennsylvania.

Edward E. Wagner acquired his early education in the public schools of Rock Rapids, Iowa, and afterward entered the law office of H. G. McMillan at that place. In May, 1893, he was admitted to the bar by the supreme court of Iowa and opened his first office at Mitchell, South Dakota. He remained there for three years and then returned to Rock Rapids, where he spent a similar period of time. In the spring of 1899 he went to Alexandria, South Dakota, and in 1900 was elected states attorney of Hanson County, serving one term of two years. In 1904 he was elected to the state senate from district No. 11 and his record as a member of the legislative body was a commendable one, his vote and influence having been always on the side of right and progress. One year after the expiration of his term in the senate Mr. Wagner was appointed by President Roosevelt United States attorney for the district of South Dakota and in this office, he did conscientious, impartial and able work for a period of five years and a half, after which he resigned and gave his entire time to his private practice. On the 1st of January, 1910, he returned to Mitchell and there formed a partnership with Harrison C. Preston, an association which continued for three years. At the end of that time Mr. Wagner moved to Sioux Falls, where he is now engaged in general practice, being ranked among the able and successful attorneys of the city.

At Rock Rapids, Iowa, July 10, 1894, Mr. Wagner was united in marriage to Miss Alice Tresslar, a daughter of Jacob Tresslar, a veteran of the Civil War, as was also the father of our subject, who served three and a half years as private in the Twenty-fourth Iowa Volunteer Infantry. Mr. and Mrs. Wagner have become the parents of three children, Hazel, Ruth and Robert.

Mr. Wagner belongs to the Dacotah, the Country and the Elks Clubs and is connected fraternally with the Knights of Pythias and the Masons. He is a member of the Presbyterian church. His political allegiance is given to the republican party, and he has always been active in public affairs, serving with credit and ability in various positions of trust and responsibility. He was enthusiastically mentioned by his many friends and admirers as a candidate for the office of United States senator recently but refused this honor, being unwilling to take part in an arduous political campaign. However; he is now the object of a strong non-partisan movement to place him upon the bench in the second judicial district.

In discussing this movement, the Sioux Falls Press in an editorial dated November 25, 1913, said: "Mr. Wagner is not only preeminently fit for a position that calls for conscience, a clear mind, knowledge of the law and courage, but he has proven that he has a keen sense of the moral values of a situation. All these requisites of a good jurist Mr. Wagner possesses, we believe, in great abundance. We have only to hark back a few months to the occasion where, as United States district attorney, he had the courage to resign rather than to be a factor in a situation that offended his conscience, violated the intent of the law and shocked his sense of values with respect to what is right and what is wrong; there we find in Mr. Wagner the qualities which all men admire and which should belong to judges more than to any other class of men. It is to be hoped that he will accept what is offered him. Of all the important matters the voters of this circuit must decide in the approaching elections, none is more vital and far-reaching in its potentialities than the election of a circuit judge. The Press is confident that E. E. Wagner measures up to the great responsibilities of the place."

As previously stated, Mr. Wagner was appointed United States district attorney for South Dakota by President Roosevelt, and tendered his resignation on the 28th of December, 1912, on account of the attitude of Mr. Wickersham, the United States attorney general, in the celebrated case of Charles L. Hyde of Pierre. During his incumbency he had tried some well-known cases. Probably the most conspicuous, because of the results which followed it, was that of Charles L. Hyde, a banker, real-estate dealer, promoter and reputed richest man in South Dakota, who was tried and convicted in the United States district court in December, 1911, of using the mails for fraudulent purposes, it being contended by the government that through circulars and letters sent through the mails he had made false statement regarding the values of Pierre real estate and had sold almost worthless lots in Pierre for two hundred dollars and three hundred dollars in cash each to eastern people who desired to invest their savings in what they believed was property which would increase rapidly in value. The trial was hard fought by both sides and the verdict was considered a great victory for the government. Mr. Hyde was sentenced to serve one year and three months in the federal penitentiary and to pay a fine of three thousand five hundred dollars and costs. Mr. Hyde made appeal for a new trial to Judge Elliott, to the circuit court of appeals, and was denied in each case. He then petitioned President Taft to pardon him. Mr. Wagner opposed the pardoning of Hyde, holding that he had been duly convicted and that no extenuating circumstances were brought out in the case, and that Hyde's wealth should not be taken into consideration. Mr. Wickersham wanted Mr. Wagner to secure a stay of commitment and Wagner refused to comply with the request, believing that, had it been the case of a poor man, no such interference with justice would have been attempted. President Taft granted Mr. Hyde immunity from imprisonment and Mr. Wagner, believing it to be a clear case of the perverting of justice because the convicted person was a man of great wealth, whereas a poor man would have been speedily incarcerated, voiced his protest against the same, and at once withdrew from the office by resignation. Such wide attention was attracted to the case that a published statement was made by the United States attorney general setting forth the reasons why the president had taken action, and this was followed by a statement from Mr. Wagner in which he fully reviewed the evidence which had led to the conviction. The case was one of the most widely discussed ever tried in South Dakota, and, however it may be regarded by the pros and cons, it clearly shows the high, unswerving principles of honor which actuated Mr. Wagner in the discharge of his duty under his oath of office.

LEVI D. WAIT

Douglas County is favored in having so able a representative of its interests as the Armour Herald, which is recognized as one of the best county newspapers to be found in the state. Of the corporation of Wait & Dana, editors and publishers of the Herald, the subject of this sketch is the senior member and president of the company. He is a native of the state of Wisconsin, having been born in Sylvan Corners, Richland County, on the 26th of June, 1867, a son of Lorenzo and Rachel (Townsend) Wait. In the family were ten children, and of the number the following seven survive: Helen, who is the wife of J. M. Cross, of Richland County, Wisconsin; Nora, who is the wife of A. P. Monnell, of Selby, Iowa; Iona, who is the widow of William Jones, and resides in Oacoma, South Dakota; Nellie, who is the wife of E. S. Wallace, of Richland County, Wisconsin; Dighton C. resides in Richland County, Wisconsin; Charles A., who is likewise a resident of that county; and Levi D., who is the immediate subject of this sketch. Lorenzo Wait was born in the city of Cleveland, Ohio, in 1829, and there he was a boyhood friend of the late President Garfield, being reared to maturity in that city. As a young man he became identified with the lake marine industry, sailing on various vessels on the Great Lakes for a number of years, after which he removed to Wisconsin and located in Richland County, where he has since maintained his home, save for a period of twelve years passed in Kimball, South Dakota, whence he and his wife returned to their old home in Wisconsin in 1894. Both are devoted members of the Methodist Episcopal church, and in politics Mr. Wait is a stanch adherent of the Democratic party.

The subject of this sketch was reared to maturity in his native county and his educational discipline was secured in the public schools. At the age of twenty years, he entered upon an apprenticeship at the printers' trade, in the office of the Flandreau Herald, at Flandreau, South Dakota, his parents having been residents of this state at the time. He continued to be identified with the publication of this paper for three years and was thereafter employed in the office of the Pipestone Star, at Pipestone, Minnesota, until 1802, when he removed to Howard, Miner County, South Dakota, where he became editor of the Howard Advance, retaining this position one year, at the expiration of which he entered into partnership with his present associate, Mr. Dana, and purchased the plant and business of the Miner County Democrat, of Howard, continuing the publication of the paper until 1898, when Mr. Dana became the sole owner of the enterprise, having purchased our subject's interest. Mr. Wait was thereafter employed for one year as a traveling commercial salesman, and he then returned to Howard and purchased the paper and business of his former partner, the publication being continued under his control for the ensuing year. In May, 1901, he came to Armour, Douglas County, and purchased the plant of the Armour Herald, and the first edition after the property came into his hands was issued under his name, as editor and publisher. A week later, however, Mr. Dana became his associate in the enterprise, and they have since successfully carried the same forward under the firm name of Wait & Dana (recently merged into a stock company). Mr. Wait is inflexible in his allegiance to the Democratic party and takes a deep interest in the questions and issues of the hour, as well as in local affairs of a public nature. He has just completed a term as alderman for the city of Armour. In 1900 he was chosen permanent secretary of the Democratic state convention at Yankton, and since that time has been identified more or less with the organization of the party in the state. Mr. Wait has devoted a great deal of time and energy the past winter to furthering the ambitions of Hon. E. S. Johnson to become national Democratic committeeman for South Dakota, and at the state convention in Sioux Falls March 30, 1904, saw his efforts rewarded by the unanimous election of Mr. Johnson to the head of the party within the state. By reason of his activity in party councils Mr. Wait is probably one of the best-known Democrats in South Dakota today, and has the respect and esteem of his party and business associates at all times. During the summer of 1903, Mr. Wait was one of the prime movers in the organization of the Publishers' Mutual Insurance Association. For Huron, now the strongest mutual insurance company in the state. Mr. Wait was elected its first president and was unanimously re-elected by the board of directors at their annual 1904 meeting. He is also serving his second term as treasurer of the South Dakota Press Association, one of the strongest bodies of newspaper men in the United States. He is a thorough churchman of the Protestant Episcopal church, of which he was made a communicant in 1900, and he is now warden of the parish in Armour.

Fraternally he is identified with the Masons, Knights of Pythias and the Modern Woodmen of America. On the 25th of February, 1893, was solemnized the marriage of Mr. Wait to Miss Lulu A. Wallace, of Kimball, this state, and they are the parents of one son, Harry W., who was born on the 8th of September, 1895. Mrs. Wait also is a communicant of the Episcopal church and is an active worker in the same.

EDWIN OLIVER WALGREN

Edwin Oliver Walgren is the secretary and treasurer of the Schwenk-Barth Brewing Company, one of the large productive industries of Yankton. He was born in Galesburg, Knox County, Illinois, January 29, 1866. His father, Charles Walgren, a native of Sweden, crossed the Atlantic to America in 1856 and at different periods worked in the pineries of Minnesota and of Arkansas but ultimately returned to his native land in 1865. There he married, after which he brought his young wife to the new world. They settled in Illinois and there Mrs. Walgren passed away in the fall of 1868, when their son Edwin Oliver was less than three years of age. The father followed farming, having purchased a tract of land in Knox County, Illinois, which he continuously cultivated and improved until 1888, when he retired from active farm life and removed to Dixon, Illinois, where he passed away in 1903.

Edwin Oliver Walgren was the eldest in his father's family. He was reared upon the home farm to the age of nineteen years and then started out in the business world, securing a position as bookkeeper after having pursued a course of study preparing him for work of that character at the Northern Illinois Normal school and Dixon Business College. His position as bookkeeper was in a general store at Dixon, where he continued for thirteen years, or until 1899, a fact unmistakably evidencing his capability, his efficiency and his trustworthiness. His thorough study and experience made him an expert accountant, and he won a wide and well merited reputation in that direction.

In 1899 Mr. Walgren arrived in Yankton, South Dakota, where he has since made his home. He was first employed in checking up for the Building & Loan Association and did work as an accountant for the county treasurer and others. In July, 1901, he embarked in the restaurant business, which he conducted for four years, or until 1905. In the meantime, he acquired an interest in the brewery which was incorporated in May, 1903. He assumed charge of the office at that date, being elected secretary and treasurer, in which connections he has since continued, contributing in large measure to the success of the company through the capable manner in which he controls its business and financial affairs.

In July, 1901, Mr. Walgren was married to Miss Maud Vore, a native of Logan, Harrison County, Iowa, and they have one son, William Edwin, who is now attending school. Mr. Walgren has advanced through both the York and Scottish Rites in Masonry since becoming a member of St. John's Lodge, No. I, F. & A. M. He also belongs to Yankton Chapter, No. I, R. A. M., of which he is a past high priest; Omego Council, No. 2, R. & S. M., of Salem, South Dakota; De Molay Commandery, No. 3, K. T.; Oriental Consistory, No. I, A. A. S. R., in which he has attained the thirty-second degree of the Scottish Rite and of which he is preceptor; and Yelduz Temple, A. A. O. N. M. S., of Aberdeen, South Dakota. He likewise has membership in the Elks Lodge, No. 994; the Eagles Aerie, No. 1486; and Phoenix Lodge, No. 34, K. P., in which he is chancellor commander. He is also connected with Yankton Council of the United Commercial Travelers and is a member of the Improved Order of Red Men, of which he was the first great sachem for South Dakota. His political indorsement is given to the republican party, but he has never sought nor desired office, preferring to give undivided attention to his business affairs. Indefatigable energy and close application have featured most strongly in his success. He has worked hard and merit has won its true reward, so that he is now one of the prosperous business men of his city.

DELBERT T. WALKER

Delbert T. Walker, superintendent of schools for Codington County and proprietor of the Watertown Commercial College, is a native of the Hawkeye state, having been born in Mount Auburn, Benton County, Iowa, on the 25th of July, 1867, and being a son of George H. and Julia S. (Gillette) Walker, the former of whom was born in England and the latter in the state of Connecticut, while they were numbered among the pioneers of Benton County, Iowa, where they still maintain their home, the father of our subject having been formerly engaged in farming and in mercantile pursuits, while for nearly a decade and a half he has served as postmaster at Mount Auburn, being one of the honored and influential citizens of the county. He came to America in 1843, and was a resident of Iowa at the time of the outbreak of the war of the Rebellion. He signalized his loyalty to the land of his adoption, since, in 1862, he enlisted as a private in Company G. Thirteenth Iowa Volunteer Infantry, with which he was in active service until the close of the war, when he received his honorable discharge. He participated in many of the most notable battles of the great conflict, having been a member of General Grant's forces at Chattanooga and Vicksburg. while later he took part in the Atlanta campaign and accompanied Sherman on the ever-memorable march to the sea.

The subject, who is the only child of his parents, completed the curriculum of the public schools of his native town, being graduated in the Mount Auburn high school as a member of the class of 1887, while later he completed courses in the commercial and normal departments of the Cedar Rapids (Iowa) Business College, being graduated in each. He also was for a time a student in the Iowa State University, at Iowa City, but did not complete a course. Mr. Walker began, teaching at the age of eighteen years, and in 1890 came to Watertown to accept the position of principal of the commercial college here, retaining the incumbency for a period of five years. after which he was for one year principal of the Curtis Business College, in St. Paul, Minnesota. He then returned to his native town, where he was principal of the public schools for one and one-half years, when he resigned and returned to Watertown, purchasing the Watertown Commercial College, which he has since conducted, having greatly amplified the functions and usefulness of the institution and brought it up to the highest standard of excellence in all its departments. He was elected county superintendent of schools in 1900, and that his course met with popular endorsement was shown in his re-election, in 1902, without opposition. He is enthusiastic in his work, a careful and conscientious executive, and has done much to further educational interests in the county. He is a member of the board of trustees of the public library of Watertown and took an active part in securing the donation for the new Carnegie library, which is to be erected in the near future, at a cost of fifteen thousand dollars.

Professor Walker is a stanch advocate of the I principles and policies of the Republican party, and fraternally is prominently identified with the Masonic order and the Knights of Pythias. In the former he has completed the round of the York Rite bodies, including the commandery of Knights Templar, while he has served as worshipful master of the blue lodge, and as recorder of Watertown Commandery, No. 7, Knights Templar, and keeper of records and seals of Trishocotyn Lodge, No. 17, Knights of Pythias, having held the latter office ever since he was constituted a Knight of Pythias with the exception of an interval of six months, while in 1893 he represented the local Masonic lodge in the grand lodge of the state, at Deadwood, and has thrice been a delegate to the grand lodge of the Knights of Pythias in South Dakota.

On the 25th of July, 1892, Professor Walker was united in marriage to Miss May A. Slattery, who was born in Ohio, being a daughter of David A. and Margaret (Jones) Slattery, the former now deceased and the latter is now a resident of Watertown, South Dakota. She had been a successful teacher in the public schools of South Dakota prior to her marriage. Professor and Mrs. Walker have two children, Blaine E. and Hazel M. Watertown Commercial College was established in 1887. The school enrolls from one hundred to one hundred and twenty-five pupils per year and is adding from fifteen to twenty percent, increase each year. The courses are commercial, shorthand and typewriting, and normal.

JAMES WALKINS

James Walkins needs no introduction to the readers of this volume, for he is well and favorably known in Sioux Falls as a member of the firm of Walkins & McDonald, one of the leading real-estate firms in the city. He was born in Brooklyn, New York, in 1862 and at the age of five years went to Tipton, Iowa, where he was reared upon a farm. Later he turned his attention to agricultural pursuits, engaging in that occupation in the vicinity of Tipton until he located in Sioux Falls. He purchased one thousand eight hundred acres of land in Minnehaha County and with Sioux Falls as his headquarters engaged extensively in farming and stock-raising, buying, selling and shipping cattle on an extensive scale.

In 1905 he turned his attention to the real-estate business and in 1909 associated himself with Charles S. McDonald, forming the present firm of Walkins & McDonald. Believing that location is as much to be considered in the real-estate business as in any other, the partners procured the very best by taking a long-term lease on their present quarters in the Cataract Hotel building on West Ninth street and, knowing that no merchant can sell goods to advantage unless he is directly interested, they began investing in city property and farm lands and today the county records show that they are the heaviest owners of Sioux Falls city property and Minnehaha county farming lands in their locality. From the very beginning their success was assured. Their personal acquaintance and reputation were such that when they formed a partnership more business came to them in a short time than it is sometimes possible to obtain in many years. As a result, they have taken the front rank among the real-estate dealers in Sioux Falls, a position usually held by a firm of greater age, but in this instance made possible by a strict adherence to good business principles. Their record of sales shows that clients to whom they have sold property often buy realty of them again and that men to whom they have sold land afterward make them their agents when they have property to sell. In the real-estate business no better indorsement of a firm can be given than this. Both Mr. Walkins and Mr. McDonald are enthusiastic allies of any scheme which has as its object the further advancement of Sioux Falls and the state of South Dakota. Each is thoroughly familiar with the conditions which have made the city and state what they are today and this knowledge is one of the most valuable assets the company has in its present line of business. Mr. Walkins gives practically all of his time and attention to the affairs of the firm and his judgment on everything connected with land values is accepted as authoritative.

At Iowa City, Iowa, Mr. Walkins married Miss Anna B. Wingert and they have become the parents of four children: Myrtle Belle, the wife of Arthur Dunn, of Sioux Falls; Earl M.; Floyd J.; and Edna Grace. Mr. Walkins is a member of the Methodist Episcopal church and belongs to the Mystic Shrine. He gives his political allegiance to the republican party but has never been active as an office seeker, preferring to concentrate his attention upon his business affairs. In these he has been most successful and much credit is due him for the position which he has attained among the substantial and representative business men of Sioux Falls.

JOSEPH MARK WALSH, M. D.

Dr. Joseph Mark Walsh is successfully engaged in the practice of medicine at Fort Pierre and enjoys a merited reputation as an able representative of his chosen calling. His birth occurred at Yankton, Dakota territory, on the 27th of July, 1877, his parents being Edward John and Ellen (Melloy) Walsh, who came to Yankton County in the late '60s and settled in the vicinity of Walshtown.

Dr. Joseph M. Walsh acquired his more specifically literary education in the schools of Yankton and Yankton College and subsequently prepared for the medical profession as a student in the University of Illinois, which institution conferred upon him the degree of M. D. on the 10th of May, 1905. Fort Pierre has since remained the scene of his professional labors, and his practice has steadily grown as he has demonstrated his skill and ability in coping with the intricate problems which continually confront the physician in his efforts to restore health and prolong life.

On the 24th of April, 1902, in Omaha, Nebraska, Dr. Walsh was united in marriage to Miss Jeanette Joslyn, a daughter of Mr. and Mrs. J. G. Joslyn, of Kingston, Wisconsin. They have a son, Francis Mark Walsh, who was born on the 10th of May, 1912; and a daughter, Bonnie, born March 11, 1914.

Dr. Walsh is a member of St. John's Lodge, No. I, A. F. & A. M., of Yankton. He is popular in both professional and social circles of his community and has won recognition as a worthy and valued native son of the Dakotas.

CYRUS WALTS

Cyrus Walts, is of sturdy German lineage, the name having originally been spelled Walz, and is a native of the state of New York, having been born in Watertown, Jefferson County, on the 24th of March, 1844, being a son of William and Louise Walts, both of whom were likewise born and reared in the Empire state, the respective families having there located in an early day. The subject was reared on a farm and early became familiar with the strenuous toil of tilling the soil, while his educational training in his youth was secured in the common schools of northern New York. This has been most effectively supplemented by personal application and judicious study in later years, as well as by the valuable lessons gained in the great school of experience. He remained identified with farm work until he had attained the age of twenty-two years, when he set forth to seek his fortunes in the west, having arrived in Sioux Falls, South Dakota, in 1869, and having here followed for a number of years his profession of surveyor and civil engineer, for which he had fitted himself while still a resident of New York. In 1872 he was chosen clerk of the United States district court, retaining this position for the long period of fifteen years, and being a valued and trusted official. For fourteen years he was a member of the board of education of Sioux Falls, having been its president for one year and having taken a deep interest in forwarding educational interests here, while for two years he served as county superintendent of schools. He was admitted to the bar of the territory in 1887, having given much time to the technical reading of the law and having thus fitted himself for the active work of the profession, though he has not practiced directly to any considerable extent. In 1898 he was elected city justice of the peace, and reelected in 1902, of which office he has since been incumbent, and in this capacity, he has gained a high reputation for fair and impartial rulings.

In politics Mr. Walts gives his allegiance to the Republican party. Fraternally he is affiliated with Minnehaha Lodge, No. 5, Ancient Free and Accepted Masons; of Sioux Falls Chapter, No. 2, Royal Arch Masons; Cyrene Commandery, No. 2, Knights Templar, and El Riad Temple of the Ancient Arabic Order of the Nobles of the Mystic Shrine. On the 15th of May 1873, was solemnized the marriage of Mr. Walts to Miss Mary A. Benton, who was born in the city of Columbus, Ohio, on the 13th of September, 1853, being a daughter of Porter W. and Harriet (Phelps) Benton. She has the distinction of having been the first teacher in the first public school in Sioux Falls, having been thus employed here during a portion of the years 1870-71. Mr. and Mrs. Walts have three children, Charles C, who is now engaged with R. G. Dun & Company Mercantile Agency as assistant manager at Buenos Ayres, South America; Harriet L., wife of George W. Stearns, managing editor of the St. Louis Globe-Democrat, and Hope V., wife of M. J. Gochey, of Duluth, Minnesota.

Prominently identified with various business and corporate interests of Aberdeen, A. L. Ward has risen by force of his ability, executive power and initiative spirit to a high place in commercial affairs of that city, where since 1885 he has made his home. He is the founder and promoter of the Ward Hotel and is connected also with the Ward-Owsley Company, wholesale and manufacturing confectioners, and his extensive interests have made him for many years a force in promoting the prosperity of the city.

Mr. Ward was born in 1861 and was taken to Linn County, Iowa, by his parents in 1866, acquiring his education in the public schools of that locality. In 1882 he came to South Dakota, where he took up government land in Beadle County, proving up his claim and continuing to reside upon his farm until 1885. In that year he came to Aberdeen and opened the first modern restaurant in the city, conducting this enterprise successfully for some years thereafter. In 1897 he erected the Ward Hotel, of which he has since been the proprietor and which under his capable and intelligent management has become one of the leading hostelries in the city. It has ninety rooms and twenty-five baths and is well furnished and completely equipped, provided with all the conveniences and accessories necessary to the comfort of the guests. Mr. Ward is interested also in the Sherman Hotel and is a director in the Aberdeen Railway, which he aided in promoting. In addition to these connections, he is also well known as one of the organizers of the Ward-Owsley Company, wholesale and manufacturing confectioners, and since the foundation of this enterprise he has given a great deal of time to its affairs. The company owns a two-story building with one-hundred-foot frontage and controls a large business in all departments, giving employment to forty people in the home plant and to four traveling salesmen.

In 1894 Mr. Ward was united in marriage to Miss Carrie H. Paulhamus, who came to Aberdeen with her mother in 1883. Mr. and Mrs. Ward have become the parents of two children, a son and a daughter. Mr. Ward is a thirty-second degree Mason, holding membership in the lodge, chapter, commandery and Shrine; is affiliated with the Knights of Pythias, and gives his political allegiance to the republican party. He has been a resident of Aberdeen for thirty years and has during that period been closely and influentially associated with business interests of the city. He has won a gratifying degree of success and his influence has been a tangible force for good in community development.

F. B. WARD

F. B. WARD, is a son of James and Levina (Barber) Ward, old residents of Jefferson County, in the Empire state. They lived at Carthage and there, in 1838, F. B. Ward was born, his early education being obtained in the schools of his native place. At a later period, he had the benefit of a course in a normal school at Albany, where he was graduated in 1859. Shortly after this event he engaged in the mercantile business and in 1874 returned to the place of his nativity at Carthage, where his parents were still living. In 1882 he decided to cast his lot with the rapidly rising commonwealth of the west and obtaining a position as surveyor with the Northwestern Railroad Company, he assisted in the survey of that line from Hawarden, Iowa, to Iroquois, South Dakota. He filed a claim on a quarter section of land in Miner County, planned a town site and named the embryonic city Carthage, in honor of the old home in New York state, where he had spent his boyhood days. The growth of the place was rapid and its development was largely due to the enterprise and business foresight of Mr. Ward. He it was who built the Palmer House and established the Plank of Carthage, the latter important event in the town's early career occurring in 1883.

This bank is the oldest in Miner County and enjoys the distinction of having weathered all the financial storms occurring during the formation period of the Dakotas, which wrecked so many other struggling financial institutions. Mr. Ward has always been an ardent Republican in politics, but, while ever ready to help along the cause by word of mouth and timely work, he has never sought political rewards and kept aloof from office seeking.

Mr. Ward's fraternal connections are with the Masonic fraternity, the Independent Order of Odd Fellows and the Benevolent and Protective Order of Elks. In 1860 Mr. Ward was united in marriage with Miss Harris, of Harrisville, New York, who shared his fortunes in the west until claimed by death, in 1892. Subsequently Mr. Ward was married to Miss Langley and has one child named Francis B.

WILLIAM WARD

William Ward, as senior member of the firm of Ward & Trux, doing business at No. 337 Douglas Street in Yankton, is conducting the largest meat business in the city. He is a native of Cambridgeshire, England, born on the 17th of February, 1852, a son of Daniel and Ann (Sherman) Ward, both natives of that section of the country, where the father carried on agricultural pursuits. He is deceased but the mother survives.

William Ward, the eldest in a family of four children, received his education in the public schools of his native land and was there reared to the age of sixteen years, at which time he emigrated to the new world, the year of his arrival here being 1868. Landing in New York he made his way to Little Falls, that state, where his uncles were located. He secured employment on a farm and was thus engaged until he had attained his majority, when he made his way to Bay City, Michigan, and there became apprenticed to the butcher's trade. In 1877 after learning the business he removed to Yankton, South Dakota, where he has since been located. His first employment there was with the firm of Wooley & Wyman and in the fall of 1879, Mr. Wooley having retired Mr. Ward purchased his interest and the firm then did business under the style of Wyman & Ward, their concern being situated at Third and Douglas streets. The business was thus continued until the fall of 1898 when the partnership was dissolved, Mr. Ward retiring from the firm. For a brief period, he visited Chicago and points in Colorado and then once more returned to Yankton to again engage in the meat business. This time he bought a half interest with Mr. Branch but after a short time the latter retired from the firm and Mr. Ward continued business alone until 1906, when Mr. Trux purchased a half interest, the establishment being now conducted under the firm style of Ward & Trux. They are the largest meat dealers in the city and keep on hand at all times the best grade of meats, doing all their own killing. Mr. Ward understands the business to the minutest detail and this coupled with his excellent management has constituted the foundation for his splendid success.

In 1884 Mr. Ward married Miss Mary Alice Parsons, a native of Illinois. He belongs to Dakota Lodge, No. I, I. O. O. F. and to Yankton Encampment, No. 2. He is also prominent in Masonic circles, belonging to St. John's Lodge, No. I, A. F. & A. M., having attained the thirty-second degree in Oriental Consistory, No. I, and being a member of Yelduz Temple of the Nobles of the Mystic Shrine at Aberdeen. His many excellent characteristics have given him high standing in the city which has been his home for almost four decades.

HENRY B. WARDMAN

Henry B. Wardman, engaged in the hardware, plumbing and sheet metal business at Deadwood, was born in Buffalo, New York, August 22, 1845, a son of William and Jane (Martin) Wardman. The father was born in Yorkshire, England, and the mother was a native of Dublin, Ireland. Mr. Wardman followed farming, and after his marriage, which was celebrated in Canada, came with his young wife to the United States, settling in Buffalo, New York, where he died in 1848. His widow long survived and passed away in Buffalo about 1883.

Henry B. Wardman was only four years of age at the time of his father's death. He attended the public schools of Buffalo and in his youthful days learned the tinner's trade in that city. In 1868 he came west, making his way to Cheyenne, Wyoming, and afterward working as a journeyman tinner to the coast. In 1878 he arrived in Deadwood, where he worked at his trade until 1884. In that year he entered into partnership with George V. Ayers in the establishment and conduct of a hardware business, in which he continued until 1898, when he sold out to Mr. Ayers and went upon the road as a traveling salesman for a wholesale hardware firm, which he represented for two years. He next went to New Mexico, where he resided for six months in order to benefit his health, which had become somewhat impaired. On the expiration of that period, he returned to Deadwood and opened a plumbing establishment. He also deals in hardware and does all kinds of tin and sheet metal work, as well as taking contracts in plumbing. He devotes his entire time to the management a conduct of this business and is also the owner of city property, for he has made judicious investments in real estate here.

Mr. Wardman has been married twice. In 1885 he wedded Miss Alma Hammond, who was born in Ohio. Her parents, Thomas B. and Belle Hammond, came to Deadwood in 1878, and after living on Centennial Prairie for a time took up their abode in the city of Deadwood. At a later date they removed to the state of Washington and the father died on a ranch near Winanche. The mother now makes her home in Winanche. Mrs. Wardman passed away in San Diego, California, and her remains were brought back to Deadwood for interment. There were two children of that marriage: Warren, who married a Miss Boase and resides in Los Angeles, California, where he is engaged in the real-estate business; and Ruth, the wife of A. B. Read, also of Los Angeles, who is engaged in the ice-manufacturing business. On the 10th of October, 1899, Mr. Wardman was again married, his second union being with Miss Catherine Phillips, who was born in Fremont, Nebraska, a daughter of Lee and Hattie (Fullenweider) Phillips, who in 1878 arrived in Deadwood, where the father engaged in the grocery business until his death. Mrs. Phillips now resides with Mr. and Mrs. Wardman.

Mr. Wardman belongs to the Masonic fraternity, is a past master of the blue lodge and has taken the degrees of the Scottish Rite and the Mystic Shrine. He is connected with the Benevolent Protective Order of Elks and attends the Christian Science church. With him opportunity has spelled success. He has worked his way steadily upward, urged on by ambition and unfaltering determination, and the prosperity which has come to him is the direct result of his own labors.

CHARLES PARKER WARREN

Charles Parker Warren, attorney at law of Huron, was born at Oronoco, Minnesota, April 28, 1873. His father, Josiah H. Warren, was both a farmer and builder and after living for a considerable period in Minnesota removed to Dakota territory in 1882, settling in Kingsbury County, where he engaged in farming until his death in 1902. His wife, who bore the maiden name of Mary A. Gibson, is now living in Highmore, South Dakota.

In their family were four children, of whom Charles Parker Warren is the third in order of birth. He was a lad of nine years when brought to this state and in the district schools he acquired his early education, later attending the high school at Iroquois, South Dakota, and the Western Normal School at Lincoln, Nebraska. He then entered the University of South Dakota, in which he pursued his classical course, and afterward became a student in the Law University of Minnesota, from which he was graduated with the class of 1901. Mr. Warren located for practice at De Smet, South Dakota, and while there residing served for two terms as states attorney, making a creditable record in that position. After a residence there of about nine years he removed to Huron in 1910, joining ex-Governor Coe I. Crawford in a partnership under the firm style of Crawford & Warren. This relation is still maintained and the firm occupies an enviable position at the bar of the state.

In his political views Mr. Warren has always been a republican since age conferred upon him the right of franchise. He is identified with several leading fraternal organizations, including the Masons, the Independent Order of Odd Fellows, the Knights of Pythias and the Benevolent Protective Order of Elks. He is a member of the Huron Commercial Club and is filling the office of president. His interest in behalf of the general welfare is manifest in many tangible and effective ways and his cooperation proves a potent force in advancing the general interests of the community. He belongs to the South Dakota State and the American Bar Associations and in his profession has steadily advanced. He worked his way through college, teaching at intervals between college terms, and the strength of character which enabled him to pursue that course has been one of the potent elements on which he has builded his later success. Since beginning the active work of the profession, he has constantly advanced, and the court records bear testimony to his ability in the practice of law.

EDWARD H. WARREN

Edward H. Warren, owner and editor of the Queen City Mail, published at Spearfish, was born in Horicon, Dodge County, Wisconsin, February 6, 1859, a son of James H. and Augusta B. (Horton) Warren. The father was born in Eden, Erie County, New York, September 4, 1820, and his wife's birth occurred in western Pennsylvania, March 12, 1831. In early life he went to Ohio and in 1845 removed to Wisconsin, settling near Milwaukee. He taught penmanship and other branches and also followed the trades of a carpenter and mason, but later in that year he returned to Ohio, where he took up the study of medicine. He also made several trips to the Allegheny mountains, gathering blazing star root and other herbs of medical value, which he took to Cincinnati and sold. Returning to Wisconsin, he settled in Dodge County, near Mayville, where he engaged in hunting, and sold deer skins, which were manufactured into mittens and gloves. He also gathered wild honey, for which he found a market, and in fact he resorted to every honorable method to secure a dollar and gain a start in life. In 1852 he entered the employ of the firm of Hamilton & Bishop, proprietors of a linseed oil mill, remaining thus employed for a year or more.

In 1859 he established his home in Trempealeau County, Wisconsin. He remained for a year at Arcadia and in 1862 went to Eau Claire, where he worked for the Daniel Shaw Lumber Company as a scaler in the summer and as head millwright in the winter months.

There he continued until May, 1866, when he built a flatboat thirty-three feet long, twelve feet wide and three feet deep. With the family aboard the boat floated down to Dubuque, where they sold the boat and by rail proceeded to Iowa Falls and thence by team to Algona, Kossuth County. They took up their abode in an old log cabin south of Algona, where a number of months were spent, and later they became residents of Algona, where the father engaged in carpenter work. In 1866 he purchased a newspaper plant of Mrs. Read and without experience in that line of work began the publication of a paper, the Upper Des Moines. In order to make ends meet he found it necessary to work at his trade of building houses, plastering or laying brick, at all of which he was proficient, and he wrote his copy for the newspaper in the evenings. During the first year or two of his careers as a newspaper publisher the only press which he had was one of the Washington types, the first one brought into Iowa. In 1868 he purchased a Ruggles job press at Fort Dodge, the first ever introduced in that county, and it did service until 1880. In 1870 the Upper Des Moines purchased a cylinder press and Mr. Warren went to Milwaukee and bought a Potter cylinder, which did good service until the Upper Des Moines ceased to exist as a separate business in 1902. When he settled in Iowa the nearest railroad was eighty miles distant and the entire country round about was sparsely settled. It was uphill work establishing a profitable newspaper, for at that time paper sold for from eight to twelve dollars per bundle. He served as postmaster at Algona, Iowa, for three years and as deputy United States revenue collector for three years. He was also county supervisor at Estherville, Emmet County, Iowa. At the time of the Civil War, he attempted to enlist but because of physical disability was not accepted.

In the summer of 1888, he made his way to the Black Hills and in January, 1889, established the Queen City mail at Spearfish, conducting it as a daily paper for five years. The daily, known as the Daily Bulletin, was discontinued in August, 1894, but the weekly edition was published. Mr. Warren remained at Spearfish until the July prior to his death and was active in the management of the paper. He passed away August 31, 1895, and his wife died on the 8th of November, 1904. They were the parents of three children. Eliza L., who was born February 2, 1848, was married November 9, 1870, at Algona, Iowa, to Hugh Waterhouse and died in 1908. Robert B., born December 1, 1850, is engaged in the printing business in Spokane, Washington.

Edwin H. Warren, the youngest of the family, attended the public schools at Algona, Iowa, and when eighteen years of age, having previously learned the printer's trade under his father, was employed as foreman in the office of the Vindicator at Estherville, Iowa. He remained in that position for eighteen months and then returned to Algona, where he continued from January, 1880, until January, 1884. He was next at St. Paul on the Pioneer Press for several years, after which he again went to Iowa and established a paper at West Bend, Palo Alto County, where he continued for a year and a half. In July, 1888, he went to Rapid City, South Dakota, where he was connected with the Daily Republican until with his father, he established the Queen City Mail at Spearfish. He has been continuously engaged in the publication of this paper since that time except for a period of three years following the sale of his plant, and he was also out of the business while in the county auditor's office. He repurchased the plant and is now actively engaged in the publication of this paper, which he publishes in a substantial building that he owns. He now devotes his entire time to the Mail and has made it a very readable and attractive journal.

On the 15th of July, 1881, Mr. Warren was united in marriage to Miss Flora C. Bates, who was born July 1, 1860, in the southeastern part of Iowa, a daughter of O. C. and Mary (Sweeting) Bates, the former a native of western Pennsylvania and the latter of Michigan. The father was a newspaper man and went to

Iowa long prior to the Civil War. Until 1885 he was continuously engaged in newspaper work at various points in Iowa. He removed from that state to Atkinson, Nebraska, where he resided until about 1900 and then came to South Dakota. He is now living retired and spends most of his time in the home of Mr. and Mrs. Warren. His wife passed away in Aberdeen, South Dakota, in 1912. He was at one time a postmaster in Iowa. To Mr. and Mrs. Warren have been born three children. James R., born June 19, 1882, and now serving as deputy postmaster at Spearfish, married May 9, 1903, Olive May Packard, of Sturgis, who was born in 1882. They have one child, Russell Edward, born February 22, 1904. Nellie G., born January 2, 1886, is a graduate of the Normal School at Spearfish and is now superintendent of schools for Lawrence County, South Dakota. Hazel, born January 3, 1890, was graduated on the completion of a special course in domestic science from the Spearfish State Normal School.

Mr. Warren belongs to the Masonic fraternity, holding membership in the lodge and chapter. He has served through all of the chairs in the former and for two terms was master of the blue lodge. He was also junior deacon pro tem of the grand lodge in Pierre, and at Huron was appointed junior warden. In 1897 he was appointed senior warden at the grand lodge in Mitchell. He took his first degree of the chapter in 1901, was exalted in January, 1902, was elected scribe in 1906 and served for two years, afterward filled the office of king for one year, then high priest for one year, and in 1912 received the degree of high priesthood at the grand lodge in Deadwood. There is no duty too arduous for him to undertake to advance the cause of Masonry and he exemplifies in his life the beneficent spirit of the craft. He is also connected with the Knights of Pythias and the Owls. Politically a stalwart republican, he served for two terms in the state legislature during the sessions of 1899 and 1901. He was also county auditor of Lawrence County for two years and was a member of the board of education of Spearfish for two years. His interest in public affairs is deep and sincere and he cooperates heartily in all measures and movements which he deems of benefit and value to the community and to the commonwealth. His life has been a busy and useful one fraught with activity in business and in behalf of public interests and his labors have been productive of good results.

FREDERICK A. WARREN

Frederick A. Warren, states attorney and an active and prominent representative of the Flandreau bar, was born at Green Bay, Wisconsin, on the 13th of August, 1877, a son of O. O. and Rasminnie Warren. The father was a lumberman of Wisconsin and on leaving that state removed to South Dakota and located on a farm northwest of Flandreau in 1878, thus becoming one of the early residents of that section. He afterward followed the occupation of carpentering and also carried on farming but has now put aside further business cares and duties and is living retired in Flandreau, where he and his wife have many friends.

In the State Normal School at Madison, Frederick A. Warren continued his education after leaving the public schools and still later was a student in Fremont College, from which he was graduated with the class of 1900. He next entered the Nebraska University, where he pursued a law course and was graduated in 1903. Immediately afterward he came to Flandreau, opened an office and entered upon the active practice of his profession. He has been successful from the start. No dreary novitiate awaited him; he was well versed in the knowledge of law and it was but a brief period before he demonstrated his ability to successfully cope with the intricate problems that continually confront the attorney. Moreover, he gave evidence of preparing his cases with great thoroughness and skill and in the presentation of his cause his arguments were sound and his deductions followed with logical sequence. He was soon accorded a liberal clientage and, in the fall of 1910, he was elected states attorney on the democratic ticket without opposition, even though this is a strong republican locality. He made such an excellent record during his first term that he was reelected in 1912.

After commencing the practice of law Mr. Warren became a member of the South Dakota Bar Association and worked faithfully in placing the association on a high plane and in recognition of his services the association unanimously elected him as its president in January, 1915. During his presidency of the bar association considerable has been accomplished in reformation of procedure and practice and in simplifying appellate procedure.

Mr. Warren was married on the 31st of May, 1906, to Miss Clara Moen, a daughter of the Rev. C. J. Moen, of the United Lutheran church. Their children are Flora, Waldo, Stanford and Eleanor.

Mr. and Mrs. Warren hold membership in the United Lutheran church and are people of genuine worth, highly esteemed by all who know them. In the year 1913 Mr. Warren was a candidate for United States attorney. Fraternally he is well known as a Mason, belonging to the lodge, chapter, commandery and to the Mystic Shrine. He is also affiliated with both the subordinate lodge and encampment of Odd Fellows. He enjoys hunting and when leisure permits indulges his taste for that sport. He is very popular and well liked, having a circle of friends almost coextensive with the circle of his acquaintances. His high standing in public regard is due to the fact that he has ever been loyal to the trusts reposed in him, that he has ever been progressive in citizenship, that he is faithful in friendship and kindly in disposition.

SAMUEL PRENTISS WATKINS

Samuel Prentiss Watkins, who stands as one of the leading members of the bar of Spink County, comes of stanch old New England stock, the genealogy in the paternal line being of English and Scotch derivation and in the maternal of English, while both families were founded in New England in the colonial epoch. Mr. Watkins was born in Cambridge, Lamoille County, Vermont, on the 22d of July, 1855. and is a son of David H. and Harriet A. (Holmes) Watkins. The father was born in Walpole, New Hampshire, whither his paternal ancestors came from Connecticut, while on his mother's side the ancestors were from England. The mother of the subject was born in Grafton, Massachusetts, with the annals of which state the family name was identified for many generations, the original progenitors in the new world having come from England.

The subject received his early education in the common schools of the old Green Mountain state and later continued his studies in the public schools of Massachusetts and in Grafton Academy, at Grafton, that state, and the Wesleyan Academy, at Wilbraham, prosecuting his educational work in these two institutions in the four years intervening between 1871 and 1876. Thereafter he was successfully engaged in teaching in Massachusetts and Vermont until 1877, when he came west and engaged in the same vocation in Minnesota, where he remained until 1879, when he came to the territory of Dakota and located in Bigstone City, in what is now Grant County, South Dakota. Two years later he removed to Ashton, Spink County, being one of the early settlers of the town and county, and here engaged in the real-estate and loan business, in which he met with success, since the section soon began to feel the beneficent effects of the strong incoming tide of immigration and advancing civilization. In the meanwhile, he had for a number of years devoted much attention to the reading of law, and on the 14th of December, 1888, he was admitted to the bar of the territory, forthwith beginning the active practice of his profession in Ashton, where he has ever since maintained his home, and where he has gained distinctive precedence and success in his profession. He at the present time maintains an independent attitude in politics, but he was a member of the first three Republican conventions after the admission of South Dakota to the Union. He has been called to the incumbency of various offices of local trust and responsibility, where he gave his best efforts in the advancing of the general welfare and material progress, and for several years he was mayor of Ashton, in which connection his administration met with uniform approval and popular endorsement.

He is affiliated with Ashton Lodge, No. 33, Ancient Free and Accepted Masons, and of Redfield Chapter, No. 20, Royal Arch Masons, at Redfield, while from 1888 to 1891 he was grand chief templar of the Independent Order of Good Templars in South Dakota. He and his wife are zealous and valued members of the Methodist Episcopal church of Ashton. On the 17th of October, 1882, was solemnized the marriage of Mr. Watkins to Miss Lilla B. Lee, who was born in Cresco, Howard County, Iowa, on the 2d of April, 1866, being a daughter of Timothy W. P. and Myra N. Lee. They have five children, Howard Lee, Myrtle May, Samuel Prentiss, Gardner H. and Elmer Leland. Timothy W. P. Lee was a native of Stanstead, Canada, and came to the territory of Dakota in 1879. He was a lawyer by profession, taking an active part in politics, and was a member of the Sioux Falls constitutional convention, and was one of the framers of the present constitution of the state of South Dakota.

BERT G. WATTSON

B. G. WATTSON, senior member of the firm of Wattson & Hulseman, hardware merchants of Chamberlain, was born in Northwood, Worth county, Iowa, September 23, 1867, and is a son of George F. and Felixine M. (Wardall) Wattson, of whose six children he is the eldest of the five now living, the others being as follows: Carrie, the wife of L. G. Gunn, of Lawton, Oklahoma; Charles, a resident of El Reno, that territory; as are also Robert and Kenneth. The father of the subject was born in Michigan, and there his mother died when he was a child, his father soon afterward removing to Iowa. There he was reared and educated, and at the age of seventeen years he enlisted as a private in Company K, Fifth Iowa Volunteer Infantry, with which he served during the major portion of the Civil War, the history of that regiment being that of his career as a valiant son of the republic. After the close of the war, he engaged in the drug business in Northwood, Iowa, where he continued to reside until 1888, when he disposed of his interests there and removed to Texas, where he engaged in railroad contracting and in the real-estate business. In 1891 he removed to El Reno, Oklahoma, where he established himself in the real-estate business, and soon after the inauguration of the late lamented President McKinley he was appointed postmaster in that place, a position which he has ever since filled, having been reappointed under President Roosevelt. He was elected a member of the Iowa state legislature in the early 'eighties, serving one term. He is a Royal Arch Mason. His devoted wife entered into eternal rest in 1894, and he later married Mrs. Adah Birney, no children having been born of this union.

Bert G. Wattson secured his early education in the public schools of his native state and then entered the Iowa State Agricultural College, at Ames, where he continued his studies, after which he was engaged in teaching for one term. He then secured a clerkship in the office of the United States Express Company at Northwood, and in September, 1886, he came to Chamberlain, South Dakota, where for the ensuing three years he was employed as clerk in the dry-goods establishment of M. W. Egleston. In the autumn of 1889 he went to Vernon, Texas, where he was assistant postmaster for one year. In 1890 he returned to Chamberlain and in the spring of the following year he was here united in marriage to Miss Mildred M. Hart, daughter of Charles B. Hart, local station agent of the Chicago, Minneapolis & St. Paul Railroad.

Soon after his marriage he removed with his bride to the state of Washington, where they remained about four months, and he then returned to Chamberlain, with the intention of entering into partnership with a friend and engaging in the dry-goods business here. But shortly after his arrival the store of his former employer, Mr. Egleston, was sold to J. W. Orcott, and our subject was engaged as manager of the enterprise, and somewhat less than a year later Mr. Egleston again engaged in business, in a new location, and Mr. Wattson again entered his employ, remaining with him about four years, or until 1892, when he was elected city auditor, of which office he continued incumbent about four years. In the fall of 1896 Mr. Wattson purchased an interest in the grocery business of Charles H. Young, and the enterprise was continued under the firm name of Wattson & Young until the fall of 1897, when the business was sold, and thereupon our subject purchased the interest of J. M. Green in the hardware business of J. M. Green & Company, the firm name being simultaneously changed to Cook & Wattson. On the 1st of January, 1903, J. F. Hulseman purchased Mr. Cook's interest, and the present firm name was adopted.

Mr. Wattson is a stanch Republican, and is identified with Chamberlain Lodge, No. 56, Free and Accepted Masons; Pilgrim Chapter, Royal Arch Masons; Chamberlain Lodge, No. 88, Ancient Order of United Workmen; Sioux Tent, No. 34, Knights of the Maccabees; and Sioux Falls Lodge, No. 262, Benevolent and Protective Order of Elks. Mr. and Mrs. Wattson have had three children, of whom two are living, George H. and Donald H. Mrs. Mildred Wattson died in April, 1900, and on March 10, 1904, Mr. Wattson married Miss Cora M. Miner, of Mitchell, South Dakota, daughter of George H. Miner.

FRANK H. WEATHERWAX

Frank H. Weatherwax, a progressive and enterprising young business man of Sioux Falls, well known as the proprietor of a first-class clothing store, was born in Spring Mountain, Ohio, May 13, 1887, a son of George A. and Sarah Ellen (Hawn) Weatherwax. In the acquirement of an education, he attended Kenyon Military Academy at Gambier, Ohio, graduating from this institution in 1904. He afterward attended Kenyon College, from which he was graduated in 1908, and two years later he removed to Sioux Falls, opening the clothing store which he has since conducted. He has a modern establishment and controls a large and representative patronage, for he keeps only goods of high quality and follows always the most practical and progressive methods.

On the 26th of January, 1911, at Springboro, Pennsylvania, Mr. Weatherwax was united in marriage to Miss Donna M. King and both are well known in social circles of Sioux Fails. Mr. Weatherwax is a member of the Methodist Episcopal church, gives his political allegiance to the republican party and belongs to the Masons, the Knights of Pythias and the Independent Order of Odd Fellows. Although still a young man he has already met with excellent success in the conduct of his interests and, being ambitious and enterprising, he will undoubtedly be carried forward into still more important relations with the business life of the community.

JOHN F. WEAVER

John F. Weaver, now serving for the third term as treasurer of Potter County, has been a resident of the county during the past three decades and was long and successfully identified with general agricultural pursuits here. His birth occurred in Pioneer, Williams County, Ohio, on the 15th of October, 1861, his parents being John M. and Caroline (Snow) Weaver, who were natives of Pennsylvania and New York respectively. The father, who followed farming throughout his entire business career, removed to Ohio with his parents when about eighteen years of age and was married in the Buckeye state. Subsequently he established his home in Michigan, where his demise occurred in January, 1900, while his wife passed away in March, 1905. John M. Weaver served in the Civil War as a ninety-day recruit in an Ohio regiment. He held some local township offices but never sought nor desired the honors and emoluments of public preferment.

John F. Weaver, the second in order of birth in a family of three children, acquired he education in his native town and also attended country schools. When nineteen years of age he secured employment as a farm hand in Ohio but at the end of about six months returned home, subsequently spending a part of his time under the parental roof and being engaged for about three years in railroad work. He was married when a young man of twenty-two years and devoted his attention to farming on the homestead place until the spring of 1885, when he came to South Dakota, locating on a farm six miles south of Lebanon. In the operation of that property, he was busily engaged until elected to the office of county treasurer in 1904 taking office January 1, 1905, and since that time his attention has been given to duties of a public nature. He served as county treasurer for two consecutive terms and was then employed as deputy treasurer until again elected treasurer in 1914, being the capable incumbent at the present time. He is likewise the vice president of the First National Bank of Gettysburg and still owns the land on which he settled when he came to this state.

On the 4th of October, 1883, Mr. Weaver was united in marriage to Miss Josephine L. Ennis, a native of Iowa and a daughter of Isaac and Harriet (Russell) Ennis, both of whom were born in New York. They came to South Dakota in May, 1884, and took up their abode on a farm six miles south and one mile east of Lebanon, whereon the father passed away in the fall of 1896. The mother now makes her home in Gettysburg with our subject. Mr. and Mrs. Weaver have six children, as follows: Ethel, the wife of Henri S. Klein, who is employed as clerk in a hardware store of Gettysburg; Blanche, the wife of Louis Klein, who is proprietor of a restaurant in Gettysburg; May, living at home, who was formerly engaged in teaching school and has also served in the capacities of deputy county treasurer and deputy county auditor; Fay, also living with her parents, who formerly taught school and is now serving as deputy register; Roy, who assists his father in his official duties; and Lloyd, who is attending school.

Mr. Weaver gives his political allegiance to the republican party and has served as school treasurer and in other public positions in addition to that of treasurer of the county, ever making a most commendable record as a faithful, reliable and trustworthy official. Fraternally he is identified with the Masonic order, belonging to the blue lodge at Gettysburg, in which he is now serving as junior deacon. He also acts as treasurer of the local organization of the Independent Order of Odd Fellows and is likewise affiliated with the Ancient Order of United Workmen. His life has been upright and honorable in every relation and he has long been numbered among the prosperous, representative and valued citizens of his community.

JOHN R. WEAVER

J. R. WEAVER, a successful merchant and representative citizen of Claremont, Brown County, was born at Eureka, Montcalm County, Michigan, on the 29th of December, 1858, and is a son of Benjamin A. and Betsy (Clark) Weaver, both of whom were born and reared in the state of New York, the former having been a son of Aaron Weaver, who was a native of Rhode Island. The last mentioned was a son of John

Weaver, who was likewise born in Rhode Island and who married a Miss Chase, whose original ancestor in America was one of two brothers who came over in the historic Mayflower, while their sister remained in England and became the wife of Sir John Townsend. Representatives of the Chase family were valiant soldiers in the Continental line during the war of the Revolution, and through their thus giving allegiance to the colonial cause they sacrificed a large estate in England. The paternal grandfather of the subject continued to reside in Troy, New York, until 1845, when he removed to Michigan and became one of the pioneers of Ionia County, where he passed the residue of his life. The father of the subject became the owner of a farm in Montcalm County, that state, where he remained until 1859, when he then removed to Ionia County, same state, then removed to Stearns County, Minnesota, being one of the pioneers of that section of the state. They passed on their way only three miles distant from the point the memorable Indian massacre at New Ulm, he and his family fortunately being unmolested. For a quarter of a century, he resided in the city of Chicago, where he was a prominent contractor and builder, finally meeting with an accident which compelled him to retire from active labors. He is now living in the home of the subject, being seventy-four years of age at the time of this writing. His present wife is living with a daughter in Chicago. They became the parents of four children, all of whom are living. The subject's mother died in July, 1861; she was the mother of four children, three of whom are dead.

John R. Weaver, the immediate subject of this review, passed his school days in Michigan, and as his mother died when he was but eighteen months of age he was reared in the home of his paternal grandfather, with whom he remained until the spring of 1885, when he came to Brown County, South Dakota, and located in Detroit township, where he took up government land and engaged in farming. Two years later, upon the completion of the line of the Great Northern Railroad through this section, he engaged in the draying and freighting business, in which line he continued operations one year, at the expiration of which he established himself in business in Claremont, where for the ensuing decade he conducted a lumber yard and also dealt in coal and farming machinery and implements, building up a most prosperous enterprise. In 1899 he disposed of his business and purchased a farm southeast of the town, where he established the family home, and thereafter he was engaged as traveling representative for the Piano Manufacturing Company until March, 1904, when he entered into partnership with his brother, James A., and became associated with him in the carrying on of the general merchandise business which the latter had established in Claremont in the preceding September, and the enterprise has been since conducted under the firm name of Weaver Brothers. They carry a large and complete stock of general merchandise and also handle farming machinery and implements, and their trade has been most satisfactory from the start and is constantly increasing in scope and importance. It may be noted in the connection that our subject's brother and partner was the first white child born on the Indian reservation across the river from Sauk Center, Minnesota, and is the offspring of the second marriage of their father.

He came to South Dakota in the autumn of 1903. In politics the subject is a stanch Republican, and fraternally is a member of the Masonic order, in which he has passed the capitular degree, and also of the Ancient Order of United Workmen, the Modern Woodmen of America and the Knights of the Maccabees. On the 31st of December, 1878, Mr. Weaver was married to Miss Janett Cole, who was born in Eureka, Montcalm County, Michigan, being a daughter of Leander T. and Sarah J. Cole, who were numbered among the pioneers of Brown County. South Dakota. Mr. and Mrs. Weaver have two children, Clarence J., who has charge of our subject's farm, previously mentioned, and Maud J., who is the wife of M. Hugh Miller, a successful young farmer of this county.

JOSEPH WEGENER

Joseph Wegener, one of the leading business men of Hecla, Brown County, is a native of the Hawkeye state, having been born in the city of Dubuque, Iowa. He was educated in private schools in Dubuque and then entered a local drug store, where he learned the science of pharmacy in a most practical way. When twenty years of age he came to South Dakota and located in Columbia, Brown County, while in the following year he took up a claim of government land. He resided on this claim until he had perfected his title to the same, and then came to Hecla and opened a drug store, gaining a representative support from the start and now having one of the most popular and attractive business places in the town. He has ever shown himself ready to give his aid and influence in support of all measures for the general good of the community, being essentially public-spirited and progressive.

Fraternally he has attained to the thirty-second degree in the Ancient Accepted Scottish Rite of Freemasonry, being thus crowned a Sublime Prince of the Royal Secret and standing high in the circles of this time-honored fraternity. He is a member of the consistory at Aberdeen, and a charter member of Humanity Lodge, Ancient Free and Accepted Masons, in Hecla, while he is also affiliated with the Ancient Arabic Order of the Nobles of the Mystic Shrine and the Ancient Order of United Workmen. Mr. Wegener was married to Miss Jennie A. Myra, and they have five children.

H. A. WELLS, D. D. S.

Since 1910 Dr. H. A. Wells has been engaged in the practice of dentistry in Aberdeen and he is numbered today among the most able representatives of his profession in the city. He was born in Verdon, South Dakota, in 1889, and is a son of Wilbur E. and Hattie (McIntyre) Wells, who came to this state from New York. The father engaged in farming during his early life, but is now active in the real-estate business, owning valuable holdings in Minnesota.

Dr. H. A. Wells acquired his early education in the public schools of Aberdeen and later entered the State University of Minnesota, graduating from the dental department in 1910. On September 10th of that year, he located in Aberdeen, where he opened an office for the practice of his profession. He has built up a large and growing patronage and his success is the best proof of his capabilities.

On the 22d of January, 1912, Dr. Wells was united in marriage to Miss Margaret Countryman, a daughter of Dr. George E. Countryman. Dr. Wells is connected fraternally with the Masonic lodge and belongs to Xi Psi Phi, a college fraternity. He is well known in professional circles, being president of the Aberdeen District Dental Society and active in the affairs of that organization. Since the beginning of his active career, he has made steady progress in his profession and is now established in a large and growing practice.

N. H. WENDELL

N. H. Wendell, the period of whose residence in Aberdeen covers a quarter of a century, was born in Albany, New York, on the 6th of November, 1868, his parents being N. D. and Jane A. (Mosher) Wendell. He acquired his education in the public schools and the military academy at Albany and subsequently secured employment on the Albany Morning Express. In 1888, when a young man of twenty years, he removed to Aberdeen, South Dakota, and became identified with the real-estate firm of Fletcher & Fisher, while afterward he spent a few years in the service of other concerns. He held the position of credit man for Jewett Brothers until 1904 and then embarked in the insurance business on his own account, conducting the same until he disposed of his interests in February, 1907, when he was appointed postmaster of Aberdeen. He ably discharged the duties of that office for four and one-half years, making an excellent and praiseworthy record.

In February, 1896, Mr. Wendell was united in marriage to Miss Jessie Huff, of Aberdeen, by whom he has four children. He gives his political allegiance to the republican party and is identified fraternally with the Masons, being past master of the blue lodge, past high priest of the chapter, past eminent commander of the Knights of Templar commandery and a member of the Mystic Shrine. He also belongs to the Benevolent Protective Order of Elks. Mr. Wendell is numbered among the leading and representative citizens of his home town, being highly esteemed for his sterling worth and as a promoter of all that tends to advance the general welfare.

CYRUS LEROY WENDT, M. D.

Dr. Cyrus Leroy Wendt, actively engaged in the practice of medicine and surgery and enjoying a creditable and deserved reputation as a physician, was born in Davis, Illinois, on the 18th day of May, 1873, and is a Born of Ernest and Fredericka (Meinzer) Wendt. The family came to South Dakota in 1875 and settled two miles south of Canton, where the father conducted a store for many years, being one of the early and leading business men of that city. At the present writing, however, he is living retired, having gained a competence which enables him to put aside business cares and enjoy a well-earned rest.

After attending the public schools of Canton, Dr. Wendt continued his studies at Brookings, South Dakota, and in the Northwestern Indiana Normal School at Valparaiso. Later he became a student in Rush Medical College of Chicago and on the 22d of May, 1895, was graduated therefrom. Still anxious to make further advancement in preparation for his life work, after completing his course he also spent seven months in the Charity Hospital of Berlin, Germany, gaining during that period the practical experience which only hospital service can bring. He then returned and located in his home town on the 1st of January, 1896, and in the intervening years to the present he has enjoyed a liberal share of the public patronage. His ability is generally recognized and it is well known that thorough study and broad reading keep him in touch with the onward march of the profession and the trend of thought in scientific medical investigation. In addition to his other interests, he is a stockholder in the Farmers Lumber Yard and still other business enterprises. He is particularly fond of livestock and has opportunity to indulge his taste in that direction. Along strictly professional lines he has been active, being an officer of the board of health and county physician. He has been physician for various life insurance companies, almost twenty in number. He has extensive land holdings in different parts of the state which he operates through the aid of promising young farmers, receiving a portion of the crop as rent.

On the 22d of December, 1896, Dr. Wendt was united in marriage to Miss Edna Dean, a daughter of Edgar and Vina Dean, and they have one child, F. Lucile, who is attending high school. Dr. Wendt and his wife hold membership in the Methodist church, are actively interested in its work and give generously to its support. He votes with the republican party but has neither sought nor held office outside of the strict path of his profession. Fraternally he is connected with Silver Star Lodge, No. 4, F. & A. M., and is in hearty sympathy with the plans and purposes of the craft. His interest centers, however, most largely upon his professional duties, which he meets with a sense of conscientious obligation. He realizes fully the responsibilities that devolve upon the practitioner of medicine and surgery and he is most careful in the diagnosis of his cases and in the care of his patients. His patronage is steadily increasing and he is today accounted one of the leading representatives of the profession in southeastern South Dakota.

ED L. WENDT

Ed L. Wendt is successfully engaged in the real-estate business at Canton as a member of the firm of Wendt & Straw and has long enjoyed an enviable reputation as one of the enterprising and progressive citizens of the town. His birth occurred in Stephenson County, Illinois, on the 25th of June, 1869, his parents being Ernest and Frederika Wendt. The family came to South Dakota in 1875, locating at Lower Canton, where the father embarked in business as a merchant. Four years later he removed to Canton and there both he and his wife still reside. The period of their residence in this state covers almost four decades and they are widely and favorably known.

Ed L. Wendt, who was a little lad of six years when he came with his parents to South Dakota, acquired his education in the public schools and at Augustana College of Canton. After putting aside his textbooks he entered his father's store as clerk and assistant and for twenty years was identified with merchandising. During this period, he also devoted considerable attention to the real-estate business and acquired quite extensive landed holdings in his locality and in other parts of the state. Eventually, when the management of his investments demanded all of his attention, he left the store and has since been associated with E. J. Straw as a member of the firm of Wendt & Straw. Success has attended his undertakings in this connection and he is widely recognized as a prosperous and enterprising business man. For seventeen years he was a member of the board of directors of the Lincoln County Bank.

On the 18th of October, 1888, Mr. Wendt was united in marriage to Miss Jessie E. Gage, of Missouri, by whom he has one daughter, Zoe Marie, who is now the wife of E. E. Subert. In his political views Mr. Wendt is independent, always supporting candidates because of their fitness rather than because of party affiliation. He has served for three years as a member of the city council and for a similar period on the school board, while for ten years he acted as treasurer of the Chautauqua Association of Canton. His religious faith is indicated by his membership in the Methodist Episcopal church, to which his wife also belongs. Fraternally he is identified with the Masonic order, holding membership in Silver Star Lodge, No. 4, F. & A. M., of Canton. Mr. Wendt is a lover of clean sport, an enthusiastic motorist and a public-spirited, loyal citizen who has ever taken a leading part in all movements instituted to advance the interests of his home city. Cordial and pleasing in address, he has made many friends who are, attracted to him not only on account of his genial characteristics but because of his recognized liberality and public spirit and his high standing in business circles.

JOHN E. WEST

John E. WEST is a native of the Empire state of the Union, having been born in the city of Syracuse, New York, on the 22d of May, 1848, and being a son of Henry and Elizabeth (Bloomer) West. He was reared in his native commonwealth and there secured a common school education. When but fifteen years of age he manifested in a significant way his loyalty to the Union, the country being then in the period of the great Civil War. In 1863 he enlisted in the Fourteenth New York Heavy Artillery, proceeding with his command to the front and taking part in a number of the most hotly contested battles incident to the farther progress of the war, among the number being Spotsylvania, the Wilderness, Petersburg and Fort Steadman, He received his honorable discharge in Washington City, 1865, having proved himself a valiant young soldier and gaining the right to be designated as a youthful veteran. He retains an interest in his old comrades in arms and perpetuates the associations of his army days by retaining membership in the Grand Army of the Republic.

After the close of the war Mr. West was variously employed in the state of New York until 1874, when he secured the position of fireman on the New York Central Railroad. Four years later he was given an engine and continued in the employ of that great system for eight years. In 1883 he entered the employ of the Chicago, Milwaukee & St. Paul Railroad, and in this connection established his residence and headquarters in Aberdeen, which has thus been his home for the past score of years, during which time he has had runs out from this point, now hauling the passenger train west of Aberdeen. He has ever been self-controlled and clear-minded in his thirty years of service as an engineer and his record has not been marred by serious accidents.

He is a popular member of the Brotherhood of Locomotive Engineers and also of the time-honored Masonic fraternity, in which he has attained the thirty-second degree of the Ancient Accepted Scottish Rite. In politics he gives his allegiance to the Republican party, taking an intelligent and lively interest in the questions and issues of the day. At Bowdle, Edmunds County, South Dakota, on the 13th of February, 1889, was solemnized the marriage of Mr. West to Miss Mamie C. Barndt, who was born at St. Mary's, Ohio, and reared at McComb, Hancock County, Ohio. They have two daughters, Florence and Helen. The parents of Mrs. West were L. T. and Louise (Crawford) Barndt. The father was born at New Lexington, Perry County, Ohio, and died at Everett, Washington, on December 7, 1903, at the age of seventy-one years. The mother, who is still living, was also born in Ohio.

CLARK S. WEST

Clark S. West is now living retired in Fullerville, enjoying a rest which he has truly earned and richly deserves. For nearly a half century he has been a resident of South Dakota, coming here in early territorial days when the work of progress and development seemed scarcely begun. He was born in Chautauqua County, New York, May 9, 1841, the family home being about twelve miles from Jamestown and an equal distance from Dunkirk. His parents were Lewis and Miranda (Hasbrook) West, who both died in Iowa. In 1854 the family removed westward, traveling by train from Buffalo to the end of the line somewhere near Johnstown, Wisconsin. The family there resided but a short time, and during the winter the father made a journey into Iowa, seeking a location. He filed on a preemption claim on the Big Cedar near where Otranto was later started, being the first settler in that township, after which he rejoined his family in Wisconsin and in the spring, they loaded their belongings into wagons drawn by oxen and began the long journey to the west, camping by the wayside at night. There were no railroads in Iowa at that time and the nearest market was at McGregor, a distance of one hundred and twenty miles. The boys often drove an ox team to the river town to market their wheat, the journey to and from that place requiring two weeks' time. Occasionally they would find, on reaching the end of their journey, that there was a line of wagons extending five miles back into the ravine, for all of the settlers over a wide territory had to go to that place to market their products. Later when the railroad had been extended to Cedar Falls, they had but eighty miles to haul their produce to market, which seemed a short distance in comparison with the trip which they had previously made.

Clark S. West remained with his father until 1867. In 1862, however, he was sent with another young man as a scout up into New Ulm County, Minnesota, after the Indian massacre there. In the fall of 1867, he came to Dakota territory and secured a preemption on section 8, Gayville township. He now has two hundred and thirty acres in Yankton County. He also secured homestead and timber claims in Hutchinson County, where he now has eight hundred acres, of which four hundred acres is under the plow. He likewise owns a half interest in his father's old farm in Iowa of one hundred and seventy-two acres. He lived here at a time when a blizzard was not an unknown thing in Dakota through the late '60s and early '70s, and also encountered the pest of locusts for several seasons, when crops were utterly or almost entirely destroyed, but the worst of all was the flood in the spring of 1881, when the water stood four and a half feet deep in his house. He had been storing his grain for four seasons and had the crops of 1877, 1878, 1879 and 1880 in the granary when the waters rose and ruined all in a night. In addition, he lost three horses, thirty head of cattle and other property, his losses amounting in all to five thousand dollars, a heavy sum for him in those days when he was just getting a start.

Mr. West was married November 8, 1863, in Faribault, Minnesota, to Miss Mary E. van Osdel, a native of Indiana, whose parents were among the earliest settlers of Yankton County and are mentioned elsewhere in this volume. Mr. and Mrs. West became the parents of two sons: Abraham Lewis, who now operates the home farm; and Jesse C, who was proprietor of a store in Fullerville, until his death, which occurred June 3, 1915, when he was forty-five years of age. Abraham L. married Ida Harris and has four children: Harry Lewis, who now has the store in Fullerville; and Walter, Edna Miranda and Lillian Irene, at home.

Mr. West is a republican in politics and has ever given stalwart support to the party. Among other offices that he has filled is that of member of the territorial council. He has been a member of the Masonic lodge since 1874 and is identified with several Masonic bodies in Yankton, having attained the thirty-second degree of the Scottish Rite. He can look back over the period of pioneer existence in Yankton County and remembers vividly the conditions brought about by many hardships and trials which had to be endured, but all this has passed and today he is a substantial and well-to-do citizen of Fullerville, his persistent labor and energy having brought to him a comfortable competence as the years have gone by in spite of the privations of pioneer times.

FRANK L. WHEELER

Frank L. Wheeler, a grain dealer of Scotland, Bon Homme County, is a native of the lake country of New York, a region famous for its beauty. His birth occurred May 20, 1859, in Seneca County, south of Seneca Falls, on the old Wheeler homestead situated on the west shore of Cayuga lake. His parents, Jonathan and Harriet (Ogden) Wheeler, were natives of the Empire state and the mother, who has now reached the advanced age of eighty-five years, is still a resident of that state, making her home in Geneva, at the foot of Seneca lake.

Mr. Wheeler of this review migrated west in the spring of 1880 and remained for a year at Winona, Minnesota, but on the 17th of May, 1881, he came to Huron, South Dakota, on the first train that made the trip with its own engine. Owing to a stretch of marshy ground transfers had to be made until a firmer track could be built and even this at places sank below the surface, the water rising behind the train as it proceeded on its way. Shortly after his arrival in South Dakota Mr. Wheeler opened a lumberyard in Hitchcock near where he took up a homestead, a pre-emption and a timber claim, remaining there until 1893. He was then for two years in business at Viborg and for three years at Howard, after which time, in 1898, he came to Scotland and entered the grain business, in which he has continued to the present time. He has a large elevator and is well equipped for handling all kinds of grain and farm produce. He also has elevators at Blaha and Plumba. His careful study of commercial and agricultural conditions and his systematic methods of carrying on his business are the causes of his gratifying success. In addition to his grain business he has other interests, including a controlling interest in the Peoples Telephone Company of Scotland.

Mr. Wheeler was united in marriage in Scotland in 1891 to Miss Ida Shaw, a daughter of Henry and Mary (Eckert) Shaw, who came to South Dakota in 1886. Mr. and Mrs. Wheeler have become parents of five children: Mary, a teacher in the Scotland schools; Floyd, who is associated in business with his father; Henry, who is now taking an engineering course at Vermillion; Frank and Harriet.

Upon coming to Scotland to reside Mr. Wheeler purchased the house in which he had been previously married. He is a member of the Masonic fraternity and has served as worshipful master and high priest. He fortunately escaped the blizzard of January 12, 1888, as he was on a visit in New York at the time. However, he had occasion to worry because of the great storm, as on his ranch at Hitchcock was a considerable herd of cattle in charge of a brother. In a little over one year from that time his farm was in the track of the worst prairie fire the Dakotas have ever known. On the 2d of April, 1889, the flames swept with appalling speed across the wide plains and at times leaped across half a mile of fire guard. The barn upon Mr. Wheeler's place was burned, but he considered himself fortunate to escape so well. With the usual American thrift and energy, he has succeeded in business and is accounted one of Scotland's respected and prosperous citizens. He is a democrat in politics and is a member of the school board, having served as its president for ten years.

JUDGE ARTHUR BUCK WHEELOCK

JUDGE ARTHUR L. WHEELOCK

No history of public interests in Sioux Falls would be complete were their failure to make prominent reference to Judge Arthur Buck Wheelock, who for twenty years was city and police justice, retiring in 1912, since which time he has enjoyed the rest to which he is justly entitled. He was born in Royalton, Vermont, April 19, 1832, a son of Peter and Chestina Eliza Smith (Buck) Wheelock. The father was also a native of Royalton, while the grandfather, Peter Wheelock, Sr., was born in Swansea, Massachusetts. He was one of the minutemen of the Revolutionary war. The ancestral line can be traced back to Ralph Wheelock, who came from Shropshire, England, in 1630, and whose son, Eleazer Wheelock, was the founder of Dartmouth College.

In taking up the personal history of Judge Wheelock we present to our readers the life record of one who is most widely and favorably known in Sioux Falls and throughout this section of the state. He has now passed the eighty-second milestone on life's journey, but in spirit and interests seems yet in his prime. In 1833 his parents removed from Royalton to Newbury, Vermont, where he was reared and educated. He remained at home until October, 1853, and then left New England with Milwaukee, Wisconsin, as his destination, having an uncle, J. S. Buck, and his maternal grandmother, Polly Buck living in that city at the time, which fact influenced him in his removal. He was afterward in Missouri and later went to Fort Bridger with a freight outfit. Subsequently he returned to Missouri, where he operated a sawmill for two years, and then again went to Milwaukee, whither his parents had removed in 1853. On the twenty-ninth anniversary of his birth — the 19th of April, 1861 — Judge Wheelock enlisted as a member of the old Milwaukee Light Guards, which command became Company A, First Wisconsin Volunteer Infantry. They responded to the president's call for three months' troops and on the expiration of that period Judge Wheelock reenlisted as a private of the Seventh Wisconsin Light Artillery for three years, or during the war. He was detailed for recruiting service and in September, 1861, was commissioned second lieutenant of the battery. Further promotion came to him in the spring of 1865, when he was made captain of the Seventh Battery, with which he served until mustered out in Milwaukee on the 20th of July, 1865. He was captured at Memphis, Tennessee, and taken to Cahaba, Alabama, August 21, 1864, by General Forrest's command and was held for two months at that place, after which he was exchanged and again engaged in active duty with his regiment. When mustered out of service he was thirty-three years of age, was six feet, two and a half inches in height and had almost Herculean strength. He is still a splendid specimen of physical manhood, bearing his eighty-two years lightly, and while he has retired from office and business life, he is still active and is keenly interested in affairs of the day.

After the war Judge Wheelock engaged in railroad building in the west from 1866 until February, 1868, when he came to the territory of Dakota and homesteaded land in Lincoln County, on which the town of Hudson is now located. The village of Hudson was first called Eden, being so named by Judge Wheelock, who donated the land for the town site. Subsequently, however, owing to the fact that its similarity to Egan caused considerable confusion, the name of the place was changed to Hudson. Judge Wheelock devoted about two decades to general agricultural pursuits and in 1888 came to Sioux Falls. He was city and police justice for twenty years, in which connection he rendered decisions strictly fair and impartial, his capable service being indicated by his long retention in office. It was not until 1912 that he retired, being then eighty years of age. He was also at one time a member of the territorial legislature and he has ever been deeply interested in matters affecting the welfare, development and upbuilding of the commonwealth. His political allegiance has ever been given to the republican party since its organization.

On the 21st of October, 1869, at Hudson, South Dakota, Judge Wheelock was united in marriage to Miss Cynthia E. Mundy, a daughter of James Martin Mundy, who was a noncommissioned officer of a Minnesota regiment and died at La Grange, Tennessee, in 1861, while defending the Union, being there buried. Judge and Mrs. Wheelock are the parents of two daughters. Mary Elsie, a graduate of All Saints School of Sioux Falls, is the wife of Maurice Blair Mayne, of Sioux City, Iowa, by whom she has two children, Kenneth Wheelock and Mary Wheelock Mayne. Alice Muriel was graduated from All Saints School and is a graduate of the Art Institute of Chicago. She resides with her parents.

The religious faith of the family is that of the Episcopal church, of which Judge Wheelock has been a member for many years. He likewise holds membership with the Dacotah Club and with the Masonic fraternity, being a Knight Templar and a member of the Mystic Shrine. Sterling qualities of manhood and citizenship have ever characterized his life and won for him the respect, confidence and goodwill of all concerned. Throughout his entire life he has been as true and loyal to his public duties as he was when he followed the old flag on the battlefields of the south, making a most creditable record as a soldier. His loyalty to the flag has ever been one of his strong characteristics and patriotism and progress might well be termed the keynote of his character.

HON. EDWIN TERRY WHITE

Hon. Edwin Terry White, mayor of Yankton, who for many years has occupied a prominent and enviable position in legal and business circles of the city, is a native son of New England, his birth having occurred at Woodstock, Vermont, on the 6th of June, 1847. His parents were Samuel and Elizabeth (Elliott) White, both of whom were natives of New Hampshire. The father was born in January, 1800, and was descended in the paternal line from Scotch-English ancestry and in the maternal line was of an old American family. The White family can trace their genealogy back to earliest colonial days, when three brothers came from England and settled in the northeastern portion of this country. One branch of the family was finally established in New Hampshire and it is to that branch that Edwin Terry White belongs. Many representatives of the name have attained prominence as history has progressed and all of the wars of the country have found its members among the participants in the struggle. They have made prominent places for themselves in military, professional and commercial circles in the various communities with which they have been identified. The grandfather of Edwin T. White was a soldier of the Revolutionary war.

Samuel White became a wood carver, serving a seven years' apprenticeship and attaining high rank as an artistic and skilled workman. Evidences of his superior ability are seen in the woodwork of the state capitol at Montpelier, Vermont. His skill gained him wide and favorable acquaintance throughout New England and there were frequent demands made upon him for work of that character. He removed from New Hampshire to Vermont and there spent his remaining days. He married Elizabeth Elliott, whose father was a soldier of the War of 1812 and became one of the pioneers of Lawrenceburg, Indiana, where he acquired a splendid estate. His death there occurred during the cholera epidemic of 1833. There were eleven children in the family of Samuel and Elizabeth White, namely: George, who was a soldier of the Sixth Vermont Regiment during the Civil War and is now deceased; John E., deceased, who was leader of a New Hampshire band in the Civil War; Stephen P., who became a member of Company C, Sixth

Vermont Infantry, and was killed in the second battle of Winchester, Virginia, September 24, 1864; Samuel G., who was a member of the same regiment and now resides in Cove, Oregon; Charles K., who makes his home in Randolph, Vermont; Edwin T., of this review; Elizabeth E., deceased; Emily B.; Frances, who has passed away; Mary C. V., whose home is in Concord, New Hampshire; and David A., deceased.

Edwin Terry White acquired his education in the public schools of his native city and started out in life for himself at the age of fourteen years. He was employed in many ways, working as a farm laborer, as a peddler and carpenter, and, carefully hoarding his earnings, he acquired a sufficient sum to enable him to meet his expenses while attending high school. He was very anxious to improve his education and throughout life has had continuous desire to broaden his knowledge and gain understanding of those things which are of vital worth to the individual and to the country. After completing his high-school course he again worked in various ways until appointed second assistant clerk of the Vermont legislature. In the meantime, beginning when eighteen years of age, he read law in the office of Converse & French, well known attorneys of Woodstock, Vermont. At the same time, he was forced to support himself, devoting his evenings to study and his days to labor. His efforts were thus considerably hampered, but his difficulty seemed to serve as an impetus for renewed effort and, continuing his reading, he was admitted to practice on his twenty-second birthday.

Immediately after being admitted to the bar Judge White started westward, going first to Cedar Rapids, Iowa, and later to Marshalltown, that state, where C. J. B. Harris, now of Yankton, was then living. In company with Mr. Harris, he came to South Dakota in 1870, arriving in Yankton on the 7th of July of that year. They formed a law partnership which was continued for a year, at the end of which time Mr. White became associated with Hon. S. L. Spink, formerly territorial delegate to congress. This firm maintained its existence for three years and made a memorable record. Judge White has since practiced alone, but has gradually abandoned the law for the conduct of an insurance, real-estate and loan business, which he manages in connection with the discharge of his official duties as mayor of Yankton and as United States commissioner. He was elected judge of the Yankton County courts in 1889 and served upon the bench for seven years, his decisions being strictly fair and impartial. He has served also as police justice, as justice of the peace and as city clerk, and in 1909 was elected mayor of Yankton, in which position he discharged his duties with such capability that he was reelected in 1910 for a term of five years under the commission form of government and is the present incumbent of that office. He is most highly esteemed and honored by reason of his able discharge of public duties. He is one of the leading republicans in his part of the state, stands very high in party councils and has always been active in support of party principles. Mr. White was one of the originators and was the secretary and treasurer of the first company in South Dakota to dig an artesian well. They completed his well in the spring of 1881, obtaining a big flow of water, and since then thousands of wells have been dug in South Dakota. Mr. White took up the subscription for the funds for this well, which was the first artesian well in South Dakota, although historians have credited the first well to another place in the state.

On the 1st of January, 1874, Mr. White was united in marriage to Miss Mary L. Bagley, of Bethel, Vermont. They have always taken a progressive interest in supporting charitable movements and they stand for that which is best for the community and for the individual. Mr. White is a member of St. John's Lodge, No. I, A. F. & A. M., of which he was worshipful master for three years. He is likewise a member of Oriental Consistory, No. I, S. P. R. S., of Yankton, in which he has been registrar for many years, and he is the secretary of the Scottish Rite Temple Association of Yankton. He is a member of De Molay Commandery, No. 3, K. T., and is an honorary thirty-third degree Mason, having been given that degree in October, 1905. He also belongs to Keystone Chapter, Order of the Eastern Star, of Yankton, and is a member of Dakota Lodge, No. I, I. O. O. F. He is today one of the best-known citizens of Yankton and his part of the state and for a long period has exerted a beneficial influence over public thought and action.

FREDERICK CARROL WHITEHOUSE

Frederick Carrol Whitehouse is senior partner of the real-estate firm of F. C. Whitehouse & Company of Sioux Falls and makes a specialty of handling farm lands and loans in which connection he has had much to do with the development and prosperity of his section of the state. In all things he has followed most progressive methods, and his energy and enterprise have brought him to the prominent position which he now fills as one of the foremost dealers in farm lands in South Dakota.

He was born in Boonesboro, Iowa, March 18, 1870, a son of Julius Frederick and Elizabeth Morris (Duckworth) Whitehouse, who in the year 1871 removed to a homestead in Cherokee County, Iowa. The father was a native of Maine and a son of Isaac Whitehouse, who was also born in the Pine Tree state. The great-grandfather, Webber Whitehouse, was a native of Holland and became the founder of the family in New England.

FREDERICK C. WHITEHOUSE

Frederick Carrol Whitehouse was reared amid the usual environment and conditions of pioneer life while upon the homestead farm in Cherokee County. At the age of thirteen, however, he left home and lived with Dr. M. F. Butler in the town of Cherokee, remaining with him for three years, during which period he attended school in Cherokee, the county seat, completing the high school course in 1887. On leaving Cherokee he went to Primghar, the county seat of O'Brien county, Iowa, where he engaged in bookkeeping for four years and was also deputy county auditor for one year. He next entered the Primghar State Bank first in the capacity of bookkeeper but in 1891 was promoted to the position of cashier, serving thus for three years. He then left the bank and began handling farm lands and loans at Primghar, remaining there until 1896, when he removed to Sioux Falls and opened his present office. He immediately became active in immigration work and his efforts have been attended with immediate, substantial and beneficial results. Hundreds of families that are now settled in various rich sections of South Dakota and are meeting with prosperity owe their present location to the influence and the arguments advanced by F. C. Whitehouse. He is himself a firm believer in Sioux Falls and the future of South Dakota and bases his belief upon thorough knowledge of the natural resources, possibilities and opportunities of the country. The offices of F. C. Whitehouse & Company are located on Main Avenue. While the firm makes a specialty of working in the immigration field, they also handle city real estate and have negotiated a number of important property transfers in Sioux Falls.

On Christmas Day of 1889, at Shellrock, Iowa, Mr. Whitehouse was united in marriage to Miss Abigail C. Blake, a daughter of George G. Blake, and their children are: Harold R., Leland B. and Marie A.

The family attend the Congregational church and Mr. Whitehouse is a republican in his political belief. He has attained the Knights Templar degree in Masonry, is a member of the Mystic Shrine and also belongs to the Knights of Pythias and Odd Fellows lodges, to the Benevolent Protective Order of Elks, the Modern Woodmen of America and the Ancient Order of United Workmen. His membership list also includes the Dacotah Club and the Commercial Club. While in Primghar he served for three terms as mayor of the city and in 1904 was elected alderman of Sioux Falls, and later a member at large of the school board of Sioux Falls. These honors have come to him unsolicited as he has never sought office nor asked a man to vote for him. He is deeply and actively interested in everything pertaining to the welfare and progress of city and state, and his efforts have been a factor in promoting civic virtue and civic pride.

FREDERICK D. WICKS

F. D. Wicks, who is presiding on the bench of the county court of Bon Homme County, an incumbency which he has retained for nearly a decade, is a native of the old Empire state of the Union, having been born in Fort Edward, Washington County, New York, on the 31st of July, 1866, and being the youngest of the seven children of Walter W. and Ellen (Kennedy) Wicks, all of whom survive except one, a brief record concerning them being as follows: William E. died at the age of forty-five years; Mary remains at the parental home; Walter J. is superintendent of the Indian school at Springfield, South Dakota; Sarah is the wife of James D. Keeting, a printer and publisher in Fort Edward, New York; Fannie is the wife of Frank B. Hall, a successful merchant of Hartford, New York; Albert H., is a cigar manufacturer and tobacconist at Fort Edward, that state; and Frederick D. is the immediate subject of this sketch. The parents are still living at the old home in Fort Edward, where the father of the subject has long been engaged in building and contracting. He is a Republican in his political proclivities and both he and his wife are members of the Episcopal church.

Judge Wicks secured his early educational training in the public schools of his native town and later supplemented this discipline by a course of study in the Fort Edward Collegiate Institute. In 1886 he began the reading of law in the office of R. O. Bascom, a prominent member of the bar of Fort Edward, and under his able preceptorship he continued his technical studies until he became eligible for admission to the bar, gaining this distinction in 1890. Soon afterward he came to South Dakota and located in Scotland, where he established himself in the practice of his chosen profession. His ability so manifested itself that his novitiate in his new field of endeavor was of short duration and he soon took a prominent place at the bar of the county, while a gratifying recognition of his personal popularity and his professional talent came only two years after he took up his abode in the town, since in 1892 he was elected county judge, of which important office he has since remained consecutively incumbent save for an interim of two years. He has a distinctively judicial mind, is well poised and impartial in his rulings, which are based on a thorough knowledge of the science of jurisprudence in its various branches, and he has dignified the bench by his able and discriminating services. He is also city attorney of Scotland, a position which he has held for four terms, and he is known as a skillful advocate and a conservative and able counsellor.

In politics the judge gives an unwavering allegiance to the Republican party, in whose cause he has rendered timely and efficient service, and both he and his wife are communicants of the Protestant Episcopal church, while fraternally he is identified with Scotland Lodge, No. 52, Free and Accepted Masons; Scotland Chapter, No. 31, Royal Arch Masons, and Oriental Consistory, No. I, Ancient Accepted Scottish Rite, in Yankton. On the 12th of November, 1895, was solemnized the marriage of Judge Wicks to Aliss Mary L. Wood, of Springfield, this county. She was born in Springfield, Bon Homme County, in 1874. Judge and Mrs. Wicks have three children, Emma, Walter and Ellen.

Since 1894 Thomas L. Wiggen has been engaged in the plumbing business in Yankton, his well-equipped establishment being located at No. 222 Capitol Avenue. He is a native of Norway, the year of his birth being 1871. His parents were Louis and Carrie (Jensen) Wiggen, the father a native of Norway and the mother of France. The son began his education in his native land but at the age of twelve years accompanied his elder brother, James, to America, their destination being Minneapolis, Minnesota. He then entered the public schools of that city, which he attended for two years, or until he was fourteen years of age. At that time, he became apprenticed to the plumber's trade, thus serving four years, and as a journeyman plumber worked at his trade in many of the principal cities of the United States. In 1894 he made his way to Yankton, South Dakota, where for a time he was employed in a similar capacity, but after four years he opened an establishment of his own at 222 Capitol Avenue. He handles all kinds of plumber's supplies and does a contracting business, his establishment being the most completely equipped for repair work in the state. He installed the heating and plumbing apparatus in the Sisters Hospital in Yankton and in Garfield school and also had the contract for laying the main sewerage throughout the city. He has likewise done much other important work along his line in Yankton and in the surrounding districts. He understands his business thoroughly and employs only skilled workmen to assist him, and this added to his honesty and fair dealing has brought to him a gratifying and substantial success.

Mr. Wiggen was married to Miss Bertrena Nelson, a native of Denmark and a daughter of Christian and Kristiana (Nelson) Nelson. The daughter accompanied her parents on their removal to South Dakota and the father for many years followed farming near Tabor, in Yankton County but he is now living practically retired. Mrs. Wiggen attended the public schools of Yankton and later the Lutheran Normal College at Sioux Falls. Mr. and Mrs. Wiggen have one daughter, Lillian. The family attend the services of the Lutheran church. Mr. Wiggen is a member of St. John's Lodge, No. I, A. F. & A. M., and has attained the thirty-second degree in Masonry, belonging to Oriental Consistory, No. I, and he is likewise a member of Yelduz Temple of the Nobles of the Mystic Shrine at Aberdeen, South Dakota. He also holds membership relations with the Ancient Order of United Workmen. Mr. Wiggen is yet a young man, alert, energetic and wide-awake, and if his present success is any criterion of what the future holds in store for him, he will undoubtedly attain much greater prosperity ere his career comes to a close.

ANDREW G. WILLIAMS

Andrew G. Williams, who has been a resident of Gettysburg, Potter County, for the past score of years, is a native of the Badger state, having been born in Portage, Columbia County, Wisconsin, on the 12th of February, 1861, and being a son of O. P. and Mary A. Williams, his father a real-estate and insurance agent. He secured his educational training in his native town, where he duly availed himself of the advantages afforded by the public schools, and continued his residence in Wisconsin until 1880, when he came to what is now the state of South Dakota and took up his residence in Gettysburg in 1884, where he now controls a large and flourishing real-estate business, his books showing at all times most desirable investments in town property and farming and grazing lands. He is one of the popular and public-spirited citizens of Gettysburg and a man of much force and initiative ability. Fraternally he has attained the thirty-second degree in Masonry, belonging to Aberdeen Consistory.

ERASTUS A. WILLIAMS

Erastus A. WILLIAMS, U. S. Surveyor General of North Dakota, came to Yankton, Dakota Territory — now South Dakota — in May, 1871, and came to the settlement then without name and now Bismarck, the capital city of North Dakota, by wagon train in 1872. It was largely through the efforts of General Williams that the town was finally given its present name. He was born at Mystic River, Conn., October 13, 1850. His father, Daniel K. Williams, was a lumber manufacturer in Wisconsin. He was a man full of energy and enterprise. He was in California in an early day, but finally settled in the lumber regions of Wisconsin. General Williams' mother's maiden name was Matilda Appleman. Like her husband, she was of old New England ancestry. Erastus was nine years old when his parents moved to Wisconsin, and his early years were spent in lumber camp surroundings, where he gained a knowledge of men and things while obtaining his school education. He went to Illinois to study law, and in 1871 was admitted to practice at Freeport, where, eleven years later, he married his wife. Immediately after his admission to the bar he struck out for the west, and landed at Yankton, as mentioned. His first employment at Bismarck was with the Northern Pacific Railroad Company, and soon afterward he entered the employ of the Lake Superior & Puget Sound Land Company. In 1872 he was elected to the lower house of the territorial legislative assembly. In 1874 and 1875 he served as assistant United States attorney, under Col. William Pound. In 1874 and 1875 he was a member of the territorial council. In the fall of 1882, he was again elected to the legislature of 1883, and chosen speaker of the house. In 1885 he was re-elected member of the house and again in 1887. Preparatory to the formation of the state of North Dakota he was elected to the constitutional convention. He was then elected a member of the first legislature of the state. In all these positions General Williams proved himself to be a man of sound judgment and of marked ability. In 1890 President Harrison appointed him U. S. Surveyor General, a position which he held for four years. In 1896 he was again elected to the legislature, and was a second time made speaker of the house. In 1898 he was again appointed V. S. Surveyor General — this time by President McKinley — a position he still holds, with his home at Bismarck, of which city he has been a resident since it was settled, general Williams is a Republican, and has been one of the most prominent and influential men of the state. He is a member of the Masonic fraternity, and prominent in political and social affairs. In 1882 he was married at Freeport, Ill., to Jennie E. Hettinger, who died in 1894. They had five children: Eva E., Matilda A., Alice J., Erastus H. and Odessa Williams.

JAMES W. WILSON

The State Agricultural College of South Dakota, at Brookings, is signally fortunate in having secured the subject of this sketch as a member of its faculty, and his efforts in the connection have not failed of due appreciation on the part of those interested in this valued institution. Professor Wilson was born on a farm near Traer, Tama county, Iowa, on the 12th of February, 1871, and his is the distinction of being a son of the present able incumbent of the office of secretary of the United States department of agriculture, James Wilson, while the maiden name of his mother was Esther Wilbur, the ancestry in the agnatic line tracing back to Scotch origin, while on the maternal side the lineage is of German extraction, the Wilbur's having early become identified with the history of the state of New York. James Wilson was numbered among the pioneers of Iowa, and so familiar to the public is the record of his life and services that a recapitulation is not demanded in this connection.

The subject of this review passed his boyhood days on the homestead farm, while his early educational discipline was secured in the district schools, which he continued to attend until he had attained the age of fifteen years, when he entered the high school at Traer, Iowa, where he continued his studies for two years, after which he returned to the home farm, where he was engaged in the caring for the livestock until he had attained his legal majority. He then, in 1893, was matriculated in the State Agricultural College of Iowa, at Ames, where he completed the prescribed four-years course in science and agriculture, being graduated with the degree of Bachelor of Science as a member of the class of 1896, while two years later his alma mater conferred upon him the degree of Master of Science. For one year he was assistant professor of animal husbandry in the same institution, and he then went to the national capital in the capacity of private secretary to his father, who had been chosen secretary of agriculture. This incumbency Professor Wilson retained for three years, during the last two of which he was a student in the law department of Georgetown University, where he attended the evening sessions. After leaving Washington he passed a year in the law office of the firm of Hubbard, Dawley & Wheeler, of Cedar Rapids, Iowa, and during the succeeding year he had charge of a farm of eight hundred acres in that state. On the 22d of May, 1902, he was chosen director of the state experiment station established at the State Agricultural College of South Dakota and was simultaneously made professor of agricultural and animal husbandry at the college and placed in charge of the farm and the college dairy. He has proved an able, discriminating and enthusiastic worker in these important capacities, and has done much to increase the prestige of the institution, while within the year 1903 will have been completed on the farm a fine barn for experimental work in his line, the building representing an expenditure of twelve thousand dollars. Professor Wilson will thus have excellent facilities for carrying on his work, including original research and experimentation, and he is certain to make his department one of great value to not only the students of the college, but to the farmers of the entire state. He is a close observer and indefatigable student, and has had the advantages of wide travel, having visited every state in the Union with the exception of two or three in New England, and having also made trips to Cuba and Jamaica.

In politics he gives his allegiance to the Republican party; his religious faith is that of the Presbyterian church, and fraternally he is identified with the Masonic order, being affiliated with lodge and chapter in Washington, D. C. and the commandery in Brookings, South Dakota.

MORRIS M. WILLIAMS

Morris M. Williams, a well-known and representative citizen of Lebanon, Potter County, was born in Portage, Wisconsin, on the 12th of October, 1865, and after there, completing the curriculum of the public schools, he entered the Northwestern Business College, in Madison, the capital of the state, where he was graduated as a member of the class of 1885. In 1885 he came to the territory of Dakota and was for one year employed as clerk in the Inter Ocean Hotel, at Mandan, in what is now North Dakota. He then, in 1886, came to Gettysburg, Potter County, South Dakota, and was there working for his brother, A. G., in the real-estate business for two years, at the expiration of which, in 1888, he came to Lebanon, where he engaged in the buying of grain for the Marfield Elevator Company, remaining with this concern twelve years, while during the latter few years of this period he was also engaged in the lumber and farming implement and machine business on his own responsibility, retiring from the grain business in 1902, while he still continued the other lines of individual enterprise, having built up a large and successful business. In 1898 he was also engaged in the general merchandise business here, as the senior member of the firm of Williams & Schneider, having a commodious store and warehouse and carrying an extensive stock of goods. He has been consecutively concerned in the real-estate business, and his books at all times show desirable investments in good farming and grazing lands, as well as town property. He has recently completed in Lebanon a fine modern residence, the same being heated by the hot-water system and having other up-to-date facilities and being one of the most attractive homes in this section of the state. In politics he is a stanch Republican but has not been ambitious for public office, though he served for a number of years as treasurer of the school district.

He is a Royal Arch Mason and also identified with the Ancient Order of United Workmen. On the 8th of August, 1890, Mr. Williams was united in marriage to Miss Frankie Carr, and they have three children, Perry R., Benjamin H. and Marjorie.

ROLLA G. WILLIAMS

Holla G. Williams, just retiring from the office of register of deeds of Codington County, is embarking in the insurance business in addition to his connection with the Codington County Abstract Company, maintaining his office in Watertown, the county seat. His life record stands in contradistinction to the old adage that a prophet is never without honor save in his own country, for Mr. Williams has won a creditable place in public regard in the city in which he was born. His natal day was August 29, 1883, his parents being George R. and Eva E. Williams. The mother was a daughter of George W. Carpenter, who came to Watertown in early pioneer times and was the first surveyor of Codington County. With the later development and improvement of this section of the state he was closely associated for many years and at the time of his death he was again filling the office of county surveyor as well as that of city engineer. He was a veteran of the Civil War. having loyally defended the Union in the darkest hour of our country's history. He passed away in 1912, at the age of seventy-six years.

It was in 1879 that George R. Williams came with his family from Berlin, Wisconsin, to South Dakota, settling near Watertown, where he homesteaded land. He afterward worked in town for R. B. Spicer, then register of deeds, for four years and on the expiration of that period was nominated on the republican ticket for the office, to which he was afterward elected for three successive terms. On his retirement he entered the abstract business, which is now conducted under the name of the Codington County Abstract Company, with his son, Holla G. Williams, as its secretary, J. Huntzicker as treasurer and manager, and Mrs. Eva Whiting, mother of the subject of this review, as the president. George R. Williams continued in the abstract business until his death, which occurred in 1907, his remains being then interred in the Watertown cemetery. He was one of the pioneers of that city, there being but a small village at the time of his arrival. As the years went on, he bore his part in the work of general advancement and improvement and became recognized as a worthy and valued citizen. In 1909 Mrs. Williams became the wife of George H. Whiting of Yankton, where they now reside.

After attending the public schools Rolla G. Williams continued his education in the Watertown Business College and when his school days were over entered the employ of the Northwestern Railroad Company, with which he remained for six months. He then spent four years with the Chicago, Milwaukee & St. Paul Railroad at Sioux Falls, South Dakota. He later was located for a time at Minot, North Dakota, in the employ of the Great Northern Railroad, and afterward at Midway, British Columbia, for the same company. Following his father's death, he returned to Watertown in 1908 and entered the abstract office of his father, taking charge of the business, and is now secretary of the company. In 1910 he was elected register of deeds — a position which his father had previously filled for several terms — entered upon the duties of the office on the 1st of January, 1911, and was afterward reelected and started upon his second term in 1913. On March 1, 1915, he entered into partnership with J. C. Miller, retiring county auditor, for the conduct of an insurance office. He made a creditable record as a public official, is successful in business, and is accounted one of the progressive young men of Codington County.

Mr. Williams is fond of outdoor life and of manly sports and when business cares permit, he enjoys spending a few hours or days, as the case may be, in the open. In his political views he is a republican and is now recognized as one of the local leaders of the party. His religious faith is that of the Baptist church and fraternally he is connected with the Masons, the Elks and the Modern Woodmen. In the first named he has advanced steadily and is now a member of the El Riad Shrine at Sioux Falls.

GEORGE N. WILLIAMSON

G. N. WILLIAMSON has been successfully engaged in the practice of law in the city of Aberdeen, Brown County, for the past twelve years, and is one of the representative members of the bar of the state.

He is a native of the state of Minnesota, having been born in Rochester, Olmsted County, on the 20th of December, 1865, and being a son of Nathan N. and Mary Williamson, the former of whom was born in the state of New York and the latter in New England, while they were remembered among the pioneers of Minnesota, the father having been for many years engaged in the contracting business at Rochester. The subject received his early educational discipline in the public schools of Oronoco and Rochester. Minnesota, and then entered the law department of the University of Minnesota. He was admitted to the bar of his native state in 1889 and the same year to that of the new commonwealth of South Dakota, since he located in Aberdeen in 1892 and here initiated the active work of his profession, in which he has been most successful, being an able trial lawyer and a duly conservative counselor, he is a close student of his profession and gives careful preparation to every cause which he presents before court or jury.

In politics he is an independent Republican and while he takes an active interest in public affairs and in the success of the party cause, he has never been ambitious for political office. He has attained the thirty-second degree in the Ancient Accepted Scottish Rite Masonry, and is also identified with the Knights of Pythias. On the 15th of April, 1896, Mr. Williamson was married to Miss May M. Mackenzie, who was born in the city of St. Paul, Minnesota, on the 3d of August, 1875, being a daughter of Alexander C. and Annie Mackenzie. Of this union have been born three children, Alan N., Marjorie and Helen.

JOHN WILLIAMSON

John Williamson, a retired gold mill manager living in Tyndall, has had a great deal of experience in different parts of the world, his business interests taking him to three continents. He was born in Medford, New Jersey, July 23, 1845, a son of Benjamin and Susanna (Hoover) Williamson, natives of England and New Jersey respectively. When he was about seven years of age the family removed to Pike County,

Missouri, where they resided until 1870. The father, being a spinner and weaver by trade, ran a custom woolen mill there. In 1870 they came to South Dakota, where John Williamson had preceded the other members of the family arriving in December, 1869. He came by rail to Sioux City, which was the end of the railroad, and from that point traveled by stage to old Bon Homme, changing horses about every ten miles. He located a claim about three and a half miles from Bon Homme and held it until 1913. In 1876 he went to the Black Hills, where he worked for about thirteen years. He did little prospecting but during his first year "grubstaked" a friend who prospected for the two but did not succeed in uncovering any profitable lead. Mr. Williamson secured a place in the mills for a time and in 1884 entered the employ of the Homestake Company, working in their mills, where his efficiency and faithfulness won him rapid promotion. He eventually became manager of milling and proved himself not only thoroughly acquainted with all processes employed but also a man of executive ability and a good judge of men. He was subsequently employed by Hyderabad Decan Company, a British mining company, as manager and for nine years was in charge of their mills at Hyderabad in the Decan district of British India. He went to his new place of duty by way of London in order to receive instructions and returned the same way that he might report and make final settlement with the company. He returned to Bon Homme County, South Dakota, but was not allowed to remain long in retirement, as the Ashantee Gold Mining Company, another British organization, secured his services as manager on the 5th of October, 1900, for a period of eighteen months. He took charge of their mills at Obossa, some one hundred and twenty miles inland from the west coast of Africa. On his journey into the interior, he was carried in a hammock by six natives. He adapted himself to the conditions of work and the class of labor employed and proved an able manager, but the enervating climate of the tropics sapped his strength and a severe attack of jungle fever so weakened him that he refused to remain after the termination of his contract. He then came to South Dakota and purchased three hundred and twenty acres near Tyndall, where he settled down and is now passing his days in retirement, enjoying the ease won by former toil.

Mr. Williamson is a republican in his political allegiance and stanchly supports the policies of that party. He has attained the thirty-second degree in the Masonic order and is a member of the Shrine. He won many friends in that organization, as he has many attractive social qualities. Although he has had extensive experience in widely separated parts of the globe, he believes that South Dakota offers opportunities the equal of those afforded by any other part of the world and he does all in his power to promote the development of the state.

JOHN H. WILLIAMSON

J. H. Williamson, a member of the state senate, from Lake County, is a native of the old Pine Tree state, having been born in the town of Stark, Somerset County, on the 30th of July, 1859, and being a son of Hon. Henry and Temperance (Boardman) Williamson, both of whom were born and reared in that same county, being scions of prominent old families of New England. The paternal grandfather of the subject was Rev. Stephen Williamson, who was born in Siasconset, Nantucket County, Massachusetts, and was a clergyman of the Freewill Baptist church and was long active in the work of the ministry. The original progenitors of the family in America came hither from England in the colonial days, and the great-grandfather of the Senator was a valiant soldier in the Continental line during the war of the Revolution, while the Rev. Stephen Williamson was in active service during the war of 1812, in which he was an officer. Patriotism and loyalty have been distinctive traits in the several generations, and the father of the subject was a stanch abolitionist in the crucial epoch culminating in the war of the Rebellion. He was physically disqualified for active, service in the field but took a prominent part in recruiting work and in sustaining those who went to the front. He was a farmer by vocation, owning and operating a large homestead in his native county, where he was held in the highest esteem and confidence. He was graduated in Hamilton College, at Clinton, New York, as a member of the class of 1847. He was a member of the state senate of Maine and also of the lower house of the legislature, was chairman of the board of selectmen of his county for fifteen years, while he served for four years as county judge and for a time as a member of the governor's council, all of which preferments indicate the influential position which was his. He was twice married, the two children of the first union being John H., the immediate subject-of this review, and Horace B., who died April 10, 1900, at Madison, South Dakota. The honored father died in 1892, at the advanced age of seventy-five years.

John H. Williamson received his preliminary educational discipline in the public schools of Stark, Maine, and then entered the Eaton School, at Norridgewock, Maine, and later the Maine Central Institute, at Pittsfield, where he completed his preparatory collegiate work, being graduated in the institution as a member of the class of 1882. He was shortly afterward matriculated in Bates College, at Lewiston, Maine, where he completed the classical course and was graduated with the degree of Bachelor of Arts, in 1886, with special honors in mathematics. In October of the same year he came to South Dakota and took up his abode in Madison, where he entered the law office of Judge William E. Howe, under whose direction he prosecuted his technical study of the law for one year, at the expiration of which he entered the law department of the University of Wisconsin, at Madison, where he took up the work in both the junior and senior classes, this being the first attempt of the sort made by any student in that celebrated institution, being graduated as a member of the class of 1888 and receiving the degree of Bachelor of Laws and being simultaneously admitted to the bar of Wisconsin by the supreme court of the state. He then went to Anoka, Minnesota, where he was for six months associated in practice with George Wyman, and at the expiration of the period noted he returned to Madison, South Dakota, where he has ever since been actively and prominently identified with the work of his profession. He served two years as police or city justice, and in 1892 was elected to the bench of the county court, retaining the office four years. In 1900 he was elected to the state senate, of which he was an active working member during the ensuing general assembly, while he was chosen as his own successor in the election of November, 1902. He is a stalwart advocate of the principles of the Republican party, and a voucher of his ability and personal popularity was that offered at the time of his first election to the senate, since he was the first Republican to have secured this preferment in the district for a decade. He was one of the organizers of the Lake Madison Chautauqua Association, of which he was the first president, holding this office eight consecutive years, and being at the present time a member of the directorate of the organization. He is vice-president of the Madison State Bank and is the owner of residence property in the town of Madison.

The Senator is identified with the Masonic fraternity, the Knights of Pythias, the Benevolent and Protective Order of Elks and the Modern Woodmen of America. He has taken an especially active interest in the State Normal School, in Madison, and both in the senate and in a private way has done much to foster the same. It should also be noted in the connection that during the general assembly of the legislature of 1902 he received the special honor of being elected president pro tern, of the senate, his intimate knowledge of parliamentary rules making him an especially capable presiding officer. On the 9th of June, 1891, Senator Williamson was united in marriage to Miss Stella L. Storms, daughter of Elisha C. and Mary (Tuttle) Storms, of Anoka, Minnesota, while she was born in Waukesha County, Wisconsin. Of this union have been born four children: Lura M., Henry S., Frank E. and J. Horace.

ALBERT W. WILMARTH

ALBERT W. WILMARTH

Albert W. Wilmarth, engaged in the practice of law at Huron, was born at Harford, Susquehanna County, Pennsylvania, February 15, 1856, and was one of twin members of a family of four children whose parents were George P. and Martha (Payne) Wilmarth, both of whom were natives of Pennsylvania. The father was a farmer by occupation and in 1885 came to this state, establishing his home in De Smet, where he remained until called to his final rest. He was descended from English ancestry, the first representatives of the family in America arriving about the time of the close of the Revolutionary war.

Albert W. Wilmarth acquired his education in the district schools near his father's home and in the high school at Harford, Pennsylvania. After reviewing the opportunities offered by various occupations, he decided to study law and in preparation for the bar began his reading at Montrose, Pennsylvania, where he studied until admitted to practice in 1879. He then opened an office in the east, where he remained in active practice until 1883, when he removed to the west, settling at Huron, Dakota territory. Immediately afterward he opened an office and now for almost a third of a century has followed his profession in Huron. It was not long before he had gained a good practice and his clientage has always been large and of a distinctively representative character. He has never been in a partnership relation and thus it has been his individual ability entirely that has brought him to a prominent place as a member of the Huron bar. For six years he filled the office of city attorney and for two years was county attorney, while for two terms he represented his district in the state legislature, leaving the impress of his individuality upon the laws enacted during that period.

On the 28th of April, 1886, Mr. Wilmarth was united in marriage to Mrs. Alma Sill, a daughter of Erasmus E. and Maria Hull, of Chicago. Mr. Wilmarth finds his chief recreation in hunting. Fraternally he is connected with the Masons, Elks, Knights of Pythias and Modern Woodmen and his political allegiance is given to the republican party, which he has always supported since age conferred upon him the right of franchise. He concentrates his energies, however, upon his law practice, which is now very extensive. At the present writing he is attorney for the James Valley and the City National Banks and represents in a professional capacity other important corporation interests. The professional work which brought him most largely into prominence perhaps was litigation in which he engaged following the admission of the state into the Union. At that time there was a contest between all the larger cities to secure the state capital and all of them issued bonds and warrants to secure money with which to aid in their contest. Huron issued bonds and warrants greatly in excess of the constitutional limit of indebtedness and sold its waterworks to acquire money for that purpose. As a result of this, money could not be secured to maintain a city government. A contest was inaugurated to set aside the spurious indebtedness and recover to the city its waterworks. Mr. Wilmarth was elected city attorney to take immediate charge of this litigation and mainly through his efforts the indebtedness in excess of the constitutional limit was annulled and the waterworks recovered to the city without the return of any money to the purchasers thereof. From that time on the standing of Mr. Wilmarth as an able and resourceful lawyer has been of the best in the state and he has by far the most extensive local practice of any attorney in Beadle County. It is said a crisis ever calls forth the latent powers and displays the real ability of an individual and Mr. Wilmarth proved equal to the occasion and gained the recognition to which his powers as a lawyer entitle him.

Edward Henry Wilson, who has been a practicing attorney of Salem, South Dakota, for more than three decades, enjoys an enviable reputation as one of the leading representatives of the profession in his section of the state. His birth occurred in New Williamsport, Pennsylvania, on the 7th of April, 1857, his parents being Evan C. and Leah (Crawford) Wilson, who were likewise natives of the Keystone state and came of Irish extraction. They passed away in Lycoming County, Pennsylvania. Throughout his active business career Evan C. Wilson devoted his attention to general agricultural pursuits.

Edward H. Wilson was reared on the home farm and acquired his early education in the common schools. Subsequently he attended Mount Union College of Mount Union, Ohio, and Starkey Seminary of Yates County, New York. The former institution conferred upon him the degree of Bachelor of Philosophy. In 1876 he took up the study of law at Williamsport, Pennsylvania, in the office of Bentley & Parker. In November, 1880, he came to South Dakota, locating in Canton, where he completed his law studies in the office of Judge O. S. Gifford. He was admitted to the bar in 1882 and in the spring of the following year came to Salem, South Dakota, where he has remained in successful practice continuously since. An excellent presence, an earnest, dignified manner, marked strength of character, a thorough grasp of the law and the ability accurately to apply its principles are factors in his effectiveness as an advocate.

In 1885 Mr. Wilson was united in marriage to Miss Ettie L. Young, of Morganville, New York, by whom he had four children, two of whom survive, namely Leon P., who is a commercial salesman residing at Fort Worth, Texas; and Leverne E., a high-school student.

Mr. Wilson is a republican in politics, loyally supporting the men and measures of that party. From 1884 until 1890 he served as territorial district attorney and also held the office of states attorney for fourteen years, from 1890. In these important positions he made a most creditable record and has been attorney for the Chicago, St. Paul, Minneapolis & Omaha Railroad since 1885. For the past twenty years he has been a member of the Salem school board and has ever taken an active and commendable part in public affairs. He is a charter member of the State Historical Society.

Fraternally Mr. Wilson is identified with the Masons, belonging to the following organizations: Fortitude Lodge, No. 73, A. F. & A. M.; Salem Chapter, No. 34, R. A. M.; Constantine Commandery, K. T.; Oriental Consistory, No. II, A. & A. S. R., of Yankton; and El Riad Temple, A. A. O. N. M. S., of Sioux Falls, South Dakota. He is likewise a member of the Ancient Order of United Workmen and Salem Lodge, No. 106, I. O. O. F., while his wife belongs to the Presbyterian church. A social nature renders him popular and his genuine worth has gained for him the high regard of many with whom he has been associated. His attention, however, is chiefly concentrated upon his profession and he is regarded as a faithful and conscientious minister in the temple of justice, who gives to his client the service of great talent, unwearied industry and wide learning, yet never forgets that there are certain things due to the court, to his own self-respect and above all to justice and a righteous administration of the law, which neither the zeal of an advocate nor the pleasure of success would permit him to disregard.

W. H. WILSON

Since 1905 W. H. Wilson has been connected with the undertaking business in Aberdeen and has now one of the well-appointed establishments of this character in the city. He was born in Illinois in 1871 and after acquiring a public-school education entered the employ of an undertaker in that state. In 1901 he removed to Aberdeen, South Dakota, where for a time he was associated with Andy Gerup in the furniture business. He was later connected with the J. V. Moore Furniture Company until 1905, when he established himself in the undertaking business. In 1909 his present building was erected containing a chapel twenty-five by one hundred and thirty feet in dimensions and with a seating capacity of one hundred and twenty-five. Mr. Wilson's establishment is well appointed and its equipment is modern. He carries a fine line of caskets and funeral supplies and a liberal patronage is accorded him, for his prices are reasonable and his integrity above reproach.

In 1895 Mr. Wilson married Miss Theresa Murphy, a native of Illinois, and they have become the parents of a son, Robert. Mr. Wilson is connected fraternally with the Masons, in which he has taken the thirty-second degree, holding membership in the blue lodge, chapter, commandery and Shrine. He belongs also to the Knights of Pythias, the Elks, the Modern Woodmen of America, and the Ancient Order of United Workmen. His political allegiance is given to the republican party. His business record deserves great commendation, for he has won success by reason of his integrity, knowledge and ability.

EDWIN R. WINANS

Edwin R. Winans, one of the leading representatives of the bar in Sioux Falls, was born in Albany, Illinois, November 4, 1874. He is a son of Aaron and Mary (Provine) Winans, the former a native of Seneca Falls, New York, who was a steamboat pilot on the Mississippi river for a number of years and died in Vermont, Illinois, in 1885. He had survived his wife six years, her death having occurred in 1879. Of their children two are yet living: Edwin R., of this review; and Ralph L., a manufacturer in Chicago.

Edwin R. Winans acquired his preliminary education in the public schools of Vermont, Illinois, and afterward entered the Illinois Wesleyan University at Bloomington, graduating in law in 1900. In 1901 he came to Sioux Falls and in the same year entered the law office of the late United States Senator A. B. Kittredge, for whom he acted as private secretary for some time. In 1903 he was taken into partnership, the firm name being Kittredge, Winans & Scott. This existed until Mr. Winans entered into partnership with P. J. Rogde, who afterward served as postmaster of Sioux Falls, and is now deceased. The latter firm was dissolved in 1911 and since that time Mr. Winans has been engaged in practice alone. He has a large and representative patronage and has made a notable reputation as a strong and forceful practitioner.

On the 26th of October, 1904, at Sioux Falls, Mr. Winans married Miss Maud R. O'Loughlin and they have a daughter, Elizabeth. Mr. Winans gives his political allegiance to the republican party. He was judge advocate general for the South Dakota State Guard for one year and is very well known in fraternal circles, having been initiated into the Masonic order according to both the Scottish and York Rites. He is past master of Unity Lodge, No. 60, F. & A. M., of Sioux Falls; is past high priest of Sioux Falls Chapter, No. 2, R. A. M.; and holds membership also in the Shrine. He belongs to the Benevolent Protective Order of Elks and is past exalted ruler of the local lodge. He has become widely known as a man of more than ordinary ability, having attained an enviable degree of success in a profession where advancement comes only as a result of individual merit.

ANDREAS A. WIPF, M. D.

Andreas A. WIPF, was born in southern Russia, on the 12th of September, 1868, being a son of Andreas and Susan (Glanzer) Wipf, to whom were born five children, namely: Sarah, who is the wife of Joseph G. Gross, of Hutchinson County; Joseph A., who is engaged in farming in this county; Susan, who is the wife of Andrew R. Hofer, a farmer of this county; Anna, who remains at the parental home; and Andreas Albert, the immediate subject of this sketch. The Wipf family traces back to Swiss origin, but has been established in Russia for fully a century, representatives of the name having removed from Switzerland into Tyrol, Austria, and thence into southern Russia, where both parents of our subject were born and reared. In 1875 they emigrated to America and came to Hutchinson County, South Dakota, where the father entered a homestead claim on Wolf creek, five miles southwest of the present town of Bridgewater, and there he improved a valuable farm, upon which he died, and where his estimable wife still continues to make her home, being numbered among the honored pioneers of the county.

Dr. Wipf was seven years of age at the time when the family came from Russia, and he was reared to maturity in South Dakota, his youthful days being devoted to working on the home farm and attending the common schools. Later he entered the Dakota University, at Mitchell, and finally was matriculated in the University of South Dakota, in Vermillion, where he continued his scholastic discipline. He then devoted three winters to teaching in the district schools, engaging in farm work during the summer seasons. In 1891 he took up the study of medicine, and in the fall of that year entered that celebrated institution. Rush Medical College, in the city of Chicago, where he completed the prescribed course under the most favorable auspices, being graduated in the spring of 1894, with the degree of Doctor of Medicine. Shortly afterward the Doctor opened an office in Freeman, where he has since been established in the practice of his profession and where he has attained distinctive prestige as an able and discriminating physician and surgeon. He is a stalwart supporter of the Republican party, but has never held office, save that of county coroner, in which capacity he served four years. He is a member of the South Dakota State Medical Society and is held in high esteem by his professional confreres.

Fraternally he is identified with Eureka Lodge, No. 71, Free and Accepted Masons; Scotland Chapter, No. 31, Royal Arch Masons; Oriental Consistory, Ancient Accepted Scottish Rite; El Riad Temple, Ancient Arabic Order of the Nobles of the Mystic Shrine, the latter two being organized in the city of Sioux Falls, and he is also affiliated with the lodge of the Ancient Order of United Workmen at Bridgewater and the camp of the Modern Woodmen of America at Menno. The Doctor is the owner of a fine farm of one hundred and eighty-five acres, located three miles northeast of Freeman, in Turner County. On the 26th of June, 1894, Dr. Wipf was united in marriage to Miss Dorothea Hoellwarth, of Hutchinson County, and they are the parents of six children, namely: Claudia, Adeline, Alice, Alfred, Lilly and Kurt.

DAVID D. WIPF

David D. Wipf is president of the First National Bank of Parkston and is one of the extensive landowners of his section of the state and has not only been active along business lines but has also left the impress of his individuality upon the political history of the state. He was born at Hutterthal, South Russia, August 4, 1872, his parents being David and Katharina (Stahl) Wipf, the former born February 5, 1846, and the latter January 21, 1854. They were reared and married in their native land and left Hutterthal for the United States on the 19th of June, 1879. They arrived in Yankton on the 8th of July of that year and the father filed on a homestead, securing the southeast quarter of section 12, township 99, range 57, in what was then Armstrong County, Dakota territory, but is now Hutchinson County. He established his residence upon the homestead and there remained until March 31, 1909, when he removed to Wells County, North Dakota, and again settled upon a farm. There his wife passed away on the 19th of May, 1911. The father has been successful in his business affairs and has given to each of his children a good start. He was, however, practically empty handed when he came from Russia, possessing at that time a capital of only six hundred and ten dollars. He possessed resolute energy, determination and ability, however, and these proved the capital upon which he has builded his prosperity, coming in time to rank with the men of affluence in his community.

David D. Wipf acquired a common-school education and in early life devoted his attention to farming, school-teaching and grain buying. Gradually in his business career he has worked his way upward and now has important commercial, financial and agricultural interests. On the 12th of January, 1909, he was elected a member of the board of directors of the First National Bank of Parkston and on the same day was selected as cashier of that institution, occupying that position until the 8th of September, 1910, on which day the board of directors reorganized and selected Mr. Wipf as president. He still occupies that office and bends his energies to the further development and upbuilding of the bank and the extension of its patronage and connections. Besides being a heavy stockholder therein, he is also a stockholder in the Menno Lumber Company and is an extensive landowner, having twenty-four quarter sections of land, four in Sully County and one in Butte County, South Dakota, two in Crook County, Wyoming, and seventeen in Duchesne County, Utah.

While Mr. Wipf's business interests have made constant demand upon his time and energies, he has yet found opportunity to cooperate in many measures for the general good and his fellow townsmen, appreciative of his worth and ability, have again and again called him to public office. He served as deputy county assessor under C. P. Hirsch in 1893, under Samuel Klaudt in 1895 and 1896, and under Jacob Haisch in 1897. He was deputy county treasurer under Christian Buechler from March 1, 1897, until January 1, 1901, and under J. M. Schaefer from the latter date until the 1st of March, 1901. In the November election of 1900 he was chosen county auditor and assumed the duties of that position on the 1st of March, 1901, serving in that capacity until the 28th of December, 1904, when he resigned. He was chosen secretary of state at the November election of 1904 and took office on the 3d of January following, remaining as the incumbent until the 5th of January, 1909. He was appointed supervisor of census for the first supervisors' district of South Dakota by President Taft on the 8th of September, 1909, and supervised the taking of the census by four hundred and fifty enumerators in as many districts between the 15th day of April, 1910, and the 15th day of June, of the same year. Preparations for the thirteenth census were begun in September, 1909, and the work was completed on December 21, 1910, that being the date of an honorable discharge signed by Hon. E. Dana Durand, director of the census. Supervisors' district No. 1 consisted of all of the state lying east of the Missouri river and had a population of four hundred and forty-three thousand, two hundred and seventy-two. In politics Mr. Wipf has always been a republican, favoring progressive policies and principles, and his influence has been a potent force in shaping the policy of his party and advancing its welfare on many occasions.

On the 1st of June, 1891, at Freeman, South Dakota, Mr. Wipf was married to Miss Katharina Wipf, a daughter of Joseph and Katharina Wipf. She was born in Johannesruh, South Russia, December 31, 1870. Her mother died in that place in 1871, after which her father married again and came with his family to what was then Armstrong County, Dakota territory, and is now Hutchinson County. Later he removed with his family to Spink County, South Dakota, where he now resides upon a farm. To Mr. and Mrs. David D. Wipf has been born a son, John D., whose birth occurred July 19, 1895, and who was graduated from the commercial department of Redfield College at Redfield, South Dakota, in June, 1912. He is now attending Yankton College.

Mr. Wipf is a Mennonite in religious faith. Fraternally he is connected with Scotland Lodge, No. 52, A. F. & A. M.; Scotland Chapter, No. 31, R. A. M.; Oriental Consistory, No. I, Valley of Yankton, in which he has attained the thirty-second degree; and Menno Camp, No. 3071, M. W. A. His activities have largely touched the general interests of society and his efforts have been a potent force in advancing the welfare and upbuilding of his portion of the state. He has largely been dependent upon his resources since starting out in life and has so directed his energies and controlled his affairs that he is a prosperous citizen and one who wields a wide influence.

JOSEPH WILHELM WIPF

The subject of this sketch comes of stanch old Swiss lineage, though his ancestors for several generations have been established in the southern portion of Russia. The original representatives proceeded from Canton Unterwalden, Switzerland, into the Tyrol, Austria, and thence into Russia. Mr. Wipf is one of the enterprising and prominent young business men of Freeman, Hutchinson County, and has been a resident of South Dakota since 1879, in which year his parents emigrated from Russia and became pioneers of this commonwealth, the father having become one of the successful farmers of Hutchinson County.

Joseph W. Wipf was born in the colony of Huterthal, southern Russia, on the 12th of August, 1869, a son of Joseph and Susanna (Wurz) Wipf, who were reared and educated in Russia, the former there learning the blacksmith trade, to which he devoted his attention for a number of years, also engaging in farming. He continued to follow the later vocation after coming to South Dakota, and he died in Hutchinson County, on the 11th of November, 1888, respected by all who knew him. His wife survived him by nearly a decade, being summoned into eternal rest on the 6th of November, 1898. Both were devoted members of the Mennonite church, and the father was a stanch Republican in politics, his life having been one of honest and earnest endeavor.

The subject of this sketch was eight years of age at the time his parents took up their abode on the pioneer farm in this county, and here he was reared to manhood, securing his early educational training in the public schools and supplementing this by a six-months course in the South Dakota State University, at Vermillion — in 1888-9. In 1896-1897 he was matriculated in the pharmaceutical department of the University of Iowa, at Iowa City, and was there graduated as a member of the class of 1897. In 1886 Mr. Wipf began teaching in the district schools of Hutchinson County, and continued in pedagogic work until 1892, in which latter year he held a clerkship as bookkeeper in the Bridgewater State Bank, while during the years 1893-4 he was bookkeeper in the hardware establishment of Meyer Brothers, in Bridgewater. Since 1897, he has been engaged in the drug business in Freeman, owning a half interest in the drug store conducted under the firm name of J. W. Wipf & Company. He also holds a half interest in the Freeman Telephone Company. In politics he gives his allegiance to the Republican party, and his religious faith is that of the Mennonite church, of which he has been a member since 1889.

Fraternally he is identified with Eureka Lodge, No. 71, Free and Accepted Masons, and Menno Camp, No. 3071, Modern Woodmen of America. On the 13th of October, 1897, was solemnized the marriage of Mr. Wipf to Miss Mary Graber, daughter of Peter and Elizabeth Graber, of Storkweather, North Dakota, and they became the parents of three children: Evelina, born November 11, 1898; Elva, born September 8. 1901, died two days later, and Edmund Filmore, born January 20, 1902.

AUGUST C. WITTE

A. C. Witte, president of the Witte Hardware Company, and one of Aberdeen's prominent citizens, was born in the city of Pein, Hanover, Germany, on July 6, 1857. His parents were August and Anna (Mueller) Witte, both natives of Germany, the former of whom died in 1875. The subject was educated in the public schools and in Hildesheim College, completing the three-years course in the latter and being graduated in 1874. He then became an apprentice in a wholesale hardware store with the purpose of preparing himself for a commercial career. He spent four years in the above establishment, and then entered the German army as a one-year volunteer, being stationed in the city of Hanover. At the end of his term of one year he was commissioned a second lieutenant. In November, 1879, he arrived in America, and proceeding to Faribault, Minnesota, he entered a hardware store, where he was employed for one year. In 1880 he engaged in the same line of business in Faribault, associating himself as a partner with A. W. Mueller, under the firm name as Mueller & Witte. This firm continued in business at Faribault until 1883, when they closed out, in order to give all their attention to their hardware business in Aberdeen which they had previously established in 1881. This co-partnership continued until the death of Mr. Mueller, in 1893, and from that time on until 1902 the subject carried on the business by himself. In the last-named year the Witte Hardware Company was organized, the subject taking in his two stepsons as active partners. The company have one of the largest and best equipped hardware establishments in South Dakota, and do a large and increasing business.

Mr. Witte has been a Republican in politics since coming to America, and during his residence in Aberdeen has been active and prominent in public affairs. In 1885 he was elected to the board of aldermen, and, with the exception of two years, has continued a member of the board, being at the present time a member from the fourth ward. His worth as a faithful city official was recognized by the people in 1902, when he was elected mayor of the city for a term of two years. His administration of the affairs of the office during the term was most satisfactory to all concerned.

Mr. Witte is a member of the Masonic fraternity, in which he has attained the thirty-second degree of the Scottish Rite, and the honor of K. C. C. H., which was bestowed upon him by the supreme council; he is at the present time commander of Albert Pike Council, No. 4, Knights of Kadosh, in this division of the order. He is also a member of the Independent Order of Odd Fellows, in which he was grand patriarch of South Dakota in 1893, having represented the grand encampment of South Dakota in the sovereign grand lodge for two years. On April 30, 1895, Mr. Witte married Mrs. Carole W. Mueller, widow of his late partner. Mrs. Witte, by her former marriage, became the mother of three children: Arthur L., Otto E. and Alma. The sons are members of the Witte Hardware Company.

Among those sterling citizens of South Dakota who have lived up to the full tension of the strenuous life on the frontier and who have likewise contributed in a significant degree to the development and upbuilding of the great and prosperous commonwealth, stands the subject of this memoir, than whom there are few to be found who have been longer resident of what is now the state of South Dakota, since he took up his abode here forty-five years ago. Mr. Wixson may be said with all consistency to be the founder of the town of Elk Point, the official center of Union County. He still resides in Elk Point and no citizen of the county is held in higher estimation than is this sturdy pioneer of pioneers.

Eli B. Wixson was born in Wayne, Steuben County, New York, on the 6th of May, 1833, a son of Daniel and Deborah (Conklin) Wixson, the former of whom was of English lineage and the latter of German, both

ELI B. WIXSON.

families having been early established in America. The subject was reared to manhood on the homestead farm, securing his early educational training in the common schools of the locality and remaining on the parental home until he had attained his legal majority. He thereafter attended for a time the academy at Dundee, New York, and shortly after leaving this institution he started for what was then considered the far west, this action being born of a spirit of adventure and a desire to discover what fortune had in store for him. He arrived in Sioux City, Iowa, in the month of May, 1856, the place being at that time a mere village of straggling order, and in 1859 he came into Dakota territory and pre-empted land in Union County, the southern portion of the town of Elk Point being located on this tract. He built the first house in the town, laying the foundation on the 22d of July, 1859. The domicile was of most primitive description, being constructed of logs and equipped with a dirt roof. Mr. Wixson located on his claim and devoted his attention to farming for several years, being one of the very first settlers in what is now a well-populated and prosperous section of the state. He was proprietor of the first hotel in Elk Point, conducting the same for a number of years, while he later erected and conducted what is now known as the Tremont House.

In 1861 Mr. Wixson enlisted in Company B, First Dakota Cavalry, being mustered in at Sioux City, Iowa, and he was in active service on the frontier in various Indian campaigns, having been for some time under command of General Sully and continuing in the service until 1865, when his company was mustered out, at Sioux City. He held the office of commissary sergeant during the entire period of his service and was a participant in many exciting and hazardous engagements with the hostile savages.

In politics the subject gives an unqualified support to the Democratic party, and he has been prominently concerned in public affairs of a local nature. He served for one term as mayor of Elk Point and was for many years a member of the town council and the school board. In 1871-72 he was elected register of deeds of Union County, being the fourth incumbent of this office, and he also held the position of county commissioner for several years, ever manifesting a lively interest in the welfare and development of his home town, county and state and evincing this interest in a practical and tangible way. In 1866 he was elected to and served with honor in the territorial legislature as a member from Union County. He is the owner of valuable realty in Elk Point, being one of its most substantial and prosperous citizens. At the time when preparation was being made for the erection of the new court house Mr. Wixson gave to the county the land on which the present fine building is located, the same having been erected in 1898, and the condition on which he donated the land was that the county seat remain perpetually in Elk Point and that the land in question should be utilized for the purpose designated. To these grounds he has since given a warranty deed to the county. He also donated the land on which the Elk Point high-school building was erected, the latter being a fine structure, containing eight rooms and basement.

Mr. Wixson was a charter member of the first Masonic lodge organized in Sioux City, Iowa, and is now affiliated with Elk Point Lodge, No. 3. Free and Accepted Masons, in Elk Point. He is without doubt the oldest Mason in the county at the present time. He also holds membership in Stephen A. Hurbert Post, No. 9, Grand Army of the Republic, in his home town. He was one of the organizers of the Old Settlers' Association of Union County and has been its president from the beginning.

In Elk Point, on the 30th of November, 1865, was solemnized the marriage of Mr. Wixson to Mrs. Clara E. Christy (nee Cook), who was born in Onondago County, New York, on August 7, 1840. They have three sons and three daughters, concerning whom we incorporate a brief record, as follows: William M. is now engaged in a flouring mill at Hawarden, Iowa; Mary D. is the wife of George Walker, of Avon, South Dakota: Franklin B. is engaged in the elevator business in Elk Point; Eli B., Jr., is engaged in the barber business in Avon, this state; Alice May is the wife of Ren Wheeler, of Aberdeen, South Dakota; and Clara, who was the wife of William Davis, died in 1894, at the age of twenty-four years. By her former marriage Mrs. Wixson had a daughter, Lottie, who is now the wife of J. W. Steckman, of Avon, this state.

LEWIS E. WOOD

L. E. WOOD, auditor of Spink County, was born near Bourbon, Marshall County, Indiana, on the 15th of August, 1853, and is a son of Daniel R. and Lydia E. (Wickersham) Wood, both of whom were born in Ohio. Daniel R. Wood was of Welsh and English extraction and the original ancestors in America were early settled in Virginia, which was the theater of so important a portion of the historic events of our nation. The mother of the subject was a representative of the old English Quaker family of Wickershams. who settled in Pennsylvania as colonists of William Penn. The parents of the subject removed from Ohio to the densely timbered region of Marshall County, Indiana, in 1851, and there literally hewed out a home in the midst of the virgin forest.

Lewis Edwin Wood, the immediate subject of this review, was reared under the sturdy discipline of the old homestead farm. His rudimentary education was secured in the district schools and was supplemented by effective courses of study in the public schools of Rochester, Indiana. He taught in the schools of his native county for three years, after which he was engaged in farming in that county until 1883, when he came to South Dakota, in company with his brothers, Joshua F. and Joseph T. He entered a homestead claim of one hundred and sixty acres, near the present town of Doland, Spink County, and here developed a valuable farm. He assisted in the organization of the first school districts in the county and in the erection of the first school buildings, while his efforts in looking to the educational interests of the new county were freely given and did not lack for popular appreciation. In 1896 he located in Doland, where he was engaged in the drug and jewelry business until 1900, disposing of his interests there upon his election to his present office. He has ever been found a stanch advocate of the principles of the Republican party, and has striven to maintain the honesty of the party and to defend it against corrupting influences. In 1895 he was elected a member of the board of county commissioners, and was re-elected in 1898. Before the expiration of his second term, he was elected to his present office of county auditor, removing with his family to Redfield in 1901. He gave a most able and satisfactory administration of the affairs of this office and was honored with reelection in the fall of 1902.

Fraternally he is identified with the Masonic order, the Knights of Pythias, the Ancient Order of United Workmen and the Modern Woodmen of America. In June, 1876, Mr. Wood was united in marriage to Miss Mary T. Kirk, who was a successful and popular teacher in the schools of their home county in Indiana. She was summoned to the life eternal in January, 1895, and is survived by her two children, Roscoe, who is now a commercial traveler for the Jewett wholesale drug house, of Aberdeen, this state, and Elma, who was graduated in shorthand and typewriting in Redfield College, and who now finds her services much in demand in the various offices in her home town. In May, 1897, Mr. Wood consummated a second marriage, being then united to Miss Eliza Richards, who was for seven years a teacher in the primary department of the graded schools of Argos, Indiana, in which state she was born and reared.

W. B. WOLCOTT

W. B. Wolcott, who is one of the leading merchants and honored citizens of White Lake, Aurora County, is a native of the Empire state of the Union, having been born in Batavia, Orleans County, New York, on the 28th of January, 1863, and being a son of J. Warren and Susan (Hayward) Wolcott, of whose six children four are living, namely: Kate M., wife of E. M. Chamberlain, of Findlay, Ohio: Nellie A., wife of E. F. Janes, of Erie County, Pennsylvania: Margaret H., a resident of Alden, New York: and W. B., the subject of this sketch. J. Warren Wolcott was born in Orleans County, New York, in 1828, his parents having emigrated thither from Connecticut, where the family was founded in the colonial epoch, the ancestry being of French Huguenot derivation. Oliver Wolcott, Jr., a great-uncle of the subject, was the first comptroller of the United States treasury and upon the death of Alexander Hamilton was appointed secretary of the treasury. The father of our subject devoted his active life to agricultural pursuits in western New York and is now living retired in the town of Alden, that state. He is a Democrat in politics and while never an office seeker he served for one or more terms as sheriff of Orleans County. His wife, who was born in Erie County, Pennsylvania, in 1830, of English ancestry, died in 1871, at the age of forty-one years, having been a devoted member of the Presbyterian church, with which her husband likewise has been identified for many years.

W. B. Wolcott was reared on the home farm and his early educational advantages were those afforded by the public schools of the city of Buffalo, New York. At the early age of fifteen years, he secured employment as clerk in a grocery in that city, and to this line of effort he there continued to devote his attention until 1883, when he came to the territory of Dakota, working on a farm in Aurora County for the first two years and then securing a position in the lumber yard of Warren Dye, of White Lake, with whom he remained two years. He then returned to the state of New York, where he remained about seventeen months, at the expiration of which, in February, 1888, he again took up his residence in White Lake, securing a clerkship in the general store of H. Hofmeister, in whose employ he continued about eleven years. In the spring of 1900 Mr. Wolcott engaged in the same line of enterprise on his own responsibility, and he has now a well-equipped store and controls a large business, the same being the result of his correct methods and marked personal popularity in the community.

He is a stanch adherent of the Republican party, and fraternally is prominently identified with the Masonic order, being a member of White Lake Lodge, No. 85, Free and Accepted Masons; Pilgrim Chapter, No. 32, Royal Arch Masons; St. Bernard Commandery, No. II, Knights Templar, at Mitchell; Oriental

Consistory, No. I, Ancient Accepted Scottish Rite, at Yankton: and El Riad Temple of the Ancient Arabic Order of the Nobles of the Mystic Shrine, in Sioux Falls, while he also holds membership in White Lake Lodge, No. 84, Independent Order of Odd Fellows. On the 25th of August, 1898, Mr. Wolcott was united in marriage to Miss Ida Ponto, of Charles City, Iowa, she being a daughter of the late Martin Ponto, a prominent farmer of that local city.

JOHN WOLZMUTH

JOHN WOLZMUTH

On the list of the enterprising merchants of Spearfish appears the name of John Wolzmuth, who is engaged in the sale of a general line of light and heavy hardware, implements, etc. He is a self-made man and has worked his way steadily upward to his present position of affluence. He started out in life empty-handed when but twelve years of age and has since depended entirely upon his own resources. Not only is he a successful merchant but he is also widely known throughout the state as one of its law makers, being now a representative to the general assembly, in which he has served for eight or nine terms. He was born in Oneida county, New York, December 27, 1850, a son of David and Katherine (Klugensmith) Wolzmuth, both of whom were born in Alsace-Lorraine, Germany, the former in 1801 and the latter in 1808. They were reared and married in that country and in 1847 bade adieu to friends and native land, sailing for America. They settled in Oneida County, New York, where the father engaged in farming, and there they spent their remaining days, Mr. Wolzmuth passing away in 1899, while his wife survived until 1904. After leaving Europe he served as a soldier in the French army.

The family of David and Katherine Wolzmuth numbered eight children, of whom John Wolzmuth, of this review, was the sixth in order of birth. He began his education as a public-school pupil and afterward attended a seminary at Whitesboro, New York, and when twelve years of age began providing for his own support, working for others in the Empire state. He was thus employed for about four years and then made his way westward to Iowa, settling in Cedar Falls, where he worked in a hardware store for about six years. He next went to Sioux City, Iowa, where he engaged in the hardware business on his own account for a number of years. On the expiration of that period, he made his way to the Black Hills in July, 1876, and was engaged in the freighting business as a member of the firm of Evans, Wolzmuth & Hornick, continuing therein for two years. He next engaged in mining until 1880, in which year he removed to Spearfish and purchased a flouring mill which he operated for twenty-four years, being thus actively and prominently identified with the manufacturing enterprises of the city. In 1890 he also engaged in the hardware business with a Mr. Valentine as a partner. That association was continued until 1892, since which time Mr. Wolzmuth has been alone as proprietor and promoter of the business, carrying a general line of light and heavy hardware, farm implements and other goods of that character. He also has mining interests and is the owner of farm lands in South Dakota, but concentrates his attention chiefly upon his mercantile affairs. His business methods are thoroughly reliable and the industry and enterprise which he displays have been the foundation upon which he has builded his prosperity.

On the 5th of June, 1881, Mr. Wolzmuth was united in marriage to Miss Margaret L. Goughonour, who was born in Adel, Iowa, a daughter of Emanuel and Jennie (Sense) Goughonour. The father was born of

German parentage and the mother of English. He was a lumberman and in 1879 left Iowa, removing with his family to Deadwood, where he engaged in the lumber business. He afterward established his home in Livingston, Montana, where he is now living retired. Mr. and Mrs. Wolzmuth have become the parents of three children: Elmore J., who married Miss Mable Allen and resides in Spearfish with his father, whom he assists in business; Roecoe V., who married Miss Nina Miller and is conducting an automobile and garage business in Spearfish; and Zella, at home.

Mr. Wolzmuth holds membership in the Masonic fraternity and has passed from the blue lodge through all of the degrees of the Scottish Rite to the Mystic Shrine. He also holds membership with the Modern Woodmen of America and attends the Congregational church. His political indorsement is given the republican party and he is one of its active workers in Lawrence County. In 1886 his fellow townsmen elected him to represent the county in the lower house of the territorial legislature and he was a member of that body when South Dakota became a state. He has served altogether for eight or nine terms and is the present incumbent in that office. He has done much to shape legislation and his reelections indicate the confidence and trust reposed in him by his fellow townsmen, who recognize that in him loyalty is combined with ability and public spirit. He also served as mayor of Spearfish for a number of terms, has been a member of the city council and was one of the first county commissioners. He served on the board of education, having in charge the public and normal schools of Spearfish until the law was changed. He is interested in everything that pertains to the public welfare, studies the questions and issues of the day and is conversant with the various phases of life in South Dakota. His work has indeed been of direct value to his community and to the commonwealth and in all of his public service he has placed the general good before personal aggrandizement.

WILLIS R. WOOD

W. R. Wood, who is engaged in the lumber business at Parker, Turner County, is a native of the Badger state, having been born on a farm in Columbia County, Wisconsin, on the 23d of October, 1859, a son of Norman I. and Julia A. (Welliver) Wood, who were pioneers of that state, where the former was a successful farmer. The parents are now living in Green Lake County, Wisconsin. After completing the curriculum of the public schools, the subject supplemented this discipline by a course of study, in the Wisconsin State Normal School at Oshkosh, this being in the year 1880. He thereafter taught school for a short time in his native state, after which he removed to Winterset, Iowa, where he was identified with the lumber business until August, 1884, when he came to Parker, South Dakota, as manager of the local interests of the Oshkosh Lumber Company, of Oshkosh, Wisconsin, which then maintained a number of lumber yards along the line of the Chicago, Milwaukee & St. Paul Railroad. He thus continued in the employ of this company about five years, at the expiration of which he became associated with Charles W. Davis, of Oshkosh, in the purchase of the interests of the afore mentioned company in Parker and Alexandria, South Dakota, and since that time the enterprise has been continued under the firm name of W. R. Wood & Company, the business having become one of no inconsiderable scope and importance. In 1895 Mr. Wood purchased of Vale P. Thielman his abstract, land and loan business, at Parker. This enterprise was established by Mr. Thielman in 1870 and was conducted by him for a quarter of a century, thus having the prestige of being the oldest of the sort in the county, its foundation having been contemporaneous with the issuing of the patent of the first quarter section of land in the county, so that it figures as a distinctively pioneer institution. In politics Mr. Wood has ever been stanchly arrayed in support of the Republican party and its principles, and while he takes a deep interest in public affairs of a local nature, he has never been a seeker of official preferment.

Fraternally he is identified with Parker Lodge, No. 30, Free and Accepted Masons; Parker Lodge, No. 88, Independent Order of Odd Fellows; and Monitor Lodge. No. 57, Knights of Pythias, all of Parker. On January 19, 1904, Mr. Wood was united in marriage to Miss E. Belle Waterbury, of Nashua, Iowa.

GEORGE W. WOODWORTH

George W. Woodworth, a farmer and stock-raiser living on section 9, Spirit Mound township, Clay County, was born in Sauk county, Wisconsin, a son of Samuel G. and Julia A. (Skinner) Woodworth. The father was born in Connecticut, of Scotch and English stock, and the mother was a native of Ohio and of German extraction. Both came west in their youth and were married in Wisconsin, where they lived from 1837 until 1856, when they removed to Minnesota, which remained their home until 1870, in which year they came to this state. The father proved up on government land on section 4, Spirit Mound township, Clay County, and operated his farm until his death, which occurred in 1881. He had survived his wife for eight years, as she passed away in 1873. They were the parents of three daughters and seven sons, five of whom are yet living, as follows: Henry W., James H., George W., Charlotte E. and Wesley C.

George W. Woodworth received his education in Wisconsin and there grew to manhood. When twenty-seven years of age he removed to Clay County, this state, and purchased a quarter section of raw prairie land. He immediately began the work of its development and improvement and the highly cultivated fields and the commodious and substantial buildings indicate how efficient his labors were. He has bought additional land from time to time and is now one of the largest landowners in the county, owning nine hundred and twenty acres, eight hundred of which is under cultivation. It is all productive, being situated in a river bottom, and his labors yield him a handsome income annually. He follows general farming, raising both grain and stock. He is also interested financially in the Farmers Elevator Company of Vermillion, of which he is a charter member. His wife owns a fine residence in Vermillion.

In 1874 Mr. Woodworth was united in marriage with Miss Perrilla Morey, a native of New York state and a daughter of Milton Morey. She accompanied her parents to Minnesota and resided there for fifteen years but in 1866 the family removed to Yankton, South Dakota. The father was a farmer and met with success. To Mr. and Mrs. Woodworth were born seven children: Ollie, who died when one year of age; Milton M., a resident of Sioux Falls, South Dakota and manager of the Western Supply House of that place; Elsie P., the wife of Fred G. Carr, a druggist of Madison, this state; Raymond F., who is financially interested in the Western Supply House of Sioux Falls, where he resides; George, deceased; Harry L., an attorney of Sioux Falls ; and Lloyd J., who is also interested in the Western Supply House of Sioux Falls.

The family are members of the Congregational church and Mr. Woodworth is a republican in his political belief. He has served on the township board on a number of occasions and is active in local public affairs. Fraternally he belongs to the Masonic order and has passed through all the chairs of the blue lodge. He is one of the representative agriculturists of his county and his energy and sound judgment have enabled him to acquire a considerable fortune, which no one begrudges him as it has been fairly and honorably won. He is public spirited in his citizenship and holds the confidence and goodwill of all who know him.

Z

JOSEPH ZITKA

Joseph Zitka, cashier of the Security Bank at Tyndall, is a native of Bohemia, where he was born on the 21st of March, 1850, being a son of Joseph and Anna (Riha) Zitka, of whose three children he is the elder of the two surviving, the other being Frances, who is the wife of Charles Vaulk, of Bon Homme County, this state. The father of the subject was a farmer in his native land, where he continued to reside until 1867, when he immigrated with his family to the United States, locating in Cedar Rapids, Iowa, where he remained about three years, after which he came as a pioneer to South Dakota, which was then still a portion of the great undivided territory of Dakota. He located in Bon Homme County, where he took up a homestead claim and again turned his attention to agricultural pursuits. He was a man of energy and excellent business judgment, and through his well-directed efforts he attained a definite success in connection with his industrial enterprise as a pioneer of this state, while he so lived as to command the respect of all who knew him. At the time of his death, which occurred in September, 1902, he was a resident of Bon Homme County, South Dakota, and his political faith was that of the Democratic party.

The subject of this sketch received his early educational discipline in his native land, being accorded the advantages of the excellent schools in the vicinity of his home, and being about seventeen years of age at the time of the family's emigration to the United States. After locating in South Dakota, he continued to be associated with his father in his farming enterprises until 1883, a partnership relation having been maintained. He early became interested in matters of public concern and eventually became a prominent factor in the local councils of the Democratic party, of whose principles and policies he has ever been a stalwart advocate. In 1872 he was elected a member of the board of county commissioners of Bon Homme County and in the ensuing year he was still further honored by being chosen to represent his district in the legislature of the territory, while in 1876 he was again elected a member of the board of county commissioners. In 1883 Mr. Zitka was elected register of deeds of Bon Homme County, having become a resident of this county in 1870, and this office he held for three consecutive terms of two years each. In 1889 he was a member of the constitutional convention, at Sioux Falls, which formulated the present admirable constitution of the state. In 1898 he was elected treasurer of Bon Homme County, and thereupon became a resident of Tyndall, the county seat having been removed to this place from Bon Homme in 1885.

In 1889 was affected the organization of the Security Bank in Tyndall and Mr. Zitka was chosen cashier of the new institution, a position of which he has ever since remained incumbent, while his discriminating management of its affairs has shown him to be an able executive and through his efforts the institution has become one of the popular and solid ones of the state. He is the owner of about fifteen hundred acres of valuable farming land in Bon Homme County.

He and his wife are communicants of the Catholic church and fraternally he is a member of Bon Homme Lodge, No. 101, Free and Accepted Masons. On the 8th of June, 1877, Mr. Zitka was united in marriage to Miss Mary Bohac, of Crete, Nebraska, and of this union have been born eight children, concerning whom we enter the following brief record: Hattie is the wife of Frank Chladek, of Hawarden, Iowa; Rose is the wife of John Herman, of Tabor, South Dakota; and Mary, Charles, Anna, Agnes, Frances and George still remain at the parental home, which is a center of refined hospitality.